해커스 텝스 READING 200% 활용법

무료 핵심포인트 인강 이용하기

PC로 이용

해커스텝스(HackersTEPS.com) 접속 ▶
상단의 [텝스 무료강의 →
텝스 리딩 강의] 클릭해 보기

모바일로 이용

해커스텝스(HackersTEPS.com) 접속 ▶
중단의 [추천 무료강의 →
텝스 리딩 무료강의] 클릭해 보기

핵심포인트 인강 바로 가기 ▶

무료 텝스 온라인 실전모의고사 이용하기

방법

해커스인강(HackersIngang.com) 접속 ▶ 상단의 [텝스 → MP3/자료 → 온라인 모의고사]
클릭 ▶ 본 교재의 [온라인 실전모의고사] 클릭해 이용하기

무료 단어암기장 및 단어암기 MP3 이용하기

방법

해커스인강(HackersIngang.com) 접속 ▶
상단의 [텝스 → MP3/자료 → 무료 MP3/자료] 클릭 ▶
본 교재의 [단어암기 MP3 & 단어장] 클릭해 다운받기

MP3/자료 바로 가기 ▶

해커스 텝스 READING

David Cho

해커스 어학연구소

시험에 나올 문제를 미리 풀어보고 싶을 땐?

해커스텝스(HackersTEPS.com)에서

텝스 적중예상특강 보기!

텝스를 철저히 분석 반영한
해커스 텝스 Reading
개정 3판을 내면서

대한민국 영어 교육의 중심, 해커스 어학연구소의 텝스(TEPS) 교재가 **베스트셀러** 자리를 지킬 수 있는 것은 여러분의 **텝스 점수 상승**, 나아가 **영어 실력 향상**을 위해 끊임없이 고민하고, 그 고민을 교재에 담아내기 때문입니다.

이러한 고민과 노력의 결실로, **최신 텝스 경향을 반영한 「해커스 텝스 Reading」 개정 3판**을 출간하게 되었습니다.

최신 텝스 경향 완벽 반영!

최신 텝스 경향을 철저히 분석하여 교재 내 모든 내용과 문제에 반영하였으며, 이에 맞는 효과적인 문제풀이 전략을 제시하였습니다. 실전보다 더 실전 같은 텝스 문제로 학습자들은 최신 시험에 대한 감각을 충분히 익히고, 보다 철저하게 실전에 대비할 수 있습니다.

기본부터 실전까지 체계적인 학습!

「해커스 텝스 Reading」은 문법, 어휘, 독해에 대한 핵심 이론을 단계에 따라 체계적으로 학습할 수 있도록 정리하였으며, 방대한 양의 실전 문제 또한 수록하고 있습니다. 다시 말해, 기본서와 실전서의 역할을 동시에 하는 교재로, 영어의 기본을 탄탄하게 다지려는 학습자부터 시험 전 실전 감각을 최대로 끌어올리려는 학습자까지 목적에 맞게 학습할 수 있습니다.

상세한 해설과 문제풀이 전략 적용을 통한 고득점 달성!

각 챕터에서 학습한 내용과 전략을 적용하는 방법을 익힐 수 있도록 모든 문제의 정확한 해석과 상세한 해설을 중요 어휘와 함께 수록하였습니다. 「해커스 텝스 Reading」으로 문제에 대한 이해도를 높이고, 전략 적용 방법을 학습하면 단기간에 텝스 고득점 달성이 가능합니다.

텝스 전문 커뮤니티 **해커스 텝스 사이트(HackersTEPS.com)**에서 교재 학습 중 궁금한 점을 다른 학습자들과 나누고, 다양한 무료 텝스 학습 자료를 함께 이용한다면, 학습 효과를 더욱 높일 수 있습니다. 또한, 실시간으로 공유하는 텝스 시험 정보를 통해 보다 효과적으로 시험에 대비할 수 있습니다.

「해커스 텝스 Reading」이 여러분의 텝스 목표 점수 달성에 확실한 해결책이 되고 영어 실력 향상은 물론, **여러분의 꿈을 향한 길**에 믿음직한 동반자가 되기를 소망합니다.

CONTENTS

GRAMMAR

해커스 텝스 Reading

OCABULARY

READING COMPREHENSION

「해커스 텝스 Reading」으로 점수 잡는 비법!

텝스 출제 유형을 철저히 파악한다!

텝스 리딩 출제 유형 한눈에 보기

텝스 리딩의 영역별 특징과 출제 유형을 철저하게 분석하여 알기 쉽게 정리하였으며, 이에 따른 문제풀이 방법 또한 제시하였습니다. 이를 통해 텝스의 **출제 유형**을 파악하는 것은 물론, **전략적인 학습**이 가능합니다.

텝스 리딩 영역별 출제 비율

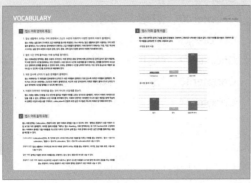

Grammar / Vocabulary / Reading 각 영역의 **문제 유형별 분석 자료**를 제시하였으며 교재 내 수록된 이론 설명, 문제에도 **텝스 분석 내용**을 반영하여 효과적으로 실전에 대비할 수 있게 하였습니다.

기본기와 실전 감각을 동시에 쌓는다!

[문법] Basic Grammar / 문법 Point

문법 영역에서는 시험에 출제되는 **핵심 문법 사항과 필수 문법 포인트**를 정리하여 텝스 문법 시험에 확실히 대비할 수 있게 하였습니다.

[어휘] 출제 경향 / Vocabulary List

어휘 영역에서는 최신 시험 출제 경향을 확인하고, **Vocabulary List**를 통해 핵심 출제 단어를 효과적으로 학습할 수 있도록 하였습니다.

[독해] 문제 / 지문 유형별 공략

독해 영역에서는 **문제, 지문 유형에 대한 출제 포인트와 문제풀이 및 지문분석 전략**을 제시하여 빠른 독해와 정답 선택 능력을 키울 수 있게 하였습니다.

Hackers Practice / Hackers Test

Hackers Practice에서는 실제 시험에 출제될 만한 문장들로 배운 내용을 간단히 확인할 수 있으며, **Hackers Test**에서는 실전 유형과 동일한 문제를 수록하여 체계적인 학습이 가능합니다.

텝스 실전모의고사

시험 전, **실전과 동일한 구성과 난이도를 반영한 텝스 실전모의고사**를 풀어봄으로써 자신의 실력을 점검하고, 실전 감각을 키울 수 있도록 하였습니다.

「해커스 텝스 Reading」으로
점수 잡는 비법!

상세한 해설로 문제풀이 전략을 익힌다!

Grammar / Vocabulary 영역 해설

교재 내 수록된 모든 문제에 대해 **정확한 해석과 상세한 해설**을 수록하였습니다. 해설에서는 각 보기가 **정답 혹은 오답이 되는 이유**와 추가적으로 알아야 할 어휘 혹은 문법 개념 등을 소개하여 문제를 쉽게 이해하고, 관련 내용을 확실하게 학습할 수 있도록 하였습니다.

Reading 영역 해설

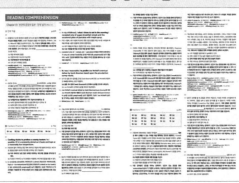

각 문제 유형에 맞는 문제풀이 전략을 적용하여 **실제 문제를 푸는 순서에 따라** 상세하게 풀이하였습니다. 이를 통해 해설을 읽는 것만으로도 **문제풀이 방법과 전략 적용 노하우**를 자연스럽게 익힐 수 있도록 하였습니다. 또한, 필수 어휘를 별도로 정리하여 어휘력을 향상시킬 수 있도록 하였습니다.

해커스만의 노하우가 담긴 학습자료를 활용한다!

들으면서 외우는 단어암기자료

시험 전 반드시 알아두어야 할 텝스 영역별 필수 어휘로 구성된 단어암기장을 단어암기 MP3와 함께 해커스인강(HackersIngang.com)에서 무료로 제공합니다. 3,000개 이상의 단어를 듣고 따라 읽으며, 쉽고 재미있는 어휘 학습이 가능합니다.

해커스 텝스 리딩 무료 동영상강의

HackersTEPS.com

본 교재로 공부하는 학습자들이 혼자서도 효과적으로 학습할 수 있도록 해커스텝스(HackersTEPS.com)에서는 무료 동영상강의를 제공하고 있습니다. 이외에도 매일 텝스 풀기, 텝스 보카 TEST 등을 통해 보다 빠른 목표 점수 달성이 가능합니다.

텝스 소개

TEPS란?

TEPS란 Test of English Proficiency developed by Seoul National University의 약자로, 서울대학교 언어교육원에서 개발하고 TEPS 관리위원회에서 주관하는 국내 개발 영어 인증 시험이다. 실제 활용하는 영어 능력을 평가함으로써, 기업체 및 공사고시 및 대학 입시 등 각종 자격 요건 평가시험으로 활용된다.

텝스의 구성

영역	파트	내용	문항 수	시간	배점
청해	Part 1	질의 응답 (하나의 문장을 듣고 이어질 응답 고르기)	10	40분	240점
	Part 2	짧은 대화 (3턴의 주고받는 대화를 듣고 이어질 응답 고르기)	10		
	Part 3	긴 대화 (6~8턴의 주고받는 대화를 듣고 질문에 알맞은 답 고르기)	10		
	Part 4	담화문 (한 명의 화자가 말하는 긴 내용을 듣고 질문에 알맞은 답 고르기) (1지문 1문항)	6		
	Part 5	긴 담화문 (한 명의 화자가 말하는 긴 내용을 듣고 질문에 알맞은 답 고르기) (1지문 2문항)	4		
어휘	Part 1	구어체 (대화문의 빈칸에 가장 적절한 어휘 고르기)	10	25분	60점
	Part 2	문어체 (단문의 빈칸에 가장 적절한 어휘 고르기)	20		
문법	Part 1	구어체 (대화문의 빈칸에 가장 적절한 답 고르기)	10		60점
	Part 2	문어체 (단문의 빈칸에 가장 적절한 답 고르기)	15		
	Part 3	대화 및 문단 (어법상 틀리거나 어색한 부분 고르기)	5		
독해	Part 1	빈칸 채우기 (빈칸에 가장 적절한 답 고르기)	10	40분	240점
	Part 2	흐름 찾기 (한 단락의 글에서 내용 흐름상 어색한 부분 고르기)	2		
	Part 3	내용 이해 (지문을 읽고 질문에 가장 적절한 답 고르기) (1지문 1문항)	13		
	Part 4	내용 이해 (지문을 읽고 질문에 가장 적절한 답 고르기) (1지문 2문항)	10		
	14개 파트		135문항	105분	600점

* 각 문항의 난이도에 따른 반응 패턴을 근거로 평가하는 문항 반응 이론 적용

시험 응시 안내

1. 원서 접수

- 인터넷 접수: www.teps.or.kr로 접속한다. 사진 파일을 미리 준비해야 하고, 응시료는 신용카드 또는 계좌이체로 결제할 수 있다.
- 방문 접수: www.teps.or.kr의 시험 접수 → 접수처 안내에서 가까운 접수처를 확인한 후 방문하여 접수, 3*4 사진 한 장과 응시료가 필요하다.

2. 응시

- 응시일: 매달 토요일과 일요일 중 1~3회
  정확한 날짜는 www.teps.or.kr로 접속 → 시험 접수 → 시험일정 안내를 통해 확인
- 준비물: 규정에 맞는 신분증(주민등록증, 운전면허증, 청소년증 등이 인정되며, 자세한 신분증 규정은 www.teps.or.kr에서 확인), 수험표, 컴퓨터용 사인펜(연필 불가), 수정테이프(수정액 사용 불가), 아날로그 손목시계
- 성적 확인: 휴대폰 문자 및 인터넷 확인 (성적 발표 일시는 시험 접수 시 확인 가능)

TEPS 응시 관련 Tips

1. 고사장 가기 전

- 준비물을 잘 챙겼는지 확인한다.
- 시험 장소를 미리 확인해 두고, 규정된 입실 시간에 늦지 않도록 유의한다.

2. 고사장 입구에서

- 수험표에 적힌 수험 번호가 배정된 고사실을 확인한다.

3. 시험 보기 직전

- 모든 영역의 시험이 끝날 때까지 휴식 시간이 없으므로 화장실은 미리 다녀온다.

4. 시험 시

- 답안을 따로 마킹할 시간이 없으므로 풀면서 바로 마킹한다.
- 연필이나 볼펜으로 먼저 마킹한 후 사인펜으로 마킹하면 OMR 카드에 오류가 날 수 있으니 주의한다.
- 정해진 영역을 푸는 시간에 다른 영역의 문제를 풀면 부정 행위로 간주되므로 주의한다.
- 대부분의 영역이 앞에는 쉬운 문제가, 뒤에는 어려운 문제가 나오므로 앞부분을 빨리 풀어 시간을 확보한다.
- 청해 시험 시 놓친 문제나 어휘 / 문법 / 독해 시험 시 풀기 어려운 문제에서 오래 머무르지 않아 다른 문제 풀 시간에 영향이 가지 않도록 한다.
- 문항 난이도, 변별도 및 영역별 특정 가중치에 따라 문항 배점이 다르므로, 어려운 문제를 많이 맞추면 높은 점수를 받을 확률이 더 높다.
- 청해 시험 시 문제지의 빈 공간에 조금씩 필기하는 것은 괜찮다.

영역별 문제 유형

어휘 & 문법

텝스 어휘 & 문법 영역은 통합 25분 동안 어휘에서 30문항, 문법에서 30문항, 총 60문항을 풀도록 구성되어 있다. 어휘 영역은 상대적으로 문제 길이가 짧기 때문에 약 10분 정도의 시간을 할애하는 것이 권장되고, 문법 영역은 Part 3에 상대적으로 길이가 긴 지문이 등장하는 것을 고려하여 약 15분의 시간을 분배하여 푸는 것이 권장된다.

어휘 (Vocabulary)

텝스 어휘 영역은 Part 1에서 10문항, Part 2에서 20문항, 총 30문항을 풀도록 구성되어 있다. Part 1에서는 구어체, Part 2에서는 문어체를 통해 어휘 능력을 평가한다. 단어의 단편적인 의미보다는 문맥에서 쓰인 상대적인 의미를 더 중요하게 다룬다.

Part 1 짧은 대화 중 빈칸 채우기

| 1번~10번 (10문항)

| A와 B의 짧은 일상 대화 내의 빈칸에 알맞은 어휘를 선택지 4개 중에 고르는 유형이다. 기본 어휘의 다양한 구어적 활용과 하나의 어휘처럼 관용적으로 굳어져 쓰이는 어구 표현을 묻는다.

> A: The lights went out!
> B: Let me _____ if anything is wrong with the electricity.
>
> (a) test
> (b) note
> (c) control
> (d) check
>
> 정답 (d)

Part 2 서술 문장 중 빈칸 채우기

| 11번~30번 (20문항)

| 한두 개의 문장 내의 빈칸에 알맞은 어휘를 선택지 4개 중에 고르는 유형이다. 일상 생활에서 흔히 접할 수 있는 안내문이나 광고문 외에도 학술 분야를 다룬 문장이 나오므로 Part 1보다 난이도가 높은 편이다.

> In some countries, private citizens are allowed to _____ a gun if they first obtain a license.
>
> (a) conduct
> (b) carry
> (c) secure
> (d) enforce
>
> 정답 (b)

문법 (Grammar)

텝스 문법 영역은 Part 1에서 10문항, Part 2에서 15문항, Part 3에서 5문항, 총 30문항을 풀도록 구성되어 있다. 구어와 문어 상황, 단문과 장문 등 다양한 상황과 길이의 문장을 통하여 문법 사항의 이해도 및 활용도를 평가한다.

Part 1 짧은 대화 중 빈칸 채우기

| 1번~10번 (10문항)

| A와 B의 짧은 대화 내의 빈칸에 어법·문법적으로 알맞은 것을 선택지 4개 중에 고르는 유형이다.

A: It's raining. You should take an umbrella with you.
B: I should, _____ I'm just driving to the bank and coming home.

(a) or
(b) for
(c) and
(d) but

정답 (d)

Part 2 서술 문장 중 빈칸 채우기

| 11번~25번 (15문항)

| 하나의 문장 내의 빈칸에 문법적으로 알맞은 것을 선택지 4개 중에 고르는 유형으로, 일상 생활, 시사, 학술 분야를 다룬 문장이 나오므로 Part 1보다 난이도가 높은 편이다.

_____ a defective television set, Alice returned it the next day.

(a) Have been bought
(b) Having bought
(c) To have bought
(d) She had bought

정답 (b)

Part 3 긴 대화나 서술 지문 중 어법·문법상 틀린 문장 찾기

| 26번~30번 (5문항)

| 네 차례 오가는 A와 B의 대화 혹은 네 개의 문장으로 이루어진 서술 지문 중 어법·문법적으로 틀린 문장을 찾는 유형이다. 지문의 길이가 길고 학술적인 내용을 다루기도 하므로 가장 어렵다고 여겨지는 파트이다.

(a) The United States has been the most significant participant in the global economy for years. (b) However, this role expected to change as more countries modernize during the twenty-first century. (c) India has recently been ranked as the second fastest emerging economy, despite still being wracked with poverty. (d) The higher the standard of living in India becomes, the closer it will come to matching the economic power of the U.S.

정답 (b) expected → is expected

영역별 문제 유형

독해 (Reading Comprehension)

텝스 독해 영역은 40분 동안 Part 1에서 10문항, Part 2에서 2문항, Part 3에서 13문항, Part 4에서 10문항, 총 35문항을 풀도록 구성되어 있다. 따라서 응시자는 1분에 1문제 꼴로 빠르게 문제를 해결해야 한다. Part 1~3은 보통 1개의 단락으로 이루어진 지문 한 개당 하나의 문제가 출제되고, Part 4는 2개 이상의 단락으로 이루어진 지문 한 개당 두 개의 문제가 출제된다. 지문은 편지/코멘트, 광고, 공지, 기사/논평 등의 실용문과 인문 · 사회 · 자연과학 등의 분야에 걸친 비전문적 학술문으로 구성되며, 일부 지문에서는 실제를 반영하는 다양한 디자인이 적용된다.

Part 1   지문 내 빈칸 완성하기

| 1번~10번 (10문항)

| 한 개의 지문 내의 빈칸에 지문의 흐름상 적절한 내용 또는 연결어를 선택지 4개 중에 고르는 유형이다. 1번~8번에는 내용을 넣는 문제가, 9번~10번에는 연결어를 넣는 문제가 나온다.

> Sugarland Corporation, located in the greater Dallas area, is accepting applications for the Shift Supervisor position at our manufacturing facility. The supervisor is responsible for coordinating the company's production team and is expected to keep in close contact with the CEO and other corporate officers. Individuals seeking this position are expected to have 15 years of industry experience and a proven leadership record at previous places of employment. Candidates unable to meet these requirements are not encouraged to apply _____.
>
> (a) to manufacture our products
> (b) to become a company officer
> (c) for this supervisory opening
> (d) for supervising the applicants
>
> 정답 (c)

Part 2   지문 흐름상 어색한 문장 찾기

| 11번~12번 (2문항)

| 다섯 문장으로 이루어진 지문 가운데 네 개의 문장이 선택지로 주어지며 이 문장 중 글의 주제와 관련이 없거나 문맥에
  맞지 않는 문장을 선택해야 한다.

From July 16 to October 9, Toronto residents will be treated to the work of photographer Annie
Leibovitz. (a) Guests at the Yonge Street Gallery can catch a glimpse of her most well-known
portraits firsthand. (b) Leibovitz has dedicated herself to photographing celebrities, and images
of several famous public figures will be displayed. (c) The exhibition will include a written narrative
of each photo shoot, describing how she conceived her shots. (d) Leibovitz has always attempted to
imbue the subjects of her pictures with a sense of vulnerability and grace.

정답 (d)

Part 3 지문 읽고 질문에 답하기 (1지문 1문항)

| 13번~25번 (13문항)

| 보통 1개의 단락으로 이루어진 지문을 읽고 질문에 대해 가장 적절한 답을 고르는 유형이다. 일반적으로 중심 내용을 묻는 문제, 세부 내용을 묻는 문제, 바르게 추론된 것을 묻는 문제 순으로 출제된다.

Sea Creatures Suffer after Rouge Bay Cleanup

In the aftermath of increased government efforts to remove illegal waste from Rouge Bay, the amount of scrap metal buried on the sea floor has decreased by 50 percent and chemical levels in the water have also fallen. The bay has not looked this unsoiled at any point in recent memory. Unfortunately, these cleanup efforts have also caused their own share of problems. The removal of large clusters of metal, instead of helping to safeguard sea creatures, has actually taken away one of their heavily used habitats.

Q Which of the following is correct about the government's waste removal efforts?

(a) They have expanded the amount of positive chemicals in the water.
(b) They have not had the desirable effect of protecting sea life.
(c) They have entirely removed the metal from the sea floor.
(d) They have been unable to impact the bay's murky appearance.

정답 (b)

Part 4 지문 읽고 질문에 답하기 (1지문 2문항)

| 26번~35번 (10문항)

| 2개 이상의 단락으로 이루어진 지문을 읽고 두 개의 문제에 대해 가장 적절한 답을 고르는 유형이다. 보통 중심 내용을 묻는 문제, 세부 내용을 묻는 문제, 바르게 추론된 것을 묻는 문제 중 두 문항이 주어진다.

The use of digital devices has risen dramatically over the last few decades, particularly among adolescents. Within this age group, most social interactions are now carried out via a screen. The effects of this shift in adolescent behavior are yet to be comprehensively analyzed, but one recent study, which questioned over a million American teenagers, observed that teens that spend more time on their phones or computers were less happy and had lower self-esteem than those who engaged in more off-screen activities.

However, somewhat surprisingly, the teenagers that did not use digital devices at all were not the happiest group; that was the group who used their phones or computers for around an hour a day. Contradicting a widespread idea about taking a complete break from technology, the researchers surmised that a limited amount of technology use per day was optimal for teenagers. They therefore recommended that teens should refrain from overusing their devices by making rules about how much screen time they allow themselves every day.

Q What is the passage mainly about?

(a) Why teens use digital devices more than other age groups
(b) How to limit the amount of time teenagers spend on screens
(c) What impact the use of technology is having on teens
(d) Why teens should try to cut down on excessive digital use

정답 (c)

Q What can be inferred from the passage?

(a) It is a common belief that quitting technology is beneficial.
(b) Addiction to social media can lead to other problems.
(c) Most people use digital devices for a few hours a day.
(d) Teenagers were more content if they didn't own a phone.

정답 (a)

수준별 학습방법

*25페이지의 진단고사를 본 후, 본인이 맞은 개수에 해당하는 레벨의 학습방법을 참고하시면 됩니다.

LEVEL 1 (진단고사 14~24점)
초보탈출,
기본 개념을 이해하라!

영어만 보면 울렁증이 생기는 당신

영어에 대한 막연한 두려움이 있거나 텝스 리딩이 거대한 벽으로 느껴지는 학습자를 위한 기초 공사

LEVEL 2 (진단고사 25~35점)
중수도약,
유형과 전략을 파악하라!

영어 공부, 하긴 했지만 원하는 점수는 멀기만 한 당신

목표 점수를 향해 힘겨운 발걸음을 떼고 있는 사람을 위한 중급 코스 진입을 위한 점수 상승 학습법

LEVEL 3 (진단고사 36~45점)
고지 점령,
실전 감각을 익혀라!

고지가 눈앞인데 좀처럼 점수가 오르지 않는 당신

몇 달을 공부해도 제자리인 점수에 가슴이 답답한 사람을 위한 실전 대비 학습법

LEVEL 4 (진단고사 46점 이상)
만점 정복
오답 패턴을 깨뜨려라!

이미 상당한 실력자이지만 더 높은 목표를 가진 당신

만점에 가까운 높은 점수를 목표로 하는 사람을 위한 고득점 학습법

법 Basic Grammar부터 꼼꼼히 보아 기본 개념을 확실히 이해한다. 포인트 설명을 꼼꼼히 학습하고 Hackers Practice를 통해 배운 내용을 확실히 이해하도록 한다.

휘 리스트에 실린 단어를 차근차근 반복적으로 암기한다.

해 Hackers Practice의 구문독해를 꼼꼼히 학습한다. 문제를 복습할 때는 문장 구조를 정확히 파악하는 연습을 한다.

해설집
해석과 해설을 꼼꼼히 본다. 해설 내의 전략을 그대로 적용하여 다시 한 번 문제를 푼다.

단어암기장
무료 단어암기 MP3로 반복해 들으며 외운다.

법 하나라도 놓치지 않겠다는 마음가짐으로 문법 포인트를 완벽하게 학습하고, Hackers Practice와 Test를 꼼꼼하게 학습한다. 복습할 때는 모든 문제의 문장 구조를 꼼꼼히 분석해본다.

휘 어휘의 뜻뿐만 아니라 어휘가 문맥 속에서 어떻게 쓰였는지를 확실히 파악하며 어휘를 암기한다.

해 문제풀이 전략을 익히고 적용하는 것을 집중적으로 학습한다. 문제를 복습할 때는 문장 구조에 따라 정확히 해석하는 연습을 한다.

해설집
해석과 해설을 꼼꼼히 본다.

단어암기장
무료 단어암기 MP3로 반복해 들으며 외운다.

법 문법 포인트를 학습한 후 Hackers Practice와 Test로 점검하되, 틀린 문제는 오답 노트를 만들어 수시로 읽는다.

휘 어휘를 빠르게 반복해 암기하고, 시간을 재고 Test를 풀어 실전 감각을 높이는데 집중한다.

해 문제풀이 전략을 익히고 적용하는 것을 집중적으로 학습한다. 문제를 복습할 때는 전략을 제대로 적용했는지 반드시 체크한다.

해설집
해석과 해설을 꼼꼼히 본다. 이때 자신이 사용한 전략과 해설집의 전략을 비교하며 복습하면 효과적이다.

단어암기장
무료 단어암기 MP3로 반복해 들으며 외운다. 하루에 2일 분량을 빨리 한 번 외운 후 다시 한 번 외우는 게 효과적이다.

법 문제를 풀면서 헷갈리거나 생소한 문법을 정리하며 학습한다.

휘 몰랐던 어휘를 빠르게 익히고, 고난도 어휘를 집중 암기한다.

해 문제를 풀 때는 반드시 시간을 재고 빠른 속도로 문제를 푼다. 틀린 문제를 살펴보아 자신이 취약한 부분이 어디인지 파악하고 그 부분에 집중해 학습한다.

해설집
틀린 문제를 모아 오답 노트를 만들어 수시로 읽는다.

단어암기장
모르는 단어만 체크해서 집중 암기한다.

성향별 학습방법

혼자 공부할 때
더 집중이 잘되는 당신이라면!

개별 학습형

교재와 홈페이지 등을 적극적으로 활용하여 실력을 쌓자!
주의! 계획을 세워 공부하고, 한 번 세운 계획은 절대 미루지 말 것

여러 사람과 함께 토론하며 공부할 때
더 이해가 잘되는 당신이라면!

스터디 학습형

팀원끼리 스터디 원칙을 정해 놓고 문제 토론도 하고 시험도 치며
실전 감각을 쌓자!
주의! 너무 긴 잡담으로 인해 휴식 시간이 늘어지지 않도록 할 것

선생님 강의를 들으며 확실하게
공부하는 것을 선호하는 당신이라면!

학원 학습형

학원 강의를 듣고, 반별 게시판을 적극 활용해 공부하며, 선생님과
상호 작용도 하면서 모르는 것을 바로 바로 해결하자!
주의! 학원 수업을 듣는다고 안심하지 말고 반드시 복습할 것.

원하는 시간, 원하는 장소에서
공부하길 원하는 당신이라면!

동영상 학습형

웹사이트 커뮤니티를 적극 활용하자!
주의! 인터넷 접속 시 절대 다른 사이트의 유혹에 빠지지 말 것.

[교]재
날짜별로 계획하여 학습 → Hackers Practice · Test로 확인 및 실전 연습 → 오답 노트 작성하며 복습

HackersTEPS.com
텝스 문제 Q&A에서 궁금증 해결 → 매일 텝스 풀기에서 연습

HackersIngang.com
무료 단어암기 MP3 파일을 다운로드 받아 암기

[교]재
스터디 계획대로 예습 → 팀원끼리 쪽지 시험 (단어, 문제 등) → 시간 재고 Hackers Practice · Test 함께 풀고 정답 확인 → 오답 관련
토론 → 오답 노트 작성하며 복습

HackersTEPS.com
텝스 문제 Q&A에서 궁금증 해결 → 매일 텝스 풀기에서 연습

HackersIngang.com
무료 단어암기 MP3 파일을 다운로드 받아 암기

[교]재
수업에 빠짐없이 참여 → 의문점은 선생님께 질문하여 해결 → 오답 노트 작성하며 복습

Hackers.ac
레벨게시판에서 선생님 및 학생들과 상호작용

HackersTEPS.com
텝스 문제 Q&A에서 궁금증 해결 → 매일 텝스 풀기에서 연습

HackersIngang.com
무료 단어암기 MP3 파일을 다운로드 받아 암기

[교]재
계획대로 학습 → Hackers Practice · Test로 확인 및 실전 연습 → 오답 노트 작성하며 복습

HackersIngang.com
강의를 보며 몰랐던 부분 확실히 학습 → 핵심 내용 노트 정리 → 모르는 부분 게시판에서 질문하기 → 무료 단어암기 MP3 파일을
다운로드 받아 암기

HackersTEPS.com
텝스 문제 Q&A에서 궁금증 해결 → 매일 텝스 풀기에서 연습

학습플랜

■ 순서 학습형 문법→어휘→독해

문법 영역 학습을 통해 영어의 기초를 다진 후, 어휘 영역 학습을 통해 어휘력을 향상시키고, 마지막으로 독해 영역을 완벽 대비한다.

		Day 1	Day 2	Day 3	Day 4	Day 5	Day 6	Day 7
1st Week	문법	진단고사 (p.25-39)	Ch.01-02 (p.46-65)	Ch.03-04 (p.66-81)	Ch.05-06 (p.82-95)	Ch.07-08 (p.96-113)	Ch.09-10 (p.114-129)	복습
2nd Week	문법	Ch.11-12 (p.132-147)	Ch.13-14 (p.148-167)	Ch.15-16 (p.170-185)	Ch.17-18 (p.186-201)	Ch.19-20 (p.204-219)	Ch.21 (p.220-227)	복습
3rd Week	어휘	Ch.01 (p.234-243)	Ch.02-03 (p.244-261)	Ch.04-05 (p.264-279)	Ch.06-07 (p.280-301)	Ch.08-09 (p.302-319)	Ch.10-11 (p.322-339)	복습
4th Week	독해	Ch.01-02 (p.348-365)	Ch.03-04 (p.366-383)	Ch.05-06 (p.384-405)	Ch.07-09 (p.406-425)	Ch.10-11 (p.426-433)	Ch.12-14 (p.434-445)	실전모의고사 (p.447-472)

학습 플랜 이용 Tip

- 4주 완성형의 경우 위의 표를 따르고 8주 완성형은 하루 분량을 2일에 나누어 학습한다.
- 2주 동안 단기로 책을 완성하기를 원하면 2일 분량을 하루에 학습한다.
- 특정 영역에 집중하여 학습하기를 원하면 원하는 영역의 1일 학습 분량을 2일에 나누어 자세히 학습한다.
- 계획한 학습 기간에 맞춰 28일로 구성된 단어암기장을 병행 학습한다.

혼합 학습형 문법 + 어휘 + 독해

매일 세 영역을 고르게 학습하여 실전 감각을 쌓는다.

		Day 1	Day 2	Day 3	Day 4	Day 5	Day 6	Day 7
1st Week	문법	진단고사 (p.25-39)	Ch.01 (p.46-53)	Ch.01 (p.54-55)	Ch.02 (p.58-65)	Ch.03 (p.66-73)	Ch.04 (p.74-81)	복습
	어휘		Ch.01 (p.234-239)	Ch.01 (p.240-243)	Ch.02 (p.244-249)	Ch.02 (p.250-253)	Ch.03 (p.254-257)	
	독해		Ch.01 (p.348-351)	Ch.01 (p.352-357)	Ch.02 (p.358-361)	Ch.02 (p.362-365)	Ch.03 (p.366-373)	
2nd Week	문법	Ch.05 (p.82-89)	Ch.06 (p.90-95)	Ch.07 (p.96-103)	Ch.08 (p.106-113)	Ch.09 (p.114-121)	Ch.10 (p.122-129)	복습
	어휘	Ch.03 (p.258-261)	Ch.04 (p.264-267)	Ch.04 (p.268-271)	Ch.05 (p.272-275)	Ch.05 (p.276-279)	Ch.06 (p.280-285)	
	독해	Ch.04 (p.374-377)	Ch.04 (p.378-383)	Ch.05 (p.384-387)	Ch.05 (p.388-393)	Ch.06 (p.394-397)	Ch.06 (p.398-405)	
3rd Week	문법	Ch.11 (p.132-139)	Ch.12 (p.140-147)	Ch.13 (p.148-157)	Ch.14 (p.158-167)	Ch.15 (p.170-175)	Ch.16 (p.176-183)	복습
	어휘	Ch.06 (p.286-289)	Ch.07 (p.292-295)	Ch.07 (p.296-299)	Ch.07 (p.300-301)	Ch.08 (p.302-305)	Ch.08 (p.306-309)	
	독해	Ch.07 (p.406-409)	Ch.07 (p.410-415)	Ch.08 (p.418-421)	Ch.09 (p.422-425)	Ch.10 (p.426-429)	Ch.11 (p.430-433)	
4th Week	문법	Ch.16 (p.184-185)	Ch.17 (p.186-193)	Ch.18 (p.194-201)	Ch.19 (p.204-211)	Ch.20 (p.212-219)	Ch.21 (p.220-227)	실전모의고사 (p.447-472)
	어휘	Ch.09 (p.310-315)	Ch.09 (p.316-319)	Ch.10 (p.322-327)	Ch.10 (p.328-331)	Ch.11 (p.332-335)	Ch.11 (p.336-339)	
	독해	Ch.12 (p.434-435)	Ch.12 (p.436-437)	Ch.13 (p.438-439)	Ch.13 (p.440-441)	Ch.14 (p.442-443)	Ch.14 (p.444-445)	

학습 플랜 이용 Tip

• 4주 완성형의 경우 위의 표를 따르고 8주 완성형은 하루 분량을 2일에 나누어 학습한다.

• 2주 동안 단기로 책을 완성하기를 원하면 2일 분량을 하루에 학습한다.

• 특정 영역에 집중하여 학습하기를 원하면 원하는 영역의 1일 학습 분량을 2일에 나누어 자세히 학습한다.

• 계획한 학습 기간에 맞춰 28일로 구성된 단어암기장을 병행 학습한다.

혼자 하기 어렵고 막막할 땐?

텝스 진단고사

* 실제 텝스 Reading 시험과 유사한 진단고사를 통해 본인의 실력을 평가해 봅니다.
  그리고 본인에게 맞는 학습방법(p.18)을 확인한 후, 본 교재를 효율적으로 학습합니다.

Part I | Questions 01~05

Choose the best answer for the blank.

01 A: What did the professor say about the exam next week?

B: I can't quite _____. Let me look at my notes.

(a) refresh
(b) recall
(c) repeal
(d) revive

02 A: Do you happen to know where my new DVD is?

B: No, I don't have a _____.

(a) thought
(b) clue
(c) prospect
(d) vision

03 A: I guess I must have _____ to sleep for a few minutes.

B: You actually slept for over an hour.

(a) rushed off
(b) faded out
(c) dropped off
(d) fallen out

04 A: You look a little _____.

B: I'm fine. I just haven't been sleeping well.

(a) over the hill
(b) under the weather
(c) on the cuff
(d) in hot water

05 A: I'd like to meet with the counselor sometime next week.

B: There's a _____ open on Monday at noon that you can take.

(a) gap
(b) slot
(c) crack
(d) section

Part II | Questions 06~15

Choose the best answer for the blank.

6 The new computer monitor can be assembled _____ with this instruction manual.

(a) effortlessly
(b) relentlessly
(c) conversely
(d) relatively

7 Road repairs in areas where people with below-average incomes live are often given _____ priority.

(a) weak
(b) base
(c) short
(d) low

8 Our restaurant _____ the right to remove any patron who is behaving inappropriately and causing a public disturbance.

(a) reserves
(b) reprimands
(c) exempts
(d) speculates

09 Investigative reporters must develop the skill of _____ information from people who are on guard.

(a) eliciting
(b) evoking
(c) provoking
(d) proclaiming

10 Celebrities often _____ products by appearing in advertisements for both print and broadcast media.

(a) endorse
(b) confirm
(c) sanction
(d) attest

11 According to the news, the storm that hit this week brought a massive snowfall that made the highways _____.

(a) attainable
(b) replaceable
(c) impeccable
(d) impassable

12 Until a more feasible plan presents itself, the current project will be _____ for the time being.

(a) baffled
(b) shelved
(c) subdued
(d) stocked

13 Check fraud continues to be one of the most popular ways for people to try to _____ money from banks.

(a) consecrate
(b) obstruct
(c) swindle
(d) deplete

14 After a dictatorship was established, a number of outspoken journalists disappeared and are presumed to have been _____.

(a) distorted
(b) placated
(c) liquidated
(d) depreciated

15 Since smoking has been banned in public buildings, the discussion regarding a smokers' room is _____.

(a) moot
(b) guileless
(c) flimsy
(d) intrepid

Part I | Questions 01~05
Choose the best answer for the blank.

1 A: Samantha seems really pleased.

B: She received nothing but praise _____ her progress report.

(a) at

(b) to

(c) on

(d) with

2 A: I don't think I can finish this pizza.

B: _____. Let's put it in the refrigerator.

(a) Either I can't

(b) Either can't I

(c) Neither I can

(d) Neither can I

3 A: Is it OK if we listen to something else?

B: Sure. I'll listen to _____ you'd prefer.

(a) that

(b) which

(c) whatever

(d) whichever

04 A: The local sculpture show was _____ more disappointing than I expected.

B: That's unfortunate to hear.

(a) so

(b) far

(c) that

(d) very

05 A: Aren't you happy that it's snowing out?

B: I am, but I don't like _____.

(a) how cold gets it during winter

(b) how cold it gets during winter

(c) how it gets cold during winter

(d) how gets it cold during winter

Part II | Questions 06~13
Choose the best answer for the blank.

06 Our eyewear shop will have your glasses
_____ in 24 hours or less.

(a) repair
(b) repairing
(c) repaired
(d) to repair

07 The high school girl's singing was like
_____ of a professional vocalist.

(a) it
(b) one
(c) her
(d) that

08 When I was in college, my siblings and I
_____ always trying to find time to talk
on the phone.

(a) am
(b) are
(c) was
(d) were

09 In 1952, the war between Taiwan and Japan
_____ after both nations signed the
Treaty of Taipei.

(a) resolved
(b) was resolved
(c) has resolved
(d) has been resolved

10 There's always _____
if you need assistance.

(a) for help someone you can reach
(b) someone for help you can reach
(c) help you can reach someone for
(d) someone you can reach for help

11 _____, knights would pay fealty
to a lord or king and serve him loyally.

(a) Medieval times
(b) In medieval time
(c) In medieval times
(d) In the medieval times

12 _____ a valid passport, visitors to
Europe can easily traverse between countries.

(a) Possess
(b) Possessing
(c) Having possessed
(d) To possess

13 New clothing styles _____
as soon as the next designs come along.

(a) can turn almost instantly unfashionable
(b) can almost unfashionable turn instantly
(c) can instantly almost turn unfashionable
(d) can turn unfashionable almost instantly

Part III | Questions 14~16

Identify the option that contains an awkward expression or an error in grammar.

14 (a) A: Is there anything you haven't done that you want to try?

(b) B: If I don't work full-time, I would compose a full symphony.

(c) A: Really? What's keeping you from pursuing that goal now?

(d) B: I need time to focus and concentrate, but I'm just too busy lately.

15 (a) A: Working twelve hours a day is so tiring.

(b) B: It would be wonderful if we had a more flexible schedule.

(c) A: Maybe I should work faster to get my tasks completed sooner.

(d) B: You'd still have the same work hours no matter how hardly you work.

16 (a) In many judicial courts, a suspected criminal is assumed to be innocent until otherwise proven to be guilty. (b) As such, it is common procedure for courts to hire prosecutors who utilizes indisputable evidence. (c) The evidence as well as a convincing argument is necessary to appeal to the sensibilities of a jury. (d) If found guilty, the defendant is convicted and sentenced to a punishment based on the severity of the crime.

Part I | Questions 01~05
Read the passage. Then choose the option that best completes the passage.

01 Doctors are now advocating _____ because bovine and porcine collagen causes allergic reactions in many patients. Collagen is a protein found in the ligament: tendons, cartilage, bones, skin and teeth of mammals. Its strength and elasticity support the bones, skin muscles and blood vessel walls. With age, however, collagen breaks down, a process that is particularly apparent in the skin, which becomes wrinkled and saggy. Doctors perform cosmetic procedures using mammalian collagen to modify the appearance of the skin. But persons with allergies to animal collage suffer from rashes or tissue swelling, which can be fatal.

(a) a transition to plant-based collagen sources
(b) the use of collagen taken from humans
(c) a reduction in cosmetic surgery procedures
(d) collagen as a treatment for allergy sufferers

02 A week-long symposium on digital rights management sponsored by the Electronic Frontier Foundation came to a close earlier today. The organization gathered representatives from the music industry, consumer rights groups, and the legal field to discuss the application of copyright law to digital music. Organizers arranged the symposium to address the rights of consumers with regard to music procured via the Internet. In recent months, several lawsuits have been filed on behalf of music companies who feel that consumers are illegally distributing intellectual property. Music fans, however, assert that

_____.

(a) filing lawsuits against consumers is bad for business
(b) music companies should provide cheaper sources of music
(c) music companies must have their rights respected
(d) transmitting music online is not a criminal act

03 The linguistic roots of the Kusunda language spoken in western Nepal are as yet unknown to researchers. Linguists compared the language to others originating in nearby Tibet and China, but found vastly different grammatical structures. In determining the roots of languages spoken throughout India and Central Asia, no connections could be found between Kusunda and any of these tongues. When examining the features of minor languages and dialects in the regions surrounding Nepal, a common lineage also could not be determined. These findings led linguists to speculate that _____.

(a) most Asian languages came from an undiscovered source
(b) Nepal's linguistic diversity is greater than previously thought
(c) Kusunda developed in isolation from neighboring languages
(d) even languages with the same roots are grammatically different

4 Although language ability typically improves in children over time, an environment rich in social interaction is necessary for its cultivation. Researcher Douglas Candland explored this notion in examining the case of feral children, who were born either in the wild or in confinement. They had experienced no contact with other humans and had no opportunities to communicate orally. Once rescued, these now-older children were still unable to communicate and could never learn to recognize or utter the most basic of commands. This research suggests that _____.

(a) older children are incapable of learning new skills quickly
(b) language ability can deteriorate without practice
(c) feral children are less intelligent than regular children
(d) language ability cannot be acquired without early interaction

5 From our teenage years, we were taught to believe that shaving causes our hair to grow back coarser and thicker than before. On the contrary, individual hairs grow back in the exact same manner after being shaven. They just feel rougher because the corners have not been worn down and softened yet like with longer-exposed hairs. _____, repeated shaving does not actually change the texture of one's hair permanently.

(a) Instead
(b) Thus
(c) Moreover
(d) Particularly

Part II | Question 06
Read the passage. Then identify the option that does NOT belong.

---

6 Herodotus was the first writer in the Western literary tradition to publish a book of history. (a) His main work was entitled *The Histories*, and was an account of the battles that took place during the Greco-Persian Wars in the fifth century BC. (b) As modern historians compare his work with other written sources and archaeological data, the accuracy of Herodotus' version is being disputed. (c) At present, scholars consider Peter Green's 1998 book to be the definitive historical record of the battles between Greece and Persia. (d) However, Herodotus' version is still widely read because of his interesting anecdotes and knack for storytelling.

Part III | Questions 07~13

Read the passage and the question. Then choose the option that best answers the question.

07 *Watch Mr. Wizard*, first aired in 1951, was one of the pioneering children's educational programs on television. The show featured easily replicable science experiments that kids could safely conduct at home. In all, 541 episodes were aired before the program was cancelled in 1965. After an extended hiatus, a Canadian-produced version called *Mr. Wizard's World*, featuring the same host, Don Herbert, ran until 2000. Even after being taken off the air, the show is fondly remembered by legions of adults who watched it during their youth.

Q   What is the passage mainly about?

   (a) The inception of educational television programming
   (b) The former popularity of televised science shows
   (c) The extensive history of the *Mr. Wizard* television series
   (d) The influence of *Mr. Wizard* on children's education

08 Personal counseling has grown much more quickly as a psychological discipline than has psychoanalysis. Counseling has a much larger scope, bringing together parts of many different fields of study and research. Counseling is also advocated by a majority of licensed psychologists whereas psychoanalysis is only advocated by a handful of doctors. A third reason for the growth of personal counseling is that the treatment course is much shorter than that required for psychoanalysis, which is usually long-term. These factors ensure that personal counseling, unlike psychoanalysis, will continue to expand.

Q   What is the main idea of this passage?

   (a) Psychoanalysis has far greater potential than personal counseling.
   (b) The scope of personal counseling indicates the need for more research.
   (c) Personal counseling is developing more quickly than psychoanalysis.
   (d) Psychologists believe that the field of psychoanalysis has not matured.

09 In our nation's prison system, the inmates' dealings with other prisoners and their interaction with guards make their surroundings as bad as or worse than the outside environment that led to their incarceration. Essentially, what is propagated is a culture of violence and fear. Accordingly, introducing an environment where respect is encouraged between prisoners and guards without resorting to authority and intimidation would break this cycle. Giving inmates an opportunity for individual growth through enrichment classes or meaningful work assignments would help as well.

Q   Which of the following is correct according to the passage?

   (a) The prison environment is better than the surroundings outside the prison.
   (b) Prisons offer those incarcerated a chance for personal improvement.
   (c) Encouraging positive interaction in prisons would improve conditions for inmates.
   (d) Eliminating violence and fear is the main goal of the prison.

Sign up to Finance Secure's Pension Fund Today

It's time to start investing in your retirement. With Finance Secure's range of pension investment packages, you can secure your future prosperity.

- Make your money work for you in a tax-favored retirement account that invests your savings.
- Only pay income tax on the money when you withdraw it after retirement. (without paying capital gains tax)
- Money can be invested in stocks, bonds, and mutual funds of your choosing.
- Split your money between various investment options to increase your profits.
- Get expert advice from Finance Secure's team of investment specialists.
- If you maintain the fund until the age of 60, you are guaranteed tax-exemption. (cashing out before 60 incurs a 10 percent penalty and capital gains tax)
- Build a nest egg for your family's future and rest easy with Finance Secure.

Visit *www.financesecure.com* for more information.

Q   Which of the following is correct according to the advertisement?

(a) Money can be divided between different opportunities for investment.
(b) All participants pay a 10 percent fee when removing their money.
(c) The Finance Secure pension fund is completely tax free.
(d) Capital gains tax will be applied to all investments at withdrawal.

The inclement weather has caused all airlines to suspend operations today. If you were unable to make your flight, the following steps should aid you in flying out at the earliest time possible. Be sure to inform your outbound airline of your situation by contacting a representative in the departure lounge. Also, keep a cell phone handy to ensure that you can be reached at any time. Avoid leaving the airport for the night if at all possible; airlines will assign early-morning openings on a first-come-first-served basis.

Q   What should those with canceled flights do?

(a) Stay apprised of changing weather conditions
(b) Remain within the confines of the airport overnight
(c) Contact airline representatives by cell phone
(d) Wait to be assigned to a flight later today

12

Dear Ms. Ortiz:

Our promotions department is delighted to reply to your letter, especially after having read about your dedicated patronage of our store over the last fifteen years. However, it is with regret that we inform you that the coupon you included cannot be used to obtain a tablet PC 9.2 free of charge. It is from a previous promotion and is no longer valid. Nonetheless, please keep in mind that our store will be holding a discount sale next week, and tablet PCs will be marked down well over fifty percent. If you have any further inquiries, feel free to write us again.

Sincerely,
Paula Morelli
Top Choice Electronics

Q   Which of the following is correct according to the letter?

(a) Ms. Morelli will redeem Ms. Ortiz's coupon for a tablet PC.
(b) Ms. Morelli will use the coupon in next week's sale.
(c) Ms. Ortiz's promotional coupon has already expired.
(d) Ms. Ortiz recently began patronizing the store.

13 Parliament has asked some of the nation's top scientists to determine whether mobile phones pose a health hazard to children who regularly use them. For several years, parents have lauded the safety aspect of the technology that keeps them connected to their kids at all times. Nevertheless, studies have found that mobile phones may not be so harmless, providing evidence that their use precipitates threefold increase in the brain's exposure to high-frequency radio waves, which concerns scientists.

Q   Which statement would the writer most likely agree with?

(a) The risk posed by mobile phones to young children is not certain.
(b) Mobile phones is the best way for parents to check on their children.
(c) Both mobile phones and regular phones release radio waves.
(d) High-frequency radio waves makes mobile phones unsafe for children.

Part IV | Questions 14~19

Read the passage and the questions. Then choose the option that best answers each question.

uestions 14-15

Hazardous Air in Beijing

Beijing has been notorious for its polluted air for many years, with skies regularly blackened by smog in what has become known as an "airpocalypse." This has not only tarnished the Chinese capital's image abroad, but has led to a serious public health problem, as the PM 2.5 particles that make up the majority of the pollution are extremely hazardous. These particles are much smaller than other forms of pollution, and can therefore bypass the respiratory system's defenses and cause health problems ranging from asthma to heart attacks and lung cancer.

In response to this problem, the Chinese government has taken a tough stance, vowing to clear Beijing's skies in the next few years. To do so, it has set strict targets for cutting the major source of pollution in the region, the burning of coal for power. The government has forced millions of homes and businesses to switch from coal to clean-burning natural gas, while also investing billions in clean energy. Whether these efforts will make the necessary difference to Beijing's smog-filled skies remains to be seen.

. Q: What is the main topic of the passage?

(a) Government attempts to lower air pollution throughout China
(b) Effects of Beijing's pollution problem and measures to reduce it
(c) Impacts of extensive air pollution on the respiratory system
(d) Beijing's international image and public health in the city

. Q: What has been done to reduce the burning of coal?

(a) Strict targets have been established for the use of clean energy.
(b) Power plants have been forced to switch to alternative forms of energy.
(c) The number of cars on the roads in Beijing has been significantly reduced.
(d) Companies have been persuaded to get their energy from cleaner sources.

WE'RE HIRING
JUNIOR GRAPHIC DESIGNERS

We're on the lookout for creative Junior Graphic Designers to join our print and digital design team. Experience in a design firm is preferred(including internship or contract roles). Training in digital design is essential. Please submit a résumé, cover letter, and two references(one personal, one professional), along with your portfolio, to jobs@designcity.com before the 14th of December.

- The position involves designing websites, posters, online advertisements, book covers, and more.
- Clients include small businesses in the Denver area as well as some major conglomerates.
- The ability to learn new skills quickly is vital. We are a fast-moving company where knowledge of cutting-edge design practices is expected.
- Working remotely is possible, but at least two days per week must be spent in-office. Hours are 9 to 5, Monday to Friday but expect to do overtime and some weekend work. Following a three-week probation period, 20 days of vacation per calendar year will be available.

16. Q: Which of the following is correct?

(a) Applicants must have experience in a graphic design company.
(b) The completion of job-related training courses is a prerequisite.
(c) All of the company's clients are located in Denver.
(d) The portfolio must include at least two pieces of digital design.

17. Q: Which of the following is NOT required for the new Junior Graphic Designers?

(a) They should design a wide selection of requested promotional material.
(b) They should be in the office for a minimum of three days per week.
(c) They are expected to learn a range of new abilities as they work.
(d) They must occasionally do some work on Saturdays or Sundays.

In 1947, the Indian Independence Act finally liberated India from British rule. It was the culmination of a long fight for independence, but it set off a wave of intense sectarian violence and created a regional dispute that continues to this day.

During the fight for independence, two political groups were at the forefront: the Indian National Congress, represented by Gandhi and Nehru, and the All-India Muslim League, led by Muhammad Ali Jinnah. While the former campaigned for a unified India, the latter demanded a completely separate Muslim-majority country. Eventually, the discord between the two resulted in the establishment of a border between Hindu-dominated India and the new Muslim country of Pakistan. The partition exacerbated preexisting tensions between Muslims and Hindus throughout the subcontinent, sparking widespread violence.

Ever since the division, conflict has repeatedly broken out between India and Pakistan. Much of the bloodshed has been caused by the location of the border, which neither side had fully agreed on before it was established. One of the main issues dividing the two countries is the status of Kashmir, historically dominated by Muslims but made part of India due to the partition. As Kashmir reveals, the problems arising from the placement of the border are far from resolved.

18. Q: Which of the following is correct according to the passage?

(a) Jinnah objected to the establishment of a Muslim country.
(b) Gandhi and Nehru were opposed to the division of India.
(c) The partition of India was followed by the Indian Independence Act.
(d) The Congress Party feared the institution of Hindu dominance.

19. Q: Which statement would the writer most likely agree with?

(a) The location of the border was not given enough consideration.
(b) The violence over partition was inevitable given the sectarian tensions.
(c) The establishment of Pakistan by the British was a costly mistake.
(d) The Kashmir dispute is evidence that the partition was necessary.

시험에 나올 문제를 미리 풀어보고 싶을 땐?

해커스텝스(HackersTEPS.com)에서
텝스 적중예상특강 보기!

GRAMMAR

GRAMMAR

1 텝스 문법 영역의 특징

1. 짧은 시간 안에 풀어내는 문법 지식을 평가한다.

텝스 어휘&문법 영역은 25분 동안 60문제(어휘 30문제, 문법 30문제)를 풀어내도록 요구한다. 문법 영역은 Part 상대적으로 길이가 긴 지문이 등장하는 것을 고려하여 약 15분의 시간을 분배하여 푸는 것이 권장된다. 짧은 시간에 은 문제를 풀어내야 하기 때문에 문법·어법상의 옳고 그름을 감각적으로 판단할 수 있어야 한다. 따라서 문법 지식의 순 암기보다는 예문을 통해 문법의 원리가 어떻게 표현되는지에 유의하며 학습하도록 한다.

2. 후반의 파트로 갈수록 난이도가 높아진다.

Part 3은 여러 문장으로 이루어진 대화나 지문의 의미를 파악하면서, 동시에 문법·어법적으로 틀린 부분을 찾아야 기 때문에 Part 1과 Part 2에 비해 난이도가 높다. 따라서 상대적으로 짧아서 읽기 쉽고 난이도가 낮은 Part 1과 Pa 를 신속하게 풀어 Part 3을 풀 시간을 확보해두도록 한다.

3. 일상생활, 캠퍼스, 직장, 시사, 학술 등 다양하고 폭넓은 주제로 출제된다.

비즈니스 같은 특정 분야를 다루는 다른 시험과는 달리, 텝스 문법은 출제 토픽의 범위가 매우 넓다. 일상생활, 캠 직장 생활은 물론 시사, 학술에 관련된 주제까지 다루기 때문에 다양한 어휘와 상황에 익숙해지도록 한다.

4. 여러 가지 문법 사항을 종합해서 답을 도출해야 하는 문제가 다수 출제된다.

텝스 문법에는 여러 가지 문법 사항을 동시에 고려해서 답을 골라야 하는 문제가 다수 출제되기 때문에 단편적인 지식을 쌓는 것만으로는 고득점을 얻을 수 없다. 따라서 다양한 문법의 상관관계에 유의하여 종합적인 학습을 하도록

Example

What _____ is that construction on the bridge requires the underpass to be closed of

(a) need to take into account
(b) needs to be taken into account
(c) is needed to take into account
(d) is needed to be taken into account

▶ 동사 need의 단수·복수와 능동태·수동태를 구별할 수 있는가와 to부정사구(to take into account)의 능동형·수동형을 구별할 는가를 함께 묻는다.

5. 문장 구조와 어순에 대해 묻는다.

보기에 들어갈 하나의 단어를 고르도록 하는 다른 시험과 달리 텝스 문법 영역에서는 괄호 안에 문장 전체나 여러 단어를 한꺼번에 채우도록 하는 문제가 출제되기 때문에 문장의 구조를 파악하여 적절한 어순으로 이루어진 보기를 고 있어야 한다. 따라서 다양한 길이와 어휘로 이루어진 문장을 분석하는 학습을 통해 문장의 구조를 보는 눈을 기르도록

Example

_____ by the insurance agents.

(a) Into consideration fully was the damage taken
(b) Consideration was fully taken into the damage
(c) The damage taken was fully consideration into
(d) The damage was fully taken into consideration

▶ 주어(The damage), 동사(was taken into consideration), 부사(fully)를 문장 구조에 맞는 어순으로 채울 수 있는가를 묻는다.

6. 숙어, 관용표현, 구어체 표현을 묻는다.

텝스 문법은 통째로 암기해야만 알 수 있는 숙어, 관용표현을 물으며, 대화로 구성된 Part 1의 경우 대화 상황에서만 쓰이는 구어체 표현도 출제된다. 따라서 자주 쓰이는 이러한 표현들을 암기해두도록 한다.

Example

A: I decided to accept the realtor's invitation to visit the house in order to see if _____.
B: Can I join you when you go there?

(a) it is worth buying
(b) it is worth to buy
(c) it being worthy to buying
(d) buying is to be worthy of

▶ 동명사구 관련 관용표현인 be worth -ing를 알고 있는가를 묻는다.

텝스 문법 출제 유형

텝스 문법에 나오는 문법 문제는 크게 문장 성분, 동사구, 준동사구, 품사, 접속사와 절, 어순과 특수구문으로 유형을 나눌수 있다. 「해커스 텝스 Reading」 문법 영역에서는 이러한 문제 유형을 여섯 가지 섹션으로 분류하여 세부적인 문법 사항과 풀이 전략을 제시한다.

문장 성분 | 주어, 동사, 목적어, 보어, 수식어 자리에 올 수 있는 것에 대해 묻는다.

동사구 | 동사의 종류, 조동사, 수, 시제, 태, 가정법 등 동사의 다양한 변화와 쓰임에 대해 묻는다.

준동사구 | to부정사, 동명사, 분사의 역할과 형태, 의미상 주어, 준동사구 사이의 쓰임 구별 등에 대해 묻는다.

품사 | 명사와 관사, 대명사, 형용사와 부사, 전치사의 역할과 관련 표현, 각 품사의 상관관계에 대해 묻는다.

접속사와 절 | 등위 접속사와 상관 접속사, 종속 접속사의 역할과 쓰임, 종속 접속사가 이끄는 명사절, 관계절, 부사절의 역할과 구조에 대해 묻는다.

어순과 특수구문 문장 | 구조에 따른 어순과 비교구문, 생략·대용 / 도치 구문의 형태와 관련 표현에 대해 묻는다.

텝스 문법 출제 비율

텝스 문법 영역의 출제 비율을 「해커스 텝스 Reading」에서 제시한 문법 사항으로 분류하면 다음과 같다.

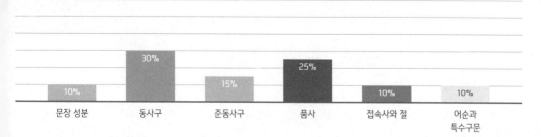

문장 성분	동사구	준동사구	품사	접속사와 절	어순과 특수구문
10%	30%	15%	25%	10%	10%

혼자 하기 어렵고 막막할 땐?

Section 1 문장성분

Chapter 01 주어·동사 / 목적어·보어 / 수식어

CHAPTER **01** 주어 · 동사 / 목적어 · 보어 / 수식어

BASIC GRAMMAR 고수로 가는 첫 걸음

1 동사는 문장에서 표현하는 동작이나 상태를, 주어는 그 동작이나 상태의 주체(누가 / 무엇이)를 가리키는 말로, 문장에 없어서는 안 될 필수 성분이다.

Tom smiled. Tom은 미소 지었다.
주어   동사

'미소 지었다'는 동작을 묘사하고 있는 smiled가 이 문장의 동사이다. 그리고 'smiled'한 주체, 즉 누가 미소 지었는지의 '누가'에 해당하는 Tom이 이 문장의 주어이다. 이와 같이 필수 성분인 주어와 동사가 모두 있어야 바른 문장이 된다.

하나의 주어와 하나의 동사가 이루는 단위를 '절'이라고 하며, 절[주어 + 동사]과 절[주어 + 동사] 사이에는 접속사가 와야 한다.

Tom smiled when he saw me. Tom은 나를 보았을 때 미소 지었다.
절1[주어1 + 동사1] 접속사 절2[주어2 + 동사2]

절1[주어1 + 동사1](Tom smiled)과 절2[주어2 + 동사2](he saw)가 한 문장 안에 접속사 없이 나란히 올 수 없다. 절과 절은 접속사(when)로 연결되어야 한다.

2 목적어는 동사의 대상을 나타내고, 보어는 주어나 목적어를 보충해주는 말로, 문장에 없어서는 안 될 필수 성분이다.

I like **music**. 나는 음악을 좋아한다.
타동사 목적어

It is **a chocolate cake**. 그것은 초콜릿 케익이다.
주어   주격보어

She made **me happy**. 그녀는 나를 행복하게 해주었다.
      목적어 목적격보어

첫 번째 문장에서 동사 like의 대상인 music이 이 문장의 목적어이다. 목적어 music이 없다면 무엇을 좋아하는지 알 수 없어 의미가 완전하지 않으므로 틀린 문장이 되며, 이렇게 목적어를 반드시 필요로 하는 동사를 타동사라 한다. 두 번째 문장에서 a chocolate cake은 주어(It)를 보충하는 주격 보어이며, 세 번째 문장의 happy는 목적어(me)를 보충하는 목적격 보어이다. 이 보어들이 없다면 It이 '무엇인지', me가 '어떠한지' 알 수 없어 틀린 문장이 된다. 이렇게 몇몇 동사들은 보어를 반드시 필요로 한다.

3 수식어는 문장에 부가적인 의미를 더해주며, 문장에 없어도 되는 부가 성분이다.

Ben is sitting on the bench. Ben이 벤치에 앉아 있다.
            수식어

주어와 동사 Ben is sitting은 문장에 없어서는 안 될 필수 성분이다. 수식어 on the bench는 필수 성분으로 이루어진 문장(Ben이 앉아 있다)에 '어디', 즉 장소에 대한 부가적인 의미를 더해주고 있다. 수식어 on the bench 없이 Ben is sitting만으로도 바른 문장이 되므로, on the bench와 같은 성분을 '수식어 거품'이라고 부르기도 한다.

1 주어 자리

주어 자리에 올 수 있는 것은 명사 역할을 하는 것들이다.

명사구	Many people **protest** animal testing by drug companies. 많은 사람들이 제약 회사에 의한 동물 실험에 반대한다.
대명사	He **got** his eyes checked last week. 그는 지난주에 눈을 검사받았다.
동명사구	Drinking a glass of milk before bed **is** a good way to sleep soundly. 자기 전에 우유 한 잔을 마시는 것은 숙면을 취하는 좋은 방법이다.
to부정사구	To become a leader **is not easy.** 지도자가 되는 것은 쉽지 않다.
명사절	What the singer wants most **is to be famous.** 그 가수가 가장 원하는 것은 유명해지는 것이다.

※ to부정사구가 주어 자리에 오는 경우는 많지 않다. to부정사구는 주로 가짜 주어 it에 대한 진짜 주어로 쓰인다. 이에 대해서는 이 Chapter의 06 '가짜 주어 구문과 명령문'에서 자세히 다룬다.

주어 자리에 동사는 올 수 없다.

~~Imagine~~ often helps children to make up stories. 상상력은 종종 아이들이 이야기를 지어내도록 돕는다.
Imagination

➡ 주어 자리에는 동사(Imagine)가 아니라 명사(Imagination)가 와야 한다.

주어는 뒤에 오는 분사구나 관계절 등의 수식을 받을 수 있다.

The award <u>given to the winner</u> includes a prize of 2,000 dollars. 우승자에게 주어지는 상은 2,000달러의 상금을 포함한다.
　주어　　　　분사구

➡ 주어(The award)가 뒤에 나온 분사구(given to the winner)의 수식을 받고 있다.

The guests <u>whom Erica invited</u> flew in for the wedding. Erica가 초대한 손님들은 결혼식을 위해 비행기를 타고 왔다.
　주어　　　　관계절

➡ 주어(The guests)가 뒤에 나온 관계절(whom Erica invited)의 수식을 받고 있다.

※ 텝스에서는 주어뿐만 아니라 주어를 뒤에서 수식하는 분사나 관계절까지 함께 묻는 문제가 주로 출제된다. 분사와 관계절에 대해서는 각각 Chapter 10과 Chapter 17에서 자세히 다룬다.

전치사구와 같은 수식어는 문장의 맨 앞에 있어도 주어가 아니다.

Of the eggs, some had cracks in their shells. 달걀 중 몇 개는 껍질에 금이 가 있었다.
　전치사구　　주어

➡ Of the eggs는 주어가 될 수 없는 전치사구이다. 이 문장의 주어는 대명사 some이다.

텝스 실전 문제

텝스 문제 이렇게 나온다

명사구 주어와 이를 수식하는 수식어를 함께 채우는 문제가 주로 나온다.

Part II

1. _____ suitable for the governorship didn't run for the election.

(a) To the politician consider
(b) The politician considered
(c) Consider the politician
(d) Considering the politician

2. _____ at Salvatore's Restaurant on a regular basis are wealthy.

(a) Who dine most customers
(b) Most customers who dine
(c) Most dines customers
(d) Of most customers dining

정답 p.9

1 동사 자리에 올 수 있는 것은 '동사'나 '조동사 + 동사'이다.

Carrie <u>completed</u> her assignment. Carrie는 숙제를 마쳤다.
　　　　동사

Because Carrie <u>must complete</u> her assignment, she can't come. Carrie는 숙제를 마쳐야 하기 때문에, 올 수 없다.
　　　　　　　　조동사 + 동사

2 동사 자리에 '동사원형 + -ing'나 'to + 동사원형'과 같은 형태는 올 수 없다.

Most students ~~regarding~~ Timothy as their leader. 대부분의 학생들이 Timothy를 그들의 리더로 여긴다.
　　　　　　　regard

▶ 동사 자리에는 '동사원형 + -ing'인 regarding이 아니라 동사 regard가 와야 한다.

Muriel was a teacher before she ~~to become~~ a writer. Muriel은 작가가 되기 전에는 선생님이었다.
　　　　　　　　　　　　　　became

▶ 동사 자리에는 'to + 동사원형'인 to become이 아니라 동사 became이 와야 한다.

※ '동사원형 + -ing'(동명사/현재분사)나 'to + 동사원형'(to부정사)을 준동사라고 부르는데, 준동사는 동사가 아닌 명사, 형용사, 부사 등의 역할을 한다. 준동사에 대해서는 Chapter 08, 09, 10에서 자세히 다룬다.

3 동사 자리에는 수, 시제, 태가 적절한 동사가 와야 한다.

Members of this fitness center ~~has~~ the privilege to use all the facilities. 이 헬스 클럽의 회원들은 모든 시설을 이용할 혜택을 가진다.
　주어　　　　　　　　　　have

▶ 주어(Members)가 복수이므로, 단수 동사인 has가 아니라 복수 동사인 have가 와야 한다.

The concert last night ~~is~~ fantastic. 어젯밤 콘서트는 환상적이었다.
　　　　시간 표현　was

▶ 과거를 나타내는 시간 표현(last night)이 있으므로, 현재 시제인 is가 아니라 과거 시제인 was가 와야 한다.

Photographic film ~~invented~~ by George Eastman in 1888. 사진 필름은 1888년에 George Eastman에 의해 발명되었다.
　　　　　　　was invented

▶ 주어인 Photographic film이 George Eastman에 의해 발명되었다는 수동의 의미이므로, 능동태인 invented가 아니라 수동태인 was invented가 와야 한다.

※ 동사의 수, 시제, 태에 대해서는 Chapter 04, 05, 06에서 자세히 다룬다.

☑ 텝스 실전 문제　　　　　　　　　　　　　　　　　　텝스 문제 이렇게 나온다

| 접속사 뒤의 동사 자리를 채우는 문제가 주로 나온다.
| 동사가 될 수 없는 형태의 보기를 제거한 후, 수, 시제, 태가 맞는 동사를 채우는 문제가 주로 나온다.

Part I

1. A: Michael decided to come to the party after all.
　 B: Miranda will be surprised if he _____ up.

　 (a) show　　　　　(b) shows
　 (c) to show　　　 (d) showing

Part II

2. After he _____ an Academy Award, the former comedy actor only accepted roles in dramas.

　 (a) win　　　　　(b) wins
　 (c) to win　　　 (d) won

정답

03 목적어 자리

목적어 자리에 올 수 있는 것은 명사 역할을 하는 것들이다.

명사구	Some Indian tribes use local plants for dyeing cloth. 어떤 인디언 부족들은 천을 염색하기 위해 토착 식물을 이용한다.
대명사	Christine invited us to her new office. Christine은 우리를 그녀의 새 사무실로 초대했다.
동명사구	He loves cooking for his family. 그는 가족을 위해 요리하는 것을 좋아한다.
to부정사구	The baby suddenly started to cry. 아기가 갑자기 울기 시작했다.
명사절	I heard that he retired last year. 나는 그가 작년에 은퇴했다고 들었다.

※ 목적어 자리에 to부정사나 동명사가 올 때는 동사에 따라 목적어를 결정해야 한다. to부정사나 동명사를 목적어로 취하는 동사에 대해서는 Chapter 08, 09에서 자세히 다룬다.

목적어 자리에 동사는 올 수 없다.

I really hate ~~bring~~ up this issue. 나는 이 문제에 대해 이야기 꺼내는 것을 정말 싫어한다.
　　　　　　bringing / to bring

▶ 목적어 자리에는 동사(bring)가 아니라 동명사(bringing)나 to부정사(to bring)가 와야 한다.

to부정사구나 that절 목적어가 목적격 보어와 함께 오면, 진짜 목적어를 목적격 보어 뒤로 보내고, 목적어가 있던 자리에 가짜 목적어 it을 써야 한다.

Laptops make to work almost anywhere possible. [×]
　　　　　　목적어 (to부정사구)　　　　　목적격보어

Laptops make it possible to work almost anywhere. [○] 노트북 컴퓨터는 거의 모든 곳에서 일하는 것을 가능하게 한다.
　　　　가짜목적어 목적격보어　　　　진짜목적어

▶ 목적어가 to부정사구(to work almost anywhere)이므로 목적격 보어(possible) 뒤로 가고, 원래 목적어 자리에 가짜 목적어 it을 써야 한다.

I thought that she didn't go to the dance weird. [×]
　　　　　목적어 (that절)　　　　　　목적격보어

I thought it weird that she didn't go to the dance. [○] 나는 그녀가 댄스 파티에 가지 않은 것을 이상하다고 생각했다.
　　　가짜목적어 목적격보어　　　　진짜목적어

▶ 목적어가 that절(that she didn't go to the dance)이므로 목적격 보어(weird) 뒤로 가고, 원래 목적어 자리에 가짜 목적어 it을 써야 한다.

☑ 텝스 실전 문제

텝스 문제 이렇게 나온다

동명사나 to부정사 목적어를 채우는 문제가 주로 나온다.
가짜 목적어와 목적격 보어, 진짜 목적어를 함께 채우는 문제가 주로 나온다.

Part I

1. A: What have you been saving all that money for?
　B: I want _____ a car to make the commute
　　to work quicker.

　(a) buy　　　　　　(b) have bought
　(c) to buy　　　　　(d) bought

Part II

2. The chief of police found _____
　the only one unaware of the change in protocol.

　(a) being embarrassing it
　(b) embarrassing to be
　(c) it embarrassing to be
　(d) to be embarrassing

정답 p.9

1 보어 자리에 올 수 있는 것은 명사 또는 형용사 역할을 하는 것들이다.

- **명사 역할을 하는 것**

  명사구   Doll Biz quickly became the world's best toy maker.   Doll Biz는 빠르게 세계 최고의 장난감 생산업체가 되었다.

  동명사구   His hobby is listening to opera at home.   그의 취미는 집에서 오페라를 듣는 것이다.

  to부정사구   What I need is to take a good break.   내게 필요한 것은 잘 쉬는 것이다.

  명사절   The important thing is that you did your best.   중요한 것은 네가 최선을 다했다는 것이다.

- **형용사 역할을 하는 것**

  형용사   Tim was upset about losing money in the stock market.   Tim은 주식 시장에서 돈을 잃은 것에 속상했다.

  분사   Daisy's younger brother always makes her worried.   Daisy의 남동생은 항상 그녀를 걱정하게 만든다.

  ※ 보어 자리에 분사가 오는 경우 현재분사인지 과거분사인지 결정해야 한다. 현재분사/과거분사 구별에 대해서는 Chapter 10에서 자세히 다룬다.

2 보어 자리에 동사나 부사는 올 수 없다.

I kept ~~wait~~ for you to come.   나는 네가 오기를 계속 기다렸다.
    waiting

▶ 보어 자리에는 동사(wait)가 아니라 형용사 역할을 하는 분사(waiting)가 와야 한다.

Ted made his teacher ~~angrily~~.   Ted는 선생님을 화나게 했다.
        angry

▶ 보어 자리에는 부사(angrily)가 아니라 형용사(angry)가 와야 한다.

3 주격 보어를 갖는 동사, 목적격 보어를 갖는 동사

주격 보어를 갖는 동사	be ~이다. ~이 되다 smell ~한 냄새가 나다 look / seem / appear ~처럼 보이다	go ~해지다. ~하러 가다 sound ~하게 들리다	keep 계속해서 ~하다 taste ~한 맛이 나다 become / get / grow / turn ~이 되다. ~해지다	remain 여전히 ~이다
목적격 보어를 갖는 동사	make ~을 –로 만들다	find ~이 –임을 알게 되다	leave ~을 –한 채로 남겨두다	keep ~을 계속 –하게 하다

I got lost on the way home.   나는 집에 오는 길에 길을 잃었다.
   주격보어

The comedian kept the audience laughing throughout the performance.   그 코미디언은 공연 내내 관객을 계속 웃게 했다.
               목적격보어

☑ 텝스 실전 문제   텝스 문제 이렇게 나온다

| 형용사와 부사를 구별하여 보어 자리를 채우는 문제가 주로 나온다.
| 현재분사와 과거분사를 구별하여 보어 자리를 채우는 문제가 주로 나온다.

Part II

1. Despite the rain and sleet caused by the hurricane, construction on the new library remains _____.

   (a) persist   (b) persistent
   (c) persistently   (d) most persistently

Part I

2. A: I heard that Nancy is behind schedule.
   B: Yes, I found her _____ overtime last night.

   (a) work   (b) to working
   (c) working   (d) worked

정답 p.

5 수식어 거품 자리

수식어 거품 자리에 올 수 있는 것들

전치사구	**At the library,** he got the very book. 도서관에서, 그는 바로 그 책을 구했다.
to부정사구	We turned away **to protect our eyes.** 우리는 눈을 보호하기 위해 고개를 돌렸다.
분사구(문)	The food **delivered from the deli** was too expensive. 그 식당에서 배달된 음식은 너무 비쌌다.
관계절	I remember one professor **who taught rather strictly.** 나는 꽤 엄격하게 가르쳤던 한 교수님을 기억한다.
부사절	**Before I left for work,** I went out for a jog. 일하러 가기 전에, 나는 조깅을 하러 나갔다.

※ 수식어 거품 자리에 분사구(문)이 오는 경우 현재분사가 올지 과거분사가 올지 결정해야 한다. 현재분사 / 과거분사 구별에 대해서는 Chapter 10에서 자세히 다룬다.

수식어 거품 자리에 동사는 올 수 없다.

~~Finds~~ himself lost, he needed to ask a stranger for directions. 길을 잃었기 때문에, 그는 낯선 사람에게 길을 물어야 했다.
Finding

▶ 수식어 거품 자리에는 필수 성분인 동사(Finds)가 아니라 분사(Finding)가 와야 한다.

필수 성분을 모두 갖춘 완전한 절의 앞뒤에는 접속사로 연결된 절이나, 수식어 거품만 더해질 수 있다.

The teenager stands more than six feet tall, ~~he surpasses~~ the height of both of his parents.
and he surpasses / surpassing

그 십대는 키가 6피트가 넘고, 그의 부모님보다 크다.

▶ 주어(The teenager)와 동사(stands)를 모두 갖춘 완전한 절에, 또 다른 절(he surpasses)이 바로 올 수 없다. 접속사(and)를 포함한 and he surpasses
가 오거나, 수식어 거품 형태인 surpassing이 와야 한다.

수식어 거품이 오는 위치

●+ 주어 + 동사	Even with the bad weather, the game was not cancelled. 나쁜 날씨에도 불구하고, 경기는 취소되지 않았다.
	수식어거품 (전치사구) / 주어 / 동사
주어 + ● + 동사	The curtains lining the windows should be cleaned yearly. 창에 다는 커튼은 해마다 세탁되어야 한다.
	주어 / 수식어거품 (분사구) / 동사
주어 + 동사 + ●	Melissa bought a new coat although it was expensive. Melissa는 비록 비쌌지만 새 코트를 샀다.
	주어 / 동사 / 목적어 / 수식어거품 (부사절)

수식어 거품 자리 찾는 순서

Companies advertising on TV must pay a commercial fee. TV에 광고를 하는 회사들은 광고료를 지불해야 한다.
　2) 주어　　3) 수식어거품 (분사구)　1) 동사

▶ 먼저 문장의 동사(must pay)를 찾은 후 주어(Companies)를 찾는다. 그 다음에 수식어 거품(advertising on TV)을 파악한다.

☑ 텝스 실전 문제

텝스 문제 이렇게 나온다

분사구(문) 수식어 거품을 채우는 문제가 주로 나온다.

Part I

1. A: How did you get all wet?
   B: _____ the street, I tripped and fell
   in a puddle.

   (a) Runs across　　(b) Running across
   (c) Ran across　　(d) I ran across

Part II

2. Trichomes are the fine hairs _____ the
   exterior of certain plants like cacti.

   (a) covers　　(b) has covered
   (c) to covering　　(d) covering

정답 p.9

06 가짜 주어 구문과 명령문

1 가짜 주어 there와 it구문

- 가짜 주어 there는 '~가 있다'를 뜻하며 'there + 동사(be, remain, exist …) + 진짜 주어(명사)' 형태를 이룬다.

There has been controversy over cloning organisms for years. 생명체를 복제하는 것에 대한 논쟁이 수년간 있어왔다.
가짜주어   동사   진짜주어 (명사)

There remains enough space for the sofa in my room. 내 방에는 그 소파를 놓을 충분한 공간이 남아 있다.
가짜주어   동사   진짜주어 (명사구)

- it은 to부정사구, that절 같은 긴 주어를 대신해서 쓰인다. 이때, it을 '가주어', 긴 주어를 '진주어'라고 한다.

It is important to get along with your classmates. 반 친구와 잘 지내는 것은 중요하다.
가짜주어   진짜주어 (to부정사구)

It is widely believed that Native Americans had supernatural powers.
가짜주어   진짜주어 (that절)
미국 원주민들이 초자연적인 능력을 지녔었다는 것이 널리 믿어진다.

- it은 사람/사물, 시간/장소 등을 강조할 때 that과 함께 쓰여, 'it – that 강조구문'을 만든다.

It was Jonathan that broke the vase. 꽃병을 깨뜨린 사람은 바로 Jonathan이었다.
강조된 내용 (사람)

It was in the eighteenth century that humans first succeeded in flying. 인간이 처음으로 하늘을 나는 데 성공한 것은 18세기였다.
강조된 내용 (시간)

🔹 고득점 포인트   강조되는 내용이 사람일 경우 that 대신 who(m), 사물일 경우 which, 시간일 경우 when, 장소일 경우 where을 쓸 수 있다.

It was Dave who arrived late last night. 어젯밤 늦게 도착한 사람은 Dave였다.
사람

It was in 1776 when the United States declared its independence. 미국이 독립을 선언한 것은 1776년이었다.
시간

2 명령문은 주어를 생략하고 동사원형으로 시작한다.

Tell me why you're late. 네가 왜 늦었는지 말해라.
동사원형

If you are interested in our items, please contact us via e-mail. 우리 제품에 관심있으시면, 이메일로 연락을 주십시오.
동사원형

☑ 텝스 실전 문제

텝스 문제 이렇게 나온다

ㅣ 'there + 동사 + 진짜 주어' 구문의 전체나 일부를 채우는 문제가 주로 나온다.
ㅣ 'it – that 강조구문'의 전체나 일부를 채우는 문제가 주로 나온다.
ㅣ 명령문 전체를 채우는 문제도 가끔 나온다.

Part I

1. A: What is the problem with the new software system?
   B: _____ with the installation.

   (a) There some errors have been
   (b) Have been some errors there
   (c) Some errors there have been
   (d) There have been some errors

Part II

2. _____ who pushed him to reach the peak of the mountain.

   (a) Climbing partner of his was
   (b) His climbing partner was it
   (c) It was his climbing partner
   (d) It his climbing partner was

정답 p.

Hackers **Practice**

중 알맞은 것을 고르세요.

(Learn / Learning) organic chemistry is a necessity if you ever hope to attend medical school.

The large tornado left many homes (destroyed / destroy) with its high winds.

Once this tree is older, it will grow (wide / widely) like the others in the forest.

It is at the carnival (where / there) spectators can watch brilliant evening fireworks during the summer.

I am not able to go to the shopping mall with you this afternoon because my house (is being inspected / being inspected) for termites today.

The old man (playing / played) a variety of homemade musical instruments performs for the crowd every Sunday.

부분이 있으면 바르게 고치세요.

The man at the bus stop started sweat as the sun's harsh rays beamed down on him.

It is a frustrating experience wait for hours in a crowded emergency room when you need treatment.

Mike thinks there is something wrong with his car, as the engine sounds very noisy.

In 1992, the prime minister of Singapore made to chew gum in a public place illegal.

The hunting scene in the movie Bambi always makes children sadly.

For Mother's Day, my brother gave our mom a bouquet of flowers pick from the neighbor's garden.

정답 p.10

Hackers **TEST**

Part I Choose the best answer for the blank.

01 A: Did you send me this package?
B: Actually, it's your parents _____ sent it.

(a) who
(b) what
(c) when
(d) which

02 A: He seems happy to be moving to London.
B: He's more _____ than I've ever seen him.

(a) excite
(b) excites
(c) excited
(d) be excited

03 A: The doctor will see your child now.
B: It's about time. He kept us _____ here for two hours!

(a) sit
(b) sat
(c) to sit
(d) sitting

04 A: You should buy this suit.
B: No thanks. It _____.

(a) looks expensive
(b) looking expensive
(c) expensive looking
(d) to look expensive

05 A: I skipped the sociology seminar today.
B: Same here. Although _____
behind his back, the lecturer rambles on forever
without saying anything substantial.

(a) ill to speak of him is rude
(b) it's rude to speak ill of him
(c) speaking it ill of him is rude
(d) rude it is to speak ill of him

06 A: What was your elementary school like?
B: I don't know. There is _____
from those days.

(a) not I have single a memory
(b) I have not a single memory
(c) have not a memory single
(d) not a single memory I have

Part II Choose the best answer for the blank.

07 Gatun Lake is the component of the Panama Ca
_____ as a reservoir for the waterway.

(a) act
(b) acting
(c) acted
(d) has acted

08 Tolstoy's novel *War and Peace* is an extended
version _____ shortly after the original v
published.

(a) rewrites
(b) rewritten
(c) rewriting
(d) to rewriting

09 Thanks to technological advances and innovatic
humans can now start _____ the
mysteries of Earth's planetary neighbors.

(a) pierce
(b) pierced
(c) to pierce
(d) having pierced

10 Because it was too hot, he left his shirt buttons
_____.

(a) undo
(b) undoing
(c) undone
(d) to undoing

The boxer took a serious blow to the head, but the doctor deemed _____, as there were no signs of a concussion.

(a) to continue the match to be safe
(b) it safe continue the match
(c) it safe to continue the match
(d) to be safe continuing

Because memories are subjective, _____ by time, feelings, and other impressions.

(a) can be distorted your events
(b) remember events by you can be distorted
(c) events you remember can be distorted
(d) your events remembered can be distorted

rt III Identify the option that contains an awkward expression or an error in grammar.

(a) A: Can you sit down for a moment so I can talk to you?
(b) B: What's the matter? It makes me sad see you unhappy.
(c) A: I don't have enough money to afford tuition this year.
(d) B: If you would like, I can help you take out an affordable loan.

(a) A: What is the time frame on the project you are working on?
(b) B: The plan, bars any sudden changes, is to have it done by May.
(c) A: If possible, I would like you to complete it sooner.
(d) B: I will let you know if I can once I talk with my supervisor.

15 (a) Galileo Galilei was an Italian astronomer who publicly supported the Copernican heliocentric model. (b) Heliocentrism asserts that the Sun, rather than the Earth, is positioned at the center of the solar system. (c) At the time, this model stood in opposition to the geocentric beliefs of the Catholic Church. (d) Few daring to stand in support of this model after Galileo was put on public trial for his heliocentric theories.

16 (a) Charles Lindbergh was of the first American aviator to fly across the Atlantic Ocean. (b) His 33 1/2-hour, nonstop flight from New York to Paris inspired people on both sides of the ocean. (c) This accomplishment, in 1927, renewed interest in the aviation industry, spurring the participation of financiers. (d) As a result, American and European airplane development grew substantially over the next decade.

Section 2 동사구

CHAPTER 02 동사의 종류

BASIC GRAMMAR 고수로 가는 첫 걸음

1 동사는 목적어를 필요로 하지 않는 자동사와 목적어를 필요로 하는 타동사로 나뉜다.

Lily **swam** in the pool. Lily는 수영장에서 수영했다.
　　　자동사

Lily **ate** a hamburger. Lily는 햄버거를 먹었다.
　　타동사　　목적어

'수영하다'를 뜻하는 동사 swam(swim의 과거형)은 목적어 없이도 의미가 완전한 자동사이다. 반면 '먹다'를 뜻하는 동사 ate(eat의 과거형)은 '무엇'을 먹었는지 대상을 나타내는 목적어(a hamburger) 없이는 문장의 의미가 완전해지지 않는 타동사이다.

2 자동사는 1·2형식 문장을, 타동사는 3·4·5형식 문장을 만든다.

① 1형식 (주어 + 자동사)

The sun **rises** in the east. 해는 동쪽에서 뜬다.
주어　　자동사

② 2형식 (주어 + 자동사 + 주격 보어)

The sky **is** clear. 하늘이 맑다.
주어　자동사　주격보어

③ 3형식 (주어 + 타동사 + 목적어)

Susan **met** Billy. Susan은 Billy를 만났다.
주어　타동사　목적어

④ 4형식 (주어 + 타동사 + 간접 목적어 + 직접 목적어)

Billy **lent** his younger sister his book. Billy는 그의 여동생에게 그의 책을 빌려주었다.
주어　타동사　　　간접목적어　　　　직접목적어

⑤ 5형식 (주어 + 타동사 + 목적어 + 목적격 보어)

She **found** the book interesting. 그녀는 그 책이 재미있다는 것을 알게 되었다.
주어　타동사　　목적어　　　목적격보어

자동사와 타동사

타동사는 목적어를 반드시 가져야 한다.

I can complete ⁀ by tomorrow. 나는 내일까지 그 일을 끝낼 수 있다.
　　　타동사　/the work
▶ 타동사(complete)는 반드시 목적어(the work)를 가져야 한다.

자동사가 목적어를 갖기 위해서는 전치사가 필요하지만, 타동사는 전치사 없이 목적어를 바로 갖는다.

You should ~~reply~~ this letter within thirty days. 당신은 이 편지에 30일 이내에 답해야 한다.
　　　reply to　목적어
▶ 자동사(reply)는 바로 뒤에 목적어를 가질 수 없기 때문에, 전치사(to)가 목적어(this letter) 앞에 와야 한다.

When the phone rings, I'm the one who ~~answers to~~ it. 전화벨이 울리면, 내가 전화를 받는 사람이다.
　　　　　　　　　　　　　　　　　　answers　목적어
▶ 타동사(answer)는 바로 뒤에 목적어를 갖기 때문에, 전치사(to) 없이 목적어(it)가 와야 한다.

혼동하기 쉬운 자동사와 타동사

의미	자동사 + 전치사 + 목적어		타동사 + 목적어	
말하다	speak to / about ~에게/~에 대해 말하다 talk to / about ~와/~에 대해 이야기하다	converse with ~와 대화하다 account for ~에 대해 설명하다	tell ~에게 말하다 discuss ~에 대해 토론하다	explain ~에 대해 설명하다
답하다	respond to ~에 답하다	reply to ~에 답하다	answer ~에 답하다	
반대하다	object to ~에 반대하다	rebel against ~에 대항하다	oppose ~에 반대하다	resist ~에 저항하다
기타	arrive at / in ~에 도착하다 agree with / to ~에 동의하다 complain about / of ~에 대해 불평하다	graduate from ~을 졸업하다 wait for ~을 기다리다 adhere to ~을 고수하다	enter ~에 들어가다 marry ~와 결혼하다 contact ~에게 연락하다	approach ~에 접근하다 resemble ~을 닮다 reach ~에 도착하다

I ~~graduated~~ college three years ago. 나는 3년 전에 대학을 졸업했다.
graduated from
▶ graduate는 자동사이므로 목적어(college)가 바로 오지 못하고 전치사(from)가 먼저 와야 한다.

We will ~~contact to~~ you within five to seven days. 우리는 5일에서 7일 이내에 너에게 연락할 것이다.
　　　　contact
▶ contact는 타동사이므로 전치사(to) 없이 목적어(you)가 바로 와야 한다.

고득점 포인트 · 자동사와 타동사의 쓰임을 모두 갖는 동사

approve of ~을 승인하다 approve ~을 승인하다	think of ~에 대해 생각하다 think ~을 생각하다	believe in ~을 믿다 believe ~을 믿다

I **thought of** going to China. [○] 나는 중국에 가는 것에 대해 생각했다.
I **thought** that you were in Florida. [○] 나는 네가 플로리다에 있다고 생각했다.

☑ 텝스 실전 문제

자동사와 타동사를 구별하여 적절한 형태의 목적어를 동사와 함께 채우
는 문제가 주로 나온다.

Part I

1. A: Do you know how to get to the café?
　B: I think so. I'll call you if I _____.

(a) it can't find　　　(b) can't find
(c) find can't　　　　(d) can't find it

Part II

2. A substantial majority of respondents
_____.

(a) agreed the decision
(b) the decision agreed
(c) agreed with the decision
(d) the decision to the agreed

정답 p.12

02 4형식 동사

1 4형식 동사는 두 개의 목적어를 취하며, 이때 목적어는 '간접 목적어(~에게) + 직접 목적어(~을/를)', 또는 '직접 목적어 ╋ 전치사 + 간접 목적어' 순서로 와야 한다.

4형식 동사	give ~에게 –을 주다	lend ~에게 –을 빌려주다	bring ~에게 –을 가져다주다
	tell ~에게 –을 말해주다	send ~에게 –을 보내주다	show ~에게 –을 보여주다
	buy ~에게 –을 사주다	ask ~에게 –을 질문하다	make ~에게 –을 만들어주다
	offer ~에게 –을 제공하다	inquire ~에게 –을 질문하다	owe ~에게 –을 빚지다

The boy's grandmother sent a gift him. [×]
<u>직접목적어</u> <u>간접목적어</u>

The boy's grandmother sent him a gift. [○] 소년의 할머니가 그에게 선물을 보냈다.
<u>간접목적어</u> <u>직접목적어</u>

The boy's grandmother sent a gift to him. [○] 소년의 할머니가 그에게 선물을 보냈다.
<u>직접목적어</u> <u>전치사 + 간접목적어</u>

▶ 위의 첫 문장은 '~을/를'로 해석되는 직접 목적어(a gift)가 '~에게'로 해석되는 간접 목적어(him)보다 먼저 나와서 틀리다. 4형식 동사(sent) 뒤┃ 두 번째 문장에서처럼 간접 목적어가 직접 목적어보다 먼저 나오거나, 세 번째 문장에서처럼 '직접 목적어 + 전치사 + 간접 목적어'(a gift to him) ┃ 로 와야 한다.

2 that절이나 의문사절을 직접 목적어로 갖는 4형식 동사

tell ~에게 –라고 말하다		
convince ~에게 –라고 확신시키다	+ 간접 목적어(사람)	+ that절/의문사절
inform / notify ~에게 –라고 알리다		

Jerry told ~~to his wife~~ that he wanted to buy a new car. Jerry는 아내에게 새 차를 사고 싶다고 말했다.
　　　　　his wife

▶ that절이나 의문사절을 직접 목적어로 갖는 4형식 동사(tell) 뒤에는 전치사 없이 간접 목적어(his wife)가 와야 한다.

고득점 포인트 that절과 의문사절을 목적어로 갖는 3형식 동사

say / mention / announce ~에게 –라고 말하다	(+ to 사람)	+ that절/의문사절
explain / describe ~에게 –라고 설명하다		

He said ~~me~~ that he would quit school. (→ to me) 그는 나에게 학교를 그만둘 거라고 말했다.
　↳ that절을 목적어로 갖는 3형식 동사(say) 뒤에는 '사람'(me)이 혼자 올 수 없고 'to + 사람'(to me) 형태로 와야 한다.

☑ 텝스 실전 문제

텝스 문제 이렇게 나온다

| 4형식 동사와 3형식 동사를 구별하여, 목적어를 적절한 형태와 순서로 동 사와 함께 채우는 문제가 주로 나온다.

Part I

1. A: I should treat you to dinner in return for helping me with my move.
   B: You don't have to. You always _____.

   (a) give to me a ride to work
   (b) a ride to work to give me
   (c) give me for a ride to work
   (d) give me a ride to work

Part II

2. When asked by a police officer, the witness _____ the shop.

   (a) described to him how the thief entered
   (b) described him how the thief entered
   (c) how the thief entered described him
   (d) how the thief to enter describing him

정답 p.1█

5형식 동사

출제빈도
★★★

5형식 동사는 '목적어 + 목적격 보어'를 취하며, 동사에 따라 다양한 형태의 목적격 보어가 올 수 있다.

명사	Brad <u>calls</u> his father captain. Brad는 그의 아버지를 대장이라고 부른다.
형용사	<u>Keep</u> yourself warm while exercising outside. 밖에서 운동하는 동안에는 몸을 따뜻하게 유지해라.
분사	I <u>found</u> my roller skate damaged. 나는 내 롤러스케이트가 망가진 것을 발견했다.
to부정사	Jerry didn't <u>expect</u> her to come. Jerry는 그녀가 올 것이라 예상하지 못했다.
동사원형	She <u>felt</u> someone sit gently beside her. 그녀는 누군가가 그녀 옆에 조용히 앉는 것을 느꼈다.

to부정사나 동사원형을 목적격 보어로 취하는 동사

to부정사를 취하는 동사		동사원형을 취하는 동사	
		사역동사	지각동사
want ~가 –하는 것을 원하다	**force** ~가 –하게 강요하다	**have** ~가 –하게 시키다	**see** ~가 –하는 것을 보다
tell ~에게 –하도록 이야기하다	**allow** ~가 –하게 허락하다	**let** ~가 –하도록 허락하다	**look at** ~가 –하는 것을 보다
urge ~가 –하도록 설득하다	**get** ~가 –하게 시키다	**make** ~가 –하게 만들다	**watch** ~가 –하는 것을 보다
cause ~가 –하게 (원인 제공)하다	**compel** ~가 –하게 강요하다		**hear** ~가 –하는 소리를 듣다
ask ~가 –할 것을 요청하다	**remind** ~에게 –하도록 상기시키다		**listen to** ~가 –하는 소리를 듣다
expect ~가 –할 것을 기대하다			**feel** ~가 –하는 것을 느끼다

The repairman <u>got</u> the copier ~~work~~ again.   정비사는 복사기가 다시 작동되도록 했다.
           to work

▶ to부정사를 목적격 보어로 취하는 동사(get)가 쓰였으므로, 동사원형(work)이 아니라 to부정사(to work)가 목적격 보어로 와야 한다.

The security guards <u>made</u> people ~~to open~~ their bags.   경비원은 사람들이 가방을 열도록 했다.
           open

▶ 동사원형을 목적격 보어로 취하는 사역동사(make)가 쓰였으므로, to부정사(to open)가 아니라 동사원형(open)이 목적격 보어로 와야 한다.

고득점 포인트

1. 지각동사는 목적격 보어로 현재분사를 취할 수 있다.
   She <u>felt</u> her cat **lie** on her feet.   그녀는 고양이가 발치에 눕는 것을 느꼈다.
   She <u>felt</u> her cat **lying** on her feet.   그녀는 고양이가 발치에 누워 있는 것을 느꼈다.

2. get, 사역동사, 지각동사 등은 목적어와 목적격 보어가 수동 관계일 때, 목적격 보어로 과거분사를 취한다.
   I <u>had</u> my nails ~~do~~. (→ done)   나는 손톱을 손질받았다.
   ↳ 사역동사(had)의 뒤에 온 목적어(my nails)와 목적격 보어가 '손톱을 손질받다'라는 의미의 수동 관계이므로, 목적격 보어 자리에 과거분사(done)가 와야 한다.

✅ 텝스 실전 문제

텝스 문제 이렇게 나온다

5형식 동사의 종류를 구별하여, 적절한 형태의 목적어와 목적격 보어를
동사와 함께 채우는 문제가 주로 나온다.

Part I

1. A: This book is fantastic! Here, you can borrow it.
   B: Please don't _____.

   (a) force read it to me
   (b) force me reading it
   (c) force me to read it
   (d) read me to it force

Part II

2. Ian _____ at the repair shop.

   (a) had his transmission of car to replace
   (b) had his car's transmission replace
   (c) had his car's transmission replaced
   (d) had his replacing car's transmission

정답 p.13

04 목적어 뒤에 as나 to be를 갖는 동사

1 regard류 동사

regard ~을 –으로 여기다			
describe ~을 –으로 묘사하다			
define ~을 –으로 정의하다			
identify ~을 –으로 확인하다	+ 목적어	+ as	+ 명사
refer to ~을 –이라고 부르다			
think of ~에 대해 –이라고 생각하다			
conceive of ~을 –이라고 생각하다			
view / see ~을 –으로 간주하다			

Most people today regard the cell phone ~~a necessary item~~. 오늘날 대부분의 사람들은 휴대 전화를 필수적인 물건으로 여긴다.
as a necessary item

▶ regard류 동사(regard)가 쓰였으므로 명사(a necessary item)가 아니라 'as + 명사'(as a necessary item)가 와야 한다.

2 think류 동사

think ~이 –이라고 생각하다			
believe ~이 –이라고 믿다	+ 목적어	+ (to be)	+ 명사·형용사
find ~이 –이라고 알다			

People think nightmares to be images of their fears. 사람들은 악몽이 그들이 가진 공포의 이미지라고 생각한다.

3 consider류 동사

consider ~을 –으로 여기다	+ 목적어	+ as	+ 명사
		+ (to be)	+ 명사·형용사

They considered the dog ~~as to be~~ a member of the family. 그들은 그 개를 가족의 일원으로 여겼다.
as / to be

▶ consider류 동사는 목적어 뒤에 as와 to be를 한꺼번에 취할 수 없다. 'as + 명사'(as a member of the family)나 'to be + 명사'(to be a memb⟩ the family) 형태로 와야 한다.

☑ 텝스 실전 문제

텝스 문제 이렇게 나온[

ㅣ동사의 종류에 따라 목적어 뒤에 as나 to be를 선택하여 동사와 함께 채
우는 문제가 주로 나온다.

Part II

1. Taxonomists _____ a rodent.

    (a) define of the squirrel
    (b) the squirrel as defined
    (c) define the squirrel as
    (d) the squirrel defined as to

Part I

2. A: Why do you never wear high heels?
    B: I don't consider _____.

    (a) that is quite practical
    (b) them quite practical
    (c) them being quite practical
    (d) that quite practical to be

정답 p.

Hackers **Practice**

§ 알맞은 것을 고르세요.

What did you (discuss / discuss about) in Mr. Ebert's history class this morning?

Parents can't expect advertisers (understand / to understand) that marketing products to children borders on the unethical.

When I mentioned that I needed a new umbrella, my brother bought (me one / for me one).

The airline offers (passengers / to passengers) a free upgrade to business class if they have accumulated enough points.

My girlfriend usually wants to go out for lunch on the weekend, but I (object / oppose) to it.

The manager informed (to me / me) that our office will be moving to a new location sometime next year.

부분이 있으면 바르게 고치세요.

realized while looking at my grandmother's picture that I resemble.

The angry customer, unhappy with the result, forced the contractor repaint the exterior of his house.

The fisherman felt a tug, but seeing it was from a little fish, he let it to go.

Most people would describe a zebra a horse-like creature with alternating black and white stripes.

John sent a postcard his friend Eric while traveling around South America.

passing car splashed water on me as I was waiting the bus.

정답 p.13

Hackers **TEST**

Part I Choose the best answer for the blank.

01 A: Do you use an alarm clock?
   B: No. I tried one, but I would never _____.

   (a) respond it   (b) responding it
   (c) respond to it   (d) respond for it

02 A: Can you _____ when you're done with it?
   B: Sure, but it might take a week or two.

   (a) lend me that book
   (b) lending me that book
   (c) that book to lend me
   (d) lend to me that book

03 A: We'll come pick you and your wife up in an hour.
   B: OK. I'll go _____.

   (a) tell her that getting ready
   (b) tell her to get ready
   (c) tell to her to get ready
   (d) tell getting ready to her

04 A: Those jackets both look good on you.
   B: Thanks, but which one _____ with these
   black shoes?

   (a) be well   (b) being well
   (c) go well   (d) goes well

05 A: I need to be absent on Monday.
   B: I'm sorry, but I _____.

   (a) another day off can't give you
   (b) can't give another day off you
   (c) can't give you another day off
   (d) can't to you give another day off

06 A: Your acceptance letter just arrived in the mail.
   B: Already? I _____ so soon.

   (a) expected not receive it
   (b) did not expect it to receive
   (c) expected to never receive it
   (d) never expected to receive it

07 A: Thanks for all your help.
   B: No problem. If you ever have anything on yo[...]
   mind, you can always _____

   (a) talk about it me
   (b) talk to me about it
   (c) to me talk about it
   (d) have talked to me about it

08 A: I spent the whole morning rearranging the s[...]
   shelves.
   B: You'd better _____ before the st[...]
   opens.

   (a) get the one last finish
   (b) get the last one finish it
   (c) get the last one finished
   (d) get the last one it finished

Part II Choose the best answer for the blank.

09 The Confederacy surrendered to the Union in 1[...]
   _____ the American Civil War to an[...]

   (a) bring   (b) brings
   (c) bringing   (d) brought

10 Researchers are studying genetic mutations to[...]
   _____ for hemophilia.

   (a) they can provide
   (b) they can provide a cure
   (c) if they can provide
   (d) if they can provide a cure

11 When inflation rises, banks demand higher
   compensation for their loans, which

   _____.

   (a) making interest rates go up
   (b) makes interest rates go up
   (c) makes interest rates to go up
   (d) makes that interest rates go up

_____ the dentist twice a year in order to prevent plaque buildup and cavities.

(a) To visit is necessary
(b) To visit it is necessary
(c) It is necessary to visit
(d) It is to visit

Vegetarians _____ a healthy alternative to animal meat.

(a) consider as tofu
(b) tofu considering as
(c) considered as to be tofu
(d) consider tofu as

The plaintiff stated that she would drop all charges if the defendant returned the money _____ _____.

(a) to her his son owed
(b) his owed her son
(c) his son owed her
(d) her his son owed

As soon as the details of the plans are completed, the city council will _____.

(a) have the old freeway demolish
(b) have the freeway old demolished
(c) have demolished the old freeway
(d) have the old freeway demolished

Scientists believe _____ Mars in this lifetime.

(a) humans impossible to colonize
(b) impossible for humans to colonize
(c) it impossible for humans to colonize
(d) to colonize impossible for humans

17 The city transportation authority decided to raise the public bus fare even though the general public _____.

(a) objected to it   (b) objecting to it
(c) objected it   (d) to object it

18 Although President Allen's tax reforms are popular, the politicians in parliament _____ _____.

(a) approve of them not at all
(b) won't approve of them at all
(c) won't at all approve them
(d) approve not at all of them

Part III Identify the option that contains an awkward expression or an error in grammar.

19 (a) A: Do you think my dad will let me borrow his car?
(b) B: It depends on how long you intend to use it.
(c) A: Well, I want to take it on a two-week trip across the country.
(d) B: You'll have to explain him why you came up with that idea.

20 (a) Vaishnavism is a religion whose followers adhere a lifestyle that they believe will allow them to break the cycle of reincarnation. (b) Vaishnavism is considered one of the world's oldest and most influential religions and has nearly 350 million devotees in India. (c) Followers of Vaishnavism worship a deity called Vishnu who preserves and protects the universe and those in it. (d) Practices of Vaishnavism include daily prayer and meditation as well as living as plainly as possible.

CHAPTER **03** 조동사

BASIC GRAMMAR 고수로 가는 첫 걸음

1 조동사는 동사 앞에 와서 동사를 돕는 역할을 한다.

I run fast. 나는 빨리 달린다.
I can run fast. 나는 빨리 달릴 수 있다.

'달리다'라는 동사 run에 조동사 can이 '가능'의 의미를 더해 '달릴 수 있다'는 뜻을 만든다. 이와 같이 조동사는 동사 앞에서 동사를 돕는 보조적인 역할을 한다.

2 조동사는 시제나 태, 부정을 표현하는 것과 동사에 보조적인 의미를 더하는 것으로 나뉜다.

① 조동사 be, have, do는 시제, 태, 부정을 표현한다.

진행	**I am** cleaning my room now.	나는 지금 내 방을 청소하는 중이다.
완료	**I have** cleaned my room for two hours.	나는 두 시간 동안 내 방을 청소했다.
수동	My room **is** cleaned by me.	내 방은 나에 의해 청소된다.
부정	**I don't** clean my room.	나는 내 방을 청소하지 않는다.

be동사는 진행 시제와 수동태를 만드는 데 쓰이고, have는 완료 시제를 나타내는 데 사용된다. do는 일반동사의 부정형을 만들기 위해 쓰인다.

② 조동사 can, will, may, must, should는 동사에 보조적인 의미를 더한다.

can	**I can** clean my room now.	나는 지금 내 방을 청소할 수 있다.
will	**I will** clean my room.	나는 내 방을 청소할 것이다.
may	**I may** clean my room tonight.	나는 오늘 밤에 내 방을 청소할지도 모른다.
must	**I must** clean my room.	나는 내 방을 청소해야 한다.
should	**I should** clean my room.	나는 내 방을 청소해야 한다.

조동사 can, will, may, must, should는 동사(clean) 앞에 와서 '~할 수 있다', '~할 것이다', '~할지도 모른다', '~해야 한다'는 보조적인 의미를 더해준다.

01 조동사 + 동사원형

조동사 can, will, may, must, should 뒤에는 반드시 동사원형이 와야 한다.

He will ~~to come~~ / ~~coming~~ / ~~comes~~ here. 그는 여기에 올 것이다.
　 조동사　　　　　come

▶ 조동사(will) 다음에는 to부정사/동명사/3인칭 단수형 동사가 올 수 없고 동사원형(come)이 와야 한다.

고득점 포인트

1. 다음과 같이 조동사처럼 쓰이는 표현들 뒤에도 동사원형을 쓴다.

ought to ~해야 한다	be going to ~할 것이다	be able to ~할 수 있다	had better ~하는 게 좋겠다
have to ~해야 한다	need to ~해야 한다	used to ~하곤 했다	dare to 감히 ~하다

You <u>had better</u> **hurry** up. 너는 서두르는 게 좋겠다.

My family <u>used to</u> **take** trips to the beach on weekends. 나의 가족은 주말에 해변으로 여행을 가곤 했다.

2. need는 일반동사로도 쓰이지만, 부정문, 의문문, 조건문 등에서 조동사로도 쓰일 수 있다.

She **needs** something to drink. 그녀는 마실 것이 필요하다.
　 일반동사

I **need** not start right now. 나는 지금 당장 출발할 필요가 없다.
　 조동사

↳ 첫 번째 문장에 쓰인 needs는 '필요하다'라는 뜻의 일반 동사이고, 두 번째 문장의 need는 '~할 필요가 있다'라는 뜻의 조동사로 뒤에 동사원형(start)이 온다. need가 조동사로 쓰이면, 일반동사인 경우와 달리 두 번째 문장에서처럼 not이 붙을 수 있다.

제안·의무·요청을 나타내는 동사·명사·형용사가 주절에 나오면, 종속절에 '(should +) 동사원형'이 와야 한다.

동사	request 요청하다 command 명령하다 desire 요구하다	ask 요청하다 order 명령하다 recommend 추천하다	suggest 제안하다 require 요구하다 insist 주장하다	propose 제안하다 demand 요구하다 move 동의하다
명사	suggestion 제안	insistence 주장	requirement 요구	pleading 간청
형용사	necessary 필수적인 advisable 바람직한	essential 필수적인 crucial 중요한	imperative 필수적인	important 중요한

The ski trainer <u>suggests</u> that a beginner ~~starts~~ on the novice slopes. 스키 강사는 초보자는 초보 슬로프에서 시작해야 한다고 제안한다.
　　　　　　　　　　　　　　　　start

▶ 주절에 제안을 나타내는 동사(suggest)가 왔으므로, 종속절에는 3인칭 단수형 동사(starts)가 아니라 should를 생략한 동사원형(start)이 와야 한다.

It was the school's <u>requirement</u> that all student ~~wore~~ uniforms. 모든 학생이 교복을 입어야 한다는 것은 학교의 요구였다.
　　　　　　　　　　　　　　　　　　　 wear

▶ 주절에 요청을 나타내는 명사(requirement)가 왔으므로, 종속절에는 과거 동사(wore)가 아니라 should를 생략한 동사원형(wear)이 와야 한다.

It is <u>important</u> that the report ~~is handed~~ in on time. 보고서는 제때 제출되는 것이 중요하다.
　　　　　　　　　　　　be handed

▶ 주절에 의무를 나타내는 형용사(important)가 왔으므로, 종속절에는 3인칭 단수형 동사(is handed)가 아니라 should를 생략한 동사원형(be handed)이 와야 한다.

☑ 텝스 실전 문제

조동사 뒤에 동사원형을 채우는 문제가 주로 나온다.
제안·의무·요청을 나타내는 주절의 종속절에 동사원형을 채우거나, 동사원형 이외의 형태가 와서 틀린 문장을 찾는 문제가 주로 나온다.

Part I

1. A: I bought a modem but I haven't set it up yet.
　 B: You ought to _____ so you can go online.

　 (a) get it installed 　　(b) getting installed it
　 (c) get it to install 　　(d) got it installed

Part III

2. (a) A: Hello, can I speak to Ms. Parker?
　 (b) B: I'm sorry. She's out of the office at the moment.
　 (c) A: I asked that she contacts me today, but she hasn't yet.
　 (d) B: I'll be sure to have her call you when she gets in.

정답 p.16

해커스 텝스 Reading

02 조동사 be · have · do

1 be동사는 과거분사와 결합하여 수동형(be + p.p.)을 만들고, have동사는 과거분사와 결합하여 완료형(have + p.p.)을 만든다.

수동형 All employees are required to dress in formal attire. 모든 직원은 정장을 입도록 요구받는다.

완료형 My family has been to Mexico for sightseeing. 우리 가족은 관광하러 멕시코에 간 적이 있다.

2 동사가 수동 의미로 쓰이면 p.p. 앞에 be동사가 오고, 완료 의미로 쓰이면 p.p. 앞에 have동사가 와야 한다.

The list of names ~~has~~ organized alphabetically. 명단은 알파벳 순으로 정리되어 있다.
　　　　　　　　　is

▶ 주어인 The list of names가 '정리되었다'는 수동의 의미이므로, p.p. 앞에는 완료형 동사를 만드는 has가 아니라 수동형 동사를 만드는 is가 와야

He ~~was~~ studied criminal psychology for eight years. 그는 8년 동안 범죄 심리학을 공부해왔다.
　　has

▶ 현재완료를 나타내는 시제 표현(for eight years)이 와서 '공부해왔다'는 완료의 의미가 되므로, p.p. 앞에는 수동형 동사를 만드는 was가 아니라 완료형 동사를 만드는 has가 와야 한다.

3 do동사는 앞에 나온 일반 동사가 반복되는 경우, 이를 대신한다.

She likes dancing, and so do(= like) I. 그녀는 춤추는 것을 좋아하고, 나도 그렇다(좋아한다).
You eat much more than Nicholas does(= eats). 너는 Nicholas보다(Nicholas가 먹는 것보다) 훨씬 많이 먹는다.
I'll take a flute lesson as you did(= took) last year. 나는 네가 작년에 그랬던 것처럼(플루트 교습을 받았던 것처럼) 플루트 교습을 받을 것이다.

▶ 위의 문장들에서 do동사(do, does, did)는 앞에 나온 일반동사(like, eats, took)를 대신한다. 단, do동사는 자신이 속한 절의 주어와 시제에 일치한다.

4 do동사는 일반동사의 부정문을 만들며, 'do / does / did + not + 동사원형'으로 와야 한다.

I ~~know not~~ where to go. 나는 어디로 가야 할지 모르겠다.
don't know

▶ 일반동사(know) 뒤에 not이 오는 것이 아니라 'do + not + 동사원형'(don't know)으로 와야 한다.

고득점포인트 1. never를 일반동사 앞에 붙여 부정문을 만들 수 있다.
　　　　　The home team **never** seems to win. 홈팀은 결코 이길 것처럼 보이지 않는다.

　　　　2. 부정문의 마지막에 at all을 붙여 '전혀'라고 부정의 의미를 강조할 수 있다.
　　　　　I **don't** hate him **at all**. 나는 그를 전혀 싫어하지 않는다.

☑ 텝스 실전 문제

텝스 문제 이렇게 나온다

| be동사와 have동사의 쓰임을 구별하여 채우는 문제가 주로 나온다.
| 일반동사를 대신하는 do동사를 채우는 문제도 가끔 나온다.

Part II

1. Many moments of the day _____ wasted on mundane activities like sleeping and cleaning.

(a) is　　　　　　(b) are
(c) has　　　　　(d) have

Part I

2. A: The subway where we live always runs late.
　 B: The bus _____, as well.

(a) does　　　　　(b) does to
(c) running　　　　(d) runs

정답 p.

3 조동사 can · will · may · must · should

★ ★ ★

can · will · may

can	능력 ~할 수 있다	Computers can save a great amount of data. 컴퓨터는 많은 양의 정보를 저장할 수 있다.
	허가 ~해도 된다	You can take a break at three o'clock. 너는 3시에 잠시 쉬어도 된다.
	요청 ~해주다	Can you bring me a paper? 내게 신문을 가져다줄래?
	강한 추측 ~일 수 있다	Earthquakes can cause large tidal waves. 지진은 큰 해일을 야기할 수 있다.
will	미래 ~할 것이다	He will respond to you by the end of the week. 그는 주말까지 네게 응답할 것이다.
	의지·고집 ~하겠다	I will go to today's concert however sick I feel. 나는 얼마나 아프든지, 오늘 콘서트에 가겠다.
	요청 ~해주다	Will you take care of my dog for me? 나 대신 내 개를 돌봐줄래요?
may	허가 ~해도 된다	Students may use the lounge after 6 p.m. 학생들은 오후 6시 이후에 휴게실을 이용해도 된다.
	약한 추측 ~일지 모른다	Susan may be right. Susan이 옳을지 모른다.

고득점 포인트

1. '허가'나 '요청'의 의미로 쓰인 문장에서 could, would, might는 더 공손한 '허가'나 '요청'을 나타내고, '추측'의 의미로 쓰인 문장에서 could와 might가 오면 더 약한 '추측'을 나타낸다.

   Could you call me later? 나중에 전화해주시겠어요?

   Grace **might** come back within an hour. Grace는 혹시 한 시간 안에 돌아올지도 모른다.

   ↳ 첫 번째 문장은 Could를 써서 '전화해줄 수 있었니?'라는 의미의 '과거' 시제를 나타내는 것이 아니라, '전화해주시겠어요?'라는 의미의 더 공손한 '요청'을 나타낸다. 두 번째 문장은 might를 써서 '돌아올지도 몰랐었다'라는 의미의 '과거' 시제를 나타내는 것이 아니라, '혹시 돌아올지도 모른다'라는 더 약한 '추측'을 나타낸다.

2. would는 지금은 그만둔 과거의 '동작'을 나타낸다. 이와 비슷하게 used to는 지금은 그만둔 과거의 '동작'이나, 지금은 그렇지 않은 과거의 '상태'를 나타낸다.

   We **would[used to]** play soccer together. 우리는 함께 축구를 하곤 했었다. (그런데 지금은 하지 않는다)

   There **used to** be a large lake 10 years ago. 10년 전에는 커다란 호수가 있었다. (그런데 지금은 없다)

must · should

must	의무 ~해야 한다	All applicants must register by noon. 모든 지원자들은 정오까지 등록해야 한다.
	강한 확신 ~임에 틀림없다	Smith must be disappointed with the test results. Smith는 결과에 실망한 것이 틀림없다.
should	의무·제안 ~해야 한다	You should visit the dentist. 너는 치과 진료를 받아야 한다.
	추측 ~일 것이다	Skies should clear up before the evening. 저녁 전에는 하늘이 갤 것이다.

☑ 텝스 실전 문제

텝스 문제 이렇게 나온다

의미상 적절한 조동사를 채우는 문제가 주로 나온다.
적절하지 않은 조동사가 와서 틀린 문장을 찾는 문제가 주로 나온다.

Part II

1. Current GPS technology _____ pinpoint one's location anywhere in the world.

   (a) must
   (b) can
   (c) should
   (d) would

Part III

2. (a) A: My apartment always feels empty when I come home.
   (b) B: Perhaps you would think about getting a puppy.
   (c) A: It may take a lot of money and effort to raise a dog, though.
   (d) B: Then consider a cat instead, since they are easier to care for.

정답 p.16

04 조동사 관련 표현

1 조동사 + have p.p.

cannot[couldn't] have p.p. ~이었을 리가 없다	**could have p.p.** ~할 수 있었다 (그런데 하지 않았다)
must have p.p. ~이었음에 틀림없다	**should have p.p.** ~했어야 했다 (그런데 하지 않았다)
may[might] have p.p. ~이었을지 모른다	

She cannot have known for sure that it would rain today. 그녀는 오늘 비가 오리라는 것을 알았을 리가 없다.

Anna must have left before I even woke up. Anna는 내가 일어나기도 전에 떠난 것이 틀림없다.

Wilson may have tried to call while you were on the phone. 네가 통화하는 동안 Wilson이 전화하려고 했을지 모른다.

You could have notified us instead of just being late. 너는 그냥 늦는 대신 우리에게 알릴 수도 있었다. (그런데 알리지 않았다)

We should have called to make a reservation. 우리는 예약을 하기 위해 전화를 했어야 했다. (그런데 전화하지 않았다)

고득점 포인트 1. cannot[couldn't] have p.p.와 mustn't have p.p.의 쓰임을 구별해야 한다.

You ~~mustn't~~ have seen a dodo. It became extinct in 1681. (→ **couldn't**) 너는 도도새를 보았을 리가 없다. 그것은 1681년에 멸종되었다.

↳ cannot[couldn't] have p.p.와 mustn't have p.p.는 둘 다 강한 부정적 추측의 의미를 가지고 있지만, 위의 문장처럼 '1681년에 멸종되었다'와 같은 정확한 근거가 있어서 논리적으로 불가능함을 나타내기 위해서는 cannot have p.p.(couldn't have seen)가 와야 한다.

2. must have p.p.와 should have p.p.의 쓰임을 구별해야 한다.

I burned my hand. I ~~mustn't~~ have taken my eyes off the iron. (→ **shouldn't**) 나는 손을 데었다. 나는 다리미에서 눈을 떼지 말았어야 했다.

↳ mustn't have p.p.는 '~하지 않았음이 틀림없다'는 뜻으로 과거에 어떤 일을 하지 않음에 대한 강한 확신을 나타낸다. 자연스러운 의미가 되기 위해서는 '~하지 말았어야 했다'는 뜻으로 과거에 한 일에 대한 후회를 나타내는 shouldn't have p.p.(shouldn't have taken)가 와야 한다.

2 조동사 관련 숙어

would rather 차라리 ~하는 게 낫다	**may[might] as well** ~하는 편이 더 낫겠다	**may well** ~하는 게 당연하다
would like to ~하고 싶다	**cannot (help) but** ~할 수밖에 없다 (= cannot help + -ing / have no choice but + to 동사원형)	

I'd rather choose another way. 나는 다른 길을 택하는 게 낫겠다.

I'd like to have Mexican food. 나는 멕시코 음식을 먹고 싶다.

I may as well go to the library. 나는 도서관에 가는 편이 더 낫겠다.

He may well think so. 그가 그렇게 생각하는 게 당연하다.

I could not but admit my fault. 나는 실수를 인정할 수밖에 없었다.

3 조동사 관련 관용표현

You can't be serious. 너 농담이지?

You must be kidding. 설마 농담이겠지.

Who wouldn't be? 누군들 그러지 않겠어?

☑ 텝스 실전 문제

텝스 문제 이렇게 나온다

| have p.p. 앞에 의미상 적절한 조동사를 채우는 문제가 주로 나온다.
| 적절한 숙어와 관용표현을 만드는 조동사를 채우는 문제도 간혹 나온다.

Part I

1. A: I threw out all the fruit in the refrigerator.
   B: It was still fresh. You _____ have wasted it.

   (a) wouldn't (b) couldn't
   (c) mustn't (d) shouldn't

2. A: Everyone around the office seems really tense.
   B: Who _____ be? We're all anticipating layoffs.

   (a) wouldn't (b) shouldn't
   (c) mustn't (d) couldn't

정답 p.

5 알맞은 것을 고르세요.

Carlos (cannot / should not) have written the letter; his spelling is much better than that.

At yesterday's meeting, the CEO proposed that the company (considers / consider) a merger with one of its competitors.

My friends and I (can / will) stay late because the teacher is forcing us to.

When I was young, my family used to (renting / rent) a cabin in the mountains where we would spend three weeks every summer.

The waiter said that he used to be a famous actor, but I (recognize not / didn't recognize) him.

There is frost on the grass, so it (needs to be / must be) freezing outside.

부분이 있으면 바르게 고치세요.

Nowadays, millions of unnecessary plastic bags have given away to people only purchasing a single item.

We would have eaten at that restaurant before, but I really cannot say for certain.

If you want the bone to heal properly, you wouldn't do any activities using your left arm.

The oven must have been preheated to 200 degrees, but Roger mistakenly set it at 400.

It is important that all of your research is completed before you meet with the committee next week.

When can you think that the repairs to the leaky roof should be finished?

정답 p.16

Hackers **TEST**

Part I Choose the best answer for the blank.

01 A: _____ we have Chinese food for dinner?
B: Sure, I'm in the mood for that myself.

(a) Do   (b) Need
(c) Must   (d) Could

02 A: I can't believe I missed the meeting!
B: You _____ have answered your phone when
I called you about it.

(a) could   (b) should
(c) must   (d) would

03 A: Did you get a haircut? You look handsome
today.
B: _____ I? Thanks for the compliment.

(a) Do   (b) Will
(c) Can   (d) Are

04 A: I think my essay is full of mistakes.
B: You'd better _____.

(a) have edit it
(b) have it edited
(c) having it to edit
(d) had have edited it

05 A: I thought you were bringing Nancy with you.
B: I was, but we had an argument earlier and she
said she _____ come.

(a) mustn't   (b) needn't
(c) wouldn't   (d) shouldn't

06 A: I thought I saw Heidi at the grocery store.
B: It _____ have been her. She's on vacation in
the Bahamas.

(a) wouldn't   (b) shouldn't
(c) mustn't   (d) couldn't

07 A: Are you going to be at Lizzie's party tonight?
B: You _____ be kidding. Not after what sh
said to me earlier.

(a) can   (b) should
(c) will   (d) must

Part II Choose the best answer for the blank.

08 The Queen _____ be able to attend the anr
remembrance commemorations due to her busy
schedule.

(a) won't   (b) shouldn't
(c) couldn't   (d) can't

09 Physicians recommend that we _____
regularly as a healthy means of weight loss, and
warn against reliance on pills, dieting, and othe
seemingly quick-fix alternatives.

(a) exercise   (b) exercised
(c) may exercise   (d) exercising

10 In the early twentieth century, Ford Model T
automobiles _____ only be started by turni
a hand crank.

(a) could   (b) must
(c) might   (d) should

11 Leaving your car lights on overnight _____ ha
drained the battery.

(a) can   (b) dare
(c) need   (d) might

12 As business has been getting slow, the manage.
decided that there _____ waiter in t
cafe at a time.

(a) needs to be one only
(b) needs to be only one
(c) need be one only
(d) need being only one

Many historians argue that after the First World War, the victorious countries _____ have imposed such harsh sanctions on Germany.

(a) shouldn't
(b) wouldn't
(c) mustn't
(d) couldn't

If you want to take advantage of the clothing sale, _____ when you go to pay.

(a) show your coupon the clerk
(b) show your coupon to the clerk
(c) your coupon to show the clerk
(d) to show your clerk the coupon

Only hours into her trip, Joan _____ cut her holiday short after receiving distressing news from home.

(a) ought to
(b) had to
(c) might
(d) can

After gathering the staff in the meeting room, the CEO _____.

(a) explained them why he was leaving the company
(b) explained to them why he was leaving the company
(c) why he was leaving the company explained to them
(d) why leaving the company explained them

As Charlesbridge County Fair is expected to be very crowded this year, it is advisable that guests _____ tickets in advance.

(a) buy
(b) bought
(c) will buy
(d) have buy

Part III Identify the option that contains an awkward expression or an error in grammar.

18 (a) A: My coworker always goes to smoke in the bathroom, refusing to do it outside.
(b) B: You should demand that he smokes outside from now on.
(c) A: I should tell the supervisor about it when I get the chance.
(d) B: Rather than telling the supervisor, you should tell your coworker how you feel.

19 (a) Leonidas was the Spartan hero immortalized for fighting bravely at Thermopylae. (b) He was reputed to have led three hundred soldiers to prevent the Persians' attack. (c) Though outnumbered, the Spartans would succeed in repelling the attack for two days, holding off their enemies. (d) On the third day, the soldiers died in battle, having saved their motherland as a result of their efforts.

20 (a) One of the earliest ancestors of whales was *ambulocetus*, which was actually able to walk on land. (b) Although this ancient ancestor of modern-day whales could leave the water, it was not primarily a land-dweller. (c) It was likely quite slow on land and therefore can have done all of its hunting under the water. (d) When swimming, its movements would have been similar to those of modern whales, making it both fast and powerful.

CHAPTER 04 주어와의 수 일치

BASIC GRAMMAR 고수로 가는 첫 걸음

1 동사는 주어에 수 일치해야 한다.

> 단수 주어 + 단수 동사
> 복수 주어 + 복수 동사

A bird sings. 새가 노래한다.
  단수주어 단수동사

Birds sing. 새들이 노래한다.
복수주어 복수동사

첫 번째 문장의 주어 A bird는 단수이고, 두 번째 문장의 주어 Birds는 복수이다. 주어가 단수인 첫 번째 문장에는 단수 동사인 sings가 오고, 주어가 복수인 두 번째 문장에는 복수 동사인 sing이 온다. 이처럼 동사는 주어에 반드시 수 일치해야 한다.

2 단수 동사는 동사의 기본형에 s나 es를 붙이고, 복수 동사는 동사의 기본형을 그대로 사용한다.

Malcolm **watches** a movie every Friday. Malcolm은 매주 금요일에 영화를 본다.
  단수주어   단수동사

They **watch** a movie every Friday. 그들은 매주 금요일에 영화를 본다.
복수주어 복수동사

Malcolm/They **watched** a movie last Friday. Malcolm은/그들은 지난 금요일에 영화를 보았다.
  단수주어 복수주어   과거동사

첫 번째 문장의 주어 Malcolm은 단수이므로 -es가 붙은 단수 동사 watches가 온다. 두 번째 문장의 주어 They는 복수이므로 기본형 watch가 그대로 온다. 그런데 동사가 과거형일 때는 단수와 복수의 형태가 같다. 따라서 세 번째 문장에서 주어가 단수(Malcolm)이든 복수(They)이든 상관없이 과거 동사 watched가 온다. 단, have동사와 be동사는 이 규칙에 따르지 않고 단수인지, 복수인지에 따라 특별한 형태를 갖는다.

기본형	단수 동사	복수 동사
have	has / had	have / had
be	am · is / was	are / were

The student **has** many things to do. 그 학생은 할 일이 많다.
  단수주어   단수동사

The students **have** many things to do. 그 학생들은 할 일이 많다.
  복수주어   복수동사

She **is / was** busy. 그녀는 바쁘다/바빴다.
단수주어 단수동사

They **are / were** busy. 그들은 바쁘다/바빴다.
복수주어   복수동사

01 단수 주어에는 단수 동사, 복수 주어에는 복수 동사

단수 주어에는 단수 동사, 복수 주어에는 복수 동사를 쓴다.

My digital watch beeps **hourly.** 내 디지털 시계는 한 시간마다 삑 소리를 낸다.
　　단수주어　　　단수동사

▶ 주어(My digital watch)가 단수이므로 단수 동사(beeps)가 온다.

Our pizzas are **more authentic than any other pizza around.** 저희 피자는 주변의 다른 어떤 피자보다도 정통 피자입니다.
　복수주어　복수동사

▶ 주어(Our pizzas)가 복수이므로 복수 동사(are)가 온다.

고득점 포인트

1. 동명사 · 명사절 주어에는 단수 동사를 쓴다.

   Running for hours ~~make~~ **me drink lots of water. (→ makes)** 몇 시간 동안 뛰는 것은 내가 물을 많이 마시게 만든다.
   　동명사구 주어

   ↳ 주어(Running for hours)가 동명사구이므로, 복수 동사(make)가 아니라 단수 동사(makes)가 와야 한다.

   What they found ~~were~~ **an old stamp collection. (→ was)** 그들이 발견한 것은 오래된 우표 수집품이었다.
   　명사절 주어

   ↳ 주어(What they found)가 명사절이므로, 복수 동사(were)가 아니라 단수 동사(was)가 와야 한다.

2. 기간 · 가격 · 길이 · 무게 등을 나타내는 명사구 주어에는 단수 동사를 쓴다.

   Three days ~~are~~ **plenty to finish a painting. (→ is)** 3일은 그림을 완성하기 충분한 시간이다.
   　주어 (기간)

   ↳ 주어(Three days)가 기간을 나타내는 명사구이므로, 복수 동사(are)가 아니라 단수 동사(is)가 와야 한다.

3. here나 there로 시작하는 문장은 동사 뒤에 나오는 진짜 주어에 동사를 수 일치시킨다.

   Here ~~stand~~ **a statue dedicated to the town's founder. (→ stands)** 그 마을의 창립자에게 헌정된 조각상이 여기에 서 있다.
   　　　　　단수명사

   ↳ 문장의 주어(a statue)가 단수이므로 단수 동사(stands)가 와야 한다.

주어와 동사 사이의 수식어 거품은 동사의 수 결정에 영향을 주지 않는다.

The researchers in this laboratory ~~studies~~ **a genetic map.** 이 연구실의 연구원들은 유전자 지도를 연구한다.
　복수주어　　　수식어 거품　　　study

▶ 수식어 거품(in this laboratory) 내의 단수 명사 laboratory는 동사의 수 결정에 영향을 주지 않는다. 주어(The researchers)가 복수이므로 단수 동사(studies)가 아니라 복수 동사(study)가 와야 한다.

☑ 텝스 실전 문제

주어에 수 일치하는 동사를 채우는 문제가 주로 나온다.
동사가 주어에 수 일치하지 않아 틀린 문장을 찾는 문제가 주로 나온다.

Part II

. Drawing portraits with realism and precision
_____ a difficult skill to acquire.

(a) is　　　　　　　　(b) are

(c) being　　　　　　(d) are being

Part III

2. (a) The surface of the planet Venus is obscured from the view of human observers due to thick layers of clouds. (b) These clouds of sulfuric acid prevents large amounts of light from penetrating the Venusian atmosphere. (c) Not only does this make the surface of the planet difficult to study, but it also makes the atmosphere unsuitable for habitation. (d) Despite these harsh conditions, many attempts have been made to send probes closer to the planet for further research.

정답 p.19

1 단수 취급하는 수량 표현에는 단수 동사를, 복수 취급하는 수량 표현에는 복수 동사를 쓴다.

단수 취급하는 수량 표현	복수 취급하는 수량 표현
one/each (+ 명사) every/the number of/one of/neither of + 명사 somebody, someone, something anybody, anyone, anything everybody, everyone, everything nobody, no one, nothing	many/several/few/both (+ of the) + 복수 명사 a number of/a couple of + 복수 명사 a range of/a variety of + 복수 명사

The number of cars ~~are~~ increasing. 자동차의 수가 증가하고 있다.
                is

▶ 단수 취급하는 수량 표현(The number of)이 주어에 쓰였으므로, 복수 동사(are)가 아니라 단수 동사(is)가 와야 한다.

A number of tourists ~~visits~~ the Modern Art Museum every year. 많은 관광객들이 매년 현대 미술관을 방문한다.
                 visit

▶ 복수 취급하는 수량 표현(A number of)이 주어에 쓰였으므로, 단수 동사(visits)가 아니라 복수 동사(visit)가 와야 한다.

2 부분 · 전체를 나타내는 표현을 포함한 주어는 of 뒤 명사에 동사를 수 일치시킨다.

부분 · 전체를 나타내는 표현	all, most, any, half, a lot, lots, some, none part, the rest, the bulk, percent, 분수	+ of	+ 단수 명사	+ 단수 동사
			+ 복수 명사	+ 복수 동사

Half of the tuition is covered by the scholarship. 학비의 절반이 장학금으로 충당된다.
        단수명사 단수동사

▶ 부분을 나타내는 표현(Half of) 뒤에 단수 명사(the tuition)가 왔으므로, 단수 동사(is)가 와야 한다.

30 percent of people under the age of 24 lack health insurance. 24세 이하 사람들의 30퍼센트는 의료 보험이 없다.
            복수명사   복수동사

▶ 부분을 나타내는 표현(percent of) 뒤에 복수 명사(people)가 왔으므로, 복수 동사(lack)가 와야 한다.

☑ 텝스 실전 문제

텝스 문제 이렇게 나온다

| 수량 표현, 부분 · 전체 표현을 포함한 주어에 수 일치하는 동사를 채우는
문제가 주로 나온다.

Part I

1. A: It feels like the subway is always becoming more crowded.
   B: And that means the number of available seats _____ decreasing.

   (a) keep   (b) keeps
   (c) kept   (d) keeping

Part II

2. More than half of the soldiers serving in the conflict _____ less than two years of combat experience.

   (a) has   (b) have
   (c) is   (d) are

정답 p.

13 접속사로 연결된 주어와 동사의 수 일치

출제빈도 ★★

and로 연결된 주어에는 복수 동사를 쓴다.

A and B A와 B	both A and B A와 B 둘 다

Water and sunshine are essential for plants. 물과 햇빛은 식물에 필수적이다.
    A and B   복수동사

▶ 두 개의 명사가 and로 연결되어 있으므로 복수 동사(are)가 온다.

고득점 포인트 두 개의 명사가 and로 연결되었어도 하나의 대상을 가리키는 경우, 주어에는 단수 동사가 와야 한다.
Ham and eggs **are** a popular brunch entree. (→ **is**) 햄과 계란 요리는 인기 있는 브런치 메뉴이다.

↳ 주어 Ham and eggs는 접속사 and로 연결되었지만, 햄과 계란을 섞어서 만든 한 종류의 요리를 지칭하므로, 복수 동사(are)가 아니라 단수 동사(is)가 와야 한다.

The famed writer and orator **teach** at Yale. (→ **teaches**) 그 유명한 작가이자 연설가는 예일대에서 가르친다.

↳ 주어 The famed writer and orator는 and로 연결되었지만, 관사(the)를 한 번만 써서 한 사람을 가리키므로, 복수 동사(teach)가 아니라 단수 동사(teaches)가 와야 한다.

or나 nor로 연결된 주어(A or / nor B)는 B에 동사를 수 일치시킨다.

A or B A나 B	either A or B A나 B 둘 중 하나	neither A nor B A와 B 둘 중 어느 것도 아닌

Some chips or a salad is enough for me. 약간의 감자칩이나 샐러드면 내게 충분하다.
    A or B   단수동사

▶ B 위치에 단수 명사(a salad)가 왔으므로 단수 동사(is)가 온다.

고득점 포인트 다음과 같은 접속사로 연결된 주어는 수 일치에 주의해야 한다.

A에 일치시키는 구문	A as well as B B뿐 아니라 A도	
B에 일치시키는 구문	not A but B A가 아니라 B	not only A but (also) B A뿐 아니라 B도

Marcy as well as her parents **prefers** to eat at home. Marcy의 부모님뿐 아니라 Marcy도 집에서 먹는 것을 선호한다.
    A as well as B   단수동사

↳ A 위치에 단수 명사(Marcy)가 왔으므로 단수 동사(prefers)가 온다.

Not only drought **but also** pests **cause** huge damage to farms. 가뭄뿐 아니라 해충도 농장에 큰 해를 끼친다.
    not only A but also B   복수동사

↳ B 위치에 복수 명사(pests)가 왔으므로 복수 동사(cause)가 온다.

☑ 텝스 실전 문제

텝스 문제 이렇게 나온다

접속사로 연결된 주어에 수 일치하는 동사를 채우는 문제가 주로 나온다.

Part I

1. A: Who's going to conduct the proceedings tonight?
   B: The director as well as her assistants _____ hosting the ceremony.

(a) is   (b) are
(c) are being   (d) have been

Part II

2. Neither the stars nor the moon _____ as bright at night as the sun is during the day.

(a) is   (b) are
(c) have   (d) have been

정답 p.19

04 주격 관계절의 선행사와 동사의 수 일치

1 주격 관계절의 동사는 선행사에 수 일치시킨다.

단수 선행사		+ 단수 동사
복수 선행사	+ 주격 관계사 (who / which / that)	+ 복수 동사

They met <u>their senior</u> who <u>has</u> experience in their field.   그들은 그들의 분야에 경험이 있는 선배를 만났다.
             단수선행사   단수동사

▶ 선행사(their senior)가 단수이므로 주격 관계절의 동사 자리에는 단수 동사(has)가 온다.

People who <u>are</u> hopeful about the future are called optimists.   미래에 대해 희망적인 사람들은 낙천주의자라고 불린다.
복수선행사   복수동사

▶ 선행사(People)가 복수이므로 주격 관계절의 동사 자리에는 복수 동사(are)가 온다.

2 관계절 앞에 명사가 여러 개 있는 경우, 무엇이 선행사인지 파악하여 관계절 내 동사의 수를 결정해야 한다.

The train for <u>the backpackers</u> who ~~wants~~ to travel at night is currently running.
           복수선행사   want

야간에 이동하기를 원하는 배낭여행객들을 위한 열차가 현재 운행 중이다.

▶ '야간에 이동하기를 원하는'이라는 의미의 관계절(who ~ at night)이 수식하는 선행사는 단수 명사(The train)가 아니라 복수 명사(the backpackers)
따라서 관계절의 동사도 단수 동사(wants)가 아니라 복수 동사(want)가 와야 한다.

<u>The book collection</u> on the shelves, which ~~consist~~ of thirty-four volumes, is worth thousands of dollars.
       단수선행사   consists

선반 위에 있는 34권으로 구성된 책 전집은 수천 달러의 가치가 있다.

▶ '34권으로 구성된'이라는 의미의 관계절(which ~ volumes)이 수식하는 선행사는 복수 명사(shelves)가 아니라 단수 명사(The book collection)
따라서 관계절의 동사도 복수 동사(consist)가 아니라 단수 동사(consists)가 와야 한다.

☑ 텝스 실전 문제

텝스 문제 이렇게 나온다

| 선행사에 수 일치하는 주격 관계절 동사를 채우는 문제가 주로 나온다.
| 주격 관계절 동사가 선행사에 수 일치하지 않아 틀린 문장을 찾는 문제가 주로 나온다.

Part II

1. A fire in the woods that _____ to spread can threaten wildlife.

    (a) is left   (b) have been left
    (c) are left   (d) have left

Part III

2. (a) Different types of food decompose at different rates, depending on a number of factors. (b) Temperature plays a large role in the decomposition process, as does humidity. (c) Fruit or other food which exist in a cold environment decomposes slower than food in warmer environments. (d) Researchers take the above factors into consideration when developing new methods of food storage.

정답 p.

중 알맞은 것을 고르세요.

My children occasionally (shouts / shout) when they hear thunder, but they aren't really afraid of much else.

Not only Polaris but many other stars (was / were) seen in the night sky.

Only a couple of companies (manufactures / manufacture) manual typewriters these days.

20 kilograms (is / are) a lot of weight for anyone to try to lose.

A visit to an art exhibition followed by some drinks (seem / seems) like a fine idea for a date.

Each member of the cast (rehearse / rehearses) four hours a day.

린 부분이 있으면 바르게 고치세요.

Here lives several members of the art museum's board of directors.

We ought to call the coach or some other person who know what time the game is.

I expected my old neighborhood to have changed, but everything remain the same as it was when I lived there.

Both cancer and heart disease causes more deaths each year than automobile accidents.

The final scenes of the movie were exciting, but the rest of the plot elements was quite boring.

What I know about biology and plants suggest that the root systems of these banyan trees are connected.

정답 p.20

Hackers **TEST**

Part I Choose the best answer for the blank.

01 A: Who is supposed to attend your graduation ceremony?
   B: My uncle as well as my parents _____ coming.

   (a) is   (b) are
   (c) has been   (d) have been

02 A: Let's go by the scenic route instead.
   B: You know, fifty kilometers of winding roads _____ almost an hour to drive.

   (a) take   (b) takes
   (c) are to take   (d) is to take

03 A: You must struggle a lot with recovering from that accident.
   B: One of my goals _____ making regular use of my legs again.

   (a) is being   (b) are being
   (c) has been   (d) have been

04 A: What do you think of my proposal?
   B: That you included visual aids _____ very impressive.

   (a) is   (b) are
   (c) do   (d) doing

05 A: I can't stand winter's chill, but summer is too hot.
   B: I agree. Neither of those seasons in this area _____ pleasant.

   (a) are   (b) is
   (c) was   (d) were

06 A: Why do you still listen to vinyl records?
   B: I like them, even though everyone I know _____ them outdated.

   (a) consider   (b) considers
   (c) is considered   (d) are considering

07 A: What did the professor say about our project outline?
   B: He suggested it _____ rewritten again bef getting his approval.

   (a) be   (b) was
   (c) being   (d) has being

Part II Choose the best answer for the blank.

08 Among the news reports broadcast yesterday _____ the story of an oil spill disaster.

   (a) is   (b) was
   (c) are   (d) were

09 Eating a balanced diet of meat, grains, and vegetables _____ important for staying in go health.

   (a) is   (b) is being
   (c) are   (d) are being

10 A cup of soup coupled with a house salad and a selection of dressings _____ a standard restaurant appetizer.

   (a) is   (b) are
   (c) is being   (d) are being

11 Almost 25 percent of Canadians _____ French as their native language.

   (a) speak   (b) speaks
   (c) is speaking   (d) are speaking

12 Here _____ most of the remains of the famous writer, Sheldon Cramer, though his hear was buried in his home town.

   (a) lie   (b) lies
   (c) to be lied   (d) lying

The fashion label is releasing clothing that _____ a new synthetic fabric.

(a) use   (b) uses
(c) using   (d) to use

Though many citizens implored the mayor to preserve the colonial townhouse, not one of their pleas _____ enough to reverse his decision.

(a) are   (b) is
(c) was   (d) were

_____ deserving of a Nobel Peace Prize is the U.N. ambassador who united people around the world with words of inspiration.

(a) Considers the only man
(b) Considering the only man
(c) The only man considered
(d) The only man considers

The high school principal, in addition to the school board, _____ currently in favor of allotting more money for sports.

(a) is   (b) are
(c) was   (d) were

Marie and Patrick think that $100 _____ enough to buy all they want.

(a) is   (b) are
(c) be   (d) were

Either ink or pencils _____ allowed for submitting a black-and-white illustration to the magazine.

(a) is   (b) has
(c) are   (d) have

Part III Identify the option that contains an awkward expression or an error in grammar.

19 (a) A: I'm never able to enroll in the economics classes I want to take.
   (b) B: It seems like the number of students majoring in economics are increasing lately.
   (c) A: This is going to make the job market in this field even more competitive.
   (d) B: The economics field is still growing, so there will be plenty of opportunities.

20 (a) The ballpoint pen, although its origins are unclear, were first patented in 1888. (b) Ink in early pens was prone to becoming clogged due to reliance on gravity to force the ink out. (c) An improved model was released in the United States in 1945, selling for $12.50 per pen. (d) Pens have since been made more affordable by the office supplies industry, which produces them in bulk.

CHAPTER 05 시제

BASIC GRAMMAR 고수로 가는 첫 걸음

1 동사는 어느 시점의 동작이나 상태를 나타내는지에 따라 다른 형태를 가지며, 이것을 동사의 시제라고 한다.

Adam **visited** me yesterday. Adam은 어제 나를 방문했다.
　　　과거시제

Adam **visits** me every day. Adam은 매일 나를 방문한다.
　　　현재시제

Adam **will visit** me tomorrow. Adam은 내일 나를 방문할 것이다.
　　　미래시제

위의 문장들에서 동사 visit은 동작이 일어나는 시점에 따라 visited, visits, will visit로 변화하고 있다. 이와 같이 시간을 나타내는 동사의 형태 변화를 시제라고 한다.

2 동사는 단순, 진행, 완료 시제로 쓰이며, 각 시제에 따라 다른 형태를 취한다.

① 단순 시제는 특정 시점에 일어나는 동작이나 상태를 나타내며, '동사 (+ s / es)', '동사 + ed', 'will + 동사'형을 취한다.

현재　　　We **play** basketball every Saturday. 우리는 매주 토요일에 농구를 한다.
과거　　　We **played** basketball last Saturday. 우리는 지난 토요일에 농구를 했다.
미래　　　We **will play** basketball next Saturday. 우리는 다음 토요일에 농구를 할 것이다.

② 진행 시제는 특정 시점에 동작이 계속 진행되고 있는 것을 나타내며, 'be + -ing'형을 취한다.

현재진행　　She **is sleeping**. 그녀는 자고 있다.
과거진행　　She **was sleeping**. 그녀는 자고 있었다.
미래진행　　She **will be sleeping**. 그녀는 자고 있을 것이다.

③ 완료 시제는 특정 시점 이전에 일어난 일이나, 기준 시점 이전부터 기준 시점까지 계속된 동작이나 상태를 나타내며, 'have + p.p.'형을 취한다.

현재완료　　Brian **has gone**. Brian은 가고 없다.
과거완료　　Brian **had gone** when I arrived. 내가 도착했을 때, Brian은 가고 없었다.
미래완료　　Brian **will have gone** by then. 그때쯤이면, Brian은 가고 없을 것이다.

1 현재 / 과거 / 미래

현재 시제는 반복되는 동작·상태 묘사, 일반적인 사실, 진리·법칙 등을 표현하는 데 사용된다.

반복적 동작·상태 He often takes long walks. 그는 종종 오래 산책한다.

▶ 오래 산책하는 반복적인 행동을 나타내기 위해 현재 시제(takes)를 쓴다.

일반적 사실 Modern technology allows for more free time. 현대 과학 기술이 더 많은 자유 시간을 가능하게 한다.

▶ 현대 과학 기술이 지닌 장점에 대한 일반적인 사실을 나타내기 위해 현재 시제(allows)를 쓴다.

진리·법칙 Water freezes when the temperature drops below 32 degrees Fahrenheit.
온도가 화씨 32도 아래로 내려가면 물이 언다.

▶ 화씨 32도 이하에서 물이 언다는 변하지 않는 법칙을 진술하기 위해 현재 시제(freezes)를 쓴다.

과거 시제는 이미 끝난 과거의 동작·상태 묘사, 역사적 사실을 표현하는 데 사용된다.

과거의 동작·상태 I took a shower last night. 나는 어젯밤에 샤워를 했다.

▶ 샤워를 한 어젯밤의 일을 나타내기 위해 과거 시제(took)를 쓴다.

역사적 사실 French colonists settled Louisiana in the 17th century. 프랑스 식민지 개척자들은 17세기에 루이지애나에 정착했다.

▶ 17세기에 프랑스 식민지 개척자들이 루이지애나에 정착한 역사적 사건을 나타내기 위해 과거 시제(settled)를 쓴다.

미래 시제는 미래의 상황에 대한 예상이나 의지를 표현하는 데 사용된다.

미래의 상황 예상 The weather will start to improve in March. 날씨가 3월에 좋아지기 시작할 것이다.

▶ 3월부터 날씨가 좋아질 것이라는 예상을 표현하기 위해 미래 시제(will start)를 쓴다.

미래에 대한 의지 I will take my son on my next trip. 나는 다음 여행에 아들을 데려갈 것이다.

▶ 다음 여행에 아들을 데려갈 것이라는 의지를 표현하기 위해 미래 시제(will take)를 쓴다.

시간이나 조건을 나타내는 부사절에서는 미래 시제 대신 현재 시제를 써야 한다.

When you ~~will finish~~ your book, I will borrow it. 네가 책을 다 읽으면, 나는 그것을 빌릴 것이다.
      finish

▶ 시간을 나타내는 When절에서는 미래를 나타내기 위해 미래 시제(will finish)가 아니라 현재 시제(finish)를 써야 한다.

고득점 포인트 1. 시간/조건의 부사절을 이끄는 접속사에는 when, before, after, as soon as, by the time, if, unless 등이 있다.
2. 명사절로 쓰인 접속사절에서는 when이나 if가 쓰였더라도 미래 시제를 그대로 사용한다.
I want to know when you **arrive** in Japan tomorrow. (→ **will arrive**) 나는 네가 내일 언제 일본에 도착할지 알고 싶다.
   ↳ when절이 동사(know)의 목적어 자리에 온 명사절이므로, 미래 시제를 나타내기 위해 현재 시제(arrive)가 아니라 미래 시제(will arrive)를 써야 한다.

📋 텝스 실전 문제

텝스 문제 이렇게 나온다

적절한 시제의 동사를 채우거나, 동사의 시제가 틀린 문장을 찾는 문제가 주로 나온다.
시간/조건을 나타내는 부사절과 명사절로 쓰인 when/if절을 구별하여 동사를 채우거나, 동사의 시제가 틀린 문장을 찾는 문제가 주로 나온다.

Part I

A: These books are due at the library tomorrow.
B: _____ them on my way to work.

(a) I return   (b) I was returning
(c) I returned   (d) I'll return

Part III

2. (a) A: The dance troupe's performance was so amazing.
(b) B: Yeah, I never thought they would come here to perform.
(c) A: I would love to go again when they will come back.
(d) B: They're going overseas, so it won't be for a while.

정답 p.22

1 현재진행 시제(am / are / is + -ing)는 현재 시점에 진행되고 있는 일을 표현한다.

The phone is ringing **now.** 지금 전화기가 울리고 있다.

▶ 현재 시점(now)에 전화가 울리는 중이라는 것을 나타내기 위해 현재진행 시제(is ringing)를 쓴다.

📌 고득점 포인트 현재진행형은 미래에 일어나기로 예정되어 있는 일이나 곧 일어나려고 하는 일을 표현하여 미래를 나타내기도 한다.
The guests are coming in half an hour. 손님들이 30분 안에 올 것이다.
I am seeing Thomas on Thursday night. 나는 목요일 밤에 Thomas를 만날 예정이다.

2 과거진행 시제(was / were + -ing)는 특정 과거 시점에 진행되고 있었던 일을 표현한다.

The rain was pouring **when I woke up.** 내가 일어났을 때 비가 퍼붓고 있었다.

▶ 특정 과거 시점(when I woke up)에 비가 퍼붓고 있는 중이었다는 것을 나타내기 위해 과거진행 시제(was pouring)를 쓴다.

3 미래진행 시제(will be + -ing)는 특정 미래 시점에 어떤 일이 진행되고 있을 것임을 표현한다.

We will be swimming **in the sea at this time tomorrow.** 내일 이 시간쯤이면 우리는 바다에서 수영하고 있을 것이다.

▶ 특정 미래 시점(at this time tomorrow)에 수영을 하고 있을 것임을 나타내기 위해 미래진행 시제(will be swimming)를 쓴다.

4 진행 시제로 쓸 수 없는 동사

감정	love 좋아하다	like 좋아하다	prefer 선호하다	hate 싫어하다	surprise 놀라게 하다	satisfy 만족시키다
상태	be ~이다	belong 속하다	have 가지다	owe 빚지다	possess 소유하다	consist 구성하다
인지	believe 믿다	know 알다	see 알다	understand 이해하다	realize 깨닫다	remember 기억하다
감각	sound ~하게 들리다	look ~처럼 보이다	seem ~인 것 같다	appear ~인 것 같다	smell ~한 냄새가 나다	taste ~한 맛이 나다
기타	need 필요하다	agree 동의하다	deny 부인하다	promise 약속하다	want 원하다	wish 바라다

I ~~was having~~ urgent business last night. 나는 어젯밤에 급한 일이 있었다.
　　had
They ~~are needing~~ your help right now. 그들은 지금 당장 너의 도움을 필요로 한다.
　　　need

▶ '가지다'라는 의미로 상태를 나타내는 동사 have와 '필요하다'는 의미의 동사 need는 진행 시제로 쓰일 수 없는 동사이므로, was having이 아니라 had를, are needing이 아니라 need를 써야 한다.

☑ 텝스 실전 문제
텝스 문제 이렇게 나온

| 적절한 시제의 동사를 채우는 문제가 주로 나온다.

Part I

1. A: How did you get that ticket?
   B: I _____ too fast and was pulled over by the police.

   (a) drive　　　　(b) was driving
   (c) will drive　　(d) am driving

Part II

2. The core of the hurricane _____ ove
   Florida during the next 24 hours.

   (a) pass　　　　　(b) passes
   (c) was passing　(d) will be passing

정답 p

3 현재완료 / 과거완료 / 미래완료

현재완료 시제(have / has + p.p.)는 과거에 시작된 일이 현재까지 계속되는 경우, 현재에 완료된 경우, 현재의 결과에 영향을 미치는 경우, 과거에서 현재에 이르는 경험을 표현한다.

계속 She has played the piano since she was in elementary school. 그녀는 초등학생 때 이래로 피아노를 쳐왔다.
> 초등학생 때 시작하여 지금까지 계속 피아노를 치고 있으므로 현재완료 시제(has played)를 쓴다.

완료 We have just finished the first chapter. 우리는 막 첫 번째 챕터를 마쳤다.
> 과거에 시작한 첫 번째 챕터를 방금 마쳤으므로 현재완료 시제(have finished)를 쓴다.

결과 He has gone to New York. 그는 뉴욕에 가고 없다.
> 그가 과거에 뉴욕에 가서 지금 여기에 없다는 결과를 나타내므로 현재완료 시제(has gone)를 쓴다.

경험 I have eaten at this restaurant before. 나는 이 식당에서 전에 먹어본 적이 있다.
> 과거에 이 식당에서 먹어봤던 경험을 나타내므로 현재완료 시제(have eaten)를 쓴다.

과거완료 시제(had + p.p.)는 특정 과거 시점 이전에 발생한 일을 표현한다.

She had planned to go on a picnic, but it was raining. 그녀는 소풍을 가려고 계획했었지만, 비가 오고 있었다.
> 비가 오고 있던 시점 이전에 소풍을 가려고 계획한 사실을 나타내기 위해 과거완료 시제(had planned)를 쓴다.

미래완료 시제(will have + p.p.)는 특정 미래 시점 이전에 시작된 일이 미래의 그 시점에 완료될 것임을 표현한다.

At this rate, our profits will have doubled in five years. 이런 속도라면, 우리의 수익은 5년 후에 두 배가 될 것이다.
> 이전의 특정 시점부터 증가하기 시작한 수익이 5년 후라는 특정 미래 시점에 두 배가 된다는 것을 나타내기 위해 미래완료 시제(will have doubled)를 쓴다.

완료진행 시제(have / has / had been + -ing)는 기준 시점 이전에 시작된 일이 기준 시점까지 계속 진행 중임을 표현한다.

I've been thinking of changing jobs since last May. 나는 지난 5월 이래로 직업을 바꾸는 것에 대해 생각해왔다.
> 직업을 바꾸는 것을 5월부터 현재까지 생각하고 있는 중임을 나타내기 위해 현재완료진행 시제(have been thinking)를 쓴다.

텝스 실전 문제

적절한 시제의 동사를 채우거나, 동사의 시제가 틀린 문장을 찾는 문제가 주로 나온다.

Part II

By the time my novel is eventually published, I _____ working on my next one already.

(a) start (b) started
(c) was starting (d) will have started

Part III

2. (a) A: What is that song you're listening to?
   (b) B: This is Beethoven's Moonlight Sonata. I'm surprised you don't know it.
   (c) A: I had listened to it many times before, but I don't recognize this part.
   (d) B: This is the second movement, which sounds different from the first and third.

정답 p.22

1 과거, 미래, 현재완료 시제와 자주 함께 쓰이는 표현들

과거	미래 · 미래완료	현재완료
yesterday last + 시간 표현 시간 표현 + ago by the time + 주어 + 과거 동사	tomorrow next + 시간 표현 by + 미래 시간 표현 by the time + 주어 + 현재 동사	yet so far since + 과거 시간 표현 over/for + 시간 표현

Joe <u>went</u> to the eye doctor <u>last week</u>.   Joe는 지난주에 안과 진료를 받았다.
    <small>과거</small>   <small>과거 시간표현</small>

▶ 과거 시간 표현(last week)이 있으므로 과거 시제(went)를 쓴다.

By the time Monday comes, I <u>will have recovered</u> from my cold.   월요일이 올 때쯤이면, 나는 감기가 다 나아 있을 것이다.
  <small>By the time + 주어 + 현재동사</small>   <small>미래완료</small>

▶ 미래 시점을 나타내는 시간 표현 'by the time + 주어 + 현재 동사'(By the time Monday comes)가 있으므로, 미래완료 시제(will have recove
쓴다.

고득점 포인트 1. 'by the time + 주어 + 과거 동사'는 과거뿐만 아니라 과거완료 시제와도 자주 함께 쓰인다.
        The movie **had** already **ended** by the time I got home.   내가 집에 도착했을 때 쯤, 영화는 이미 끝났다.

        2. 최상급 표현을 포함한 선행사를 수식하는 관계절에 완료 시제가 자주 쓰인다.
        Ben is <u>the tallest man</u> I **have** ever **seen**.   Ben은 내가 본 사람 중 가장 키가 크다.
          ↳ 최상급 표현(the tallest)이 포함된 명사를 수식하고 있으므로 관계절의 동사는 현재완료 시제(have seen)를 쓴다.

2 주절의 시제가 과거일 경우 종속절에는 과거나 과거완료가 온다.

I ordered the sofa (that) I ~~see~~ in the catalogue.   나는 제품 목록에서 본 소파를 주문했다.
  <small>과거</small>   saw

▶ 주절의 시제가 과거(ordered)이고 종속절에서 '내가 소파를 본' 것 역시 과거 시점에 일어난 일이므로, 종속절의 동사는 현재 시제(see)가 아니
시제(saw)가 와야 한다.

He said that he ~~has witnessed~~ the criminal deed.   그는 범죄 행위를 목격했다고 진술했다.
  <small>과거</small>   had witnessed

▶ 주절의 시제가 과거(said)이고 종속절에서 '그가 범죄 행위를 목격한' 것은 주절에서 일어난 일보다 더 이전 시점에 일어난 일이므로, 현재완료 시
witnessed)가 아니라 과거완료 시제(had witnessed)가 와야 한다.

☑ 텝스 실전 문제

<small>텝스 문제 이렇게 나</small>

| 시간 표현에 시제 일치하는 동사를 채우는 문제가 주로 나온다.
| 주절에 시제 일치하는 종속절 동사를 채우는 문제가 주로 나온다.

Part I

1. A: What do you think of this new piece?
   B: It's the most beautiful song _____ yet.

  (a) you're writing   (b) you had written
  (c) you've written   (d) you've been writing

Part II

2. The woman came home and saw that her husba
  _____ the stew and set the table alread

  (a) has boiled   (b) had boiled
  (c) will boil   (d) is boiling

<small>정답</small>

중 알맞은 것을 고르세요.

The Summer Olympics (take place / are taking place) every four years, with the host city alternating continents each time.

Our bookstore (has sold / has been selling) the last copy of the book in stock.

You had better take your umbrella, since it (was raining / is raining) outside.

The value of the company's stock (dropped / drops) and people are selling it in large amounts.

City officials predict that the protesters (have / will have) left the area by tomorrow.

Eleanor returned home and discovered that Scott (has been cooking / had been cooking) dinner for the past two hours.

부분이 있으면 바르게 고치세요.

I finish the laundry now, and then I can meet my colleagues at the party.

Maggie will be waiting for me when my flight arrives this evening.

I'm having something special to give you as a baby shower gift.

The magazine *Stars* said that the former child actor has earned over five million dollars before he retired at age 14.

You will read the entire book by next Friday if you keep going at this rate.

The ticket counter will be on your left as soon as you will enter the airport.

정답 p.23

Hackers **TEST**

Part I Choose the best answer for the blank.

01 A: I can't believe I didn't get any mail today.
   B: Don't you know mail never _____ on Sundays?

   (a) come   (b) comes
   (c) came   (d) have come

02 A: Did you enjoy your vacation?
   B: Unfortunately no, as things didn't turn out the way I _____.

   (a) plan   (b) had planned
   (c) have planned (d) was planning

03 A: What time will the ceremony tomorrow finish?
   B: It will finish at noon if it _____ on time.

   (a) begins   (b) began
   (c) has begun   (d) will have begun

04 A: _____ if he'll ever call me back.
   B: You can't keep waiting. You should move on.

   (a) I wondered
   (b) I wondering
   (c) I've been wondered
   (d) I've been wondering

05 A: Judy, are you still asleep?
   B: I _____, but I already woke up.

   (a) will just nap
   (b) am just napping
   (c) was just napping
   (d) will just have napped

06 A: I can't give you a firm answer right away.
   B: Then I _____ it later this week.

   (a) anticipated
   (b) have anticipated
   (c) will be anticipating
   (d) was going to anticipate

07 A: What were you about to say?
   B: I _____ about something, b now I can't remember it.

   (a) will think
   (b) will have thought
   (c) am thinking
   (d) was thinking

Part II Choose the best answer for the blank.

08 As the term _____ next week, the school will hold a special assembly for all stude

   (a) is finishing   (b) finishing
   (c) finished   (d) has finished

09 The student had stayed up for two nights in preparation for his final exam, but he accidenta _____ on the day of the test.

   (a) overslept   (b) oversleeps
   (c) has overslept (d) will oversleep

10 Over the last few years, many elevators and escalators _____ installed in subwa stations to aid the elderly and disabled.

   (a) had been   (b) have been
   (c) will be   (d) will have been

11 After watching the suitors perform a courtship dance, the female hummingbird decides which _____ most suitable among them.

   (a) is   (b) are
   (c) have been   (d) has been

Although the underage kids were drinking alcohol in the neighborhood park, _____ that provoked the neighbors to call the police.

(a) their noise-making was it
(b) it was their noise-making
(c) noise-making of theirs was
(d) was it their noise-making

When asked who would play in the game on Friday, the manager said he _____ his players yet.

(a) hadn't chosen
(b) won't have been choosing
(c) hadn't been choosing
(d) won't have chosen

If the payment goes as planned, the money _____ to the real estate agent's account by the time the bank closes.

(a) was deposited
(b) is being deposited
(c) was being deposited
(d) will have been deposited

Robert had spent almost the entire day poring over the riddle before he finally _____ it.

(a) solve   (b) solved
(c) has solved   (d) will have solved

The average price of a house has fallen ever since the government _____ plans to invest in affordable public housing.

(a) revealed   (b) had revealed
(c) has revealed   (d) was revealing

Part III Identify the option that contains an awkward expression or an error in grammar.

17 (a) A: This was such a hectic week for me.
   (b) B: What had you been doing that's kept you so busy?
   (c) A: A million different things had to be dealt with.
   (d) B: I hope you have everything straightened out now.

18 (a) A: Mom, didn't you say we would go out for dinner?
   (b) B: I did, but your father came home and now he is sleeping a while.
   (c) A: Do you remember if he said when he wakes up?
   (d) B: Probably soon, but if you're hungry, have an apple while you wait.

19 (a) Aristotle believed that three modes of persuasion constitutes the basis of rhetoric.
   (b) Ethos refers to one's authority on a subject and how qualified one is to speak about it.
   (c) Connecting to the audience and appealing to their emotions is what is meant by pathos.
   (d) Logic and data, or logos, proves most persuasive, since it deals with proven facts.

20 (a) Virtual universities are available online to facilitate those who want to take academic courses remotely. (b) Eliminating the need for physical attendance, they are designed to let students study at their own pace. (c) Some programs give students assignments to be completed, while others offer lectures through video. (d) Regardless of their format, virtual universities are expected to make higher education more accessible once they will reach a wider audience.

CHAPTER 06 능동태·수동태

BASIC GRAMMAR 고수로 가는 첫 걸음

1 능동태는 '주어가 ~하다'라는 의미로 주어가 행위의 주체가 되며, 수동태는 '주어가 ~되다 / 당하다'라는 의미로 주어가 행위의 대상이 된다. 수동태 동사의 기본 형태는 'be + p.p.'이다.

능동태 I **made** this cake. 내가 이 케이크를 만들었다.

수동태 This cake **was made** by me. 이 케이크는 나에 의해 만들어졌다.

위의 첫 번째 문장은 '내가 만들었다'라는 의미로 주어인 '내'가 '만들다'는 행위의 주체인 능동태 문장이고, 두 번째 문장은 '이 케이크는 만들어졌다'라는 의미로 주어인 '케이크'가 '만들다'는 행위의 대상이 되는 수동태 문장이다.

	기본형	진행형	완료형
능동태의 형태	동사의 현재/과거/미래형	be + -ing	have + p.p.
수동태의 형태	be + p.p.	be being + p.p.	have been + p.p.

2 능동태 문장의 목적어가 문장의 주어 자리로 오면 수동태 문장이 된다.

능동태 Austen wrote this novel. Austen이 이 소설을 썼다.
　　　　　　주어　능동태동사　목적어

수동태 This novel was written by Austen. 이 소설은 Austen에 의해 쓰였다.
　　　　　　주어　　수동태동사　　by + 행위의 주체

3 능동태 문장의 목적어가 수동태 문장의 주어가 되므로, 목적어를 갖는 타동사만이 수동태가 될 수 있고, 목적어를 갖지 않는 자동사는 수동태가 될 수 없다.

The movers should ~~be arrived~~ within forty minutes. 운송업자들이 40분 내에 도착할 것이다.
　　　　　　　　　　arrive

위 문장의 동사 arrive는 자동사이므로 목적어를 갖지 않고, 따라서 수동태로 쓰일 수 없다.

의미상 수동태로 쓸 수 있는 것처럼 혼동되는 자동사에는 remain(~인 채로 남아 있다), range(범위에 이르다), arise(발생하다), occur(일어나다), take place(일어나다), result(결과로서 생기다 / 끝나다), turn out(~으로 밝혀지다), belong(속하다) 등이 있다.

01 능동태 · 수동태 구별

타동사는 능동태일 때는 반드시 목적어를 갖지만, 수동태일 때는 목적어를 갖지 못한다.

Cars ~~are needed~~ regular maintenance. 자동차는 정기적인 관리를 필요로 한다.
    need   목적어

▶ 동사 뒤에 목적어(regular maintenance)가 있으므로, 수동태 동사(are needed)가 아닌 능동태 동사(need)가 와야 한다.

The library will ~~renovate~~. 도서관은 수리될 것이다.
         be renovated

▶ 타동사 뒤에 목적어가 없으므로, 능동태 동사(renovate)가 아닌 수동태 동사(be renovated)가 와야 한다.

고득점 포인트 감정을 나타내는 동사 역시 동사 뒤에 목적어가 있는지 여부에 따라 능동태·수동태를 구별한다.

The new world record **was excited** the spectators. (→ excited) 세계 신기록이 관중들을 흥분시켰다.

  ↳ 동사 뒤에 목적어(the spectators)가 있으므로, 수동태 동사(was excited)가 아닌 능동태 동사(excited)가 와야 한다. excite는 '흥분하다'가 아니라 '흥분시키다'라는 뜻의 타동사이므로 목적어를 갖는다.

Alice **excited** about her new shoes. (→ **was excited**) Alice는 그녀의 새 구두에 흥분했다.

  ↳ 동사 뒤에 전치사구(about her new shoes)만 있고, 목적어가 없으므로, 능동태 동사(excited)가 아닌 수동태 동사(was excited)가 와야 한다.

to부정사의 동사와 관계절의 동사도 목적어 여부에 따라 능동태·수동태를 구별한다.

The lawyers were unable ~~to be reached~~ an agreement. 변호사들은 합의에 도달할 수 없었다.
               to reach   목적어

▶ to부정사 뒤에 목적어(an agreement)가 있으므로, to부정사의 수동형(to be reached)이 아닌 to부정사의 능동형(to reach)이 와야 한다.

The accounting report had ~~to finish~~ by Monday. 회계 보고서는 월요일까지 마쳐져야 한다.
              to be finished

▶ to부정사 뒤에 목적어가 없으므로, to부정사의 능동형(to finish)이 아닌 to부정사의 수동형(to be finished)이 와야 한다.

The announcer who ~~is delivered~~ the evening news will retire. 저녁 뉴스를 전하는 아나운서는 은퇴할 것이다.
         delivers   목적어

▶ 관계절의 동사 뒤에 목적어(the evening news)가 있으므로, 수동태 동사(is delivered)가 아닌 능동태 동사(delivers)가 와야 한다.

They took in the dog that ~~found~~ under the porch. 그들은 현관 아래에서 발견된 개를 집에서 지내게 했다.
               was found

▶ 관계절의 동사 뒤에 목적어가 없으므로, 능동태 동사(found)가 아닌 수동태 동사(was found)가 와야 한다.

☑ 텝스 실전 문제

| 동사의 능동태·수동태를 구별하여 채우거나, 동사의 태가 틀린 문장을 찾는 문제가 주로 나온다.

Part II

1. The woman's tonsils, which had been causing her chronic illness, needed ＿＿＿＿＿＿ for her to recover.

  (a) remove   (b) removed
  (c) to remove   (d) to be removed

Part III

2. (a) With wings attached to their forearms, bats are the only mammals with the natural ability to fly. (b) Though most bats feast on insects or fruit, some bats take blood from their prey. (c) They are typically nocturnal creatures that sleep during the day, and often upside down. (d) They equipped with the ability to locate prey based on the echoes of the sounds they emit.

정답 p.25

1 목적어를 두 개 갖는 4형식 동사가 수동태가 되는 경우, 목적어 중 한 개가 수동태 동사 뒤에 남는다.

능동태	He gave Dan a pen. 그는 Dan에게 펜을 주었다.
	간접목적어 직접목적어
간접 목적어가 주어로 간 수동태	Dan was given a pen. Dan은 펜을 받았다.
직접 목적어가 주어로 간 수동태	A pen was given to Dan. 펜은 Dan에게 주어졌다.

▶ 간접 목적어(Dan)가 주어로 간 수동태 문장에서는 직접 목적어(a pen)가 수동태 동사(was given) 뒤에 그대로 남는다. 이때 뒤에 남은 직접 목적어를 목적어로 생각해 능동태 동사를 쓰지 않도록 주의한다. 직접 목적어(a pen)가 주어로 간 수동태 문장에서는 수동태 동사(was given) 뒤에 '전치사 + 간접 목적어'(to Dan)가 온다.

2 목적어와 목적격 보어를 갖는 5형식 동사가 수동태가 되는 경우, 목적격 보어는 수동태 동사 뒤에 남는다.

· 목적격 보어가 '명사구'인 5형식 동사의 수동태

능동태	They consider Jessica a sister. 그들은 Jessica를 자매로 여긴다.
	능동태 동사 목적어 목적격 보어
수동태	Jessica is considered a sister. Jessica는 자매로 여겨진다.
	주어 수동태 동사 목적격 보어

▶ 목적어(Jessica)가 주어로 가서 수동태 문장이 되는 경우, 목적격 보어(a sister)는 수동태 동사(is considered) 뒤에 그대로 남는다. 이때 뒤에 남은 목적격 보어를 목적어로 생각해 능동태 동사를 쓰지 않도록 주의한다.

· 목적격 보어가 '분사'인 5형식 동사의 수동태

능동태	Henry found the vase broken. Henry는 꽃병이 깨진 것을 발견했다.
	능동태 동사 목적어 목적격 보어
수동태	The vase was found broken. 꽃병이 깨진 것이 발견되었다.
	주어 수동태 동사 목적격 보어

▶ 목적어(the vase)가 주어로 가서 수동태 문장이 되는 경우, 목적격 보어(broken)는 수동태 동사(was found) 뒤에 그대로 남는다.

· 목적격 보어가 'to부정사구'인 5형식 동사의 수동태

능동태	I asked them to turn down the volume. 나는 그들에게 볼륨을 줄여달라고 요청했다.
	능동태 동사 목적어 목적격 보어
수동태	They were asked to turn down the volume. 그들은 볼륨을 줄여달라고 요청받았다.
	주어 수동태 동사 목적격 보어

▶ 목적어(them)가 주어로 가서 수동태 문장이 되는 경우, 목적격 보어(to turn down the volume)는 수동태 동사(were asked) 뒤에 그대로 남는다.

☑ 텝스 실전 문제

텝스 문제 이렇게 나온다

| 4형식 문장의 수동태 동사를 채우는 문제가 주로 나온다.
| 5형식 문장의 수동태 동사를 채우거나, 분사나 to부정사 목적격 보어를 수동태 동사와 함께 채우는 문제가 주로 나온다.

Part I

1. A: Sylvia _____ a seat in the council last week.
   B: She must be excited.

   (a) offers
   (b) offered
   (c) is offered
   (d) was offered

Part II

2. Sports drinks _____ the body more effectively than water or regular juice.

   (a) think to hydrate
   (b) are thought to hydrate
   (c) thinks to be hydrate
   (d) is thought to be hydrated

정답 p.2

Hackers **Practice**

중 알맞은 것을 고르세요.

An author from Spain (considers / is considered) the most prolific writer of the 21st century.

The company's line of products (ranges / is ranged) from mobile phone cards to low-cost air tickets.

I thought the dinner was delicious, but the chunks of potatoes needed (to cut / to be cut) a bit smaller.

After they demolished the building, dozens of rats (saw / were seen) scurrying across the street.

Any person who works with statistics (is regarded / regards) computers as an essential tool of their trade.

I (surprised / was surprised) to find out that he was ten years older than me.

된 부분이 있으면 바르게 고치세요.

The use of too much wasabi is overpowered the other flavors in a piece of sushi.

The luxury car in the driveway is belonged to my cousin Rick who has been employed in the financial firm for only a year.

Tomorrow's solar eclipse expects to be visible to over 70 million people.

Michelle is a good friend who is appreciated everywhere she goes.

Elections for the United States House of Representatives are occurred once every two years.

The fireworks were delighted the guests who were being seated along the riverside.

Hackers **TEST**

제한 시간: 10분

Part I Choose the best answer for the blank.

01 A: You've been here for years and you're still an assistant?
B: Yes, but by this time next year, I _____.

(a) promote
(b) have promoted
(c) will be promoting
(d) will have been promoted

02 A: The shop you newly opened looks smaller than the old one.
B: Indeed, but the number of items it carries _____ the same.

(a) remain   (b) remains
(c) is remained   (d) are remained

03 A: You finally get to take a vacation next week.
B: Yes, but I _____ to take a flight for eight hours.

(a) scare   (b) am scared
(c) was scaring   (d) have been scared

04 A: Please give me one more chance.
B: I'm sorry. All of your chances _____.

(a) used up
(b) been used up
(c) have been used up
(d) will have been used up

05 A: Wasn't there any food remaining from the party last night?
B: Because there were so many guests, _____.

(a) none left   (b) none was left
(c) none had left   (d) none had been left

Part II Choose the best answer for the blank.

06 Despite an extensive trial to which many witness had come to testify, a verdict _____ rath quickly.

(a) reach   (b) reached
(c) was reached   (d) were reached

07 The quiet yet brilliant calculus student in the bac _____ the first forty digits of pi b heart.

(a) to be believed
(b) believed to know
(c) was believed to know
(d) is believed to be known

08 The paucity of average snowfall in recent years _____ many ski resorts to lose business.

(a) causes   (b) is caused
(c) has caused   (d) has been caused

09 Before becoming a prominent stage actor, Phillip Silver abandoned the name he _____ at birt and took on a pseudonym.

(a) gives   (b) gave
(c) have given   (d) was given

10 A number of citizens _____ to rally behi the idealistic young candidate.

(a) was begun   (b) were begun
(c) has begun   (d) have begun

11 The Web site's plans to redesign its main page a media content _____ the effort of a skilled professional.

(a) require   (b) requires
(c) is required   (d) are required

Because certain issues had yet to be resolved, it _____ that the board reconvene in two weeks.

(a) suggests   (b) suggested
(c) is suggested   (d) was suggested

John Locke's theories about human nature _____ the basis of modern democratic thought.

(a) constitute   (b) constitutes
(c) is constituting   (d) are constituted

Mr. Williams _____ his students due to the fact that he had locked his keys in his car for the second time in one week.

(a) laughed at   (b) was laughed at
(c) was laughed by   (d) was laughed at by

Marie Curie _____ the Nobel Prize in 1903 for having discovered radioactivity.

(a) formally awards   (b) formally awarded
(c) was formally awarded (d) is formally awarding

Of all natural energy sources, petroleum _____ the most on a global scale up to now.

(a) has consumed   (b) has been consumed
(c) will consume   (d) will be consumed

18 (a) A: What is that crowd by the bookstore entrance doing?
(b) B: They are waited for the book signing to begin.
(c) A: Is anyone allowed to get an autograph?
(d) B: Yes, but you have to purchase a book first.

19 (a) Modern evolutionary theory based on the findings of unique animal fossils. (b) For example, scientists have discovered fossils of animals that resemble small whales with hind legs. (c) These fossils date back to an era in which whales are not known to have lived. (d) Therefore, the theory has posited that these animals are the evolutionary ancestors of modern whales.

20 (a) The term "mushrooming" is derived from the ability of some mushrooms to reach full size in a short span of time. (B) One example, the *Parasola plicatilis*, takes several days to develop cells that can quickly absorb water. (c) These mushrooms are arisen over the course of a single night after heavy rain and disappear the next day after releasing spores. (d) This quick-blooming trait exists only in certain mushrooms, as other species develop at a slower rate.

t III Identify the option that contains an awkward expression or an error in grammar.

(a) A: Has the administration looked at my proposal yet?
(b) B: It is being considering and you will be notified within the hour.
(c) A: Since I have a meeting to attend, can I be contacted about it later?
(d) B: Of course. Please leave your number and the time when you can be reached.

정답 p.26

CHAPTER **07** 가정법

BASIC GRAMMAR 고수로 가는 첫 걸음

1 가정법 문장은 현재나 과거의 상황을 반대로 가정해보거나, 일어날 가능성이 희박한 일이 미래에 일어날 경우를 가정해보는 문장이다.

If I were free, I would go out for dinner. 만약 내가 한가하다면, 저녁 식사를 하러 나갈 텐데.
If it should rain tomorrow, we will not go hiking. (혹시라도) 내일 비가 온다면, 우리는 하이킹을 가지 않을 것이다.

첫 번째 문장은 현재의 상황을 반대로 가정하는 가정법 문장으로, 현재 한가하지 않지만 한가한 상황을 가정해보는 것이다. 두 번째 문장은 일어날 가능성이 희박한 일이 미래에 일어날 것이라고 가정하는 가정법 문장으로, 내일 비가 올 가능성은 거의 없지만 비가 올 경우를 가정해보는 것이다.

2 가정법은 대개 If로 시작하며, 특별한 시제를 사용한다.

If I knew him, I would say hello to him. 내가 그를 안다면, 그에게 인사를 할 텐데.
　　　과거　　　　조동사의 과거형 + 동사원형
If I had known him, I would have said hello to him. 내가 그를 알았다면, 그에게 인사를 했을 텐데.
　　　과거완료　　　　조동사의 과거형 + have p.p.

가정법 문장에서는 첫 문장에서처럼 '현재' 상황의 반대를 가정하기 위해 If절에 '과거 시제'(knew)를 쓰고, 주절에 '조동사의 과거형 + 동사원형'(would say)을 쓴다. 또한, '과거' 상황의 반대를 가정하기 위해서는 두 번째 문장에서처럼 If절에 '과거완료 시제'(had known)를 쓰고, 주절에 '조동사의 과거형 + have p.p.'(would have said)를 쓴다.

If절이 없어도, 특별한 시제로 쓰인 문장이 '현재'나 '과거'의 상황을 반대로 가정하는 문장이 될 수 있다.

I would go to the party, but I'm busy. 나는 파티에 가고 싶지만, 바쁘다.
He could have met me, but he wanted to finish his paper. 그는 나를 만날 수도 있었지만, 논문을 마치기를 원했다.

3 가정법 문장은 If로 시작하는 조건절 문장과 구별해야 한다.

가정법　　**If it were not cold, I could go hiking.** 춥지 않다면, 하이킹을 갈 수 있을 텐데. (사실은 춥다)
조건절　　**If you are cold, you can close the window.** 네가 춥다면, 창문을 닫아도 된다. (추울 수도 있고 아닐 수도 있다)

첫 번째 문장과 같이 특정한 상황을 반대로 가정하는 것이 아니라, 사실이거나 일어날 가능성이 있는 일에 대해 말하는 두 번째 문장의 If절(If you are cold)을 조건절이라고 한다. 특별한 시제를 사용하는 가정법 문장과는 다르게, 조건절 문장에서는 주어의 인칭과 시제에 따라 동사의 형태가 바뀐다.

1 가정법 과거 · 과거완료

출제빈도 ★★★

가정법 과거

| 현재 상황을 반대로 가정 | If + 주어 + 과거동사 (be동사는 were),   주어 + would/should/could/might + 동사원형 |

If I spoke Spanish, I ~~can work~~ in South America. 만약 내가 스페인어를 한다면, 남미에서 일할 수 있을 텐데. (스페인어를 못해서 일할 수 없다)
과거동사   could work
▶ 현재 스페인어를 못하지만 스페인어를 한다고 가정하는 가정법 과거 문장이므로, 주절에 can work가 아니라 could work가 와야 한다.

If we were married, we ~~will move~~ out of the city. 만약 우리가 결혼한 상태라면, 도시 밖으로 이사를 갈 텐데. (결혼을 안해서 이사를 못 간다)
과거동사   would move
▶ 현재 결혼한 상태는 아니지만 결혼한 상태라고 가정하는 가정법 과거 문장이므로, 주절에 will move가 아니라 would move가 와야 한다.

고득점포인트 가정법 If절에 be동사가 오는 경우, I/he/she/it 등의 주어 뒤에는 were 대신 was를 쓰기도 한다.
If Joshua **were / was** nicer, he might make more friends. 그가 더 상냥하다면, 더 많은 친구를 사귈 수도 있을 텐데.

가정법 과거완료

| 과거 상황을 반대로 가정 | If + 주어 + had p.p.,   주어 + would/should/could/might + have p.p. |

If someone had arrived at the door, I ~~would hear~~ the doorbell ring. 누군가 왔었다면, 나는 초인종이 울리는 것을 들었을 텐데.
had p.p.   would have heard
▶ 과거에 누군가 오지 않았지만 왔었다고 가정하는 가정법 과거완료 문장이므로, 주절에 would hear가 아니라 would have heard가 와야 한다.

If Melissa had told me earlier about the concert, I ~~might be~~ able to go.
had p.p.   might have been
Melissa가 그 콘서트에 대해서 더 일찍 말했다면, 나는 갈 수도 있었을 텐데.
▶ 과거에 Melissa가 콘서트에 대해 더 일찍 말하지 않았지만 더 일찍 말했다고 가정하는 가정법 과거완료 문장이므로, 주절에 might be가 아니라 might have been이 와야 한다.

☑ 텝스 실전 문제

텝스 문제 이렇게 나온다

가정법 과거나 과거완료의 동사구를 채우는 문제가 주로 나온다.
if절과 주절에 쓰인 동사의 짝이 틀린 가정법 과거나 과거완료 문장을 찾는 문제가 주로 나온다.

Part I

1. A: You took so long to answer my text message.
   B: I _____ my phone sooner if I had known it was so urgent.

   (a) checked   (b) would check
   (c) have checked   (d) would have checked

Part III

2. (a) The Sun appears yellow in color when seen from Earth, but if viewed from outer space, it actually glows a bright white. (b) This is because Earth's atmosphere blocks a part of the spectrum of visible light coming from the Sun. (c) It scatters the Sun's short-wavelength colors, such as green, blue and violet. (d) Therefore, if the Earth had no atmosphere, the Sun will appear a very bright white in color.

정답 p.28

1 가정법 미래

가능성이 희박한 미래 가정	If + 주어 + should + 동사원형, 주어 + will / can / may would / should / could / might + 동사원형
	If + 주어 + were to + 동사원형, 주어 + would / should / could / might + 동사원형

If it <u>should rain</u> tomorrow, we ~~meet~~ at your house instead. (혹시라도) 만약 내일 비가 온다면, 우리는 대신에 너의 집에서 만날 것이다.
<u>should + 동사원형</u>   will meet

▶ should를 이용한 가정법 미래 문장이므로, 주절에 meet가 아니라 will meet이 와야 한다.

If I <u>were to quit</u> my job, my family ~~will be~~ shocked. (혹시라도) 만약 내가 일을 그만 둔다면, 가족들이 충격을 받을 것이다.
<u>were to + 동사원형</u>   would be

▶ were to를 이용한 가정법 미래 문장이므로, 주절에 will be가 아니라 would be가 와야 한다.

고득점 포인트 'If + 주어 + should + 동사원형, 명령문'은 문제가 발생하거나 도움이 필요할 경우 해결책을 제시하는 표현으로 사용된다.
If you should have any problems, please report them to customer service. 문제가 생기면, 고객 서비스센터에 알려주시기 바랍니다.

2 혼합 가정법

If + 주어 + had p.p., 주어 + would / should / could / might + 동사원형	만약 (과거에) ~했었더라면 (지금) ―할 텐데

If I had done my homework, I ~~could have gone~~ to a movie <u>now</u>. 내가 숙제를 했었더라면, 지금 영화를 보러 갈 수 있을 텐데.
     could go

▶ If절에 과거의 사실을 반대로 가정하는 가정법 과거완료 시제(had done)가 왔지만, 주절에서는 현재 상황을 반대로 표현하고 있으므로 가정법 과거 (could have gone)가 아니라 가정법 과거(could go)가 와야 한다. 이때, 주절에는 now와 같이 '현재'임을 나타내는 단서가 함께 오기도 한다.

If Tiffany had not quit playing the violin, she ~~might~~ still ~~have had~~ a music career.
     might   have

Tiffany가 바이올린 연주를 그만두지 않았더라면, 여전히 음악 활동을 할 텐데.

▶ If절에 과거의 사실을 반대로 가정하는 가정법 과거완료 시제(had not quit)가 왔지만, 주절에서는 현재 상황을 반대로 표현하고 있으므로 가정법 과거 료(might still have had)가 아니라 가정법 과거(might still have)가 와야 한다.

☑ 텝스 실전 문제
텝스 문제 이렇게 나온ㄷ

| 가정법 미래나 혼합 가정법 문장의 동사구를 채우는 문제가 주로 나온다.

Part I

1. A: I will take the bus to your house tonight from work.
   B: If you should miss the bus, I _____ you up.

   (a) have picked   (b) can pick
   (c) could have picked   (d) have been picking

Part II

2. If Jack had not injured his ankle, he _____ a professional soccer player now.

   (a) had been   (b) has been
   (c) was being   (d) would be

정답 p.2

3 If가 생략된 가정법

가정법 문장에서 If가 생략될 수 있으며, 이때 주어와 동사의 자리가 바뀌는 도치가 일어난다.

과거	If + 주어 + 과거동사/were, → 과거동사/were + 주어,	주어 + would/should/could/might + 동사원형
과거완료	If + 주어 + had p.p., → Had + 주어 + p.p.,	주어 + would/should/could/might + have p.p.
미래	If + 주어 + should + 동사원형, → Should + 주어 + 동사원형,	주어 + will/can/may would/should/could/might + 동사원형

If I were wealthy, I would travel the world. 내가 부자라면, 세계를 여행할 텐데.
→ Were I wealthy, I would travel the world.
▶ 가정법 문장의 If가 생략되면서, 동사(Were)가 주어(I)보다 앞에 온다.

If Brian had practiced harder, he could have been a professional pianist. Brian이 더 열심히 연습했다면, 전문 피아니스트가 됐을 수 있었을 텐데.
→ Had Brian practiced harder, he could have been a professional pianist.
▶ 가정법 문장의 If가 생략되면서, 조동사(Had)가 주어(Brian)보다 앞에 온다.

If you should have time tomorrow, we could go to the park. (혹시라도) 내일 시간이 있으면, 우리는 공원에 갈 수 있어.
→ Should you have time tomorrow, we could go to the park.
▶ 가정법 문장의 If가 생략되면서, 조동사(Should)가 주어(you)보다 앞에 온다.

If가 생략된 가정법 관용구문

과거	Were it not for + 명사 (= If not for/Without)	~가 아니라면, ~가 없다면	현재 상황의 반대
과거완료	Had it not been for + 명사 (= If not for/Without)	~가 아니었다면, ~가 없었다면	과거 상황의 반대

Were it not for the snow, the traffic would be going smoothly. 눈이 안 오면, 교통이 원활할 텐데.
[If it were not for the snow/If not for the snow/Without the snow]
▶ 'Were it not for + 명사(the snow)'는 If가 생략된 가정법 관용구문으로, If not for나 Without으로 바꿔 쓸 수 있다.

Had it not been for your help, I would not have been able to move the furniture.
네 도움이 없었더라면, 나는 가구를 옮기지 못했을 것이다.
[If it had not been for your help/If not for your help/Without your help]
▶ 'Had it not been for + 명사(your help)'는 If가 생략된 가정법 관용구문으로 If not for나 Without으로 바꿔 쓸 수 있다.

텝스 실전 문제

If가 생략되어 도치된 가정법 문장의 동사구를 채우는 문제가 주로 나온다.
If가 생략된 가정법 관용구문을 채우는 문제가 가끔 나온다.

Part II

1. _____, John would stay at work to finish his report.

(a) That it were not late
(b) Were not for it that late
(c) Were it not that late
(d) It was not that late

2. _____ the stormy weather, all flights would have run on time.

(a) For (b) Without
(c) If for (d) Not for

정답 p.29

1 I wish / I would rather 가정법

I wish	과거	I wish + 주어 + 과거 동사	~하면 좋을 텐데	현재 상황의 반대
	과거완료	I wish + 주어 + had p.p.	~했다면 좋을 텐데	과거 상황의 반대
I would rather	과거	I would rather + 주어 + 과거 동사	~하면 좋을 텐데	현재 상황의 반대
	과거완료	I would rather + 주어 + had p.p.	~했다면 좋을 텐데	과거 상황의 반대

I wish I were **with you.** 내가 너와 함께 있다면 좋을 텐데.
I wish I had been **with you.** 내가 너와 함께 있었다면 좋을 텐데.

I would rather he stayed. 그가 머물러 있다면 좋을 텐데.
I would rather he had stayed. 그가 머물러 있었다면 좋았을 텐데.

2 If only 가정법

과거	If only + 주어 + 과거 동사	~만 하면 좋을 텐데	현재 상황의 반대
과거완료	If only + 주어 + had p.p.	~만 했다면 좋았을 텐데	과거 상황의 반대

If only I were **not allergic.** 내가 알레르기만 없다면 좋을 텐데.
If only you had realized **what was wrong.** 무엇이 잘못 되었는지 네가 알기만 했다면 좋을 텐데.

포인트 고득점 If only 가정법은 주절과 함께 쓰기도 한다.
I could cook more often if only I had more time. 시간만 더 있다면, 나는 더 자주 요리할 수 있을 텐데.
If only I had known you were with her, I wouldn't have been so worried. 네가 그녀와 함께 있는 것만 알았다면, 내가 그렇게 걱정하지 않았을 텐

3 as if / as though 가정법

과거	as if / as though + 주어 + 과거 동사	마치 ~한 것처럼	현재 상황의 반대
과거완료	as if / as though + 주어 + had p.p.	마치 ~했던 것처럼	과거 상황의 반대

She talks as if/ as though she knew **everything.** 그녀는 마치 모든 것을 아는 것처럼 말한다.
Jacey talks as if/ as though she had met **Johnny Depp.** Jacey는 마치 조니 뎁을 만났던 것처럼 말한다.

4 It's (about / high) time 가정법

과거	It's (about / high) time + 주어 + 과거 동사	~해야 할 때이다	현재 상황의 반대

It's about/ high time he switched **careers to one he likes better.** 그가 더 좋아하는 것으로 직업을 바꿔야 할 때이다.

☑ 텝스 실전 문제
텝스 문제 이렇게 나온

| I wish / I would rather 가정법 문장의 동사구를 채우는 문제가 주로 나
온다.
| as if / as though 가정법 문장의 동사구를 채우는 문제가 가끔 나온다.

Part I

1. A: I found a great sale at my local grocery.
   B: I wish my grocery _____ regular sales.

   (a) will have   (b) has
   (c) had   (d) have had

Part II

2. Sofia treats her dog as if it _____ a person.

   (a) were to   (b) were
   (c) has been   (d) has to be

정답 p.

Hackers **Practice**

알맞은 것을 고르세요.

really wish our family's house (is / were) as nice as my friend Billy's mansion.

(have gone / would go) rock climbing with you today if I hadn't sprained my ankle.

t's high time the restaurant (treated / treats) regular customers better.

f the student (had studied / studied) more, he might have been able to pass the class.

He reacts to losing as if it (were / has been) the end of the world.

f an earthquake (was to / were to) happen right now, this building would surely collapse.

부분이 있으면 바르게 고치세요.

Have the shoes cost only twenty dollars less, she would have bought them.

f we watched more movies at home, I will buy a flat-screen television.

Were it not for the rain clouds on the horizon, I would play basketball outside.

Were there any problems with your new computer, our store's technicians will fix it free of charge.

'd rather you won't shut the window – the fresh air is invigorating.

f a decision were made earlier, then we wouldn't be facing such big problems right now.

Hackers **TEST**

Part I Choose the best answer for the blank.

01 A: It's a good thing you stayed inside tonight.
    B: If I _____ out there, I would've frozen to
       death.

(a) go   (b) went
(c) have gone   (d) had gone

02 A: Can we use your parents' car?
    B: I would rather we _____.

(a) didn't   (b) mustn't
(c) couldn't   (d) shouldn't

03 A: Are you going to buy that dress?
    B: I would if only I _____ completely broke
       after shopping yesterday.

(a) aren't   (b) weren't
(c) haven't been   (d) won't

04 A: Are you going to visit me at my beach house
       this weekend?
    B: I _____ if my parents weren't visiting me
       from out of town.

(a) am   (b) was
(c) will   (d) would

05 A: I like the new blue exterior of your house.
    B: Thanks, but I wish it _____ a bit lighter.

(a) is   (b) be
(c) were   (d) will be

06 A: I wish you had come to my party.
    B: If I hadn't gone to visit my parents, I
       _____ it.

(a) could attend
(b) could be attending
(c) could have attended
(d) could have been attended

07 A: Thanks for fixing the heater.
    B: Not at all. Call us at the front desk
       _____ further problems.

(a) you should have
(b) should you have
(c) were you having
(d) had you have

08 A: I told you to buy stock from that company. N
       it's doing really well.
    B: It _____ wise to do it, but I had t
       pay back my student loan then.

(a) was
(b) would be
(c) will have been
(d) would have been

09 A: It is about time you _____ a job.
    B: Don't worry. I have an interview tomorrow.

(a) got   (b) to get
(c) getting   (d) having got

Part II Choose the best answer for the blank.

10 My father acts as though he _____ a big
    sports star in his youth.

(a) is   (b) will be
(c) has been   (d) had been

11 Without the arrival of European explorers, the
    many native tribes of the American continents
    _____ from foreign disease and conques

(a) don't die   (b) not dies
(c) would not die   (d) would not have d

Despite the origin of its name, the wolverine _____ in the weasel family rather than in that of the wolf.

(a) classifies (b) is classifying
(c) is classified (d) are classified

If China's economy _____ collapse, the world economy would go with it.

(a) was to (b) were to
(c) will be to (d) had been to

Charles _____ here earlier, had he anticipated the heavy rush hour traffic and left for work by seven.

(a) were (b) had been
(c) would be (d) would have been

The deliveryman _____ have brought two large pizzas, but he only brought one by accident.

(a) may (b) might
(c) should (d) will

_____ the lifeguard, the current would have swept away the kids on the float.

(a) Been for had it not
(b) Had it not been for
(c) If it haven't been for
(d) It had not been for

If massive amounts of oil had not been spilled into the Yellow Sea, it _____ safer to swim in today.

(a) was (b) has been
(c) would be (d) should have been

18 _____ to marry between races, the majority of the world's population will eventually have mixed racial backgrounds.

(a) Humans should continue
(b) If humans had continued
(c) Should humans continue
(d) Were humans continue

Part III Identify the option that contains an awkward expression or an error in grammar.

19 (a) A: You seem rather annoyed. What's the matter?
(b) B: I drove to Abel's to buy a grill, but found it was out of business.
(c) A: I heard Abel's closed down this past weekend.
(d) B: If I was told sooner, I wouldn't have wasted my time.

20 (a) The transistor is a semiconductor device that is used to boost or direct the flow of an electric current or electronic signal. (b) It is a component that is found in nearly every instrument or machine used in the twenty-first century. (c) Telephones, radios, computers and many other electronic gadgets are completely useless without the transistor. (d) Were it not for the transistor, there have been none of the numerous devices that we use and take for granted today.

정답 p.30

혼자 하기 어렵고 막막할 땐?

해커스텝스(**HackersTEPS.com**)에서
스타강사의 무료 동영상강의 보기!

Section 3 준동사구

CHAPTER 08 to부정사

BASIC GRAMMAR 고수로 가는 첫 걸음

1 to부정사(to + 동사원형)는 동사에서 나왔다. 그러나 문장에서 동사 역할이 아니라 명사, 형용사, 부사 역할을 한다.

I **to read** books. [×]
I <u>like</u> **to read** books. [○] 나는 책 읽는 것을 좋아한다.
I bought many <u>books</u> **to read.** [○] 나는 읽을 책을 많이 샀다.
I'll <u>go</u> to the library **to read** books. [○] 나는 책을 읽기 위해서 도서관에 갈 것이다.

위 문장들에서 볼 수 있듯이 to부정사는 동사 역할을 하지 못한다. to부정사(to read)는 동사(like)의 목적어로 쓰여 명사 역할을 하거나, 명사(books)를 수식하는 형용사 역할을 하거나, 동사(go)를 수식하는 부사 역할을 한다.

이처럼 동사원형에 to가 붙어 문장에서 다양한 품사로 사용되는 to부정사는 품사가 정해져 있지 않다는 뜻으로 '부정사'라고 불린다. to 없이 쓰인 동사원형은 그에 상응하여 '원형 부정사'라고도 불린다.

2 to부정사는 동사의 성질을 여전히 가지고 있어서, 목적어나 보어를 가질 수 있고 부사의 수식을 받을 수 있다.

He wants **to play <u>the violin</u>.** 그는 바이올린을 켜고 싶어 한다.
　　　　　　　　目적어

He wants **to be <u>a violinist</u>.** 그는 바이올리니스트가 되고 싶어 한다.
　　　　　　　　보어

He needs **to exercise <u>regularly</u>.** 그는 규칙적으로 연습할 필요가 있다.
　　　　　　　　부사

첫 번째 문장에서 to부정사(to play)는 목적어(the violin)를 갖고, 두 번째 문장의 to부정사(to be)는 보어(a violinist)를 가지며, 세 번째 문장의 to부정사(to exercise)는 부사(regularly)의 수식을 받는다. 이와 같은 'to부정사 + 목적어 / 보어 / 부사'의 형태를 'to부정사구'라고 부른다.

01 to부정사의 역할

출제빈도 ★★

to부정사는 명사·형용사·부사 역할을 한다.

· 명사처럼 주어, 목적어, 보어 자리에 온다.

주어	**To eat less** is a method of losing weight. 덜 먹는 것은 몸무게를 줄이는 방법이다.
목적어	I want **to reserve a table**. 테이블 하나를 예약하고 싶습니다.
주격 보어	The key to life for many is **to live happily**. 많은 사람에게 인생에서 중요한 것은 행복하게 사는 것이다.
목적격 보어	Her secretary told me **to call back later**. 그녀의 비서는 내게 나중에 다시 전화하라고 말했다.

· 형용사처럼 명사를 수식한다.

명사 수식	She has a meeting **to attend**. 그녀는 참석할 회의가 있다.

· 부사처럼 목적, 이유, 결과 등을 나타낸다.

목적	I'll go to England **to visit my family**. 나는 가족을 방문하기 위해 영국에 갈 것이다.
이유	I'm happy **to see you again**. 너를 다시 만나서 기쁘다.
결과	He has grown up **to be a physicist**. 그는 자라서 물리학자가 되었다.

고득점 포인트

1. to부정사는 진짜 주어와 진짜 목적어 자리에도 올 수 있다.

It is recommended **to keep** a record of your expenses. 지출에 대해 기록해두는 것이 권장된다.
가짜주어   진짜주어

He always makes it a goal **to beat** his previous marathon record. 그는 항상 자신의 이전 마라톤 기록을 갱신하는 것을 목표로 삼는다.
    가짜목적어   진짜목적어

2. 'be + to부정사'는 예정, 의무, 의도, 운명, 가능의 의미를 나타낸다.

예정	The new sofa **is to be delivered** tomorrow afternoon. 새 소파는 내일 오후에 배달될 예정이다.
의무	Customer service operators **are to be polite** on the phone. 고객 서비스 센터 직원들은 통화 시 친절해야 한다.
의도	If you **are to save** money, you should eat out less. 돈을 모으고자 한다면, 외식을 덜 해야 한다.
운명	Men **are to die**. 사람은 죽기 마련이다.
가능	Staff members **are to choose** between either getting a money bonus or extra time off. 직원들은 상여금을 받거나 추가적으로 휴가를 내는 것 중에 선택할 수 있다.

3. to부정사가 목적을 나타낼 때는 to 대신 in order to나 so as to를 쓸 수 있다.

I climbed the mountain **so as to[in order to]** get the best view of the valley. 나는 계곡의 가장 좋은 경치를 보기 위해서 산을 올랐다.

to부정사 자리에 동사는 올 수 없다.

I forgot ~~call~~ you last night. 나는 어젯밤에 네게 전화하기로 한 것을 잊었다.
    to call

▶ 동사(forgot)의 목적어가 되기 위해서 동사(call)가 아니라 명사 역할을 하는 to부정사(to call)가 와야 한다.

The professor emphasized the need ~~attend~~ every class. 교수는 매 수업 출석할 필요성을 강조했다.
    to attend

▶ 명사(the need)를 수식하기 위해서 동사(attend)가 아니라 형용사 역할을 하는 to부정사(to attend)가 와야 한다.

☑ 텝스 실전 문제

텝스 문제 이렇게 나온다

명사·형용사·부사 역할을 하는 to부정사를 채우는 문제가 주로 나온다.

Part I

1. A: I heard that the society's founder will be at the seminar.
   B: Yes, I actually asked her _____ a speech.

   (a) give   (b) giving
   (c) to give   (d) to giving

Part II

2. Beachgoers often cover their skin with sunscreen _____ from burning.

   (a) prevent it   (b) to prevent it
   (c) prevents it   (d) to being prevented

정답 p.31

1 to부정사는 'to + 동사원형'의 형태를 갖는다.

These walls were built ~~to blocking~~ traffic noise.　이 벽은 교통 소음을 차단하기 위해 세워졌다.
　　　　　　　　　　　to block
▸ to부정사에서 to 뒤에 -ing형(blocking)은 올 수 없고 동사원형(block)이 와야 한다.

2 to부정사의 부정형은 to 앞에 not을 붙인다.

They preferred ~~to not sell~~ their house until April.　그들은 4월까지 집을 팔지 않고 싶어했다.
　　　　　　　　not to sell
▸ to부정사(to sell)의 부정형을 만들기 위해서 not은 to 뒤가 아니라 앞에 와야 한다.

3 to부정사의 수동형은 'to be p.p.', 진행형은 'to be -ing', 완료형은 'to have p.p.' 이다.

He doesn't want to be included in the discussion.　그는 토론에 포함되는 것을 원하지 않는다.
▸ 그가 포함되는 것이므로, to부정사의 수동형(to be included)을 쓴다.

Meredith seems to be making an important phone call.　Meredith는 중요한 전화를 하고 있는 것처럼 보인다.
▸ 전화를 하는 동작이 진행 중임을 나타내기 위해, to부정사의 진행형(to be making)을 쓴다.

I am sorry to have kept you waiting.　너를 기다리게 해서 미안하다.
▸ '기다리게 한' 시점이 '미안함을 느끼는(am sorry)' 시점보다 이전이므로, to부정사의 완료형(to have kept)을 쓴다.

4 문장의 주어와 to부정사의 행위 주체가 달라서 to부정사의 의미상 주어가 필요한 경우, 'for + 명사' 또는 'for + 대명사의 목적격'을 to 앞에 쓴다.

The goal of this workshop is ~~the staff~~ to improve teamwork.　이 연수의 목적은 직원들이 팀워크를 향상시키는 것이다.
　　　　　　　　　　　for the staff
▸ 문장의 주어(The goal)와 to부정사의 행위 주체가 다르므로, to부정사의 의미상 주어로 명사(the staff)가 아니라 'for + 명사'(for the staff)를 써야 한

It's a good idea ~~to be for her~~ in charge of promoting the new product line.　그녀가 신제품 홍보를 담당하는 것은 좋은 생각이다.
　　　　　　　　　for her to be
▸ to부정사의 의미상 주어(for her)는 to부정사 뒤가 아니라 앞에 와야 한다.

고득점 포인트 nice, kind, rude, cruel, (in)considerate, (im)polite 등과 같이 사람의 성격이나 성질을 나타내는 형용사 뒤에 오는 to부정사의 의미상 주어는 'of + 명사' 또는 'of + 대명사의 목적격'으로 쓴다.
It was considerate ~~for Mr. Bishop~~ to let everyone go home early. (→ of Mr. Bishop)
↳ 사람의 성격을 나타내는 형용사(considerate) 뒤에 오는 to부정사의 의미상 주어는 'for + 명사(for Mr. Bishop)'가 아니라 'of + 명사'(of Mr. Bishop)를 써야 한다

☑ 텝스 실전 문제　　　　　　　　　　　　　　　　텝스 문제 이렇게 나온다

| 올바른 형태의 to부정사를 채우거나 to부정사의 형태가 틀린 문장을 찾는 문제가 주로 나온다.
| to부정사의 의미상 주어를 채우는 문제가 가끔 나온다.

Part II

1. Students must pass a comprehensive exam and undergo a rigorous interview to _____ the university.

(a) having been admitted to
(b) being admitted to
(c) be admitted to
(d) admit to

Part I

2. A: Jodie did a really good job on her presentation with John.
   B: Yes, it was smart _____ to choose John as her partner.

(a) of her　　　　　(b) by her
(c) for her　　　　 (d) with her

정답 p.3

to부정사를 취하는 동사

동사 + 목적어(to부정사)				
~하기를 원하다	want to	need to	wish to	hope to	expect to
~하기를 계획·결정하다	plan to	aim to	decide to	intend to	
~하기를 제안·약속·거절하다	offer to	ask to	promise to	agree to	refuse to
기타	fail to ~하지 못하다	afford to ~할 수 있다	serve to ~하기 알맞다	pretend to ~한 체하다	happen to 우연히 ~하다
	manage to (간신히) ~해내다		hesitate to ~하기 주저하다		force to ~하도록 강요하다

동사 + 목적어 + 목적격 보어(to부정사)				
~가 -하기를 원하다	want 목 to	need 목 to	expect 목 to	invite 목 to	require 목 to
~가 -하게 부추기다	cause 목 to	persuade 목 to	convince 목 to	encourage 목 to	ask 목 to
~가 -하게 강요하다	force 목 to	compel 목 to	get 목 to	tell 목 to	pressure 목 to
~가 -하게 허락하다	allow 목 to	permit 목 to	enable 목 to	forbid 목 to ~을 금하다	
~가 -하라고 알려주다	remind 목 to	advise 목 to	warn 목 to	recommend 목 to	

동사 + 주격 보어(to부정사)		
remain to 아직 ~해야 한다	seem to ~인 것 같다	appear to ~인 것처럼 보이다

The employer <u>expects</u> to hire nine new clerks. 고용주는 9명의 새 점원을 고용하기를 원한다.
She <u>wants</u> <u>him</u> to buy flowers for her birthday. 그녀는 생일에 그가 꽃을 사주기를 원한다.
We <u>seem</u> to work together better than before. 우리는 전보다 더 함께 잘 일하는 것 같다.

'명사 + to부정사'로 쓰는 표현

ability to ~할 능력	chance to ~할 기회	need to ~할 필요	right to ~할 권리	plan to ~하려는 계획
attempt to ~할 시도	opportunity to ~할 기회	way to ~할 방법	effort to ~하려는 노력	decision to ~하려는 결정
authority to ~할 권한	readiness to ~할 의향	time to ~할 시간	wish to ~하려는 바람	claim to ~에 대한 주장

The holiday break gave him a <u>chance</u> to catch up on his sculpting. 휴가는 그에게 그가 조각을 마무리할 기회를 주었다.

'형용사 + to부정사'로 쓰는 표현

be able to ~할 수 있다	be eager to 몹시 ~하고 싶다	be pleased to ~해서 기쁘다	be difficult to ~하기 어렵다
be likely to ~할 것 같다	be anxious to 몹시 ~하고 싶다	be delighted to ~해서 기쁘다	be dangerous to ~하기 위험하다
be ready to ~할 준비가 되다	be willing to 기꺼이 ~하다	be about to 막 ~하려 하다	be certain to ~할 것이 확실하다

The old man is <u>able</u> to tell when it will rain. 그 노인은 언제 비가 올지 알 수 있다.

☑ 텝스 실전 문제
텝스 문제 이렇게 나온다

to부정사와 함께 쓰는 동사·명사·형용사 뒤에 to부정사를 채우는 문제
가 주로 나온다.

Part I

1. A: Why are you mad at Sandra?
   B: She promised _____ my CD but still hasn't.

   (a) to return (b) return
   (c) returns (d) returning

Part II

2. Though swans navigate aquatic terrain by gliding
   on the surface of water, they lack the ability
   _____ underneath the surface.

   (a) swim (b) swam
   (c) to swim (d) swimming

정답 p.32

1 사역동사(make, let, have) + 목적어 + 원형 부정사

His parents let him ~~to see~~ the hockey game. 그의 부모는 그가 하키 경기를 보는 것을 허락했다.
　see

▶ 사역동사 let의 목적격 보어로 to부정사(to see)가 아니라 원형 부정사(see)가 와야 한다.

고득점 포인트 1. '목적어가 목적격 보어 되다'라는 의미의 수동 관계이면 목적격 보어로 원형 부정사가 아닌 과거분사가 와야 한다.
　　She had her wisdom teeth ~~remove~~. (→ **removed**) 그녀는 사랑니를 뽑았다.
　　↳ 사랑니가 '제거하다'가 아니라 '제거되다'라는 의미이므로, 목적격 보어로 원형 부정사(remove)가 아니라 과거분사(removed)가 와야 한다.

　2. 동작의 '진행'을 나타낼 때, 사역동사 have의 목적격 보어로 현재분사가 올 수도 있다.
　　The band had everyone in the audience **dancing** throughout the concert. 그 밴드는 콘서트 내내 관객 모두를 춤을 추고 있도록 만들었다.
　　↳ '관객 모두가 춤을 추고 있도록 만들었다'라는 '진행'의 의미를 나타내기 위해 사역동사 have의 목적격 보어로 현재분사(dancing)가 올 수 있다.

2 준 사역동사 help (+ 목적어) + 원형 부정사 / to부정사

Swimming **helps** (to) improve physical appearance. 수영은 외모를 개선시키는 것을 돕는다.
Rachel **helped** Felix (to) prepare for his bar exam. Rachel은 Felix가 변호사 시험을 준비하는 것을 도왔다.

▶ 준 사역동사 help의 목적어와 목적격 보어로 원형 부정사(improve, prepare)와 to부정사(to improve, to prepare) 모두 올 수 있다.

3 지각동사(hear, see, watch, notice … 등) + 목적어 + 원형 부정사 / 현재분사

We **saw** them fight outside. 우리는 그들이 밖에서 싸우는 것을 보았다.
We **saw** them fighting outside. 우리는 그들이 밖에서 싸우고 있는 것을 보았다.

▶ 지각동사(saw)의 목적격 보어로 원형 부정사(fight)와 현재분사(fighting)가 모두 올 수 있다. 현재분사가 쓰였을 경우, 동작의 진행을 강조한다.

고득점 포인트 '목적어가 목적격 보어 되다'라고 수동으로 해석되면, 목적격 보어로 원형 부정사나 현재분사가 아닌 과거분사가 와야 한다.
I heard the winner ~~announce / announcing~~. (→ **announced**) 나는 우승자가 발표되는 것을 들었다.
↳ '우승자가 발표하다'가 아니라 '우승자가 발표되다'라고 수동으로 해석되므로, 목적격 보어로 원형 부정사(announce)나 현재분사(announcing)가 아니라 과거분사(announced)가 와야 한다.

☑ 텝스 실전 문제

| 사역동사의 목적격 보어 자리에 원형 부정사나 과거분사를 채우는 문제가 주로 나온다.
| 지각동사의 목적격 보어 자리에 원형 부정사나 현재분사를 채우는 문제가 가끔 나온다.

Part II

1. Medieval crusaders traveled the world to make their ideology ＿＿＿＿＿ to all unconverted nations.

(a) known　　(b) knowing
(c) know　　(d) to known

Part I

2. A: Have you heard ＿＿＿＿＿?
　B: No, but someone told me he's amazing.

(a) Jeremy a cappella sing
(b) sing a cappella Jeremy
(c) Jeremy sing a cappella
(d) singing a cappella Jeremy

정답 p.3

Hackers **Practice**

§ 알맞은 것을 고르세요.

Each one of the people waiting outside hopes (to enter / enter) the popular nightclub.

Douglas had the new patio (to make / made) by a carpenter friend of his.

After analyzing their options for several days, the Taylor family finally made a decision (to buy / buy) a new car.

Now that I've read the guidebook, I'm feeling really anxious (going / to go) on my trip to Poland.

The dog needs (to wash / to be washed) at least once a week to prevent lice from infesting its hair.

We should persuade some of the new employees (joining / to join) us for dinner and drinks this weekend.

부분이 있으면 바르게 고치세요.

Before today's meeting, I had never heard the boss to scream at an employee like that.

t is a good idea carry a pen and paper with you at all times.

A partnership agreement with a local resident is required a nonresident to buy land in many countries.

My son often pretends sleeping when I check in on him after his bedtime.

My sister decided to not attend the local university despite having received a scholarship.

know many people dislike John, but I am compelled to include him in our picnic plans.

Hackers **TEST**

Part I Choose the best answer for the blank.

01 A: I'm not feeling good today. Maybe I should stay
     home.
   B: Can you really afford _____ any more classes?

   (a) miss   (b) missed
   (c) to miss   (d) been missing

02 A: How long will it take to repair my sink?
   B: The plumber said he would get the water pipes
      _____ by Thursday.

   (a) fix   (b) fixed
   (c) fixing   (d) to fix

03 A: Jack already knows we're planning a surprise
     party for him.
   B: He _____ if you hadn't told him!

   (a) didn't know
   (b) hasn't known
   (c) won't know
   (d) wouldn't have known

04 A: How do you want to proceed with organizing
     the project deadline?
   B: The best way to determine a date
      _____ and discuss it.

   (a) to meet is for the team
   (b) is for the team to meet
   (c) to meet is the team for
   (d) is to meet the team for

05 A: When can I come back and pick up my car?
   B: Maintenance shouldn't take long, so it can be
     ready whenever _____.

   (a) to completing it
   (b) to complete it by you
   (c) you want to complete
   (d) you want it completed by

06 A: I'm being sued by one of my clients.
   B: You should ask _____
     about your options.

   (a) your lawyer advising you thoroughly
   (b) your lawyer to advise you thoroughly
   (c) your lawyer advising thoroughly
   (d) advising you thoroughly to your lawyer

07 A: It took three hours and we're only halfway do
   B: Come on, we've got to have this project ___

   (a) finish   (b) to finish
   (c) finished   (d) finishing

08 A: Was the train crowded this morning?
   B: I didn't take it. Since it was warm out, I decic
      _____ instead.

   (a) to walk   (b) walking
   (c) to be walking   (d) to have walked

09 A: My computer froze while I was typing and I l
     the data.
   B: I'd advise _____ in the future.

   (a) you to save often   (b) often saving to do
   (c) you saving often   (d) often you save

Part II Choose the best answer for the blank.

10 Professional waiters learn how to balance platt
   and glasses on a tray _____ them.

   (a) as not dropping so   (b) so as not to drop
   (c) not to drop so   (d) to drop not as so

11 If a flashlight won't light up, it means the bulb
   _____.

   (a) it needs to replace
   (b) needs to be replaced
   (c) replaced is needing
   (d) is needing to be replaced

A socialist revolutionary, Ernesto "Che" Guevara embraced strong convictions and a determination that made him _____ around the world as an idealist.

(a) celebrating   (b) celebrated
(c) to celebrate   (d) having celebrated

The reaction of iron and oxygen with the inclusion of moisture causes _____.

(a) rust to form
(b) rust to be forming
(c) to form the rust
(d) to be formed in the rust

Punctuality and diligence _____ looked well upon by employers.

(a) is   (b) are
(c) is being   (d) are to being

The audience, who rose from their seats in applause after the finale, wanted _____ an encore performance.

(a) give   (b) to give
(c) to be given   (d) having given

Competition makes _____ decent jobs without a college degree.

(a) young adults difficult to obtain
(b) difficult for young adults to obtain
(c) to obtain difficult for young adults
(d) it difficult for young adults to obtain

This year's Carter prize is _____ to a deserving student from the Engineering department.

(a) to award   (b) awading
(c) to be awarded   (d) to have awarded

18 The capacity of young children to be clever and resourceful is _____.

(a) to be not underestimate
(b) not to be underestimated
(c) to not be underestimating
(d) not to be underestimating

Part III Identify the option that contains an awkward expression or an error in grammar.

19 (a) A: Hello. I would like to have this roll of film developing.
(b) B: How many copies would you like of each picture?
(c) A: Two, please. When will the photos be ready to be picked up?
(d) B: Just leave the film here overnight and you can pick them up tomorrow.

20 (a) The 2004 Olympics brought contemporary designs and new technology to the city of Athens. (b) New venues built for the various events were designed by some of the world's leading architects. (c) Construction costs for Olympic facilities and stadiums came to nearly nine billion euros, one ninth of that being for security. (d) In addition, modern transportation services were required to be implementing in the city to prepare for the influx of tourists.

CHAPTER 09 동명사

BASIC GRAMMAR 고수로 가는 첫 걸음

1 동명사(동사원형 + -ing)는 동사에서 나왔다. 그러나 문장에서 동사 역할이 아니라 명사 역할을 한다.

I **jogging** in the morning. [×]
I like **jogging** in the morning. [○]   나는 아침에 조깅하는 것을 좋아한다.

동명사(jogging)는 동사에서 나왔지만 동사 역할을 하지 못한다. 동명사는 동사(like)의 목적어처럼 명사 역할을 한다.

2 동명사는 동사의 성질을 여전히 가지고 있어서, 목적어나 보어를 가질 수 있고 부사의 수식을 받을 수 있다.

Luke enjoys **writing poems**.   Luke는 시 쓰는 것을 즐긴다.
　　　　　　　목적어

Becoming a poet is his dream.   시인이 되는 것이 그의 꿈이다.
　　　　　보어

He is famous for **writing well**.   그는 글을 잘 쓰는 것으로 유명하다.
　　　　　　　　　　부사

첫 번째 문장에서 동명사(writing)는 목적어(poems)를 가지고, 두 번째 문장의 동명사(becoming)는 보어(a poet)를 가진다. 세 번째 문장에서는 동명사(writing)가 부사(well)의 수식을 받고 있다. 이와 같은 [동명사 + 목적어 / 보어 / 부사]의 형태를 '동명사구'라고 부른다.

1 동명사의 역할

동명사는 명사 역할을 하며 주어, 목적어, 보어 자리에 온다.

주어	Cooking is a practical skill to learn. 요리는 배워두면 실용적인 기술이다.
동사의 목적어	Meredith dislikes washing dishes. Meredith는 설거지하는 것을 싫어한다.
전치사의 목적어	Despite feeling sleepy, Marcus continued to study. 졸림에도 불구하고, Marcus는 공부를 계속했다.
보어	Teresa's worry is coming to class late. Teresa의 걱정은 수업에 늦는 것이다.

동명사 자리에 동사는 올 수 없다.

Sam began ~~practice~~ yoga. Sam은 요가를 연습하기 시작했다.
           practicing

▶ 동사(began)의 목적어 자리이므로, 동사(practice)가 아니라 동명사(practicing)가 와야 한다.

She is worried about ~~be~~ late. 그녀는 늦는 것에 대해 걱정한다.
             being

▶ 전치사(about)의 목적어 자리이므로, 동사(be)가 아니라 동명사(being)가 와야 한다.

텝스 실전 문제

동사의 목적어나 전치사의 목적어 자리에 동명사를 채우는 문제가 주로 나온다.
동명사 자리에 동사가 와서 틀린 문장을 찾는 문제가 가끔 나온다.

Part I

A: What did you do on the weekend?
B: I finished _____ my house.

(a) paint   (b) painted
(c) painting   (d) to painting

Part III

2. (a) A: I hate driving because I easily get lost when I'm at the wheel.
(b) B: That was my problem till I began to depend on use a GPS to find my way.
(c) A: Maybe I should get one installed in my car.
(d) B: You should! They don't cost that much and they're a big help.

정답 p.35

1 동명사의 부정형은 동명사 앞에 not을 붙인다.

He regretted ~~joining not~~ the baseball team. 그는 야구팀에 가입하지 않은 것을 후회했다.
　　　　　　　not joining

▶ 동명사(joining)의 부정형을 만들기 위해서 not은 동명사의 뒤가 아니라 앞에 와야 한다.

2 동명사의 수동형은 'being p.p.', 완료형은 'having p.p.'이다.

I imagined being awarded the grand prize. 나는 대상을 받는 것을 상상했다.

▶ 대상을 수여받는 것이므로, 동명사의 수동형(being awarded)을 쓴다.

She apologized for having missed my call. 그녀는 내 전화를 못 받았던 것에 대해 사과했다.

▶ '전화를 받지 못한(miss)' 시점이 '사과를 한(apologized)' 시점보다 이전이므로, 동명사의 완료형(having missed)을 쓴다.

3 문장의 주어와 동명사의 행위 주체가 달라 동명사의 의미상 주어가 필요한 경우, '명사의 소유격' 또는 '소유격 대명사'를 명사 앞에 쓴다.

Debra will never forgive Ben's canceling the dinner party. Debra는 Ben이 저녁 파티를 취소한 것을 결코 용서하지 않을 것이다.

▶ 문장의 주어(Debra)와 동명사(canceling)의 행위 주체가 다르므로 동명사의 의미상 주어가 필요하고, 이때 명사의 소유격(Ben's)을 써야 한다.

~~She~~ missing class will hurt her grades. 그녀가 수업을 빠진 것은 그녀의 성적에 타격을 줄 것이다.
Her

▶ 문장의 주어(missing class)와 동명사(missing)의 행위 주체가 다르므로 동명사의 의미상 주어가 필요하고, 이때 주격(She)이 아니라 소유격(Her)이어야 한다.

🔹 고득점 포인트　일상적인 대화에서는 동명사의 의미상 주어로 목적격 대명사를 쓸 수도 있다.
Would you mind **my[me]** smoking? 제가 담배를 피워도 되겠습니까?

☑ **텝스 실전 문제**　　　　　　　　　　　　　　　　　텝스 문제 이렇게 나온

| 올바른 형태의 동명사를 채우는 문제가 주로 나온다.
| 동명사의 의미상 주어와 동명사를 함께 채우는 문제가 주로 나온다.

Part II

1. Despite _____ by millions of viewers every week, the show is less popular than it was in its first season.

(a) being watched　　(b) to be watched
(c) to being watched　(d) having been watched

Part I

2. A: Are you talking to Paul again?
　 B: No, I'm still angry at _____ my birthda

(a) his forgotten　　(b) forgetting by him
(c) he forgot　　　　(d) his having forgotten

정답 r

3 동명사를 목적어로 취하는 동사

동명사만 목적어로 취하는 동사

제안·고려	suggest -ing -을 제안하다	recommend -ing -을 추천하다	consider -ing -을 고려하다	
중지·연기	stop -ing -을 그만두다	finish -ing -을 끝내다	quit -ing -을 그만두다	
	discontinue -ing -을 중지하다	give up -ing -을 포기하다	postpone -ing -을 연기하다	
부정적 의미	dislike -ing -을 싫어하다	deny -ing -을 부인하다	mind -ing -을 꺼리다	avoid -ing -을 피하다
기타	enjoy -ing -을 즐기다	imagine -ing -을 상상하다	allow -ing -을 허락하다	keep -ing -을 계속하다

Michael finished ~~to write~~ his screenplay. Michael은 시나리오 쓰는 것을 끝냈다.
　　　　　　　　writing
▶ 동명사만 목적어로 취하는 동사(finish)가 쓰였으므로, 목적어로 to부정사(to write)가 아니라 동명사(writing)가 와야 한다.

동명사와 to부정사 둘 다 목적어로 취하는 동사

• 동명사가 목적어일 때와 to부정사가 목적어일 때 문장의 의미 변화가 없는 경우

시작하다/계속하다	begin 시작하다	start 시작하다	continue 계속하다	
좋아하다/싫어하다	like 좋아하다	love 좋아하다	prefer 선호하다	hate 싫어하다

We like swimming / to swim. 우리는 수영하는 것을 좋아한다.
▶ like는 동명사(swimming)와 to부정사(to swim) 둘 다 목적어로 취할 수 있으며, 이때 의미의 차이는 없다.

• 동명사가 목적어일 때와 to부정사가 목적어일 때 문장의 의미 변화가 있는 경우

	-ing (과거 의미)	to부정사 (미래 의미)
remember	-한 것을 기억하다	-할 것을 기억하다
forget	-한 것을 잊다	-할 것을 잊다
regret	-한 것을 후회하다	-하게 되어 유감스럽다

Larry remembered fixing the lamp. Larry는 램프를 고친 것을 기억했다. (이미 고쳤다)
Larry remembered to fix the lamp. Larry는 램프를 고칠 것을 기억했다. (아직 고치지 않았다)
▶ remember는 동명사(fixing)와 to부정사(to fix) 둘 다 목적어로 취하지만, 동명사 목적어는 '과거'를, to부정사 목적어는 '미래'를 의미한다.

고득점 포인트
1. try도 뒤에 동명사와 to부정사를 모두 목적어로 가질 수 있으며, 이때 의미 변화가 있다.
Jacob tried eating Kimchi. Jacob은 김치를 (시험 삼아) 먹어봤다. 　　Jacob tried to eat Kimchi. Jacob은 김치를 먹어보려 노력했다.
↳ try 뒤의 동명사(eating)가 오면 '(시험 삼아) ~을 해보다'라는 의미이고, to부정사(to eat)가 오면 '~하려고 노력하다'라는 의미의 차이가 있다.

2. stop 뒤에 온 to부정사는 부사적 용법으로 '목적'을 의미한다.
Cindy stopped crying. Cindy는 울음을 멈췄다. 　　　　　　　　Cindy stopped to stretch. Cindy는 기지개를 켜기 위해 멈췄다.
↳ stop 뒤의 동명사(crying)는 목적어로 '~하는 것을 멈추다'라는 의미이고, to부정사는 목적어가 아니라 부사적 용법으로 '~하기 위해 (하던 일을) 멈추다'라는 의미이다.

☑ 텝스 실전 문제

텝스 문제 이렇게 나온다

동명사와 to부정사를 구별하여 동사 뒤에 의미에 맞게 채우는 문제가 주로 나온다.
동명사를 목적어로 취하는 동사 뒤에 to부정사가 목적어로 와서 틀린 문장을 찾는 문제가 주로 나온다.

Part II

. After six hours of driving in traffic, the woman had to stop _____.

(a) rest 　　　　　　　　(b) resting
(c) rested 　　　　　　　(d) to rest

Part III

2. (a) A: Will you be having a soda too?
　 (b) B: No thanks. I'd prefer to have water instead.
　 (c) A: I thought you always used to get soda when we'd go out.
　 (d) B: I did, but I quit to drink it because of the caffeine.

정답 p.35

1 동사(구) + 전치사 to + -ing

contribute to -ing -에 공헌하다	look forward to -ing -을 고대하다	object to -ing -에 반대하다
lead to -ing -의 원인이 되다	admit (to) -ing -을 인정하다	confess to -ing -을 고백하다
be committed to -ing -에 전념하다	be dedicated to -ing -에 헌신하다	be devoted to -ing -에 헌신하다
be used to -ing -에 익숙하다	be accustomed to -ing -에 익숙하다	be attributed to -ing -의 탓이다
get around to -ing -할 시간을 내다	come down to -ing -으로 설명되다	be close to -ing 거의 다 -하다

Angela is <u>looking forward to</u> ~~ski~~ this winter. Angela는 올 겨울 스키타는 것을 고대하고 있다.

                                       skiing

▶ look forward 뒤에 쓰인 to는 전치사이므로, 동사원형(ski)이 아니라 동명사(skiing)가 와야 한다.

The employees <u>objected to</u> ~~work~~ longer hours. 직원들은 더 오랜 시간 일하는 것에 반대했다.

                              working

▶ object 뒤에 쓰인 to는 전치사이므로, 동사원형(work)이 아니라 동명사(working)가 와야 한다.

2 동명사구 관용 표현

go -ing -하러 가다	be worth -ing -할 가치가 있다	keep (on) -ing 계속 -하다	feel like -ing -하고 싶다
be busy -ing -하느라 바쁘다	on[upon] -ing -하자마자	end up -ing 결국 -하다	
cannot help -ing -하지 않을 수 없다 (= have no choice but + to부정사)		spend + 시간/돈 + (in) -ing -하는 데 시간/돈을 쓰다	
have difficulty[trouble, a problem] (in) -ing -하는 데 어려움을 겪다		It's no use[good] -ing -해도 소용 없다	
when it comes to -ing -에 관한 한		What do you say to -ing? -하지 않겠어?	

I cannot help watching the news when it comes on. 나는 뉴스가 나오면 뉴스를 보지 않을 수 없다.

Sheila and her husband spend their afternoon sitting in the cool shade under the tree.

Sheila와 그녀의 남편은 나무 아래 시원한 그늘에 앉아서 오후를 보냈다.

☑ 텝스 실전 문제

텝스 문제 이렇게 나온다

| 동명사 관련 표현에 동명사를 채우는 문제가 주로 나온다.
| 전치사 to 뒤에 동명사가 아니라 동사가 와서 틀린 문장을 찾는 문제도 가끔 나온다.

Part I

1. A: I don't think it's worth _____ at the mall on Saturday.

   B: Yeah, it will be too crowded.

   (a) hang out   (b) to hang out
   (c) hanging out   (d) of hanging out

Part III

2. (a) A: Did you see that Amy got a bouquet of flowers this morning?
   (b) B: I did, but nobody seems to know who they're from.
   (c) A: You mean that no one has confessed to sen them to her?
   (d) B: Yes. It seems like Amy must have a secret admirer.

정답 p.3

Hackers **Practice**

§ 알맞은 것을 고르세요.

After running for twenty miles, the marathon runner started (become / becoming) exhausted.

I like (employing / being employed) by a Fortune 500 company, because I feel my role is important.

When Sally talked to me about him, I was really impressed by (his having behaved / having him behaved) in a gentlemanlike way.

It is best to avoid (to drive / driving) downtown during rush hour if at all possible.

In spite of (earning / to earn) twice as much money as I do, Sarah still lives such a thrifty life.

Children who have trouble (focusing / to focus) in groups are highly likely to misunderstand the behavior of others.

부분이 있으면 바르게 고치세요.

Do you mind of me taking a seat at your table?

She hates playing tennis, but I'm sure she'll be willing to play a game of croquet with you.

The driver denied to have been driving under the influence when he was caught.

The construction laborers were used to work in extremely humid weather.

The students were undoubtedly excited about going not to school today.

I think it's safe to say that Paul regrets to fight with you about the project.

정답 p.35

Hackers **TEST**

Part I Choose the best answer for the blank.

01 A: How about we walk to the food store instead of drive?
   B: That's fine with me. I don't mind _____ a little exercise.

   (a) get   (b) getting
   (c) to get   (d) to be gotten

02 A: One of my contacts fell out but I can't find it.
   B: _____ for it. Just buy some new ones.

   (a) Looking is no use
   (b) To look is no use
   (c) It's no use looking
   (d) I am no use looking

03 A: I remember your _____ The Star-Spangled Banner at the ceremony last year.
   B: Thanks, I hope you enjoyed it.

   (a) sang   (b) had sang
   (c) singing   (d) to sing

04 A: Tell me what Nick told you.
   B: I can't. I promised _____ a living soul.

   (a) didn't tell   (b) telling not
   (c) not telling   (d) not to tell

05 A: Have you noticed how organized Karen is?
   B: I haven't seen anyone _____ on her work.

   (a) concentrating hard so
   (b) concentrate so hard
   (c) to concentrate so hard
   (d) hard so concentrating

06 A: Are you prepared for your test tomorrow?
   B: I think so, and I really don't feel like _____ my notes again.

   (a) review   (b) reviewing
   (c) to review   (d) to reviewing

07 A: There's an art convention this weekend that I was planning to sign up for.
   B: I think I'll register _____ it as well.

   (a) to attend   (b) attending
   (c) for attend   (d) to attending

08 A: My granddaughter works as a news anchorwoman.
   B: Wow, I can't imagine _____
   _____.

   (a) she has that famous been
   (b) her being that famous
   (c) her having been that famous
   (d) that famous her being

09 A: What are you looking up online?
   B: I'm trying _____ which bank to invest in

   (a) deciding   (b) decided
   (c) to decide   (d) to be decided

Part II Choose the best answer for the blank.

10 Besides _____ for the local newspaper, he al
   bartends at night.

   (a) written   (b) writing
   (c) to write   (d) being written

11 The state legislature recommends _____
   paper in order to reduce the number of trees cu
   down.

   (a) recycle   (b) recycling
   (c) to recycle   (d) to recycling

12 By the fact of _____ all over the wal
   Albert knew his daughter had found the marker

   (a) she coloring   (b) her colored
   (c) her having colored (d) colored by her

Despite _____ the weather reports, the coach told his football team that they would practice in the rain.

(a) have seen   (b) having seen
(c) to have seen   (d) having been seen

Most of our staffs are busy _____ the recent project.

(a) finishing up   (b) to finish up
(c) being finished up (d) to be finishing

Once it started raining, everyone began _____ for cover.

(a) ran   (b) running
(c) having run   (d) to be running

Many people enjoy _____ as a form of entertainment and aerobic exercise.

(a) danced   (b) dancing
(c) to dance   (d) having danced

In spite of the figure skater's excellent score, she ended up _____ to the championship.

(a) not going   (b) not being gone
(c) not to go   (d) not to going

The new traffic law only allows _____ along the main street after 6 p.m.

(a) parking   (b) to parking
(c) to be parking   (d) to be parked

Part III Identify the option that contains an awkward expression or an error in grammar.

19 (a) A: I heard you took off a semester to work as a waiter.
   (b) B: Yes, I needed the money to buy myself a car.
   (c) A: Now that you're back at school, do you still have your job?
   (d) B: No, I stopped to work after I had saved up enough money.

20 (a) Working long hours while doing very little physical movement can result in Carpal Tunnel Syndrome(CTS). (b) This condition is mainly caused by tension experienced in the wrist, which can bring about chronic pain in the hand and lower arm. (c) Activities that wear out the wrist, such as typing at a keyboard for hours at a time, may lead to CTS. (d) In order to loosen the muscles in the wrist, doctors suggest to take frequent breaks.

CHAPTER 10 분사

BASIC GRAMMAR 고수로 가는 첫 걸음

1 분사(동사원형 + ing / 동사원형 + ed)는 동사에서 나왔다. 그러나 문장에서 동사 역할이 아니라 형용사 역할을 한다.

I **exciting** movies. [×]
I watched **exciting** movies. [○] 나는 흥미진진한 영화를 보았다.

The movies **exciting**. [×]
The movies were **exciting**. [○] 그 영화는 흥미진진했다.

분사(exciting)는 동사(excite)에서 나왔지만 동사 역할을 하지 못한다. 분사는 두 번째 문장에서처럼 명사(movies)를 수식하거나, 네 번째 문장에서처럼 보어 자리에 온다.

2 분사는 동사의 성질을 여전히 가지고 있어서, 목적어나 보어를 가질 수 있고 부사의 수식을 받을 수 있다.

She has a friend **learning Spanish**. 그녀는 스페인어를 배우는 친구가 있다.
　　　　　　　　　　　　　　목적어

The singer, **feeling tense**, couldn't sing his song. 긴장을 느꼈던 가수는 노래를 부를 수 없었다.
　　　　　　　　　　보어

The girl **walking slowly** is my sister. 천천히 걷고 있는 그 소녀는 내 여동생이다.
　　　　　　　　　　부사

첫 번째 문장에서 분사(learning)는 목적어(Spanish)를 가지고, 두 번째 문장의 분사(feeling)는 보어(tense)를 가진다. 세 번째 문장에서는 분사(walking)가 부사(slowly)의 수식을 받고 있다.

3 분사구문은 문장에서 부사절 역할을 하는 수식어 거품이다.

When she met her friend again, Karen was so pleased.
Meeting her friend again, Karen was so pleased. 그녀의 친구를 다시 만났을 때, Karen은 너무나 기뻤다.

두 번째 문장에서처럼 분사구문(Meeting her friend again)은 첫 번째 문장의 부사절(When she met her friend again)과 같이, 완전한 문장(Karen was so pleased)에 붙어 '친구를 다시 만났을 때'와 같은 부가적 의미를 더하며, 문장에 없어도 되는 부가성분인 수식어 거품이다.

01 분사의 역할

분사는 형용사 역할을 한다.

· 형용사처럼 명사 앞이나 뒤에서 명사를 수식한다.

명사 앞 수식　　In the silence she heard the ticking <u>clock</u>.　고요함 속에서 그녀는 똑딱거리는 시계 소리를 들었다.
　　　　　　　　　　　　　　　　　　　　　　　　　　명사

　　　▶ 분사(ticking)는 명사(clock)를 앞에서 수식한다.

명사 뒤 수식　　There is a long list of <u>people</u> scheduled for interviews.　인터뷰 예정인 사람들의 긴 명단이 있다.
　　　　　　　　　　　　　　　　　　　　명사

　　　▶ 분사구(scheduled for interviews)는 명사(people)를 뒤에서 수식한다.

· 형용사처럼 주격 보어나 목적격 보어로 쓰인다.

주격 보어　　That game looks entertaining.　그 게임은 재미있어 보인다.
　　　　　　　　주어　　　동사　　　주격보어

　　　▶ 분사(entertaining)가 동사(looks) 뒤에서 주격 보어로 쓰여 주어의 상태를 나타낸다.

목적격 보어　　Mrs. Smith looked at the footprints left in the snow.　Mrs. Smith는 눈에 남겨진 발자국을 보았다.
　　　　　　　　주어　　　동사　　　　목적어　　　목적격보어

　　　▶ 분사(left)가 목적어(the footprints) 뒤에서 목적격 보어로 쓰여 목적어의 상태를 나타낸다.

고득점 포인트 분사와 to부정사의 의미상 차이에 주의해야 한다.
The man ~~to leave~~ the restaurant forgot to pay. (→ **leaving**)　식당에서 나온 그 남자는 돈 내는 것을 잊었다.
The child ~~to leave~~ alone fell asleep. (→ **left**)　혼자 남겨진 아이는 잠이 들었다.

　　┗ 명사(The man) 뒤에 형용사처럼 쓰여 명사를 수식하는 to부정사(to leave)는 '~(해야) 할'이라는 미래 의미를 나타낸다. 따라서 첫 번째 문장은 '식당에서 나올 남자가 돈 내는 것을 잊었다'라는 어색한 의미가 되고, 두 번째 문장은 '혼자 남겨질 아이가 잠이 들었다'라는 어색한 의미가 된다. '미래'의 의미를 나타내는 것이 아니라면 to부정사(to leave)가 아니라 분사(leaving, left)가 명사를 수식해야 한다.

분사 자리에 동사는 올 수 없다.

The books ~~order~~ online arrived one week later.　온라인으로 주문된 그 책은 일주일 후에 도착했다.
　　　　　　ordered

▶ 동사(order)가 명사(books)를 수식할 수 없으므로, 형용사 역할을 하는 분사(ordered)가 와야 한다.

She became ~~acquaint~~ with the others quickly.　그녀는 다른 사람들과 빠르게 친해졌다.
　　　　　　acquainted

▶ 동사(acquaint)가 주격 보어 자리에 올 수 없으므로, 형용사 역할을 하는 분사(acquainted)가 와야 한다.

☑ 텝스 실전 문제

텝스 문제 이렇게 나온다

형용사처럼 명사를 수식하거나, 보어 자리에 쓰인 분사를 채우는 문제가
주로 나온다.

Part I

1. A: You seem surprised to see me.
   B: Actually, I'm _____ you chose to come.

   (a) delight　　　　　(b) delighted
   (c) to delight　　　 (d) have delighted

Part II

2. In his new work, the playwright referenced many
   historical figures _____ in classical Latin
   literature.

   (a) feature　　　　　(b) to featuring
   (c) featured　　　　 (d) had featured

정답 p.38

1 분사구문은 시간, 이유, 조건 등을 나타내는 부사절 역할을 한다.

시간   Writing the cover letter, he tried to tailor it to the company.
      (= When he wrote the cover letter)
      자기 소개서를 쓸 때, 그는 그 회사에 맞추려고 노력했다.

이유   Finding herself lost, she asked a passerby for directions.
      (= Because she found herself lost)
      그녀는 자신이 길을 잃은 것을 알았기 때문에, 지나가는 사람에게 방향을 물어보았다.

조건   Held steady, the ship will be able to navigate through the storm.
      (= If it is held steady)
      균형이 잡히면, 배는 폭풍을 뚫고 항해할 수 있을 것이다.

고득점 포인트   부사절 역할을 하지 않는 분사구문들도 존재한다.

1. 분사구문은 문장에서 and로 대등하게 연결된 절의 역할을 하기도 한다.
   The awards ceremony will be held on Thursday, **honoring outstanding individuals**.
                                 (= and it will honor outstanding individuals)
   시상식은 목요일에 개최될 것이고, 뛰어난 사람들에게 영예를 줄 것이다.

2. 'with + 목적어 + 분사' 구문을 이용하여 동시에 일어나는 상황이나 이유를 나타내기도 한다.
   동시상황   Anne waited outside with the car running.   Anne은 자동차의 시동을 켠 채로 밖에서 기다렸다.
           ↳ Anne이 밖에서 기다리는 것과 자동차의 시동을 켠 채로 있는 것은 동시에 일어나는 상황이다.

    이유   With the river flooded, the roads were not safe for travel.   강이 침수되어, 여행하기에 도로가 안전하지 않았다.
           ↳ 강이 침수된 것은 도로가 안전하지 않은 것의 이유이다.

2 동사는 분사구문 자리에 올 수 없다.

~~Ride~~ the bus, I read a book.   버스를 타고 가면서, 나는 책을 읽었다.
Riding
   ▶ 문장에 부가적 의미를 더하는 분사구문 자리이므로, 동사(Ride)가 아니라 분사(Riding)가 와야 한다.

~~Hide~~ in the shadows, the tiger was ready to attack.   그늘에 가려진 채, 호랑이는 공격할 준비를 했다.
Hidden
   ▶ 문장에 부가적 의미를 더하는 분사구문 자리이므로, 동사(Hide)가 아니라 분사(Hidden)가 와야 한다.

☑ 텝스 실전 문제

텝스 문제 이렇게 나온다

| 분사 구문 전체나 일부를 채우는 문제가 주로 나온다.

Part I

1. A: How is your new job going?
   B: A lot better. _____, I figured out
      how to better manage my workload.

   (a) Getting myself organized
   (b) Got myself organized
   (c) I got myself organized
   (d) Had got myself organized

Part II

2. _____ daily, vitamins can help regulate one's
   diet.

   (a) Take   (b) Taken
   (c) Took   (d) To take

정답 p.

03 분사구문의 형태와 의미상 주어

분사구문은 –ing나 p.p.형의 분사로 시작한다.

You should show your sales receipt, returning clothing. 옷을 환불할 때, 구매 영수증을 보여주어야 한다.

Dressed in appropriate attire, you will be admitted to the dance hall. 적절한 복장을 입는다면, 댄스홀에 입장이 허가될 것입니다.

고득점
포인트 분사구문의 뜻을 분명하게 하기 위해 부사절 접속사가 분사구문 앞에 올 수 있다.

Please show your sales receipt **when returning clothing.**

ㄴ '~할 때'라는 뜻을 분명하게 하기 위해 분사구문(returning clothing) 앞에 접속사(when)가 왔다.

If dressed in appropriate attire, you will be admitted to the dance hall.

ㄴ '만약 ~라면'이라는 뜻을 분명하게 하기 위해 분사구문(dressed in appropriate attire) 앞에 접속사(If)가 왔다.

분사구문의 부정형을 쓸 때는 분사 앞에 not이나 never를 붙인다.

Not getting through, she hung up and called again. 연결이 되지 않았기 때문에, 그녀는 전화를 끊고 다시 걸었다.

Never considered safe, the park was closed off at night. 결코 안전하다고 여겨지지 않기 때문에, 공원은 밤에 폐쇄되었다.

분사구문의 완료형은 having p.p.이고, 주절의 동사보다 이전의 시점에 일어난 일을 나타낸다.

Having taken a vacation, she came back refreshed and energized. 휴가를 갔다온 후, 그녀는 원기가 회복되고 활기가 넘쳐서 돌아왔다.

▶ '휴가를 간' 시점이 '돌아온(came back)' 시점보다 이전이므로, 분사의 완료형(Having taken)을 쓴다.

주절의 주어와 분사구문의 행위 주체가 달라 분사구문의 의미상 주어가 필요한 경우 '명사'를 분사구문 앞에 쓴다.

Ending late, the staff decided to get dinner together. [×]
　　　주절의 주어

The meeting ending late, the staff decided to get dinner together. [○] 회의가 늦게 끝났기 때문에, 직원들은 함께 저녁을 먹기로 결정했다.
　분사구문의 주어　　　　주절의 주어

▶ 의미상 '늦게 끝난 것'의 주체가 주절의 주어(the staff)가 아니므로, 분사구문의 의미상 주어(The meeting)가 분사구문 앞에 와야 한다.

고득점
포인트 의미상 주어가 we, you, they, people 등과 같이 일반적인 사람을 가리킬 때는 이를 생략하고 쓸 수 있다. 이렇게 의미상 주어를 생략하고 관용적으로 쓰는 표현을 비인칭 독립분사구문이라고 한다.

considering ~을 고려하면	broadly / frankly / generally speaking 대체적으로 / 솔직하게 / 일반적으로 (말해서)
seeing that ~이기 때문에	granting that 비록 ~이라고 하더라도

If we consider the number of people living in this building, it is very quiet. 이 건물에 사는 사람들의 수를 고려하면, 매우 조용하다.

→ **Considering** the number of people living in this building, it is very quiet.

☑ 텝스 실전 문제

텝스 문제 이렇게 나온다

분사구문 전체나 일부를 올바른 형태로 채우는 문제가 주로 나온다.
주절의 주어와 다른, 분사구문의 의미상 주어가 오지 않아서 틀린 문장을 고르는 문제가 가끔 나온다.

Part I

1. A: Did you tell him how you really feel?
   B: Yes. Before _____ everything to him, I had kept him at a distance.

   (a) explain　　　　(b) to explain
   (c) explaining　　　(d) to explaining

Part III

2. (a) A: Losing weight, you helped me a lot by constantly encouraging me to exercise regularly.
   (b) B: I just wanted to give you the support necessary to reach your goal.
   (c) A: Without your help, I would still be unfit and depressed.
   (d) B: As you can see, exercising is good for not only your mind but also your body.

정답 p.38

04 현재분사 vs. 과거분사 ★★

1 분사가 명사를 수식하는 경우, 수식받는 명사와 분사가 능동 관계면 현재분사, 수동 관계면 과거분사가 와야 한다.

I received a letter ~~informed~~ me to pick up a package at the post office. 나는 우체국에서 소포를 가져가라고 알리는 편지를 받았다.
명사   informing

▶ 수식받는 명사(a letter)와 분사가 '편지가 알려주다'라는 의미의 능동 관계이므로, 과거분사(informed)가 아니라 현재분사(informing)가 와야 한다.

The audience enjoyed the aria ~~singing~~ at the opera. 관객들은 오페라에서 불려지는 아리아를 즐겼다.
명사   sung

▶ 수식받는 명사(the aria)와 분사가 '노래가 불려지다'라는 의미의 수동 관계이므로, 현재분사(singing)가 아니라 과거분사(sung)가 와야 한다.

2 분사가 주격 보어이거나 목적격 보어일 경우, 주어와 보어 또는 목적어와 보어가 능동 관계면 현재분사, 수동 관계면 과거분사가 와야 한다.

The lecture on evolution seems ~~interested~~. 진화에 대한 강의는 흥미로운 것 같다.
주어   interesting

▶ 주어(The lecture)와 분사가 '강의가 흥미롭게 하다'라는 의미의 능동 관계이므로, 과거분사(interested)가 아니라 현재분사(interesting)가 와야 한다.

Jessie found the entire building ~~remodeling~~. Jessie는 건물 전체가 개조된 것을 발견했다.
목적어   remodeled

▶ 목적어(the entire building)와 분사가 '건물이 개조되다'라는 의미의 수동 관계이므로, 현재분사(remodeling)가 아니라 과거분사(remodeled)가 와야 한다.

3 분사구문의 경우, 주절의 주어와 분사구문이 능동 관계면 현재분사, 수동 관계면 과거분사가 와야 한다.

~~Rescued~~ a child from a well, the man broke his arm. 우물에 빠진 아이를 구하다가, 그 남자는 팔이 부러졌다.
Rescuing   주절의 주어

▶ 주절의 주어(the man)와 분사구문이 '그가 아이를 구하다'라는 의미의 능동 관계이므로, 과거분사(Rescued)가 아니라 현재분사(Rescuing)가 와야 한다.

~~Decorating~~ in lights, the tree looked beautiful. 조명으로 장식되어 있기 때문에, 그 나무는 아름다워 보였다.
Decorated   주절의 주어

▶ 주절의 주어(the tree)와 분사구문이 '나무가 장식되다'라는 의미의 수동 관계이므로, 현재분사(Decorating)가 아니라 과거분사(Decorated)가 와야 한다.

고득점포인트 'with + 목적어 + 분사' 구문의 경우, with의 목적어와 분사가 능동 관계면 현재분사, 수동 관계면 과거분사가 와야 한다.
With people **preferring** cell phones, land lines are less common. 사람들이 휴대 전화를 선호해서, 일반 전화는 덜 일반적이다.
Nicole is listening to music with her eyes **closed**. Nicole은 눈을 감은 채로 음악을 듣고 있다.

↳ 첫 번째 문장에서 with의 목적어(people)와 분사가 '사람들이 선호하다'라는 의미의 능동 관계이므로 현재분사(preferring)가 와야 하고, 두 번째 문장은 with의 목적어(her eyes)와 분사가 '그녀의 눈이 감기다'라는 의미의 수동 관계이므로 과거분사(closed)가 와야 한다.

☑ 텝스 실전 문제

텝스 문제 이렇게 나온다

| 수식어 거품 자리에 현재분사와 과거분사를 구별하여 채우는 문제가 주로 나온다.
| 현재분사와 과거분사 선택이 틀린 문장을 고르는 문제가 주로 나온다.

Part II

1. _____ herself of her morning appointment, the woman set her alarm to go off at seven.

(a) Reminding   (b) Reminded
(c) To reminding   (d) She reminded

Part III

2. (a) When listening to music, the ear recognizes both the pitch and timbre of the sound. (b) Pitch describes a sound wave's frequency, indicating how high or low a note sounds. (c) Timbre refers to the unique type of sound producing when a particular instrument is played. (d) When pitch and timbre are combined, the ear can distinguish which notes are made by which instruments.

정답 p.3

중 알맞은 것을 고르세요.

Spanish is one of many languages (write / written) in the Western alphabet.

It will be impossible to get around, (not having / having not) a car and all.

Nitrogen is the element (making / made) up the majority of the atmosphere.

(Exposed / Expose) to the summer sun, crayons will quickly melt and turn into a sloppy mess.

(Checking / Having checked) all of the contents for the presentation thoroughly, Rick is full of confidence.

I wanted to play at the basketball tournament, but I injured my leg while (to lift / lifting) weights at the gym.

린 부분이 있으면 바르게 고치세요.

When the police arrived, the suspect was found beat the victim.

Hoped to earn money for her upcoming trip, Rhonda began working a second job at a convenience store.

Her phone having been left in the office, she couldn't respond to the call.

The cyclone was responsible for massive amounts of property damage, it left millions of people without working electricity or water.

Children staying outdoors having played will have fewer allergies than those staying indoors.

Boracay, considering one of the nicest islands in the Philippines, is where the tour group will arrive tomorrow.

Hackers **TEST**

Part I Choose the best answer for the blank.

01 A: I'm taking the GRE test next week.
   B: _____ you, I don't doubt that you're well
   prepared.

   (a) Know   (b) Known
   (c) Knowing   (d) To be known

02 A: Are you going to be Katie's maid of honor at her
   wedding?
   B: _____, how can I refuse her?

   (a) To be asked   (b) Been asked
   (c) To being asked (d) Having been asked

03 A: Is my cooking good?
   B: _____, what you do is that you use a
   little too much pepper.

   (a) Cook   (b) Cooking
   (c) You cook   (d) When you cook

04 A: What happened to your bike's tires?
   B: I popped them _____ over some broken
   glass.

   (a) ride   (b) to ride
   (c) riding   (d) have ridden

Part II Choose the best answer for the blank.

05 Many people wave or stick out their thumbs when
   _____ a taxi.

   (a) signal   (b) signaled
   (c) signaling   (d) to signal

06 _____, children are able to acquire
   two or more languages while still young as long as
   they have meaningful exposure to each language.

   (a) Speaking generally   (b) Generally speaking
   (c) Speak generally   (d) Being spoken generally

07 Not _____ a jazz performance before, Ryan
   asked Kelly if he could accompany her to one on
   Saturday.

   (a) seen   (b) seeing
   (c) had seen   (d) having seen

08 New Orleans, _____ land below sea level, w
   eventually be completely flooded by rising sea
   levels.

   (a) occupy   (b) occupying
   (c) occupied   (d) to occupy

09 Cambria knife company demonstrates its produc
   in stores with numerous people _____
   which improves sales.

   (a) watched
   (b) watching
   (c) have watched
   (d) have been watching

10 On Groundhog Day, the remaining length of wir
   is predicted when the groundhog is observed
   _____ from its burrow.

   (a) spring   (b) sprang
   (c) springing   (d) sprung

11 Recently, many parents are considering installin
   web filtering software _____
   from obscene material.

   (a) shield their children
   (b) to shield their children
   (c) shielded their children
   (d) have shielded their children

12 When the flock of geese _____ up north felt
   icy chill coming, they commenced their journey
   warmer climates.

   (a) live   (b) living
   (c) lived   (d) to have lived

afety inspectors recently surveyed forty
lementary schools, _____ that many of the
uildings' fire alarms were not functional.

a) found   (b) it finds
c) finding   (d) have found

_____ by the singers he saw at the
pera, Daniel hired a trainer to begin giving him
rivate voice lessons.

a) Inspired   (b) His inspiring
c) He was inspired   (d) Will be inspiring

_____, the family had to endure
he cold until a new supply was delivered.

a) Using up their oil
o) Used up their oil
c) Being used up their oil
d) Having used up their oil

_____ to Spain for five years, Darren
urrently works near his hometown in Utah again.

a) To be transferred
o) It is transferred
c) Being transfer
d) Having been transferred

III Identify the option that contains an awkward
expression or an error in grammar.

a) A: Since there's a 45-minute wait, we should
   find another restaurant.
o) B: We'd better stay, having seen that we're
   already here.
c) A: But it'll be an hour until we eat since we'll
   still have to order.
d) B: It'll probably be the same at every other
   restaurant, though.

18 (a) A: Even though my GPA isn't high enough,
      I want to apply for the scholarship.
   (b) B: You will automatically be disqualified if you
      try.
   (c) A: It's not fair that the qualifications they made
      were so strict.
   (d) B: But those are the guidelines setting by a
      committee of academics.

19 (a) Minos was the fabled Greek king who ruled the
   island of Crete on which the minotaur was kept.
   (b) Though possessing the body of a human, the
   minotaur was born with the head of a bull.
   (c) Each year, Minos would have seven women
   and children sending to the minotaur as offerings.
   (d) When the hero Theseus confronted the
   minotaur, he was able to kill it and escaped from
   Crete.

20 (a) The job of air traffic controllers requires
   organizational skills, an exceptional memory, and
   the ability to work well under pressure.
   (b) Operating from the control tower and from the
   ground, they coordinate the takeoff and landing
   schedules of aircraft. (c) Controllers manage
   runway traffic and help navigate each plane to
   the intended point of takeoff. (d) Coordinating the
   landing with the pilots, planes are able to land on
   the correct runway at the appointed time.

정답 p.39

시험에 나올 문제를 미리 풀어보고 싶을 땐?

Section 4 품사

CHAPTER 11 명사와 관사

BASIC GRAMMAR 고수로 가는 첫 걸음

1 명사는 사람이나 사물, 추상적인 개념 등을 나타내는 단어이다.

student   dog   computer   sun   water   love   belief   America

2 명사는 셀 수 있는 명사(가산 명사)와 셀 수 없는 명사(불가산 명사)로 나뉜다.

① 가산 명사

보통명사	일반적인 사람, 사물의 이름·명칭	boy, teacher, customer, book, desk, ...
집합명사	여러 개체가 모여 이룬 하나의 집합	family, people, police, team, audience, ...

② 불가산 명사

고유명사	특정한 사람이나 사물의 이름	Korea, Seoul, Jane, Christmas, ...
추상명사	실제 형태 없이 추상적으로 존재하는 개념	math, information, pleasure, peace, ...
물질명사	형태가 정해져 있지 않은 기체나 액체 등	air, oil, salt, water, ...

3 관사는 명사 앞에 쓰여 명사의 의미를 한정하며 부정관사와 정관사로 나뉜다.

① 부정관사(a / an)는 명사 앞에서 '정해지지 않은 하나의'라는 뜻으로 쓰인다.
There is **a table** in my room. 내 방에는 하나의 탁자가 있다.
부정관사(a)는 명사(table) 앞에 와서 '특별히 정해지지 않은 하나의 탁자'라는 의미를 나타낸다.

② 정관사(the)는 명사 앞에서 '이미 언급한', '특별히 정해진'이라는 뜻으로 쓰인다.
I bought **the table** from my cousin. 나는 그 탁자를 내 사촌에게서 샀다.
정관사(the)는 명사(table) 앞에 와서 '이미 언급한 그 탁자'라는 의미를 나타낸다.

명사는 문장 내에서 주어, 목적어, 보어 자리에 온다.

주어	Malnutrition can lead to sickness. 영양실조는 질병을 야기할 수 있다.
타동사의 목적어	Officials noted the improvement in education. 공무원들은 교육에 있어서의 개선에 주목했다.
전치사의 목적어	Lucy asked about the furniture that was on sale. Lucy는 판매 중인 가구에 대해 물었다.
보어	Mr. Fein is the president of this company. Mr. Fein은 이 회사의 회장이다.

명사는 다음의 품사 앞이나 뒤에 나온다.

관사 + 명사 + 전치사	The structure of seaplanes allows them to land on water. 수상 비행기의 구조는 그것들이 물 위에 착륙할 수 있도록 해준다.
형용사/분사 + 명사	The resort hotel features a <u>beautiful</u> beach. 그 휴양지 호텔은 아름다운 해변을 특징으로 한다.
소유격 + (형용사 +) 명사	You have <u>my eternal</u> gratitude for everything you've done. 당신이 해주신 모든 것에 대단히 감사드립니다.
명사 + 명사 [복합명사]	The next customer may proceed to the checkout counter. 다음 손님은 계산대로 오셔도 좋습니다.

명사 자리에 동사는 올 수 없다.

We told the driver to step on the ~~accelerate~~. 우리는 운전사에게 엑셀을 밟으라고 말했다.
　　　　　　　　　　　　　　　　accelerator

▶ 전치사(on)의 목적어 자리이면서 관사 뒤에 위치하므로, 동사(accelerate)가 아니라 명사(accelerator)가 와야 한다.

It wasn't my ~~intend~~ to stay late at the office, but I had to. 사무실에 늦게까지 있는 것은 내 의도가 아니었지만, 나는 그래야만 했다.
　　　　　　intention

▶ be동사(wasn't)의 보어 자리이면서 소유격 뒤에 위치하므로, 동사(intend)가 아니라 명사(intention)가 와야 한다.

☑ **텝스 실전 문제**　　　　　　　　　　　　　　　텝스 문제 이렇게 나온다

주어, 목적어, 보어 자리에 명사를 채우는 문제가 주로 나온다.
명사 자리에 동사가 와서 틀린 문장을 찾는 문제가 가끔 나온다.

Part I

. A: I feel guilty that my older brother always treats me to meals.
　B: It's just the general ＿＿＿＿＿＿＿＿.

　(a) expected by elders　　(b) expected for elders
　(c) expectation for elders　(d) elders expect

Part III

2. (a) A: I don't know how to make my puppy stay quiet while I'm sleeping.
　(b) B: It's a good idea to put her in a cage whenever she barks.
　(c) A: Really? I would never use one, as it seems cruel and inhumane.
　(d) B: Before offering your criticize, you should see what trainers say.

정답 p.41

02 가산 명사 · 불가산 명사

1 가산 명사는 반드시 관사와 함께 쓰이거나 복수형으로 쓰여야 한다.

The child fed ~~duck~~ at the pond. 그 아이는 연못에 있는 한 마리의 오리에게/오리들에게 먹이를 주었다.
      a duck / ducks

▶ duck은 가산 명사이므로, 관사도 없고 복수형도 아니면 틀리다. 가산 명사는 반드시 관사를 붙인 형태(a duck)나 복수형(ducks)으로 써야 한다.

2 불가산 명사는 부정관사와 함께 쓰일 수 없고, 복수형으로 쓰일 수 없다.

Security officers at the airport scan ~~a luggage / luggages~~. 공항 경비원들은 화물을 조사한다.
                                luggage

▶ luggage는 불가산 명사이므로, 앞에 부정관사가 올 수 없고 복수형으로도 쓰일 수 없다.

포인트 불가산 명사인 물질명사는 앞에 단위를 붙여 센다.

물질명사 앞 단위표현	a cup of (two cups of)	a piece of (two pieces of)	a sheet of (two sheets of)	a bottle of (two bottles of)	a bundle of (two bundles of)	a pack of (two packs o

She woke up and got herself ~~waters~~. (→ **two cups of water**) 그녀는 일어나서 물 두 잔을 마셨다.
    물질명사(water)는 복수형으로 쓸 수 없으므로, 복수형의 단위표현(two cups of)을 붙여 세야 한다.

3 혼동하기 쉬운 가산 명사 · 불가산 명사

가산 명사	a price 가격 a noise 소음	a workplace 일터 measures 수단·대책	a result / an outcome 결과 belongings 소지품
불가산 명사	furniture 가구 population 인구	information 정보 equipment 장비	news 뉴스 politics 등의 학문 이름 정치학

~~Price~~ have gone up across the board in the food industry. 식품 산업에서 전반적으로 가격이 상승해왔다.
Prices

▶ price는 가산 명사이므로 관사도 없고 복수형도 아니면 틀리다. 따라서 Price가 아니라 Prices가 와야 한다.

The encyclopedia contains ~~an information~~ on world population density. 백과사전은 세계 인구밀도에 관한 정보를 담고 있다.
                               information

▶ information은 불가산 명사이므로 부정관사가 올 수 없다. 따라서 an information이 아니라 information이 와야 한다.

포인트 가산 · 불가산일 때 의미가 다른 명사

가산	a light 조명	a room 방	times 시대
불가산	light 빛	room 여지, 공간	time 시간, 시기

He closed the blinds so that ~~a light~~ would not enter the room. (→ **light**) 그는 빛이 방에 들어 오지 않도록 블라인드를 내렸다.
    light는 '빛'이라는 의미로 쓰이면 불가산 명사이므로, 부정관사가 올 수 없고 복수형으로도 쓰일 수 없다.

☑ 텝스 실전 문제

| 가산 명사와 불가산 명사를 구별하여, 필요한 경우 관사까지 함께 채우는 문제가 주로 나온다.
| 가산 명사와 불가산 명사를 혼동하여 관사나 명사의 단수/복수 선택이 틀린 문장을 찾는 문제가 주로 나온다.

Part I

1. A: Let's go on a camping trip this weekend.
   B: I'd like to, but I really don't have _____ .

  (a) time   (b) a time
  (c) one time   (d) times

Part III

2. (a) The New York Stock Exchange is the largest stock exchange in the world. (b) It can be found o[n] Wall Street, which is the heart of the city's financia[l] district. (c) Not only is it the hub of American trade and commerce, but its activity has an internationa[l] impact. (d) Whatever happens to NYSE has a significant effect on the global economies. 정답 p.4

3 부정관사

부정관사는 가산 단수 명사 앞에만 오며, 복수 명사나 불가산 명사 앞에는 올 수 없다.

He will apply to ~~an~~ exchange <u>programs</u>. 그는 교환 학생 프로그램에 지원할 것이다.

He will apply to an exchange <u>program</u>.

➡ 부정관사(a/an)는 복수 명사 앞에 올 수 없으므로, 부정관사(an)가 삭제되거나, 복수 명사(programs) 대신 단수 명사(program)가 와야 한다.

The transportation of goods to and from warehouses is aided by ~~a~~ <u>machinery</u>.
창고를 오가는 상품의 수송은 기계에 의해 도움을 받는다.

➡ 부정관사(a/an)는 불가산 명사(machinery) 앞에 올 수 없으므로, 부정관사(a)는 삭제되어야 한다.

고득점 포인트 부정관사 a/an은 단수 가산 명사 앞에서 '~당', '~마다'라는 의미로 쓰이기도 한다.
Carlos tries not to spend more than eighty dollars **a** <u>week</u>. Carlos는 일주일당 80달러 이상 쓰지 않으려고 노력한다.

부정관사 관련 숙어 표현

a series of 일련의	a range of 일정한 범위의	a variety of 다양한
a part of 일부분의	a portion of 일부의	a bit of 약간의
a maximum of 최대의	a capacity of 최대한의	a number of 많은

Each car model is available in a range of colors. 각각의 차 모델은 일정한 색상 범위 내에서 구입이 가능하다.

부정관사 관련 관용표현

That's a shame!(= What a shame!) 정말 안타깝다!

It's a pity!(= What a pity!) 정말 안됐구나!

Can I ask you a favor? 부탁 좀 해도 될까요?

What a coincidence! 우연의 일치군요!

It's not a big deal. 별일 아니야.

Have a good time! 즐거운 시간 보내세요!

Let's take a walk. 산책을 하자.

✓ 텝스 실전 문제

부정관사 관련 숙어 표현이나 관용표현을 채우는 문제가 주로 나온다.

Part II

The newest high-powered digital cameras are equipped with changeable lenses and _____ _____.

(a) a series of digital effects
(b) a digital effects series
(c) a digital of series effects
(d) digital series of effects

Part I

2. A: Our home team isn't going to make it to the finals.
   B: It's _____. I thought they had a chance.

(a) pity   (b) a pity
(c) the pity   (d) some pity

정답 p.42

1 정관사는 가산 단수·복수 명사와 불가산 명사 모두의 앞에 온다.

Alan bought his wife the <u>necklace</u> she wanted. Alan은 그의 부인에게 그녀가 원하는 목걸이를 사주었다.
가산 단수명사

She used a telescope to view the <u>moons</u> of Mars. 그녀는 화성의 위성들을 보기 위해 망원경을 사용했다.
가산 복수명사

We advise guests not to drink the <u>water</u>. 우리는 손님들에게 그 물을 마시지 말라고 충고한다.
불가산명사

🏆 고득점
포인트 정관사가 형용사 앞에 오는 경우 '~한 사람들/것들'이라는 의미의 명사구가 된다.
There are marked parking spaces for **the handicapped. (= handicapped people)** 장애인들을 위해서 구획된 주차 공간이 있다.

2 정관사와 함께 쓰이는 표현

the + 최상급 + 명사	She is the tallest member on the basketball team. 그녀는 농구팀에서 가장 키가 큰 선수다.
the + 서수 + 명사	Thanksgiving is the fourth Thursday of November. 추수감사절은 11월 넷째 목요일이다.
the + same + 명사	The man ordered the same meal as his wife. 그 남자는 그의 부인과 같은 식사를 주문했다.
the + only + 명사	Friday is the only day the gym isn't crowded. 금요일은 체육관이 붐비지 않는 유일한 날이다.
the + very (+ same) + 명사	A stereo was the very (same) gift Danielle had wanted. 스테레오는 Danielle이 원했던 바로 그 (똑같은) 선물이었다.
the + top/middle/bottom	The hikers reached the top of the mountain. 그 도보 여행자는 산 꼭대기에 도달했다.
by the + 단위/수량표현	Our employer pays us by the hour. 고용주는 우리에게 시간당 급여를 지급한다.
the + 유일한 것	The sun rises in the east. 해는 동쪽에서 뜬다.

3 정관사 관련 관용표현

That's the case. 사실은 그렇다.
That's the spirit. 바로 그 자세야.
What's the occasion? 무슨 좋은 일이 있어?
I'm on the phone. 나는 통화 중이야.
What's the matter? 무슨 일이야?
What's the problem? 무슨 일이야?
That's the problem. 그게 바로 문제야.
Do you have the time? 몇 시입니까?

☑ 텝스 실전 문제

텝스 문제 이렇게 나온다

| 정관사와 함께 쓰이는 표현을 채우는 문제가 주로 나온다.
| 정관사가 빠져서 틀린 문장을 찾는 문제가 주로 나온다.

Part I

1. A: Should I call you Jeff or Jeffrey?
   B: Since we have _____ name, I'll be Jeffrey and you be Jeff.
   (a) same   (b) a same
   (c) the same   (d) each same

Part III

2. (a) A: There are so many ice cream flavors to choose from.
   (b) B: How about marshmallow fudge? I've neve tried that one before.
   (c) A: Which one is that? I don't see it among all those in the display.
   (d) B: Look at the second row from top, next to t vanilla.

정답 p

중 알맞은 것을 고르세요.

As a result of the accident, the man on the bicycle has requested an (apologize / apology).

Because the two candidates were evenly matched, (outcome / the outcome) was in doubt until the results were officially announced.

The organic supermarket on the corner sells (the variety of / a variety of) delicious fruits and vegetables.

Robotics will become an increasingly important field as robots gradually are introduced to the homes of the world's (population / populations).

From what I remember, (a / the) 9:30 a.m. meeting is with the director of Midland Chemical.

After hearing the window break, John went outside to investigate (a noise / the noise).

린 부분이 있으면 바르게 고치세요.

His father cut down enough trees for bundle of firewoods to keep the house warm.

Sometimes I feel like my best friend is only person I can trust.

I was fortunate to have saved ten thousand dollars towards college tuition.

I would offer to let you ride with us, but we really don't have a room in the car.

The new development in the historical district strikes a good balance between ancient and modern.

Amy couldn't help but exclaim "what the coincidence!" when we saw each other across the airplane aisle.

정답 p.42

해커스 텝스 Reading

Hackers **TEST**

Part I Choose the best answer for the blank.

01 A: Oh, the remote just needs new batteries.
    B: Aha! So that's _____ problem.

(a) a   (b) any
(c) each   (d) the

02 A: Do you want to come with me to the Yankees
    game?
    B: Wow. That really is _____ offer.

(a) generous   (b) a generous
(c) each generous   (d) any generous

03 A: Was your business meeting a success?
    B: It never took place, as there was _____
    about the location.

(a) a mistake   (b) mistake
(c) the mistake   (d) other mistake

04 A: This is the Baltimore directory. Can I help you?
    B: Yes, I'd like _____ about five-star hotels
    in the area.

(a) information   (b) informations
(c) an information (d) the information

05 A: It's so tough to score a goal.
    B: If you _____ an opening, you should take
    the shot.

(a) saw   (b) see
(c) had seen   (d) will see

06 A: That book had too much violence.
    B: Well, _____ of the story was that violence
    doesn't solve anything.

(a) point   (b) a point
(c) any point   (d) the point

07 A: I'm sorry I knocked over your books. Let me pi
    them up.
    B: I'll get them. It's not _____ big deal.

(a) a   (b) the
(c) some   (d) very

Part II Choose the best answer for the blank.

08 Many kinds of _____ are utilized for
    mixing and enhancing music in a recording studi

(a) equipment   (b) the equipment
(c) equipments   (d) some equipment

09 With the hurricane approaching, dark and ominc
    rain clouds encroached from the horizon to fill
    _____.

(a) sky   (b) a sky
(c) all sky   (d) the sky

10 Special honor was given to _____ first
    passenger of the new luxury cruise ship.

(a) a   (b) one
(c) some   (d) the

11 I wasn't sure which dress to put on for the prom
    but John said to wear _____ one that I
    bought yesterday.

(a) a blue   (b) the blue
(c) each blue   (d) blue

12 Alex's company was launching a new product or
    Friday so it was certain to be _____.

(a) a too hectic week
(b) a hectic week
(c) hectic week
(d) too much hectic week

The members of the jury were instructed to review all _____ they had seen before coming to a decision.

(a) evidence   (b) evidences
(c) the evidence   (d) the evidences

The United Kingdom was in _____ in 1941 following Germany's conquest of France and Belgium.

(a) a difficult position
(b) the difficult position
(c) some difficult position
(d) difficult position

John's friends often told him he should be a singer, but he ignored _____ due to his lack of confidence.

(a) advice   (b) advices
(c) an advice   (d) the advice

The new family SUV model provides _____ for more passengers and more luggage than the old compact model.

(a) room   (b) rooms
(c) a room   (d) each room

Steven Spielberg is probably _____ director who has remained consistently successful since the 1970s.

(a) only   (b) an only
(c) the only   (d) all only

18 Regardless of physical build, both _____ _____ can compete equally in tests of intelligence and logical reasoning.

(a) weak and strong
(b) a weak and strong
(c) some weak and some strong
(d) the weak and the strong

19 She knew how to get to the embassy due to the fact of _____ there before.

(a) she walked   (b) her walked
(c) her having walked   (d) walking by her

Part III Identify the option that contains an awkward expression or an error in grammar.

20 (a) Taxonomy is the process through which different types of animals are classified. (b) This process helps scientists determine the evolutionary relationships between organisms with similar traits. (c) The most specific category is species, into which a group of animals is classified based on notable characterizes. (d) For example, while present-day humans belong to the species *Homo sapiens*, primitive humans who first learned to walk standing erect were classified as *Homo erectus*.

CHAPTER **12** 대명사

BASIC GRAMMAR 고수로 가는 첫 걸음

1 대명사는 앞서 나온 명사가 반복되는 것을 막기 위해 앞의 명사를 대신하여 사용된다. 따라서 대명사는 명사처럼 문장에서 주어, 목적어, 보어 역할을 한다.

I love <u>my brothers</u>. **They** love me, too.　나는 내 형제들을 사랑한다. 그들 또한 날 사랑한다.

두 번째 문장의 주어 역할을 하는 They는 앞에 나온 명사(my brothers)가 반복되는 것을 막기 위해 대신 쓴 대명사이다.

2 대명사는 쓰임에 따라 인칭대명사, 재귀대명사, 지시대명사, 부정대명사로 나뉜다.

① 인칭대명사(I, you, she, he, it, they 등)는 사람이나 사물을 가리킨다.

<u>Connie</u> went to graduate school because **she** wanted to study more.
Connie는 더 공부하기를 원했기 때문에 대학원에 진학했다.

she는 사람 Connie를 대신해서 쓴 인칭대명사이다.

② 재귀대명사(myself, yourself, himself, herself 등)는 인칭대명사에 -self(selves)를 붙여 '- 자신'을 뜻한다.

재귀용법　　<u>Andy</u> looked at **himself** in the mirror.　Andy는 거울 속의 자신을 쳐다봤다.
강조용법　　<u>Roy</u> **himself** said that he had lied.　Roy는 자신이 거짓말을 했다고 직접 말했다.

첫 번째 문장의 himself는 목적어 자리에서 주어 Andy를 대신한다. 이처럼 목적어가 주어와 같은 사람이나 사물을 지칭할 때 목적어 자리에 재귀대명사(himself)를 쓰는데, 이때 재귀대명사는 생략할 수 없다.

두 번째 문장의 himself는 주어인 Roy를 강조하기 위해 쓰였다. 이처럼 주어나 목적어를 강조할 때 강조하는 대상 바로 뒤나 문장 맨 뒤에 재귀대명사를 쓰는데, 이때 재귀대명사는 생략할 수 있다.

③ 지시대명사(this / these, that / those)는 특정 사물을 가리켜 '이것(들)', '저것(들)'이라는 뜻을 나타낸다. 또한 명사 앞에서 '이 ~', '저 ~'와 같은 뜻의 지시형용사로 쓰이기도 한다.

I don't like movies like **this**.　나는 이것 같은 영화들을 좋아하지 않아.
I don't like **this** movie.　나는 이 영화를 좋아하지 않아.

첫 번째 문장의 this는 '이것'이라는 뜻의 지시대명사이고, 두 번째 문장의 this는 명사(movie) 앞에 온 '이 ~'라는 뜻의 지시형용사이다.

④ 부정대명사(some, any 등)는 막연한 사람, 사물, 수량 등을 나타낸다. 또한 명사 앞에서 '어떤 ~', '몇몇의 ~' 등의 뜻을 가진 부정형용사로 쓰이기도 한다.

Some of the students are wearing glasses.　학생들 중 몇몇은 안경을 쓰고 있다.
Some students are wearing glasses.　몇몇의 학생들은 안경을 쓰고 있다.

첫 번째 문장의 some은 '몇몇'이라는 뜻의 부정대명사이고, 두 번째 문장의 some은 '몇몇의 ~'라는 뜻의 부정형용사이다.

1 인칭대명사 / 재귀대명사

출제빈도 ★★

인칭대명사와 재귀대명사의 종류

인칭	수/성		인칭대명사				재귀대명사
			주격	소유격	목적격	소유대명사	
1인칭	단수		I	my	me	mine	myself
	복수		we	our	us	ours	ourselves
2인칭	단수		you	your	you	yours	yourself
	복수		you	your	you	yours	yourselves
3인칭	단수	남성	he	his	him	his	himself
		여성	she	her	her	hers	herself
		사물	it	its	it	–	itself
	복수		they	their	them	theirs	themselves

고득점 포인트 대명사 it은 날짜, 시간, 요일, 날씨, 거리 등을 표현할 때 해석하지 않는 비인칭 주어로도 사용된다.
It is extremely hot in here. 여기는 매우 덥다.

인칭대명사의 용법

주격	주어자리	He hasn't returned from the store. 그는 가게에서 돌아오지 않았다.
소유격	명사 앞 (~의)	The suggestion to take a shortcut was my idea. 지름길로 가자는 제안은 나의 생각이었다.
목적격	타동사의 목적어 자리	I'll show you around the apartment. 내가 너에게 아파트를 안내해줄게.
	전치사의 목적어 자리	Sal carried the books for her. Sal은 그녀를 위해 책을 옮겼다.
소유대명사	'소유격 + 명사' 자리 (~의 것)	The bed by the window will be yours. 창문 옆의 침대는 네 것이 될 것이다.

재귀대명사 관련 관용표현

전치사 + 재귀대명사

by oneself 홀로, 혼자 힘으로(= alone, on one's own)	in spite of oneself 자기도 모르게	of itself 저절로
for oneself 혼자 힘으로	beside oneself 이성을 잃고, 흥분하여	in itself 자체로, 본질적으로
to oneself 독점하여	between ourselves 우리끼리 이야긴데	

동사 + 재귀대명사 (+ 전치사)

indulge oneself in ~에 빠지다	help oneself (to) (~을) 마음대로 먹다	blame oneself 자책하다
make oneself at home 편하게 지내다		

The guitarist practiced by himself until his band arrived. 그 기타리스트는 그의 밴드가 도착할 때까지 홀로 연습했다.

Everyone at the party can help themselves to the food at the buffet. 파티에 온 사람들은 뷔페 음식을 마음대로 먹을 수 있다.

📝 텝스 실전 문제

텝스 문제 이렇게 나온다

인칭과 격에 맞는 인칭대명사를 채우는 문제가 주로 나온다.
재귀대명사 관련 표현을 채우는 문제가 가끔 나온다.

Part II

After Mary gave birth to a boy, her husband wanted the child to be named after _____.

(a) his   (b) he

(c) him   (d) it

Part I

2. A: Isn't he weird sitting alone in the cafeteria?
   B: Actually, he likes _____.

   (a) eating despite himself
   (b) eating by himself
   (c) eat of himself
   (d) eat with himself

정답 p.44

1 지시대명사 that / those는 앞에 나온 명사를 대신하며, 이때 반드시 뒤에서 수식어(전치사구, 관계절, 분사)의 수식을 받는

Ms. Crawford's <u>novel</u> sold better than ~~this~~ of her rival. Ms. Crawford의 소설은 그녀의 라이벌의 것보다 더 잘 팔렸다.
　　　　　　명사　　　　　　　　　　　　that　수식어

▶ 지시대명사가 앞에 나온 명사(novel)를 대신하므로, this가 아니라 that이 와야 한다.

Additional <u>measures</u> should be taken besides ~~these~~ <u>that already exist.</u> 이미 존재하는 것들 이외에 추가적인 조치가 취해져야 한다.
　　　　　　명사　　　　　　　　　　　　　　　　those　수식어

▶ 지시 대명사가 앞에 나온 명사(measures)를 대신하므로, these가 아니라 those가 와야 한다.

2 지시대명사 those는 '~한 사람들'이라는 뜻으로, 이때 반드시 뒤에서 수식어(전치사구, 관계절, 분사)의 수식을 받는다.

~~They~~ found <u>trespassing on private property</u> will be fined. 사유지에 침입한 것으로 밝혀진 사람들에게는 벌금이 부과될 것이다.
Those　　　　　수식어

▶ 뒤에 나오는 수식어구의 수식을 받아 '~한 사람들'이라는 뜻이 되어야 하므로, They가 아니라 Those가 와야 한다.

3 지시형용사 this / that은 단수 명사 앞에, these / those는 복수 명사 앞에 쓰여 '이 ~', '저 ~'의 의미를 갖는다.

That <u>window</u> needs to be cleaned. 저 창문은 닦일 필요가 있다.
　　단수명사

These <u>potato chips</u> always make me thirsty. 이 포테이토칩은 항상 나를 목마르게 한다.
　　　복수명사

☑ 텝스 실전 문제

| 앞에 나온 명사와 수 일치하는 지시대명사를 채우는 문제가 주로 나온다.
| '~한 사람들'이라는 뜻으로 those를 채우는 문제가 주로 나온다.

Part I

1. A: Let me see the notes you took in history class last semester.
   B: But my class's work was different from _____ of yours.

   (a) this　　　　(b) that
   (c) these　　　(d) those

Part II

2. _____ holding business-class plane tickets should proceed to the check-in area at this time.

   (a) This　　　　(b) That
   (c) Those　　　(d) These

정답 p

GRAMMAR | 명사

one / another / other

· one(ones)은 정해지지 않은 가산 명사를 대신한다.

Our new coffee machine works better than the last one. 우리의 새 커피 자판기는 예전 것보다 더 잘 작동한다.

· another는 '이미 언급한 것 이외의 또 다른 하나'라는 뜻의 대명사, 형용사로 쓰인다.

If you don't like this plan, I have another. 만약 네가 이 계획이 싫다면, 나는 또 다른 계획이 있다.

We have another pair of shoes in the back. 뒤에 또 다른 신발 한 켤레가 있다.

· others는 '이미 언급한 것 이외의 것들 중 몇몇'이라는 뜻의 대명사로 쓰이고, other는 형용사로 복수 명사 앞에 쓰인다.

Children need to play with others. 아이들은 다른 아이들과 함께 놀 필요가 있다.

The magazines are stocked with other books. 잡지는 다른 책들과 함께 쌓여 있다.

· the other(s)는 '정해진 것 중 남은 것 전부'라는 뜻의 대명사로 쓰이고, the other는 형용사로도 쓰인다.

I own one of her albums, but I don't have the others yet. 나는 그녀의 앨범 중 하나를 소장하고 있지만, 나머지 것들은 갖고 있지 않다.

The left pedal accelerates, and the other pedal brakes. 왼쪽 페달은 가속을 시키고, 나머지 한 페달은 감속을 시킨다.

고득점 포인트 each other, one another는 '서로서로'라는 뜻으로 사용된다.

Those tennis partners are a good match for **each other**. 저 테니스 파트너들은 서로서로에게 좋은 상대이다.

They introduced themselves to **one another**. 그들은 서로서로를 소개했다.

some은 '몇몇(의), 약간(의)'라는 뜻의 대명사와 형용사로 주로 긍정문에 쓰이고, any는 '몇몇(의), 조금(의)'라는 뜻의 대명사와 형용사로 주로 부정문, 의문문, 조건문에 쓰인다.

The weather is cloudy only some of the time. 가끔씩만 구름이 낀 날씨다.

I don't have any idea what happened. 무슨 일이 일어났는지 나는 조금도 모르겠다.

고득점 포인트 1. 'some + 명사', something, somebody, someone은 긍정문에, 'any + 명사', anything, anybody, anyone은 의문문이나 부정문에 쓰인다.

Some birds are flightless. 어떤 새들은 날지 못한다.　　　　　Is there **anyone** home? 집에 누구 있습니까?

2. some이 의문문에 쓰이면 권유나 요청의 의미를 나타내고, any가 긍정문에 쓰이면 '어떤 ~이라도/누구라도'라는 의미이다.

Can I offer you **some** tea? 차를 좀 드릴까요?

Any doctor will say that too much drinking is not good for health. 어떤 의사라도 과도한 음주는 건강에 좋지 않다고 말할 것이다.

no와 none '아무 ~도 −않다'라는 뜻으로, 대명사인 none은 혼자 명사 자리에, 형용사인 no는 명사 앞에 온다.

There were five bottles left, but now there are none. 5개의 병이 남아 있었지만, 지금은 아무것도 남아 있지 않다.

The tourists had to navigate the trail with no map. 여행자들은 지도 없이 산길을 여행해야만 했다.

해커스 텝스 Reading

☑ 텝스 실전 문제

텝스 문제 이렇게 나온다

적절한 부정대명사나 부정형용사를 채우는 문제가 주로 나온다.

Part II

1. It is one thing to talk about skydiving and _____ to go out and do it.

   (a) each　　　　　　　(b) others

   (c) another　　　　　　(d) these

Part I

2. A: We're running out of wood for the fireplace.

   B: There's _____ more by the shed outside.

   (a) some　　　　　　　(b) any

   (c) another　　　　　　(d) further

정답 p.45

1 대명사는 그것이 지시하는 명사에 수 일치해야 한다.

	단수	복수
인칭대명사	he/his/him, she/her/her, it/its/it	they/their/them
재귀대명사	himself, herself, itself	themselves
지시대명사	this, that	these, those

The <u>book</u> had sold millions of copies and was on ~~their~~ fifth printing. 그 책은 수백만 부가 팔려서 5판 인쇄에 들어갔다.
 its

▶ 대명사가 지시하는 명사(book)가 단수이므로, 복수 대명사(their)가 아닌 단수 대명사(its)가 와야 한다.

<u>Sam</u> prepared lunch for the children by ~~themselves~~. Sam은 혼자 힘으로 아이들을 위한 점심을 준비했다.
 himself

▶ 대명사가 지시하는 명사(Sam)가 단수이므로, 복수 대명사(themselves)가 아닌 단수 대명사(himself)가 와야 한다.

This grocery's <u>vegetables</u> are fresher than ~~that~~ of its competitor. 이 식료품점의 채소들은 다른 경쟁점들의 그것들보다 더 신선하다.
 those

▶ 대명사가 지시하는 명사(vegetables)가 복수이므로, 단수 대명사(that)가 아닌 복수 대명사(those)가 와야 한다.

2 대명사는 그것이 지시하는 명사에 성·인칭이 일치해야 한다.

<u>Mr. Jackson</u> will show you ~~her~~ new invention. Mr. Jackson은 네게 그의 새 발명품을 보여줄 것이다.
 his

▶ 대명사가 지시하는 명사(Mr. Jackson)가 남성이므로, her가 아니라 his가 와야 한다.

Tommy told me that his new <u>restaurant</u> will open ~~my~~ doors soon. Tommy는 그의 새 레스토랑이 곧 개점할 것이라고 내게 말했다.
 its

▶ 대명사가 지시하는 명사(restaurant)가 3인칭 사물이므로, my가 아니라 its가 와야 한다.

☑ 텝스 실전 문제

텝스 문제 이렇게 나온다

| 지시하는 명사에 수 일치하는 대명사를 채우는 문제가 주로 나온다.
| 지시하고 있는 명사에 일치하지 않는 대명사가 와서 틀린 문장을 찾는 문제가 가끔 나온다.

Part II

1. If one wants to be an expert on movies, putting a significant amount of time, energy and money into _____ is necessary.

(a) another   (b) it
(c) that   (d) them

Part III

2. (a) Being of the flatfish family, flounder lead a horizontal existence by swimming parallel to the ocean floor. (b) Their two eyes are located on one side of the body, depending on which side is favored. (c) At birth, the young have an eye on each side, but either the left or right eye eventually migrates to the opposite side. (d) As a result, adult fish swim horizontally in order to look out for predators above it.

정답 p.4

알맞은 것을 고르세요.

The actor's fan was overwhelmed to have her T-shirt signed by (him / it).

In much of the southern hemisphere, (it / that) is hot throughout December and cold in June.

Wines made from grapes grown in France are generally considered better than (those / these) produced in other countries.

The computer virus the man wrote made copies (of itself / by himself) and spread to thousands of computers.

Are (some / any) good documentaries being shown on television this evening?

Ranked the fastest and most reliable printer of (their / its) class, the Starlight-200 is trusted by business establishments around the world.

부분이 있으면 바르게 고치세요.

They who submit their applications by December 1 will be eligible for early admission.

An effective method of studying and retaining information for one student may not necessarily bring the same benefits to other.

The design on the cover of our copies of the book is not the same as those on yours.

It was impossible to walk with no flashlight to illuminate the path in front of me.

The deer were found grazing in the same spot as it were yesterday.

Do you really plan to wear these ugly pair of shoes to the dance club tonight?

정답 p.45

Hackers **TEST**

Part I Choose the best answer for the blank.

01 A: Do you only carry old editions of this encyclopedia?
B: No, we also have some new _____ up front.

  (a) one   (b) ones
  (c) those   (d) thing

02 A: What do you think about the corruption in the government?
B: I honestly don't have _____ thoughts on the matter.

  (a) any   (b) those
  (c) much   (d) some

03 A: Did you take any pictures of the bears at the zoo?
B: They were hibernating, so there were _____ to see.

  (a) some   (b) neither
  (c) less   (d) none

04 A: If we go out, won't your daughter need a babysitter?
B: She's old enough to take care of _____.

  (a) herself   (b) himself
  (c) yourself   (d) ourselves

05 A: Did you see those customers arguing in the store?
B: No, but I heard _____ from outside.

  (a) any   (b) one
  (c) them   (d) each

06 A: I heard that Jeremy was elected as the new class president.
B: Really? We should ask him _____ the gym.

  (a) renovate   (b) renovating
  (c) to renovate   (d) to renovating

07 A: I love sailing so much that I'm renting a boat this summer.
B: We used to own _____, but we hardly ever used it.

  (a) one   (b) each
  (c) many   (d) some

08 A: Do you usually buy lunch every day?
B: No, I like _____

  (a) make lunch of myself
  (b) making lunch for myself
  (c) made lunch with myself
  (d) having made lunch in myself

Part II Choose the best answer for the blank.

09 The cry of hyenas is different and distinct from _____ of wolves.

  (a) this   (b) that
  (c) these   (d) those

10 Due to factors such as environment and upbringing, some infants learn how to walk so _____ than _____.

  (a) ones   (b) other
  (c) others   (d) another

11 Family members rely on _____ for companionship, conversation, security, and emotional support.

  (a) each   (b) another
  (c) the other   (d) one another

12 Primo Mouth Rinse contains more antibacterial cleansing agents and has a longer-lasting flavor than other mouthwash brands of _____ kind.

  (a) its   (b) our
  (c) them   (d) those

As more college graduates compete in the job market for the same jobs, the number of unemployed workers _____.

(a) are increased   (b) are increasing
(c) is increased   (d) is increasing

Vehicles that run on diesel fuel are less environmentally friendly than _____ that run on electricity.

(a) this   (b) that
(c) these   (d) those

Kenneth ran ahead of Shelly to hold a seat for _____ at the stadium.

(a) she   (b) her
(c) hers   (d) it

Last seen in 1986, Halley's Comet will not make _____ to human beings until 2061.

(a) another appearance
(b) another appearances
(c) the other appearance
(d) other appearances

III   Identify the option that contains an awkward expression or an error in grammar.

(a) A: I think we're all out of fruit at home.
(b) B: The bananas are on sale. These large cluster looks pretty ripe.
(c) A: That one seems to have bruises on the outside. Maybe someone dropped it.
(d) B: This store needs to take better care of its products.

18 (a) A: Is there anything you see that I can get you?
   (b) B: I wonder if you have any Hawaiian slice.
   (c) A: Had you only come ten minutes sooner, we might have still had some available.
   (d) B: In that case, I'll just be getting slice of pepperoni and sausage.

19 (a) The flying fox is not the name of a mammal, but rather a type of fish commonly found in aquarium tanks. (b) It lives near the floor of its environment fed on green algae and various types of vegetations. (c) As a dweller of aquarium communities, it can comfortably coexist among other species of fish. (d) However, in groups, flying foxes are known to become territorial.

20 (a) The Markum and Hillier smartphones look so similar at first glance that it is hard to tell one from the others. (b) However, once you start using them, it is easy to see how very different they really are. (c) The Markum has a simple interface, and also has many applications that come preinstalled, including maps. (d) The Hillier, a less popular phone, is not as user-friendly and does not have as much free software.

정답 p.46

CHAPTER **13** 형용사와 부사

BASIC GRAMMAR 고수로 가는 첫 걸음

1 형용사는 명사를 수식하여 한정하는 역할을 하거나, 보어로서 명사의 성질과 상태를 설명하는 역할을 한다.

She spoke in a gentle <u>voice</u>. 그녀는 부드러운 목소리로 말했다.
Her <u>voice</u> was gentle. 그녀의 목소리는 부드러웠다.

첫 번째 문장에서는 형용사 gentle이 명사(voice)를 수식하여 '부드러운 목소리'라는 의미를 만든다. 두 번째 문장에서는 형용사 gentle이 명사(voice)의 성질을 '목소리가 부드러웠다'라는 의미로 설명한다.

2 부사는 명사를 제외한 나머지 품사(형용사, 동사, 부사)를 수식하거나, 구, 절, 문장 전체를 수식하는 역할을 한다.

She spoke in a very <u>gentle</u> voice. 그녀는 매우 부드러운 목소리로 말했다.
She <u>spoke</u> gently. 그녀는 부드럽게 말했다.
She spoke so <u>gently</u>. 그녀는 매우 부드럽게 말했다.
Amazingly, <u>she spoke so gently</u>. 놀랍게도, 그녀는 매우 부드럽게 말했다.

첫 번째 문장의 부사 very는 형용사(gentle)를 수식하여 '매우 부드러운'이라는 의미를 만들고, 두 번째 문장의 부사 gently는 동사(spoke)를 수식하여 '부드럽게 말했다'라는 의미를 만든다. 세 번째 문장의 부사 so는 부사(gently)를 수식하여 '매우 부드럽게'라는 의미를 만들고, 네 번째 문장의 부사 Amazingly는 문장 전체(she spoke so gently)를 수식하여 '놀랍게도, 그녀는 매우 부드럽게 말했다'는 의미가 된다.

3 형용사는 주로 -able / -ible, -al, -tive, -ous, -ful, -y로 끝나고, 부사는 주로 '형용사 + ly' 형태를 가진다.

형용사	probable	magical	active	dangerous	successful	heavy
부사	probably	magically	actively	dangerously	successfully	heavily

그러나 -ly로 끝나는 형용사들이 있으므로 이들을 부사로 혼동하지 않도록 주의해야 하며, -ly로 끝나지 않는 부사들도 주의해서 익혀두어야 한다.

-ly로 끝나는 형용사	costly	deadly	elderly	friendly	likely	lively
-ly로 끝나지 않는 부사	ahead	even	just	right	still	well

1 형용사 자리

형용사는 명사를 수식하거나 보어 자리에 온다.

· 명사를 수식할 때

(관사 +) (부사 +) 형용사 + 명사   That's a pretty good guess. 그건 꽤 훌륭한 추측이야.

형용사 + 복합명사   Our conductor has great leadership skills. 우리 지휘자는 뛰어난 통솔력을 지니고 있다.

명사 + 형용사   The airline had no more seats available. 그 항공사에는 더 이상 이용 가능한 좌석이 없었다.

· 보어 자리에 올 때

주격 보어   The sun is bright. 태양이 밝다.

목적격 보어   They painted the house brown. 그들은 집을 갈색으로 칠했다.

고득점 포인트

1. 명사를 수식하는 자리나 보어 자리에는 형용사 외에 분사 역시 올 수 있으므로, 형용사와 분사의 의미 차이에 주의해야 한다.

The mayor suggested a ~~practiced~~ plan to deal with rising crime. (→ **practical**) 시장은 증가하는 범죄를 해결할 실질적인 계획을 제안했다.

  ↳ 명사(plan)를 수식하는 분사 practiced는 '실행된'이라는 뜻이므로 문맥에 어울리지 않는다. '실질적인'이라는 의미의 형용사 practical이 문맥상 적절하다.

The technician is ~~depending~~ when there's a computer problem. (→ **dependable**) 컴퓨터 문제가 있을 때 그 기술자는 믿을 수 있다.

  ↳ 보어 자리에 온 분사 depending은 '의존하는'이라는 뜻이므로 문맥에 어울리지 않는다. '믿을 수 있는'이라는 의미의 형용사 dependable이 문맥상 적절하다.

2. 형용사는 명사를 주로 앞에서 수식하지만, -able/-ible로 끝나는 형용사는 명사를 뒤에서 수식할 수 있으며, -where, -thing, -one, -body로 끝나는 명사는 항상 뒤에서 수식한다.

The scientist tried every way possible. 그 과학자는 가능한 모든 방법을 시도해보았다.

We need to go somewhere quiet. 우리는 조용한 어딘가로 갈 필요가 있다.

형용사 자리에 명사나 부사는 올 수 없다.

The fitness trainer has a ~~health~~ body. 그 헬스 트레이너는 건강한 신체를 갖고 있다.
         healthy

▶ 명사(body)를 수식하기 위해서는 명사(health)가 아니라 형용사(healthy)가 와야 한다.

Despite the winter, we are experiencing ~~mildly~~ temperatures this week. 겨울임에도 불구하고, 우리는 이번 주에 온화한 기후를 보내고 있다.
                mild

▶ 명사(temperatures)를 수식하기 위해서는 부사(mildly)가 아니라 형용사(mild)가 와야 한다.

텝스 실전 문제

형용사 자리에 명사나 부사가 와서 틀린 문장을 찾는 문제가 주로 나온다.

Part III

1. (a) Criminal court jurors must be careful not to make any haste judgments. (b) Making sure that culpable criminals are given the sentences they deserve is of great importance. (c) However, it is more crucial to ensure that innocents are not wrongly convicted for crimes they did not commit. (d) The legal system exists to make this distinction, but it is not without error.

2. (a) A: I think we're lost. Do you know which road this is?
   (b) B: It appears to be the detour route, which should take roughly forty minutes to drive.
   (c) A: Do you know any shortcuts that are quickly to take?
   (d) B: The only alternative at this point would be to turn around and go back.

정답 p.48

1 가산 명사 · 불가산 명사 앞에 오는 수량 표현

가산 명사 앞		불가산 명사 앞	가산 · 불가산 명사 앞	
단수 명사 앞	복수 명사 앞			
a / an 하나의	one of ~ 중 하나 each of ~의 각각	little 거의 없는	no 어떤 ~도 –아니다	all 모든
each 각각의	both 둘 다의 many 많은	a little 적은	more 더 많은	most 대부분
one 하나의	several 몇몇의 numerous 많은	less 더 적은	some 몇몇의, 어떤	any 어떤
every 모든	various 다양한 a variety of 다양한 ~	much 많은	lots of 많은 ~	a lot of 많은
another 또 다른	a couple of 몇몇의 a number of 많은 ~	a great deal of 많은 ~	plenty of 많은 ~	other 다른
a single 하나의	few 거의 없는 fewer 더 적은	a large amount of 많은 ~		
either 어느 한쪽의	a few 적은 any number of 많은, 얼마든지			
neither 어느 ~도 –않다				

There are ~~little~~ countries that have not joined the United Nations. UN에 가입하지 않은 나라는 거의 없다.
        few ─────────

▶ countries는 가산 명사이므로, 불가산 명사 앞에 오는 little이 아니라 가산 명사 앞에 오는 few가 와야 한다.

고득점 포인트 1. every가 '~마다'라는 뜻으로 쓰일 때는 뒤에 '숫자/few + 복수 명사'가 올 수 있다.
    We visit our grandmother **every** 2 weeks. 우리는 2주마다 할머니를 찾아뵌다.

    2. another 뒤에는 복수 명사가 바로 올 수 없지만, '숫자/few + 복수 명사'는 올 수 있다.
    The manager will be at our subsidiary for **another** few months. 관리자는 앞으로 몇 달 동안 우리 자회사에 있을 것이다.

2 수량 표현 + of the + 명사

one / two 하나/둘	each 각각	some / any 몇몇	
many / much 다수	most 대부분	several 몇몇	+ of the + 명사
none 하나도 ~않다	(a) few 약간 (거의 ~않다)	(a) little 약간 (거의 ~않다)	
all 전부	both 둘 다	(a / the) half 절반	

One ~~of / the~~ benefits of solar power is its lack of pollution. 태양열 발전의 이점 중 하나는 오염이 없는 것이다.
   of the

▶ 수량 표현(One)과 명사(benefits) 사이에는 of나 the 둘 중 하나만은 올 수 없고, of와 the가 함께 와야 한다.

고득점 포인트 1. all, both, half는 of 없이 'all / both / half + the + 명사'로 쓸 수 있다.
    All (of) the parking spaces on this street are metered. 이 거리의 모든 주차 공간은 미터제이다.

    2. 명사 앞에 the 대신 소유격 대명사가 올 수 있다.
    All of our employees have business cards. 우리 직원 모두 명함을 갖고 있다.

☑ 텝스 실전 문제
텝스 문제 이렇게 나온

| 가산 명사 · 불가산 명사에 적절한 형용사 관련 수량 표현을 채우는 문제
가 주로 나온다

Part I

1. A: Can you help me redecorate my bedroom?
   B: Sure, I can offer _____ suggestions.

  (a) a few   (b) a little
  (c) much   (d) every

Part II

2. Many listeners complain that radio stations dev
_____ to airing commercials and provi
too little musical content.

  (a) half of time   (b) half a the time
  (c) the half of time   (d) half the time

정답 p

동사를 수식할 때 부사 자리

- 부사는 '동사 + 목적어'의 앞이나 뒤에 온다.

She completely <u>forgot her wedding anniversary</u>. 그녀는 결혼 기념일을 완전히 잊어버렸다.

Ben <u>treats his customers</u> well. Ben은 그의 손님을 잘 대접한다.

- 진행형 · 완료형 · 수동형 동사를 수식할 때 부사는 '조동사 + -ing/p.p.' 사이나 그 뒤에 온다.

[조동사 + 동사] 사이   The auditorium <u>has</u> clearly <u>reached</u> its full capacity. 강당은 명백히 최대 수용 인원에 달했다.

[조동사 + 동사] 뒤   The film crew <u>is editing</u> currently. 영화사 직원들은 현재 편집 중이다.

> **고득점 포인트** just, still, long 등 -ly로 끝나지 않는 몇몇 특수한 부사들은 '조동사 + -ing/p.p.' 사이에는 올 수 있지만 뒤에는 올 수 없다.
> They ~~were talking still~~ about their next plan.(→ **were still talking**) 그들은 여전히 다음 계획에 대해서 이야기하고 있었다.
> └ 부사 still은 '조동사 + -ing/p.p.'(were talking)의 뒤가 아니라 were와 talking 사이에 와야 한다.

동사 이외의 것을 수식할 때 부사는 수식 받는 것 앞에 온다.

형용사 · 분사 앞   The tour package is highly <u>recommended</u>. 그 여행 패키지는 매우 권장된다.

부사 앞   The new coffee grinder works really <u>well</u>. 새 커피 분쇄기는 정말 잘 작동한다.

전치사구 앞   The award ceremony will begin exactly <u>at three</u>. 시상식은 정확히 3시에 시작할 것이다.

문장 앞   Typically, <u>wild bears will avoid humans</u>. 대체로, 야생 곰은 사람들을 피할 것이다.

부사 자리에 형용사는 쓸 수 없다.

We were ~~fortunate~~ able to get tickets. 우리는 운 좋게도 표를 구할 수 있었다.
       fortunately

➤ 형용사(able)를 수식하기 위해서는 형용사(fortunate)가 아니라 부사(fortunately)가 와야 한다.

📝 텝스 실전 문제   텝스 문제 이렇게 나온다

동사를 수식하는 부사와 동사구를 함께 채우는 문제가 주로 나온다.
부사 자리에 형용사가 와서 틀린 문장을 찾는 문제가 가끔 나온다.

Part II

The fire marshal _____ with the station's slow response time, so he will change the policy.

(a) has felt long angry   (b) has felt angry long
(c) has long felt angry   (d) has long angry felt

Part III

2. (a) A: The DVD keeps skipping when I put it in the player.
(b) B: It might play good after the scratches are removed.
(c) A: Do you have anything that can get rid of scratches?
(d) B: Yes, I bought a special device for it just recently.

정답 p.48

1 강조 부사는 '매우, 너무' 등의 의미를 더해 수식하는 대상을 강조하는 부사이다.

very 매우	**much** 너무, 많이	**so** (긍정적·부정적 의미로) 매우, 너무	**too** (부정적 의미로) 너무
right 바로	**just** 막, 그저, 정말	**only** 단지, 겨우	**even** ~조차, 심지어 ~까지도
pretty 꽤, 제법	**well** 잘, 훨씬	**quite** 꽤, 상당히	**ever** 항상, 도대체
enough 충분히	**way** (대화 표현에서) 너무, 훨씬	**much / even / still / far / a lot / by far** (비교급 앞에서) 훨씬	

Thank you very much. 대단히 감사합니다.
New laptop computers continue to get even smaller. 새로운 노트북 컴퓨터들은 계속 훨씬 더 작아지고 있다.

2 강조 부사는 보통 형용사나 부사를 앞에서 강조한다.

We thought Murphy's introductory speech was just fine. 우리는 Murphy의 소개 연설이 정말 괜찮았다고 생각했다.
He came over to pick me up pretty early. 그는 나를 꽤 일찍 데리러 왔다.

3 특수한 자리에 쓰이는 강조 부사

· quite는 'a(n) + 형용사 + 명사'를 앞에서 강조한다.
My apartment required quite a large deposit. 내 아파트는 꽤 많은 보증금을 요구했다.

· enough는 동사와 형용사를 뒤에서 강조한다.
She is smart enough to get any job she wants. 그녀는 그녀가 원하는 어떤 직업이든 구할 수 있을 만큼 충분히 똑똑하다.

· well, right, way는 전치사구를 앞에서 강조한다.
Temperatures tonight will be well below zero. 오늘 밤 기온은 영도 훨씬 이하로 떨어질 것이다.
The bank is located right beside the post office. 은행은 우체국 바로 옆에 위치하고 있다.
My score is way above average. 내 점수는 평균을 훨씬 넘는다.

· even은 명사, 동사, 전치사구를 앞에서 강조한다.
Even water can be harmful to drink in large amounts. 물조차 많은 양을 마시면 해로울 수 있다.
The new restaurant even offers a 10 percent discount in addition to free dessert.
그 새로운 식당은 무료 후식에 더해 10퍼센트 할인을 제공하기까지 한다.
In some areas of the Arctic, it's bright even at night during summer. 북극의 몇몇 지역에서는 여름 동안 심지어 밤에도 환하다.

· just와 only는 명사나 전치사구를 앞에서 강조한다.
It's just a rerun of last week's episode. 그것은 단지 지난주 방영분의 재방송일 뿐이다.
Breakfast is available only until 10 a.m. 아침 식사는 오전 10시까지만 이용 가능합니다.

· ever는 의문사를 뒤에서 강조한다.
I wonder who ever will be the next chairman. 나는 도대체 누가 다음 의장이 될지 궁금하다.

☑ 텝스 실전 문제
텝스 문제 이렇게 나온

| 적절한 강조 부사를 채우는 문제가 주로 나온다.

Part I

1. A: Those two are always arguing.
   B: I don't know what _____ they fight for.

   (a) never   (b) ever
   (c) still   (d) least

Part II

2. Marathon races take _____ a long time t(
   complete.

   (a) so   (b) much
   (c) very   (d) quite

정답 p

05 빈도 부사

빈도 부사는 얼마나 자주 일이 발생하는지를 의미하는 부사이다.

always 항상	almost 거의	often 자주	frequently 종종	usually 보통
sometimes 때때로	hardly / rarely / seldom / scarcely / barely 거의 ~않다	never 결코 ~않다		

When the refrigerator is opened, its light always turns on. 냉장고가 열리면, 불빛이 항상 켜진다.

I usually go to sleep around 11:30. 나는 보통 11시 30분 쯤에 잔다.

빈도 부사는 보통 일반동사 앞, 또는 be동사나 조동사의 뒤에 와야 한다.

Janet often <u>visits</u> her grandparents. Janet은 자주 그녀의 조부모님을 방문한다.

You <u>are</u> sometimes too straightforward. 너는 때때로 너무 솔직하다.

I <u>can</u> hardly <u>bear</u> my boss. 나는 상사를 거의 견딜 수 없다.

hardly, rarely, seldom, scarcely, barely는 부정의 의미로 not과 같은 부정어와 함께 올 수 없다.

Steve ~~is rarely not~~ late for his appointments. Steve는 약속에 거의 늦지 않는다.
　　　is rarely

▶ 빈도 부사 rarely는 이미 부정의 뜻을 담고 있으므로 부정어 not이 함께 쓰일 수 없다.

🎯 고득점
포인트 부정 부사가 문장의 맨 앞에 오면 주어와 동사의 자리가 바뀌는 도치가 일어난다. 도치에 대해서는 Chapter 21에서 자세히 다룬다.
He **never** goes home before midnight. 그는 자정 전에는 결코 집에 가지 않는다.
주어　　　동사
→ **Never** does he go home before midnight.
　　　　동사 주어

☑ 텝스 실전 문제

빈도 부사를 동사와 함께 올바른 위치에 채우는 문제가 주로 나온다.
부정의 의미를 지닌 빈도 부사가 부정어와 함께 와서 틀린 문장을 찾는
문제가 가끔 나온다.

Part II

1. Inherited genetic physical traits, such as height or hair color, _____.

   (a) usually differ between family members
   (b) between family members are differing usually
   (c) are differing family members between usually
   (d) are usually between family members differ

Part III

2. (a) A: I can't believe what you're wearing tonight.
   (b) B: Do you have a problem with my jeans and sneakers?
   (c) A: Your outfit is hardly not appropriate for this restaurant.
   (d) B: I didn't know we would be eating at such a nice place.

정답 p.48

1 형태가 유사해서 혼동을 주는 형용사와 부사

late (형) 늦은	hard (형) 힘든, 단단한	near (형) 가까운	high (형) 높은	most (형) 대부분의, 가장 많은
(부) 늦게	(부) 열심히, 심하게	(부) 가까이, 근처에	(부) 높게	(부) 가장 많이
lately (부) 최근에	hardly (부) 거의 ~않다	nearly (부) 거의	highly (부) 매우	mostly (부) 대체로, 주로
				almost (부) 거의

During the storm, the rain was coming down ~~hardly~~. 폭풍이 치는 동안에, 비가 심하게 왔다.
              hard

▶ '비가 심하게 왔다'는 의미가 되어야 문맥상 자연스러우므로 hardly가 아니라 hard가 와야 한다.

Apes are ~~hard~~ as intelligent as humans. 원숭이는 거의 인간만큼 똑똑하지 않다.
        hardly

▶ '거의 똑똑하지 않다'는 의미가 되어야 문맥상 자연스러우므로 hard가 아니라 hardly가 와야 한다.

고득점 포인트 형용사와 부사로 모두 쓰이는 단어들도 주의해서 익혀두도록 한다.

early (형) 이른/(부) 일찍	fast (형) 빠른/(부) 빨리	far (형) 먼/(부) 멀리	long (형) 긴/(부) 오래, 오랫동안

She has **long** curly hair. 그녀는 긴 곱슬머리를 가지고 있었다.
I won't stay very **long**. 나는 아주 오래 머물지 않을 것이다.
↳ 첫 번째 문장의 long은 명사(hair)를 수식하는 형용사이고, 두 번째 문장의 long은 동사(stay)를 수식하는 부사이다.

2 쓰임이 유사해서 혼동을 주는 형용사와 부사

· **형용사 such vs. 부사 so**
The professor spoke ~~such~~ quietly that I couldn't hear her. 교수님이 너무 조용히 말씀하셔서 나는 그녀의 말을 알아 들을 수가 없었다.
              so   부사
I've never seen ~~so~~ things. 나는 그러한 것은 전혀 본 적이 없다.
            such   명사

▶ 부사(quietly)를 수식하는 것은 부사이므로 such가 아니라 so가 와야 한다. 반면, 명사(things)를 수식하는 것은 형용사이므로 so가 아니라 such가
  야 한다.

· **either vs. neither**
He doesn't know the way, ~~neither~~. 그 역시 방법을 알지 못한다.
                    either
He doesn't know the way, and ~~either~~ do I. 그는 방법을 알지 못한다. 그리고 나 역시 알지 못한다.
                        neither

▶ 부정문의 마지막에 와서 '~ 역시 아니다'는 의미를 나타내기 위해서는 neither가 아니라 either가 와야 한다. 반면, 부정문 뒤에 이어지는 절이나,
  의 첫머리에서 '~ 역시 아니다'는 의미를 나타내기 위해서는 either가 아니라 neither가 와야 한다.

☑ 텝스 실전 문제

텝스 문제 이렇게 나온다

| 형태나 쓰임이 유사해서 혼동을 주는 형용사와 부사를 구별하여 채우는
문제가 주로 나온다.

Part II

1. Coffee drinks are _____ made of water or milk, while consisting of only a small percentage of genuine coffee.

   (a) most   (b) the most
   (c) the mostly   (d) mostly

Part I

2. A: Why are you so late?
   B: The bus took _____ long to come that I just decided to walk instead.

   (a) so   (b) such
   (c) just   (d) even

정답 p.4

중 알맞은 것을 고르세요.

A (rare / rarely) drawing from Picasso can be worth millions of dollars.

The party would have been much quieter if (fewer / less) people had attended.

The weather forecast mentioned that it would (probable / probably) rain tomorrow.

I have (many / a lot of) work to do before I can leave the office.

After playing in the mud, the dog's paws were (too / even) dirtier than they had been.

My youngest sister has grown (near / nearly) eight inches in the past year.

긴 부분이 있으면 바르게 고치세요.

The advertisement offered 3 DVDs for free, but I would have to pay thirty dollars for any added discs.

Because he just arrived from Bangladesh, he can hard speak the local language.

They had bought just milk, but they already ran out.

The company is announcing its profits later, and they are expected to be well below expectations.

I've never been to India neither, so you're not the only one who hasn't seen the Taj Mahal.

She realized she wasn't enough fast to win the race.

정답 p.49

Hackers **TEST**

Part I Choose the best answer for the blank.

01 A: Did you hear that loud storm last night?
   B: It was only supposed to be a passing shower, but there was _____ much thunder.

   (a) ever   (b) so
   (c) only   (d) really

02 A: We spent too much money this month.
   B: You're right. We eat out _____ too often.

   (a) way   (b) well
   (c) such   (d) pretty

03 A: Can you turn the music up a little more?
   B: Are you sure? I think it's _____ loud already.

   (a) enough   (b) far
   (c) much   (d) quite

04 A: Heller's *Catch-22* is an excellently plotted book.
   B: I know. It's like he wanted _____ to build upon the one before, one by one.

   (a) chapter   (b) the chapter
   (c) any chapter   (d) each chapter

05 A: Is there any way I can improve my job conditions at the meat factory?
   B: Unfortunately, there is _____.

   (a) no way that you can
   (b) a way you can not do
   (c) you can not a way
   (d) that doing no way

06 A: I'm so angry that they're building a mall right in the heart of town.
   B: Honestly, I _____.

   (a) either care for it
   (b) neither care for it
   (c) don't care for it, either
   (d) don't care for it, neither

07 A: Were there many positive responses to the questionnaire about our customer service?
   B: Yes, _____ papers sent back said peo[ple] think we are doing a good job.

   (a) most the   (b) most of
   (c) most of the   (d) the most of

08 A: That painting is incredibly striking.
   B: The colors are _____ brilliant that I feel li[ke] I need to squint to look at it.

   (a) so   (b) such
   (c) much   (d) too

09 A: Are you thinking of buying a Blu-Ray Disc player?
   B: I don't think so. Its price is _____ exorbita[nt].

   (a) also   (b) much
   (c) too   (d) well

10 A: What did Gordon say when you called?
   B: It was noon and he _____! Can you believe it?

   (a) has woken up just
   (b) was just waking up
   (c) just waking up
   (d) had him woken up

Part II Choose the best answer for the blank.

11 In South Korea, the executive branch is structure[d] so that a new president is elected _____ five years.

   (a) all   (b) the
   (c) each   (d) every

12 Fitness trainers advocate that aerobic training is _____ healthier than anaerobic training.

   (a) much   (b) too
   (c) very   (d) well

The miniaturization of technology makes modern appliances look similar to _____ in science fiction movies.

(a) that   (b) this
(c) those   (d) these

A local philanthropist offered _____ toward the renovation of the public park.

(a) quite a generous donation
(b) a quite generous donation
(c) quite generous a donation
(d) quite a donation generous

The police chief ordered that _____ bystanders stand back from the burning building.

(a) much   (b) all
(c) little   (d) either

Taiwan represents _____ million people and continues to petition to join the United Nations.

(a) few   (b) many
(c) every   (d) several

t III Identify the option that contains an awkward expression or an error in grammar.

(a) A: Where do you imagine yourself living in ten years?
(b) B: I think I might possible settle down in Maine.
(c) A: Why? Do you really like small towns and seafood that much?
(d) B: I've lived in big cities my whole life, so eventually I'd like to move away.

18 (a) A: Hello. I wonder if I can speak to Dr. Phillips.
(b) B: He's busy in a meeting at the moment. Would you like to make an appointment?
(c) A: I just need to speak to him for a few minutes if possible.
(d) B: I'll tell him and make sure he returns your call lately.

19 (a) The expanding Gobi Desert poses a problem to China and those countries in its vicinity. (b) China has already begun to combat this change in an effort to plant thousands of trees. (c) Tree fences are known to catch blowing sand in order to protect farmland and habitats. (d) Today, trees are being still planted to block blowing sand, but results have yet to be seen.

20 (a) The Native American flute, which possesses a distinct sound, has become popularly recognized of late. (b) Its original purpose served only personal occasions, such as for spiritually healing or meditation. (c) In the 1960s, the flute began to enter popular music for the unique ambience it creates. (d) Today, the flute is featured in all manner of performance, utilized across various genres of music.

정답 p.49

CHAPTER 14 전치사

BASIC GRAMMAR 고수로 가는 첫 걸음

1 전치사는 명사 앞에 와서 장소, 시간 등을 나타낸다.

I met him **at** <u>the bus stop</u>. 나는 버스 정류장에서 그를 만났다.
She usually gets up early **in** <u>the morning</u>. 그녀는 대개 아침에 일찍 일어난다.

첫 번째 문장의 at은 '~에서'라는 장소의 의미를 나타내고, 두 번째 문장의 in은 '~에'라는 시간의 의미를 나타낸다. 이때 전치사 뒤에 있는 명사 the bus stop, the morning을 전치사의 목적어라고 하고 '전치사 + 전치사의 목적어'를 '전치사구'라고 한다.

2 전치사구는 명사를 수식하는 형용사 역할이나, 동사를 수식하는 부사 역할을 한다.

<u>The book</u> **on the desk** is mine. 책상 위의 그 책은 내 것이다.

He <u>slept</u> **for 2 hours**. 그는 2시간 동안 잤다.

첫 번째 문장에서 전치사구(on the desk)는 명사(The book)를 수식하는 형용사 역할을 한다. 두 번째 문장의 전치사구(for 2 hours)는 동사(slept)를 수식하는 부사 역할을 한다.

01 전치사 자리

전치사는 명사 역할을 하는 것 앞에 온다.

명사   They took many pictures in <u>Singapore</u>. 그들은 싱가포르에서 많은 사진을 찍었다.

대명사(목적격)   I offered to pay for <u>them</u>. 나는 그들 대신 지불할 것을 제안했다.

동명사   He excels at <u>debating</u> with others. 그는 다른 이들과의 토론에 있어 탁월하다.

명사절   She's not positive about <u>what I suggested</u>. 그녀는 내가 제안했던 것에 대해 긍정적이지 않다.

고득점 포인트 '전치사 (+ 관사) (+ 부사) (+ 형용사) + 명사'처럼 관사나 형용사, 부사가 전치사와 명사 사이에 올 수 있다.

The lawyer slyly answered the question **in a roundabout manner**. 변호사는 질문에 우회적으로 교묘하게 대답했다.
전치사 + 관사 + 형용사 + 명사

Online auction sites have let people search for items **in a completely new way**.
전치사 + 관사 + 부사 + 형용사 + 명사

온라인 경매 사이트는 사람들이 완전히 새로운 방식으로 상품을 검색할 수 있도록 해주었다.

전치사는 의문사절과 관계대명사절에서 의문사와 관계대명사 앞에 올 수 있다.

To <u>whom</u> are you mailing this package? 누구에게 이 소포를 보내십니까?
의문사

Please follow the guidelines about <u>which</u> you've been instructed. 당신이 지시받아왔던 지침을 따라주세요.
관계대명사

고득점 포인트 대화 상황에서는 전치사가 의문사절과 관계절의 맨 뒤에 남을 수 있다.

Who(m) are you mailing this package **to**?

└ '누구에게'라는 의미를 나타내기 위해 전치사가 의문사 앞에 와서 To whom이 되어야 하지만, 대화 상황에서는 의문사만 문장 앞에 나오고 전치사는 의문사절의 마지막에 남을 수 있다.

Please follow the guidelines <u>which</u> you've been instructed **about**.

└ 관계대명사(which)가 지칭하는 것은 the guidelines이다. '지침에 대해서'라는 의미를 나타내기 위해 전치사는 관계대명사 앞에 와서 about which가 되어야 하지만, 대화 상황에서는 관계대명사만 앞에 나오고 전치사는 관계절의 맨 뒤에 남을 수 있다.

형용사적 용법으로 쓰여 명사를 수식하는 to부정사 뒤에 전치사가 올 수 있다.

I need a sofa ~~to sit~~ in my living room. 나는 거실에 앉을 소파가 필요하다.
            to sit on

▶ to부정사(to sit)의 동사(sit)와 to부정사가 수식하는 명사(a sofa)가 전치사(on) 없이 바로 연결될 수 없으므로 전치사(on)가 필요하다.

☑ 텝스 실전 문제

텝스 문제 이렇게 나온다

전치사구를 올바른 순서로 채우는 문제가 주로 나온다.
의문사절과 관계대명사절에서 전치사의 위치가 틀린 문장을 찾는 문제가
가끔 나온다.

Part II

1. The deforestation of the Earth's tropical rainforests is occurring _____.

(a) worrying a pace at

(b) worrying pace at a high

(c) at a worrying pace

(d) at high a pace worry

Part III

2. (a) A: I seem to be a little lost and need help.

(b) B: How can I be of assistance to you?

(c) A: Which building is in the conference?

(d) B: Alvin Hall, which is down this road and on the left.

정답 p.51

1 시간을 나타내는 전치사

in	월 · 연도 · 시간(~ 후에)	in January 1월에	in 2008 2008년에	in five hours 5시간 후에
	계절 · 세기	in spring 봄에	in the twenty-first century 21세기에	
	오전/오후/저녁	in the morning / in the afternoon / in the evening 오전에/오후에/저녁에		
at	시각 · 시점	at 3 o'clock 3시에	at the beginning of class 수업 시작에	
	정오/밤/새벽	at noon / at night / at dawn 정오에/밤에/새벽에		
on	날짜 · 요일 · 특정일	on May 1 5월 1일에	on Monday 월요일에	on Independence Day 독립 기념일에

The Berlin Wall fell in 1989. 베를린 장벽은 1989년에 무너졌다.
We have a dinner reservation at 7:30 p.m. 우리는 오후 7시 30분에 저녁 식사 예약이 있다.
Cinco de Mayo is a Mexican holiday celebrated on May 5. 신코 데 마요는 5월 5일에 기념되는 멕시코의 휴일이다.

고득점 포인트 next, last, this, that, one, every, each, some, any, all 등을 포함한 시간 표현 앞에는 보통 전치사 in/at/on이 오지 않는다.
See you ~~on~~ next Friday. 다음 주 금요일에 보자. I stayed up ~~at~~ all night. 나는 밤새 깨어 있었다.

2 장소를 나타내는 전치사

in	(상대적 큰 공간) 내의 장소	in the world 세계에	in the room 방에
at	지점 · 번지	at the station 역에	at 31 Park Avenue Park 가 31번지에
on	표면 위 · 일직선상의 지점	on the shelf 선반 위에	on the street 길에

There is a statue of Christopher Columbus in Central Park. 센트럴 파크에는 크리스토퍼 콜럼버스의 동상이 있다.
Please check your luggage at the counter. 짐은 카운터에 맡겨주십시오.
We installed a satellite dish on the roof. 우리는 지붕 위에 위성 안테나를 설치했다.

3 in / at / on 숙어 표현

in	in time 제때에	in place 제자리에	in order 정돈되어	in one's opinion ~의 의견으로는
at	(all) at once 즉시	at a 형 pace/speed ~한 속도로	at a 형 price ~한 가격으로	at the age of ~의 나이로
	at times 때때로	at the rate of ~의 비율로	at a charge of ~의 비용 부담으로	at one's convenience ~가 편한 때
	at least 적어도	at the latest 늦어도	at one's expense ~의 비용으로	at a disadvantage 불리한 입장에
on	on time 정시에	on the list of ~의 목록에	on a regular basis 규칙적으로	on sale 판매 중인, 할인 중인

We arrived in time to get the train. 우리는 기차를 타기에 제때에 도착했다.
Airlines allocate a few tickets at a low price. 항공사들은 약간의 표를 낮은 가격에 배분한다.
Running on a regular basis can slow the effects of aging. 규칙적으로 달리는 것은 노화를 늦출 수 있다.

☑ 텝스 실전 문제
텝스 문제 이렇게 나온다

| 문맥에 맞게 전치사 in/at/on을 채우는 문제가 주로 나온다.
| in/at/on 숙어 표현이 틀린 문장을 찾는 문제가 가끔 나온다.

Part I

1. A: What did you order _____ the restaurant?
   B: I had chicken parmesan over pasta.

   (a) at   (b) on
   (c) for   (d) of

Part III

2. (a) Researchers believe that long-distance runners can improve their speed by running slower. (b) This may sound counter-intuitive, but it has to do with how runners train in preparation for a race.
(c) Scientists suggest that athletes run in a steady pace that is a little slower than they would normally run. (d) Runners can then last a little longer, which will help them to build up cardiovascular strength.

정답 p.5

3 전치사 선택 2: 시점 · 기간

시점을 나타내는 전치사

since ~ 이래로 until / by ~까지	from ~부터 before / prior to ~ 전에	+ 시점	since 2000 2000년 이래로 until 11 / by 11 11시까지	from March 3월부터 before Friday / prior to Friday 금요일 전에

I haven't seen my parents since January.   나는 1월 이래로 부모님을 뵙지 못했다.

고득점
포인트 by는 '상태 · 동작의 완료'를, until은 '상태 · 동작의 지속'을 의미한다.

The lunch special is available **by** two o'clock. (→ until)   점심 특선은 2시까지 이용 가능합니다.

↳ '점심 특선이 2시까지 이용 가능하다'는 '상태의 지속'을 의미하므로 by가 아니라 until이 와야 한다.

Make sure to give me a call ~~until~~ noon. (→ by)   정오까지 반드시 내게 전화를 해라.

↳ '정오까지 전화를 해라'라는 '동작의 완료'를 의미하므로 until이 아니라 by가 와야 한다.

기간을 나타내는 전치사

for / during ~ 동안 over / throughout ~ 동안, ~ 내내 within ~ 이내에	+ 기간	for a week 일주일 동안 over the summer 여름 동안, 여름 내내 within ten days 10일 이내에	during holidays 휴일 동안 throughout a year 1년 동안, 1년 내내

We exercised every day over the summer.   우리는 여름 내내 매일 운동을 했다.

고득점
포인트 for와 during은 둘 다 '~ 동안'을 뜻하지만 for는 숫자를 포함한 시간 표현 앞에 와서, '얼마나 오래 지속되는가'를 나타내고, during은 명사 앞에 와서 '언제 일어나는가'를 나타낸다.

I will be volunteering in India **during** five weeks. (→ for)   나는 5주 동안 인도에서 자원봉사를 하고 있을 것이다.

↳ '5주 동안 자원봉사를 할 것'이라는 의미로 숫자를 포함한 시간 표현(five weeks) 앞에 와야 하므로, during이 아니라 for가 와야 한다.

The Pope will be visiting London **for** August. (→ during)   교황이 8월 동안 런던을 방문할 것이다.

↳ '8월 동안 런던을 방문할 것'이라는 의미로 명사(August) 앞에 와야 하므로, for가 아니라 during이 와야 한다.

텝스 실전 문제

문맥에 맞게 시점 · 기간을 나타내는 전치사를 채우는 문제가 주로 나온다.

Part II

The national mint will release new bills that will replace the existing currency _____ next month.

(a) on   (b) until
(c) from   (d) to

Part I

2. A: How long does that MP3 player last?

B: It can play music nonstop _____ almost 25 hours.

(a) during   (b) on
(c) to   (d) for

정답 p.52

1 위치를 나타내는 전치사

above / over ~ 위에	He felt like he was flying above / over the clouds. 그는 구름 위로 날고 있는 것처럼 느꼈다.
below/under/underneath ~ 아래에	She dropped her contact lens below / under / underneath the table. 그녀는 탁자 아래로 그녀의 콘택트 렌즈를 떨어뜨렸다.
beside / next to ~ 옆에	There's a bookshelf beside / next to the desk. 책상 옆에 책장이 있다.
between / among ~ 사이에	Scarlet stood between two people. Scarlet이 두 사람 사이에 섰다.
around ~의 여기저기에, ~ 주위에 near ~ 근처에	We walked for a while around the park. 우리는 잠시 동안 공원 여기저기를 걸었다. Is there a bank near the airport? 공항 근처에 은행이 있습니까?
within ~ 내에	A yearly barbecue is held within the community. 매년 바비큐 파티가 지역사회 내에서 개최된다.

 between은 '둘 사이'에 쓰여서 위치와 시간의 '사이'를 의미하고, among은 '셋 이상'의 그룹 '사이'를 의미한다.
His car was parked ~~among~~ two vans. (→ **between**) 그의 차는 두 대의 밴 사이에 주차되어 있었다.
ㄴ '두 대의 밴 사이'를 의미하므로 among이 아니라 between이 와야 한다.
Many weeds sprouted ~~between~~ the flowers. (→ **among**) 많은 잡초들이 꽃들 사이에서 자라났다.
ㄴ '셋 이상의 꽃들 사이'를 의미하므로 between이 아니라 among이 와야 한다.

2 방향을 나타내는 전치사

from ~로부터, ~에서 to ~에게, ~으로 for ~을 향해 toward ~쪽으로	I got a letter from Thomas. 나는 Thomas로부터 편지를 받았다. He wrote a complaint to the editor. 그는 편집자에게 불만을 써서 보냈다. She has already started for Boston. 그녀는 이미 보스턴을 향해 출발했다. The storm is blowing toward the south. 폭풍은 남쪽으로 불고 있다.
up ~ 위로 down ~ 아래로	Take the escalator up three floors. 에스컬레이터를 타고 위로 세 층 가세요. Room 205 is located down the hall. 205호는 복도 끝에 위치해 있다.
across ~을 가로질러 along ~을 따라	With binoculars she could see across the lake. 쌍안경으로 그녀는 호수를 가로질러 볼 수 있었다. Palm trees were planted along the road. 야자 나무는 길을 따라 심어져 있었다.
into ~ 안으로 out of ~ 밖으로	She stepped into the car. 그녀는 차 안으로 들어갔다. Andrew drove out of the parking lot. Andrew는 주차장 밖으로 운전해 나갔다.

3 위치·방향을 나타내는 전치사 관련 표현

across the world 전 세계적으로	under discussion 토론 중인	under control 통제 하에 있는
all over the world 전 세계적으로	under consideration 고려 중인	under pressure 압력을 받고 있는
around the world 전 세계적으로	under way 진행 중인	under the name of ~의 이름으로

There are riots in the poor countries all over the world[across the world / around the world].
전 세계적으로 가난한 국가들에서 폭동이 일어난다.

☑ 텝스 실전 문제

텝스 문제 이렇게 나온

| 문맥에 맞게 위치·방향을 나타내는 전치사를 채우는 문제가 주로 나온다.

Part II

1. The natives of Rapa Nui had strategically placed stone figures _____ the island.

(a) over   (b) to
(c) under   (d) around

Part I

2. A: I've started reading Buddhist texts.
   B: Oh, you must be interested in finding the path _____ enlightenment.

(a) at   (b) to
(c) for   (d) along

정답 p

5 전치사 선택 4: 이유 · 양보 · 목적 / of / ~에 관하여

출제빈도
★★

이유 · 양보 · 목적을 나타내는 전치사

because of due to owing to	~ 때문에	The game was canceled because of rain. 그 경기는 비 때문에 취소되었다. There is a 45-minute delay due to heavy traffic. 많은 교통량 때문에 45분의 지연이 있다. The trial was halted owing to defendant's health. 피고인의 건강 때문에 재판은 중지되었다.
despite in spite of	~에도 불구하고	Despite / In spite of strong winds, the plane experienced a smooth takeoff. 강한 바람에도 불구하고, 비행기는 부드럽게 이륙했다.
for	~을 위해	The couple went to Hawaii for their honeymoon. 그 커플은 신혼여행을 위해 하와이에 갔다.

A of B

의미상 A가 동사, B가 주어	the graduation of our daughter 우리 딸의 졸업 (← 우리 딸이 졸업하다) the spinning of the Earth 지구의 회전 (← 지구가 회전하다)
의미상 A가 동사, B가 목적어	the planning of a new project 새 프로젝트의 계획 (← 새 프로젝트를 계획하다) the renovation of a house 집의 개조 (← 집을 개조하다)
A와 B가 동격	the hope of meeting his idol 그의 우상을 만난다는 희망 (← 희망 = 그의 우상을 만나는 것) the land of China 중국 대륙 (← 대륙 = 중국)
A가 B의 부분 · 소속	the point of the argument 논쟁의 요점 (← 그 논쟁 중 중요한 점) the center of town 도시의 중심 (← 도시에 속한 중심 지역)

'~에 관하여'라는 의미의 전치사

| about | of | as to | regarding | with / in regard to | with respect to |
| over | on | as for | concerning | with / in reference to | |

We have never heard of that institute. 우리는 그 단체에 관하여 들어본 적이 없다.

Canada takes no position with respect to the constitutional status of the Indian reservation.
캐나다는 인디언 보호 구역의 헌법상의 지위에 관하여 아무 입장도 취하지 않는다.

✍ 텝스 실전 문제

텝스 문제 이렇게 나온다

문맥에 맞게 전치사를 채우는 문제가 주로 나온다.

Part II

1. _____ a traffic accident on the road that delayed Alfred's commute to work, he still arrived five minutes early.

(a) Thanks to   (b) Contrary to
(c) In spite of   (d) On behalf of

2. The Amazon Rainforest is home to over three thousand different species _____ fish.

(a) of   (b) for
(c) in   (d) about

정답 p.52

1 기타 전치사

except (for)	~을 제외하고	Everyone was able to attend except (for) Craig. Craig를 제외하고 모두가 참석할 수 있었다.
by	~에 의해	The winner is determined by a lottery. 당첨자는 제비 뽑기에 의해 결정된다.
	~을 타고	They journeyed to the island by motorboat. 그들은 모터보트를 타고 섬으로 여행했다.
	~만큼	The company's stock dropped by fifteen percent. 그 회사의 주식은 15퍼센트만큼 떨어졌다.
through	~을 통해	A language is best acquired through practical use. 언어는 실제 사용을 통해 가장 잘 습득된다.
	~을 통과하여	We traveled through the state. 우리는 그 주를 통과하여 지나갔다.
with	~을 가지고	She amused herself with her cell phone. 그녀는 휴대 전화를 가지고 놀았다.
	~와 함께	Jacob studied for the exam with his tutor. Jacob은 개인 교사와 함께 시험 공부를 했다.
without	~ 없이	I drink coffee without cream. 나는 크림 없이 커피를 마신다.
as	~로서	She is working as a manager at the shop. 그녀는 그 가게에서 매니저로 일하고 있다.
like	~처럼	Like drawing, painting requires an eye for beauty. 데생처럼, 회화도 미에 대한 안목을 필요로 한다.
unlike	~와 달리	Speaking, unlike writing, improves social skills. 말하기는 쓰기와 달리 사교 기술을 발전시킨다.
against	~에 반(대)하여	Citizens took a firm stand against the new tax bill. 시민들은 새로운 세금 법안에 반대하여 강경한 자세를
beyond	~을 넘어	The sheep never stray beyond the pasture. 양들은 절대 목장을 넘어서 돌아다니지 않는다.
for	~에 비해서	It is cool for August. 8월인 것에 비해서 시원하다.
apart from	~을 제외하고	Apart from the worker who is sick, everyone is at work today. 아픈 직원을 제외하고 오늘 모두 출
	~뿐만 아니라	Apart from taking notes, Kurt will be explaining the meeting agenda. 기록하는 것뿐만 아니라, Kurt는 회의 안건을 설명할 것이다.

2 동사·형용사·명사와 함께 쓰이는 전치사

동사 + 전치사	account for ~을 설명하다 consist of ~으로 구성되다 depend / rely on ~에 의존하다 credit A with B A에게 B의 공이 있다고 여기다	cope with ~을 다루다 provide A with B A에게 B를 공급하다 associate A with B A를 B에 관련시키다 accuse A of B A를 B로 고발·비난하다	contribute to ~에 기여하다 pertain to ~에 속하다, ~과 관련되다 add A to B A를 B에 더하다 put A into B A를 B에 쏟아 붓다
형용사 + 전치사	similar to ~와 비슷한 identical to ~와 동일한	consistent with ~와 일관된 comparable with ~와 비교되는	absent from ~에 불참한 responsible for ~에 책임 있는
명사 + 전치사	access to ~에의 접근·출입 exposure to ~에의 노출 favor of ~의 호의, ~에 대한 찬성	effect / influence on ~에 대한 영향 opinion on ~에 대한 의견 question about ~에 대한 질문	respect for ~에 대한 존중 cause / reason for ~의 원인·이유 decrease / increase in ~의 감소

Bread usually consists of flour, water, salt, fat, and yeast. 빵은 보통 밀가루, 물, 소금, 기름, 효모로 구성된다.

Peaches are identical to nectarines, with the exception of their skin. 복숭아는 껍질을 제외하면, 천도복숭아와 동일하다.

Courtney's engagement announcement was the cause for the celebration. Courtney의 약혼 발표가 축하의 이유였다.

☑ 텝스 실전 문제

| 문맥에 맞게 전치사를 채우는 문제가 주로 나온다.
| '동사 + 전치사' 표현을 채우는 문제가 주로 나온다.

Part II

1. After the successful negotiations, the lawyer exited the meeting _____ enthusiasm for the future of his career.

(a) for (b) in
(c) of (d) with

Part I

2. A: What was the argument between the marketi director and our manager?

B: The marketing manager accused the boss _____ suggesting that the ad campaign isn' very good.

(a) of (b) out
(c) with (d) for

정답 p

Hackers **Practice**

알맞은 것을 고르세요.

The manager said it would be difficult to choose (between / among) so many highly qualified candidates.

(Regarding / Apart from) noticing what's on the surface, a psychologist must be able to dig deep into a patient's psyche.

The big construction project should be completed (by / until) the end of the year.

The eighth annual job fair for graduating seniors will be held (in / on) October 8, 2008.

The Beatles is a famous musical group that is still loved (around / on) the world.

The value of the Euro has risen (for / by) over one hundred percent in recent years.

부분이 있으면 바르게 고치세요.

Because trans fats are bad health for, many cities are making laws to ban their use in restaurants.

t goes for Hinduism to eat beef because cows are regarded as holy.

hope to visit my old university roommate at his home along the coast at some point for my trip.

Firefighters must be properly protected to cope with the extremely dangerous conditions.

Only members of the executive committee have access for the organization's investment portfolio.

The choice to associate the Democratic and Republican parties of donkey and elephant symbols started with the political cartoons of Thomas Nast.

Hackers **TEST**

Part I Choose the best answer for the blank.

01 A: I gained a lot of weight _____ the winter.
    B: Really? You look the same to me.

    (a) by   (b) for
    (c) over   (d) across

02 A: I've decided not to keep this jacket.
    B: Then you should take it back _____ where
    you bought it.

    (a) from   (b) at
    (c) to   (d) by

03 A: Can I open the window?
    B: I'd rather you not. There's construction outside
    and the dust will pass _____ it.

    (a) in   (b) for
    (c) onto   (d) through

04 A: I can't get my basketball.
    B: Is it stuck _____ the roof again?

    (a) in   (b) on
    (c) at   (d) with

05 A: I need you to pick up eggs and milk today.
    B: Then add eggs and a gallon of milk _____
    the grocery list.

    (a) at   (b) to
    (c) inside   (d) among

06 A: This is my dad's signature.
    B: Really? I think you signed it _____ his name
    on your own.

    (a) into   (b) onto
    (c) over   (d) under

Part II Choose the best answer for the blank.

07 Pairing children _____ the same behavior
    ensures a better chance that they will get along
    well.

    (a) for   (b) about
    (c) in   (d) with

08 We would appreciate if all questions were held
    _____ the end of the lecture.

    (a) by   (b) until
    (c) to   (d) after

09 Insect and rodent habitats located _____
    topsoil face destruction during periods of heavy
    rain and flooding.

    (a) through   (b) underneath
    (c) behind   (d) beside

10 Among the scientific community, there have been
    many opinions _____ the "big bang."

    (a) what ignited   (b) what ignited on
    (c) on what ignited   (d) for what ignited

11 The faulty air conditioner made a loud buzzing
    sound _____ the day.

    (a) within   (b) inside
    (c) before   (d) throughout

12 Our new paper supplier will cut shipping costs
    _____ twelve percent.

    (a) by   (b) for
    (c) of   (d) through

13 Thanks to easily accessible news on the Internet,
    many young teens today are politically
    knowledgeable _____ their age.

    (a) by   (b) over
    (c) in   (d) for

The committee had to put _____ organizing the gala in the short time they had.

(a) a lot of effort into
(b) a lot of effort for
(c) effort about a lot
(d) into a lot of effort

_____, an essay is still likely to contain errors that may be better spotted by an outside party.

(a) Be meticulously written
(b) Writing meticulously
(c) Written meticulously
(d) Having meticulously written

The students spent _____ after class everyday reviewing their notes.

(a) time   (b) a time
(c) every time   (d) one time

t III Identify the option that contains an awkward expression or an error in grammar.

(a) A: What are you planning during tomorrow night?
(b) B: My friends invited me to go bowling with them.
(c) A: Since you're going, is it OK if I come, too?
(d) B: Yes, but make sure you're ready to go at seven.

(a) A: Were you able to find any parking spaces located near the movie theater?
(b) B: I'm afraid not. The nearest available spot was over two blocks away.
(c) A: That's no good. The show ends kind of late and I don't want to walk by the dark.
(d) B: If you prefer, I can get the car myself and come pick you up. It's no problem.

19 (a) Before 1961, it was unusual for men and women to dance without touching one another. (b) The release of Chubby Checker's "The Twist" changes the way people danced worldwide. (c) It was one of the first dances to popularize dance moves independent of a partner. (d) Today, most dancing does not require a partner and can be performed by oneself.

20 (a) Pumice pertains at igneous rock formed by the sudden cooling of volcanic lava. (b) Since ancient Roman times, it has been incorporated into construction materials and used in landscaping. (c) Pumice is popular when it comes to skin care, since its abrasive properties can remove dead skin cells and calluses. (d) Finely ground pumice can also be found in household products such as paint removers and glass polishers.

정답 p.53

Section 5 접속사와 절

CHAPTER **15** 등위 접속사와 상관 접속사

BASIC GRAMMAR 고수로 가는 첫 걸음

1 등위 접속사는 단어와 단어, 구와 구, 절과 절을 대등하게 연결한다.

Fruit is delicious and healthy. 과일은 맛있고 건강에 좋다.
　　　　　　단어　　　　단어

The gardener takes care of the main lawns and the back gardens. 정원사는 큰 잔디밭과 뒤뜰을 가꾼다.
　　　　　　　　　　　　　　구　　　　　　　　　구

Jane cleaned the room and Mike did the dishes. Jane은 방을 청소했고 Mike는 설거지했다.
　　　　절　　　　　　　　　절

등위 접속사 and는 첫 번째 문장에서 단어와 단어를, 두 번째 문장에서는 구와 구를, 세 번째 문장에서는 절과 절을 대등하게 연결하고 있다.

2 상관 접속사는 둘 이상의 단어가 짝을 이루어 쓰이는 접속사로 단어와 단어, 구와 구, 절과 절을 대등하게 연결한다.

Both you and I should attend the meeting. 너와 나 둘 다 그 모임에 참석해야 한다.
　　　단어　　단어

You can come here either by bus or on foot. 너는 여기에 버스를 타거나 걸어서 올 수 있다.
　　　　　　　　　　　구　　　　구

Neither what he has nor how he looks is attractive to me. 그의 재산도 그의 외모도 나에겐 매력적이지 않다.
　　　　절　　　　　　절

상관 접속사(Both A and B, either A or B, Neither A nor B)가 첫 번째 문장에서 단어와 단어를, 두 번째 문장에서는 구와 구를, 세 번째 문장에서는 절과 절을 연결하고 있다.

01 등위 접속사

등위 접속사의 종류

and 그리고	or 또는	but 그러나	yet 그러나	so 그래서	for 왜냐하면 (~기 때문에)

The newly designed glasses are light but expensive. 새롭게 디자인된 안경은 가벼우나 비싸다.

My cat knocked over a vase, so I had to clean up the pieces. 내 고양이가 꽃병을 넘어뜨려서, 나는 파편들을 치워야 했다.

고득점 포인트 1. 3개의 단어나 구, 절은 'A, B, + 등위 접속사 + C' 형태로 연결해야 한다.

The doctor specializes in the ears, nose, **and** throat. 그 의사는 귀, 코와 목에 관해 전문이다.

2. 등위 접속사로 연결된 구나 절에서 반복되는 단어는 생략할 수 있다.

This new windbreaker is perfect for rainy **(weather)** or windy weather. 이 새 점퍼는 비가 오거나 바람이 부는 날씨에 완벽하다.

For good oral hygiene, be sure to brush, **(to)** floss, **and (to)** use fluoride.
청결한 구강 위생을 위해, 반드시 양치하고, 치실 청소를 하고, 그리고 불소를 사용해라.

Clare will explain the agenda and **(Clare will)** lead the meeting. Clare는 안건을 설명하고 회의를 이끌 것이다.

등위 접속사 없이 단어와 단어, 구와 구가 바로 연결될 수 없다.

After the semester is finished, students ‿and‿ professors should complete a survey.

학기가 끝난 후에, 학생들과 교수들은 설문 조사를 마쳐야만 한다.

▶ 두 개의 단어(students와 professors)가 접속사 없이 바로 쓰일 수 없으므로, 등위 접속사(and)가 두 단어 사이에 와야 한다.

Attendees can make a donation through our organization's website ‿or‿ by visiting our office.

참가자들께서는 저희 기관의 웹 사이트나 저희 사무실에 방문하셔서 기부하실 수 있습니다.

▶ 두 개의 구(through our organization's website와 by visiting our office)가 접속사 없이 바로 연결될 수 없으므로, 등위 접속사(or)가 두 전치사구 사이에 와야 한다.

등위 접속사는 문맥에 맞는 것을 선택해야 한다.

He couldn't find his watch, ~~and~~ so he bought a new one. 그는 그의 시계를 찾을 수 없어서, 새 것을 샀다.

▶ '시계를 찾을 수 없어서 새 것을 샀다'라는 문맥이 되어야 하므로, and가 아니라 so가 와야 한다.

주어가 and로 연결되면 복수 동사를 쓰고, or로 연결되면 마지막 주어에 수를 일치시킨다.

My brother and sister are going to visit me this afternoon. 나의 형과 누나는 오늘 오후에 나를 방문할 것이다.

▶ 두 개의 주어(My brother와 sister)가 and로 연결되었으므로 복수동사(are)가 온다.

The manager or the employees have to contact the authorities in the case of an emergency.
경영자 또는 직원들은 비상시에 당국에 연락해야 한다.

▶ 두 개의 주어(The manager와 the employees)가 or로 연결되었고, 마지막 주어가 복수이므로 복수 동사(have)가 온다.

☑ 텝스 실전 문제

의미가 적절한 등위 접속사를 채우는 문제가 주로 나온다.
단어와 단어, 구와 구 사이에 등위 접속사가 빠져 틀린 문장을 찾는 문제가 주로 나온다.

Part I

1. A: Why aren't you eating that salmon?
   B: It's uncooked, _____ it has far too many bones.

   (a) yet   (b) and
   (c) or   (d) for

Part III

2. (a) Bruxism occurs when people grind their teeth tighten their jaw, often while sleeping. (b) This unconscious action is not a learned habit, but results from the mouth's chewing reflex. (c) Tooth enamel, gradually worn away by the grinding, can wear to the point of uneven alignment and lead to pain while chewing. (d) Though lacking a cure, bruxism can be reduced with the use of dental guards to be worn during sleep.

정답 p.55

02 상관 접속사

1 상관 접속사의 종류

both A and B A와 B 둘 다	either A or B A 또는 B 중 하나
not A but B A가 아니라 B	neither A nor B A도 B도 아닌
not only A but (also) B A뿐만 아니라 B도 (= B as well as A)	

She is not only the society's leader but also its founder. 그녀는 모임의 리더일 뿐만 아니라 창립자이다.

Neither cans nor bottles should be placed in this receptacle. 캔도 병도 이 저장소에 두면 안됩니다.

2 상관 접속사는 짝이 맞는 것끼리 써야 한다.

Both the buses ~~or~~ the trains are running late. 버스와 기차 둘 다 늦고 있다.
　　　　　　　and

▶ Both와 짝을 이루어 올바른 상관 접속사가 되는 것은 or이 아니라 and이다.

Not only wine ~~and~~ cocktails are available. 와인뿐만 아니라 칵테일도 이용 가능하다.
　　　　　　but (also)

▶ Not only와 짝을 이루어 올바른 상관 접속사가 되는 것은 and가 아니라 but (also)이다.

3 상관 접속사로 연결된 주어와 동사의 수 일치

항상 복수 동사를 쓰는 주어	both A and B			
동사를 B에 일치시키는 주어	not A but B	either A or B	neither A nor B	not only A but (also) B

Both paper and plastic items need to be recycled. 종이와 플라스틱 품목 모두 재활용될 필요가 있다.

▶ 주어가 상관 접속사 Both A and B로 연결되었으므로, 복수 동사(need)가 온다.

Either credit cards or cash is an acceptable form of payment. 신용 카드 또는 현금이 허용되는 결제 수단이다.

▶ 주어가 상관 접속사 Either A or B로 연결되었으므로, B의 단수 명사 cash에 일치하는 단수 동사(is)가 온다

☑ 텝스 실전 문제

| 짝이 맞는 상관 접속사를 채우는 문제가 주로 나온다.
| 상관 접속사로 연결된 주어에 수 일치하는 동사를 채우는 문제가 주로 나온다.

Part II

1. Musical conductors have to coordinate not only with the orchestra pit _____ also with the actors on stage.

   (a) and　　　　　(b) but

   (c) or　　　　　 (d) as

Part I

2. A: It seems like both you and your sons _____ along with the new babysitter.

   B: Yes, she is very nice and diligent.

   (a) get　　　　　(b) gets

   (c) is getting　　(d) has get

정답 p.5

Hackers **Practice**

중 알맞은 것을 고르세요.

It is his most popular album, (yet / since) I haven't seen a copy of it in stores.

Either popcorn (or / nor) drinks are selling on the first floor by the ticket counter.

You should dress warmly, (so / for) there's a cold front coming through the region.

Neither my cousin Eddie nor his parents (has / have) ever been to Chicago.

In the event of an accident, it is wise to contact not only the police (and / but) also your insurance company.

Both 'Merlot' (and / or) 'Shiraz' are popular types of grapes used to produce red wine.

부분이 있으면 바르게 고치세요.

The 'Heavenly Blues', the 'Flying Saucers', the 'Pearly Gates' are three of the most common cultivars of morning glory flowers.

A bottle of perfume or some flowers are the perfect choice for a Mother's Day present.

I knew the restaurant would be busy on a Friday evening, since I made reservations earlier in the week.

Not only Iraq but also several other countries uses the dinar as currency.

Many elementary school science classes learn that baking soda and vinegar reacts when mixed.

An elephant's trunk is used to pick things up communicate with others in its group.

정답 p.55

Hackers **TEST**

Part I Choose the best answer for the blank.

01 A: How did you like Florida?
   B: The weather was cloudy, _____ the beaches were beautiful.

   (a) and   (b) as
   (c) for   (d) but

02 A: Did you hear about the fight during the baseball game?
   B: Yeah. Not only both teams but also the umpire _____ involved.

   (a) was   (b) were
   (c) has   (d) have

03 A: Do you feel like having Italian for dinner?
   B: OK, I _____ mind some pasta.

   (a) didn't   (b) couldn't
   (c) wouldn't   (d) shouldn't

04 A: We ought to get going, _____ the restaurant seems to be closing now.
   B: Let's find a café to go to instead.

   (a) so   (b) or
   (c) but   (d) for

05 A: Have you reached a decision yet?
   B: Yes. I'm going to sell my old minivan _____ buy a new SUV.

   (a) and   (b) but
   (c) since   (d) because

06 A: What do you think of _____ being hired as a company promoter?
   B: I believe she will adapt herself quickly.

   (a) she   (b) her
   (c) hers   (d) herself

07 A: Do you want me to proofread your report?
   B: Yes. I just finished it, _____ I'll send it to you now.

   (a) but   (b) or
   (c) so   (d) as

Part II Choose the best answer for the blank.

08 The Easter Bunny is associated with the Easter holiday, _____ its origin remains unclear.

   (a) so   (b) and
   (c) yet   (d) as

09 Passengers are asked to use neither portable electronic devices _____ cell phones during takeoff and landing.

   (a) or   (b) nor
   (c) and   (d) but

10 Many English-speaking students choose either Spanish _____ French as their second language.

   (a) or   (b) and
   (c) but   (d) as

11 Neither chemistry nor physics _____ been able to sufficiently explain why fire has a brightly glowing flame.

   (a) has   (b) have
   (c) are   (d) is

12 Hybrid automobiles not only run on gasoline, _____ are simultaneously powered by electricity generated by a rechargeable battery.

   (a) and   (b) but
   (c) so   (d) though

t III Identify the option that contains an awkward expression or an error in grammar.

(a) A: Why are you looking for the doctor's office number?
(b) B: I don't remember if my appointment is this week or the next.
(c) A: Don't they usually call the patients first to remind them?
(d) B: That's true, but I guess there's no need to call them.

(a) A: Did you hear that Tony was involved in a car accident?
(b) B: No, this is the first time I've heard about it. Is everything OK?
(c) A: He's fine but his car was completely totaled.
(d) B: That's shocking bad news, considering he bought that car last month.

15 (a) In order to organize a fitness training schedule and follow it through, discipline, determination, moderation are necessary. (b) Such a regimen is important for losing weight, toning muscle, and staying in shape. (c) At least half the time should be allotted to aerobic exercise, which may include running, swimming, or bicycling. (d) In addition to the activities mentioned above, lifting weights is a method of building muscle strength through anaerobic exercise.

16 (a) This is the transit authority regarding the approach of this vehicle to the upcoming stop at Madison Station. (b) The platform is shorter than the train's full length and only the first eight cars will be able to exit and board. (c) We ask that passengers in the last car and second car for the last move toward the front if they disembark.
(d) The transit authority thanks you for listening and hopes that you will continue to use our services.

CHAPTER **16** 명사절

BASIC GRAMMAR 고수로 가는 첫 걸음

1
명사절은 문장 내에서 명사 역할을 하는 절로 명사처럼 주어, 목적어, 보어 역할을 하는 필수 성분이다.

Whether it will rain tomorrow is important. 내일 비가 올지 안 올지가 중요하다.
I heard **that you got a new job.** 나는 네가 새 직장을 얻었다고 들었다.
That is **what I need.** 그것이 내가 필요한 것이다.

첫 번째 문장에서 명사절 Whether it will rain tomorrow는 주어 역할을, 두 번째 문장에서 명사절 that you got a new job은 목적어 역할을 하고 있으며, 세 번째 문장에 쓰인 명사절 what I need는 보어 역할을 하고 있다. 이와 같이 명사절은 명사처럼 문장의 필수 성분인 주어, 목적어, 보어로 쓰인다.

2
명사절은 '명사절 접속사 (+ 주어) + 동사'로 이루어진다.

I don't know **if I can help you.** 내가 널 도울 수 있을지 모르겠다.
What makes him angry is her lies. 그를 화나게 하는 것은 그녀의 거짓말이다.

첫 번째 문장에서 목적어로 쓰인 명사절은 '명사절 접속사(if) + 주어(I) + 동사(can help)'로 이루어져 있다. 두 번째 문장에서 주어로 쓰인 명사절은 '명사절 접속사(What) + 동사(makes)'로 이루어져 있다.

명사절 접속사에는 that, if, whether, 의문사(who, what, which, when, where, how, why), 복합관계대명사(whoever, whatever, whichever) 등이 있다.

1 명사절 자리와 쓰임

명사절은 명사처럼 주어, 목적어, 보어 자리에 온다.

주어　　　Whoever owns the van parked outside **needs to move it.**
밖에 주차된 밴을 소유한 사람이 누구든 그것을 옮겨야 한다.

동사의 목적어　　Larry heard that we planned a surprise party for him. Larry는 우리가 그를 위한 깜짝 파티를 계획했다는 것을 들었다.

전치사의 목적어　The police looked into what had started the fire. 경찰은 무엇이 화재를 일으켰는지 주의 깊게 살펴봤다.

보어　　　Today's topic is how one should invest in the stock market. 오늘의 주제는 어떻게 주식 시장에 투자해야 하는지에 대한 것이다.

고득점 포인트　that이 이끄는 명사절은 4형식 동사의 직접 목적어 자리에도 온다.
The doctor told Chris **that his leg would be fully healed in three weeks.** 그 의사는 Chris에게 그의 다리가 3주 후에 완치될 것이라고 말했다.
　　　　　4형식동사　　간접목적어　　　　　　　　　　직접목적어

명사절 접속사 자리에 대명사는 올 수 없다.

She reported ~~them~~ the date for the meeting would have to be rescheduled. 그녀는 회의 날짜가 재조정되어야 할 것이라고 보고했다.
　　　　　　that

▶ 대명사(them)는 절(the date ~ rescheduled)을 이끌 수 없으므로 접속사가 와야 한다. 동사(reported)의 목적어가 될 수 있는 명사절을 이끌기 위해서는 명사절 접속사(that)가 와야 한다.

명사절 내의 동사 자리에 준동사는 올 수 없다.

The teacher suggested that they ~~checking~~ over their answers. 선생님은 그들이 답을 확인할 것을 제안했다.
　　　　　　　　　　　　　　check

▶ 명사절(that they ~ answers) 내의 동사 자리에 준동사는 올 수 없으므로, checking이 아니라 check가 와야 한다.

✍ 텝스 실전 문제

명사절 전체나 명사절 접속사를 목적어 자리에 채우는 문제가 주로 나온다.

Part I

1. A: We really need to have dinner together sometime.
   B: I agree, but I don't know _____.

   (a) available
   (b) when available
   (c) when being available
   (d) when I'll be available

Part II

2. Peter participated in the demonstration, even though he did not fully understand _____ was being protested.

   (a) those　　　　　(b) them
   (c) what　　　　　(d) him

정답 p.57

1 that이 이끄는 명사절은 문장에서 주어, 동사의 목적어, 보어로 쓰인다.

주어	That the home team lost **didn't upset us much.** 홈팀이 졌다는 것이 우리를 많이 화나게 하지는 않았다.
동사의 목적어	**They believed** that she was innocent. 그들은 그녀가 결백하다고 믿었다.
보어	**The first rule of bicycle safety is** that you should always wear a helmet. 자전거 안전에 관한 첫 번째 수칙은 항상 헬멧을 써야 한다는 것이다.

> **고득점 포인트** 1. except that, in that 등과 같이 관용적으로 쓰는 경우를 제외하고, that절은 전치사의 목적어로 쓰이지 않는다.
> I think of **that he is a little bossy.** [×]
> I think **that he is a little bossy.** [○] 나는 그가 약간 권위적이라고 생각한다.
>
> 2. that절은 the fact, the idea, the news 등의 명사 뒤에 와서 명사와 같은 기능을 하는 동격절로 쓰일 수 있다.
> The fact **that our record player still works** is amazing. 우리의 전축이 아직 작동한다는 사실이 놀랍다.

2 that절을 취하는 동사와 형용사

that절을 취하는 동사	say / tell that ~라고 말하다 suppose that ~라고 가정하다 think that ~라고 생각하다 know that ~인 것을 알다 report that ~라고 보고하다 believe that ~라고 믿다 show that ~인 것을 보여주다 imagine that ~라고 상상하다
that절을 취하는 형용사	be sure / convinced that ~라고 확신하다 be aware that ~을 알고 있다 be glad that ~해서 기쁘다 be happy that ~해서 기쁘다 be sorry that ~해서 유감이다 be afraid that ~해서 유감이다

Rising sea levels show that **ice caps are melting.** 상승하는 해수면은 만년설이 녹고 있다는 것을 보여준다.

The guard was sure that **he had locked the door.** 경비원은 그가 문을 잠갔다고 확신했다.

> **고득점 포인트** 발화·인식·감정 등에 관련된 동사(say, think 등), 형용사(sure, glad 등) 뒤에 쓰인 that은 생략할 수 있다.
> **Rising sea levels** show **(that)** ice caps are melting.
> **The guard was** sure **(that)** he had locked the door.

☑ 텝스 실전 문제

텝스 문제 이렇게 나온다

| 생략된 that을 포함한 명사절 전체를 채우는 문제가 주로 나온다.
| 동격절의 that을 채우는 문제가 가끔 나온다.

Part II

1. Technology enthusiasts need to accept the fact _____ flying cars will not become the standard of transportation in this generation.

(a) that   (b) what
(c) which   (d) whatever

Part I

2. A: Do you think you will find your wallet?
   B: _____.

(a) I don't lose I suppose
(b) I don't believe I will
(c) I don't believe losing
(d) I don't suppose of that I will

정답 p.

3 명사절 접속사 2: if와 whether

if나 whether가 이끄는 명사절은 '~인지 아닌지'를 의미하며, 문장에서 주어, 목적어, 보어로 쓰인다.

주어	Whether it's going to snow or not **is my concern.** 눈이 올지 안 올지가 내 관심사이다.
동사의 목적어	**I don't know** if she ever got my message. 그녀가 내 메시지를 받았는지 아닌지 나는 모른다.
전치사의 목적어	**The couple argued about** whether they should move out of the city.
	그 부부는 그들이 도시를 떠나 이사를 해야 할지 말아야 할지에 대해 논쟁을 했다.
보어	**My worry is** whether this vehicle is safe. 나의 걱정거리는 이 차가 안전한지 아닌지이다.

고득점 포인트

1. if가 이끄는 명사절은 주어 자리나 전치사의 목적어 자리에 쓰일 수 없다.
   ~~If~~ I pass this interview is crucial. (→ **Whether**) 내가 이 면접을 통과할 수 있을지 없을지가 중요하다.
   └ if절(If I pass this interview)은 주어 자리에 올 수 없으므로, If가 아니라 Whether가 와야 한다.
   The jury was confused about ~~if~~ he was guilty. (→ **whether**) 배심원은 그가 유죄인지 무죄인지 혼란스러웠다.
   └ if절(if he was guilty)은 전치사(about)의 목적어 자리에 올 수 없으므로, if가 아니라 whether가 와야 한다.

2. if는 '만약 ~이라면'이라는 뜻의 부사절 접속사로, whether는 '~이든지 아닌지'라는 뜻의 부사절 접속사로도 쓰인다.
   I will take a taxi home **if it's still raining.** 만약 여전히 비가 오면 나는 택시를 타고 집에 가겠다.
   Whether it's feasible or not, we're going ahead with the project. 그것이 가능하든 불가능하든지 간에, 우리는 그 프로젝트를 진행할 것이다.

whether와 if는 'whether A or B', 'if A or B'로 자주 쓰인다.

Ms. Fine asked the clerk whether / if the gift shop accepts credit card or only cash.
Ms. Fine은 선물 가게에서 신용 카드를 받는지 현금만 받는지 점원에게 물었다.

The news report didn't mention whether / if vehicles on the highway could use the bridge or had to take a detour.
뉴스 보도에서는 고속도로 위의 자동차들이 다리를 이용할 수 있는지 우회해야 하는지 언급하지 않았다.

고득점 포인트

'whether or not'은 쓸 수 있지만, 'if or not'은 붙여 쓸 수 없다.
Tommy isn't sure ~~if~~ or not Charlotte likes him. (→ **whether**) Tommy는 Charlotte이 그를 좋아하는지 아닌지 확신할 수 없다.
└ if or not은 붙여 쓸 수 없으므로, if가 아니라 whether가 와야 한다.

if와 whether는 불확실한 사실을 나타내는 반면, that은 확실한 사실을 나타낸다.

Billy didn't know ~~that~~ the shop closes at 10:00 p.m., so he called the shop.
    if / whether
Billy는 그 상점이 밤 10시에 닫는지 아닌지 몰라서, 상점에 전화를 했다.

▶ '상점에 전화를 했다(called the shop)'는 사실로 보아 '상점이 10시에 닫는지 아닌지' 불확실하다는 의미가 되어야 하므로, that이 아니라 if나 whether가 와야 한다.

Billy didn't know ~~if~~ / ~~whether~~ the shop closed at 10:00 p.m., so he couldn't buy her present.
                    that
Billy는 그 상점이 밤 10시에 닫는 몰라서, 그녀의 선물을 살 수 없었다.

▶ '선물을 살 수 없었다(couldn't buy her present)'는 사실로 보아 '상점이 10시에 닫는다'는 확실한 사실을 몰랐다는 의미가 되므로, if나 whether가 아니라 that이 와야 한다.

☑ 텝스 실전 문제

명사절 접속사 자리에 if나 whether를 채우는 문제가 주로 나온다.

Part II

1. Alison stuck her hand outside the window to check _____ it had stopped raining and the temperature had cooled.

(a) and   (b) for
(c) while   (d) if

Part I

2. A: I heard that a major distributor wants to buy your company.
   B: It's true. I'm thinking about _____ I should sell it to them or remain in business.

(a) that   (b) how
(c) if   (d) whether

정답 p.58

1 의문대명사 who, whose, what, which는 명사절을 이끌며, 그 자체가 명사절 내의 주어나 목적어, 보어 역할을 하므로, 에는 주어나 목적어, 보어가 없는 불완전한 절이 온다.

Who <u>set fire to the house</u> hasn't been determined. 누가 그 집에 불을 질렀는지는 밝혀지지 않고 있다.

▶ 의문대명사(Who)가 그것이 이끄는 명사절 내에서 주어 역할을 하므로, 뒤에 주어가 없는 불완전한 절(set fire to the house)이 온다.

He couldn't decide what <u>he should wear to the conference</u>. 그는 회의에 무엇을 입고 가야 할지 결정할 수 없었다.

▶ 의문대명사(what)가 그것이 이끄는 명사절 내에서 목적어 역할을 하므로, 뒤에 목적어가 없는 불완전한 절(he should wear to the conference)이

포인트 1. what, which는 둘 다 '무엇'을 의미하지만, 가리키는 대상의 범위가 특정하게 정해져 있을 때는 which를 쓴다.
No one could tell **what** is the original between the two paintings. (→ **which**) 두 그림 중에서 무엇이 진품인지 누구도 구별하지 못했다.
└ '두 그림 중에서'라고 특정한 범위의 대상이 정해져 있으므로 what이 아니라 which가 와야 한다.

2. 의문사가 이끄는 명사절 중에는, 다른 문장 안에 의문문을 포함해서 질문을 하는 '간접 의문문'이 포함된다. 간접 의문문에 대해서는 Chapter 19에서 히 다룬다.
I wonder **who he is**. 나는 그가 누구인지 궁금하다.

2 의문형용사 whose, what, which는 뒤에 나온 명사를 수식하면서 명사절을 이끌며, '의문형용사 + 명사' 형태로 명사절 의 주어나 목적어, 보어 역할을 하므로, 뒤에는 주어나 목적어, 보어가 없는 불완전한 절이 온다.

Please tell me which color <u>suits me better</u>. 어떤 색깔이 내게 더 잘 어울리는지 말해주세요.

▶ '의문형용사 + 명사'(which color)가 그것이 이끄는 명사절 내에서 주어 역할을 하므로, 뒤에 주어가 없는 불완전한 절(suits me better)이 온다.

포인트 의문형용사 what은 little, few와 함께 관용적으로 '적지만 전부'라는 의미로 쓰인다.
She sent Tommy **what little** money she had. 그녀는 적지만 그녀가 가진 돈 전부를 Tommy에게 보냈다.

3 의문부사 when, where, how, why는 명사절을 이끌며, 절 내에서 부사 역할을 하므로 뒤에는 완전한 절이 온다.

Professor Stein couldn't remember where <u>he left his keys</u>. Stein 교수는 그가 어디에 열쇠를 뒀는지 기억할 수 없었다.

▶ 의문부사(where)는 그것이 이끄는 명사절 내에서 부사 역할을 하므로, 뒤에 완전한 절(he left his keys)이 온다.

4 '의문사 + to부정사'는 명사절 자리에 오며 '의문사 + 주어 + should + 동사원형'으로 바꿀 수 있다.

He didn't know what to write[what he should write] for his report. 그는 그의 보고서에 무엇을 써야 할지 몰랐다.

포인트 to부정사 앞 의문사 자리에 whether 역시 올 수 있다.
You need to choose **whether to apply for a loan**. 너는 대출을 신청할지 결정할 필요가 있다.

☑ 텝스 실전 문제

텝스 문제 이렇게 나온다

| 명사 앞에 적절한 의문형용사를 채우는 문제가 주로 나온다.
| 의문사절 전체나 '의문사 + to부정사'를 채우는 문제가 주로 나온다.

Part I

1. A: There's one woman who comes in and always pays in change.
   B: I think I know _____ customer you're talking about.

   (a) who   (b) whom
   (c) which   (d) whose

Part II

2. The engineering supervisor was summoned to th work site to show _____.

   (a) the laborers what to do
   (b) the laborers to do what
   (c) what the laborers do to
   (d) what to do the laborers

정답 p.

5 명사절 접속사 4: 복합관계대명사

복합관계대명사가 이끄는 명사절은 문장에서 주어, 목적어, 보어로 쓰이며, 이때 복합관계대명사는 '대명사 + 관계대명사' 역할을 한다.

주어 Whatever[Anything that] you suggest **is fine with me.** 당신이 제안하는 것이 무엇이든 나는 좋다.

목적어 **You may select** whichever[anything that] you prefer. 너는 네가 선호하는 어떤 것이든 고를 수 있다.

보어 **You can become** whoever[anyone who] you want to be. 너는 네가 되고 싶은 누구든 될 수 있다.

고득점 포인트
1. whatever와 whichever는 뒤에 나오는 명사를 수식하는 복합관계형용사로도 쓰인다.
   I'll join **whichever** team has an opening. 나는 공석이 있는 어느 팀에든 가입할 것이다.
2. 복합관계대명사절은 부사절로도 쓰인다. 이에 대해서는 Chapter 18에서 자세히 다룬다.
   Whatever you decide to major in, I will support your decision. 네가 전공하려는 것이 무엇이든, 나는 네 결정을 지지할 것이다.

복합관계대명사는 그 자체가 명사절 내의 주어나 목적어, 보어 역할을 하므로, 뒤에 주어나 목적어, 보어가 없는 불완전한 절이 온다.

Whatever tastes best **is what we should order.** 가장 맛이 좋은 것이 무엇이든 우리가 주문해야만 하는 것이다.

Review the applicants and choose whomever you want. 지원자들을 검토하고 당신이 원하는 누구든 선택하세요.

어떤 복합관계대명사를 쓸지는 복합관계대명사의 격과 의미에 따라 결정한다.

	주격		목적격	
사람	whoever 누구든		who(m)ever 누구든	
사물	whatever 무엇이든	whichever 어느 것이든	whatever 무엇이든	whichever 어느 것이든

We can have ~~whoever~~ you're in the mood for. 우리는 네가 마음 내켜 하는 무엇이든 먹을 수 있다.
　　　　　whatever
▶ '무엇이든'이라는 의미가 되어야 하므로 사람을 가리키는 whoever가 아니라 사물을 가리키는 whatever가 와야 한다.

복합관계대명사를 쓸지 의문사를 쓸지는 문맥에 따라 결정된다.

I'd be willing to buy ~~which~~ is still available. 남은 것이 어느 것이든 나는 기꺼이 살 것이다.
　　　　　　　　whichever
▶ '남은 것이 어느 것이든'이라는 의미가 되어야 하므로 의문사(which)가 아닌 복합관계대명사(whichever)가 와야 한다.

She doesn't know ~~whoever~~ will go there with her. 그녀는 누가 그녀와 함께 거기에 갈지 모른다.
　　　　　　　who
▶ '누가 그녀와 함께 거기에 갈지'라는 의미가 되어야 하므로 복합관계대명사(whoever)가 아닌 의문사(who)가 와야 한다.

✍ 텝스 실전 문제

텝스 문제 이렇게 나온다

복합관계대명사와 의문사를 구별하여 채우는 문제가 주로 나온다.
격과 의미가 맞지 않은 복합관계대명사가 와서 틀린 문장을 찾는 문제가 가끔 나온다.

Part I

A: I'm having trouble deciding between history and business as a major.

B: I'll support _____ fits your goals and personal interests.

(a) which 　　　　　(b) what

(c) whatever 　　　　(d) whichever

Part III

2. (a) A: Today is the debate for the class president candidates.

(b) B: I'm excited to see how they will both fare in a public forum.

(c) A: I don't care who wins as long as they express their points well.

(d) B: But most people will vote for whomever they feel won the debate.

정답 p.58

1 what절은 문장 내에서 명사 역할만 하지만, that절은 명사, 형용사, 부사 역할을 모두 할 수 있다.

· **명사 역할을 하는 what절**

He <u>misunderstood</u> what I said. 그는 내가 말한 것을 오해했다.

▶ 동사(misunderstood)의 목적어 자리에 온 what절은 명사 역할을 하는 명사절이다.

· **명사, 형용사, 부사 역할을 하는 that절**

명사 역할   Deborah <u>said</u> that she could help me with painting. Deborah는 내가 그림 그리는 것을 도울 수 있다고 말했다.

             ▶ 동사(said)의 목적어 자리에 온 that절은 명사 역할을 하는 명사절이다.

형용사 역할   Jupiter is the largest <u>planet</u> that orbits the sun. 목성은 태양 주위를 도는 가장 큰 행성이다.

             ▶ 명사(planet)를 뒤에서 수식하는 that절은 형용사 역할을 하는 형용사절(관계절)이다.

부사 역할   The governor was <u>so</u> firm that no one could dissuade him. 주지사는 너무나 확고해서 아무도 그를 단념시킬 수 없었다.

             ▶ so 뒤에 오는 that절은 문장 내에서 부사 역할을 하는 부사절이다.

2 what절과 that절이 명사절로 쓰일 때, what은 불완전한 절을 이끌고, that은 완전한 절을 이끈다.

~~That~~ is included in the prize is a seven-day vacation in the Bahamas. 상품에 포함된 것은 바하마에서의 7일간의 휴가이다.
What

▶ 접속사 뒤에 주어가 없는 불완전한 절(is included in the prize)이 이어지므로, That이 아니라 What이 와야 한다.

It seems ~~what~~ the garage door needs to be fixed. 차고 문은 수리될 필요가 있는 것 같다.
         that

▶ 접속사 뒤에 완전한 절(the garage door needs to be fixed)이 이어지므로, what이 아니라 that이 와야 한다.

☑ 텝스 실전 문제

| 명사절 접속사 what과 that을 구별하여 채우는 문제가 주로 나온다.

Part I

1. A: What are you doing?
    B: I'm laying traps for the cockroaches _____ live in the cracks of my apartment's walls.

    (a) that   (b) what
    (c) where   (d) whichever

Part II

2. _____ many full-time urban workers find relaxing is the occasional vacation to tropical climates.

    (a) What   (b) When
    (c) Which   (d) That

정답 p

알맞은 것을 고르세요.

The most amazing part of the story is (it / what) happened to him after he met the president.

The clouds in the sky make me wonder (if / that) it is going to rain.

It appears (what / that) the new wing of the building will be finished this month.

One task of a manager is to solve (what / whatever) problems come up in the office.

When I met my neighbor Mrs. Shue at the store, she asked me (how / where) my plans to study in France were progressing.

Existentialism is a philosophy proposing the idea (that / whether) individuals are the only ones capable of giving their lives meaning.

부분이 있으면 바르게 고치세요.

It's such a complex game that I don't know how I to play it.

When analyzing his technique, you must consider that he has never been formally trained.

At this point, you should decide if or not you want to go straight.

That concerns doctors about the medicine is that it has too many side effects.

The coach promised to buy whatever scored a goal an ice cream cone after the game.

He didn't know what answer to pick since they all seemed possible.

정답 p.58

Hackers **TEST**

 제한 시간: 10분

Part I Choose the best answer for the blank.

01 A: I'm looking for three more members to join an acting group I started.
   B: I'll ask my friends to see _____ any of them are interested.

   (a) if   (b) for
   (c) and   (d) while

02 A: It seems like most of the staff showed up for the Halloween party.
   B: Are you sure? With those costumes, I can't recognize _____ anyone is.

   (a) who   (b) which
   (c) whom   (d) whoever

03 A: The amount of this bill seems much higher than it should be.
   B: I think _____.

   (a) has to be some mistakes
   (b) there has to be some mistake
   (c) some mistake there is
   (d) it has to be mistakes

04 A: I didn't realize that salt is so important for storing food.
   B: It is. Salt is _____ keeps bacteria from forming.

   (a) that   (b) which
   (c) how   (d) what

05 A: Will everyone still be on the team next season?
   B: Everyone except Jacob. Please tell the coach _____.

   (a) he isn't returning
   (b) isn't he returning
   (c) to it his not returning
   (d) his returning to it not

06 A: Pam just had a baby. Should I call her or go t her house?
   B: It doesn't matter. _____ w congratulate her.

   (a) What necessary that it is
   (b) What's necessary is that
   (c) That's what is necessary
   (d) It is necessary what

07 A: Have you heard _____ for the tour?
   B: I think it's at the entrance to the palace.

   (a) are we where supposed to gathered
   (b) where we are supposed to gather
   (c) we are supposed to gather where
   (d) gathering where we are supposed to

Part II Choose the best answer for the blank.

08 Max needed his keys to drive to work, but he couldn't remember _____ he had left them.

   (a) which   (b) what
   (c) where   (d) who

09 Psychological studies have shown that people ir group situations tend to agree with _____ opinion they think has the most support.

   (a) what   (b) whose
   (c) which   (d) whichever

10 If a cure for smallpox _____ developed centuries earlier, native societies might not have been killed by foreign plagues.

   (a) be   (b) were
   (c) has been   (d) had been

The disposal crew came to remove _____ the demolished restaurant hadn't been burned to cinders by the fire.

(a) which little
(b) which little of
(c) what little of
(d) what little of it

_____ tree branches litter the ground is evidence of last night's storm.

(a) Once
(b) As
(c) What
(d) That

The minister in charge of the investigation said he wondered _____ change the public's view of politicians.

(a) how would the case
(b) the case would
(c) would the case how
(d) how the case would

Many teens do not yet know _____ to choose as their future occupations.

(a) what
(b) why
(c) that
(d) how

_____ on the honor roll does not discourage her from continuing to work hard.

(a) That Meriam is no longer
(b) That no longer is Meriam
(c) It is that Meriam is no longer
(d) It is Meriam that is no longer

The Wentworths drove to the beach to show their children _____.

(a) like what the coast was
(b) like what was the coast
(c) what was the coast like
(d) what the coast was like

Part III Identify the option that contains an awkward expression or an error in grammar.

17 (a) A: You ought to try investing in the stock market.
   (b) B: Having seen that many stocks are in freefall, I must decline.
   (c) A: It's only risky if you don't invest wisely.
   (d) B: You will have to teach me the best strategies.

18 (a) A: Are you done with your world history paper yet?
   (b) B: Yeah, I made a few last-minute edits last night. How about you?
   (c) A: I've been thinking about changing the topic to the Persian Empire. Are you familiar with it?
   (d) B: Of course. It was the largest ancient empire established in where is now Iran.

19 (a) Virgil's *Aeneid* chronicles the adventures of the Trojan Aeneas after Troy is destroyed by the Greeks. (b) The Greeks hide inside a wooden horse, a gift given to Troy as a peace offering and meant to bring its people fortune. (c) After the horse is brought inside the city walls, the Greeks emerge and attack the Trojans. (d) When Aeneas hears the news what Troy is under attack, it is too late, so he flees the city with his family.

20 (a) First seen in 1966, the Golden Toad is an extinct species of toad native to Costa Rica. (b) Very little is known about this bright, yellow toad, as it was last sighted in 1989. (c) A researcher discovered the toads mating in the forest and observed that they lay eggs underground keep them hidden in small water reservoirs. (d) The species may have died out because warmer temperatures caused pools where the eggs were stored to dry up.

정답 p.59

CHAPTER 17 관계절

BASIC GRAMMAR 고수로 가는 첫 걸음

1 관계절은 문장 내에서 관계절 앞의 명사를 수식하는 형용사 역할을 하는 수식어 거품이다.

The man **whom you saw yesterday** is my brother. 네가 어제 보았던 그 남자는 내 형이다.
I love the tree **which my wife planted**. 나는 내 아내가 심은 나무를 좋아한다.

첫 번째 문장의 whom you saw yesterday와 두 번째 문장의 which my wife planted는 형용사 역할을 하여 각각 앞에 있는 명사 The man과 the tree를 수식하는 수식어 거품이다. 이렇게 형용사 역할을 하는 절을 '관계절'이라 하고, 관계절의 수식을 받는 명사를 '선행사'라고 부른다.

2 관계절은 '관계대명사 (+ 주어) + 동사', '관계부사 + 주어 + 동사'로 이루어진다.

Your parents are the people **who love you the most**. 네 부모님은 널 가장 사랑하는 사람들이다.
I remember the day **when my daughter was born**. 나는 내 딸이 태어난 날을 기억한다.

첫 번째 문장에서 선행사 the people을 수식하는 관계절은 '관계대명사(who) + 동사(love)'로 이루어져 있고, 두 번째 문장에서 선행사 the day를 수식하는 관계절은 '관계부사(when) + 주어(my daughter) + 동사(was born)'로 이루어져 있다.

관계대명사에는 who, whom, which, that이 있고, 관계부사에는 when, where, why, how가 있다.

3 관계절은 앞의 명사를 한정하는 한정적 용법과, 앞의 명사에 대해 부가 설명을 하는 계속적 용법으로 쓰인다.

한정적 용법   Sean keeps two dogs **which are six months old**. Sean은 6개월된 개 2마리가 있다.
계속적 용법   Sean keeps two dogs, **which are six months old**. Sean은 개가 2마리 있는데, 이 개들은 6개월이 되었다.

한정적 용법으로 쓰인 첫 번째 문장의 경우 관계절(which are six months old)이 선행사(two dogs)를 한정하고, 계속적 용법으로 쓰인 두 번째 문장의 경우 관계절은 선행사에 대한 부가 설명을 한다. 첫 번째 문장의 경우 Sean에게 개 2마리 외에 다른 개가 더 있을 수 있는 반면, 두 번째 문장의 경우 Sean이 기르는 개는 단 2마리뿐이라는 의미 차이가 있다.

01 관계절 자리와 쓰임

관계절은 수식어 거품으로 선행사 뒤에 온다.

The man who delivers our mail **comes at the same time every day.** 우리의 우편물을 배달하는 남자는 매일 같은 시간에 온다.
　선행사

She got on the bus, which goes to the airport. 그녀는 버스를 탔는데, 그것은 공항으로 간다.
　　　　　선행사

관계절을 이끄는 관계사와 명사절을 이끄는 명사절 접속사를 구별해야 한다.

I met the woman ~~what~~ **was my teacher in high school.** 나는 고등학교 때 내 은사님이셨던 여자분을 만났다.
　　　　　　　that / who

▶ 명사(the woman)를 수식하기 위해 형용사 역할을 하는 관계절이 와야 하므로, 명사절 접속사(what)가 아니라 관계사(that / who)가 와야 한다.

The technician knows ~~that~~ **went wrong with the phone network.** 기술자는 전화 통신망에 무엇이 잘못되었는지 안다.
　　　　　　　　　　what

▶ 동사(knows)의 목적어 자리에 오기 위해서 명사 역할을 하는 명사절이 와야 하므로, 관계사(that)가 아니라 명사절 접속사(what)가 와야 한다.

관계절 내의 동사 자리에 준동사는 올 수 없다.

Customers who ~~purchasing~~ **a pair of pants can get a second pair free.** 바지 한 벌을 구매한 고객들은 공짜로 한 벌을 더 얻을 수 있다.
　　　　　　　purchase

▶ 관계절(who ~ a pair of pants)의 동사 자리에는 준동사(purchasing)가 올 수 없고 동사(purchase)가 와야 한다.

**고득점
포인트** 관계절의 동사는 관계절의 주어 또는 선행사와 수, 태가 맞아야 한다.
　　We will sign a contract with the clients **who** **accepts** **our offer. (→ accept)** 우리는 우리의 제안을 받아들이는 의뢰인들과 계약할 것이다.
　　　⎣ 관계절의 선행사(the clients)가 복수이므로, 단수 동사(accepts)가 아니라 복수 동사(accept)가 와야 한다.
　　Many subway stations are equipped with elevators, **which** **designed** **to help the disabled. (→ were designed)**
　　많은 지하철 역에는 엘리베이터가 갖춰져 있고, 이것은 장애인들을 돕기 위해 고안된 것이다.
　　　⎣ 관계절의 선행사(elevators)와 동사(design)가 '엘리베이터가 고안되다'라는 의미의 수동 관계이므로, 능동태 동사(designed)가 아니라 수동태 동사(were designed)
　　가 와야 한다.

☑ 텝스 실전 문제

관계사를 채우거나 관계절 내에 올바른 형태의 동사를 채우는 문제가
주로 나온다.

Part I

1. A: Have you met him before?
　B: I think so. Isn't he the man _____ comes
　　to deliver express packages?

　(a) if　　　　　　　　(b) whether
　(c) what　　　　　　　(d) who

Part II

2. Scientists have found much information in ape
　DNA that genetically _____ to human
　beings.

　(a) links them　　　　(b) linking them
　(c) to link themselves　(d) link it to themselves

정답 p.61

1 관계대명사는 선행사의 종류와 관계절 내에서 그것이 하는 역할에 따라서 선택해야 한다.

선행사 격	주격	목적격	소유격
사람	who	whom	whose
사물·동물	which	which	of which / whose
사람·사물·동물	that	that	–

I carpool with <u>two women</u> who / that <u>work</u> near my office.   나는 내 사무실 근처에서 일하는 두 여성과 차를 함께 탄다.

▶ 선행사(two women)가 사람이고, 관계절 내에서 동사(work)의 주어 역할을 하므로, 사람을 가리키는 주격 관계사 who가 온다.

He will lend me <u>the CD</u> which / that I <u>requested</u>.   그는 내가 요청했던 CD를 나에게 빌려줄 것이다.

▶ 선행사(the CD)가 사물이고 관계절 내에서 동사(requested)의 목적어 역할을 하므로, 사물을 가리키는 목적격 관계사 which가 온다.

Companies prefer <u>applicants</u> whose <u>ideas</u> are creative.   기업들은 생각이 창의적인 지원자들을 선호한다.

▶ 선행사(applicants)가 사람이고 관계절 내에서 ideas가 누구의 것인지 나타내므로, 사람을 가리키는 소유격 관계사 whose가 온다.

I watched a documentary, <u>the topic</u> of which / whose <u>topic</u> was WWII.   나는 다큐멘터리를 보았는데, 그것의 주제는 제2차 세계 대전이었다.

▶ 선행사(a documentary)가 사물이고 관계절 내에서 the topic이 무엇의 주제인지 나타내므로, 사물을 가리키는 소유격 관계사 of which가 온다. 단, '명사 + of which'(the topic of which)는 'whose + 명사'(whose topic)로 바꾸어 쓸 수 있다.

고득점 포인트

1. 목적격 관계대명사와 '주격 관계대명사 + be동사'는 생략할 수 있다.
   She bought the camera **(which / that)** she saw at the store.   그녀는 상점에서 봤던 카메라를 샀다.
   We're preparing a meal **(that is)** fit for a king.   우리는 왕에게 걸맞은 식사를 준비하고 있다.

2. 계속적 용법으로 쓰인 관계대명사 which는 앞 문장 전체를 선행사로 받아 부가 설명을 할 수 있다.
   <u>The professor assigned no homework</u>, which relieved the students.   교수님은 아무 숙제도 내주지 않았는데, 이것은 학생들의 부담을 덜어주었다.

3. 계속적 용법으로 쓰인 관계절에는 선행사에 관계 없이 관계대명사 that이 올 수 없다.
   The restaurant, ~~that~~ closed last year, has been turned into a bookstore. (→ which)   그 식당은 작년에 문을 닫았는데, 서점으로 바뀌었다.

2 관계대명사 바로 뒤에 '주어 + know / said / think / feel / hope' 등의 어구가 삽입될 수 있으며, 이는 관계대명사의 격 선택에 아무런 영향을 미치지 않는다

Jeremy is the person ~~whom~~ I think used your computer.   내가 생각하기에는, Jeremy가 네 컴퓨터를 사용했던 사람이다.
             who

▶ 선행사(the person)가 관계절 내에서 동사(used)의 주어 역할을 하므로, 목적격 관계대명사가 아니라 주격 관계대명사가 와야 한다. I think는 삽입된 로 관계대명사의 격 선택에 아무런 영향을 미치지 않는다.

☑ 텝스 실전 문제

텝스 문제 이렇게 나온다

| 선행사의 종류와 격에 맞는 관계대명사를 채우는 문제가 주로 나온다.

Part II

1. The police arrested the suspect _____ they believed had committed the crime.

   (a) who   (b) whom
   (c) which   (d) what

2. She admired the art of Van Gogh, _____ paintings evoked in her feelings of melancholy an wistfulness.

   (a) which   (b) whose
   (c) of which   (d) whom

정답 p.6

3 전치사 + 관계대명사 / 수량 표현 + 관계대명사

전치사 + 관계대명사

· 앞 문장과 공통의 명사가 뒷 문장에서 전치사의 목적어일 때 관계대명사 앞에 전치사가 온다.

She introduced her friends to the man. + She was engaged to him. 그녀는 친구들을 그 남자에게 소개했다. + 그녀는 그와 약혼했다.

She introduced her friends to the man to whom she was engaged. 그녀는 친구들을 그녀와 약혼한 남자에게 소개했다.

▶ 앞 문장의 the man을 가리키는 him이 전치사(to)의 목적어이므로, 관계대명사(whom) 앞에 전치사가 와서 to whom이 된다.

고득점 포인트 1. 대화 표현에서는 전치사가 관계절의 뒤에 남을 수 있다.
   She introduced her friends to **the man whom** she was engaged **to**.

2. 전치사 뒤에 관계대명사 that은 올 수 없다.
   She introduced her friends to the man to ~~that~~ she was engaged. (→ whom)
   ↳ 전치사(to) 뒤에 that은 올 수 없다. 선행사(the man)에 일치하는 whom이 와야 한다.

· '전치사 + 관계대명사'에서 전치사는 선행사 또는 관계절의 동사에 따라 결정된다.

We attended a convention at which everyone exchanged business cards. 우리는 모든 사람들이 명함을 교환했던 컨벤션에 참석했다.
　　　　　　　(= at the convention)

▶ 문맥상 '컨벤션에서'라는 뜻이 되어야 하므로, 전치사 at이 관계대명사 앞에 온다.

This is the examination for which I've been preparing. 이것은 내가 준비해오고 있는 시험이다.
　　　　　　　　(= for the examination)

▶ 동사 prepare는 전치사 for와 짝을 이루어 '~을 준비하다'라는 의미가 되므로, 전치사 for가 관계대명사 앞에 온다.

· '전치사 + 관계대명사' 뒤에는 완전한 절이 온다.

This is the suspect to whom the police asked many questions. 이 사람은 경찰이 많은 질문을 했던 용의자이다.

▶ '전치사 + 관계대명사'(to whom) 뒤에 '주어(the police) + 동사(asked) + 목적어(many questions)'로 이루어진 완전한 절이 왔다.

수량 표현 + 관계대명사

one / each several	some / any half	the rest many / much / most	all / both	+ of	+ 관계대명사	(which / whom whose + 명사)

The company promoted six employees. + All of the employees had joined the company two years ago.
그 회사는 6명의 직원을 승진시켰다. 　　+ 그 직원들은 모두 2년 전에 입사했었다.

→ The company promoted six employees, and all of them had joined the company two years ago.

→ The company promoted six employees, all of whom had joined the company two years ago.

☑ 텝스 실전 문제

텝스 문제 이렇게 나온다

'수량 표현 + 관계대명사'를 채우는 문제가 주로 나온다.
관계대명사 앞에 전치사가 빠지거나, 불필요한 전치사가 와서 틀린 문장을 찾는 문제가 주로 나온다.

Part II

. The strike for increased wages consisted of hundreds of immigrants, _____ were earning less than minimum wage.

(a) most of them　　(b) most of whom
(c) they were　　　 (d) who being

Part III

2. (a) Computers used to be the primary method which people were able to access the Internet. (b) Today, most technological devices can connect to the Internet without the need for wires. (c) Cell phones are among the smallest devices that can visit Web sites and download files. (d) This trend of universal connectivity reflects the public's desire to have online access from any place at any time.

정답 p.61

1 선행사의 종류에 따라 관계부사를 선택해야 한다.

선행사	관계부사
시간 (time, day, week, year 등)	when
장소 (place, park, house 등)	where
이유 (the reason)	why
방법 (the way)	how

March is the time when flowers start to bloom. 3월은 꽃이 피기 시작하는 시기이다.

The island where they spent their vacation was very beautiful. 그들이 휴가를 보냈던 섬은 매우 아름다웠다.

고득점
포인트 1. 관계부사 when, where, why는 선행사와 관계부사를 모두 쓰거나, 둘 중 하나를 생략한다. 단, how의 경우 선행사 the way와 how 중 하나는 반드시 한다.

The architect described **the reason why[the reason / why]** the bridge had become unstable.
건축가는 그 다리가 불안정해진 이유를 설명했다.

She knows ~~the way how~~ we can get uptown quickly. (→ **the way / how**) 그녀는 우리가 주택가로 빨리 갈 수 있는 방법을 안다.

⌐ 첫 번째 문장의 관계부사(why)는 선행사(the reason)와 함께 the reason why로 쓰거나, 둘 중 하나를 생략하고 쓸 수 있다. 반면 두 번째 문장의 선행사 the way와 how는 함께 쓸 수 없으므로, the way나 how 중 하나만 와야 한다.

2. 관계부사 whereby는 선행사의 종류에 관계없이 '~에 의한(by which)' 등의 의미로 관계절을 연결한다.

We set up a plan **whereby[by which]** we can increase our sales. 우리는 판매를 증가시킬 수 있는 계획을 세웠다.

(= We set up a plan. + We can increase our sales by it.)

2 관계부사는 '전치사 + 관계대명사'로 바꾸어 쓸 수 있다.

The truck driver missed the moment when[at which] he could have made a left turn.
트럭 운전사는 좌회전할 수 있었던 순간을 놓쳤다.

Deforestation is the reason why[for which] some animal species have become extinct.
산림 벌채는 몇몇 동물의 종이 멸종된 이유이다.

3 관계부사 뒤에는 완전한 절이 오는 반면, 관계대명사 뒤에는 불완전한 절이 온다.

Tuesday is the only day ~~which~~ I visit the city. 화요일은 내가 그 도시를 방문하는 유일한 날이다.
                  when

▶ 뒤에 주어(I), 동사(visit), 목적어(the city)를 갖춘 완전한 절이 왔으므로, 관계대명사(which)가 아니라 관계부사(when)가 와야 한다.

We visited the house ~~where~~ he bought. 우리는 그가 산 집에 방문했다.
                   which / that

▶ 뒤에 타동사(bought)의 목적어가 없는 불완전한 절이 왔으므로, 관계부사(where)가 아니라 목적격 관계대명사(which / that)가 와야 한다.

☑ 텝스 실전 문제

텝스 문제 이렇게 나온

| 선행사에 맞는 관계부사를 채우는 문제가 주로 나온다.
| 선행사에 맞지 않는 관계부사가 와서 틀린 문장을 찾는 문제가 가끔 나온다.

Part II

1. The annual book sale event is taking place at all avenues _____ participating bookstores are located.

(a) what   (b) when

(c) where   (d) why

Part III

2. (a) In the thirteenth century, the Mexica tribe settled in what is known today as the Valley of Mexico. (b) They built the city Tenochtitlan, which served as the center of the Aztec Empire for the next two centuries. (c) In the sixteenth century, foreign explorers arrived and brought diseases that decimated the Aztec population. (d) The Azte Empire collapsed in 1521, where they were conquered by the Spanish.

정답 p.

중 알맞은 것을 고르세요.

Sherry was not able to find the type of light bulb (that / what) was needed for the ceiling light in her bathroom.

The experiments performed in the lab, (which / that) is only for authorized personnel, are highly volatile and require radiation suits.

He had coffee with the man (who / what) had been his college roommate.

Many tourists visited the art gallery (in which / which) Picasso's works were being displayed.

The era predating modern technology is known as the Middle Ages, (when / where) people lived without electricity and indoor plumbing.

This is the biggest house for sale (that / who) still falls within your price range.

| 부분이 있으면 바르게 고치세요.

Prisms are transparent objects which light is refracted to produce an array of colors.

In Rome in 64 AD, a great fire spread through fourteen Roman districts, Nero's palace, and the Temple of Vesta, all of them were destroyed.

The orange oakleaf butterfly has special coloration that camouflaging it from being seen by predators.

The linguistics department offered a large merit-based scholarship for that Tamara applied.

No artist better represents the movement of pop art than Andy Warhol, whose style continues to influence modern artists.

I forgot to visit the doctor's office where I had scheduled to take a medical checkup at yesterday.

정답 p.62

Hackers **TEST**

Part I Choose the best answer for the blank.

01 A: Why do you take that bus when it's so slow?
   B: It's the only one by my apartment _____ goes near the office.

   (a) that   (b) what
   (c) who   (d) where

02 A: I would appreciate if you could seat us sooner.
   B: If you'll wait, I'll see _____ I can do.

   (a) which   (b) that
   (c) what   (d) how

03 A: What happened to the manager?
   B: He made a controversial and unpopular policy change _____ he was pressured into resigning.

   (a) that   (b) which
   (c) in which   (d) for which

04 A: I can't believe we have to cancel the baseball game.
   B: _____ replaced, we haven't had enough time to reorganize.
   (a) Our coach been
   (b) Our coach was
   (c) Our coach having been
   (d) Having our coach been

Part II Choose the best answer for the blank.

05 Young workers, especially those _____ have to raise infant children, often don't get enough sleep.

   (a) who   (b) whom
   (c) of whom   (d) of which

06 Chicks are hatched from eggs _____ hens sit incubating them for an average of 21 days.

   (a) that   (b) what
   (c) from which   (d) upon which

07 _____ the Earth burn up in the atmosphere before they can strike its surface.

   (a) Most of asteroids approaching
   (b) Of all asteroids approaching
   (c) Approaches by most asteroids
   (d) Most asteroids that approach

08 Some products that utilize rubber include erasers, spandex, balloons, tires, and putty, all of _____ possess varying degrees of elasticity.

   (a) that   (b) who
   (c) what   (d) which

09 Chuck Berry helped define rock and roll with many famous tunes, _____ was "Johnny B. Goode."

   (a) that the most influential
   (b) what the most influential
   (c) the most influential of which
   (d) the most influential of whom

10 The nonprofit organization, _____ Deborah Applebee is a founder, has made much progress in preserving various endangered species.

   (a) in that   (b) for what
   (c) of which   (d) with whom

11 Many patients prefer clinical physicians to holistic healers, _____ methods seem more spiritual than scientific.

   (a) that   (b) whose
   (c) which   (d) of what

vidence that dinosaurs once existed can be seen
n their fossils, _____
n ancient sediment and stone.

a) of which preserved are the examples
b) the examples of which are preserving it
c) the examples preserving it are
d) the examples of which are preserved

he topics included in the seminar, _____ was
ttended by 200 guests, covered stem cell research
nd cloning.

a) who   (b) that
c) which   (d) where

1 2006, more than 10 million illegal immigrants
ntered the U.S., _____
ettled in California.

a) around 25 percent of whom
b) whom around 25 percent of them
c) around them 25 percent of whom
d) 25 percent around of whom

Many American homes in the West _____
_____ was once settled by various Native
American tribes.

a) inhabit the same land that
b) inhabits that the same land
c) that the same land inhabits
d) the same land inhabits that

raphing calculators feature a host of functions,
_____ the ability to visually
isplay formulas on a grid.

a) is not the least of which
b) the least which is not
c) which is not the least
d) not the least of which is

17 The preservation of sequoia trees is the reason
_____ the Redwood National Parks were
established.

(a) which   (b) in what
(c) whatever   (d) for which

Part III Identify the option that contains an awkward
expression or an error in grammar.

18 (a) A: Is Leslie the one for which car is a blue SUV?
(b) B: I think so. Did something happen that she
needs to know?
(c) A: No, it's just that its lights were left on.
(d) B: I'll go tell her that she needs to turn them off.

19 (a) There has been speculation that if a disaster
were to occur that wipes out the human
population, cockroaches would survive it. (b) It
is their ability to withstand limited resources and
harsh environments affects how likely it is that
they would endure. (c) Their high resistance to
radiation is what leads scientists to believe that
they could overcome the effects of nuclear war.
(d) Whether or not cockroaches would be the only
species to come out of such a situation remains to
be seen.

20 (a) Vitamin C plays an essential role in the diet of
mammals, and human beings in particular.
(b) Because humans lack the ability to synthesize
vitamin C from glucose, they must consume it.
(c) Its role as an antioxidant helps fight oxidative
stress and aids the circulatory system. (d) A
deficiency in one's skin and teeth can result from
scurvy, after which an insufficient amount of
vitamin C may cause.

CHAPTER **18** 부사절

BASIC GRAMMAR 고수로 가는 첫 걸음

1 부사절은 문장 내에서 시간, 조건 등을 나타내며 부사 역할을 하는 수식어 거품이다.

I was not at home **when Blair visited me.** Blair가 나를 방문했을 때 나는 집에 없었다.
If you are free, let's play chess. 만약 네가 한가하다면, 체스를 하자.

부사절 when Blair visited me와 If you are free는 문장에서 각각 시간과 조건을 나타내며, 부사 역할을 하는 수식어 거품이드
로, 없어도 문장이 성립한다.

2 부사절은 '부사절 접속사 + 주어 + 동사'로 이루어진다.

Because he is diligent, his boss raised his pay. 그가 근면하기 때문에, 그의 사장은 그의 봉급을 올려줬다.

위 문장의 부사절은 '부사절 접속사(Because) + 주어(he) + 동사(is)'로 이루어져 있다. 부사절 접속사에는 when, if, because
although, whatever 등이 있다.

단, 부사절의 동사가 be 동사일 경우, 부사절 접속사 뒤의 '주어 + 동사'를 생략할 수 있다.

You can use my car, **if (it is) necessary.** 필요하다면 너는 내 차를 쓸 수 있다.

01 부사절 자리와 쓰임

부사절은 수식어 거품 자리, 주로 필수 성분 앞이나 뒤에 온다.

While she was on a flight to Germany, <u>she listened to music</u>. 독일행 비행기를 타고 가는 동안에, 그녀는 음악을 들었다.
　　　　　　　　　　　　　　　　　　　　필수성분 (주어 + 동사)

<u>She listened to music</u> while she was on a flight to Germany.
필수성분 (주어 + 동사)

부사절은 문장에서 부사 역할을 하며, 명사 역할을 하는 명사절과 구별된다.

부사절 We can order the book for you if it's not in stock. 만약 그 책의 재고가 없다면, 우리는 당신을 위해 주문할 수 있습니다.
▶ if가 이끄는 절은 '조건'을 나타내는 부사 역할을 하므로, 없어도 문장이 성립되는 부가 성분이다.

명사절 Bill didn't know if he could prepare his report in time. Bill은 그가 보고서를 제때 준비할 수 있을지 몰랐다.
▶ if가 이끄는 절은 동사(know)의 목적어 자리에 와서 명사 역할을 하므로, 문장 성립을 위한 필수 성분이다.

부사절은 명사를 뒤에서 수식하는 형용사 역할을 하는 관계절과 구별된다.

부사절 Gerald dropped his cell phone when he stepped out of the taxi. Gerald는 택시에서 내릴 때 휴대 전화를 떨어뜨렸다.
▶ when이 이끄는 절은 '언제 발생했는가'라는 부가적 의미를 더하는 부사 역할을 한다.

관계절 Noon is the time when the sun is at its highest point. 정오는 태양이 가장 높은 지점에 있는 시간이다.
▶ when이 이끄는 절은 명사(the time) 뒤에서 명사를 수식하는 형용사 역할을 한다.

부사절 내의 동사 자리에 준동사는 올 수 없다.

She took a shower after she ~~having~~ dinner. 그녀는 저녁을 먹은 후에 샤워를 했다.
　　　　　　　　　　　　　　had
▶ 부사절(after ~ dinner) 내의 동사 자리에 준동사는 올 수 없으므로, having이 아니라 had가 와야 한다.

🔺고득점 포인트 부사절 접속사는 절 앞에 오는 것이 원칙이지만, 분사구문 앞에 오기도 한다.
When <u>going on vacation</u>, you should take some medicine along. 휴가를 갈 때, 너는 약간의 의약품을 가져가야 한다.
　　　　분사구문
The shelf will be sturdy **if** <u>assembled correctly</u>. 제대로 조립된다면 선반은 튼튼할 것이다.
　　　　　　　　　　　　　분사구문
↳ 부사절 접속사(When, if)가 분사구문(going on vacation, assembled correctly) 앞에 왔다.

☑ 텝스 실전 문제

텝스 문제 이렇게 나온다

수식어 거품 자리에 부사절을 채우는 문제가 주로 나온다.
부사절 접속사 뒤에 분사(구문)을 채우는 문제가 주로 나온다.

Part I

1. A: Why are you so late?
   B: _____, I realized that I had forgotten to set my radio alarm clock.

   (a) When woke up　　(b) When I woke up
   (c) What woke up　　(d) What I woke up

Part II

2. When _____ a place to live, there are numerous factors to consider.

   (a) find　　　　　　(b) finding
   (c) having found　　(d) to find

정답 p.65

1 시간을 나타내는 부사절 접속사

when ~일 때, ~할 때 as ~함에 따라, ~할 때 while ~하는 동안	When I was a student, my hair was longer. 학생이었을 때, 내 머리는 더 길었다. As winter approaches, daylight hours grow shorter. 겨울이 다가옴에 따라, 낮이 점점 짧아진다. While everyone was sleeping, Jim watched TV. 모두 자는 동안, Jim은 TV를 보았다.
before ~하기 전에 until ~할 때까지	She slowed the car down before she pulled into the driveway. 차도로 진입하기 전에 그녀는 차의 속도를 낮추었다. Do not cross the road until the light changes. 신호등이 바뀔 때까지 길을 건너지 마라.
after ~한 후에 since ~한 이래로	A winner was selected after the votes were tallied. 당선자는 득표수가 계산된 후에 선출되었다. I've been practicing golf since I saw a professional tournament. 나는 프로 경기를 본 이래로 골프 연습을 해오고 있다.
as soon as ~하자마자	I will shut off the TV as soon as the program ends. 나는 그 프로그램이 끝나자마자 TV를 끌 것이다.

포인트 ^{고득점} as와 since는 '~이므로'라는 뜻의 이유를 나타내는 접속사로, while은 '반면에'를 뜻하는 접속사로 쓰이기도 한다.

As / Since we live in globalized world, it's important to learn a foreign language.
우리가 국제화된 세계에서 살기 때문에, 외국어를 배우는 것이 중요하다.

A caribou can walk right after its birth, **while** a human cannot even stand up.
삼림순록은 태어난 직후 바로 걸을 수 있는 반면에, 인간은 설 수조차 없다.

2 조건을 나타내는 부사절 접속사

if 만약 ~라면 unless 만약 ~아니라면(= if ~ not)	We should have a picnic tomorrow if it doesn't rain. 만약 비가 안 오면, 우리는 내일 소풍을 갈 것이다. I can meet you for dinner unless I have to work late. 만약 내가 늦게까지 일해야 하지 않는다면, 너를 만나 저녁 식사를 할 수 있다.
provided / providing (that) ~하면, ~하는 경우에 as long as ~하는 한, ~하면	You can sleep over provided (that) you don't mind the couch. 소파를 싫어하지 않으면, 너는 소파에서 자도 된다. I can drive you home as long as it's not too far away. 거리가 너무 멀지 않으면, 너를 차로 집에 데려다 줄 수 있다.
once 일단 ~하자, 일단 ~하면	A crowd gathered once the fireworks began. 일단 불꽃놀이가 시작되자 사람들이 모였다.
in case ~(의 경우)에 대비하여	I brought two pens in case you forgot. 네가 잊었을 경우에 대비해서 펜을 두 개 가져왔다.

☑ 텝스 실전 문제

텝스 문제 이렇게 나온

| 시간 · 조건을 나타내는 부사절 접속사를 채우는 문제가 주로 나온다.

Part I

1. A: When will you submit the first draft?
   B: I'm sorry, but it will take at least another week _____ the draft is ready.

   (a) after   (b) since
   (c) while   (d) before

Part II

2. The farm vegetation will dry up and die, _____ the long drought comes to an end and the rainy season arrives.

   (a) in case   (b) as
   (c) unless   (d) once

정답 p.

양보를 나타내는 부사절 접속사

although, though, 비록 ~이지만 even if, even though	Though it may seem childish, I still watch cartoons. 비록 유치해 보일지도 모르지만, 나는 여전히 만화를 본다.
whereas, while 반면에	I love spending money, whereas my friend tries to save every penny. 나는 돈 쓰는 것을 좋아하는 반면에, 내 친구는 한푼이라도 아끼려고 노력한다.

고득점 포인트 as가 '비록 ~이지만'이라는 의미의 양보를 나타내는 부사절 접속사로도 쓰일 수 있으며, 이때 보어가 as 앞에 와야 한다.
Young as Charlie is, he's smart. 비록 Charlie는 어리지만, 그는 영리하다.
↳ as가 '비록 ~이지만'이라는 양보의 의미로 쓰이면 보어(Young)가 as 앞에 와야 한다.

이유를 나타내는 부사절 접속사

because, as, since ~기 때문에	We buy bottled water because the tap water is not fit to drink. 수돗물이 마시기에 적합하지 않기 때문에, 우리는 생수를 산다.
now (that) ~이니까	Now that the winter is coming, we should plan a ski trip. 겨울이 오고 있으니까, 우리는 스키 여행을 계획해야 한다.
in that ~라는 점에서	The story is an abridged edition in that some scenes have been removed. 몇 장면들이 제거되었다는 점에서 그 이야기는 요약본이다.

기타 접속사

in order that ~ can / may / will = so that ~ can / may / will ~하도록	Please keep the window open in order that the room will cool down. = Please keep the window open so that the room will cool down. 방이 서늘해지도록 창문을 계속 열어두세요.
lest ~ should ~하지 않도록	Let your coffee cool off for a few moments, lest it should burn your mouth. 커피에 입이 데지 않도록, 잠깐 동안 식히세요.
so that (~해서 그 결과) ~하다	I submitted an additional report so that I got extra credit. 나는 부가적인 보고서를 제출해서 추가 점수를 받았다.
so / such ~ that 매우 ~해서 –하다	The sponge was so dirty that it had to be replaced. 스펀지는 매우 더러워서 교체되어야 했다.
as if, as though 마치 ~처럼	He felt as if everyone on the train was watching him. 그는 마치 기차 안의 모든 사람들이 그를 쳐다보고 있는 것처럼 느꼈다.
(just) as, (just) like ~처럼	They went to the park (just) like they do every Saturday. 그들은 매주 토요일에 하는 것처럼 공원에 갔다.
except that, but that ~을 제외하고	These new glasses are nice, except that they're too expensive. 이 새 안경은 너무 비싸다는 점을 제외하고는 좋다.
whether ~이든 아니든, ~이든 –이든	Whether he comes or not, we will start on time. 그가 오든 안 오든, 우리는 정각에 출발할 것이다.

☑ 텝스 실전 문제

텝 스 문 제 이 렇 게 나 온 다

양보 · 이유 · 기타 부사절 접속사를 채우는 문제가 주로 나온다.

Part I

1. A: Are you sure you want to buy a book that's in such poor condition?
   B: I'll take it, _____ it's falling apart.

   (a) even if   (b) so that
   (c) once   (d) while

Part II

2. Many students often get part-time jobs _____ they need extra spending money.

   (a) because   (b) though
   (c) unless   (d) whether

정답 p.65

해커스 텝스 Reading

1 복합관계대명사와 복합관계부사가 이끄는 절은 문장 내에서 부사 역할을 한다.

복합관계대명사	복합관계부사
whatever 무엇이/무엇을 ~하든 상관없이 who(m)ever 누가/누구를 ~하든 상관없이 whichever 어느 것이/어느 것을 ~하든 상관없이	whenever 언제 ~하든 상관없이 wherever 어디로/어디에서 ~하든 상관없이 however 어떻게 ~하든 상관없이

Whoever parked in the street, please move your vehicle. 누가 거리에 주차를 했든 상관없이, 차를 빼주세요.

Wherever I eat, it seems prices have gone up. 내가 어디에서 먹든 상관없이, 가격이 오른 것 같다.

🔺고득점 복합관계대명사 whatever, who(m)ever, whichever는 문장 내에서 주어, 목적어, 보어 역할을 하는 명사절도 이끈다.
포인트 **Whatever** Mr. Moor suggests always helps me a lot. Mr. Moor가 무엇을 제안하든 항상 내게 많은 도움이 된다.
Sandra won't forgive **whoever** spoiled her garden. Sandra는 누가 그녀의 정원을 망쳤든 용서하지 않을 것이다.
The dessert is **whichever** you'd like. 디저트는 어떤 것이든 네가 먹고 싶은 것이다.

2 복합관계대명사와 복합관계부사는 'no matter + 의문사'로 바꾸어 쓸 수 있다.

Whatever[No matter what] you buy online, it's important to make sure that the seller is credible.
네가 온라인에서 무엇을 사든 상관없이, 판매자가 신용할 수 있는 사람인 것을 확인하는 것이 중요하다.

However[No matter how] tall he is, he doesn't want to be a basketball player.
그가 얼마나 키가 크든 상관없이 그는 농구 선수가 되기를 원하지 않는다.

3 however는 'however + 형용사/부사 + 주어 + 동사'로 쓰인다.

I can always find a seat on the bus, however crowded it may be. 버스가 얼마나 붐비든, 나는 항상 좌석을 찾을 수 있다.

☑ **텝스 실전 문제**   텝스 문제 이렇게 나온

| 적절한 복합관계대명사나 복합관계부사를 채우는 문제가 주로 나온다.
| 'no matter + 의문사' 절을 채우는 문제가 주로 나온다.

Part I

1. A: I'm worried about the future.
   B: _____ your career takes you, I'm sure you
      will be doing something you enjoy.

   (a) Whichever   (b) Whenever
   (c) However   (d) Wherever

Part II

2. It is admirable to stand up for one's ideals
   _____.

   (a) no matter those beliefs may be
   (b) no matter may be those beliefs
   (c) no matter what those beliefs may be
   (d) no matter what may be those beliefs

정답 p.

Hackers **Practice**

알맞은 것을 고르세요.

She was just outside the school when she (saw / seeing) her son drive past.

The excited crowd cheered the speaker for five minutes (since / after) the speech ended.

She was sweating as she practiced yoga, (even though / whereas) the temperature was quite low.

I can guarantee you a position at our company, (so that / provided that) your background check doesn't reveal any negative information.

Nobody deserves such treatment, (however / whichever) annoying you think he may be.

Once the movie had finished, he felt (if / as if) he was going to cry.

부분이 있으면 바르게 고치세요.

If you choosing to buy a new computer, you should consider memory and processor speed the most important features.

Until their mom brought out the cookies, the children ate every last one.

As nervous I am, I still think I'll receive a perfect score on the examination.

Give me a call and I'll pick you up no matter you arrive when.

As long as you stay along the right side of the street, you can't miss the apartment building.

The driver was so that tired he couldn't keep from closing his eyes behind the wheel.

Hackers **TEST**

Part I Choose the best answer for the blank.

01 A: How can I improve my grades?
   B: _____ you stick around after class, there is a review session.

   (a) If   (b) Though
   (c) Unless   (d) Since

02 A: I can't believe my car broke down.
   B: _____ you had gotten it inspected, the problem still might have occurred.

   (a) While   (b) However
   (c) Before   (d) Even if

03 A: Is it possible to change my flight reservation?
   B: You can, _____ the later flight hasn't been filled.
   (a) once   (b) unless
   (c) in that   (d) provided that

04 A: Can I help you with one of those suitcases?
   B: _____, I don't want you to hurt your back.

   (a) Are they as heavy
   (b) As heavy they are
   (c) Heavy as they are
   (d) They are as heavy

05 A: I'm going to take my umbrella with me.
   B: _____ you forget, I'll bring another one in the car.

   (a) Unless   (b) So that
   (c) In order that (d) In case

06 A: I need to talk to you once you're done cleaning.
   B: OK. I'll find you as soon as I _____.

   (a) finish   (b) finished
   (c) am finishing (d) will finish

07 A: I'm heading to the cafeteria to grab a coffee
   B: _____ you're going, could you get m an espresso?

   (a) As long as   (b) As soon as
   (c) By the time   (d) In order that

Part II Choose the best answer for the blank.

08 _____ they are sophisticated or juvenile, people of all tastes have interests they would consider to be guilty pleasures.

   (a) Since   (b) Unless
   (c) Whether   (d) While

09 _____ the lease is approved, the prospecti tenant will be able to officially move into the r apartment.

   (a) Once   (b) While
   (c) Though   (d) Now

10 Sound travels at 343 meters per second in air, _____ it travels more than four times fast in water.

   (a) just like   (b) whereas
   (c) rather than   (d) as if

11 _____ university football coaches want is players being chosen for the professional leagu

   (a) That   (b) What
   (c) Whom   (d) Whichever

12 _____ the store is going out of business, everything is being discounted by 50 to 75 perc

   (a) For   (b) With
   (c) Since   (d) As long as

_____ oxygen is necessary for humans to live and breathe, carbon dioxide is just as important because plants need it to produce the oxygen that humans consume.

(a) While   (b) Since
(c) Before   (d) Because

_____ the issue may be, it is always important to hear both sides of a debate.

(a) However   (b) Whenever
(c) Whichever   (d) Whatever

_____ data storage units and online databases grow in capacity, CDs and DVDs will begin to disappear.

(a) Although   (b) Until
(c) Unless   (d) As

The woman would receive monthly phone calls from her traveling son, _____ he was.

(a) however   (b) whenever
(c) wherever   (d) whichever

It is worth putting one's full effort into one's work _____.

(a) what no matter may involve the work
(b) no matter the work may involve what
(c) what the work may involve no matter
(d) no matter what the work may involve

Part III Identify the option that contains an awkward expression or an error in grammar.

18 (a) A: Paul, do you want to see a movie with me later?
   (b) B: I can't go out tonight because I need to work on my thesis.
   (c) A: But you still have two months since you have to turn it in.
   (d) B: Yes, but it's longer and more difficult to write than other papers.

19 (a) This is a public announcement regarding acts of vandalism and theft at the Newark Public Library. (b) Recently, many of the library's books have gone missing or have had multiple pages removed. (c) Whereas these acts are discontinued, new security measures will be taken to monitor visitors while browsing. (d) It is our wish that visitors treat the books with consideration while freely making use of the library's resources.

20 (a) Yeast is a fungus that is a required ingredient both in baking and alcohol fermentation. (b) Fermentation is the process in which sugars are converted into carbon dioxide, yielding an altered composition. (c) Baking products obtain their leavened state from dough inside that yeast produces pockets of carbon dioxide bubbles. (d) Alcohol results from the yeast that converts the sugars of malted grain into ethanol, the chemical term given to alcohol.

시험에 나올 문제를 미리 풀어보고 싶을 땐?

해커스텝스(HackersTEPS.com)에서
텝스 적중예상특강 보기!

Section 6 어순과 특수구문

CHAPTER **19** 어순

BASIC GRAMMAR 고수로 가는 첫 걸음

1 문장 성분이나, 여러 가지 품사들이 일정한 순서대로 나열되어야 바른 문장이 되며, 이때의 일정한 순서를 '어순'이라 한다.

<u>Harry</u> <u>wrote</u> <u>a letter</u>. Harry는 편지를 썼다.
　주어　동사　목적어

<u>She's reading</u> <u>a</u> <u>very</u> <u>thick</u> <u>book</u>. 그녀는 매우 두꺼운 책을 읽고 있다.
　　　　　관사　부사　형용사　명사

첫 번째 문장은 '주어 + 동사 + 목적어' 순으로 쓰여 바른 문장이다. 그러나 만약 순서를 바꿔 "Wrote Harry a letter."나 "Harry a letter wrote."로 쓰면 어순이 지켜지지 않아 틀린 문장이다.

두 번째 문장의 a very thick book은 '관사 + 부사 + 형용사 + 명사' 순으로 쓰여 바르다. 그러나 만약 순서를 바꿔 'very a thick book'이나 'a very book thick' 등으로 쓰면 어순이 지켜지지 않아 틀리다.

2 문장의 종류에 따라 어순이 다르다.

① 평서문은 '주어 + 동사'를 기본 어순으로 한다.
I live in San Francisco. 나는 샌프란시스코에 산다.

② 명령문은 주어 You를 생략하고 동사원형으로 시작한다.
(You) **Do** your homework now. 지금 네 숙제를 해라.

③ 의문문은 조동사나 be동사가 주어 앞에 온다. 일반 동사의 의문문은 do동사가 주어 앞에 오고, 주어 뒤엔 동사원형이 온다.
Can Aden speak French? Aden은 프랑스어를 말할 수 있니?
Is Elizabeth likely to agree with us? Elizabeth가 우리에게 동의할 것 같니?
Did Ethan go for a walk? Ethan은 산책을 갔니?

④ 감탄문은 '주어 + 동사' 앞에 'How + 형용사/부사'나 'What + (a/an +) 형용사 + 명사'가 온다.
How tall he is! 그는 키가 크구나!
What a beautiful dress it is! 그것은 정말 아름다운 드레스구나!

3 수식하는 말은 수식받는 대상을 바로 앞뒤에서 수식한다.

I want to drive the <u>very</u> <u>fast</u> <u>car</u> <u>in his garage</u>. 나는 그의 차고 안에 있는 매우 빠른 차를 운전하기를 원한다.

부사(very)는 형용사(fast)를 앞에서 수식하고, 형용사(fast) 역시 명사(car)를 앞에서 수식한다. 그리고 전치사구(in his garage)는 명사(car)를 뒤에서 수식한다.

1 평서문·명령문의 어순

문장 형식에 따른 평서문의 기본 어순

1형식: 주어 + 동사	The phone rang. 전화가 울렸다.
2형식: 주어 + 동사 + 보어	We are a team. 우리는 한 팀이다.
3형식: 주어 + 동사 + 목적어	She rode a bicycle. 그녀는 자전거를 탔다.
4형식: 주어 + 동사 + 간접 목적어 + 직접 목적어	He told me a story. 그는 내게 이야기를 해주었다.
5형식: 주어 + 동사 + 목적어 + 목적격 보어	I consider you my tutor. 나는 당신을 내 개인 교사로 여긴다.

고득점 포인트 준동사구(to부정사구, 동명사구, 분사구)나 접속사절(명사절, 관계절, 부사절)의 어순 또한 기본 어순을 바탕으로 한다.

It's important to get lots of rest so as not **to get sick**. 아프지 않기 위해서 충분한 휴식을 취하는 것이 중요하다.
to부정사 (2형식: 동사 + 보어)

Jeff said **that he wanted me to go over his report**. Jeff는 내가 그의 보고서를 검토해주길 원한다고 말했다.
명사절 (5형식: 주어 + 동사 + 목적어 + 목적격보어)

평서문의 부정문은 '조동사 + not / never + 동사' 순으로 온다.

She couldn't eat dinner because she was too busy. 그녀는 너무 바빠서 저녁을 먹을 수 없었다.

She hasn't eaten dinner yet. 그녀는 아직 저녁을 먹지 않았다.

고득점 포인트 평서문의 동사가 일반동사인 경우 부정문은 'do/does/did + not + 동사원형' 순으로 쓰거나, 'never + 일반동사' 순으로 쓴다.
He **doesn't pay** in cash. 그는 현금으로 지불하지 않는다.   He **never pays** in cash. 그는 결코 현금으로 지불하지 않는다.

절이나 동사를 수식하는 부사구나 전치사구는 절의 맨 앞이나 마지막에 온다.

Yesterday morning there was a strong earthquake. 어제 아침에 강력한 지진이 있었다.

My family has run this company for generations. 우리 가족은 몇 대에 걸쳐서 이 회사를 운영해오고 있다.

▶ 위의 문장들처럼 절(there was a strong earthquake)을 수식하는 부사구(Yesterday morning)나, 동사(has run)를 수식하는 전치사구(for generations) 는 절의 맨 앞이나 마지막에 와야 한다.

고득점 포인트 명사를 수식하는 전치사구는 명사의 바로 뒤에 오므로, 이를 절이나 동사를 수식하는 전치사구와 혼동하지 않도록 주의한다.
The island **across the lake** is famous for its unique ecosystem. 호수 건너편의 섬은 독특한 생태계로 유명하다.

↳ 전치사구(across the lake)가 수식하는 것은 명사 The island이므로, 절의 맨 앞이나 마지막이 아니라 명사 바로 뒤에 온다.

명령문은 주어 없이 동사원형으로 시작한다.

Explain to me why you were absent from the last class. 지난 수업에 결석한 이유를 내게 설명해라.
동사원형

✏️ 텝스 실전 문제

평서문을 문장 형식에 따라 올바른 어순으로 채우는 문제가 주로 나온다.
부정문을 올바른 어순으로 채우는 문제가 주로 나온다.

Part II

Many cafés provide a connection to the Internet so that _____.

(a) can customers access to it more conveniently
(b) customers can access it more conveniently
(c) access can customers more conveniently it
(d) customers access to it more conveniently

Part I

2. A: What did you think of the concert?
   B: Even though I like that type of music, _____.

   (a) I didn't enjoy it   (b) I not enjoyed it
   (c) I not did enjoy it   (d) I enjoyed not it

정답 p.68

1 의문문의 어순

· 조동사가 있는 경우: (의문사 +) 조동사 + 주어 + 동사

When did the mail arrive? 언제 편지가 도착했니?

Can you believe **Tommy got a scholarship**? 너는 Tommy가 장학금을 받았다는 것을 믿을 수 있니?

· 조동사가 없는 경우: (의문사 +) 동사 + 주어

When are you **able to come**? 너는 언제 올 수 있니?

Are you **free this Sunday**? 이번 주 일요일에 한가하니?

> 고득점 포인트 의문형용사 what과 which 뒤에는 명사가 올 수 있고, 의문부사 how 뒤에는 형용사나 부사가 올 수 있다.
> **Which** <u>room</u> did she enter? 그녀가 어느 방에 들어갔니?
>   명사
> **How** <u>long</u> should I wait? 제가 얼마나 오래 기다려야 하나요?
>   부사

2 간접 의문문은 다른 문장 안에 포함된 의문문으로 '의문사 + 주어 + 동사' 순으로 온다.

I heard why the professor quit. 나는 그 교수가 그만둔 이유를 들었다.

Tell me which courses you will take. 네가 어떤 수업을 들을 건지 내게 말해줘.

> 고득점 포인트 think, believe, imagine, suppose, suggest 등이 동사로 쓰인 의문문에 간접 의문문이 포함되면 의문사가 문장의 맨 앞으로 온다.
> Do you <u>think</u>? + **What** are they planning? 당신은 생각하나요? + 그들은 무엇을 계획하고 있나요?
> → Do you <u>think</u> **what** they are planning? [×]
> → **What** do you <u>think</u> they are planning? [○] 당신은 그들이 무엇을 계획하고 있다고 생각하나요?
> ↳ 동사가 think인 의문문에 간접 의문문(what they are planning)이 포함되었으므로, 의문사(what)는 문장의 맨 앞으로 온다.

3 감탄문은 'How + 형용사/부사 + 주어 + 동사', 'What + (a/an +) 형용사 + 명사 + 주어 + 동사' 순으로 온다.

How gracefully she dances! 그녀는 아주 우아하게 춤을 추는구나!

What cute babies you have! 당신의 아기들은 매우 귀엽군요!

> 고득점 포인트 1. 'How + 형용사'와 'What + a(n) + 형용사 + 명사' 뒤의 '주어 + 동사'는 생략할 수 있다.
> How noisy **(they are)**! 그들은 매우 시끄럽구나!
> What a nice day **(it is)**! 오늘은 날씨가 매우 좋구나!
> 2. 감탄문에서도 that절이나 to부정사 같은 긴 주어가 쓰이면 가짜주어 it을 사용할 수 있다.
> How refreshing <u>it is</u> that the subway trains are equipped with air conditioners! 지하철이 에어컨을 구비하고 있다니 참 상쾌하구나!
>   가짜주어   진짜주어

☑ 텝스 실전 문제

| 간접 의문문을 올바른 어순으로 채우거나, 간접 의문문의 어순이 틀린 문장을 찾는 문제가 주로 나온다.
| 감탄문을 올바른 어순으로 채우는 문제가 주로 나온다.

Part I

1. A: Is this a plum or a peach?
   B: I can't tell _____.

   (a) that is what   (b) that what is
   (c) what is that   (d) what that is

Part II

2. _____ should dim the ligh
   and use warm hues to set such a mellow mood!

   (a) How it is soothing that the lounge
   (b) How soothing the lounge is
   (c) How the lounge is soothing
   (d) How soothing it is that the lounge

정답 p

03 명사를 수식하는 여러 요소들의 어순

여러 품사가 함께 명사를 수식하는 경우의 어순

관사 (+ 부사) + 형용사 + 명사	**She took** a very long trip. 그녀는 매우 긴 여행을 했다.
소유격 (+ 부사) + 형용사 + 명사	**I am envious of** his particularly interesting job. 나는 그의 특히 흥미로운 직업을 부러워한다.
지시/수량형용사 (+ 부사) + 형용사 + 명사	**Don't waste your time on** that absurdly long line. 저 터무니없이 긴 줄에서 시간 낭비하지 마.
	Many shy people **don't enjoy attending large parties.**
	수줍음을 타는 많은 사람들은 큰 파티에 참석하는 것을 즐기지 않는다.

명사 앞에 명사를 수식하는 형용사가 여러 개 올 경우의 어순

순서	수	판단·태도	크기·길이·형태	색깔·원료
서수, last, next	three, ten	beautiful, remarkable	big, long, round	red, leather

Take the <u>first</u> <u>two</u> <u>small</u> <u>blue</u> <u>pills</u> in the packet before you sleep tonight.
　　　　순서　수　크기　색깔　명사

오늘 밤 자기 전에 포장 안에 든 첫 번째 두 개의 작은 파란색 알약을 먹어라.

▶ 4개의 형용사가 순서(first), 수(two), 크기(small), 색깔(blue) 순으로 명사(pills)를 수식한다.

고득점 포인트 명사를 수식하는 형용사가 여러 개일 경우에도 지시/수량형용사가 맨 앞에 온다.
　　　　We looked at **those** <u>beautiful</u> <u>ceramic</u> <u>vases</u>. 우리는 그 아름다운 도자기 꽃병들을 보았다.
　　　　　　　　　　지시형용사　　판단　　원료　　명사
　　　　We looked at **some** <u>beautiful</u> <u>ceramic</u> <u>vases</u>. 우리는 몇몇의 아름다운 도자기 꽃병들을 보았다.
　　　　　　　　　　수량형용사　　판단　　원료　　명사

-thing, -body, -one으로 끝나는 명사는 형용사가 뒤에서 수식한다.

<u>Everything</u> recyclable had to be taken. 재활용할 수 있는 모든 것이 가져와져야 한다.
↑

I've never seen <u>anybody</u> unfriendly here. 나는 여기서 불친절한 누구도 본 적이 없다.
　　　　　　　　　↑

I need <u>someone</u> reliable. 나는 믿을 만한 누군가가 필요하다.
　　　　↑

▶ 수식을 받는 명사가 Everything, anybody, someone이므로, 형용사(recyclable, unfriendly, reliable)가 명사를 뒤에서 수식한다.

☑ 텝스 실전 문제

명사를 수식하는 여러 형용사를 올바른 어순으로 채우거나, 명사를 수식하는 여러 형용사의 어순이 잘못된 문장을 찾는 문제가 주로 나온다. -thing, -body, -one으로 끝나는 명사와 이를 수식하는 형용사를 올바른 어순으로 채우는 문제도 가끔 나온다.

Part II

1. The commander ordered the _____ to demonstrate the new exercise.

(a) front four first soldiers
(b) first soldiers four in the front
(c) soldiers in the front first four
(d) first four soldiers in the front

Part III

2. (a) When going on an outdoor adventure such as camping, it's important to bring only what is needed. (b) Some campers bring items that aren't necessary and then find themselves weighed down with much baggage. (c) An important item to bring is a tent, as this will protect the camper from the elements as well as from small many animals roaming in the area. (d) For just one camper, a small, bright-colored, waterproof tent is adequate.

정답 p.68

1 enough는 명사 앞에 오거나, 형용사나 부사 뒤에 온다.

enough + 명사	He didn't have enough <u>money</u>. 그는 충분한 돈을 갖고 있지 않았다.
형용사/부사 + enough	You aren't being <u>careful</u> enough. 너는 충분히 신중을 기하고 있지 않고 있다.
	He is prepared <u>well</u> enough for the job. 그는 그 일을 위해 충분히 잘 준비되었다.
형용사 + enough + 명사	She didn't have a <u>long</u> enough <u>résumé</u>. 그녀는 충분히 긴 이력서를 갖고 있지 않았다.

포인트 ^{고득점} enough는 '형용사/부사 + enough + to부정사' 순으로 와서 '~하기에 충분히 −하다'라는 의미로 쓰인다.
He is **tall enough to reach** the basketball hoop. 그는 농구 골대에 닿을 만큼 충분히 키가 크다.

2 so는 'so + 형용사 + a(n) + 명사' 순으로, such는 'such + a(n) + 형용사 + 명사' 순으로 와야 한다.

We picked ~~such~~ <u>perfect</u> a <u>day</u> for hiking. 우리는 하이킹하기에 아주 완벽한 날을 골랐다.
    so

▶ '형용사 + a(n) + 명사'(perfect a day)의 어순이므로 앞에 such가 아니라 so가 와야 한다.

I've never seen ~~so~~ a <u>beautiful</u> <u>sunset</u>. 나는 그렇게 아름다운 일몰을 본 적이 없다.
    such

▶ 'a(n) + 형용사 + 명사'(a beautiful sunset)의 어순이므로 앞에 so가 아니라 such가 와야 한다.

포인트 ^{고득점} as, that, too는 so와 같이 'as/that/too + 형용사 + a(n) + 명사' 순으로, quite는 such와 같이 'quite + a(n) + 형용사 + 명사' 순으로 쓴다.
It's **as brilliant a plan** as any. 그것은 어느 것 못지 않게 멋진 계획이다.
She didn't expect to get **that short a haircut**. 그녀는 그렇게 머리를 짧게 자르게 될지 예상하지 못했다.
He is **too stubborn a competitor** to back down. 그는 너무나 완강한 경쟁 상대여서 단념시킬 수 없다.
It was **quite an educational seminar**. 그것은 꽤 교육적인 세미나였다.

3 '동사 + 부사'로 이루어진 구동사의 목적어가 대명사인 경우 '동사 + 대명사 + 부사' 순으로 와야 한다.

He took sunglasses with him, and ~~put on them~~ at the beach. 그는 선글라스를 가져와서, 해변에서 썼다.
                put them on

▶ 구동사(put on)의 목적어가 대명사(them)이므로 put on them이 아니라 put them on의 어순으로 와야 한다.

포인트 ^{고득점} 구동사의 목적어가 명사인 경우 '동사 + 부사 + 명사', '동사 + 명사 + 부사'의 두 어순 모두 쓸 수 있다.
He **put on** <u>sunglasses</u>. [○] 그는 선글라스를 썼다.
He **put** <u>sunglasses</u> **on**. [○]

☑ 텝스 실전 문제

텝스 문제 이렇게 나온다

| so나 such를 관사, 형용사, 명사 등과 함께 올바른 어순으로 채우는 문제
가 주로 나온다.
| '동사 + 대명사 + 부사' 어순을 바르게 채우는 문제가 주로 나온다.
| enough를 명사, 형용사, 부사 등과 함께 올바른 어순으로 채우는 문제가
가끔 나온다.

Part II

1. Charles Darwin's theory of evolution and the
origin of man was _____ concept
that many refused to accept it.

   (a) shocking such a   (b) shocking a such
   (c) such shocking   (d) such a shocking

Part I

2. A: I haven't made a decision about your offer yet.
   B: Then _____ while you're away this
      weekend.

   (a) thinking it over   (b) think it over
   (c) think over it   (d) thinking over it

정답 p.6

알맞은 것을 고르세요.

The boss called me into her office to ask how (the project was / was the project) going.

(How / What) a strange coincidence it is that we bought the same outfit for the wedding!

The musicians played (enough loudly / loudly enough) in the concert hall to be heard across the street.

How (it is exciting / exciting it is) that our team won the championship game!

Normally I like his movies, but his (three last / last three) films have been disappointing.

My grandfather has never caught (so / such) gigantic a fish until now.

부분이 있으면 바르게 고치세요.

Santa Monica is the lovely city along the California coast that we have called home since 1968.

Judging by the sound your car is making, there's probably wrong something with the engine.

Do you believe who was responsible for the mistake, Aaron or Becky?

She bought round some red tomatoes to include in the salad.

To thank you for your hard work, I'd like to take out you for drinks tomorrow night.

The television show was unpopular because of its subject matter, which was to children not interesting.

정답 p.69

Hackers TEST

Part I Choose the best answer for the blank.

01 A: How long will it take Stacy to arrive?
   B: I'm not sure because I don't know _____.

   (a) where does she live
   (b) where lives she
   (c) where she lives either
   (d) where lives she either

02 A: Was I really the first to leave the party?
   B: Yes, everyone else _____.

   (a) left there after you
   (b) left there you after
   (c) after you there left
   (d) there you left after

03 A: My Internet connection didn't work at all last week.
   B: Why _____? It was just installed.

   (a) down was it   (b) down was it being
   (c) it was being down   (d) was it down

04 A: Why didn't you say anything to me when I passed you in the hallway?
   B: I was talking to my professor and _____.

   (a) intended not ignore you
   (b) intended to never ignore you
   (c) did not intend you to ignore
   (d) never intended to ignore you

05 A: _____ relief it is to be done with work today.
   B: Yes, but tomorrow is another day.

   (a) What great a   (b) What a great
   (c) How a nice   (d) How nice is

06 A: Could you turn up the heater full blast so the car warms up?
   B: OK, I'll _____.

   (a) turn awhile on it   (b) turn it awhile on
   (c) turn on it awhile   (d) turn it on awhile

07 A: Your room is a mess. Don't you ever clean it?
   B: _____, my mother?

   (a) Do you think who you are
   (b) Do you think who are you
   (c) Who do you think are you
   (d) Who do you think you are

08 A: There is _____ for
   B: Sure, give me one minute to finish what I'm do

   (a) I need to check something
   (b) something I need you to check
   (c) I need you to check something
   (d) something do you need me to check

09 A: It seems like we sold a lot of T-shirts. How m money do you think we made?
   B: The profits from the sales will likely not be v high after _____

   (a) the shirts in the cost are factored
   (b) factored the cost of the shirts is in
   (c) the cost of the shirts is factored in
   (d) factored in are the cost of the shirts

Part II Choose the best answer for the blank.

10 Carol is planning to go again to the luxury hote that _____.

   (a) she stayed last year at
   (b) she stayed at last year
   (c) last year she stayed at
   (d) last year she stayed

11 This 16th-century masterpiece has attracted numerous buyers even though no one knows _____.

   (a) who it was painted by
   (b) who was painted it by
   (c) who by was painted it
   (d) who was painted by it

It is difficult for many people to read while riding in a moving vehicle without _____ or straining their eyes.

(a) becoming too tired
(b) becoming tired too
(c) too tired becoming
(d) too becoming tired

Johnson's Car Garage provides _____ as any in Michigan at rates that are affordable for everybody.

(a) as a reliable repair service
(b) as reliable a repair service
(c) very reliable repair service
(d) any reliable repair service

No one can say _____ to abandon figuration in his artwork and commit to abstraction.

(a) what inspired for sure Jackson Pollock
(b) Jackson Pollock what inspired for sure
(c) for sure what inspired Jackson Pollock
(d) for sure Jackson Pollock what inspired

Senator Lawrence accused her political rival of not telling _____ about the threat from international terrorism.

(a) the public what he intended to do
(b) the intention he had to do
(c) what he intended to the public
(d) what intentions he had the public

The Apollo 13 spacecraft _____ to use its gravity as momentum to fling it back toward Earth.

(a) flew close enough to the Moon
(b) was flying enough close to the Moon
(c) to the Moon flew close enough
(d) to the Moon was flying closer

17 Having amassed a fortune as an investment banker, Max will _____.

(a) for his retirement a luxurious marble mansion
(b) buy a luxurious marble mansion for his retirement
(c) buy marble luxurious a mansion for his retirement
(d) a marble luxurious his retirement buy mansion

Part III Identify the option that contains an awkward expression or an error in grammar.

18 (a) A: How did the meeting go? Did many people object to the plans for developing a new prototype car?
(b) B: Well, there were opposing viewpoints very few expressed. Most agreed with the idea.
(c) A: What about the director? I know he had some concerns about the cost of beginning from scratch.
(d) B: He did, but the engineering team convinced him of the overall worth of starting over again.

19 (a) A: Yesterday afternoon I had so a pleasant surprise.
(b) B: Did you have a stroke of good luck?
(c) A: Actually, I found out that I won 250 dollars in the lottery.
(d) B: That definitely sounds like good luck to me.

20 (a) Fingertips often leave behind raised ridges of oil from the skin. (b) Sweat glands in the fingers produce an oily solution that coats the ridges and makes the pattern of ridges in a fingerprint stand out. (c) Fingerprinting powder can highlight these oils, but it does not work as well with prints made by other substances. (d) As a result, most fingerprinting powders are unable to highlight fingerprints by oil not created.

정답 p.70

CHAPTER **20** 비교 구문

BASIC GRAMMAR 고수로 가는 첫 걸음

1 비교 구문은 둘 이상의 대상을 수량이나 성질 면에서 비교하는 구문이며, 다음 세 가지로 나뉜다.

① 원급 구문은 두 대상이 동등함을 나타낸다.
Brandy is **as tall as** Ashley. Brandy는 Ashley만큼 키가 크다.

② 비교급 구문은 두 대상 중 하나가 우월함을 나타낸다.
Kenneth is **taller than** Ashley. Kenneth는 Ashley보다 키가 더 크다.

③ 최상급 구문은 셋 이상의 대상 중 하나가 가장 우월함을 나타낸다.
Kenneth is **the tallest** one in the group. Kenneth는 그 집단에서 가장 키가 큰 사람이다.

위의 세 문장이 형용사 tall로 비교되고 있는 것과 같이, 비교 구문에서는 여러 대상의 '성질'을 비교하는 경우가 많으므로 성질을 나타내는 품사인 형용사나 부사가 비교 구문에 나오게 된다.

2 원급, 비교급, 최상급에서 형용사와 부사는 각각 다른 형태를 가진다.

① 1음절 단어 또는 -er, -y, -ow, -some으로 끝나는 2음절 단어

원급(일반형태)	비교급(원급 + er)	최상급(원급 + est)
tall	taller	tallest
easy	easier	easiest

② -able, -ful, -ous, -ive로 끝나는 2음절 단어 또는 3음절 이상의 단어

원급(일반형태)	비교급(more + 원급)	최상급(most + 원급)
useful	more useful	most useful
dangerous	more dangerous	most dangerous

③ 불규칙한 형태를 가지는 단어

원급	비교급	최상급
good / well	better	best
bad / ill	worse	worst
many / much	more	most
little	less	least
late	later / latter	latest / last

1 원급

'~만큼 –한'이라는 의미로 두 대상의 동등함을 나타내는 원급 표현은 'as + 형용사 / 부사의 원급 + as'를 쓴다.

His skin was as cold as ice. 그의 피부는 얼음만큼 차가웠다.

Chris held the baby as carefully as he could. Chris는 그가 할 수 있는 한 조심스럽게 아기를 안았다.

고득점 포인트 1. as ~ as 사이가 형용사 자리인지 부사 자리인지는 as, as를 지우고 구별한다.

After midnight, the house was as ~~quietly~~ as could be. (→ quiet) ← After midnight, the house was **quietly**. (→ quiet)
자정 후에 그 집은 더없이 조용했다.
└ '조용하다'는 의미의 보어로 쓰이고 있으므로, 부사(quietly)가 아니라 형용사(quiet)가 와야 한다.

She moved as ~~quiet~~ as she could. (→ quietly) ← She moved ~~quiet~~. (→ quietly) 그녀는 가능한 조용하게 움직였다.
└ '조용하게'라는 의미로 동사(moved)를 수식하고 있으므로, 형용사(quiet)가 아니라 부사(quietly)가 와야 한다.

2. '~만큼 –하지 않은'을 의미하는 경우 'not + as[so] ~ as'로 쓴다.

Your commute is **not as long as** mine is. 너의 통근거리는 내 통근거리만큼 멀지 않다.

'~만큼 많은 / 적은 –'을 나타내는 원급 표현은 'as + many / much / few / little + 명사 + as'를 쓴다.

She buys as many CDs as she can listen to. 그녀는 그녀가 들을 수 있을 만큼 많은 CD를 산다.

She uses as little heat as she can during the winter. 그녀는 겨울 동안 할 수 있는 한 적은 난방을 사용한다.

고득점 포인트 as ~ as 사이의 수량 형용사는 뒤의 명사가 가산 명사인지 불가산 명사인지에 유의하여 선택한다.

They had as ~~much~~ children as their parents did. (→ many) 그들은 그들의 부모님이 낳았던 만큼 많은 아이들을 낳았다.
└ 가산 명사(children) 앞이므로 much가 아니라 many가 와야 한다.

We bought as ~~many~~ food as we could for the feast. (→ much) 우리는 연회를 위해 살 수 있는 만큼 많은 음식을 샀다.
└ 불가산 명사(food) 앞이므로 many가 아니라 much가 와야 한다.

'~배 만큼 –하다'는 의미를 나타내기 위해 '배수사 + as + 원급 + as'를 쓴다.

The second room is twice as big as the first one. 두 번째 방은 첫 번째의 두 배만큼 크다.

고득점 포인트 배수사 자리에 퍼센트, 분수 등의 '부분'을 나타내는 표현이 올 수 있다.

Female workers earn **80 percent** as much as their male counterparts. 여성 근로자들은 남성 근로자들의 80퍼센트만큼 돈을 번다.

☑ 텝스 실전 문제

텝스 문제 이렇게 나온다

'as + 형용사 / 부사 + as'를 채우거나 'as + 형용사 / 부사 + as'의 형태가
틀린 문장을 찾는 문제가 주로 나온다.
'as + many / much / few / little + 명사 + as'를 채우는 문제가 가끔 나온다.

Part III

(a) A: I understand you asked Bruce to take over
the Parrotti account. Why didn't you ask
Allison to?

(b) B: Bruce has no other projects to work on right
now. Allison already has the Vigora job.

(c) A: Yes, but Bruce is not competent at
bookkeeping as Allison is, and Parrotti is a
major account for us.

(d) B: I understand, but our only other option is to
reassign some of Allison's work, which could
cause major delays.

Part II

2. Though they may receive steep fines, parents in
China are technically allowed to have as _____
children as they wish.

(a) much   (b) more

(c) many   (d) less

정답 p.71

1 '~보다 −한'이라는 의미로 두 대상 중 한쪽이 우월함을 나타내는 비교급 표현은 '형용사/부사의 비교급 + than'을 쓴다.

The new cell phone model is more expensive than the last model. 신형 휴대 전화 모델은 지난 모델보다 더 비싸다.

She spoke louder than the other guests. 그녀는 다른 손님들보다 더 크게 말했다.

고득점 포인트 '~보다 덜 −한'을 의미하는 경우 'less + 형용사/부사 + than'을 쓴다.
My new laptop is **less bulky than** my old one. 나의 새 노트북 컴퓨터는 예전 것보다 부피가 더 작다.

2 '~보다 더 많은/적은 −'을 나타내기 위해 비교급 표현 'more/fewer/less + 명사 + than'을 쓴다.

More women than men major in psychology. 남자보다 더 많은 여자들이 심리학을 전공한다.

3 '더 ~할수록, 더 −하다'는 의미를 나타내기 위해 'the + 비교급 + 주어 + 동사 ~, the + 비교급 + 주어 + 동사 −'를 쓴다.

The healthier you are, the longer you will live. 네가 더 건강할수록, 더 오래 살 것이다.
　　the + 비교급 + 주어 + 동사　　　the + 비교급 + 주어 + 동사

▶ '더 건강할수록 더 오래 산다'는 의미를 나타내기 위해, 'the + 비교급 + 주어 + 동사, the + 비교급 + 주어 + 동사'의 구조를 쓴다.

4 하나의 사람이나 사물이 가진 두 가지 성질이나 성격을 비교할 때는 'more + 원급 + than + 원급' 형태로 쓴다.

Bernard is ~~slier~~ than wise. Bernard는 현명하다기 보단 교활하다.
　　　　　more sly

▶ 한 사람(Bernard)의 성격에 대해 현명한지 교활한지를 비교하고 있으므로, 비교급 slier가 아니라 'more + 원급'인 more sly가 와야 한다.

5 비교급을 강조하기 위해서 much, even, still, far, a lot, by far 등이 비교급 표현 앞에 온다.

My daughter is much taller than she was a year ago. 내 딸은 일 년 전보다 훨씬 더 키가 크다.

▶ 비교급(taller)을 강조하여 '훨씬'이라는 의미를 나타내기 위해 부사 much가 쓰였다.

고득점 포인트 1. 부사 any는 보통 부정문과 의문문, 조건절에서 '조금도', '조금은'이라는 의미로 비교급을 강조한다.
Chloe doesn't feel **any** better today. Chloe는 오늘 기분이 조금도 더 나아지지 않았다.

2. 부사 still은 비교급을 뒤에서도 수식할 수 있다.
The pool is nice, but the sauna is **better still**. 수영장이 멋지지만, 사우나가 훨씬 더 좋다.

3. 비교급을 강조하는 표현으로 very, too, so, that 등의 부사는 올 수 없고, 이러한 부사들 뒤에는 원급이 와야 한다.
Eating moderately is ~~very~~ better than eating a lot. (→ **much/even/still**) 적당히 먹는 것은 많이 먹는 것보다 훨씬 더 좋다.
Tying a shoelace isn't that ~~easier~~. (→ **easy**) 구두 끈을 묶는 것은 그렇게 쉽지 않다.

└ 비교급(better)을 강조하기 위해 very가 아니라 much/even/still 등의 부사가 와야 하고, 부사 that 뒤에는 비교급(easier)이 아니라 원급(easy)이 와야 한다.

☑ 텝스 실전 문제
텝스 문제 이렇게 나온다

| 형용사나 부사의 비교급 표현을 채우는 문제가 주로 나온다.
| 비교급을 강조하는 표현을 채우는 문제가 주로 나온다.

Part I

1. A: The temperature really dropped after the sun went down.
   B: The darker the sky gets, _____.

   (a) it seems to feel the colder
   (b) the colder it seems to feel
   (c) the colder feel it to seems
   (d) it seems the colder to feel

Part II

2. Police have made the city streets _____ safer than they were a decade earlier.

   (a) very　　　　　　(b) much
   (c) well　　　　　　(d) most

정답 p

3 최상급

'~ 중에 가장 -한'이라는 의미로 셋 이상의 대상 중 하나가 가장 우월함을 나타내는 최상급 표현은 '형용사 / 부사의 최상급 + of ~ / in ~ / that절'을 쓴다.

Abraham Lincoln is often considered the greatest of all the U.S. presidents.
링컨은 종종 역대 미 대통령들 중에 가장 훌륭한 대통령으로 간주된다.

The Anderson House is the oldest building in Canada.   Anderson House는 캐나다에서 가장 오래된 건물이다.

This is the cheapest apartment that I have found.   이것은 내가 발견한 것 중에 가장 저렴한 아파트이다.

고득점 포인트

1. 최상급 뒤에 오는 명사가 무엇인지 명확할 경우, 명사를 생략할 수 있다.
   He is **the tallest (player)** of all the players in his team.   그는 그의 팀 선수들 중에서 가장 키가 큰 선수이다.

2. 최상급 뒤의 that절에는 주로 현재완료 시제가 온다.
   The SR-71 is **the fastest** jet that the pilots have ever flown.   SR-71은 조종사들이 비행해본 제트기들 중에 가장 빠른 제트기이다.

'최상급 + 명사' 앞에는 반드시 the나 소유격이 와야 한다.

Hitting a homerun was the / my greatest achievement.   홈런을 친 것은 (나의) 가장 큰 성취였다.
　　　　　　　　　　　　　the　소유격　　　최상급 + 명사

'~ 번째로 가장 -한'이라는 의미를 나타내기 위해 'the + 서수 + 최상급'을 쓴다.

Brazil is the fifth largest country in the world by territory.   브라질은 영토로 치면 세계에서 다섯 번째로 가장 큰 나라이다.

최상급을 강조하기 위해서 by far, quite 등이 최상급 표현 앞에 온다.

It was by far the hardest test that I had ever taken.   그것은 내가 치러본 시험 중 단연코 가장 어려운 시험이었다.

☑ 텝스 실전 문제

형용사나 부사의 최상급 표현을 the나 서수 등과 함께 채우는 문제가 주로 나온다.
최상급을 강조하는 표현을 채우는 문제도 가끔 나온다.

Part II

1. Having reached 119 years of age, Sarah Knauss became _____ human being known to have lived.

   (a) the oldest third　　(b) third the oldest
   (c) the third oldest　　(d) oldest the third

Part I

2. A: Why did you ask John to join your team?
   B: He's _____ the most talented athlete.

   (a) as ever　　(b) even
   (c) of all　　(d) by far

정답 p.72

1 원급 · 비교급 형태로 최상급 의미를 만드는 표현

- no other 단수 명사/nothing ~ as + 원급 + as (어떤 다른 –도 ~만큼 ~하지 않다)
  no other 단수 명사/nothing ~ 비교급 + than (어떤 다른 –도 ~보다 더 ~하지 않다)
  No other subject is as boring to him as history. 어떤 다른 과목도 그에게 역사만큼 지루하지는 않다.
  Nothing is more boring to him than history. 어떤 다른 것도 그에게 역사보다 더 지루하지는 않다.

- 비교급 + than any other + 단수 명사 (어떤 다른 –보다 더 ~한)
  History is more boring to him than any other subject. 역사는 그에게 어떤 다른 과목보다 더 지루하다.

- have + never/hardly/rarely + p.p. + 비교급 (더 ~해 본 적이 없다)
  I have rarely been busier than I am this week. 나는 이번 주보다 더 바빠 본 적이 없다.

2 원급 · 비교급 · 최상급 관련 표현

원급	as soon as possible 가능한 빨리 as ~ as can be 더없이	Deliver this package as soon as possible. 이 소포를 가능한 빨리 배달해라. Today the weather is as hot as can be. 오늘 날씨는 더없이 덥다.
비교급	more than 보다 더 많은/이상 less than 보다 더 적은/이하 no later than ~까지는 no longer 더 이상 ~않다 no sooner ~ than - ~하자마자 –하다 other than ~말고, ~않은	Exercise more than 30 minutes a day. 하루에 30분 이상 운동해라. Less than half of the class was present. 학급의 반 이하가 출석했다. Be back no later than 7 p.m. 저녁 7시까지는 돌아와라. She no longer needs braces. 그녀는 더 이상 치아 교정기를 필요로 하지 않는다. No sooner had we started driving than the engine failed. 우리가 출발하자마자 엔진이 고장 났다. Other than mysteries, I enjoy romance novels. 추리소설 말고 나는 연애소설을 즐긴다.
최상급	at least 적어도 at best 잘해야, 기껏해야 at most 기껏해야, 많아야 the world's + 최상급 세계에서 가장 ~한 one of the + 최상급 가장 ~한 –중 하나	Brush your teeth at least three times a day. 적어도 하루에 세 번 이를 닦아라. Your car will only run for three more years at best. 너의 차는 잘해야 3년 남짓 운행할 수 있을 것이다. It takes at most fifteen minutes to fill out this survey. 이 설문 조사를 기입하는 데는 기껏해야 15분이 걸린다. They sell the world's finest wine. 그들은 세계에서 가장 훌륭한 와인을 판다. He is one of the greatest poets. 그는 가장 위대한 시인 중 하나다.

3 비교 구문 관련 관용표현

I can't agree with you more. 너에게 전적으로 동의한다.   It couldn't be better. 더할 나위 없이 좋다.

☑ 텝스 실전 문제

텝스 문제 이렇게 나온

│ 원급 · 비교급 형태로 최상급 의미를 만드는 표현을 채우는 문제가 주로 나
온다.
│ 원급 · 비교급 · 최상급 관련 표현이 틀린 문장을 찾는 문제가 가끔 나온다.

Part II

1. _____ as much damage to human
lungs as do carcinogens.

   (a) Substances cause
   (b) Any substance causes
   (c) Any other substances cause
   (d) No other substance causes

Part III

2. (a) The Great Pyramid of Giza is the largest and
oldest pyramid in Egypt. (b) Situated in the Giza
Necropolis, it can be found surrounded by severa
smaller pyramids. (c) The Great Pyramid is believ
to have taken more than twenty years to assemb
by tens of thousands of workers. (d) Not until
nearly four thousand years after its completion
was it surpassed as the world's taller structure.

정답 p.

중 알맞은 것을 고르세요.

We are all hoping for as (little / less) rain as possible during our trip to the Caribbean.

No other sport has (more / most) popularity than soccer in Brazil.

The playground of your school is (as twice / twice as) large as that of mine.

Garry Kasparov is considered the (greater / greatest) of all chess masters to ever play the game.

The average giraffe has a life expectancy three times as (short / shortly) as an elephant's.

Because he's been ill so often lately, I was surprised that he felt much (healthy / healthier) today.

부분이 있으면 바르게 고치세요.

I had absolutely no idea she was that better of a computer programmer.

The Mona Lisa is arguably one of the more well-known paintings in the world.

Being kind to others has always been his most important goal in life.

The longer the argument with my husband lasted, the more I became disappointed.

The residents of the flooded neighborhood were asked to evacuate their homes as sooner as possible.

The professor's lecture lasted too longer than any of the students had expected.

Hackers **TEST**

Part I Choose the best answer for the blank.

01 A: This apartment needs a lot of cleaning.
B: Indeed. I couldn't agree with you _____.

(a) much   (b) more
(c) good   (d) better

02 A: I don't like how angry your dog looks when it barks.
B: Don't be afraid. She's _____.

(a) friendlier than fiercer
(b) friendlier than is she fiercer
(c) more friendly rather than fierce
(d) more friendly than fierce

03 A: Sherry always has a smile on her face lately.
B: That's because she's as excited about graduating _____ she is about starting her new job.

(a) as   (b) for
(c) than   (d) so

04 A: Has your class been _____ better since you hired that tutor?
B: Yes. I finally understand the material.

(a) so   (b) any
(c) that   (d) more

05 A: Margaret asked the manager to put off the meeting.
B: Really? That's _____.

(a) so a relief   (b) so relief a
(c) such a relief   (d) a such relief

06 A: What do you think of your new camera?
B: It's great. _____ it would be.

(a) I expected it than smaller
(b) I expected it's smaller than
(c) It's smaller than I expected
(d) It's smaller I expected than

Part II Choose the best answer for the blank.

07 The deeper you descend underwater, _____ t light becomes.

(a) dim   (b) dimmer
(c) the dimmer   (d) it is dimmer

08 This summer felt _____ any w had previously experienced.

(a) as warm than   (b) than warmer
(c) warmer than   (d) more than warm

09 The crater given the name of Apollo is _____
_____.

(a) the large on the Moon
(b) of the larger on the Moon
(c) one of large on the Moon
(d) one of the largest on the Moon

10 The scientist's eccentric ideas about the civil rig of robots are as divorced from reality _____

(a) as can be   (b) as can be it
(c) it can be   (d) it can be as

11 The party's members were thrilled to win so ma seats in the Senate, but _____ the news that they had overturned the majority.

(a) still was better
(b) still better it was
(c) it was still better
(d) better still was

12 This medication should only be taken once every evening _____ otherwise instructed by your physician.

(a) if   (b) unless
(c) because   (d) meanwhile

The governor suggested that juvenile delinquency could be _____ the state's school system has ever faced.

(a) greater threat
(b) greatest threat
(c) the greater threat
(d) the greatest threat

Lin Yu-chin is _____ man ever verified, and currently the record holder for those still living.

(a) shortest the second
(b) the shortest second
(c) second the shortest
(d) the second shortest

Scientists worry that the world's population is expanding at _____ rate than there is enough food to provide for.

(a) the fast
(b) the faster
(c) a much faster
(d) a much more fast

_____ about your feelings, the more others will doubt your sincerity.

(a) Are you being honest less
(b) The less honest you are
(c) The less honest are you
(d) As you are honest less

t III Identify the option that contains an awkward expression or an error in grammar.

(a) A: Help me decide which wallpaper would look best in my kitchen.
(b) B: I think this shade of blue would match the interior well.
(c) A: No, it's much dark and would create a gloomy atmosphere.
(d) B: It's just a little darker than what you have in your kitchen right now.

18 (a) A: Earl, I'm surprised to see you at work already.
(b) B: I arrive here at 6:30 every morning.
(c) A: Really? Why do you need to get here so earlier?
(d) B: It gives me time to prepare for my daily tasks.

19 (a) A type of hot air balloon called the hopper balloon was designed to carry a single occupant.
(b) Replacing the customary basket, a harness or seat suspends the passenger below the balloon.
(c) Because of this design, the hopper is small when compared to standard hot air balloons.
(d) The envelope volume of regular hot air balloons is fifteen times large than that of hoppers.

20 (a) B and T cells play a central role in the human immune system by protecting the body against harmful diseases. (b) Humans born with B and T cell immunodeficiency face a more severe risk from viruses than those with no deficiency. (c) By lacking proper defenses, those with immune deficiencies are likely to become much ill after contracting diseases. (d) The best way to ensure the survival of infants with this deficiency is through bone marrow transplants.

CHAPTER **21** 생략 · 대용 / 도치

BASIC GRAMMAR 고수로 가는 첫 걸음

1 같은 어구가 반복될 때, 반복을 피하기 위해 반복되는 어구 자체를 삭제하는 것을 생략, 다른 말로 대신하는 것을 대용이라고 한다.

① 생략: 반복되는 어구를 완전히 지운다.
  I finished the exam earlier than you finished the exam. 나는 네가 시험을 끝냈던 것보다 더 일찍 시험을 끝냈다.
  → I finished the exam earlier than you. 나는 너보다 더 일찍 시험을 끝냈다.

  첫 번째 문장에서 반복되는 똑같은 어구(finished the exam)를 생략하여 두 번째 문장처럼 쓸 수 있다.

② 대용: 반복되는 어구를 하나의 다른 단어로 대신한다.
  Martin believes that we need a new car, but I don't think that we need a new car.
  Martin은 우리에게 새 차가 필요하다고 생각하지만, 나는 우리에게 새 차가 필요하다고 생각하지 않는다.
  → Martin believes that we need a new car, but I don't think so.
  Martin은 새로운 차가 필요하다고 생각하지만, 나는 그렇게 생각하지 않는다.

  첫 번째 문장에서 반복되는 어구(that we need a new car)를 so로 대신하여 두 번째 문장처럼 쓸 수 있다.

2 주어와 동사의 위치가 바뀌는 것을 도치라고 하며, 도치는 주로 특정한 말을 강조하기 위해 문장의 맨 앞으로 이동 시킬 때 일어난다.

Steve was never happier than when he got promoted. Steve는 그가 승진했을 때보다 더 행복했던 적은 없었다.
주어 동사

Never was Steve happier than when he got promoted.
동사 주어

조동사(have/be동사 포함)가 있는 경우는 조동사가 주어 앞으로 나가지만, 조동사 없이 일반동사만 있을 경우에는 do동사(do/does/did)가 앞으로 나가고 그 자리에 있던 일반동사는 원형으로 바뀐다.

You can enter the library only after 10 a.m. 당신은 오전 10시 이후에만 도서관에 들어올 수 있습니다.
→ Only after 10 a.m. can you enter the library.

Benny rarely eats out. Benny는 거의 외식하지 않는다.
→ Rarely does Benny eat out.

01 절에서의 생략·대용

등위 접속사로 연결된 절에서 반복되는 어구는 모두 생략할 수 있다.

The Enlightenment was an era of intellectualism and of social reform. 계몽주의는 지성주의와 사회적 개혁의 시대였다.
                                                    (the Enlightenment was an era)

▶ 등위 접속사(and)로 연결된 절에서 the Enlightenment was an era가 반복되므로, 이를 생략하고 of social reform만 쓴다.

The store lights need to be turned on during the day, but not left on at night.
                                        (the store lights need) (to be)

가게의 전등은 낮 동안엔 켜져 있을 필요가 있지만, 밤에는 켜놓을 필요가 없다.

▶ 등위접속사(but)로 연결된 절에서 the store lights need to be가 반복되므로, 이를 생략하고 left on at night만 쓴다.

의문사절에서 의문사 뒤에서 언급한 내용이 반복되면 의문사만 쓰고 반복되는 내용은 생략한다.

A: Flyers say that a new restaurant will open soon. 전단지에 새로운 음식점이 곧 개점한다고 써 있어.
B: But they don't say when. 하지만 전단지에 언제 개점하는지는 써 있지 않아.
                (the new restaurant will open)

▶ 의문사(when) 뒤에 앞서 언급한 내용(a new restaurant will open)이 반복되므로, 의문사만 쓰고 이를 생략한다.

고득점 포인트 의문사 why, '의문사 + to부정사'의 경우에는 의문사 뒤에 not이 올 수 있다.
A: Can I take next Monday off? 제가 다음 주 월요일에 쉴 수 있나요?
B: I don't see why not. 나는 당신이 다음 주 월요일에 왜 쉴 수 없는지 모르겠네요. (당연히 휴가를 낼 수 있다)
      (you can) (take next Monday off)
↳ why 뒤에 앞서 언급한 내용(Can I take next Monday off)이 부정문으로 반복되고 있으므로, why not을 쓰고 반복되는 내용은 생략한다.

hope, guess, be afraid, think, suppose 등의 동사 뒤에서 앞서 언급한 내용이 that절로 반복될 때, that절이 긍정문이면 so로, 부정문이면 not으로 대신한다.

A: Will it rain tomorrow? 내일 비가 올까?
B: I hope so / not. (← that it will rain tomorrow / that it won't rain tomorrow) 내일 비가 오길 바라. / 내일 비가 오지 않기를 바라.

▶ hope 뒤에서 앞서 언급한 내용(it will / won't rain tomorrow)이 that절로 반복되므로, that절이 긍정문인 경우 so로, 부정문인 경우 not으로 대신한다.

고득점 포인트 know, be sure 뒤에서 앞서 언급한 내용이 that절로 반복되면 that절 자체를 생략하거나 it으로 대신한다.
A: There will be a fire drill today. 오늘 화재 대피 훈련이 있을 거야.
B: Yes, I know (it). (← that there will be a fire drill today) 응, 나도 오늘 화재 대피 훈련이 있을 것이라는 걸 알아.
↳ 동사 know 뒤에서 앞서 언급한 내용(there will be a fire drill today)이 that절로 반복되므로, that절 전체를 생략하거나 it으로 대신한다.

✅ 텝스 실전 문제

텝스 문제 이렇게 나온다

절에서 반복된 어구를 생략하고 채우는 문제가 주로 나온다.
반복되는 어구를 대신하는 so나 not을 채우는 문제가 주로 나온다.

Part II

The men and women who gave their lives in the Vietnam Conflict will be forever honored and their memory _____.

(a) forgets not   (b) forgetting not
(c) won't forgot   (d) not forgotten

Part I

2. A: I've never cooked steak before, so I'm afraid I might burn it.
   B: I sure _____.

(a) hope not   (b) hope so not
(c) don't hope it   (d) hope it not

정답 p.75

1 조동사 뒤에 앞에 나온 어구가 반복되면, 조동사까지만 쓰고 반복되는 내용은 생략한다.

A: Do you <u>have any change</u>? 잔돈 조금 있니?

B: Sorry, I <u>don't</u>. 미안, 나는 약간의 잔돈도 없어.
(have any change)

▶ 조동사(don't) 뒤에 앞에 나온 어구(have any change)가 반복되므로, don't만 쓰고 나머지는 생략한다.

She'll <u>come</u> as soon as she <u>can</u>. 그녀는 그녀가 올 수 있는 한 빨리 올 것이다.
(come)

▶ 조동사(can) 뒤에 앞에 나온 어구(come)가 반복되므로, can만 쓰고 나머지는 생략한다.

2 일반동사 이하에 앞에 나온 어구가 반복되면, 동사는 'do / does / did'를, 동사 뒤에 나오는 어구는 so로 대신하는데, 이때 so는 생략할 수 있다.

They <u>upgraded their Internet service</u> because everyone else did (so). (← <u>upgraded their Internet service</u>)
다른 모든 사람들이 인터넷 서비스 품질을 향상시켰기 때문에 그들도 인터넷 서비스 품질을 향상시켰다.

▶ 일반동사(upgraded) 이하에 앞에 나온 어구가 반복되므로 동사는 did로, 동사 이하 내용은 so로 대신한다. 이때 so는 생략할 수 있다.

고득점 포인트 앞에 나온 어구가 be동사 뒤에서 명사, 형용사 보어로 올 때, 이를 so로 대신하며, 이때 so는 생략할 수 있다.
A: He's <u>frustrated</u> that he lost his phone. 그는 그의 전화기를 잃어버려서 좌절했다.
B: Who wouldn't **be (so)**? (← **be** <u>frustrated</u>)? 좌절하지 않을 사람이 누가 있겠어?

ㄴ be동사 뒤에 앞서 언급된 형용사 보어(frustrated)가 반복되므로 so로 대신하거나 생략한다.

3 to부정사에서 to 뒤에 앞에 나온 어구가 반복되면, to로 대신하며, 이 경우 to를 '대부정사'라 한다.

A: Let's <u>go out for hamburgers</u>. 햄버거 먹으러 가자.

B: Because of my diet, I'm not able to. (← to <u>go out for hamburgers</u>) 내 식이요법 때문에 나는 햄버거 먹으러 갈 수가 없어.

▶ to 이하에 앞에 나온 어구(go out for hamburgers)가 반복되므로 to로 대신한다.

고득점 포인트 1. to 뒤에 반복되는 동사가 be동사일 경우에는 to be까지 쓰고 반복되는 내용은 생략한다.
A: Wasn't Maria <u>blonde</u>? Maria는 금발 아니었니?
B: She used **to be**. Now she dyed her hair black. 그랬었지. 지금은 머리를 검정으로 염색했어.
(blonde)

2. be ready, try 등 독립적으로 흔히 쓰이는 표현 뒤의 to부정사 이하가 앞에 나온 어구의 반복이면 to까지 모두 생략할 수 있다.
A: You should <u>search online for internship opportunities</u>. 너는 인턴십 고용 기회를 위해 온라인으로 검색을 해야 해.
B: OK, I will **try (to)**. 그래, 인턴십 고용 기회를 위해 온라인으로 검색해볼게.
(search online for internship opportunities)

ㄴ try 뒤에 쓰인 to부정사 이하에 앞에 나온 어구(search online for internship opportunities)가 반복되므로 to 이하를 생략하거나, to까지 모두 생략할 수 있다.

☑ 텝스 실전 문제

텝스 문제 이렇게 나온다

| 조동사나 to부정사 뒤에 반복되는 어구를 생략하고 조동사나 to부정사를 채우는 문제가 주로 나온다.
| to부정사에서의 대용 형태가 틀린 문장을 찾는 문제도 가끔 나온다.

Part I

1. A: Did you move out of your apartment yet?
   B: No, I _____. Can you come over to help me?

   (a) don't   (b) didn't
   (c) wasn't   (d) move out

Part III

2. (a) A: It would be nice if we went to the cinema,
          it's showing *Casablanca* on the big screen.
   (b) B: I'd like to do, but wouldn't it be cheaper ju
          to watch it on TV?
   (c) A: It's not about the cost. It's about the
          experience. I think it would be romantic.
   (d) B: OK, it does sound like a worthwhile thing t
          do.

정답 p.

3 도치 구문 1: 조동사 도치

부정이나 제한을 나타내는 부사(구/절)가 강조되어 문장의 맨 앞으로 나오면, 조동사와 주어가 도치되어 '조동사 + 주어 + 동사'의 어순이 된다.

부정을 나타내는 부사(구)	never 결코 ~않다	hardly / seldom / rarely / little 거의 ~않다	
	at no time 결코 ~않다	no sooner ~ than - ~하자마자 -하다	not until ~하고서야 비로소 -하다
	on no account 결코 ~않다	nowhere 어디에서도 ~않다	nor / neither ~도 역시 -않다
	by no means 결코 ~않다	under no circumstance 어떤 일이 있어도 ~않다	
제한을 나타내는 부사(구/절)	not only ~일 뿐 아니라	only + 부사구/절 오직 ~	

No sooner he had seen the police than he ran away. [×]
No sooner <u>had he seen</u> the police than he ran away. [○] 그는 경찰을 보자마자 도망쳤다.
　　　　　조동사 주어　동사
▶ 부정을 나타내는 부사구(No Sooner)가 문장의 맨 앞에 왔으므로 '조동사 + 주어 + 동사' 순으로 와야 한다.

Only after the show ended Ethan did notice he had sat in gum. [×]
Only after the show ended <u>did Ethan notice</u> he had sat in gum. [○] 공연이 끝난 후에야 Ethan은 그가 껌을 깔고 앉은 것을 알아 차렸다.
　　　　　　　　　　　　조동사　주어　동사
▶ 제한을 나타내는 'only +부사절'(Only after the show ended)이 문장의 맨 앞에 왔으므로 '조동사 + 주어 + 동사' 순으로 와야 한다.

고득점 포인트 neither는 부사이므로 2개의 절을 연결할 때 따로 접속사를 필요로 하지만, nor는 접속사로도 쓰이므로 혼자 절을 연결한다.

Diane can't stand the winter cold, and ~~nor~~ can she stand the summer heat. (→ **neither**)
Diane은 겨울의 추위를 참을 수 없고, 여름의 더위도 참을 수 없다.

Steven doesn't celebrate Thanksgiving, ~~neither~~ does he celebrate New Year's. (→ **nor**)
Steven은 추수감사절을 경축하지 않고, 새해의 첫 날도 경축하지 않는다.

↳ 첫 번째 문장은 접속사(and)가 있으므로 부사인 neither가 와야 하고, 두 번째 문장은 접속사가 없으므로, 접속사 역할을 하는 nor가 와야 한다.

'역시 그렇다'라는 표현인 so, neither / nor 뒤에는, 조동사와 주어가 도치되어 '조동사 + 주어'의 어순이 된다.

Glenda can make a fancy dress and <u>so can I</u>. Glenda는 고급 의상을 만들 수 있고, 나 역시 그렇다.
　　　　　　　　　　　　　　　　조동사 주어
▶ so를 사용해 앞의 말에 대해서 '~ 역시 그렇다'라는 의미를 나타내므로, '조동사 + 주어'(can I) 순으로 와야 한다.

Abigail was not taught to swim by Mr. Bill and <u>neither was I</u>. Abigail은 Mr. Bill에게 수영을 배우지 않았고, 나 역시 그렇다.
　　　　　　　　　　　　　　　　　　　　　　　　　조동사 주어
▶ neither를 사용해 앞의 말에 대해서 '~ 역시 그렇다'라는 의미를 나타내므로, '조동사 + 주어'(was I) 순으로 와야 한다.

고득점 포인트 앞의 말이 긍정문이면 so가, 부정문이면 neither/nor가 와야 한다.
I can write with both hands and **so** can my mother. 나는 양손으로 쓸 수 있고, 나의 엄마 역시 그렇다.
She doesn't like to go to the mall and **neither / nor** do I. 그녀는 쇼핑몰에 가는 것을 좋아하지 않고, 나 역시 그렇다.

↳ 첫 번째 문장은 앞의 말이 긍정문(I can write ~ hands)이므로 so가, 두 번째 문장은 부정문(She doesn't like ~ the mall)이므로 neither나 nor가 와야 한다.

☑ 텝스 실전 문제

텝스 문제 이렇게 나온다

'부정/제한을 나타내는 부사구/절 + 조동사 + 주어' 도치 구문을 채우는 문제가 주로 나온다.
'so/neither + 조동사 + 주어' 도치 구문을 채우는 문제가 주로 나온다.

Part II

1. Though Tamara disliked large families, _____ that one day she would have seven children of her own.

(a) little did she know　(b) little knew she
(c) she knew little　　　(d) she did little knew

2. Jane has never tried shark's fin soup and _____.

(a) so did I　　　　　(b) did I so
(c) neither have I　　(d) I have neither

정답 p.75

1 장소나 방향 등을 나타내는 부사(구)가 강조되어 문장의 맨 앞에 나올 때, 주어와 동사가 도치되어 '동사 + 주어'의 어순이 된다.

<u>Across the street</u> my best friend lives. [×]

<u>Across the street</u> <u>lives</u> <u>my best friend</u>. [○] 길 건너편에 내 가장 친한 친구가 산다.
      　　　　　　　　동사　　주어

　▶ 장소를 나타내는 부사구(Across the street)가 문장의 맨 앞에 왔으므로, '동사 + 주어' 순으로 와야 한다.

<u>There</u> the neighbor's dog goes. [×]

<u>There</u> <u>goes</u> <u>the neighbor's dog</u>. [○] 저기 이웃집 개가 지나간다.
　　　　동사　　　주어

　▶ 방향을 나타내는 부사(There)가 문장의 맨 앞에 왔으므로, '동사 + 주어' 순으로 와야 한다.

고득점 포인트

　1. 부사구 뒤에 콤마(,)가 있을 때는 도치가 일어나지 않는다.
　　On the roof, the rooster crows. 지붕 위에서, 수탉이 운다.

　2. 주어가 대명사일 경우 도치가 일어나지 않는다.
　　Here comes it. [×]
　　Here it comes. [○] 여기로 그것이 온다.
　　↳ 주어가 대명사(it)이므로, 장소를 나타내는 부사 Here가 문장의 맨 앞에 나와도 도치가 일어나지 않아, '주어 + 동사' 순으로 와야 한다.

2 형용사, 분사 보어가 강조되어 문장의 맨 앞에 나올 때, 주어와 동사가 도치되어 '동사 + 주어'의 어순이 된다.

<u>Undisturbed</u> the temple was near the construction area. [×]

<u>Undisturbed</u> <u>was</u> <u>the temple</u> near the construction area. [○] 공사 구역 근처에 절은 조용했다.
　　　　　　　동사　　주어

　▶ 보어(Undisturbed)가 강조되어 문장의 맨 앞에 왔으므로, '동사 + 주어' 순으로 와야 한다.

☑ 텝스 실전 문제

텝스 문제 이렇게 나온다

| '장소/방향을 나타내는 부사구 + 동사 + 주어' 도치 구문을 채우는 문제가 주로 나온다.
| 보어 강조 도치 구문의 어순이 틀린 문장을 찾는 문제가 가끔 나온다.

Part I

1. A: I'd like to meet your family.
　B: _____ right now. Let me introduce you to him.

　(a) Comes my husband here
　(b) Comes here my husband
　(c) Here my husband comes
　(d) Here comes my husband

Part III

2. (a) Ornithopters are aircraft that are distinguishe[d] from planes due to possessing wings that flap. (b) Aviators have tried building ornithopters capable of holding human passengers for long distances. (c) Unfortunately, such attempts have met with little success and are unlikely to succee[d] in the near future. (d) Even less likely the idea of turning ornithopters into a public mode of huma[n] transportation is.

정답 p.

해커스 텝스 Reading

중 알맞은 것을 고르세요.

Chris hasn't arrived at work yet, and (so / neither) has Terry.

Joe doesn't want to meet tomorrow, but I would (love to / love to do).

Karen thinks Lindsay is perfect for the job, and (so I do / so do I).

Most of the people at the rally came only because their friends (did / did it so).

I don't think I'll be able to complete the report by the deadline, but I'll (try / try to do).

Most students accepted into Ivy League universities get good grades, are active in school clubs, and (they do / do) volunteer work in the community.

부분이 있으면 바르게 고치세요.

My parents won't let me skateboard because they think it's dangerous, but I think so not.

At no time employees are allowed to visit unauthorized Internet sites at work.

The buyer wants to meet right now, but I won't be able until after 6:00.

Inside their one-person tents, the mountain climbers rested.

At first I was embarrassed because I couldn't sing very well, neither could she.

Gentle the breeze was as it blew along the coastline of the island.

정답 p.76

Hackers **TEST**

Part I Choose the best answer for the blank.

01 A: Shall we leave now?
   B: Yes, we are _____.

  (a) ready   (b) ready it
  (c) ready to do   (d) ready to it

02 A: No one in class can solve this problem.
   B: _____, and he's an expert.
  (a) The professor can't do
  (b) The professor can't so
  (c) Neither can the professor
  (d) Neither the professor can do

03 A: I haven't played tennis in years.
   B: Nor _____ I.

  (a) have   (b) had
  (c) haven't   (d) hadn't

04 A: Is it OK if we eat out tonight?
   B: I don't see why _____.

  (a) we not do   (b) don't we
  (c) don't   (d) not

05 A: The lawn needs some water to make it green
    again.
   B: The garden _____ as well.

  (a) needs   (b) needs to
  (c) does to   (d) does

06 A: Did you notice that taxi fares went up recently?
   B: _____ of public transportation,
    and now it's bad everywhere.

  (a) Did so the cost   (b) The cost did so
  (c) So the cost did   (d) So did the cost

07 A: Perry doesn't like his new job.
   B: He acts like nothing _____

  (a) for him is right   (b) he's right for it
  (c) is right for him   (d) is he's right for

08 A: Laura has been gone from work for almost a
    week. Do you think she'll come in tomorrow?
   B: She never said anything to me on the phone,
    but I guess _____.

  (a) so   (b) it is
  (c) it is so   (d) so it is

Part II Choose the best answer for the blank.

09 Billy wanted to wear his new beige suit, but he
   decided that it was _____ outfit
   the memorial.

  (a) casual a too   (b) a casual too
  (c) too casual an   (d) casual too an

10 My sister asked me to make a speech at my
   parents' 40th anniversary party, but I didn't
   _____.

  (a) want to do   (b) want to
  (c) want   (d) want do so

11 Melissa was not sure whether she passed the te
   because only the night before _____
   studying.

  (a) had she started   (b) does she start
  (c) she had started   (d) she does start

12 The Star of David is an emblem of Judaism and
   _____.

  (a) as well as of Israel
  (b) the nation Israel
  (c) of the nation of Israel
  (d) of Israel as well as

The jurors have not concluded their deliberations, _____ to one verdict or the other.

(a) nor they have gravitated
(b) nor have they gravitated
(c) have they neither gravitated
(d) neither they have gravitated

Isaac Asimov was very prolific and _____.

(a) a literary award winner
(b) awarded winner literary
(c) awarding winner was literary
(d) was literary to awarding winner

Due to a disappointing initial order, the publisher informed retailers that only under very unlikely circumstances _____.

(a) the book reprints
(b) the book is reprinted
(c) would the book reprinted
(d) would the book be reprinted

_____ a husband or father as dedicated to his family as Roger.

(a) There have never been
(b) There has never been
(c) Never there have been
(d) Never there has been

_____ than she began work on *Orlando*.

(a) *To the Lighthouse* had Virginia Woolf published no sooner
(b) *To the Lighthouse* no sooner had Virginia Woolf published
(c) No sooner *To the Lighthouse* Virginia Woolf had published
(d) No sooner had Virginia Woolf published *To the Lighthouse*

Part III Identify the option that contains an awkward expression or an error in grammar.

18 (a) A: Aren't you coming to the cast party after the play?
(b) B: I really can't. I have work scheduled very early the next day.
(c) A: You could just stop by for an hour or so.
(d) B: I won't be able since the play ends at 11 and I have to wake up at 5:30.

19 (a) Visitors to the Westwood Mountain camp grounds have recently reported sightings of a wild black bear. (b) Yesterday, one of our wildlife rangers confirmed those reports after she witnessed the bear herself. (c) Although the camp grounds will remain open, we ask that all visitors travel the grounds with a caution. (d) Further announcements will be made public as the situation develops and more information is known.

20 (a) The Tokyo metropolitan subway system consists primarily of two major networks. (b) Tokyo Metro is one such network, jointly owned by both the Japanese government and the Tokyo metropolitan government. (c) The other is commonly referred to as "Toei," meaning that it is operated solely by the city government. (d) Only recently there was a concerted effort to coordinate commuter transportation between both services.

혼자 하기 어렵고 막막할 땐?

해커스텝스(**HackersTEPS.com**)에서
스타강사의 무료 동영상강의 보기!

VOCABULARY

VOCABULARY

1 텝스 어휘 영역의 특징

1. 일상 생활에서 쓰이는 구어 표현에서 고난도 수준의 어휘까지 다양한 범위의 어휘가 출제된다.

텝스 어휘는 실용 영어 구사력과 고급 어휘력을 동시에 측정한다. Part 1에서는 일상 생활에서 많이 사용되는 구어들이 출제되고, Part 2에서는 문어체에서 다뤄지는 고급 어휘들이 출제된다. 이에 대비하기 위해서는 가정, 직장, 학서 쓰이는 실용 영어 표현의 쓰임과 경제, 정치, 문화, 과학 등의 다양한 분야의 어휘에 익숙해져야 한다.

2. 짧은 시간 안에 풀어내는 어휘 능력을 평가한다.

텝스 어휘&문법 영역에는 통합 25분이 주어진다. 어휘 영역은 문법 영역에 비해 상대적으로 문제 길이가 짧기 때약 10분 정도의 시간을 할애하는 것이 권장된다. 10분 정도의 시간에 30문제를 풀기 위해서는, 문제를 읽자마자 속있고 정확하게 문제를 풀어낼 수 있어야 하며, 모르는 문제에서 시간을 낭비하기보다는 아는 문제 중심으로 재빨어나갈 수 있도록 시간을 효과적으로 배분해야 한다.

3. 뒤로 갈수록 난이도가 높은 문제들이 출제된다.

텝스 어휘에서는 각 파트별로 앞부분에서 난이도가 쉬운 어휘들이 출제되고 뒤로 갈수록 어려운 어휘들이 출제된다히 Part 2의 20~30번에는 고난도의 어휘가 출제되므로, 비교적 쉬운 앞부분부터 차례로 재빨리 풀어나가서 난이높은 뒷부분에 시간을 할애할 수 있도록 해야 한다.

4. 어휘의 단편적인 의미만을 묻는 것이 아니라 쓰임새를 묻는다.

텝스 어휘는 대화나 단문을 주고 빈칸에 들어갈 적절한 어휘를 고르는 방식으로 출제된다. 따라서 어휘의 의미만답을 고를 수 없고, 문맥에서 쓰인 의미를 파악해야 한다. 어휘의 단편적인 의미뿐만 아니라 짧은 예문을 함께 학여 정확한 쓰임과 뉘앙스를 기억하고, collocation과 관용적 표현 같은 어구들은 하나의 어휘로 암기해두어야 한

2 텝스 어휘 출제 유형

텝스 어휘 문제는 Collocation, 관용적 표현, 일반 어휘로 유형을 나눌 수 있으며, 의미·형태상 혼동하기 쉬운 어휘답 보기로 자주 출제된다. 이러한 출제 유형을 「해커스 텝스 Reading」 어휘 영역에서는 네 가지 Section으로 구성텝스 어휘에서 출제된 기출 어휘들을 리스트로 다루고 있으며 실제 텝스 어휘 문제와 유사한 실전 문제를 통해 학습을 확인할 수 있다.

Collocation | collocation(연어), 즉 '단어와 단어 사이의 자연스러운 어울림'을 이루는 어휘를 묻는 유형이다. '동사 + 명collocation, '형용사 + 명사'의 collocation, '명사 + 명사'의 collocation으로 나눌 수 있다.

관용적 표현 | 일상 생활에서 구어적으로 하나의 어휘로 굳어져 쓰이는 표현을 묻는 유형이다. 이디엄, 일상 대화 표현, 구동나눌 수 있다.

일반 어휘 | 문맥상 적절한 의미의 어휘를 묻는 유형이다. 동사, 명사, 형용사와 부사로 나눌 수 있다.

혼동하기 쉬운 어휘 | 의미가 비슷하지만 쓰임새가 다르거나, 철자가 유사한 어휘들이 보기로 함께 제시되어 혼동을 주는 이묻는 유형이다. 의미상 혼동하기 쉬운 어휘와 형태상 혼동하기 쉬운 어휘로 나눌 수 있다.

텝스 어휘 출제 비율

텝스 어휘 영역의 문제 구성을 출제 유형별로 구분하여 그래프로 나타내면 다음과 같다. 또한 어휘를 품사별로 구분하여 출제 비율을 살펴보면 두 번째 그래프와 같다.

유형별 출제 비율

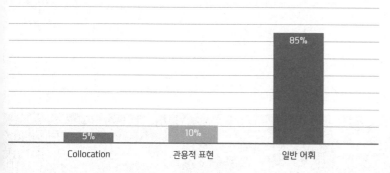

품사별 출제 비율

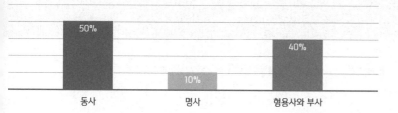

시험에 나올 문제를 미리 풀어보고 싶을 땐?

해커스텝스(HackersTEPS.com)에서
텝스 적중예상특강 보기!

Section 1 Collocation

CHAPTER 01 '동사 + 명사' Collocation

take medicine : 약을 먹다

아픈 친구와 약국에 간 마음씨 좋은 텝식씨, 약을 사고 take medicine하겠다는 친구에게 "Take? Eat! Eat! 가져가지 말고 얼른 여기서 먹으라고!!"라며 재촉한다. 하지만 '약'이든 '밥'이든 '먹다'라고 하는 우리말과 달리, 영어에서 명사 medicine과 어울려 '약을 먹다'라는 의미를 만드는 동사는 eat이 아니라 take. 이와 같이 동사와 명사 사이에는 함께 쓰일 때만 뜻이 통하는 collocation이 있다. 텝스 어휘에 출제되는 '동사 + 명사' collocation을 덩어리째 익혀보자.

■ 출제 경향

· '동사 + 명사' collocation 문제는 매 시험 평균적으로 1~2문제 정도 출제되며, Part 1과 Part 2에서 비슷한 비율로 출제된다.

· '동사 + 명사'의 collocation에서는 명사보다 동사를 묻는 문제가 주로 출제된다. 예를 들면, 'answer the phone(전화를 받다)'의 collocation에서 동사 answer를 답으로 묻는다.

■ 예제

Part I

A: Would you mind my sitting here?
B: Not at all! _____ a seat.

(a) Pass   (b) Apply
(c) Take   (d) Catch

> A: 제가 여기에 좀 앉아도 될까요?
> B: 그럼요! 앉으세요.

해설 | 빈칸 뒤의 명사 seat(좌석)과 어울려 쓰이는 동사는 (c) Take(취하다)이다. take a seat은 '자리에 앉다'라는 뜻이다. pass(전달하다), apply(바르다, 적용하다), catch(잡다)는 seat과 어울려 쓰이지 않는다.
정답 | (c) Take

Part II

The environment plays a major _____ in determining where people will choose to live.

(a) action   (b) role
(c) duty   (d) section

> 환경은 사람들이 살 곳을 선정하는 데 중요한 역할을 한다.

해설 | 빈칸 앞의 동사 play(수행하다)와 어울려 쓰이는 명사는 (b) role(역할)이다. play a role은 '역할을 하다'라는 뜻이다. action(행동), duty(의무), section(부분)은 play와 어울려 쓰이지 않는다.
정답 | (b) role

~ake
취하다, 타다, 복용하다

01 take a lesson[course] 수업을 듣다

I am thinking about taking swing dance lessons next months.
나는 다음 달에 스윙 댄스 수업을 듣는 것을 고려하고 있다.

02 take the initiative 앞장서서 하다, 솔선하다

Maria is outgoing and takes the initiative in introducing herself to others.
Maria는 외향적이어서 앞장서서 다른 사람들에게 자기소개를 한다.

03 take a risk 위험을 무릅쓰다

Businessmen must sometimes take risks when they start new ventures.
사업가들은 새로운 사업을 시작할 때 때때로 위험을 무릅써야 한다.

04 take a supplement[pill] 영양제를[알약을] 복용하다

If a diet is balanced, most people need not take vitamin supplements.
균형 잡힌 식사를 한다면, 대부분의 사람들은 비타민 영양제를 복용할 필요가 없다.

05 take the subway[elevator] 지하철을[엘리베이터] 타다

The quickest way to get downtown is to take the subway.
시내로 가는 가장 빠른 방법은 지하철을 타는 것이다.

~ake
만들다, 하다

06 make a living 생계를 꾸리다

His Internet business became successful enough for him to make a living off of it.
그의 인터넷 사업은 그가 생계를 꾸려 나갈 수 있을 정도로 성공했다.

07 make a fuss 수선을 떨다

Young kids usually make a fuss over hairstyle and fashion.
어린 청소년들은 대개 헤어스타일과 옷차림에 대해 수선을 떤다.

08 make an exception 예외를 두다

The company agreed to make an exception for an applicant who submitted his résumé late.
그 회사는 이력서를 늦게 제출한 지원자에 대해서 예외를 두는 것에 동의했다.

09 make an apology 사과하다

The mayor made a public apology for his inappropriate comments.
시장은 그의 부적절한 논평에 대해 공개 사과를 했다.

10 make a mistake 실수하다

He made a mistake filling out the form and had to start all over again.
그는 양식을 작성하다가 실수해서 처음부터 다시 시작해야 했다.

~o
하다, (이익 · 손해를) 끼치다

11 do the laundry 빨래하다

She spent the entire morning doing the laundry and ironing her clothes.
그녀는 아침 내내 빨래하고 옷을 다리미질하며 시간을 보냈다.

12 do one's hair 머리를 손질하다

My friends generally spend a great deal of time doing their hair before going out.
내 친구들은 대체로 외출하기 전에 머리를 손질하는 데 많은 시간을 소모한다.

13 do harm (=do damage) 해를 끼치다

Pesticides are known to do harm to the environment.
농약은 환경에 해를 끼치는 것으로 알려져 있다.

run

ⓥ 실시하다, 경영 · 관리하다,
(광고를) 내다, (열을) 내다

14 run a test 검사하다

The doctor will run some tests to determine the cause of your symptoms.
의사가 당신의 증상의 원인을 알아내기 위해 몇 가지 검사를 할 것이다.

15 run a business 사업하다

The beauty of the Internet is the possibility of running a business with little money.
인터넷의 장점은 적은 돈으로 사업할 수 있다는 것이다.

16 run an advertisement 광고를 내다

It can be expensive to run an advertisement in a major newspaper.
주요 신문에 광고를 내는 것은 비싸다.

17 run a fever 열이 나다

She felt fine during the day, but by evening she was running a fever.
그녀는 낮 동안에는 괜찮았지만 저녁이 되자 열이 나기 시작했다.

meet

ⓥ 충족시키다

18 meet one's needs[demand] 요구를 충족시키다

Our customer service team excels at meeting the needs of our clients.
저희 고객 서비스팀은 고객의 요구를 충족시키는 데 뛰어납니다.

19 meet a deadline 마감 기한에 맞추다

The team will work over the weekend to meet the deadline.
그 팀은 마감 기한에 맞추기 위해 주말 동안 일할 것이다.

deliver

ⓥ 전달하다, 분만시키다, 말하다

20 deliver a message 메시지를 전달하다

The congressman will deliver a message on global warming.
그 의원은 지구 온난화에 대한 메시지를 전달할 것이다.

21 deliver a baby 아기를 분만시키다

The doctor delivered the baby ten hours after the woman went into labor.
의사는 여자가 진통을 시작한지 10시간 후에 아기를 분만시켰다.

22 deliver a speech[a lecture, an address] 연설하다, 강의하다

He was very nervous when he delivered a speech last week.
그는 지난주에 연설했을 때 매우 긴장했다.

23 deliver a verdict 평결을 내리다

The jury delivered a guilty verdict at the trial of the accused kidnapper.
배심원들은 기소된 유괴범에 대한 재판에서 유죄 평결을 내렸다.

receive

ⓥ 받다

24 receive a refund 환불받다

If you are dissatisfied with the product for any reason, you will receive a full refund.
어떤 이유로든 제품에 대해 불만족하시면, 전액 환불받으실 수 있습니다.

25 receive a scholarship 장학금을 받다

Those who maintain an A average are eligible to receive a scholarship.
평균 A를 유지하는 이들에겐 장학금을 받을 자격이 주어진다.

raw
이끌어 내다

26 draw praise 칭찬을 이끌어 내다

The newspaper columnist drew praise for his perceptive comments.
신문 시사 평론가는 통찰력 있는 논평으로 칭찬을 이끌어 냈다.

27 draw a conclusion 결론을 이끌어 내다

Scientists have drawn the conclusion that Mars once had water.
과학자들은 화성에 한때 물이 있었다는 결론을 이끌어 냈다.

ll
채우다, 조제하다

28 fill a position 충원하다, 자리를 채우다

The accounting director retired and now we have to fill the position.
회계 부서장이 퇴임해서 현재 우리는 충원해야 한다.

29 fill a prescription 처방전대로 약을 조제하다

Could you fill this prescription for me?
이 처방전대로 약을 조제해주시겠습니까?

atch
병에) 걸리다, 잡아타다,
) 보다

30 catch (a) cold[a disease] 감기에[병에] 걸리다

She always catches colds during the winter season.
그녀는 겨울이면 항상 감기에 걸린다.

31 catch a flight 비행기를 타다

I caught a flight to visit family in Los Angeles.
나는 로스앤젤레스에 있는 가족을 방문하기 위해 비행기를 탔다.

32 catch a glimpse 얼핏 보다

The birdwatcher was able to catch a glimpse of the warbler before it flew away.
그 조류 관찰자는 휘파람새가 날아가버리기 전에 그것을 얼핏 볼 수 있었다.

old
개최하다, 지니다

33 hold a meeting[conference] 회의를 열다

The company manager held a conference to discuss a new project.
기업의 관리자는 새 프로젝트에 대해 논의하기 위해 회의를 열었다.

34 hold a grudge 원한을 품다

Despite his repeated apologies, she is still holding a grudge.
그의 반복된 사과에도 불구하고, 그녀는 여전히 원한을 품고 있다.

reak
기다, 깨뜨리다

35 break a law 법을 위반하다

A motorist who drives through a red light is breaking the law.
빨간 불을 무시하고 운전하는 운전자는 법을 위반하는 것이다.

36 break a record 기록을 경신하다

Barry Bonds broke the record for the greatest number of home runs in baseball.
Barry Bonds가 야구에서 최다 홈런 기록을 경신했다.

37 break the silence 침묵을 깨다

The only witness to the crime broke the silence and told the police what he had seen.
범죄의 유일한 목격자가 침묵을 깨고 경찰에게 그가 본 것을 이야기했다.

VOCABULARY | Collocation

해커스 팁스 Reading

둘 중 적절한 어휘를 골라 ∨ 표를 하세요.

01 ○ cast
   ○ throw a ballot   투표하다

02 ○ brew
   ○ mince tea   차를 끓이다

03 ○ give
   ○ make a stop   멈추다

04 ○ match
   ○ set the alarm   알람을 맞추다

05 ○ travel
   ○ admire the scenery   경치를 감상하다

06 ○ wear
   ○ apply moisturizer   보습제를 바르다

07 ○ operate
   ○ perform a machine   기계를 작동하다

08 ○ fetch
   ○ raise a question   문제를 제기하다

09 ○ defeat
   ○ impel the enemy   적을 무찌르다

10 ○ transmit
   ○ transfer a message   메시지를 보내다

11 ○ score
   ○ enter a goal   골을 넣다, 득점하다

12 ○ supply
   ○ support weight   무게를 지탱하다

13 follow ○ instructions   지시에 따르다
          ○ options

14 ○ pay
   ○ devote one's life   헌신하다

15 ○ conduct
   ○ arrange an investigation   조사·수사하다

16 ○ decorate
   ○ celebrate the new year   새해를 경축하다

17 ○ show
   ○ display a sign   징조를 보이다

18 ○ result
   ○ cause inconvenience   불편을 끼치다

19 ○ defend
   ○ deter crime   범죄를 억제하다

20 raise ○ trusts   모금하다
         ○ funds

○ defer ○ convey	a point	요점을 전달하다
take a	○ leave ○ break	휴식을 취하다
○ adapt ○ audit	a course	청강하다
make a	○ fortune ○ wealth	큰돈을 벌다
have	○ issue ○ trouble	애를 먹다
○ damage ○ cause	death	죽게 하다
○ call ○ uphold	a meeting	회의를 소집하다
○ spread ○ sprinkle	water	물을 뿌리다
○ accept ○ admit	an apology	사과를 받아들이다
○ practice ○ exercise	one's right	권리를 행사하다
○ make ○ bring	an excuse	변명하다
take	○ measures ○ means	조치를 취하다
○ draw ○ fetch	attention	주의를 끌다
do a	○ mercy ○ favor	부탁을 들어주다
○ break ○ answer	a habit	습관을 고치다
have a	○ crunch ○ hunch	대충 짐작하다
○ hold ○ press	one's breath	숨을 죽이다
○ regulate ○ apply	a law	법을 적용하다
○ change ○ modify	the subject	화제를 바꾸다
○ decide ○ reach	an agreement	합의에 도달하다

41	○ impose ○ inflict	a ban	금지하다
42	○ apply ○ handle	a situation	상황을 처리하다
43	○ entail ○ address	an issue	문제를 거론하다
44	○ launch ○ disperse	an attack	공격을 시작하다
45	○ make ○ work	an accusation	고소하다, 비난하다
46	○ weigh ○ measure	the consequences	결과를 숙고하다
47	○ crop ○ mow	the lawn	잔디를 깎다
48	○ draw ○ commit	suicide	자살하다
49	○ resolve ○ dissolve	the issue	문제를 해결하다
50	○ lose ○ drop	one's appetite	식욕을 잃다
51	○ strike ○ contract	a deal	거래하다
52	○ throw ○ create	a party	파티를 열다
53	○ raise ○ boost	sales	판매를 증진하다
54	○ wrap ○ pack	a bag	가방을 싸다
55	○ fight ○ overcome	obstacles	장애를 극복하다
56	○ turn ○ make	a right	우회전하다
57	○ conserve ○ preserve	energy	에너지를 절약하다
58	○ supply ○ offer	advice	충고하다
59	○ take ○ hold	a rally	집회를 열다
60	○ give ○ hand	a lift	차로 태워 주다

중 적절한 어휘를 골라 빈칸에 넣으세요.

regain	retain
recall	resume

| 61 | _____ health | 건강을 되찾다 |
| 62 | _____ work | 일을 다시 시작하다 |

reject	pass
skip	miss

| 63 | _____ class | 수업에 빠지다 |
| 64 | _____ an opportunity | 기회를 놓치다 |

sustain	spare
save	remain

| 65 | _____ the details | 자세하게 이야기하지 않다 |
| 66 | _____ growth | 성장을 유지하다 |

dismiss	detach
disclose	desert

| 67 | _____ an employee | 직원을 해고하다 |
| 68 | _____ a source | 출처를 밝히다 |

swing	click
ring	strike

| 69 | _____ a pose | (사진의) 포즈를 취하다 |
| 70 | _____ a bell | 벨을 누르다 |

release	discharge
publish	issue

| 71 | _____ the brake | 브레이크를 풀다 |
| 72 | _____ a visa | 비자를 발급하다 |

deserve	protect
reserve	resume

| 73 | _____ the right | 권리를 갖다 |
| 74 | _____ one's privacy | 사생활을 보호하다 |

extend	exploit
expand	exaggerate

| 75 | _____ a deadline | 마감 기한을 연장하다 |
| 76 | _____ the territories | 영토를 확장하다 |

hold	place
apply	make

| 77 | _____ an order | 주문하다 |
| 78 | _____ a difference | 차이를 낳다 |

reach	file
draw	stand

| 79 | _____ a suit | 소송을 제기하다 |
| 80 | _____ a pinnacle | 정점에 도달하다 |

정답 p.79

Hackers **TEST**

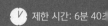

Part I Choose the best answer for the blank.

01 A: Do you think we'll be able to _____ the
    11:30 flight?
    B: Don't worry. We still have time.

  (a) depart   (b) catch
  (c) move   (d) leave

02 A: Shall we go out for coffee?
    B: Why don't we just stay home? I can _____
    some tea.

  (a) brew   (b) broil
  (c) blend   (d) stew

03 A: I don't know the first thing about _____ a
    business.
    B: For one thing, you need capital to get it
    started.

  (a) following   (b) attending
  (c) running   (d) chasing

04 A: The editor's assistant position needs to be
    _____ by next week.
    B: Then I'll review our recent applicants and
    choose the best one.

  (a) made   (b) brought
  (c) met   (d) filled

05 A: A shopper made a(n) _____ against one of
    our clerks.
    B: What was it about? I hope it's nothing serious.

  (a) failure   (b) accusation
  (c) confusion   (d) effort

06 A: Should we catch a bus to the museum?
    B: Actually, it'd be quicker to _____ the
    subway.

  (a) hold   (b) enter
  (c) board   (d) take

07 A: You have an exam this morning, right? I hope
    you ate breakfast.
    B: I couldn't eat. I've _____ my appetite.

  (a) lost   (b) broken
  (c) fled   (d) quit

08 A: I heard that the jury already _____ their
    verdict.
    B: Really? Is he innocent or guilty?

  (a) delivered   (b) transformed
  (c) deprived   (d) transmitted

Part II Choose the best answer for the blank.

09 The internationally renowned painter has never
    _____ a formal art course in her life.

  (a) spent   (b) borrowed
  (c) taken   (d) learned

10 The bank _____ clients' privacy by requiring
    security code to access each account.

  (a) contains   (b) withholds
  (c) protects   (d) restricts

High school students who graduate at the top of the class usually _____ a scholarship for university study.

(a) derive   (b) receive
(c) collect   (d) undertake

The university reminded students that their enrollment may be deferred if they fail to _____ the deadline for tuition payments.

(a) carry   (b) meet
(c) have   (d) bring

A special committee is going to _____ an investigation into workplace safety at the factory.

(a) conduct   (b) report
(c) involve   (d) hinder

A meeting of the executive committee was _____ to discuss several issues about the company's growth.

(a) taken   (b) admitted
(c) held   (d) uttered

Stanley decided to make a _____ as a freelance writer instead of getting a full-time job.

(a) surviving   (b) raising
(c) working   (d) living

16 Every year many of those who work or study abroad come back to their hometown to _____ the new year with their families.

(a) dedicate   (b) regulate
(c) maneuver   (d) celebrate

17 Organizations make use of different types of media to _____ their messages to the public.

(a) beguile   (b) preclude
(c) deliver   (d) convert

18 The candidate _____ praise for his strong and convincing arguments during the televised political debates.

(a) picked   (b) took
(c) caught   (d) drew

19 After recovering from a bad case of the flu, Larry took another day off to fully _____ his health.

(a) resume   (b) return
(c) revive   (d) regain

20 Environmentally conscious citizens can take the _____ to organize civilian cleanup committees.

(a) prescription   (b) priority
(c) initiative   (d) assignment

정답 p.80

CHAPTER 02 '형용사 + 명사' Collocation

a pop quiz : 깜짝 쪽지 시험

내일 pop quiz를 본다는 긴급 정보에 밤새 리한나와 저스틴 비버의 히트곡을 암기한 텝식씨, 어랏, 근데 공부한 게 하나도 안 나왔잖아? 텝식씨가 백지를 내야 했던 이유는 pop quiz는 팝송에 대한 시험이 아니라 '예고 없이 갑자기 보는 시험'을 뜻하기 때문. 그럼 surprise quiz가 아니냐고 텝식씨는 항변하지만 형용사와 명사 사이에도 함께 쓰일 때만 뜻이 통하는 collocation이 있다. 이처럼 텝스 어휘에 출제되는 '형용사 + 명사' collocation을 덩어리째 익혀보자.

■ 출제 경향

· '형용사 + 명사' collocation 문제는 매 시험 평균적으로 1~2문제 정도 출제되며, Part 1에 주로 나오고 Part 2에는 간혹 출제된다.

· '형용사 + 명사'의 collocation에서는 명사보다 형용사를 묻는 문제가 더 많이 출제된다. 예를 들면, 'sore throat(목감기)'의 collocat 에서 형용사 sore를 답으로 묻는다.

■ 예제

Part I

A: Do you know how to change a(n) _____ tire?
B: I have no idea. You'd better call the auto repair shop.

A: 펑크 난 타이어를 교체하는 방법을 알아요?
B: 모르겠어요. 자동차 정비소에 전화하는 편이 좋겠어요.

(a) empty   (b) scant
(c) dead   (d) flat

해설 | 빈칸 뒤의 명사 tire(타이어)와 어울려 쓰이는 형용사는 (d) flat(펑크 난, 바람이 빠진)이다. a flat tire는 '펑크 난 타이어'라는 뜻이다. empty(빈), scant(부족한), dead(죽은
tire와 어울려 쓰이지 않으므로 답이 될 수 없다.

어휘 | auto repair shop 자동차 정비소

정답 | (d) flat

Part II

A broad range of technical _____ is needed in order to be successful and competitive in the online business world.

온라인 비즈니스 세계에서 성공하고 경쟁력을 지니려면 광범위 전문 기술이 필요하다.

(a) skills   (b) assets
(c) credits   (d) means

해설 | 빈칸 앞의 형용사 technical(전문의, 기술적인)과 어울려 쓰이면서 '성공하고 경쟁력을 지니려면 광범위한 전문 _____이 필요하다'라는 문맥에 적절한 명사는 (a) skills 이다. technical skills는 '전문 기술'이라는 뜻이다. credit(신용)은 technical과 어울려 쓰이지 않으며, asset은 '자산', means는 '수단'이라는 뜻이다.

어휘 | range[reindʒ] 범위   competitive[kəmpétətiv] 경쟁력 있는

정답 | (a) skills

a common interest 공통의 관심사, 공동의 이익

Automobile companies share a common interest in improving safety measures.
자동차 회사들은 안전 조치를 개선하고자 하는 공통의 관심사를 공유한다.

modern conveniences 현대적 편의 용품·시설, 문명의 이기

Domestic life has been made easy through modern conveniences.
가정 생활은 현대적 편의 용품을 통해 편리해졌다.

an outside line 외부로 거는 전화

To get an outside line from this phone, you must dial '9' first.
이 전화기에서 외부로 전화를 걸려면, 먼저 '9'를 눌러야 한다.

a sharp contrast 현저한 차이

Readers have noted a sharp contrast between the author's earlier writings and his present works.
독자들은 작가의 초기 작품들과 현재 작품들 사이의 현저한 차이를 발견했다.

a once-in-a-lifetime opportunity 평생에 단 한 번뿐인 기회

Observing a total solar eclipse may be considered a once-in-a-lifetime opportunity.
개기일식을 관찰하는 것은 평생에 단 한 번뿐인 기회로 여겨질 수 있다.

a natural habitat 자연 서식지

Human activity has resulted in the destruction of animals' natural habitats.
인류의 활동은 동물 자연 서식지의 파괴를 초래했다.

a last resort 최후의 수단

Many farms use pesticides as a last resort if safer methods prove unsuccessful.
많은 농장들이 더 안전한 방법이 비효과적인 경우에 최후의 수단으로서 농약을 사용한다.

full name 성과 이름

Please write your full name on the application form.
신청서에 귀하의 성과 이름을 모두 써 주십시오.

a painful headache 괴로운 두통

I had such a painful headache that I was unable to concentrate on my work.
너무 괴로운 두통이 있어서 내 일에 집중할 수 없었다.

a perfect fit 딱 맞는 것·사람

The shoes were a perfect fit this morning, but they now feel a little tight.
신발이 오늘 아침에는 딱 맞았었는데, 지금은 약간 꼭 끼는 것 같다.

a strong indication 뚜렷한 조짐·증거

There is a strong indication that the economy will experience a downturn by year's end.
연말에 경제가 침체를 겪으리라는 뚜렷한 조짐이 있다.

a daunting task 힘겨운 일

Looking for a good but affordable apartment can be a daunting task.
좋지만 가격이 저렴한 아파트를 찾는 것은 힘겨운 일이다.

13 stifling heat 숨막히는 더위

Residents in this city go to the beach to get away from the stifling heat in summer.
이 도시의 시민들은 여름에 숨막히는 더위를 피하기 위해 해변으로 간다.

14 a volatile market (가격·가치가) 심하게 변동하는 시장

In a volatile market, investors tend to prefer more stable investments.
가격이 심하게 변동하는 시장에서, 투자자들은 좀 더 안정적인 투자를 선호하는 경향이 있다.

15 bodily fluids 체액

Infectious diseases can be passed on from one person to another through bodily fluids.
전염병은 체액을 통해 한 사람에게서 다른 사람에게로 전염될 수 있다.

16 a sudden change 급격한 변화·변경

A sudden change in climate may have led to the extinction of dinosaurs.
기후의 급격한 변화가 공룡의 멸종을 초래했을지도 모른다.

17 a feasible plan 실현 가능한 계획

The manager wants us to make a feasible plan for meeting product demand.
관리자는 우리가 상품 수요를 충족시킬 수 있는 실현 가능한 계획을 세우기를 원한다.

18 an endangered species 멸종 위기에 처한 종

Once nearly extinct, the gray wolf is now no longer an endangered species.
한때 거의 멸종했던 회색늑대는 현재는 더 이상 멸종 위기에 처한 종이 아니다.

19 an exhaustive list 총망라된 목록

The Web site provides an exhaustive list of films made in the 1960s.
그 웹 사이트는 1960년대에 제작된 영화의 총망라된 목록을 제공한다.

20 a late fee 연체료

Students need to pay a late fee on borrowed books that are overdue.
학생들은 연체된 대여 도서에 대해서 연체료를 지불해야 한다.

21 a connecting flight 연결편, 연결 비행기

Since there is no direct flight to Tokyo, you need to take a connecting flight.
도쿄로 가는 직항편이 없기 때문에, 연결편으로 갈아타셔야 합니다.

22 a distinctive characteristic 두드러진 특징

A distinctive characteristic of many snakes is their inability to tolerate cold weather.
많은 뱀의 두드러진 특징은 추운 날씨를 견디지 못한다는 점이다.

23 sick leave 병가

I had to give my employer a doctor's note for my three-day sick leave.
나는 3일간의 병가를 위해 고용주에게 의사의 진단서를 제출해야 했다.

24 temporary relief 일시적인 완화·경감

The medication provides temporary relief from the symptoms of a cold.
그 약은 감기 증상을 일시적으로 완화시켜준다.

a natural aversion 선천적 반감, 당연한 반감

Most people have a natural aversion to insects and worms.
대부분의 사람들은 선천적으로 곤충과 벌레를 싫어한다.

abject poverty 극도의 빈곤

A large number of people in third world countries know what abject poverty is.
제3세계 국가에서 살아가는 다수의 사람들은 극도의 빈곤이 무엇인지 알고 있다.

a regular guest 단골 손님

As a regular guest, you may avail of discounted accommodations and other perks.
단골 손님으로서, 귀하께서는 숙박 시설 할인과 다른 특혜를 누리실 수 있습니다.

a competitive price 경쟁력 있는 가격

The new grocery store offers customers a wide variety of products at competitive prices.
새로운 식료품 가게는 고객들에게 매우 다양한 상품을 경쟁력 있는 가격으로 제공한다.

an indelible impression 잊을 수 없는 인상

The young genius poet made an indelible impression on the reporter who interviewed him.
젊은 천재 시인은 그를 인터뷰한 기자에게 잊을 수 없는 인상을 남겼다.

an indigenous species 토착종

The brown bear is an indigenous species in the country and is protected by law.
불곰은 그 국가의 토착종이며 법에 의해 보호받는다.

an astute observation 날카로운 관찰력

In his book, the novelist made astute observations about the nature of human beings.
그의 책에서, 소설가는 인간의 본성에 대한 날카로운 관찰력을 보여주었다.

a good deed 선행

Not everyone wants to be recognized for a good deed they have done.
모든 사람이 자신이 베푼 선행이 알려지기를 원하는 것은 아니다.

prompt service 신속한 서비스

A company can win a customer's loyalty with reliable and prompt service.
회사는 믿을 만하고 신속한 서비스를 통해 고객의 충성을 얻을 수 있다.

a reasonable price 합리적인 가격

You can buy trendy clothing at a reasonable price at the mall.
당신은 그 쇼핑몰에서 합리적인 가격으로 최신 유행의 옷을 살 수 있습니다.

a unilateral decision 독단적인 결정

The president has made unilateral decisions to conduct military strikes on other countries.
대통령은 다른 국가들에 군사 공격을 하기로 독단적인 결정을 내렸다.

a collaborative effort 공동 작업, 공동의 노력

The self-help book about online businesses was a collaborative effort by several Internet entrepreneurs.
온라인 비즈니스에 대한 그 자기개발서는 몇몇 인터넷 기업가들이 공동 작업한 것이었다.

둘 중 적절한 어휘를 골라 ∨ 표를 하세요.

01 ○ **innate**
   ○ **exotic** plants   외래 식물

02 a ○ **hasty**
     ○ **flimsy** decision   성급한 결정

03 overseas ○ **status**
            ○ **demand**   해외 수요

04 ○ **explosive**
   ○ **colossal** growth   폭발적인 성장

05 illegal ○ **substances**
           ○ **contents**   (마약 등의) 불법 약물

06 side ○ **actions**
        ○ **effects**   부작용

07 in ○ **broad**
      ○ **whole** daylight   대낮에

08 a secret ○ **follower**
            ○ **admirer**   남몰래 흠모하는 사람

09 a medical ○ **screening**
             ○ **checkup**   건강 검진

10 a(n) ○ **perfect**
        ○ **amicable** stranger   전혀 만나본 적 없는 사람

11 ○ **affable**
   ○ **disposable** income   가처분 소득

12 a ○ **prospective**
     ○ **perspective** student   예비 학생

13 a ○ **lethal**
     ○ **mortal** dose   치사량

14 a ○ **long**
     ○ **lousy** face   시무룩한 얼굴

15 foreign ○ **currency**
           ○ **provision**   외화

16 immune ○ **organism**
          ○ **system**   면역 체계

17 the final ○ **destination**
             ○ **terminal**   최종 목적지

18 a ○ **close**
     ○ **tight** acquaintance   친지

19 cardiac ○ **seizure**
           ○ **arrest**   심장 마비

20 a ○ **concerted**
     ○ **connected** effort   협력

a ○ **fragile**
○ **lame** excuse   궁색한 변명

○ **profound**
○ **convivial** gratitude   깊은 감사

a strong ○ **likelihood**
○ **liability**   높은 가능성

○ **frugal**
○ **moral** values   도덕적 가치

○ **classified**
○ **franchised** ads   신문의 광고란

a ○ **slim**
○ **dead** end   막다른 골목, 궁지

a ○ **brute**
○ **wild** guess   대충의 추측, 어림짐작

○ **formal**
○ **solemn** attire   정장

the ○ **upper**
○ **higher** hand   우세, 우위

a(n) ○ **error**
○ **false** alarm   허위 경보

real ○ **territory**
○ **estate**   부동산

the cutting ○ **verge**
○ **edge**   최첨단

a(n) ○ **avid**
○ **fervid** reader   열렬한 독자

economic ○ **appraisals**
○ **sanctions**   경제적 제재 · 봉쇄

a(n) ○ **aged**
○ **senior** citizen   노령자, 노인

the ○ **bottom**
○ **ground** line   최종 결과, 결론

○ **capital**
○ **principal** punishment   사형

○ **national**
○ **domestic** products   국산품

○ **rave**
○ **rough** review   극찬

a ○ **get-up**
○ **wake-up** call   (호텔의) 모닝콜

41 a ○ **favorite** music 대중음악
    ○ **popular**

42 pressing ○ **need** 절실한 필요
    ○ **wish**

43 ○ **developing** country 개발 도상국
    ○ **progressing**

44 a ○ **powerful** showing 좋은 성과
    ○ **strong**

45 ○ **distressful** drought 심각한 가뭄
    ○ **severe**

46 ○ **hard-line** policy 강경책
    ○ **hard-won**

47 ○ **inclement** weather 궂은 날씨
    ○ **serene**

48 ○ **heavy** story 과장된 이야기
    ○ **tall**

49 a ○ **drastic** standard 엄격한 기준
    ○ **rigorous**

50 environmental ○ **conservation** 환경 보존
    ○ **defense**

51 a(n) ○ **hapless** matter 긴급한 사안
    ○ **urgent**

52 ○ **public** school 공립 학교
    ○ **communal**

53 intellectual ○ **property** 지적 재산권
    ○ **occupancy**

54 ○ **mental** health 정신 건강
    ○ **physical**

55 a ○ **close** examination 엄밀한 검사
    ○ **tight**

56 ○ **identical** twins 일란성 쌍둥이
    ○ **identified**

57 public ○ **speech** 공개 연설
    ○ **debate**

58 international ○ **renown** 국제적 명성
    ○ **goodwill**

59 ○ **preferred** customer 우대 고객
    ○ **ordinary**

60 working ○ **class** 노동자 계층
    ○ **level**

음 중 적절한 어휘를 골라 빈칸에 넣으세요.

bare	frozen
naked	cold

61 the _____ eye 육안
62 _____ feet 겁, 공포

prior	initial
former	previous

63 _____ notice 사전 공지
64 the _____ stage 초기

enigmatic	unidentified
unlisted	unforgettable

65 an _____ object 미확인 물체
66 an _____ number 전화번호부 미등록 번호

strong	sharp
keen	strident

67 a _____ dresser 옷을 잘 입는 사람
68 a _____ insight 예리한 통찰력

tough	rigid
grand	total

69 the _____ distance 총 거리
70 a _____ subject 어려운 과목

resignation	sojourn
acquittal	recession

71 a brief _____ 짧은 체류
72 an economic _____ 경기 침체

precious	vicious
previous	tedious

73 a _____ engagement 선약
74 a _____ circle 악순환

excessive	outside
exclusive	further

75 a(n) _____ club (회원제) 고급 단체
76 a(n) _____ question 추가 질문

sore	stuffy
upset	dull

77 a(n) _____ throat 목감기
78 a(n) _____ nose 코 막힘

rapid	busy
quick	swift

79 a _____ question 간단한 질문
80 a _____ signal 통화 중 신호음

정답 p.81

VOCABULARY | Collocation

해커스 펍스 Reading

Hackers **TEST**

Part I Choose the best answer for the blank.

01 A: Do you think Jerry is the right man for our
   company?
   B: Definitely. He's a perfect _____ for the job.

   (a) position   (b) fit
   (c) example   (d) case

02 A: The woman who checked in this morning — is
   she a VIP?
   B: Yes, you could say that. She's a _____
   guest at this hotel.

   (a) regular   (b) profuse
   (c) fastidious   (d) fellow

03 A: I think there's something wrong with this
   phone.
   B: Oh, you have to dial 9 to get an outside
   _____.

   (a) operator   (b) line
   (c) number   (d) signal

04 A: We're going to have the staff lunch today
   instead of tomorrow.
   B: That's a rather _____ change, but it's fine
   with me.

   (a) rushing   (b) scant
   (c) sudden   (d) nimble

05 A: Back so soon! Did you have a great time during
   your brief _____?
   B: I sure did! I only wish it had been longer.

   (a) impunity   (b) intermission
   (c) moratorium   (d) sojourn

06 A: I'm sure our flight will be cancelled.
   B: In this _____ weather, I wouldn't be surpris

   (a) temporal   (b) inclement
   (c) pretentious   (d) pleasant

07 A: Corey is such a _____ dresser.
   B: Well, he spends most of his salary on clothes.

   (a) sharp   (b) special
   (c) sterile   (d) succinct

08 A: Are you really going to volunteer to conduct t
   training workshop?
   B: I realize it's a(n) _____ task, but someo
   has to do it.

   (a) vigilant   (b) irresistible
   (c) daunting   (d) ostentatious

09 A: We shouldn't take modern _____ for
   granted.
   B: You're right. I can't imagine living without air
   conditioning.

   (a) conveniences   (b) creations
   (c) facilities   (d) benefits

10 A: I can't stand this _____ heat.
   B: Why don't we get something cold to drink?

   (a) fervid   (b) stifling
   (c) desolate   (d) frivolous

t II Choose the best answer for the blank.

Having been content with her previous car, the customer was searching for a new model in the _____ vein.

(a) equal (b) same
(c) coordinate (d) parallel

The company set up a quality control division to ensure that its _____ standards are met during production.

(a) educational (b) unmistakable
(c) rigorous (d) double

Employees are entitled to use sick _____ if an illness or injury prevents them from performing their duties.

(a) leave (b) favor
(c) break (d) absence

Working as a reporter at the *Daily Inquirer* is considered a once-in-a-lifetime _____ for new journalism graduates.

(a) accident (b) happening
(c) liability (d) opportunity

Hundreds of animal species are endangered because their natural _____ is being destroyed either by man or by natural disasters.

(a) habitat (b) dominance
(c) province (d) homestead

16 Reluctant to make a(n) _____ decision that would affect global security, the president consulted with other world leaders.

(a) managerial (b) sovereign
(c) unilateral (d) appropriate

17 After carefully examining the patient, the doctor recommended that surgical removal of the organ should be a last _____.

(a) stake (b) insurance
(c) resort (d) repose

18 The use of simple tools by apes is a strong _____ of their common ancestry with humans.

(a) observation (b) medication
(c) location (d) indication

19 World financial markets have become _____ in recent weeks, owing to the stock market crash.

(a) acute (b) volatile
(c) futile (d) fertile

20 The board of directors unanimously agreed to accept any _____ plan that would cut costs.

(a) altruistic (b) legible
(c) dubious (d) feasible

정답 p.82

CHAPTER 03 '명사 + 명사' Collocation

a desk job : 사무직

이력서를 쓰던 텝식씨, 희망 직무란에서 멈칫. 사무직을 뭐라고 하지? 사무는 회사 일이니까……. 회사는 company, company job? 어쩐지 어색한데? 당연하다. 사무직은 생산직이나 영업직에 비해 책상에 앉아서 하는 일이란 뜻에서 책상 + 일 = desk job이라 한다. 텝식씨처럼 어색한 표현을 만드는 일을 피하려면 함께 쓰일 때만 뜻이 통하는 명사와 명사의 어울림을 알아야 한다. 텝스 어휘에서 출제되는 '명사 + 명사' collocation을 덩어리째 익혀보자.

■ 출제 경향

· '명사 + 명사' collocation 문제는 간혹 출제되는 유형으로 Part 1과 Part 2에 모두 출제된다.

· 주로 'lunch break(점심 시간)'와 같이 '명사 + 명사' 형태로 출제되며, 'token of appreciation(감사의 표시)'처럼 '명사 + 전치사 + 명사' 형태의 collocation을 묻는 경우도 있다.

■ 예제

Part I

A: When is the _____ time for Flight AA325?
B: It's 6:30 and you will depart from Gate 15.

(a) plane
(b) boarding
(c) liftoff
(d) flying

A: AA325편의 탑승 시각이 언제인가요?
B: 6시 30분이고 15번 탑승구에서 출발할 예정입니다.

해설 | 빈칸 뒤의 명사 time(시간)과 어울려 쓰여 '탑승 시각'을 나타내는 명사는 (b) boarding(탑승)이다. boarding time은 '탑승 시각'이라는 뜻이다. plane(비행기), liftoff(이륙), flying(비행)은 time과 어울려 쓰이지 않으므로 답이 될 수 없다.

어휘 | flight[flait] 항공편 gate[geit] 탑승구

정답 | (b) boarding

Part II

In the 1950s, to increase the _____ rate among its citizens, the Chinese government began to simplify thousands of Chinese characters.

(a) literacy
(b) employment
(c) admittance
(d) acquisition

국민의 식자율을 증진하기 위해, 1950년대에 중국 정부는 수천의 한자를 단순화하기 시작했다.

해설 | 빈칸 뒤의 명사 rate(비율)와 어울려 쓰이면서 '_____ 비율을 증진하기 위해 한자를 단순화하기 시작했다'라는 문맥에 적절한 명사는 (a) literacy(읽고 쓸 줄 앎)이다. literacy rate는 '식자율, 읽고 쓸 수 있는 사람의 비율'이라는 뜻이다. employment(고용), admittance(입장, 입학), acquisition(획득)은 '식자율'이라는 의미로 rate와 어울려지 않는다.

어휘 | simplify[símpləfài] 단순하다 Chinese character 한자

정답 | (a) literacy

a lunch break 점심 시간

I need to finish this report before going on my lunch break.
전 점심 시간 시작 전에 이 보고서를 마쳐야 해요.

an information desk 안내 데스크

You can get more details about the conference at the information desk.
회의에 대한 추가 세부 사항은 안내 데스크에서 얻으실 수 있습니다.

sales volume 판매량

Unlike the demand for new books, the sales volume of used books is increasing.
새 책에 대한 수요와는 달리, 중고 서적의 판매량은 증가하고 있다.

a standing ovation 기립 박수

The singer received a standing ovation for her outstanding performance.
그 가수는 뛰어난 공연으로 기립 박수를 받았다.

a wall outlet 전기 콘센트

My apartment doesn't have enough wall outlets for all of my appliances.
내 아파트에는 모든 전자 제품을 꽂을 만큼 충분한 전기 콘센트가 없다.

gas emissions (온실)가스 배출

Greenhouse gas emissions have dramatically increased in the past hundred years.
온실가스 배출이 지난 100년간 극적으로 증가했다.

an aisle seat 통로 쪽 좌석

Can I have an aisle seat on the flight if it's available?
가능하다면 기내에서 통로 쪽 좌석에 앉을 수 있을까요?

a delivery charge 배송료

To ship your order overnight, the delivery charge will be twenty dollars.
주문 물품의 익일 배송을 원하시면, 배송료는 20달러입니다.

a complaint department 고객 불만 처리 부서

If you want a refund for the product, please contact the complaint department.
상품에 대해 환불받고 싶으시면, 고객 불만 처리 부서로 연락해주십시오.

a drug overdose 약물 과다 복용

A drug overdose can be prevented by discussing the proper dosage with your doctor.
의사에게 적정 복용량을 상의하면 약물 과다 복용을 방지할 수 있다.

a water shortage 물 부족

The drought is expected to cause a serious water shortage this year.
가뭄이 올해 심각한 물 부족을 일으킬 것으로 예상된다.

climate change 기후 변화

Many scientists believe that climate change is caused by increasing greenhouse gases in the atmosphere.
많은 과학자들은 대기 중의 온실가스 증가로 인해 기후 변화가 발생된다고 믿는다.

VOCABULARY | Collocation

해커스 텝스 Reading

13 a speed limit 제한 속도

Speed limits are enforced by governments to reduce traffic accidents.
제한 속도는 교통사고를 줄이기 위해 정부에 의해 시행된다.

14 order status 주문 처리 상황

Most online shopping sites provide a link to check your order status.
대부분의 온라인 쇼핑몰은 주문 처리 상황을 확인할 수 있는 링크를 제공한다.

15 tooth decay 충치

Tooth decay results when acid from bacteria destroy the surface of the teeth.
충치는 박테리아로부터 발생한 산이 치아의 표면을 파괴하면 발생한다.

16 job prospects 취업 전망

Job prospects in the field of education remain bright for this year.
올해 교육계의 취업 전망은 여전히 희망적이다.

17 a token of appreciation 감사의 표시

I treated him to dinner as a token of appreciation for helping me move.
이사를 도와준 것에 대한 감사의 표시로 나는 그에게 저녁을 대접했다.

18 a student loan 학자금 대출

Please submit an application to become eligible for a student loan.
학자금 대출을 받으시려면 신청서를 제출하세요.

19 leg room (좌석에서) 다리를 뻗는 공간

Business class seats generally have more leg room than economy class seats.
비즈니스석은 대개 일반석보다 다리를 뻗을 수 있는 공간이 넓다.

20 voter turnout 투표율

Voter turnout in the last election was only 62 percent of those eligible to vote.
지난 선거의 투표율은 유권자의 62퍼센트에 불과했다.

21 snow flurries 눈보라

The weather forecaster predicted snow flurries for the weekend.
기상 예보관은 주말에 눈보라를 예측했다.

22 credit standing 신용 상태

A good way to improve your credit standing is to pay all your bills on time.
신용 상태를 개선하는 좋은 방법은 모든 청구서를 제때 납부하는 것이다.

23 a customs declaration 세관 신고

Flight passengers are required to submit a customs declaration form.
항공기 승객들은 세관 신고서를 제출해야 한다.

24 room temperature 상온

This medicine should be stored at room temperature.
이 약은 상온에서 보관되어야 한다.

VOCABULARY | Collocation

해커스 텝스 Reading

다음 적절한 어휘를 골라 ∨ 표를 하세요.

a job	○ **opening** ○ **blank**	일자리, 공석
relief	○ **effort** ○ **move**	구호 활동
a price	○ **degree** ○ **range**	(상품 · 증권 등의) 가격 범위
working	○ **terms** ○ **hours**	근무 시간
the night	○ **shift** ○ **switch**	(주야 교대제의) 야간 근무
home	○ **instruments** ○ **appliances**	가전 제품
a ○ **traveler** ○ **commuter** train		통근 열차
press	○ **deliberations** ○ **credentials**	(출입을 허가하는) 기자증
the ○ **expiration** ○ **annihilation** date		유효 기한, 유통 기한
graduation	○ **qualifications** ○ **requirements**	졸업 요건
a ○ **smash** ○ **crash** hit		(책 · 영화 등의) 대성공
a traffic	○ **jam** ○ **cram**	교통 체증
energy	○ **savings** ○ **sources**	에너지원
a flu	○ **plague** ○ **epidemic**	유행성 독감
a fire	○ **drill** ○ **exercise**	화재 대피 훈련
a ○ **turning** ○ **striking** point		전환점
a ○ **wave** ○ **ripple** effect		파급 효과
○ **fringe** ○ **extra** benefits		급여 외 이익, 복리후생
market	○ **share** ○ **division**	시장 점유율
a(n) ○ **expecting** ○ **waiting** list		대기자 명단

21 a hunger ○ strike
        ○ struggle   단식 투쟁

22 a shopping ○ plunge
            ○ spree   흥청망청 쇼핑하기

23 a ○ house call
     ○ home   왕진, 가정 방문 판매

24 a tax ○ deficit
        ○ return   납세 신고(서)

25 a fairy ○ tale
          ○ fable   동화

26 a ○ costume rehearsal
     ○ dress   최종 연습

27 a point of ○ view
             ○ opinion   관점

28 power ○ outage
        ○ leakage   정전

29 ○ land mail
   ○ surface   (육상) 보통 우편

30 a ○ circulation desk
     ○ rotation   도서관의 대출 · 반납 창구

31 a(n) ○ apex meeting
        ○ summit   정상 회담

32 a(n) ○ exchange rate
        ○ currency   환율

33 a(n) ○ district code
        ○ area   지역 번호

34 a bank ○ statement
         ○ document   은행 거래 내역서

35 a food ○ section
         ○ stand   음식 가판대

36 an election ○ movement
              ○ campaign   선거 운동

37 a letter of ○ trust
              ○ credit   신용장

38 an age ○ class
         ○ group   연령층

39 a ○ price tag
     ○ money   가격표

40 a ○ homecoming party
     ○ housewarming   집들이

중 적절한 어휘를 골라 빈칸에 넣으세요.

place	refectory
lounge	chamber

41 a parking _____   주차 공간

42 a passenger_____   승객 휴게실

congestion	sickness
strain	discomfort

43 a muscle _____   근육 경직

44 motion _____   멀미

gap	lag
crack	drag

45 a generation _____   세대 차이

46 jet _____   시차로 인한 피로

provision	transition
acquisition	manipulation

47 service _____   서비스 제공

48 a(n) _____ period   과도기

expectancy	regulations
emergency	expectations

49 life _____   기대 수명

50 safety _____   안전 수칙

attention	attraction
amusement	amazement

51 a tourist _____   관광 명소

52 an _____ park   놀이 공원

address	number
directory	residence

53 a forwarding _____   이사 후의 변경 주소

54 _____ assistance   전화번호 안내

mortgage	coverage
cover	charge

55 insurance _____   보험 보상 (범위)

56 the _____ price   정가

chicken	turkey
tiger	goose

57 a paper _____   겉으로만 강한 사람

58 _____ bumps   (추위·공포로 인한) 소름

withdrawal	departure
farewell	leave

59 a _____ of absence   휴가, 휴직

60 a _____ party   송별회

정답 p.84

VOCABULARY | Collocation

해커스 탭스 Reading

Hackers **TEST**

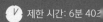

Part I Choose the best answer for the blank.

01 A: Would you prefer to sit by the window?
   B: I'd rather have a(n) _____ seat if that's all right with you.

   (a) inward   (b) border
   (c) aisle   (d) core

02 A: Why don't you try shopping online? It's so convenient!
   B: I don't want to pay the delivery _____ that gets added to the bill.

   (a) price   (b) tax
   (c) debt   (d) charge

03 A: It's noon. Aren't you taking your lunch _____?
   B: I'll just grab a sandwich. I need to finish this report by 2 p.m.

   (a) rest   (b) cycle
   (c) pause   (d) break

04 A: Excuse me. Could you direct me to the lost and found?
   B: I'm sorry. You might want to ask at the _____ desk.

   (a) information   (b) counsel
   (c) instruction   (d) notification

05 A: What's this gift for?
   B: Consider it a _____ of my appreciation for all your assistance.

   (a) badge   (b) token
   (c) clue   (d) receipt

06 A: How come you and Greg always carpool to work?
   B: We're both concerned about greenhouse gas _____.

   (a) secretion   (b) emissions
   (c) radiation   (d) ejections

07 A: These new theater seats are nice and soft, aren't they?
   B: Yeah, and they also provide plenty of leg _____.

   (a) room   (b) place
   (c) spot   (d) space

08 A: Where did you go this morning?
   B: The dentist's office. I had tooth _____ and was causing me pain.

   (a) breach   (b) fault
   (c) lag   (d) decay

09 A: It seems the recession has reached its peak this year.
   B: There go my job _____ for the future.

   (a) prospects   (b) standards
   (c) liabilities   (d) unemployment

10 A: The book I bought has the last chapter missing.
   B: Then you'd better call the complaint _____.

   (a) committee   (b) branch
   (c) ministry   (d) department

A: We've got to come up with a way to increase our sales _____.
B: We could try advertising more.

(a) point
(b) measure
(c) volume
(d) boundary

A: That performance was just marvelous! I never knew she had such a powerful voice!
B: Yes, she really deserved a standing _____.

(a) sensation
(b) ovation
(c) consideration
(d) adulation

II Choose the best answer for the blank.

When doctors work the night _____ in a hospital, they are often compensated with a higher salary.

(a) stint
(b) time
(c) section
(d) shift

Customers may check the _____ of their order on the company's Web site.

(a) status
(b) position
(c) stage
(d) portion

To apply for a student _____, students must first complete the form and submit all the necessary documents.

(a) lease
(b) loan
(c) debit
(d) debt

16 Make sure to disconnect the vacuum cleaner from the wall _____ when it is not in use.

(a) channel
(b) excerpt
(c) outlet
(d) device

17 Every continent on Earth is impacted by water _____, but the sub-Saharan countries suffer the most from this problem.

(a) mains
(b) shortages
(c) supplies
(d) resources

18 The evening news reported that a female celebrity is in a coma from an accidental drug _____.

(a) overdose
(b) immunity
(c) deprivation
(d) depression

19 Scientists are arguing whether the present-day climate _____ is caused by human activity or is a natural occurrence.

(a) change
(b) forecast
(c) system
(d) model

20 The public's growing distrust of politicians is a reason for the decline in voter _____ over the years.

(a) aftermath
(b) lineup
(c) output
(d) turnout

정답 p.84

혼자 하기 어렵고 막막할 땐?

Section 2 관용적 표현

CHAPTER **04** 이디엄

bite the bullet : 고통을 참다

충치 치료를 받으러 치과에 간 텝식씨, 간호사가 bite the bullet하라는 말에 화들짝. 총알을 깨물라니, 치아 건강을 위한 관리법 중 하나인가? 철분, 칼슘 보강? 그게 아니라 bite the bullet은 전쟁 중 마취 없이 수술을 받아야 했던 환자들이 고통을 참기 위해 총알을 입에 물었던 것에서 비롯된 것으로 '고통을 꾹 참다'라는 뜻. 이처럼 둘 이상의 단어가 모여 새로운 의미를 갖게 된 이디엄을 유래와 함께 익혀보자.

■ 출제 경향

· 이디엄 문제는 매 시험 평균적으로 1~2문제 정도 출제되며, 대부분 Part 1에서 나오고 Part 2에는 간혹 출제된다.
· 단어들이 모여 새로운 뜻을 나타내는 이디엄은 'a piece of cake(쉬운 일)'처럼 이디엄 전체를 답으로 묻는 문제들이 출제된다. 또한 단어들이 뜻을 유지한 채 함께 쓰이는 이디엄은 이디엄 중 한 단어를 묻는다. 예를 들면, 'without reservation(주저 없이)'의 이디엄에서 reservation을 답으로 묻는다.

■ 예제

Part I

A: Isn't it my turn to pay for lunch?
B: No, it's OK. I'll _____ this time.

(a) make mincemeat   (b) cook the books
(c) pick up the tab   (d) eat humble pie

A: 내가 점심 값을 낼 차례 아냐?
B: 아냐, 괜찮아. 이번엔 내가 계산할게.

해설 | '내가 점심 값을 낼 차례가 아니냐'라는 A의 질문에 B는 '아니다, 이번에 내가 _____하겠다'라고 대답하고 있다. 따라서 문맥상 빈칸에는 '(식대를) 계산하다, 값을 치르는 뜻의 (c) pick up the tab이 들어가는 것이 자연스럽다. cook the books는 '장부를 조작하다', make mincemeat은 '찍소리 못하게 하다', eat humble pie은 '굴욕을 감수하다'라는 뜻으로 답이 될 수 없다.

어휘 | turn[təːrn] 차례, 순서   tab[tæb] 계산서, 청구서

정답 | (c) pick up the tab

Part II

Riders are advised to remain seated while the Ferris wheel is in _____.

(a) routine   (b) motion
(c) function   (d) progress

회전 관람차가 움직이는 동안에 탑승객들은 좌석에 앉아 있어야 한다.

해설 | '회전 관람차가 _____하는 동안에는 좌석에 앉아 있어야 한다'라는 문맥에서 in _____의 빈칸에는 '움직이고 있는, 작동 중인'이라는 이디엄을 완성하는 (b) motion(작동)이 들어가는 것이 자연스럽다. routine은 '판에 박힌 일, 일상', function은 '기능', progress는 '진행'이라는 뜻이다.

어휘 | Ferris wheel 회전 관람차

정답 | (b) motion

들이 모여 새로운 뜻을 나타내는 이디엄

a piece of cake 아주 쉬운 일

유래 a piece of cake은 '케이크 한 조각'이라는 뜻으로 '케이크 한 조각을 먹는 것처럼 아주 하기 쉬운 일'을 나타낸다. 우리말의 '누워서 떡 먹기'와 비슷한 의미로 다른 표현으로는 a walk in the park(공원에서 쉬엄쉬엄 산책하듯 쉬운 일)가 있다.

The professional skier found the mountain's steepest slope to be a piece of cake.
프로 스키 선수는 그 산의 가장 가파른 경사를 아주 쉬운 일이라고 생각했다.

a blessing in disguise 전화위복, 불운처럼 보이는 행운

유래 blessing은 '축복', disguise는 '변장'이라는 뜻이므로 a blessing in disguise는 '불행으로 변장하고 찾아온 축복'이라는 의미이다. 즉, '처음에는 불행한 일처럼 여겨지지만 지나고 나서 보면 오히려 결과적으로 좋은 일'을 의미하는 표현이다.

Missing the bus was a blessing in disguise because it crashed into a truck seconds later.
버스가 몇 초 뒤에 트럭에 부딪혔기 때문에 그 버스를 놓친 것은 전화위복이었다.

jump the gun 성급하게 행동하다

유래 jump the gun은 '총 소리가 나기도 전에 뛰어나가다'라는 뜻이다. 육상 대회에서 선수들이 출발을 알리는 총 소리가 울리기 전에 미리 출발하는 것에서 유래한 표현으로 '성급 하게 일을 시작하거나 행동하다'라는 의미로 쓰인다.

Until there is concrete evidence, do not jump the gun by making assumptions.
구체적인 증거가 있을 때까지, 억측해서 성급하게 행동하지 말아라.

keep one's ear to the ground 소문에 귀를 기울이다

유래 keep one's ear to the ground는 '땅바닥에 귀를 대다'라는 뜻이다. 인디언들이 땅바닥에 귀를 대고 소리를 들어 적의 침입을 미리 알 수 있었던 것에서 비롯한 표현으로 '소 문이나 여론의 동향에 주의를 기울인다'는 의미를 갖는다.

We need to track changes in the industry, so keep your ear to the ground.
우린 업계의 변화를 파악할 필요가 있으니 소문에 귀를 기울이도록 하세요.

keep ~ under one's hat ~을 비밀로 하다

유래 keep ~ under one's hat은 모자 속에 중요한 것을 숨기듯 '비밀을 유지하다'라는 뜻이다. 참고로, 반대되는 표현은 spill the beans(비밀을 누설하다)이다.

I'd like you to keep this information under your hat.
이 정보는 비밀로 해주시면 좋겠어요.

keep one's fingers crossed 행운을 빌다, 좋은 결과를 빌다

유래 keep one's fingers crossed는 '손가락을 교차시키다'라는 뜻이다. 아프리카 원주민들이 검지와 중지를 교차시켜 십자가 모양을 만드는 것이 마귀를 쫓아내고 행운을 가져온 다고 믿었던 것에서 비롯한 표현으로 '행운을 빌다', '좋은 결과를 빌다'라는 의미를 갖는다.

Keep your fingers crossed that the university will accept me.
내가 대학에 합격하도록 행운을 빌어줘.

on the tip of one's tongue 기억이 날 듯 말 듯 생각나지 않는

유래 on the tip of one's tongue은 '혀의 끝에'라는 뜻으로 뭔가 기억이 날 듯 말 듯 입에서 뱅뱅 돌기만 할 뿐 생각나지 않을 때 쓰는 표현이다.

The name of the guy standing by the door is on the tip of my tongue.
문가에 서 있는 저 남자의 이름이 기억이 날 듯 말 듯 생각나지 않는다.

call the shots (상황을) 지휘하다, 주도권을 쥐고 있다

유래 call the shots는 '공의 방향을 외치다'라는 뜻이다. 포켓 당구에서 어떤 공을 구멍에 넣겠다고 미리 밝힌 뒤, 공을 넣는 데 실패할 경우 상대편에게 기회를 넘겨줘야 하는 것에 서 비롯한 표현으로 '(상황을) 지휘하다', '주도권을 쥐고 있다'라는 의미이다.

The new manager said he would call the shots in the office from now on.
그 새로운 관리자는 지금부터 그가 사무실을 지휘할 것이라고 말했다.

follow suit 남이 하는 대로 따라 하다, 선례를 따르다

유래 suit은 '카드 짝패의 한 벌'을 뜻하는 말로 follow suit은 카드 놀이에서 남이 낸 패와 같은 짝패를 내는 것처럼 '남이 하는 대로 따라 하다', '선례를 따르다'라는 의미이다.

My sister joined a health club nearby, and I soon followed suit.
여동생이 근처 헬스클럽에 가입했고, 나도 곧 따라 했다.

단어들이 뜻을 유지한 채 함께 쓰이는 이디엄

10 make it (제시간에) 도착하다

Although traffic was backed up for miles, I was able to make it to the meeting.
몇 마일에 걸쳐 차들이 막혀 있었지만, 나는 제시간에 회의에 도착할 수 있었다.

11 in hindsight = in retrospect 지나고 보니, 돌이켜 보면

In hindsight, I should have reserved the hotel room earlier since it's peak season.
지나고 보니, 성수기이니까 나는 호텔 객실을 일찍 예약했어야 했다.

12 live beyond one's means 분수에 넘치는 생활을 하다

Some people live beyond their means by spending more than they can afford.
어떤 이들은 형편보다 더 많이 지출해서 분수에 넘치는 생활을 한다.

13 no matter what the cost 어떤 희생을 치르더라도

Vince said he wanted to get the promotion no matter what the cost.
Vince는 어떤 희생을 치르더라도 승진하고 싶다고 말했다.

14 at one's convenience 편한 때에

My schedule is wide open, so we can pick a time to meet at your convenience.
내 일정은 완전히 비어 있으니까, 네가 편한 때에 우리가 만날 시간을 정할 수 있다.

15 help oneself to ~을 마음대로 먹다

Please help yourself to the refreshments provided.
제공된 다과를 마음대로 드십시오.

16 without reservation 주저 없이, 조건 없이

The spectators cheer without reservation whenever a marathoner reaches the finish line.
관중들은 마라톤 주자들이 결승선에 도착할 때마다 주저 없이 환호한다.

17 fall out with ~와 사이가 틀어지다

Brian fell out with Susan over her high credit-card bill.
Brian은 Susan의 많은 신용카드 청구 금액 때문에 그녀와 사이가 틀어졌다.

18 take one's pick 마음에 드는 것을 선택하다

Moviegoers can take their pick from seats that are still available.
영화 관람객들은 아직 비어있는 좌석들 중에서 마음에 드는 것을 선택할 수 있다.

19 on a whim 충동적으로

I moved to San Francisco on a whim, but it turned out to be a good decision.
나는 충동적으로 샌프란시스코로 이사했지만, 그것이 좋은 결정이었던 것으로 드러났다.

20 slip one's mind 잊어버리다

I was supposed to meet Steve for lunch, but it completely slipped my mind.
나는 점심에 Steve를 만나기로 되어 있었지만, 완전히 잊어버렸다.

Hackers **Practice**

다음 중 적절한 어휘를 골라 ∨ 표를 하세요.

a wide ○ **degree** of   다양한 ~
        ○ **range**

under the ○ **weather**   몸 상태가 좋지 않은
           ○ **pressure**

fall out of ○ **favor**   인기를 잃다
             ○ **target**

in a good ○ **emotion**   기분이 좋은
           ○ **mood**

cut to the ○ **subject**   본론으로 들어가다
            ○ **chase**

on one's last ○ **hands**   기진맥진하여, 다 죽어가며
               ○ **legs**

make ○ **ends** meet   수입과 지출의 균형을 맞추다
      ○ **means**

over the ○ **bottom**   과장된
          ○ **top**

sit on the ○ **bench**   중립적인 태도를 취하다
            ○ **fence**

off the top of one's ○ **brain**   즉석에서 생각나는 대로
                      ○ **head**

come a long ○ **way**   크게 발전하다
             ○ **road**

break the ○ **coldness**   서먹서먹한 분위기를 깨다
           ○ **ice**

on ○ **sake** of   ~을 대신해서
    ○ **behalf**

not to ○ **mention**   ~은 말할 것도 없이
        ○ **comment**

to no ○ **pursuit**   헛되이, 보람 없이
       ○ **avail**

on the ○ **spot**   즉석에서
        ○ **point**

be all ○ **toes**   서투르다
        ○ **thumbs**

be in the same ○ **boat**   처지가 같다, 같은 상황에 있다
                ○ **ship**

behind the ○ **scenes**   은밀하게
            ○ **stages**

over the ○ **slope**   전성기가 지난
          ○ **hill**

21 on the ○ home ○ house (음식 등이) 무료로 제공되는

22 take a ○ rain ○ snow check 다음을 기약하다

23 get the ○ picture ○ sketch 이해하다

24 make a(n) ○ scene ○ act 소란을 피우다

25 at the ○ instant ○ moment 지금 당장은

26 on ○ purpose ○ motive 고의로

27 ○ speak ○ show volumes 많은 것을 시사하다

28 lose one's ○ anger ○ temper 화를 내다

29 in the ○ bag ○ box 확실한

30 in one's ○ shoes ○ clothes ~의 입장이 되어

31 on ○ speaking ○ talking terms with ~와 말을 주고받는 사이인

32 be ○ dead ○ firm set against ~에 단호히 반대하다

33 be ○ done ○ completed with 끝내다, 마치다

34 be one's own ○ boss ○ worker 자기 사업하다, 독립하다

35 up in ○ arms ○ guns 분개하여

36 a sight for ○ sore ○ dull eyes 보아서 즐거운 사람 · 것

37 give someone a ○ credit ○ break ~을 너그러이 봐주다

38 go through the ○ top ○ roof 치솟다, 급등하다

39 out of ○ town ○ place (출장 · 여행으로) 집을 떠나 있는

40 ○ push ○ pull out all the stops 최대한 노력하다, 있는 힘을 다하다

중 해석에 맞는 적절한 어휘를 골라 빈칸에 넣으세요.

cut my teeth	play it by ear	face the music
keep an eye on	had a ball	cost an arm and a leg

I _____ on the music of Elton John when I was in my early teens.

나는 십대 초반에 Elton John의 음악을 **처음으로 접했다**.

Could you _____ the baby while I buy some milk at the store?

상점에서 우유를 살 동안 아기를 **지켜봐 주시겠어요**?

Vacationing in Hawaii would probably _____.

하와이에서 휴가를 보내는 것은 **돈이 많이 들** 것이다.

I didn't have time to book a place to stay in advance, so let's just _____.

미리 숙박할 곳을 예약할 시간이 없었으니 그냥 **임기응변으로 대처해보자**.

The factory has to _____ for emitting pollutants into the air.

그 공장은 공기 중으로 오염 물질을 방출한 것에 대해 **비난을 들어야** 한다.

They _____ at the party and didn't notice what time they went home.

그들은 파티에서 **신나게 즐겼고**, 몇 시에 집으로 돌아갔는지 알지 못했다.

start from scratch	down in the dumps	take the cake
out of the blue	a shot in the dark	spill the beans

After failing his driving test, Jonathan was _____.

운전면허 시험에 떨어지고 나서, Jonathan은 **낙담했다**.

Your theory about the missing jewelry is nothing more than _____.

분실된 보석에 대한 네 가설은 **추측**에 지나지 않는다.

I've seen bad traffic in my lifetime, but today's traffic really does _____.

살면서 교통 정체를 많이 봐 왔지만, 오늘 정체는 정말 **대단하다**.

Without any prior notice, Charles quit his job _____.

Charles는 아무런 사전 통보도 없이 **갑자기** 직장을 그만두었다.

Tabloids pay people to _____ on how celebrities live.

대중 신문은 사람들이 유명 인사의 삶에 대해 **비밀을 누설하도록** 돈을 지불한다.

After losing all his money to gambling, he had no choice but to _____.

도박에서 돈을 다 잃은 후, 그는 **처음부터 새로 시작하는** 수 밖에 없었다.

정답 p.86

Hackers **TEST**

Part I Choose the best answer for the blank.

01 A: At this rate, we'll never _____ it to the
   airport on time.
   B: Take it easy. We still have two hours.

   (a) make   (b) take
   (c) gain   (d) arrive

02 A: Who's the guy who won the best actor award?
   B: Wait! His name is _____.

   (a) on the tip of my tongue
   (b) leaving me in the cold
   (c) catching me red-handed
   (d) getting it by rote

03 A: I'll leave my bag here while I go to the
   restroom. Could you _____?
   B: Of course!

   (a) burst at the seams
   (b) pass the torch
   (c) pull away from it
   (d) keep an eye on it

04 A: There's a great second-hand car in the ads
   today. And the price is right!
   B: Well, you'd better _____ that no one's
   bought it yet.

   (a) lay down the law
   (b) hit the spot
   (c) keep your fingers crossed
   (d) beat your brains out

05 A: I think next week's exam will be
   _____.
   B: I'm not so sure. It covers some difficult material.

   (a) salt in the wound
   (b) a fly in the ointment
   (c) a piece of cake
   (d) a bull in a china shop

06 A: Can we _____ on dinner
   tomorrow?
   B: No problem. Let's reschedule for sometime n
   week.

   (a) turn the table
   (b) make a killing
   (c) take a rain check
   (d) break the ice

07 A: Don't worry. You'll do better on the next test
   B: I know, but in _____ I should have stuc
   more.

   (a) knowledge   (b) opposition
   (c) recognition   (d) hindsight

08 A: You'd better not share this information with
   anyone.
   B: Don't you trust me? I know how to
   _____.

   (a) lose my shirt
   (b) knock my socks off
   (c) keep it under my hat
   (d) tighten my belt

09 A: It looks like our company might not survive.
   could lose my job.
   B: Well, it could be _____. You
   might find a higher paying position.

   (a) a pain in the neck
   (b) the cream of the crop
   (c) a blessing in disguise
   (d) a walk in the park

10 A: Which fashion trends are companies promoti
   this year?
   B: I don't know, but I'll _____

   (a) save my breath
   (b) keep my ear to the ground
   (c) kick up my heels
   (d) hold my tongue

A: Serena seems to live beyond her _____.
B: I agree. I guess that's why she doesn't have any money saved up.

(a) means (b) assets
(c) regard (d) status

A: What a performance!
B: That really _____. No one can compare with her.

(a) takes the cake
(b) beats a dead horse
(c) plays by the book
(d) gives the green light

A: You look _____ these days.
B: I know. Nothing seems to cheer me up.

(a) on the go
(b) out of the blue
(c) up a tree
(d) down in the dumps

A: You should have waited longer before selling all your stocks.
B: Yeah, I guess I _____, didn't I?

(a) passed the buck
(b) hit the mark
(c) buried the hatchet
(d) jumped the gun

A: When are your office hours?
B: Tomorrow afternoon, from 3 to 7, so please stop by at your _____.

(a) comfort (b) convenience
(c) suitability (d) satisfaction

Part II Choose the best answer for the blank.

16 Jacob decided to travel to Europe on a _____, so not very many people knew about his plan.

(a) whim (b) date
(c) budget (d) roll

17 Many business establishments have capitalized on the fact that people want to maintain their youthful appearance no matter what the _____.

(a) worth (b) option
(c) cost (d) kind

18 Inspired by the firefighters' courage, the bystanders pitched in without _____ to help clear the wreckage.

(a) resurrection (b) redemption
(c) redundancy (d) reservation

19 During Thanksgiving, people usually _____ themselves to holiday food with little consideration given to how much they consume.

(a) serve (b) support
(c) help (d) grant

20 If you are unfamiliar with table manners at a formal dinner, observe what others do and follow _____.

(a) suit (b) action
(c) style (d) nature

정답 p.87

Chapter 04 이디엄 **271**

CHAPTER 05 일상 대화 표현

Be my guest. : 좋을 대로 하세요.

학교 퀸카 Jessica에게 펜을 빌려 달라고 한 텝식씨, 미소 지으며 답하는 그녀. 이게 웬 떡, Be my guest라며 그녀가 초대를 한다! 오브 코올~~스! 그대가 원한다면 언제든지 그대의 손님이 되어 주겠어. 하지만 그녀가 흥분한 텝식씨를 보며 식겁한 이유는 Be my guest가 초대하는 표현이 아니라 '좋을 대로 하세요'라는 뜻이었기 때문. 이와 같은 대화 표현은 텝스 어휘는 물론, 텝스 청해와 일반 회화에서도 활용할 수 있으니 알아둔다면 일석 삼조! 그럼 두 사람의 대화를 통해 다양한 일상 대화 표현들을 익혀보자.

■ 출제 경향

· 일상 대화 표현 문제는 매 시험 평균적으로 1~2문제 정도 출제되며, 모두 Part 1에서 출제된다.

· 일상 대화 표현 문제에서는 하나의 문장으로 굳어진 일상 대화 표현 중 한 단어를 묻는다. 예를 들면, 'Stay on the line(전화를 끊지고 기다리세요)'이라는 표현에서 line을 답으로 묻는다.

■ 예제

Part I

A: Did your situation at work improve?
B: Yes, I was finally able to get that raise I wanted.
   Thanks for _____.

(a) getting   (b) telling
(c) asking   (d) looking

A: 직장에서의 상황은 좀 나아졌나요?
B: 네, 마침내 원하던 대로 월급을 인상받게 되었어요. 물어봐ᅦ 고마워요.

해설 | A의 질문에 B가 대답한 후 '_____해서 고맙다'라고 감사를 표현하고 있다. 따라서 문맥상 빈칸에는 '물어봐줘서 고맙다'라는 표현인 'Thanks for asking'을 완성하 asking이 들어가는 것이 자연스럽다.

어휘 | situation[sìtʃuéiʃən] 상황, 상태   improve[imprú:v] 나아지다   get a raise 월급을 인상받다

정답 | (c) asking

Hold the line. 전화를 끊지 말고 기다리세요.

A: May I speak to Mrs. Donovan, please?
B: Certainly. Please hold the line.

A: Mrs. Donovan과 통화할 수 있을까요?
B: 물론이죠. 전화를 끊지 말고 기다리세요.

What a pity! = It's a pity! 정말 안됐구나! 불쌍해라!

A: I heard Jennifer hurt her leg.
B: What a pity! Is it serious?

A: Jennifer가 다리를 다쳤다고 들었어.
B: 정말 안됐구나! 심각하대?

I already have plans. 난 다른 계획이 있어.

A: How about going to the movies with me tonight?
B: Thanks, but I'll pass. I already have plans.

A: 오늘 밤 나랑 영화 보러 가는 거 어때?
B: 고맙지만, 사양할게. 난 다른 계획이 있어.

It's been ages. 정말 오랜만이야.

A: Hey, George! It's been a while!
B: Yeah, it's been ages since I saw you last.

A: 야, George! 오랜만이다!
B: 응, 마지막으로 본 후로 정말 오랜만이야.

I don't have a clue. = I have no idea. = I don't have the faintest idea. 난 전혀 모르겠어.

A: Do you have any idea why the police are on campus?
B: I don't have a clue.

A: 캠퍼스에 왜 경찰들이 있는지 혹시 아니?
B: 난 전혀 모르겠어.

I've been keeping busy. 난 그동안 바빴어.

A: Hey, Mark. How have you been?
B: Oh, I've been keeping busy with work.

A: 안녕, Mark. 어떻게 지냈니?
B: 아, 일 때문에 난 그동안 바빴어.

You can't miss it. 쉽게 찾으실 거예요.

A: Excuse me, but where is the nearest subway station?
B: It's just around the corner. You can't miss it.

A: 실례지만, 가장 가까운 지하철역이 어딘가요?
B: 모퉁이를 돌면 바로 있어요. 쉽게 찾으실 거예요.

That sounds like a good idea. = That sounds great. 그거 좋은 생각이네요.

A: Why don't we plan a surprise party for Jamie?
B: That sounds like a good idea!

A: Jamie를 위한 깜짝 파티를 계획하는 게 어떨까?
B: 그거 좋은 생각이다!

Catch you later. 나중에 또 보자.

A: I have to go to the library, so I'll meet you at the gym at 5.
B: OK. Catch you later.

A: 난 도서관에 가야 하니까, 5시에 체육관에서 만나자.
B: 알았어. 나중에 또 보자.

Don't give it another thought. 신경 쓰지 마세요.

A: I'm really sorry. I lost the pen I borrowed from you.
B: That's OK. Don't give it another thought.

A: 정말 미안해요. 당신한테 빌린 펜을 잃어버렸어요.
B: 괜찮아요. 신경 쓰지 마세요.

No harm done. 괜찮아요.

A: Oh, no! I forgot to tell you that Brian called!
B: Forget it. No harm done.

A: 아, 어쩌지! Brian이 전화했다고 네게 얘기하는 걸 깜빡했어!
B: 신경 쓰지 마. 괜찮아.

It's a surprise to see you. 만나서 뜻밖이에요.

A: Hi, Jim. You are the last person I expected to see here.
B: Oh, Hi! It's quite a surprise to see you here too.

A: 안녕, Jim. 여기서 만나게 될 줄은 정말 몰랐는걸.
B: 아, 안녕! 여기서 만나게 되다니 정말 뜻밖이다.

13　Thanks for the offer.　호의는 감사합니다.

A: I'm going out to get a snack. Do you want something?
B: Thanks for the offer, but I just ate.

A: 간식을 사러 갈 거예요. 뭐 필요한 거 있어요?
B: 호의는 감사하지만, 전 방금 먹었어요.

14　It's my pleasure.　천만에요.

A: Thanks for dropping me off at the station.
B: Think nothing of it. It's my pleasure.

A: 역까지 태워줘서 고마워요.
B: 별말씀을요. 천만에요.

15　Take your time.　천천히 해.

A: I'll get off the phone soon. Just give me a minute.
B: That's OK. Take your time.

A: 금방 전화 끊을 거야. 잠시만 기다려줘.
B: 괜찮아. 천천히 해.

16　Let's have a toast!　건배합시다!

A: Why don't we open up some wine and celebrate?
B: Why not? Let's have a toast!

A: 와인을 따고 축배를 드는 게 어때요?
B: 좋아요! 건배합시다!

17　It's very sweet of you.　정말 친절하네요.

A: I'll watch your son if you can't find a babysitter.
B: That's very sweet of you to say.

A: 보모를 찾을 수 없다면 내가 당신의 아들을 돌봐줄게요.
B: 그렇게 말해주다니 정말 친절하네요.

18　(I) Can't complain.　그럭저럭 잘 지내고 있어.

A: Hey, Randy. How are things with you?
B: I can't complain.

A: 안녕, Randy. 어떻게 지내니?
B: 그럭저럭 잘 지내고 있어.

19　I'll have to put you on hold.　전화를 연결해드릴 때까지 기다려주세요.

A: I need to speak to Mr. Brown.
B: OK, but I'll have to put you on hold for a few minutes.

A: Mr. Brown과 통화하고 싶은데요.
B: 네, 하지만 전화를 연결해드릴 때까지 잠시만 기다려주세요.

20　Hold your horse.　침착해 [진정해].

A: Hurry up! We might be late!
B: Just hold your horses. We can take our time a little.

A: 서둘러! 우린 늦을지도 몰라!
B: 잠깐 침착해 봐. 우리는 여유가 좀 있어.

21　You read my mind.　내 마음을 잘 아는군요.

A: I'm going to close the window. It's freezing in here.
B: You read my mind.

A: 내가 창문을 닫을게. 여기는 너무 춥다.
B: 내 마음을 잘 아는구나.

22　I'd appreciate that.　그렇게 해주시면 고맙겠습니다.

A: Do you want me to help you take out the garbage?
B: I'd really appreciate that. Thanks.

A: 쓰레기 내다 버리는 걸 도와줄까요?
B: 그렇게 해주면 고맙겠어요. 감사해요.

23　Can I ask you a favor?　부탁 좀 해도 될까요?

A: Can I ask you a favor?
B: Of course. What is it?

A: 부탁 좀 해도 될까요?
B: 물론이죠. 뭔데요?

24　I'll treat you.　제가 살게요.

A: I don't have my wallet on me.
B: I'll treat you.

A: 저에게는 지갑이 없어요.
B: 제가 살게요.

Hackers **Practice**

둘 중 적절한 어휘를 골라 ∨ 표를 하세요.

○ **Imagine** ○ **Fancy** meeting you here.	여기서 만나다니 뜻밖이네요.	
It's no ○ **bother** ○ **failure** at all.	전혀 귀찮지 않아요.	
So ○ **far** ○ **long** , so good.	지금까지 그럭저럭 지냈어요.	
Keep me ○ **posted** ○ **noted** .	계속 소식을 알려줘.	
It's not my ○ **error** ○ **fault** .	그건 내 잘못이 아니야.	
Don't get me ○ **wrong** ○ **false** .	오해는 하지 마세요.	
What ○ **makes** ○ **brings** you here?	여긴 웬일이세요?	
On second ○ **thought** ○ **idea**	다시 생각해보니	
Long time no ○ **meet** ○ **see**	오랜만이야.	
He's not my ○ **kind** ○ **type** .	그는 내 취향이 아니에요.	
I don't ○ **mind** ○ **object** at all.	나는 전혀 개의치 않아요.	
As far as I'm ○ **involved** ○ **concerned**	나로서는	
Look who's ○ **talking** ○ **saying** .	사돈 남 말 하네.	
Can I have a ○ **word** ○ **saying** with you?	저와 이야기 좀 할까요?	
You can't be ○ **earnest** ○ **serious** .	설마 농담이겠지.	
Could you ○ **take** ○ **receive** a message?	메시지를 전해주시겠습니까?	
How are ○ **stuff** ○ **things** with you?	어떻게 지내요?	
Let me be the ○ **authority** ○ **judge** of that.	그건 내가 판단할 일이야.	
Get it off your ○ **chest** ○ **heart** .	솔직하게 터놓고 얘기해 봐.	
If you'll ○ **excuse** ○ **please** me	실례가 되지 않는다면	

VOCABULARY | 관용적 표현

해커스 텝스 Reading

21 ○ **take**
   ○ **come** to think of it
생각해보니

22 if my memory ○ **serves**
                ○ **reminds** me right
내 기억이 맞다면

23 Not that I ○ **know**
             ○ **think** of.
내가 알기로는 그렇지 않아요.

24 Let's ○ **call**
         ○ **quit** it a day.
오늘은 이만 끝냅시다.

25 I can't ○ **allow**
           ○ **help** it.
어쩔 수 없어요.

26 What are you ○ **trying**
                ○ **getting** at?
넌 도대체 무슨 말을 하려는 거니?

27 the way I ○ **see**
             ○ **look** it
내가 보기에는

28 Let me put it another ○ **word**
                         ○ **way** .
달리 바꾸어 말해볼게요.

29 It's none of your ○ **business**
                     ○ **matter**
그건 네가 상관할 일이 아니야.

30 Did I make myself ○ **bright**
                     ○ **clear** ?
무슨 말인지 알겠어요?

31 Shake a ○ **leg**
            ○ **foot** !
서둘러!

32 I beg your ○ **excuse**
              ○ **pardon** ?
다시 한 번 말씀해주세요.

33 You can ○ **say**
           ○ **tell** that again.
동감이야.

34 Over my dead ○ **soul**
                 ○ **body** !
절대로 안 돼!

35 By all ○ **means**
          ○ **ways** .
좋고말고요.

36 No ○ **kidding**
       ○ **joking** !
설마! 그럴 리가!

37 Don't ○ **say**
          ○ **mention** it.
천만에요.

38 I'm ○ **telling**
       ○ **meaning** you.
정말이야. 믿어줘.

39 It ○ **depends**
      ○ **manages** .
상황에 따라 달라요.

40 No ○ **worry**
      ○ **doubt** about it.
틀림없어. 당연하지.

중 해석에 맞는 적절한 문장을 골라 빈칸에 넣으세요.

Apology accepted	**That's the spirit**	**Way to go**
You bet	**That figures**	**Beats me**

A: I lost my cell phone, so I couldn't reach you.
B: _____.

A: I just need to push myself a little harder.
B: _____!

A: I'm sorry I was rude to you yesterday.
B: _____.

A: Do you know the name of the song that's playing?
B: _____.

A: Are you coming to Mindy's farewell party?
B: _____.

A: I made it to the competition finals!
B: _____!

A: 휴대 전화를 잃어버려서, 네게 연락할 수가 없었어.
B: 그러면 그렇지.

A: 난 스스로를 좀 더 채찍질해야겠어.
B: **바로 그 자세야!**

A: 어제 네게 무례하게 굴어서 미안해.
B: **사과를 받아줄게.**

A: 넌 지금 나오는 노래 제목을 아니?
B: **전혀 모르겠어.**

A: 넌 Mindy의 환송회에 갈 거니?
B: **당연하지.**

A: 내가 결승전까지 올라갔어!
B: **잘했어!**

What's the occasion	**What a shame**	**Not on your life**
What a coincidence	**Never mind**	**No sweat**

A: Thank you for moving my new sofa.
B: _____.

A: I got black ink all over my white shirt.
B: _____!

A: _____?
B: My brother's graduation ceremony is today.

A: Can I borrow your car for a month-long trip?
B: _____.

A: I'm also on my way to the supermarket.
B: _____!

A: What were you about to say?
B: _____.

A: 내 새 소파를 옮겨줘서 고마워요.
B: 식은 죽 먹기였어요.

A: 내 하얀 셔츠에 검정색 잉크를 다 쏟았어.
B: 정말 안타깝다!

A: 무슨 좋은 일 있어요?
B: 내 남동생 졸업식이 오늘이에요.

A: 한 달 동안의 여행에 네 차를 빌릴 수 있을까?
B: 절대로 안 돼.

A: 나도 슈퍼마켓에 가는 길이에요.
B: 우연의 일치네요!

A: 넌 무슨 말을 하려던 거였니?
B: 신경 쓰지 마.

정답 p.88

Hackers **TEST**

Part I Choose the best answer for the blank.

01 A: Mr. Burke is not at his desk now. Do you want me to page him?
   B: Thanks for the _____, but I'll just wait.

   (a) advice   (b) sympathy
   (c) treat   (d) offer

02 A: I cannot believe I failed my driving test again!
   B: What a _____! You practiced almost every day for two weeks.

   (a) pity   (b) lie
   (c) mercy   (d) mistake

03 A: Can I speak to Mrs. Ross?
   B: Sure. Could you hold the _____ while I connect you with her?

   (a) line   (b) ring
   (c) phone   (d) tone

04 A: Why don't we rent a movie and watch it at home tonight?
   B: That _____ great!

   (a) looks   (b) shows
   (c) sounds   (d) feels

05 A: I decided to enter the marathon. I'd really like to finish the whole race this time.
   B: That's the _____!

   (a) soul   (b) wish
   (c) spirit   (d) pleasure

06 A: You're lending me your notes? That's really n of you. Thank you!
   B: It's my _____. I'm glad I could help.

   (a) comfort   (b) approval
   (c) respect   (d) pleasure

07 A: Do you know if the company director is resigning this year?
   B: No, I don't have the _____ idea.

   (a) faintest   (b) weakest
   (c) thinnest   (d) deepest

08 A: Bill! Do you remember me from Jacksonville High School?
   B: Right! Steve! It's a _____ to see you!

   (a) fortune   (b) doubt
   (c) desire   (d) surprise

09 A: I'm sorry for not visiting you while you were
   B: No need to worry about it. There's no _____ done.

   (a) apology   (b) excuse
   (c) harm   (d) loss

10 A: Well, I need to get going. It's time for class to start.
   B: All right. I'll _____ you later.

   (a) expect   (b) greet
   (c) catch   (d) gather

A: Larry! Long time no see! What have you been up to?
B: Oh, I've been _____ busy.

(a) working   (b) spending
(c) keeping   (d) coming

A: You look familiar. Have we _____ before?
B: I don't think so. I'm not from around here.

(a) met   (b) struck
(c) known   (d) passed

A: Excuse me. Can you direct me to the Benson Building?
B: Just turn left at the intersection. It's the blue building. You can't _____ it.

(a) omit   (b) miss
(c) ignore   (d) fail

A: I apologize for being late. I'll make it up to you.
B: Don't give it another _____. It's water under the bridge.

(a) idea   (b) thought
(c) time   (d) minute

A: Should I hurry so we can get to the station on time?
B: _____ your time. The train doesn't leave for another hour.

(a) Hold   (b) Allow
(c) Take   (d) Save

16 A: Why don't we eat out for dinner tonight?
B: You _____ my mind. I was going to ask you.

(a) read   (b) reminded
(c) guessed   (d) noticed

17 A: Here, let me help you with those bags.
B: That's so nice of you. I'd really _____ that.

(a) deserve   (b) attribute
(c) appreciate   (d) depreciate

18 A: Don't you think you're watching too much TV?
B: It's none of your business. Let me be the _____ of that.

(a) defendant   (b) plaintiff
(c) witness   (d) judge

19 A: Keep me _____ about how your move goes.
B: Sure. I'll get in touch with you as soon as things have settled.

(a) posted   (b) cared
(c) charged   (d) related

20 A: What do you think of my pumpkin pie?
B: Don't get me _____, you're a great cook. I'm just not a fan of pumpkin.

(a) risky   (b) messy
(c) wrong   (d) tough

VOCABULARY | 관용적 표현

해커스 텝스 Reading

정답 p.89

CHAPTER 06 구동사

brush up : 복습하다

영어 회화 수업을 듣던 텝식씨, 다음 시간에 꼭 brush up해오라는 선생님 말씀에 고민하는데⋯⋯. brush는 빗질하는 거고, up은 위로니까⋯⋯. 아하, 올백머리를 하라는 거군! 곱게 빗어 넘긴 머리로 수업 시간 내내 꿀먹은 벙어리가 된 텝식씨는 brush가 부사 up과 함께 '복습하다'라는 의미가 된다는 걸 몰랐던 것. 이처럼 동사는 전치사나 부사와 결합해서 새로운 의미를 가진 구동사가 된다. 카멜레온처럼 변신하는 동사들에 부사와 전치사의 의미로 접근하여 구동사를 쉽게 익혀보자.

■ 출제 경향

· 구동사 문제는 매 시험 평균적으로 1~2문제 정도 출제되며, Part 1에 주로 나오고 Part 2에는 간혹 출제된다.

· 대부분의 구동사 문제는 'cut back on(줄이다)'처럼 구동사 전체를 묻지만, 'rely on(의지하다)'의 동사 rely를 답으로 묻는 것처럼 사의 동사를 묻기도 한다.

■ 예제

Part I

A: That was a terrible accident that Jonathan had.
B: I know. He's lucky he's going to _____.

(a) bail out   (b) pull through
(c) work out   (d) pick up

> A: Jonathan이 겪은 사고는 끔찍했어요.
> B: 맞아요. 그가 회복할 거라니 운이 좋네요.

해설 | 'Jonathan이 겪은 사고가 끔찍했다'라는 A의 말에 B는 '그가 _____할 거라니 운이 좋다'라고 대답하고 있다. 따라서 문맥상 빈칸에는 '회복하다, 중병이나 중상을 이겨라는 뜻의 (b) pull through가 들어가는 것이 자연스럽다. bail out은 '손을 떼다, 책임을 회피하다', work out은 '해결하다, 운동하다', pick up은 '(차로) 태우다'라는
어휘 | terrible[térəbl] 끔찍한   accident[ǽksədənt] 사고
정답 | (b) pull through

Part II

Poor planning caused the factory to _____ behind in production for this quarter.

(a) lag   (b) drag
(c) wane   (d) crawl

> 잘못된 계획으로 인해 공장의 이번 분기 생산량이 뒤쳐지게 되

해설 | '잘못된 계획으로 인해 이번 분기의 생산량이 _____하게 되었다'라는 문맥에서 빈칸에는 behind와 함께 쓰여 '뒤쳐지다'라는 구동사를 완성하는 (a) lag가 들어가는
연스럽다. drag는 '질질 끌다', wane은 '작아지다', crawl은 '기어가다'라는 뜻이다.
어휘 | production[prədΔ́kʃən] 생산량, 생산   quarter[kwɔ́:rtər] 분기
정답 | (a) lag

01 take in 속이다, 구독하다

Many people are taken in by online scams designed to steal their personal information.
많은 사람들은 그들의 개인 정보를 훔치기 위해 고안된 온라인 신용 사기에 속는다.

02 turn in ~을 제출하다, 잠자리에 들다

Students are expected to turn in the final paper by the due date.
학생들은 기말 보고서를 예정일까지 제출해야 한다.

You can stay up and watch TV, but I'm going to turn in for the night.
넌 늦게까지 자지 않고 TV를 봐도 되지만, 난 잠자리에 들 거야.

03 work out 성취되다, 잘 되어가다

Despite my detailed itinerary, none of my vacation plans worked out.
나의 자세한 여행 계획에도 불구하고, 내 휴가 계획 중 어느 것도 성취되지 않았다.

04 sort out ~을 해결하다, 정리하다

It took the technician hours to get the printer error sorted out.
기술자가 프린터의 오류를 해결하는 데 몇 시간이 걸렸다.

05 fill out ~을 기입하다, 작성하다

Customers who fill out this survey will receive future discounts.
이 설문지를 작성하는 고객은 추후에 할인을 받게 됩니다.

06 set out 시작하다, 출발하다

After much preparation, we were ready to set out on our journey.
많은 준비 후에, 우리는 여행을 시작할 준비가 되었다.

07 dart out 빠르게 뛰쳐 나가다

The sprinter darted out from the starting blocks before everyone else.
그 단거리 주자는 다른 모든 사람보다 먼저 출발대로부터 빠르게 뛰쳐 나갔다.

08 make out ~을 알아보다, 이해하다

My grandparents' wedding picture was so old that I could barely make out their faces.
조부모님의 결혼 사진이 너무 오래되어서 나는 그분들의 얼굴을 거의 알아볼 수 없었다.

09 run out of ~을 다 써버리다, 바닥나다

We've run out of mayonnaise, so I'll go pick some up later.
마요네즈가 떨어졌으니, 내가 나중에 사러 갈게요.

10 get along (with) (~와) 사이좋게 지내다

I cannot get along with her because her interests are too different from mine.
그녀의 관심사는 내 것과 너무 달라서 나는 그녀와 사이좋게 지낼 수 없다.

11 come along 잘 진행되다

The highway renovation project is coming along according to plan.
고속도로 보수 작업은 계획대로 잘 진행되고 있다.

12 go along (with) (~에) 찬성하다, 동조하다

The staff is expected to go along with whatever the manager says.
직원들은 경영자가 무엇을 말하든 찬성할 것으로 예상된다.

up

up은 '~위로'라는 뜻으로 아래에서 위로 상승·증가하는 동작을 나타내며, 눈에 보이는 결과를 나타내거나, 동사의 의미를 강조하여 '완전히'라는 의미를 갖는다.

13 work up ~을 불러일으키다, 북돋우다

We worked up an appetite after painting the house the whole morning.
아침 내내 집에 페인트칠을 하고 나자, 우리는 입맛이 돌았다.

14 crack up 웃음을 터뜨리다

That sitcom on TV is so funny that I crack up the entire time it's on.
그 TV 시트콤이 너무 재미있어서 내내 웃게 된다.

15 blow up 화를 내다

The boss blew up at us for submitting the report late.
상사는 보고서를 늦게 제출한 것에 대해 우리에게 화를 냈다.

16 let up 누그러지다

I hope the rain will let up this weekend so that we can go hiking.
이번 주말에 등산을 갈 수 있게 비가 그치면 좋겠다.

17 stay up 밤 늦게까지 자지 않다

You won't do well on your exam if you stay up chatting on the Internet.
인터넷에서 채팅을 하면서 밤 늦게까지 자지 않으면 시험을 잘 치를 수 없을 것이다.

18 break up 헤어지다

The couple broke up due to irreconcilable differences after four years of marriage.
그 부부는 극복할 수 없는 성격 차이로 4년의 결혼 생활 후 헤어졌다.

19 pick up ~을 익히다, (사람·물건을) 도중에 태우다

She picked up useful marketing tactics during her summer internship.
그녀는 여름 인턴쉽 기간 동안 유용한 마케팅 방법들을 익혔다.

Would you like me to pick you up at the airport?
제가 당신을 공항으로 태우러 가주길 원하나요?

20 end up 결국 ~으로 끝나다

If we keep walking in this direction, we'll end up in the next town over.
만약 우리가 이 방향으로 계속 걸어간다면, 결국 옆 동네에 도착할 수 있을 것이다.

21 show up 나타나다, (모임에) 나오다

I was supposed to have a date with Jake last night, but he didn't show up.
난 어젯밤 Jake와 데이트하기로 되어 있었지만, 그는 나타나지 않았다.

down

down은 up과 반대로 위에서 아래로 움직이는 동작을 나타내며, 정도·속도·범위의 감소와 '건강이 쇠약해진'의 의미를 갖는다.

22 narrow down (범위를) 좁히다

We have narrowed down the number of remaining contestants to only three.
우리는 남은 경쟁자들의 수를 단 세 명으로 좁혔다.

23 come down with ~의 병에 걸리다

The exam was postponed because half of the class came down with the flu.
학급의 반이 감기에 걸려서 시험이 연기되었다.

over

over는 '~너머로'의 의미로, '~을 능가하여'를 뜻하거나, 행동의 완료를 나타낸다.

24 get over ~을 극복하다

The hopeful applicant was able to get over her rejection and keep applying to jobs.
그 희망에 찬 지원자는 탈락을 극복하고 계속 지원할 수 있었다.

25 pull over (차를) 길가에 세우다

The driver had to pull over because the car's trunk suddenly popped open.
트렁크가 갑자기 열려서 운전자는 차를 길가에 세워야 했다.

n

은 '(~의 면에) 접촉하여'라
의미로, 옷을 입은 상태나 동
ㅣ계속·지속 또는 사람·사
ㅐ 대한 의존을 뜻한다.

26 try on ~을 입어보다

I'd love to try on that blue sweater in the shop window.
상점 쇼윈도에 있는 저 파란색 스웨터를 입어보고 싶어요.

27 catch on 이해하다, 알아듣다

The professor used visual examples so the students could catch on easier.
교수는 학생들이 더 쉽게 이해하도록 시각 자료를 사용했다.

28 rely on ~에 의지하다

The more you grow to trust your friends, the more you rely on them.
친구에 대한 신뢰가 커질수록, 그들에게 더 의지하게 된다.

ff

는 on과 반대로 '~로부터 떨
서'라는 뜻으로, '~에서 벗
서, 일탈하여' 혹은 '~을 제
여'라는 의미를 갖는다.

29 round off ~을 마무리 짓다

They rounded off the evening with coffee and dessert at a café.
그들은 카페에서 커피와 디저트로 저녁 시간을 마무리했다.

30 stop off 도중에 들르다

Can you stop off at the bakery today on your way home from work?
오늘 퇴근해서 집에 오는 길에 빵집에 들러줄래요?

31 call off ~을 취소하다

The baseball game wasn't called off, even though it was raining heavily.
비가 많이 내렸지만 야구 경기는 취소되지 않았다.

32 lay off ~를 해고하다

Nearly half of our employees were laid off after the company merger.
기업 합병 이후에 직원의 거의 절반이 해고되었다.

33 shake off (나쁜 것을) 떨쳐내다

Rachel couldn't shake off the feeling that something bad was about to happen.
Rachel은 곧 무언가 나쁜 일이 벌어질 것 같은 기분을 떨쳐낼 수 없었다.

cross

oss는 '~을 통과하여'의 뜻
'~을 관통하여', '~을 가로
서'라는 의미를 갖는다.

34 get across 이해시키다

The teacher could get nothing across to his students eager for summer vacation.
선생님은 여름 방학에 들떠 있는 학생들에게 아무것도 이해시킬 수 없었다.

35 come across ~를 우연히 만나다

I came across a childhood friend in the supermarket.
나는 어린 시절 친구를 슈퍼마켓에서 우연히 만났다.

way

ay는 '~로부터 멀리'라는 뜻
멀어지는 동작을 나타낸다.

36 shy away from ~을 부끄러워서 피하다

James keeps to himself and tends to shy away from group lunches.
James는 혼자 다니고 점심 회식을 부끄러워서 피하는 경향이 있다.

37 carry away 흥분시키다

Carol got carried away during a sale and spent too much money.
Carol은 세일 기간 동안 흥분해서 돈을 너무 많이 썼다.

Hackers **Practice**

풀면서 외우는 기출 어휘

둘 중 적절한 어휘를 골라 V 표를 하세요.

01 ○ hang onto
   ○ root for   a team   팀을 응원하다

02 ○ beef up
   ○ run up against   a difficulty   어려움에 맞닥뜨리다

03 be ○ held up
      ○ stopped off   in traffic   교통 체증 때문에 꼼짝 못하다

04 ○ boil down to
   ○ come up with   an idea   아이디어를 생각해내다

05 be ○ cut out for
      ○ turn out for   the job   일에 적임이다

06 ○ lay off
   ○ drop out   of school   학교를 중퇴하다

07 The curtains ○ take back
                ○ go up   커튼이 올라간다.

08 ○ check in
   ○ sign in   the luggage   짐 수속을 하다

09 ○ abide by
   ○ hang on   the law   법을 지키다

10 ○ slip away
   ○ straighten up   a room   방을 정돈하다

11 The alarm ○ turns off
             ○ goes off ·   알람이 울린다.

12 ○ hang out
   ○ get around   with friends   친구들과 어울리다

13 ○ move up
   ○ get away   for a while   잠시 휴가를 떠나다

14 ○ cut back on
   ○ go down with   expenses   비용을 줄이다

15 ○ revolve
   ○ strike   around a theme   주제를 중심으로 전개되다

16 ○ catch on
   ○ drop by   the office   사무실에 들르다

17 ○ look up
   ○ check up   a word in a dictionary   사전에서 단어를 찾아보다

18 ○ iron
   ○ mess   things up   일을 망치다

19 ○ get down to
   ○ settle on to   business   본격적으로 일에 착수하다

20 be ○ tied up
      ○ pulled off   at the moment   지금은 바빠서 꼼짝할 수 없다

○ **bring up**
○ **break out**   an issue   문제를 제기하다

○ **turn out**
○ **check out**   a book   (도서관에서) 책을 대출하다

○ **blow off**
○ **pass over**   a class   수업을 빼먹다

○ **blow over**
○ **turn down**   an offer   제안을 거절하다

○ **cut down on**
○ **go down with**   smoking   흡연을 줄이다

○ **show off**
○ **dress up**   for the occasion   특별한 일에 맞게 옷을 차려입다

○ **pass out**
○ **fall through**   for a while   잠시 기절하다

○ **touch on**
○ **roll in**   a topic   주제를 간단히 언급하다

○ **dish out**
○ **eat out**   at a restaurant   식당에서 외식하다

○ **gloss over**
○ **stave off**   recession   경기 침체를 피하다

○ **count on**
○ **care about**   someone   ~에게 의지하다

Hard work   ○ **gives out**
               ○ **pays off** ·   노력이 성과를 낸다.

○ **sign up**
○ **set in**   for a class   수강 신청하다

○ **catch onto**
○ **call for**   help   도움을 요청하다

○ **lounge away**
○ **set back**   one's time   빈둥거리며 시간을 보내다

○ **bring down**
○ **wrap up**   a deal   거래를 결말짓다

○ **dwell on**
○ **abound in**   past mistakes   과거의 실수에 연연하다

○ **pass away**
○ **do without**   a car   차 없이 지내다

○ **break in**
○ **fall for**   a new pair of shoes   새 신발을 신기 시작하다

○ **go back on**
○ **make off with**   one's word   약속을 지키지 않다

41 It doesn't
- ○ **add up**
- ○ **clear up** ·

그건 말이 되지 않는다.

42
- ○ **back up on**
- ○ **fill in for** someone

~를 대신하다

43 A plan
- ○ **fell through**
- ○ **threw out** ·

계획이 실패했다.

44
- ○ **delve into**
- ○ **go by** the background of a case

사건의 배경을 철저히 조사하다

45
- ○ **make up**
- ○ **decide on** one's mind

결심하다

46
- ○ **break into**
- ○ **blow over** a bank

은행에 침입하다

47
- ○ **act up**
- ○ **loosen up** a little

긴장을 약간 풀다

48
- ○ **take after**
- ○ **turn into** one's mother

어머니를 닮다

49
- ○ **burn down**
- ○ **wear out** a house

집을 전소시키다

50
- ○ **Go for**
- ○ **Push through** it!

힘 내! 한번 도전해봐!

51
- ○ **stick to**
- ○ **catch on** the original plan

원래 계획을 고수하다

52
- ○ **rummage about**
- ○ **sneak in** the fridge

냉장고를 뒤지다

53
- ○ **come over**
- ○ **run into** a truck

트럭에 충돌하다

54 all
- ○ **booked up**
- ○ **called for**

예약이 다 찬

55
- ○ **follow in**
- ○ **stick up** one's footsteps

~의 선례를 따르다

56 Would you
- ○ **take in**
- ○ **care for** something to drink?

마실 것 좀 드릴까요?

57
- ○ **turn in**
- ○ **cut in** on a conversation

대화에 끼어들다

58 Stop
- ○ **taking after**
- ○ **picking on** me.

날 그만 괴롭혀.

59
- ○ **clear up**
- ○ **close down** a factory

공장을 폐쇄하다

60
- ○ **let on about**
- ○ **spell out** an issue

문제에 대해 간결하게 설명하다

중 해석에 맞는 적절한 어휘를 골라 빈칸에 넣으세요.

put up with	wind up	rack up
figure out	make up for	clean up

I can't _____ how to install this new computer software.

나는 이 새 컴퓨터 소프트웨어를 설치하는 방법을 **이해할** 수 없다.

I'll be late tomorrow, but I'll work overtime this week to _____ it.

난 내일 늦게 올 예정이지만, 이번 주에 그것을 **보충하기** 위해 초과 근무할 거예요.

Sharon said she would _____ the mess after cooking.

Sharon은 요리한 후에 어질러 놓은 것을 **치우겠다**고 말했다.

You'll _____ an enormous phone bill if you keep calling overseas.

네가 해외에 전화를 계속한다면 전화 요금이 엄청나게 **쌓이게** 될 것이다.

How do you _____ that leaky faucet?

너는 저렇게 물이 새는 수도를 어떻게 **참고 견디니**?

Pay attention to where you're going or you'll _____ getting lost.

네가 가고 있는 곳에 집중하지 않으면 **결국** 길을 잃고 말 것이다.

break down	cheer up	calm down
bump into	come by	catch up with

I hope this old car doesn't _____ in the middle of the road.

이 낡은 차가 도로 중간에서 **고장 나지** 않기를 바란다.

When you're upset, what do you usually do to _____?

당신은 화가 나면, **진정하기** 위해 주로 무엇을 하나요?

I slowed my bicycle in order to let her _____ me.

나는 그녀가 나를 **따라잡을** 수 있도록 자전거 속도를 늦췄다.

Please _____ the store to pick up your new computer.

새 컴퓨터를 가져가시려면 상점에 **들러주시기** 바랍니다.

To _____ Susan, I'm thinking of buying her a gift.

Susan을 **기운 나게 하기** 위해, 나는 그녀에게 선물을 사주려고 한다.

I really didn't expect to _____ Gina at the wedding.

나는 결혼식에서 Gina를 **우연히 만나리라고는** 정말 예상하지 못했다.

정답 p.91

Hackers **TEST**

Part I Choose the best answer for the blank.

01 A: You don't look so good today.
   B: I know. I think I'm _____ a cold.

   (a) coming down with
   (b) getting away with
   (c) turning over to
   (d) looking down on

02 A: Dad, can I _____ and watch the late
      night movie?
   B: No, you can't. It's time you went to bed.

   (a) watch out   (b) settle on
   (c) hang onto   (d) stay up

03 A: I need to _____ my clothes at the dry
      cleaners.
   B: Don't take too long. We'll be late for the party.

   (a) run off   (b) cut back
   (c) pick up   (d) push down

04 A: What do I need to do to apply for a loan?
   B: The first thing you have to do is _____
      this form.

   (a) write down   (b) bring up
   (c) fill out   (d) come across

05 A: I heard you're going to hike to the summit.
   B: Yes, I plan to _____ first thing in the
      morning.

   (a) ease up   (b) set out
   (c) bust up   (d) run through

06 A: I can't read the small print in the contract. Ca
      you _____?
   B: Nope. Let's get a magnifying glass.

   (a) make it out   (b) put it through
   (c) cut it off   (d) call it forth

07 A: The advertisement looks like our competitor's
   B: I agree. Let's try to _____ something
      more original.

   (a) look up to   (b) come up with
   (c) do away with   (d) make up for

08 A: Hey, it's past midnight. Are you still working
      the report?
   B: Don't worry. I'll _____ for the night as
      soon as I finish.

   (a) flip out   (b) turn in
   (c) drop down   (d) dig in

09 A: When Edward told that story, I laughed so ha
      that I almost choked on my drink.
   B: Yeah, I _____ whenever he's aroun

   (a) set down   (b) pull off
   (c) crack up   (d) turn over

10 A: I asked my boss for a promotion, but was
      denied.
   B: I'm sorry to hear it didn't _____.

   (a) work out   (b) push in
   (c) turn back   (d) pay off

A: Maxine _____ at Bob for some small thing yesterday.
B: What did he possibly say to make her so upset?

(a) switched off   (b) missed out
(c) got along   (d) blew up

A: I don't think the rain is going to _____ soon.
B: Don't worry. We can stay inside and still enjoy ourselves.

(a) cut out   (b) let up
(c) get by   (d) pass away

A: Is there anything you want me to get while I'm at the supermarket?
B: Actually, we're going to _____ cereal pretty soon.

(a) boil down to   (b) hold on to
(c) run out of   (d) put up with

A: No one wants to join the debate contest.
B: Well, a lot of people _____ from speaking in public.

(a) shy away   (b) break out
(c) talk back   (d) slow down

A: I heard Phil was devastated by his recent breakup.
B: That's true. But he'll _____ it soon enough.

(a) fall for   (b) pass through
(c) count on   (d) get over

16 A: The Internet has been down for over an hour.
B: Yeah, our technicians are trying to _____ the problem.

(a) check up   (b) make up
(c) sort out   (d) look out

17 A: Have you asked Kimberly out on a date?
B: No, I haven't been able to _____ the courage to talk to her.

(a) work up   (b) crash into
(c) throw away   (d) bail out

18 A: Who are you _____?
B: The visiting side is better, but I'm still loyal to the home team.

(a) acting on   (b) pitching in
(c) rooting for   (d) sticking up

Part II Choose the best answer for the blank.

19 After months of careful investigation, the police detectives have _____ down the list of suspects to two individuals.

(a) broken   (b) boiled
(c) narrowed   (d) turned

20 The book _____ around the experiences of soldiers who fought in the trenches during the Second World War.

(a) orbits   (b) settles
(c) loiters   (d) revolves

정답 p.92

시험에 나올 문제를 미리 풀어보고 싶을 땐?

해커스텝스(**HackersTEPS.com**)에서
텝스 적중예상특강 보기!

Section 3 일반 어휘

CHAPTER **07** 동사

Don't push me : 나 좀 밀지 말라고~

"Don't push me ~♪" 노래방에서 폼 잡으며 팝송을 부르던 텝식씨 왈, 이 노래는 만원 버스에서 날 밀지 말라고 호소하는 내용이라나? 친구들에게 톡톡히 망신을 당한 텝식씨에게 잘못이 있었다면 push에는 '밀다' 말고 '강요하다'라는 뜻도 있다는 걸 몰랐다는 것. 이처럼 텝스 어휘에서는 다양한 의미를 가진 동사의 쓰임을 묻는 경우가 빈번하다. 그럼 이제 이미 알고 있는 동사의 뜻은 다양하게, 몰랐던 동사는 새롭게 익혀보자.

■ 출제 경향

· 동사 문제는 어휘 영역에서 가장 많이 출제되는 문제 중 하나로 매 시험 평균적으로 10문제 이상 출제된다. 또한 Part 1보다 Part 2C 더 많이 출제된다.

· 기본 동사들이 지닌 1차적 의미 외에도 다양한 의미를 묻는 문제들이 출제된다.
  예) keep(몸에 지니다), run(광고를 내다), ask(초대하다), get(데려오다), take(시간이 걸리다) 등

· 다의어 동사의 의미를 묻는 문제들이 출제되기도 한다.
  예) promote(장려하다, 승진시키다), recognize(인정하다, 알아보다) 등

■ 예제

Part I

A: What issues were brought up at the meeting?
B: Sorry, but it's a tad early to _____ them at this time.

(a) speak
(b) utter
(c) discuss
(d) propose

A: 회의에서 어떤 문제들이 제기되었나요?
B: 미안하지만 현재로선 그것들에 대해 논하기 약간 이르네요.

해설 | 회의 내용을 묻는 A의 질문에 B는 '미안하지만 현재로선 _____하는 것이 이르다'라고 대답하고 있다. 따라서 문맥상 빈칸에는 '어떤 문제에 대해 논하다'를 의미하는 discuss가 들어가는 것이 자연스럽다. speak은 단순히 '말하다'의 의미로 '~에 대해 말하다'라고 표현하려면 목적어(them) 앞에 전치사 of나 about을 써야 하며, ut '입 밖에 내어 표현하다', propose는 '제안하다'의 의미로 답이 될 수 없다.

어휘 | issue [íʃuː] 문제, 논점 **bring up** ~을 제기하다 **a tad** 약간

정답 | (c) discuss

Part II

Airport security officials _____ passengers more carefully after receiving a threat over the telephone.

(a) cajoled
(b) snared
(c) forged
(d) frisked

공항 보안 관리들은 전화로 협박을 받은 후 더 주의 깊게 승객들을 몸수색했다.

해설 | '전화로 협박을 받은 후 더 주의 깊게 승객들을 _____했다'라는 문맥에서 빈칸에는 '(흉기·마약 따위의 조사를 위해 몸을 더듬어) 몸수색하다'라는 의미의 (d) frisked가 가는 것이 자연스럽다. cajole은 '감언이설로 꾀다', snare는 '함정에 빠뜨리다', forge는 '위조하다'라는 뜻으로 답이 될 수 없다.

어휘 | **security official** 보안 담당 관리 **passenger** [pǽsəndʒər] 승객

정답 | (d) frisked

promote [prəmóut] 장려하다, 승진시키다

The professor wrote a book promoting family values and traditional principles.
교수는 가족의 가치와 전통적인 원칙을 장려하는 책을 썼다.

She was promoted and given a raise for her years of service.
그녀는 수년간의 근무로 승진하고 봉급을 인상받았다.

strike [straik] 부딪치다, 갑자기 충격을 주다

Lightning strikes the Empire State Building at least one hundred times a year.
1년에 적어도 백 번 가량 번개가 엠파이어 스테이트 빌딩에 부딪친다.

migrate [máigreit] 이동하다, 이주하다

Electronic receivers are used to track the path of migrating dolphins.
전자 수신기는 이동하는 돌고래들의 경로를 추적하는 데 사용된다.

adjust [ədʒʌ́st] 조절하다

Make sure to adjust the rearview mirrors before you start to drive.
운전을 시작하기 전에 반드시 백미러를 조절하세요.

benefit [bénəfìt] 이익을 얻다, 이롭다

Everyone who attends the session on insurance will benefit from the information.
보험에 대한 회의에 참석하는 모든 사람들은 그 정보에서 이익을 얻을 것이다.

cater [kéitər] 음식을 제공하다, 요구를 채워주다

With over two hundred guests, it was hard to find someone to cater our wedding.
200명 이상의 하객으로 인해, 우리 결혼식에 음식을 제공할 사람을 찾기가 어려웠다.

obtain [əbtéin] 획득하다, 얻다

Many medical students put in ten years of studying to obtain a medical degree.
의학 학위를 획득하기 위해서 많은 의대생이 10년의 시간을 학업에 쏟는다.

limit [límit] 제한하다

A tighter system of checks and balances in the government will help limit excess spending.
정부의 더 엄격한 견제와 균형 체계가 과도한 지출을 제한해줄 것이다.

brag [bræg] 자랑하다, 허풍떨다

People who brag about their achievements can be very tiresome.
그들의 성취에 대해 자랑하는 사람들은 매우 성가실 수 있다.

console [kənsóul] 위로하다, 위안하다, 격려하다

Jake consoled Sharon after her father passed away from cancer.
Jake는 Sharon의 아버지가 암으로 돌아가신 후에 그녀를 위로했다.

topple [tápl] (건물 등이) 무너지다, 뒤엎다

Despite leaning dangerously in the wind, the tower did not topple.
바람에 위험하게 기울어졌음에도 불구하고, 그 탑은 무너지지 않았다.

impose [impóuz] 지우다, 강요하다

This restaurant has imposed a smoking ban in response to customer complaints.
이 식당은 고객 항의에 대한 대처로 흡연을 금지했다.

13 **eradicate**[irǽdəkèit] 근절하다, (병·해충을) 박멸하다

The police have sworn to eradicate all criminal activity from the neighborhood.
경찰은 지역 내 모든 범죄 활동을 근절할 것이라고 단언했다.

The dog was given medication to eradicate parasites from its body.
기생충을 몸에서 박멸하기 위해 개는 약물을 투여받았다.

14 **continue**[kəntínjuː] 계속되다, 이어지다

After a stop at the gift shop, the tour will continue.
기념품 상점에서 잠시 멈춘 후, 견학이 계속될 것입니다.

15 **strand**[strænd] ~을 오도가도 못하게 하다, 좌초시키다

The cancellation of the flight left hundreds stranded at the airport overnight.
그 비행편의 결항은 수백 명을 밤새 공항에서 오도가도 못하게 했다.

16 **accommodate**[əkámədèit] 편의를 도모하다

Our information desk is available twenty-four hours to accommodate guests' needs.
저희 안내 데스크는 투숙객들의 편의를 도모하기 위해 24시간 이용 가능합니다.

17 **constitute**[kánstitjùːt] ~이 되는 것으로 여겨지다, 구성하다

Collecting personal information without consent constitutes theft.
동의 없이 개인 정보를 수집하는 것은 절도죄로 여겨진다.

18 **bombard**[bɑmbáːrd] (질문 등을) 퍼붓다

The actor was bombarded with questions about his upcoming movie.
배우는 곧 개봉할 영화에 대한 질문 공세를 받았다.

19 **apprehend**[æprihénd] 체포하다, 파악하다, 이해하다

Two weeks after the murder, the main suspect still hadn't been apprehended.
그 살인 사건의 2주 후에도, 유력 용의자는 여전히 체포되지 않았었다.

20 **address**[ədrés] 강연하다, 연설하다

Dr. Walker is supposed to address an audience at a conference on human gene sequences next week.
Walker 박사는 다음 주에 인간 유전자 배열에 대한 학회에서 강연을 하기로 되어 있다.

21 **convulse**[kənvʌ́ls] 교란시키다

Paris was convulsed by student protests in May of 1968.
1968년의 5월에 파리는 학생 시위에 의해 교란되었다.

22 **necessitate**[nəsésətèit] ~을 필요하게 하다, 피할 수 없게 하다

The new environmental regulations will necessitate a change in the company's recycling policy.
새로운 환경 규제들은 회사의 재활용 정책에 변화를 필요하게 할 것이다.

23 **besiege**[bisídʒ] 포위하다, 공격하다

The capital was besieged for a month before finally falling to enemy forces.
그 수도는 마침내 적군에게 무너지기 전까지 한달 동안 포위당했다.

usurp[ju:sə́:rp] (권력 등을) 빼앗다

The national government should not usurp the powers of city governments.
중앙 정부는 시 정부의 권한을 빼앗아서는 안 된다.

chastise [tʃæstáiz] 벌하다, 몹시 비난하다

The school chastised the bullies, but this did not stop the violence.
학교측에서 다른 학생들을 괴롭히는 학생들에게 벌을 내렸지만, 이것은 폭력을 멈추지 못했다.

obfuscate[ɑbfʌ́skeit] 흐리게 하다

During the debate, one speaker obfuscated the issue by citing unrelated examples.
토론 중, 한 토론자가 관련 없는 예시를 언급해서 논점을 흐렸다.

laud[lɔːd] 극찬하다

The queen of England lauded the opera singer for his wonderful performance.
영국 여왕은 오페라 가수의 훌륭한 공연을 극찬했다.

entrench[intréntʃ] 굳게 자리잡다

A feeling of hopelessness has entrenched itself in the minds of frustrated soldiers.
무력감이 좌절한 병사들의 마음에 굳게 자리잡았다.

extenuate[iksténjuèit] (잘못·벌 등을) 가볍게 하다

His being ill with the flu extenuated his late submission of a term paper.
그가 독감에 걸려 아팠던 것은 학기말 보고서를 늦게 제출한 잘못을 가볍게 했다.

dabble[dæbl] 취미 삼아 해보다

David is a lawyer by profession, but he dabbles in painting when he finds the time.
David는 변호사가 직업이지만, 시간이 나면 취미 삼아 그림을 그린다.

vacillate[væsəlèit] 망설이다, 주저하다

Mildred has been vacillating between painting the walls yellow or green.
Mildred는 벽을 노란색으로 칠할지 녹색으로 칠할지 망설여왔다.

liquidate[líkwidèit] 제거하다, 죽이다

Fifteen terrorists were liquidated during the antiterrorist operations.
테러리스트 15명이 반테러리즘 작전 중 제거되었다.

stymie[stáimi] 방해하다

The company thought of setting up a complaints forum, but lack of support stymied the plan.
기업은 불만 사항 토론회를 개최하려고 했지만, 호응의 부족이 계획을 방해했다.

incite[insáit] (어떤 감정을) 불러일으키다, 조장하다

Terrorist acts in developed countries incite fear around the world.
선진국에서 발생하는 테러 행위들은 전 세계적으로 공포심을 불러일으킨다.

bestow[bistóu] 수여하다, 증여하다

The queen bestowed the author the title of "honorary citizen."
여왕은 그 작가에게 '명예시민'이라는 칭호를 수여했다.

VOCABULARY | 일반 어휘

해커스 텝스 Reading

Hackers **Practice**

둘 중 표시된 단어에 적절한 해석을 고르세요.

01 **adopt** a language 　　　　　　　　　　언어를 　ⓐ 채택하다 ⓑ 습득하다

02 **conceal** one's embarrassment 　　　당혹감을 　ⓐ 감추다 ⓑ 느끼다

03 **counter** an attack 　　　　　　　　　　공격에 　ⓐ 대비하다 ⓑ 대항하다

04 **create** new jobs 　　　　　　　　　　　일자리를 　ⓐ 창출하다 ⓑ 보호하다

05 **feature** an article on the exhibit 　　전시회에 대한 기사를 　ⓐ 크게 다루다 ⓑ 작성하다

06 **move** that the meeting adjourn 　　휴회를 　ⓐ 선언하다 ⓑ 제안하다

07 **declare** goods purchased abroad 　해외에서 구매한 물품을 　ⓐ 반환하다 ⓑ 세관 신고하다

08 **enact** a law 　　　　　　　　　　　　　법률을 　ⓐ 제정하다 ⓑ 준수하다

09 **initiate** a system 　　　　　　　　　　제도를 　ⓐ 개혁하다 ⓑ 시작하다

10 **exploit** employees 　　　　　　　　　노동력을 　ⓐ 착취하다 ⓑ 활용하다

11 **interpret** a poem 　　　　　　　　　　시를 　ⓐ 낭송하다 ⓑ 해석하다

12 **notice** a difference 　　　　　　　　　차이점을 　ⓐ 알아채다 ⓑ 설명하다

13 **propagate** seismic waves 　　　　　지진파를 　ⓐ 전달하다 ⓑ 감지하다

14 **endorse** a product 　　　　　　　　　상품을 　ⓐ 개발하다 ⓑ 추천하다

15 **reclaim** the suitcase 　　　　　　　　여행 가방을 　ⓐ 되찾다 ⓑ 부치다

16 **absorb** sunlight 　　　　　　　　　　　태양빛을 　ⓐ 반사하다 ⓑ 흡수하다

17 **resolve** a crisis 　　　　　　　　　　　위기를 　ⓐ 해결하다 ⓑ 가져오다

18 **emancipate** slaves 　　　　　　　　　노예를 　ⓐ 해방하다 ⓑ 억류하다

19 **spot** prey 　　　　　　　　　　　　　　먹이를 　ⓐ 발견하다 ⓑ 낚아채다

20 **dismiss** a class 　　　　　　　　　　　수업을 　ⓐ 편성하다 ⓑ 파하다

21 **deny** a refund 　　　　　　　　　　　　환불을 　ⓐ 거절하다 ⓑ 요청하다

22 **contribute** to global warming 　　지구 온난화에 　ⓐ 기여하다 ⓑ 대처하다

23 **sterilize** in boiling water 　　　　　끓는 물에 　ⓐ 살균하다 ⓑ 데치다

24 **house** over 1 million books 　　　백만 여권의 도서를 　ⓐ 기증하다 ⓑ 소장하다

25 **separate** trash for recycling 　　재활용을 위해 쓰레기를 　ⓐ 수거하다 ⓑ 분리하다

26 be **sentenced** to 5 years in prison 　징역 5년 형을 　ⓐ 선고받다 ⓑ 복역하다

27 feel **piqued** 　　　　　　　　　　　　감정이 　ⓐ 누그러지다 ⓑ 상하다

28 the birth rate **plummets** 　　　　출생률이 　ⓐ 급감하다 ⓑ 상승하다

29 **coax** someone into going 　　　사람을 　ⓐ 가도록 강요하다 ⓑ 구슬려서 가게 하다

30 the exchange rate **fluctuates** 　환율이 　ⓐ 오르내리다 ⓑ 안정되다

exceed the budget	예산을　ⓐ 초과하다　ⓑ 확대하다
penetrate a person's mind	사람의 마음을　ⓐ 사로잡다　ⓑ 꿰뚫어 보다
inherit a gene	유전자를　ⓐ 물려받다　ⓑ 조작하다
disperse seeds	종자를　ⓐ 퍼뜨리다　ⓑ 재배하다
be **reprimanded** for misconduct	위법 행위로　ⓐ 기소되다　ⓑ 질책받다
deposit debris	잔해를　ⓐ 퇴적시키다　ⓑ 치워 버리다
rain **pelts**	비가　ⓐ 퍼붓다　ⓑ 그치다
levy a tax	세금을　ⓐ 환급하다　ⓑ 부과하다
oil prices **skyrocket**	유가가　ⓐ 안정되다　ⓑ 급등하다
hail a cab	택시를　ⓐ 불러 세우다　ⓑ 탑승하다
smuggle drugs	마약을　ⓐ 밀수하다　ⓑ 남용하다
recuperate from an operation	수술을 받고　ⓐ 상태가 악화되다　ⓑ 회복하다
exonerate someone from an accusation	결백을　ⓐ 입증하다　ⓑ 주장하다
be **committed** to helping people	사람들을 돕는 데　ⓐ 협조하다　ⓑ 전념하다
deplete resources	자원을　ⓐ 고갈시키다　ⓑ 확보하다
savor wine	와인을　ⓐ 음미하다　ⓑ 숙성시키다
curb population growth	인구 증가를　ⓐ 장려하다　ⓑ 억제하다
emerge as a global power	강대국으로　ⓐ 부상하다　ⓑ 평가되다
inculcate respect for elders	어른에 대한 공경을　ⓐ 가르쳐주다　ⓑ 배우다
exaggerate the benefits of the product	상품의 장점을　ⓐ 과장하다　ⓑ 부각시키다
remove a tattoo	문신을　ⓐ 제거하다　ⓑ 새겨 넣다
update a policy	정책을　ⓐ 지지하다　ⓑ 개정하다
treat people differently	사람들을 다르게　ⓐ 대우하다　ⓑ 평가하다
specify how people should behave	사람들의 행동해야 하는 방식을　ⓐ 지정하다　ⓑ 변화시키다
achieve a goal	목표를　ⓐ 달성하다　ⓑ 설정하다
establish a market	시장을　ⓐ 형성하다　ⓑ 주도하다
deviate from the path	길에서　ⓐ 방황하다　ⓑ 빗나가다
resist infection	감염에　ⓐ 저항하다　ⓑ 노출하다
insert a contact lens	콘택트 렌즈를　ⓐ 소독하다　ⓑ 끼워 넣다
condemn the property	부동산을　ⓐ 몰수하다　ⓑ 매각하다

둘 중 적절한 어휘를 골라 ∨ 표를 하세요.

61 ○ pare
   ○ vent   one's anger   화를 터뜨리다

62 ○ hold
   ○ take   an Olympics   올림픽을 개최하다

63 ○ allay
   ○ allege   one's concern   근심을 가라앉히다

64 ○ embrace
   ○ cherish   one's memory   추억을 고이 간직하다

65 ○ diagnose
   ○ prescribe   antibiotics   항생제를 처방하다

66 ○ lapse
   ○ jumble   into cliché   진부하게 흘러가다

67 ○ falsify
   ○ invalidate   one's educational background   학력을 위조하다

68 ○ crack
   ○ break   a large bill   고액 지폐를 잔돈으로 바꾸다

69 ○ redeem
   ○ retain   for cash   현금으로 상환하다

70 be ○ flattered
      ○ harnessed   by compliments   칭찬에 우쭐해지다

71 ○ cajole
   ○ skirt   the law   법망을 피하다

72 ○ baffle
   ○ stunt   growth   성장을 저해하다

73 ○ apply
   ○ attach   a bandage   붕대를 감다

74 ○ swindle
   ○ elongate   money   돈을 사기 쳐서 빼앗다

75 ○ taper
   ○ flaunt   wealth   부유함을 과시하다

76 ○ grab
   ○ snap   a bite to eat   재빨리 먹다

77 can't ○ face
         ○ stand   noise   소음을 참을 수 없다

78 Can you ○ direct
          ○ transport   me to my seat?   제 좌석으로 안내해주시겠습니까?

79 Are you ○ expecting
          ○ forwarding   anybody?   누군가를 기다리고 계신가요?

80 Please ○ link
         ○ connect   me with Mr. Wright.   Mr. Wright와 전화를 연결해주십시오.

○ **pursue** ○ **engage**	a career	경력에 종사하다
○ **tally** ○ **charge**	expenses	비용을 합산하다
○ **enroll** ○ **reserve**	in a course	강좌를 등록하다
○ **mediate** ○ **rescind**	a contract	계약을 무효로 하다
○ **postpone** ○ **reinstate**	a meeting	회의를 연기하다
○ **defend** ○ **eliminate**	crime	범죄를 제거하다
○ **locate** ○ **transfer**	a call	전화를 돌려주다
○ **extol** ○ **exude**	confidence	자신감을 발산하다
○ **serve** ○ **state**	as a reference	참고가 되다
○ **accede** ○ **incline**	to the throne	왕위에 오르다
○ **audit** ○ **observe**	Christmas	크리스마스를 경축하다
○ **manufacture** ○ **fabricate**	evidence	증거를 조작하다
○ **satiate** ○ **reimburse**	the travel expenses	여행 경비를 상환해주다
○ **tackle** ○ **assuage**	one's anger	화를 진정시키다
○ **accumulate** ○ **balance**	the budget	수지타산을 맞추다
○ **flunk** ○ **unravel**	an exam	시험을 낙제하다
○ **progress** ○ **develop**	cancer	암에 걸리다
○ **confirm** ○ **concede**	a reservation	예약을 확인하다
○ **placate** ○ **shelve**	a program	계획을 보류하다
○ **veer** ○ **span**	eastward	동쪽으로 방향이 바뀌다

정답 p.94

VOCABULARY | 알맞은 어휘

해커스 탭스 Reading

Hackers **TEST**

Part I Choose the best answer for the blank.

01 A: Take whichever vegetables you'd like.
   B: Thanks. I like broccoli but can't _____ asparagus.

   (a) stand   (b) force
   (c) apply   (d) demand

02 A: I heard that you got _____.
   Congratulations!
   B: Thanks, but now I'm absolutely swamped with work.

   (a) proceeded   (b) promoted
   (c) rewarded   (d) restored

03 A: Hello. I'm calling to speak with Professor Williams.
   B: Please hold while I _____ you.

   (a) convey   (b) extend
   (c) transfer   (d) contact

04 A: This chair seems a little too high for me.
   B: Then, _____ the height of the chair to suit you.

   (a) conform   (b) adjust
   (c) arrange   (d) upgrade

05 A: Did you know that salmon hatch in freshwater streams and then _____ to the sea?
   B: Really? I thought only birds did long-distance traveling.

   (a) migrate   (b) wander
   (c) roam   (d) traverse

06 A: Should I wear a suit and tie today or dress casually?
   B: Just stop _____ and make a decision.

   (a) tantalizing   (b) vacillating
   (c) fluctuating   (d) disapproving

Part II Choose the best answer for the blank.

07 Thomas Pynchon is perhaps most famous for h tendency to _____ publicity, despite his massive literary success.

   (a) occupy   (b) shun
   (c) instill   (d) appall

08 It was during the warmest month of the year tl drought _____ all the cornfields in the Midwest region.

   (a) swayed   (b) forced
   (c) struck   (d) rushed

09 The boycott of the cosmetic company's product _____ for months until the company decide stop testing its products on animals.

   (a) continued   (b) survived
   (c) granted   (d) pursued

10 A bibliography allows interested readers to _____ more detailed information on rel topics.

   (a) exceed   (b) obtain
   (c) reclaim   (d) reckon

During the Cold War, Russian spies were often accused of trying to _____ democracy in America.

(a) neglect   (b) subvert
(c) concoct   (d) revolve

Most people don't realize that it is important to _____ the gears of mechanical appliances regularly.

(a) fluctuate   (b) lubricate
(c) motivate   (d) instigate

Students in their senior year will _____ from choosing elective courses related to their majors to broaden their range of knowledge.

(a) convert   (b) lure
(c) falter   (d) benefit

A traffic accident this morning _____ the late arrival of several employees.

(a) tempered   (b) exempted
(c) extenuated   (d) coalesced

The medical instruments and other equipment to be used for the surgical procedure should be _____ first.

(a) deodorized   (b) sterilized
(c) baptized   (d) tranquilized

16 Even after he became famous for his ideas in linguistics, Noam Chomsky _____ in political writing, having had dozens of essays published.

(a) conferred   (b) procured
(c) wobbled   (d) dabbled

17 Great authors are frequently _____ posthumously for works that failed to garner attention while they were still alive.

(a) denounced   (b) buttressed
(c) lauded   (d) sublimated

18 The feminist movement played a role in _____ women from gender biases at home and at work.

(a) dismissing   (b) emancipating
(c) disconnecting (d) separating

19 The former manager of Maritime Oil discovered a loophole through which he _____ the company out of thousands of dollars.

(a) frittered   (b) scoured
(c) alleged   (d) bilked

20 The Wildlife Conservation Commission has _____ the government for not doing more to protect endangered species on the island.

(a) chastised   (b) beseeched
(c) maltreated   (d) assaulted

정답 p.95

VOCABULARY | 일반 어휘

해커스 텝스 Reading

CHAPTER **08** 명사

> **volume of traffic : 교통 소리 크기?**
>
> 외출 준비를 하던 텝식씨, 오늘 volume of traffic이 엄청나다는 뉴스를 듣고 귀마개를 준비하는데……. 한여름 꽉 막힌 도로에서 구마개를 끼고 땀을 뻘뻘 흘려야 했던 텝식씨는 volume에 흔히 아는 '소리 크기' 말고도 '양'이라는 뜻도 있다는 사실을 몰랐던 것. 따라서 volume of traffic은 '교통 소리 크기'가 아니라 '교통량'이라는 뜻이 된다. 어휘의 다양한 의미를 묻는 텝스 어휘를 위해서는 명사역시 다양한 의미를 함께 알아두어야 한다. 그럼 이제 이미 아는 명사의 뜻은 다양하게, 몰랐던 명사는 새롭게 익혀보자.

■ 출제 경향

· 명사 문제는 매 시험 평균적으로 4문제 정도 출제되며, Part 1과 Part 2에서 비슷한 비율로 출제된다.

· 일상 생활에서 쓰이는 명사의 활용을 묻는 문제들이 자주 출제된다.
  예) level(층), line(사람들의 줄), exit(출구), block(도로의 구획) 등

· 다의어 명사의 의미를 묻는 문제들이 출제되기도 한다.
  예) extension(구내 전화, 날짜의 연기), draft(외풍, 초안) 등

■ 예제

Part I

A: Good morning. Is this where I get my boarding pass?
B: No, you have to check in at the other _____ of the airport.

(a) place   (b) end
(c) spot   (d) position

A: 안녕하세요. 여기가 탑승권을 받는 곳인가요?
B: 아니요, 공항의 다른 쪽 끝에서 탑승 수속을 하셔야 합니다

해설 | 여기서 탑승권을 받을 수 있는지 묻는 A의 질문에 B는 '공항의 다른 _____에서 탑승 수속을 해야 한다'라고 대답하고 있다. 따라서 문맥상 빈칸에는 '끄트머리, (방 등의) 다른 곳'을 의미하는 (b) end가 들어가는 것이 자연스럽다. 참고로, end에는 '결말, 마지막'이라는 뜻도 있다.
어휘 | boarding pass 탑승권   check in 탑승 수속하다
정답 | (b) end

Part II

The producers decided to stop broadcasting the show after _____ fell to less than one percent.

(a) viewership   (b) spectators
(c) turnout   (d) congregation

시청률이 1퍼센트 이하로 하락하자 제작자들은 방송을 중단하로 결정했다.

해설 | _____이 1퍼센트 이하로 하락하자 제작자들은 방송을 중단하기로 결정했다'라는 문맥에서 빈칸에는 '시청률, (텔레비전 프로그램의) 시청자 수'라는 뜻의 (a) viewersh 어가는 것이 자연스럽다. spectator는 '구경꾼, 관객', turnout은 '출석자 수, 투표자 수', congregation은 '모임, 회합'이라는 뜻이다.
어휘 | producer[prədʒúːsər] (영화 · TV의) 제작자, 프로듀서   broadcast [brɔ́ːdkæst] 방송하다
정답 | (a) viewership

vacancy [véikənsi] 빈방

Because of the holiday weekend, the motel had no vacancies.
주말 연휴 때문에, 모텔에는 빈방이 없었다.

qualm [kwɑːm] 양심의 가책, 마음의 꺼림칙함

The lawyer had no qualms about defending some of the biggest criminal organizations.
그 변호사는 몇몇의 가장 거대한 범죄 조직들을 변호하는 것에 관해 아무런 양심의 가책도 없었다.

umbrage [ʌ́mbridʒ] 불쾌감, 그림자

The prime minister took umbrage at the suggestion he was controlled by his advisors.
그 수상은 그가 그의 고문들에 의해 조정당한다는 의견에 불쾌감을 드러냈다.

subscription [səbskrípʃən] (정기 간행물의) 구독

Your subscription will expire in three months if you don't renew it now.
지금 갱신하시지 않으면 3개월 후에 귀하의 구독이 만료됩니다.

transition [trænzíʃən] 변천, 변화

The country is undergoing an economic transition from socialism to capitalism.
그 국가는 사회주의에서 자본주의로의 경제적 변천을 겪고 있다.

reticence [rétisəns] 과묵함

Certain cultures value reticence and politeness far more than others.
특정 문화들은 다른 것들보다 과묵함과 예의를 훨씬 더 가치 있게 여긴다.

acceptance [əkséptəns] 인정, 승인

Sometimes acceptance of the truth is more difficult than a convenient lie.
때로는 진실을 인정하는 것이 편리한 거짓말보다 어렵다.

controversy [kántrəvəːrsi] 논쟁, 논란

Some magazines have created a controversy by expressing viewpoints that are anti-religious.
일부 잡지는 반종교적인 관점을 표현함으로써 논쟁을 불러일으켰다.

necessity [nəsésəti] 필수품

Many underclass families cannot even afford the basic necessities of life.
많은 최하층 가정들은 생활 필수품조차 살 여유가 없다.

perception [pərsépʃən] 인식

Naturalists have a different perception of global warming than oil companies do.
자연주의자들은 지구 온난화에 대해 정유 회사와 인식을 달리 한다.

incentive [inséntiv] 자극, 동기

Evaluation bonuses act as incentives for salespeople to work harder.
성과급은 영업 사원들이 더 열심히 일하도록 하는 자극으로서 역할을 한다.

scarcity [skéərsəti] 부족

Korea relies heavily on foreign trade due to a scarcity of natural resources.
한국은 천연 자원의 부족 때문에 해외 무역에 크게 의존한다.

VOCABULARY | 일반 어휘

해커스 텝스 Reading

13 denomination [dinàmənéiʃən] 액면 금액, 명칭

The highest denomination banknote is going to be withdrawn from circulation this month.
가장 높은 액면 금액의 지폐는 이번 달에 유통이 중단될 것이다.

14 glitch [glitʃ] (컴퓨터의) 오류, (기계의) 사소한 결함

Every computer suddenly shut down due to a glitch in the network.
네트워크의 오류로 인해 모든 컴퓨터가 갑자기 종료되었다.

15 prescription [priskrípʃən] 처방(전)

Many patients fail to follow the instructions on their prescription.
많은 환자들은 그들의 처방전에 적혀 있는 지시 사항을 따르지 않는다.

16 retort [ritɔ́ːrt] 반박, 말대꾸

His point was so sharp that I could not think of a single retort.
그의 요점은 아주 예리해서 나는 반박을 한마디도 생각해낼 수 없었다.

17 correlation [kɔ̀ːrəléiʃən] 상관관계, 상호 관련

A correlation exists between a climate's rainfall and the number of species that inhabit it.
한 기후대의 강우량과 그곳에 서식하는 종의 수 사이에는 상관관계가 존재한다.

18 counterpart [káuntərpàːrt] 대응하는 사람·것

The U.S. president fulfills different tasks from his Russian counterpart.
미국의 대통령은 러시아의 대응자(대통령)와 다른 업무를 수행한다.

19 gratuity [grətjúːəti] 팁, 봉사료

Some of the staff at the hotel make a tidy sum from gratuities.
그 호텔의 일부 직원들은 팁으로 상당한 금액의 돈을 번다.

20 nuisance [njuːsns] 성가신 것, 폐

Having to traverse icy roads is such a nuisance.
얼어붙은 도로를 가로질러야 하는 것은 너무 성가시다.

21 prominence [prámənəns] 두드러짐, 탁월함

The group came to prominence after performing on a television show.
그 그룹은 텔레비전 쇼에서 공연한 뒤로 두각을 나타냈다.

22 repercussion [rìːpərkʌ́ʃən] (주로 부정적인) 반향, (간접적인) 영향

Violence against those conducting peaceful protests will have repercussions against the government.
평화적인 시위 활동을 하고 있는 사람들에 대한 폭력은 정부에 대한 부정적인 반향을 일으킬 것이다.

23 inception [insépʃən] 시작, 발단

The inception of wireless technology has revolutionized the communications industry.
무선 기술의 시작은 통신 산업에 급격한 변화를 가져왔다.

24 credence [kríːdəns] 신빙성

Unexplained phenomena give credence to the existence of the supernatural.
설명되지 않는 현상들은 초자연적인 존재에 신빙성을 더한다.

Hackers **Practice**

풀면서 외우는 기출 어휘

굵게 표시된 단어에 적절한 해석을 고르세요.

contents of a bag	가방의 ⓐ 소재 ⓑ 내용물
ask for an **extension** of the deadline	마감 기한의 ⓐ 연장 ⓑ 단축 을 요청하다
scientific **achievement** in the last century	지난 세기의 과학적 ⓐ 발전 ⓑ 성과
It's your **turn** to speak.	당신이 이야기할 ⓐ 주제 ⓑ 순서 입니다.
follow one's **instincts**	ⓐ 본능 ⓑ 규정 대로 행동하다
a **remedy** for anxiety and depression	불안 및 우울증의 ⓐ 치료 요법 ⓑ 증상의 발현
a car with good **mileage**	ⓐ 연비가 ⓑ 성능이 좋은 차
a manned space **mission**	유인 우주선 ⓐ 기술 개발 ⓑ 비행 임무
subject to a **penalty**	ⓐ 과태료가 ⓑ 추가 요금이 부과되는
spectators at a football match	축구 시합의 ⓐ 심판 ⓑ 관중
the **paradox** of modern technology	현대 기술의 ⓐ 모순 ⓑ 혜택
an airport **concourse**	공항의 ⓐ 휴게실 ⓑ 중앙 광장
an **agenda** for a conference	회의의 ⓐ 결론 ⓑ 의제
breach of contract	계약의 ⓐ 위반 ⓑ 이행
cover **liabilities**	ⓐ 손해 ⓑ 죄과 를 보상하다
be arrested on **bribery** charges	ⓐ 뇌물 수수 ⓑ 절도 혐의로 체포되다
the **aftermath** of the war	전쟁의 ⓐ 여파 ⓑ 중단
political **clout**	정치적 ⓐ 영향력 ⓑ 위기
diagnosis of lung cancer	폐암 ⓐ 치료법 ⓑ 진단
maintain **poise**	ⓐ 침묵 ⓑ 평정 을 유지하다
a movie **sequel**	영화의 ⓐ 속편 ⓑ 원작
an **influx** of foreign capital	해외 자본의 ⓐ 유입 ⓑ 유치
follow the **itinerary**	ⓐ 여정 ⓑ 규정 을 따르다
the meeting **venue**	회의 ⓐ 일정 ⓑ 장소
the **obituary** section	ⓐ 부고 ⓑ 논설 란
act as a **deterrent**	ⓐ 촉매제 ⓑ 방해물 로서 작용하다
exercise **leverage**	ⓐ 특권 ⓑ 영향력 을 행사하다
the **legacy** of civilizations	문명의 ⓐ 유산 ⓑ 몰락
an **inauguration** speech	ⓐ 퇴임 ⓑ 취임 연설
a valuable **asset** to a company	회사의 귀중한 ⓐ (인재와 같은) 자산 ⓑ 투자자

VOCABULARY | 일반 어휘

Chapter 08 명사 **305**

둘 중 적절한 어휘를 골라 V 표를 하세요.

31 a high ○ **rate** / ○ **mode** of inflation — 고도의 인플레이션

32 a(n) ○ **royalty** / ○ **heir** to the throne — 왕위 계승자

33 the ○ **gist** / ○ **core** of a story — 이야기의 요점

34 college ○ **alumni** / ○ **colleagues** — 대학 동문

35 a one-year ○ **treaty** / ○ **warranty** on a camera — 카메라의 1년 품질 보증서

36 feel a ○ **draft** / ○ **current** in the room — 방의 외풍을 느끼다

37 a full-time ○ **tinker** / ○ **earner** — 정규직 봉급자

38 on ○ **exposure** / ○ **display** — 전시 중인

39 offer one's ○ **grievances** / ○ **condolences** — 조의를 표하다

40 suffer from ○ **dehydration** / ○ **hypochondria** — 우울증을 겪다

41 without a ○ **hitch** / ○ **glitch** — 문제 없이

42 generate ○ **revenue** / ○ **surplus** — 수익을 창출하다

43 the ○ **solution** / ○ **treatment** of malaria — 말라리아 치료법

44 have a(n) ○ **hunch** / ○ **itch** — 예감이 들다

45 go through a ○ **mode** / ○ **phase** — 단계를 겪다

46 an ○ **explosion** / ○ **outbreak** of disease — 발병

47 make a ○ **deviation** / ○ **detour** — 우회하다

48 prosecute an ○ **offender** / ○ **incinerator** — 범법자를 기소하다

49 time ○ **inhibitions** / ○ **constraints** — 시간적 제약

50 a child ○ **kindling** / ○ **prodigy** — 신동

current	○ **stature** ○ **status**	현재 상태
a violin	○ **virtuoso** ○ **novice**	바이올린 명연주가
have a	○ **bypass** ○ **layover**	(항공편이) 경유하다
in	○ **conjunction** ○ **correlation** with	~와 함께
have a	○ **thirst** ○ **craving**	열망하다
take	○ **precautions** ○ **preventatives**	조심하다
have a quick	○ **temper** ○ **rage**	성미가 급하다
a firm	○ **rebel** ○ **rebuttal**	단호한 반박
tender one's	○ **resignation** ○ **restriction**	사표를 제출하다
parental	○ **guidance** ○ **prudence**	부모의 지도
including	○ **utilities** ○ **facilities**	공과금을 포함하여
a	○ **tally** ○ **slot** on the schedule	일정의 빈 시간
the general	○ **collusion** ○ **consensus**	일반적인 여론, 전반적인 합의
a	○ **flight** ○ **level** of stairs	한 줄로 이어진 계단
have good	○ **velocity** ○ **ventilation**	공기가 잘 통하다
○ **terms** ○ **affairs** of a contract		계약 조건
a	○ **discord** ○ **disparity** in the distribution of wealth	부의 분배의 불균형
hotel	○ **amenities** ○ **accessories**	호텔의 편의 시설
have a	○ **turnover** ○ **hangover**	숙취를 겪다
calcium	○ **deficiency** ○ **efficiency**	칼슘 부족

정답 p.97

Hackers **TEST**

Part I Choose the best answer for the blank.

01 A: I'd like to send this package to China.
B: Well, you should state the _____ of the
package on the box.

(a) contents   (b) substances
(c) resources   (d) fillings

02 A: Very many people today turn to cosmetic
surgery.
B: I know. It's turned into a real _____.

(a) difference   (b) opposition
(c) misunderstanding (d) controversy

03 A: I'd like to make a reservation for a single room
for this weekend.
B: I'm sorry, sir, but we don't have any _____
at this time.

(a) openings   (b) situations
(c) vacancies   (d) possibilities

04 A: There's a _____ coming in through the
window.
B: Would you like me to close it?

(a) whiff   (b) draft
(c) blast   (d) blow

05 A: I have to get a magazine from the newsstand.
B: You'd save yourself time and money if you got
a(n) _____ instead.

(a) sequence   (b) prescription
(c) subscription   (d) alternation

06 A: My computer crashed again! What a
_____!
B: Maybe you should ask a technician to look at

(a) downturn   (b) hazard
(c) blockage   (d) nuisance

Part II Choose the best answer for the blank.

07 While some companies consider network securit
a big expense, few would disagree that it is a
_____.

(a) luxury   (b) necessity
(c) bonus   (d) preference

08 Because of a manufacturing _____, the
latest model of the smartphone had to be recall

(a) dent   (b) glitch
(c) fake   (d) loophole

09 Because of the pervasive use of harmful pesticid
the town faced a(n) _____ of organic
vegetation.

(a) opulence   (b) scarcity
(c) density   (d) amenity

10 The growth of budget airlines and package
holidays have meant that previously exotic
destinations are now within the _____ o
ordinary people.

(a) grip   (b) hold
(c) grasp   (d) clasp

The protagonist of Robert Penn Warren's novel lies continually to get ahead, making him a _____.

(a) hypocrite
(b) misanthropist
(c) pugilist
(d) apostate

The company's financial _____ were found to be based on a misinterpretation of its customer data.

(a) projections
(b) peregrinations
(c) processions
(d) perambulations

Chasing prey over many kilometers, wild dogs rely on _____ rather than strength or speed to hunt successfully.

(a) patronage
(b) persistence
(c) profundity
(d) prodigality

In mythology, the god of love, Cupid, is the Roman _____ of Eros, the Greek god of love.

(a) conversion
(b) completion
(c) counterpart
(d) companion

For university graduates about to enter the working world, the _____ from student to employee is a difficult one to adjust to.

(a) modification
(b) variation
(c) commemoration
(d) transition

16 Copernicus' idea of a sun-centered universe found _____ with astronomers of his time but was rejected by the public.

(a) adherence
(b) abhorrence
(c) acceptance
(d) arbitration

17 During election campaign debates, presidential candidates sometimes give memorable _____ to their opponents' comments.

(a) oaths
(b) retorts
(c) defenses
(d) doctrine

18 A number of studies have determined that there is a direct _____ between sugar intake and diabetes.

(a) correlation
(b) comparison
(c) illustration
(d) identification

19 Imposing high interest rates on loans for small businesses can have huge _____ on this sector of the economy.

(a) determinations
(b) repercussions
(c) retaliations
(d) conclusions

20 Customers can buy over-the-counter medicines as well as _____ medication at a 24-hour pharmacy.

(a) prescription
(b) regulation
(c) consultation
(d) specification

VOCABULARY | 일반 어휘

해커스 텝스 Reading

CHAPTER 09 형용사와 부사

Smoke-free Zone : 흡연 자유 구역?

담배 연기를 유난히 싫어하는 텝식씨, 까페에서 "Smoke-free Zone"을 애써 피해 다른 쪽에 가서 앉았는데……. 그런데 텝식씨 옆에서 버젓이 담배를 피우는 이 사람들 좀 보게? 이봐요, 담배는 Smoke-free Zone에서 피우셔야죠! 하지만 free에는 '자유로운' 말고도 '~이 없는'이라는 뜻도 있으니 Smoke-free Zone은 '흡연 자유 구역'이 아니라 '흡연 금지 구역'이란 말씀. 이처럼 텝스 어휘에서는 형용사와 부사의 여러 의미를 묻는 문제들이 출제된다. 그럼 이미 아는 형용사와 부사의 뜻은 다양하게, 몰랐던 어휘는 새롭게 익혀보자.

■ 출제 경향

· 형용사와 부사 문제는 매 시험 평균적으로 5~10문제 정도 출제된다. Part 1보다 Part 2에서 더 많이 출제되며, 부사보다 형용사의 출제 비율이 훨씬 높다.

· 다의어 형용사의 의미를 묻는 문제들이 출제되기도 한다.
  예) available(이용 가능한, 시간이 비어 만날 수 있는), critical(비판적인, 중대한)

■ 예제

Part I

A: How much longer are you going to feel _____ about not having been promoted?
B: I'll be OK in a little while.

(a) outsourced   (b) underhanded
(c) downhearted   (d) offbeat

A: 승진하지 못한 것에 대해서 얼마나 더 오래 낙담해 있을 생각이야?
B: 조금 지나면 괜찮아질 거야.

해설 | '승진하지 못한 것에 대해서 얼마나 더 오래 _____할 생각이냐'라는 문맥에서 빈칸에는 '낙담한'이라는 뜻의 (c) downhearted가 들어가는 것이 자연스럽다. outsourced는 '외주에서 제작한', underhanded는 '비밀의, 인원이 모자란', offbeat은 '색다른'이라는 뜻으로 답이 될 수 없다.

정답 | (c) downhearted

Part II

Young people today are more _____ in international affairs than they were two decades ago.

(a) dependent   (b) unavailable
(c) compatible   (d) knowledgeable

오늘날의 젊은이들은 20년 전의 젊은이들에 비해 국제 정세에 대해 더 잘 알고 있다.

해설 | '오늘날의 젊은이들이 과거에 비해 국제 정세에 대해 더 _____하다'라는 문맥에서 빈칸에는 '잘 알고 있는'이라는 뜻의 (d) knowledgeable이 들어가는 것이 자연스럽다. dependent는 '의존적인', unavailable은 '(사람이) 부재한, 손에 넣을 수 없는', compatible은 '양립할 수 있는'이라는 뜻으로 답이 될 수 없다.

어휘 | international affairs 국제 정세   decade[dékeid] 10년

정답 | (d) knowledgeable

rash [ræʃ] 경솔한, 성급한

Quitting his job was a rash decision that Max regretted immediately.
그의 직장을 그만둔 것은 Max가 즉시 후회한 경솔한 결정이었다.

flexible [fléksəbl] 탄력적인, 융통성 있는

Our office hours are flexible during the semester to accommodate student needs.
저희 영업시간은 학생들의 요구를 충족시키기 위해 학기 중에 탄력적으로 운영됩니다.

critical [krítikəl] 비판적인, 중요한, 중대한

Most reviewers considered the play mediocre, but one was especially critical.
대부분의 비평가들이 그 연극을 보통이라고 여겼지만, 한 사람은 특히 비판적이었다.

It is critical that boats store life jackets in case of an emergency.
비상 사태에 대비하여, 보트는 구명조끼를 비축하는 것이 중요하다.

available [əvéiləbl] 이용·입수 가능한, 시간이 비어 만날 수 있는

Information on scholarships is available on the university's Web site.
장학금에 대한 정보는 대학 웹 사이트에서 이용 가능합니다.

No one is available to take your call, so please leave a message.
아무도 전화를 받을 수 없으니, 메시지를 남겨주시기 바랍니다.

misleading [mislídiŋ] 오해를 불러일으키는, 허위의

The news report contains a number of misleading statements that should be clarified.
그 뉴스 보도는 반드시 밝혀져야 할 많은 오해를 불러일으키는 진술을 담고 있다.

credible [krédəbl] 믿을 만한, 설득력이 있는

When writing an academic essay, make sure that the sources you cite are credible.
학술적인 에세이를 쓸 때, 당신이 인용하는 정보원이 믿을 만하다는 것을 반드시 확인하라.

prolific [prəlífik] 다작의

Ms. Oates is a prolific novelist, having published 36 novels in 34 years.
Ms. Oates는 34년간 36편을 출간했던 다작하는 작가이다.

idyllic [aidílik] 전원적인, 목가적인

People want to lead an idyllic lifestyle in a rural setting after retiring.
사람들은 퇴직 후에 시골에서 전원적인 삶을 살고 싶어한다.

vacant [véikənt] 비어 있는

A property developer has purchased the vacant lot on Pine Street to build a condominium.
한 부동산 개발업자는 분양 아파트를 짓기 위해 Pine 로의 비어 있는 부지를 구입했다.

alert [ələ́ːrt] 정신이 또렷한, 기민한

Despite her serious head injury, she remains alert and communicative.
심각한 머리 부상에도 불구하고, 그녀는 여전히 정신이 또렷하고 말을 잘하는 상태이다.

VOCABULARY | 기출 어휘

해커스 텝스 Reading

11 detrimental[dètrəméntl] 해로운, 불리한

Prolonged exposure to the sun without sunblock can be detrimental to one's skin.
자외선 차단제를 바르지 않고 태양에 오래 노출되어 있으면 피부에 해로울 수 있다.

12 complimentary[kàmpləméntəri] 무료의

All participants on the tour will receive a complimentary handbag.
여행의 모든 참가자들께서는 무료 핸드백을 받으실 것입니다.

13 consistent[kənsístənt] 일치하는, 일관된

The design colors of the store are not consistent with those on the logo.
상점의 디자인 색상은 로고의 색상과 일치하지 않는다.

14 filthy[fílθi] 더러운, 불결한, 부도덕한

Numerous reviews of the hotel claim the rooms are disgustingly filthy.
그 호텔의 무수한 후기들은 방들이 진절머리나게 더럽다고 말한다.

15 impertinent [impə́ːrtənənt] 무례한, 주제넘은

Most people find it intolerable to be asked impertinent questions.
대부분의 사람들은 무례한 질문을 받는 것을 참지 못한다.

16 reclusive[riklúːsiv] 은둔하는, 쓸쓸한

After a major scandal, the celebrity became reclusive and hid himself from the media.
대대적인 추문 이후, 그 유명 인사는 은둔하여 언론에서 자취를 감추었다.

17 viable[vaiəbl] 실용적인, (계획이) 실행 가능한

Though cheaper, cutting back the number of pages in our magazine is not a viable alternative.
더 경제적이긴 하지만, 우리 잡지의 페이지 수를 줄이는 것은 실용적인 대안이 아니다.

18 redundant[ridʌ́ndənt] (표현이) 장황한, 불필요한

The politician's new campaign speech was redundant and repetitive.
정치인의 새 선거 공약 연설은 장황하고 반복적이었다.

19 eligible[élidʒəbl] 자격 요건을 갖춘, 받을(할) 자격이 있는

Students and seniors are often eligible for transportation discounts.
학생들과 연장자들은 종종 교통 할인을 받을 자격 요건을 갖춘다.

20 copious[kóupiəs] 다량(다수)의, 풍부한, 많은

The copious amounts of sugar found in most softdrinks pose health risks.
대부분의 청량 음료에서 발견되는 다량의 설탕은 건강 위협을 제기한다.

21 repentant[ripéntənt] 후회하고 있는

Although Maxwell felt repentant about stealing from his parents, he didn't admit to the crime.
Maxwell은 그의 부모에게서 도둑질한 것에 대해 후회했지만, 그는 범죄를 시인하지는 않았다.

22 effortlessly[éfərtlisli] 노력하지 않고, 쉽게

She solved that difficult mathematical equation almost effortlessly.
그녀는 그 어려운 수학 방정식을 거의 노력도 하지 않고 풀어냈다.

distraught[distrɔ́:t] 심란한, 슬픔으로 제정신이 아닌

Judy was very distraught after her luggage was stolen at the airport.
공항에서 짐 가방을 도난당한 후 Judy는 매우 심란했다.

articulate[ɑːrtíkjulət] (사람이) 말을 분명하게 잘하는

I hate speaking in public as I'm not very articulate.
나는 말을 분명하게 잘하지 않기 때문에 대중 앞에서 말하는 것을 싫어한다.

impromptu[imprɑ́mptju:] 즉흥적인, 즉석의

Her impromptu performance at the piano underscored just how talented she was.
그녀의 즉흥적인 피아노 연주는 그녀가 얼마나 재능이 있는지를 분명히 보여주었다.

hackneyed[hǽknid] 진부한

The novel was criticized for being a hackneyed rehash of a familiar plotline.
그 소설은 익숙한 줄거리의 진부한 재탕인 점에 대해 비판받았다.

fretful[frétfəl] 조마조마해 하는, 초조해 하는

The little girl becomes fretful whenever her mother picks her up late.
그 어린 소녀는 엄마가 자신을 데리러 늦게 올 때면 조마조마해 한다.

adroit[ədrɔ́it] 능숙한

John Williams is one of the most adroit classical guitarists in the world.
John Williams는 세계에서 가장 능숙한 클래식 기타리스트 중 하나이다.

stringent[stríndʒənt] 엄격한, 가혹한

Safety measures need to be stringent to prevent accidents.
안전 수칙은 사고를 방지하기 위해 엄격할 필요가 있다.

innocuous[inɑ́kjuəs] 악의 없는, 무해한

An innocuous e-mail can also carry a link to a destructive computer virus.
악의 없는 이메일도 해로운 컴퓨터 바이러스의 링크를 옮길 수 있다.

ostentatious[àstəntéiʃəs] 과시하는, 자랑 삼아 드러내는

Sylvia's dress was colorful and ostentatious, whereas everyone else wore black and white.
다른 이들은 모두 검정색과 흰색을 입은 반면, Sylvia의 드레스는 화려하고 과시적이었다.

malicious[məlíʃəs] 악의적인, 심술궂은

People don't see the harm of malicious gossip until they become a victim of it.
사람들은 악의적인 가십의 희생자가 되어보기 전에는 그것의 해악을 모른다.

fastidious[fæstídiəs] 까다로운

Because Peter is fastidious about what he eats, he never has lunch at the cafeteria.
Peter는 먹는 것에 대해 까다롭기 때문에, 절대로 구내 식당에서 점심을 먹지 않는다.

impeccable[impékəbl] 흠잡을 데 없는, 완벽한

Your timing really is impeccable, since you showed up exactly at seven.
넌 정확히 7시에 나타났으니, 너의 타이밍은 아주 흠잡을 데 없다.

VOCABULARY | 일반 어휘

해커스 펍스 Reading

Hackers **Practice**

둘 중 표시된 단어에 적절한 해석을 고르세요.

01 an **obedient** child   ⓐ 말을 잘 듣는 ⓑ 장난꾸러기인   아이

02 **tepid** water   ⓐ 미지근한 ⓑ 펄펄 끓는   물

03 **resistant** to drugs   약물에   ⓐ 중독된 ⓑ 내성이 있는

04 look **vulnerable**   ⓐ 연약해 ⓑ 유연해   보이다

05 a **barren** desert   ⓐ 광대한 ⓑ 불모의   사막

06 a **valid** parking pass   ⓐ 유효한 ⓑ 무료의   주차 이용권

07 **extraneous** information   ⓐ 핵심적인 ⓑ 관련 없는   정보

08 lead a **secluded** life   ⓐ 자급자족하는 ⓑ 은둔하는   삶을 살다

09 feel **overjoyed**   매우   ⓐ 흥분하다 ⓑ 기뻐하다

10 **durable** materials   ⓐ 내구성이 강한 ⓑ 구하기 쉬운   소재

11 **cohesive** writing   ⓐ 설득력이 떨어지는 ⓑ 논리적으로 긴밀한   글

12 an **extinct** species   ⓐ 멸종한 ⓑ 야생화된   종

13 a **taciturn** person   ⓐ 과묵한 ⓑ 예민한   사람

14 **suited** for the job   일에   ⓐ 잘 적응하는 ⓑ 적임인

15 a **spectacular** view   ⓐ 보기 드문 ⓑ 장관의   광경

16 the **cumulative** effects   ⓐ 누적되는 ⓑ 기대되는   효과

17 a **pathetic** score   ⓐ 대략적인 ⓑ 형편없는   점수

18 a **predictable** result   ⓐ 예측 가능한 ⓑ 불분명한   결말

19 a **controversial** figure   ⓐ 존경받는 ⓑ 논란이 있는   인물

20 a **drastic** action   ⓐ 과감한 ⓑ 효과적인   조치

21 keep **current** with trends   ⓐ 최신의 ⓑ 급진적인   경향을 유지하다

22 a **chronic** disease   ⓐ 만성 ⓑ 급성   질환

23 a **reliable** product   ⓐ 신뢰할 수 있는 ⓑ 사용이 편리한   제품

24 an **assiduous** student   ⓐ 성실한 ⓑ 평범한   학생

25 an **arbitrary** action   ⓐ 결단력 있는 ⓑ 독단적인   행동

26 a **gregarious** personality   ⓐ 사교적인 ⓑ 낙관적인   성격

27 **confidential** information   ⓐ 기밀의 ⓑ 전문적인   정보

28 a **fraudulent** claim   ⓐ 강경한 ⓑ 허위의   주장

29 a **moot** point   ⓐ 논쟁의 소지가 있는 ⓑ 해결할 수 없는   문제

30 take **tentative** measures   ⓐ 잠정적인 ⓑ 근본적인   조치를 취하다

a **pervasive** problem	ⓐ 만연한 ⓑ 근본적인 문제
a **strategic** method	ⓐ 경제적인 ⓑ 효과적인 방법
a **lavish** affair	ⓐ 소박한 ⓑ 화려한 파티
an **evasive** statement	ⓐ 애매모호한 ⓑ 주제와 무관한 진술
a **ludicrous** situation	ⓐ 어색한 ⓑ 우스꽝스러운 상황
defensive driving	ⓐ 방어 ⓑ 양보 운전
a **hypothetical** question	ⓐ 유도적인 ⓑ 가정에 입각한 질문
obsolete equipment	ⓐ 노후한 ⓑ 불충분한 장비
abnormal behavior	ⓐ 무례한 ⓑ 이상 행동
a **steadfast** faith	ⓐ 확고한 ⓑ 도덕적인 신념
significantly increase	ⓐ 갑자기 ⓑ 현저하게 증가하다
an **intrepid** explorer	ⓐ 대담한 ⓑ 모험적인 탐험가
a **hostile** environment	ⓐ 불리한 ⓑ 쾌적한 환경
a **marginal** effect	ⓐ 엄청난 ⓑ 제한적인 효과
a **belated** birthday present	ⓐ 때늦은 ⓑ 약소한 생일 선물
a **mutual** feeling	ⓐ 충동적인 ⓑ 상호적인 감정
an **integral** part	ⓐ 필수불가결한 ⓑ 부수적인 부분
be **prone** to infection	감염에 ⓐ 걸리기 쉬운 ⓑ 저항성이 높은
an **apprehensive** glance	ⓐ 불안한 ⓑ 측은한 시선
report the speech **verbatim**	연설을 ⓐ 신속하게 ⓑ 글자 그대로 보도하다
resist **vigorously**	ⓐ 끊임없이 ⓑ 맹렬히 저항하다
a **congenial** colleague	ⓐ 말이 많은 ⓑ 마음이 맞는 동료
rigorously assess	ⓐ 정확하게 ⓑ 비판적으로 평가하다
degrading to women	여성을 ⓐ 위협하는 ⓑ 폄하하는
be **scarce** of food	식량이 ⓐ 부족하다 ⓑ 다 떨어지다
exempt from paying taxes	과세에서 ⓐ 면제된 ⓑ 우대된
be booked **solid**	예약이 ⓐ 완전히 다 차다 ⓑ 확정되다
a **genial** personality	ⓐ 상냥한 ⓑ 소심한 성격
a **credulous** person	ⓐ 믿음이 가는 ⓑ 잘 속는 사람
virtually impossible	ⓐ 사실상 ⓑ 통계상으로 불가능한

둘 중 적절한 어휘를 골라 ∨ 표를 하세요.

61 ○ concerned
   ○ interested in buying a car 차를 사는 데 관심이 있는

62 ○ scared
   ○ beaten of flying 비행기 타는 것을 두려워하는

63 a ○ tempting
     ○ touching movie 감동적인 영화

64 The scarf is ○ becoming
              ○ matching on you. 스카프가 당신에게 잘 어울려요.

65 an ○ unanimous
      ○ unilateral decision 만장 일치의 결정

66 look ○ alike
       ○ copied 닮아 보이다

67 fully ○ qualified
        ○ identified 충분히 자격을 갖춘

68 a(n) ○ opulent
        ○ renowned mansion 호화로운 저택

69 ○ trivial
   ○ convivial matters 사소한 일

70 live ○ worldwide
       ○ abroad 해외에서 살다

71 pay ○ dearly
      ○ highly 큰 대가를 치르다

72 a ○ multicultural
     ○ worldwide country 다문화 국가

73 ○ baffled
   ○ disruptive behavior 방해되는 행동

74 serve a ○ compulsory
          ○ probationary period 수습 기간을 거치다

75 a(n) ○ succinct
        ○ intermittent connection (전화나 인터넷의) 때때로 끊기는 접속

76 a ○ complicated
     ○ frustrated question 풀기 어려운 문제

77 a ○ reticent
     ○ torpid personality 말이 없는 성격

78 ○ doleful
   ○ radiant with joy 기쁨에 얼굴이 환한

79 a(n) ○ unpretentious
        ○ presumptuous lifestyle 소박한 생활 방식

80 a(n) ○ obtuse
        ○ stark difference 극명한 차이

a
- ○ malignant
- ○ malleable
tumor

악성 종양

- ○ preparing
- ○ expecting
a baby

임신 중인

feel
- ○ relieved
- ○ agitated

안도하다

- ○ intrinsic
- ○ indigenous
plants

토착 식물

hold
- ○ valid
- ○ good

유효하다

You are
- ○ cordially
- ○ willingly
invited.

귀하를 정중히 초대합니다.

an
- ○ ulterior
- ○ inferior
motive

저의, 숨은 동기

- ○ allergic
- ○ alleged
to peanuts

땅콩에 알레르기가 있는

a fully
- ○ furnished
- ○ accommodated
apartment

모든 가구가 갖추어진 아파트

Make yourself
- ○ relaxed
- ○ comfortable ·

(자기 집처럼) 편하게 생각하세요.

- ○ stuffy
- ○ sultry
weather

무더운 날씨

a(n)
- ○ adamant
- ○ vulgar
decision

단호한 결심

a(n)
- ○ effusive
- ○ deliberate
attempt

고의적인 시도

an
- ○ irrevocable
- ○ irksome
mistake

돌이킬 수 없는 실수

a
- ○ fiery
- ○ tedious
temper

불 같은 성격

get
- ○ serial
- ○ straight
As

전과목에서 A를 받다

- ○ accredited
- ○ pirated
software

불법 복제 소프트웨어

- ○ forensic
- ○ formulaic
evidence

법의학적 증거

- ○ affected
- ○ influenced
area

피해 지역

a
- ○ distinguished
- ○ sophisticated
scholar

저명한 학자

정답 p.100

Hackers **TEST**

Part I Choose the best answer for the blank.

01 A: I shouldn't have taken an early morning class.
      It's hard for me to stay _____.
   B: It might be a good idea to start your day with
      some coffee.

   (a) keen   (b) alert
   (c) brisk   (d) deft

02 A: Wow! Celine looks fabulous in that dress.
   B: Yeah, she has _____ taste when it comes
      to fashion.

   (a) inexplicable   (b) inconspicuous
   (c) incredulous   (d) impeccable

03 A: I was shocked that Eugene asked Mr. Peterson
      such an indelicate question.
   B: I know. I couldn't believe how _____ he
      was.

   (a) irrelevant   (b) inconsistent
   (c) imperative   (d) impertinent

04 A: My parents plan to retire and move to the
      countryside.
   B: That seems like a(n) _____ lifestyle.

   (a) provident   (b) invalid
   (c) idyllic   (d) corpulent

05 A: It turns out I'll be attending college in Italy next
      semester.
   B: Lucky you. I've always wanted to study
      _____.

   (a) abroad   (b) global
   (c) further   (d) outside

06 A: I'd like to see the dentist.
   B: Of course. Let me see when she's _____

   (a) amicable   (b) malleable
   (c) pliable   (d) available

Part II Choose the best answer for the blank.

07 Tabloid newspapers focus on publishing _____
   and often unfounded rumors about the private
   lives of celebrities.

   (a) lurid   (b) squeamish
   (c) pious   (d) piqued

08 An investigation of human rights violations is
   under way at the refugee camp, where conditions
   are reported to be _____.

   (a) irate   (b) dire
   (c) surly   (d) shrewd

09 Lost in the woods at night, Peter said his flashlight
   had been _____ to finding his way back.

   (a) identical   (b) hypocritical
   (c) skeptical   (d) critical

10 The negotiations seemed _____, but the
   parties finally came up with a compromise they
   could both agree on.

   (a) inaccessible   (b) indivisible
   (c) inconsolable   (d) interminable

Prose relies far more on the denotative signification of words than poetry, which achieves its allusive power through _____ language.

(a) perceptive
(b) cumulative
(c) connotative
(d) nominative

She created a succinct summary of the lengthy report by removing all of the _____ details.

(a) extraneous
(b) applicable
(c) outrageous
(d) permeable

People who spend too many hours alone and deliberately avoid the company of others are considered _____.

(a) affable
(b) gregarious
(c) reclusive
(d) congenial

The new video game may appear _____, but it is probably one of the most addictive games on the Internet today.

(a) gratuitous
(b) inoperative
(c) innocuous
(d) restorative

Having become too popular, J. D. Salinger escaped from the public eye to live on a(n) _____ estate in New Hampshire.

(a) secluded
(b) indistinct
(c) avaricious
(d) rudimentary

16 Although it is generally accepted that smoking is _____ to one's health, this knowledge does not always convince smokers to kick the habit.

(a) dispensable
(b) indulgent
(c) profligate
(d) detrimental

17 The most disturbing images of war are those of _____ people who have lost loved ones to death or imprisonment.

(a) exuberant
(b) distraught
(c) taciturn
(d) punctilious

18 The Tasmanian devil is a(n) _____ animal from Australia, known for its enormous appetite and frightening appearance.

(a) ferocious
(b) veracious
(c) audacious
(d) vivacious

19 All employees are expected to complete their work in a timely fashion and abide by _____ office guidelines.

(a) impetuous
(b) miscreant
(c) annihilated
(d) stringent

20 A spokesperson clarified a decision made by the firm's board of directors at an _____ press conference this morning.

(a) inveterate
(b) impromptu
(c) intractable
(d) instinctive

혼자 하기 어렵고 막막할 땐?

해커스텝스(HackersTEPS.com)에서
스타강사의 무료 동영상강의 보기!

Section 4 혼동하기 쉬운 어휘

CHAPTER 10 의미상 혼동하기 쉬운 어휘

sign : 서명이 아니라고?

신장개업을 앞둔 텝식씨. 이제 눈에 잘 띄는 sign만 붙이면 된다기에 멋들어진 본인의 서명을 가게 앞에 떡 붙인 텝식씨. 그런데 간판은 대체 어디에 붙이지? 텝식씨의 가게가 간판도 없이 개업하게 된 이유는 흔히 '서명'이라고 알고 있는 sign이 사실은 '간판, 표지, 신호'라는 뜻이기 때문. '서명'을 뜻하려면 signature나 autograph를 사용해야 한다. 텝스 어휘에는 sign, signature, autograph처럼 의미가 유사해서 혼동을 주는 보기들이 함께 출제된다. 의미가 비슷한 어휘들을 함께 묶어 영문 의미와 예문을 통해 뉘앙스의 차이를 익혀보자.

■ 출제 경향

· 의미상 혼동하기 쉬운 어휘들은 주로 collocation과 일반 어휘 문제에서 보기로 출제되며, Part 1과 Part 2에서 비슷한 비율로 출제
· bother, disturb, annoy와 같이 모두 우리말로 '방해하다'로 해석되지만 미묘한 의미상의 차이를 지니는 어휘들이 보기로 함께 제된다.

■ 예제

Part I

A: I'm sorry I'm late. Have you been waiting long?
B: Oh, no, it's OK. We're on a very _____ schedule.

(a) flexible   (b) elastic
(c) moderate   (d) stretched

A: 늦어서 미안해요. 오래 기다렸나요?
B: 오, 아니에요. 괜찮아요. 우리의 일정은 아주 유연하답니다.

해설 | 빈칸 뒤의 명사 schedule(일정)과 어울려 쓰이는 형용사는 (a) flexible(유연한, 탄력적인)이다. elastic(탄력적인)도 비슷한 의미로 상황과 변화에 따라 용이하게 바뀔 성질을 나타내지만, schedule, deadline(마감 기한)과 같이 일정을 나타내는 명사와 함께 쓰이지 않는다. moderate(적당한), stretched(늘어난)는 schedule과 어 이지 않아 답이 될 수 없다.

정답 | (a) flexible

Part II

Any _____ involving the misuse of company property must be reported to the supervisor.

(a) incident   (b) accident
(c) event   (d) adventure

기업 소유물의 오용과 관련된 모든 사고는 관리자에게 보고되야 한다.

해설 | '기업 소유물의 오용과 관련된 모든 _____는 관리자에게 보고되어야 한다'라는 문맥에서 빈칸에는 '사고'를 나타내는 (a) incident가 들어가는 것이 자연스럽다. accic '사고'라는 의미로 쓰이지만 교통사고처럼 '인명이나 재산 피해를 수반한 뜻하지 않게 우연히 발생한 사고'를 가리키며, incident는 '그 자체로는 심각하지 않지만 중대 로 발전할 가능성이 있는 사건, 또는 미리 계획되거나 의도된 사건'을 가리킨다. event는 '행사', adventure는 '모험'이라는 뜻이다.

어휘 | involve[inválv] 관련시키다   misuse[misjú:s] 오용, 악용   property[prápərti] 소유물, 자산   supervisor[sú:pərvàizər] 관리자

정답 | (a) incident

-격 · 비용

01 cost[kɔːst] 비용, 경비

n. The amount of money required to obtain something
'물건을 사거나 만드는 데 드는 비용'을 의미한다.

Various expenses make the cost of living high in urban areas.
다양한 지출이 도시 지역에서 생활비를 비싸게 한다.

02 fee[fiː] 수수료, 요금

n. Money paid for a service or any other intangible purchase
'교육 · 의료처럼 전문적인 서비스에 대한 수수료'나 'membership fee(회비)', 'registration fee(등록비)', 'late fee(연체료)'처럼 '공식적인 절차에 대해 개인이나 단체에 지불하는 요금'을 의미한다.

The museum asks for a suggested entrance fee of five dollars.
박물관은 5달러의 권장 입장료를 낼 것을 요청한다.

03 charge[tʃɑːrdʒ] 청구 금액, 요금

n. Additional money required outside of the original purchase amount
'delivery charge(배송비)', 'extra charge(추가 요금)'처럼 '서비스, 시간, 노력에 대해 청구된 요금'을 의미한다.

When the service charge is not included in the bill, it is customary to tip.
서비스 이용료가 계산서에 포함되어 있지 않을 때는 팁을 주는 것이 관례적이다.

04 fare[fɛər] 교통 요금

n. The amount required for a single trip using public transportation
'운송 수단을 이용하는 요금', '운임', '통행료'를 의미한다.

The subway fare has risen by 100 percent in the past decade.
지난 10년간 지하철 요금이 2배로 상승했다.

05 price[prais] 가격

n. The amount of money required to purchase an item
'상품을 구매할 때 지불해야 하는 돈의 양', 즉 '상품의 가격'을 의미한다.

Prices were reduced on specialty items after the holiday.
연휴 후에 특수 상품의 가격이 하락했다.

06 pay[pei] 봉급, 임금

n. The amount of money earned by an employee
가장 일반적으로 '봉급으로 받는 돈'을 의미한다.

Although the pay is low, the benefits are worthwhile.
비록 봉급은 적지만, 수당이 상당하다.

할 만하다

07 afford[əfɔːrd] ~할 여유가 있다

v. To have the ability or willingness to pay for something
'(경제적 · 시간적으로) ~할 여유가 있다'라는 뜻이다.

The restaurant's menu was more expensive than they could afford.
식당의 메뉴는 그들이 지불할 수 있는 것보다 더 비쌌다.

08 deserve[dizə́ːrv] ~을 받을 만하다

v. To be worthy of a particular, usually positive, outcome
'~을 할[받을] 만하다', '~할 가치가 있다'라는 뜻이다.

The director felt the actors got more credit than they deserved.
감독은 배우들이 받아야 할 것 이상으로 평가받았다고 느꼈다.

처리하다

09 handle[hǽndl] 처리하다, 다루다

v. To be capable of successfully completing an undertaking
'문제를 다루다', '처리하다', '논하다'라는 의미로 쓰인다.

The new intern was able to handle **all the various tasks given to her.**
새 인턴 사원은 그녀에게 주어진 다양한 업무를 모두 처리할 수 있었다.

10 manage[mǽnidʒ] 이럭저럭 해내다

v. To be able to achieve a goal, usually through difficult means
'이럭저럭 용케 해내다', '간신히 하다'라는 뜻으로 to부정사와 자주 함께 쓰인다.

I managed **to find a new apartment closer to my company.**
나는 회사에서 가까운 새 아파트를 이럭저럭 찾아낼 수 있었다.

11 conduct[kəndʌ́kt] (업무를) 수행하다

v. To initiate and maintain control of a particular process
'업무를 수행하거나 처리하다', '계속 진행되게 하다'라는 의미로 쓴다.

The police conducted **an investigation of the crime scene.**
경찰은 범죄 현장을 수사했다.

빌리다

12 borrow[bárou] 빌리다

v. To use another person's possession with the intent of returning it later
'돌려줄 것을 전제로 임시로 빌리다'라는 뜻이다.

Could I borrow **your pen for a minute?**
제가 잠시 당신의 펜을 빌릴 수 있을까요?

13 lend[lend] 빌려주다

v. To allow another person to use one's possession
'일정 기간 동안 다른 사람에게 무엇을 빌려주다'라는 뜻이다.

Could you lend **me your pen for a minute?**
잠시 당신의 펜을 제게 빌려주실 수 있나요?

14 rent[rent] (돈을 내고) 빌리다, 빌려주다

v. To temporarily use another's possession in exchange for money
'차량 · 집 · 방 등을 일정 기간 돈을 내고 빌리다' 또는 '돈을 받고 빌려주다'라는 뜻이다.

Visitors can rent **a car when they arrive at the airport.**
방문객들은 공항에 도착하면 차를 빌릴 수 있다.

모으다

15 assemble[əsémbl] 조립하다

v. To put together various parts in order to form a complete whole
'기계나 부품을 조립하여 ~으로 만들다'라는 의미로 쓰인다.

All the outdoor furniture at Steve's home was assembled **from packaged kits.**
Steve 집의 모든 야외 가구는 조립 완성 제품으로 조립된 것이다.

16 compile[kəmpáil] (자료를) 수집하다

v. To bring together and organize a set of documents or information
'자료를 수집하거나 집계하다', '자료를 수집하여 책을 편찬하다'라는 의미로 쓰인다.

Historians compile **large amounts of data to accurately portray past events.**
역사가들은 과거 사건을 정확하게 묘사하기 위해 많은 양의 자료를 수집한다.

17 accumulate [əkjúːmjulèit] 모으다, 축적하다

v. To gather or be gathered in an increasing quantity over a period of time
'돈이나 정보 등을 (장기간에 걸쳐 조금씩) 모으다'라는 의미로 쓰인다.

Kimberly put half her pay in the bank every month and soon accumulated a large sum.
Kimberly는 매달 월급의 절반을 저금했고, 얼마 안 되어 많은 돈을 모았다.

18 appoint [əpóint] 임명하다

v. To officially designate a person for a particular office or position
'사람을 업무·직위에 공식적으로 임명하다'라는 뜻이다.

Leslie was appointed as the new treasurer of the committee.
Leslie는 위원회의 새 회계 담당자로 임명되었다.

19 allot [əlát] 배정하다, 할당하다

v. To distribute a limited resource amongst several parties
'사람에게 특정한 몫을 나누어 할당하다, 분배하다'라는 뜻이다.

Housing is allotted to those that are registered for fall classes.
숙소는 가을 학기를 등록한 학생들에게 배정된다.

20 assign [əsáin] 할당하다, 임명하다

v. To give a specific task or duty to another person
'업무·임무를 할당하다', '사람을 직위·부서에 임명하다'라는 뜻이다.

The regional manager was assigned to direct the company's overseas branch.
지역 관리자가 기업의 해외 지점을 관리하도록 업무를 할당 받았다.

21 nominate [námənèit] 지명하다, 임명하다

v. To propose a candidate for a job or a position
'어떤 일자리나 직위에 알맞은 후보자를 지명하다'라는 의미로 쓰인다.

The President is authorized to nominate qualified individuals for various government positions.
대통령은 여러 관직에 적합한 인재들을 지명할 권한이 있다.

22 interrupt [ìntərʌ́pt] 방해하다, 중단하다

v. To unexpectedly stop or suspend a continuous process or action
'말·흐름·진행의 도중에 끼어들어 중단시키거나 방해하다'라는 뜻이다.

I hope I'm not interrupting your conversation.
제가 당신의 대화를 방해한 게 아니었으면 좋겠네요.

23 disturb [distə́ːrb] 방해하다, 어지럽히다

v. To interrupt what a person is doing and upset him or her
'(작업 등의) 진행 중인 일을 방해하다'라는 의미로 쓰인다.

I crept around on tiptoes in order not to disturb other people in the room.
나는 방 안에 있는 다른 사람들을 방해하지 않기 위해 발끝으로 살금살금 걸었다.

24 bother [báðər] 괴롭히다, 귀찮게 하다

v. To intrude upon or disturb someone, usually over an unimportant matter
'폐를 끼쳐 귀찮게 하다', '폐·걱정을 끼쳐 상대방의 마음을 어지럽히다'라는 뜻이다.

I'm sorry to bother you, but please turn your radio down.
귀찮게 해서 미안하지만, 라디오 소리 좀 줄여주세요.

다음 중 적절한 어휘를 골라 ∨ 표를 하세요.

01 take an alternative
○ **track**
○ **curb**
○ **route**
다른 경로를 이용하다

02 ○ **age**
○ **turn** red
○ **switch**
붉게 변하다

03 ○ **hatch**
○ **breed** from an egg
○ **bloom**
알에서 부화하다

04 ○ **replace**
○ **substitute** honey for sugar
○ **change**
설탕 대신 꿀을 이용하다

05 He can be
○ **relied**
○ **believed.**
○ **trusted**
그는 신뢰할 수 있는 사람이다.

06 search for human
○ **remnants**
○ **leftovers**
○ **remains**
유해를 수색하다

07 ○ **imprint**
○ **sculpt** a statue
○ **engrave**
상을 조각하다

08 ○ **pledge**
○ **sanction** to support
○ **cooperate**
지원하기로 서약하다

09 ○ **amass**
○ **tally** a credit card
○ **charge**
신용 카드로 대금을 청구하다

10 ○ **legislate**
○ **institute** someone for murder
○ **prosecute**
살인죄로 기소하다

11 ○ **remain**
○ **last** silent
○ **hold**
침묵을 유지하다

12 ○ **mingle**
○ **fuse** together
○ **blend**
합쳐져서 하나가 되다

13 ○ **limit**
○ **border** on expenses
○ **margin**
지출 경비의 한도

14 ○ **alter**
○ **change** one's flight
○ **convert**
비행기를 갈아타다

15 a ○ **union**
○ **coalition** between two companies
○ **merger**
두 기업 간의 합병

give a(n) ○ definite ○ unyielding answer   확답을 하다
         ○ solidified

a(n) ○ base ○ source of information   정보의 출처
     ○ origin

change ○ trails ○ lanes   차선을 변경하다
       ○ ways

○ commit
○ accomplish suicide   자살하다
○ execute

○ settle
○ install a program   프로그램을 설치하다
○ establish

a ○ vital ○ lethal dose   치사량
  ○ mortal

○ waning
○ receding hairline   점점 더 벗겨지는 머리
○ declining

○ marginal
○ subliminal to the subject   주제에서 벗어난
○ peripheral

We ○ accept ○ receive credit cards.   저희는 신용 카드를 받습니다.
   ○ admit

to be ○ meticulous ○ detailed   구체적으로 말하자면
      ○ specific

○ generous
○ abundant natural resources   풍부한 자연 자원
○ prolific

a(n) ○ genuine ○ original diamond ring   진짜 다이아몬드 반지
     ○ truthful

○ stock
○ shove for an exam   시험 때문에 벼락치기하다
○ cram

reach a ○ sentence ○ verdict   (배심원들이) 평결을 내리다
        ○ prosecution

down to ○ earth ○ ground   현실적인
        ○ land

31	○ exude ○ emit ○ shed	light on	~을 명백히 하다, ~을 해명하다
32	give ○ access ○ reach ○ approach	to	~에 접근을 허용하다
33	Please ○ remember ○ remind ○ memorize	her to call me.	그녀에게 내게 전화하라고 상기시켜 주세요.
34	a blind ○ place ○ zone ○ spot		시야에서 보이지 않는 부분, 맹점
35	a bank ○ balance ○ account ○ deposit		은행 예금 계좌
36	○ seek ○ locate ○ find	employment	일자리를 찾다
37	○ ingest ○ graze ○ gorge	on grass	풀을 뜯다
38	○ succeed ○ inherit ○ enthrone	an emperor	황제의 지위를 잇다
39	That ○ fits ○ matches ○ suits	me.	(일정 · 형편이) 저에게 잘 맞습니다.
40	a dress ○ code ○ rule ○ law		특정 상황에서 요구되는 옷차림, 복장 규정
41	○ personal ○ individual ○ intimate	calls	사적인 통화
42	military ○ subsidy ○ budget ○ stipend		국방 예산
43	rest in ○ ease ○ comfort ○ peace		편안히 잠들다
44	stop ○ abruptly ○ inadvertently ○ unwittingly		급작스럽게 중지하다
45	○ discard ○ release ○ dismiss	a charge	혐의를 기각하다

다음 중 해석에 맞는 적절한 어휘를 골라 빈칸에 넣으세요.

seats openings	Are there any available _____ on the flight to San Francisco? 샌프란시스코행 항공편에 이용 가능한 **좌석**이 있나요?
edged **flanked**	The president took the stage, _____ by two of his closest advisors. 대통령은 가까운 보좌관 두 명을 **양옆에 대동**하고 무대 위에 올랐다.
escort **guide**	The user's manual will help _____ you through the setup process. 사용 설명서는 당신에게 설치 과정을 **안내해줄** 것입니다.
match **blend**	Those dark gray shoes _____ your new dress perfectly. 그 짙은 회색 신발은 네 새 옷과 완벽하게 **어울린다**.
corrupting **deteriorating**	The global environment is _____ at an alarming rate. 지구 환경은 급속도로 **악화되고** 있다.
link **connect**	Could you _____ me with the sales department, please? 영업 부서에 **연결해**주시겠습니까?
engaged **committed**	The diplomats have been _____ in negotiations for the past three days. 외교관들은 지난 3일간 협상에 **참여하고** 있다.
complete **finish**	The gardeners will need additional supplies before they can _____. 정원사들은 일을 **끝마치기** 전에 추가적인 물품을 필요로 할 것이다.
banned **discouraged**	The customer who didn't pay his bar tab was _____ from the establishment. 술값을 치르지 않은 손님이 식당에 출입이 **금지되었다**.
delayed **caught**	I left late and was _____ by rush hour traffic. 나는 늦게 출발해서 혼잡 시간의 교통량 때문에 **지체되었다**.
deviated **sidetracked**	The freighter suspiciously _____ from its usual path of delivery. 화물차는 의심스럽게도 평소의 배달 경로에서 **벗어났다**.
possible **available**	A service representative will be _____ to speak with you in five minutes. 서비스 담당자가 5분 내에 귀하와 이야기**할 수 있을** 것입니다.

정답 p.103

Hackers TEST

제한 시간: 6분 40초

Part I Choose the best answer for the blank.

01 A: Why are you unsatisfied with your current job?
B: I want a position with higher _____.

(a) pay   (b) money
(c) budget   (d) cost

02 A: Do you want me to help you move your luggage?
B: Thank you, but I can _____ it myself.

(a) afford   (b) handle
(c) control   (d) serve

03 A: I'm not sure I can _____ my boyfriend anymore.
B: Why? Did he lie to you or something?

(a) trust   (b) confide
(c) commit   (d) promise

04 A: Will I have to pay extra if I have the desk delivered?
B: Actually, the _____ is already included in your bill.

(a) check   (b) fare
(c) charge   (d) subsidy

05 A: I just bought a bicycle that comes with instructions on how to put it together.
B: Let me help you _____ it!

(a) fabricate   (b) compile
(c) assemble   (d) knot

06 A: I don't see Jack much anymore. He's always away on business.
B: Yeah, I noticed that myself. Maybe he's trying to _____ wealth.

(a) congregate   (b) accumulate
(c) compile   (d) combine

07 A: Why don't you get dressed for the party tonight? You said you were going!
B: I have a test on Friday. Stop _____ me

(a) teasing   (b) bothering
(c) upsetting   (d) insulting

08 A: I'm sorry for calling at this late hour. Am I _____ anything?
B: No, it's quite all right. I'm still awake.

(a) harassing   (b) interfering
(c) agitating   (d) interrupting

09 A: It's almost lunch time already! I don't think I can _____ to wait any longer.
B: Billy promised to show up. Give him five more minutes.

(a) deserve   (b) maintain
(c) afford   (d) postpone

10 A: Could I _____ your car this weekend?
B: Why? Where do you need to go?

(a) lease   (b) lend
(c) owe   (d) borrow

A: What do the figures look like for last quarter?
B: I'm still in the middle of _____ the statistics.

(a) compiling   (b) itemizing
(c) assembling   (d) featuring

A: I cannot believe the _____ they are charging us for this cup of coffee.
B: I know. They nearly doubled it.

(a) price   (b) sum
(c) fee   (d) value

A: I've worked overtime for four weeks in a row.
B: I know. You really _____ some time off.

(a) concede   (b) deserve
(c) compensate   (d) assign

A: Wasn't it hard to find this place?
B: Yeah, I almost got lost coming here, but thankfully I _____ to find it.

(a) handled   (b) conducted
(c) maneuvered   (d) managed

A: How was the movie that you _____ yesterday?
B: It was great! I should have seen it sooner.

(a) leased   (b) lent
(c) rented   (d) owed

16 A: Did you know that John was _____ editor of the student paper?
B: I expected that, since he's written for it for years.

(a) approved   (b) assigned
(c) granted   (d) appointed

Part II Choose the best answer for the blank.

17 Paleontology experts recently discovered the _____ of an ancient fossilized skull that did not belong to any known prehistoric creatures.

(a) residues   (b) remains
(c) particles   (d) monuments

18 Computer error caused the popular online site to mistakenly _____ international customers a tax that only domestic residents should pay.

(a) burden   (b) accuse
(c) charge   (d) blame

19 Jenifer was _____ to the Board by the chief executive officer, but whether she will become a member remains to be seen.

(a) addressed   (b) constituted
(c) nominated   (d) allotted

20 Buildings and other structures that are not carefully maintained on a regular basis _____ very quickly.

(a) adulterate   (b) deteriorate
(c) contaminate   (d) prolapse

CHAPTER **11** 형태상 혼동하기 쉬운 어휘

> ## transfer : 역에서 변신을 하라고?
>
> 지하철을 탄 텝식씨. 인천 방면으로 가실 분은 이번 역에서 transfer하라는 안내 방송에 화들짝. transfer? 인천으로 가려면 변신을 하라고? 결국 내려야 할 곳에서 내리지 못하고 다음엔 변장을 하고 오리라 굳게 다짐한다. 텝식씨가 닫히는 지하철 문을 바라보기만 해야 했던 이유는 형태가 비슷한 어휘인 transfer(갈아타다)와 transform(변신하다)을 혼동했기 때문. 텝스 어휘에서는 형태가 매우 비슷해서 혼동을 주는 어휘들이 보기로 함께 출제된다. 형태상 유사한 어휘들을 함께 묶어 익혀보자.

■ 출제 경향

· 형태상 혼동하기 쉬운 어휘들은 대부분 Part 2에서 나오고 Part 1에는 간혹 출제되며, 일반 어휘 문제의 보기로 자주 출제된다.

· 보기 4개의 형태가 모두 비슷하거나 보기 4개 중 각각 2개씩 비슷한 형태의 보기가 제시된다. 또한 '-ment', '-tion', '-ble' 등의 접가 같은 어휘들이나, 're-', 'trans-', 'ex-' 등의 접두사가 같은 어휘들이 출제된다.

■ 예제

Part I

A: I'm sorry, but I'll need to see some _____.
B: Will my passport do?

(a) verification
(b) certification
(c) identification
(d) authorization

A: 죄송하지만, 신분증을 보여 주셔야겠습니다.
B: 여권이면 될까요?

해설 | _____을 보여 주셔야겠습니다'라는 A의 말에 B가 '여권이면 되겠느냐'라고 대답하고 있다. 따라서 문맥상 빈칸에는 '신분증'이라는 뜻의 (c) identification이 들어가야 자연스럽다. verification은 '확인, 증명', certification은 '증명, 보증', authorization은 '허가, 인증'이라는 뜻으로 답이 될 수 없다.

정답 | (c) identification

Part II

The chief executive officer often claims that his success is _____ to the support his wife gave him over the past twenty years.

(a) accessible
(b) susceptible
(c) practicable
(d) attributable

최고 경영자는 그의 성공이 지난 20년간 그의 아내가 베푼 원분이라고 종종 주장한다.

해설 | '그의 성공이 지난 20년간 아내가 베푼 원조 _____이다'라는 문맥에서 빈칸에는 '~덕분인, ~때문인'이라는 뜻의 (d) attributable이 들어가는 것이 자연스럽다. acce은 '접근하기 쉬운', susceptible은 '영향을 받기 쉬운', practicable은 '실행 가능한'이라는 뜻으로 답이 될 수 없다.

어휘 | **chief executive officer** (기업의) 최고 경영 책임자(CEO)　**claim**[kléim] 주장하다, 단언하다　**support**[səpɔ́ːrt] 원조, 지지

정답 | (d) attributable

uce

키다

re-

아닌

x-

로

eption

수락

01 induce[indʒúːs] 야기하다

Penicillin has been known to induce allergic reactions in some patients.
페니실린은 몇몇 환자들에게 알레르기 반응을 야기하는 것으로 알려져왔다.

02 produce [prədʒúːs] 생산하다, 만들어내다

American manufacturers produced thousands of combat planes during the second world war.
미국의 제조업체들은 제2차 세계 대전 동안 수천 대의 전투기를 생산했다.

03 irreplaceable[ìripléisəbl] 다른 것과 대체할 수 없는, 둘도 없는

This clock is an irreplaceable heirloom from my grandfather.
이 시계는 내 할아버지로부터 물려 받은 둘도 없는 가보이다.

04 irretrievable [ìritríːvəbl] 회복할 수 없는, 돌이킬 수 없는

The argument between the two was so vicious that it caused an irretrievable breakdown in their relationship.
두 사람의 말다툼은 너무 심각해서 그들의 관계에 회복할 수 없는 와해를 가져왔다.

05 irrevocable [irévəkəbl] 변경할 수 없는, 돌이킬 수 없는

The election committee said that their decisions, once made, are irrevocable.
선거 위원회는 그들의 결정이 한 번 내려지고 나면 변경될 수 없다고 말했다.

06 irrelevant[iréləvənt] 관계없는, 무관한

The attorney attempted to obfuscate the truth by dragging in irrelevant arguments.
변호사는 무관한 논쟁을 끌어들여 진실을 흐리게 하려고 시도했다.

07 exude[igzjúːd] 발산하다, 스며 나오게 하다

A leader must exude confidence and enthusiasm.
리더는 자신감과 열정을 발산해야 한다.

08 extol[ikstóul] 크게 칭찬하다, 격찬하다

The organization was extolled for its contribution to helping humanity.
그 단체는 인류를 도운 공헌으로 크게 칭찬받았다.

09 exhale[ekshéil] 숨을 내쉬다

Remember to exhale deeply while meditating to reduce stress.
스트레스를 줄이기 위해서 명상하는 동안 숨을 깊게 내쉬는 것을 기억하라.

10 expose [ikspóuz] 폭로하다, 드러내다

The investigative report exposed the animal abuse in several factory farms.
그 폭로 보도 기사는 몇몇 공장식 농장에서 발생하는 동물 학대에 대해 폭로했다.

11 inception[insépʃən] 도입, 시작, 발단

The GPS system was made available to the public shortly after its inception.
GPS 시스템은 도입 직후 대중이 이용할 수 있게 되었다.

12 perception[pərsépʃən] 인식, 지각, 견해

Schizophrenia is a mental disorder characterized by a distorted perception of reality.
정신 분열증은 왜곡된 현실 인식으로 특징 지어지는 정신 질환이다.

-tribute
주다

13 attribute[ətríbju:t] ~ 덕분으로 하다, ~탓으로 하다

The crew attributed their success to strong teamwork and coordination.
직원들은 그들의 성공을 강한 팀워크와 협동 덕분이라고 했다.

14 contribute[kəntríbju:t] ~의 한 원인이 되다, 기여하다

Long-term smoking contributes to increased incidence of heart disease.
장기간의 흡연은 심장병 발병률 증가의 한 원인이 된다.

15 distribute[distríbju:t] 분배하다, 배달하다

The shipping trucks distribute produce to the city's grocers every morning.
운송 트럭들은 매일 아침 도시의 식료 잡화상들에게 농산물을 배달한다.

-(t)ible
할 수 있는

16 compatible[kəmpǽtəbl] 양립할 수 있는, 호환 가능한

The new computer model is compatible with all the latest technology.
신형 컴퓨터 모델은 모든 최신 기술과 호환 가능하다.

17 susceptible[səséptəbl] 감염되기 쉬운, 영향 받기 쉬운

Not dressing warmly in winter can make one susceptible to illness.
겨울에 따뜻하게 옷을 입지 않으면 질병에 감염되기 쉬워진다.

18 reprehensible[rèprihénsəbl] 비난받을 만한, 괘씸한

To do a good deed for the sake of being recognized is reprehensible.
인정받기 위해 선행을 베푸는 것은 비난받을 만하다.

19 visible[vízəbl] 눈에 보이는

The entire city is visible from the mountaintop.
산꼭대기에서는 도시 전체가 눈에 보인다.

20 legible[lédʒəbl] (글자를) 읽을 수 있는, 읽기 쉬운

His cursive handwriting is barely legible to others.
그의 필기체는 다른 사람들이 거의 읽을 수 없다.

21 tangible[tǽndʒəbl] (근거 등이) 명백한, 만져서 알 수 있는

There is no tangible evidence to prove that he is guilty.
그가 유죄라고 증명할 명백한 만한 물증은 없다.

22 eligible[élidʒəbl] 적격의, 자격이 있는

Honor roll students may be eligible for a scholarship.
우등생들은 장학금을 받을 자격이 있을 것이다.

23 feasible[fí:zəbl] 실현 가능한

It doesn't seem feasible for the economy to recover right away.
경제가 당장 회복되는 것은 실현 가능해 보이지 않는다.

24 plausible[plɔ́:zəbl] 그럴듯한, 정말 같은

James' theory was interesting, but didn't seem plausible.
James의 가설은 흥미롭긴 하지만, 그럴듯해 보이진 않았다.

Hackers **Practice**

중 적절한 어휘를 골라 ∨ 표를 하세요.

I almost didn't
- ○ recollect
- ○ **recognize** you.
- ○ recoup

거의 당신을 못 알아봤네요.

- ○ inject
- ○ **insert** medicine into a vein
- ○ instill

정맥에 약을 주사하다

I can
- ○ synthesize
- ○ **sympathize** with you.
- ○ synchronize

당신의 기분을 잘 이해합니다.

an ethnically
- ○ different
- ○ **diffuse** neighborhood
- ○ diverse

다양한 인종이 사는 지역

I can't
- ○ **recall**
- ○ repeat his name.
- ○ replace

그의 이름이 기억나지 않는다.

- ○ inject
- ○ reject an economic growth rate
- ○ **project**

경제 성장률을 예측하다

- ○ notify
- ○ justify one's identity
- ○ **verify**

신분을 증명하다

- ○ advocate
- ○ **alleviate** pain
- ○ agitate

고통을 덜어주다

- ○ **inspire**
- ○ transpire confidence
- ○ conspire

자신감을 불어넣다

be
- ○ collaborate
- ○ commiserate with
- ○ **commensurate**

~에 상응하다

suffer from
- ○ **dyslexia**
- ○ dementia
- ○ euthanasia

난독증을 앓다

- ○ confer
- ○ confirm to a change
- ○ **conform**

변화에 순응하다

contain
- ○ conservatives
- ○ **preservatives**
- ○ preventatives

방부제를 함유하다

- ○ **expedite**
- ○ exempt the delivery
- ○ exonerate

배달을 신속히 처리하다

local
- ○ anemia
- ○ anorexia
- ○ **anesthesia**

국소 마취

VOCABULARY | 혼동하기 쉬운 어휘

해커스 텝스 Reading

○ deny
16 ○ **deify**   a government   정부에 반항하다
○ **defy**

○ **predication**
17 the average annual   ○ **premonition**   연평균 강수량
○ **precipitation**

○ **benevolence**
18 a ○ **beneficiary**   to a young pianist   젊은 피아니스트의 후원자
○ **benefactor**

○ **continuous**
19 for three ○ **consecutive**   years   3년 연속으로
○ **concurrent**

○ **contention**
20 feel ○ **contribution**   회한을 느끼다
○ **contrition**

○ **retain**
21 ○ **sustain**   nutrients   영양분을 얻다
○ **obtain**

○ **council**
22 the city ○ **counsel**   시의회
○ **consul**

○ **difference**
23 make no ○ **distinction**   차이가 없다
○ **discrepancy**

○ **conservation**
24 alcohol ○ **consumption**   음주 소비량
○ **confrontation**

○ **predominance**
25 ○ **prevalence**   of obesity   비만의 만연
○ **preference**

○ **disagreement**
26 racial ○ **discrimination**   인종 차별
○ **disengagement**

○ **altercation**
27 provide an ○ **alteration**   대안을 제시하다
○ **alternative**

○ **proverbial**
28 a ○ **pernicious**   influence   해로운 영향
○ **provisional**

○ **sludge**
29 ○ **splurge**   on luxuries   사치품에 돈을 펑펑 쓰다
○ **surge**

○ **inscrutable**
30 an ○ **invincible**   contract   이해할 수 없는 계약서
○ **inimitable**

중 해석에 맞는 적절한 어휘를 골라 빈칸에 넣으세요.

converged conversed	A large crowd _____ at the school when the president paid a visit. 대통령이 방문하자 거대한 군중이 학교에 **모여들었다.**
improvise supervise	Actors are not allowed to _____ dialogues when performing on stage. 배우들이 무대 위에서 **즉석으로** 대사를 **지어내는** 것은 허용되지 않는다.
bleary barren	Very few who have trekked through this _____ desert have come out alive. 이 **황량한** 사막을 여행해서 살아나온 사람은 거의 없다.
enhanced enabled	The money he inherited _____ him to study abroad. 그가 물려받은 재산은 그가 유학하는 것을 **가능하게 해주었다.**
posture stature	Maintaining a good _____ can prevent lower back problems. 좋은 **자세를** 유지하는 것은 허리 문제를 방지할 수 있다.
included precluded	A buffet breakfast is _____ in the room rate. 아침 식사 뷔페가 객실료에 **포함되어** 있습니다.
portable potable	The newly constructed well provided _____ water to the entire village. 새로 건설된 우물이 마을 전체에 **마실 수 있는** 물을 제공했다.
hefty hectic	Lisa rarely found time to exercise due to her _____ schedule. Lisa는 그녀의 **너무 바쁜** 일정 때문에 운동할 시간이 거의 없었다.
gazed gaped	I _____ at my son sleeping peacefully after the long trip. 나는 긴 여행 이후에 평화롭게 잠든 내 아들을 **가만히 바라보았다.**
frigid furious	The summer monsoon often brings _____ downpours to the region. 여름 계절풍은 종종 지역에 **격렬한** 호우를 일으킨다.
transient transparent	Economists see rapidly growing inflation as a _____ phenomenon. 경제학자들은 물가 급속도로 상승하는 것을 **일시적인** 현상으로 본다.
diversion divergence	Frank considered reading a novel a pleasant _____ from his work. Frank는 소설을 읽는 것이 그의 업무로부터의 즐거운 **기분 전환**이라고 생각했다.

정답 p.106

Hackers **TEST**

 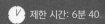

Part I Choose the best answer for the blank.

01 A: Do you have a _____ hairstyle in mind?
B: Not yet. I'm still looking at this hairstyle guide.

(a) similar   (b) particular
(c) spectacular   (d) singular

02 A: Some magazine covers really offend my sensibilities.
B: Yes, a lot of people think the editors of those periodicals are truly _____.

(a) amicable   (b) laudable
(c) deductible   (d) reprehensible

03 A: It didn't snow this year because it snowed too much last year.
B: That doesn't sound like a(n) _____ explanation.

(a) liable   (b) plausible
(c) portable   (d) eligible

04 A: The employees aren't _____ optimism about the upcoming merger.
B: Yeah, I hear a lot of people are going to get laid off.

(a) exerting   (b) exuding
(c) excreting   (d) exalting

05 A: The CEO doesn't think the new marketing strategy is _____.
B: I agree. It doesn't take our production schedule into consideration.

(a) feasible   (b) susceptible
(c) available   (d) conceivable

Part II Choose the best answer for the blank.

06 The production software _____ us to prepare our presentation well before the deadline.

(a) supported   (b) suppressed
(c) enlarged   (d) enabled

07 The depletion of the ozone layer _____ to the melting of icecaps and glaciers in the polar regions.

(a) attributes   (b) contributes
(c) distributes   (d) disperses

08 Bacteria are so small that they are _____ on with the aid of a microscope.

(a) palpable   (b) visible
(c) tangible   (d) affordable

09 The relief organization has been _____ food and medical supplies in the areas affected the catastrophic hurricane.

(a) distributing   (b) contributing
(c) rebutting   (d) reiterating

10 Freud's _____ of dream symbolism ha significant impact on the field of psychoanalysi

(a) desecrations   (b) inceptions
(c) perceptions   (d) annihilations

Feeling their personalities were no longer _____ with one another, the couple mutually agreed to end their relationship.

(a) affable (b) pliable
(c) predictable (d) compatible

Scorpions have the ability to _____ venom into their prey from the poisonous tips of their tails.

(a) infest (b) inject
(c) invert (d) incise

The aromatic oils _____ a medicinal effect when used on the skin or dispersed into the air through a diffuser.

(a) reduce (b) defuse
(c) produce (d) infuse

To obtain a refund, the item must be returned along with the original sales receipt or a(n) _____ photocopy, within 30 days of purchase.

(a) legible (b) agreeable
(c) viable (d) suitable

Ms. Forster is in charge of verifying whether the applicants are _____ for the position they are interested in.

(a) perfunctory (b) dilatory
(c) eligible (d) accessible

16 The demonstrators _____ at the town center after being forced to disperse near the Capitol.

(a) converged (b) concurred
(c) digressed (d) diverted

17 Einstein _____ his achievement more to the quality of his imagination than to his ability as a physicist.

(a) attributed (b) contributed
(c) enshrined (d) enthroned

18 Newborn and premature infants are _____ to infection because of their limited ability to produce antibodies.

(a) susceptible (b) compatible
(c) permeable (d) immeasurable

19 The medicine contains a mild sedative, and may _____ sleep in individuals who have never taken it.

(a) impart (b) inflict
(c) impose (d) induce

20 The exploitation of natural resources in the region has caused _____ changes to the environment.

(a) irretrievable (b) irreducible
(c) irremissable (d) irrelevant

시험에 나올 문제를 미리 풀어보고 싶을 땐?

해커스텝스(HackersTEPS.com)에서
텝스 적중예상특강 보기!

READING
COMPREHENSION

READING COMPREHENSION

1 텝스 독해 영역의 특징

1. 텝스 독해에는 실용문과 학술문이 출제된다.

텝스 독해에는 편지, 광고 등 일상생활과 관련된 실용문과 인문학, 사회과학, 자연과학 등과 관련된 비전문적 학술문이
출제된다. 각 지문 유형별로 지문 Flow가 유사한 경우가 많고 자주 등장하는 어휘가 존재하므로, 지문 Flow와 출제
휘를 학습하면 지문의 내용을 이해하고 앞으로 전개될 내용을 예측하는 데 도움이 된다.

2. 텝스 독해는 짧은 시간 내에 해결해야 하는 속도화 시험이다.

텝스 독해 영역의 35문제를 해결하는 데 주어지는 시간은 40분이므로 수험생은 1분에 1문제 비율로 문제를 해결해야
다. 따라서 평소 주어진 시간 내에 문제를 푸는 연습을 하고, 모르는 문제는 과감히 넘긴 뒤 남는 시간을 활용하여
하는 것이 신속한 문제 풀이에 효과적이다.

3. 텝스 독해는 정확한 독해 능력을 측정한다.

텝스 독해 지문에는 길고 복잡한 문장이 자주 등장하므로 수험생은 문장의 구조를 신속히 파악하여 내용을 정확하게
해할 수 있어야 한다. 따라서 독해 지문에 자주 나오는 대표적인 구문들을 미리 학습하고, 길고 복잡한 문장을 의미 단
로 끊어 읽는 연습을 하는 것이 정확한 독해 및 문제 풀이에 도움이 된다.

2 텝스 독해 출제 유형

텝스에 나오는 독해 문제는 크게 문제 유형과 지문 유형으로 나누어 접근할 수 있다. 「해커스 텝스 Reading」 독해 영
에서는 문제 유형을 Section 1, 지문 유형을 Section 2에서 다루고 있다. Section 1에서는 텝스 독해의 문제 유형을 일
가지로 나누어 설명하고 있으며, Section 2에서는 지문 유형을 실용문 네 가지, 학술문 세 가지로 나누어 설명하고 있다

문제 유형별 공략

텝스 독해의 문제 유형은 빈칸에 문장의 일부·전체 넣기, 연결어 넣기, 어색한 문장 골라내기, 중심 내용 문제, 육하원칙
제, Correct 문제, 추론 문제 유형으로 나눌 수 있다.

지문 유형별 공략

텝스 독해의 지문 유형은 실용문의 경우 편지/코멘트, 광고, 공지, 기사/논평으로, 학술문의 경우 인문학, 사회과학, 자
과학으로 나눌 수 있다.

텝스 독해의 출제 비율

텝스 독해 영역의 출제 비율을 문제 유형과 지문 유형으로 구분하여 살펴보면 다음과 같다.

문제 유형별 출제 비율

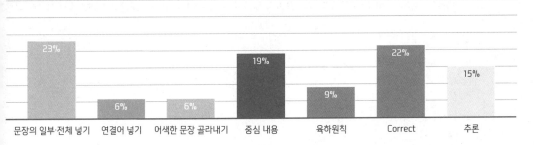

문장의 일부·전체 넣기	연결어 넣기	어색한 문장 골라내기	중심 내용	육하원칙	Correct	추론
23%	6%	6%	19%	9%	22%	15%

지문 유형별 출제 비율

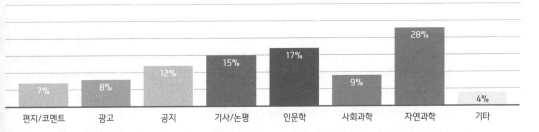

편지/코멘트	광고	공지	기사/논평	인문학	사회과학	자연과학	기타
7%	8%	12%	15%	17%	9%	28%	4%

4 텝스 독해에 꼭 필요한 핵심 스킬

1. 복잡한 문장 정확하게 파악하기

텝스 독해에는 어려운 구문이 자주 등장하여 문장이 길고 복잡하며 의미를 이해하기 어려운 경우가 많다. 그러나 지문에 자주 나오는 구문은 정해져 있는 편이므로, 이를 학습해두면 빠르고 정확하게 문장의 구조와 의미를 파악하여 답을 찾아낼 수 있다. 이러한 구문을 다음과 같이 분류하여 Hackers Practice의 구문독해 연습에서 자세히 다루었다.

· 주어
· 목적어 · 보어
· 비교 · 강조 · 동격
· 분사
· 분사 구문
· 관계절
· 접속사

2. 중요한 정보 위주로 읽기

텝스 독해 지문 내의 정보가 모두 똑같이 중요한 것은 아니며 중요한 부분과 덜 중요한 부분으로 나뉜다. 따라서 중요한 정보를 담은 부분을 자세히 읽고, 이를 보충하는 나머지 부분은 빠르게 읽어 넘겨야 지문의 큰 줄기를 신속하게 파악하며 정확한 정답을 찾는 데 큰 도움을 받을 수 있다. 보통 중요한 정보가 나오는 부분은 다음과 같으며, 중요한 정보 위주로 지문을 읽었을 때 정답을 가장 쉽게 찾을 수 있는 중심 내용 문제 챕터(Chapter 04)의 전략과 문제 해설을 통해 학습하고 적용해볼 수 있다.

· thus, so, accordingly와 같이 결론을 이끄는 연결어 다음 부분
· however, on the contrary와 같이 대조되는 말을 이끌거나 내용을 전환할 때 쓰이는 연결어 다음 부분
· Recent studies show that과 같이 연구 결과에 해당하는 내용을 이끄는 표현 다음 부분

문제풀이 적용하기

Rubies and sapphires are popular with both buyers and counterfeiters. A one-carat purple sapphire commonly sells well over one thousand dollars. Recently, well-designed imitations of these gemstones manufactured at a fraction of the cost are flooding the market and customers may not be getting what they pay for. **So, when buying an expensive piece of gemstone jewelry, confirm its authenticity with an expert and have an independent appraisal done.**

Q   What is the main point of the passage?
(a) Consumers must be on the lookout for counterfeit gems.
(b) Rubies and sapphires are the most popular gemstones.

▶ 가짜 보석이 시장에 넘쳐나고 있다는 내용을 빠르게 훑어 읽다가, 결론을 이끄는 연결어 So 다음에 나온 '보석을 살 때는 진품 확인하라'라는 내용을 자세히 읽는다. 이 내용을 담고 있는 (a)가 지문의 요점이므로 정답이다.

3. 바르게 paraphrase된 정답 찾기

텝스 독해에서는 지문의 내용이 그대로 정답에 나오지 않고 바뀌어 표현되어, 즉 paraphrase되어 나오는 경우가 많으므로 바르게 paraphrase된 문장을 찾는 연습을 하는 것이 매우 중요하다. 이러한 연습을 paraphrase가 가장 많이 사용되는 육하원칙 문제 챕터(Chapter 05)와 Correct 문제 챕터(Chapter 06) 내의 Hackers Practice 유형 연습에서 해볼 수 있고, Hackers Test 문제의 해설을 통해 적용해볼 수 있다.

문제풀이 적용하기

> Experience the hidden treasures of Jamaica with a guided tour by Wailer Vacations. Your ten-day **tour, departing from Kingston,** will take you around the exterior of the island, with stopovers in Ocho Rios, Negril, and a three-night stay at a spa and resort in Montego Bay. Opportunities for snorkeling and climbing are numerous, so those interested should make plans to bring the proper equipment.

Q   Which of the following is correct according to the advertisement?
   (a) Snorkeling equipment will be provided for interested travelers.
   (b) Travelers will embark on their tour from Kingston.

▶ 지문의 tour, departing from Kingston(킹스턴에서 출발하는 여행)이 embark on ~ tour from Kingston(킹스턴에서 여행을 시작한다)으로 바르게 paraphrase된 (b)가 정답이다. (a)의 equipment will be provided(장비가 제공될 것이다)라는 말은 지문의 should ~ bring the proper equipment(적절한 장비를 가져와야 한다)를 잘못 paraphrase했으므로 오답이다.

혼자 하기 어렵고 막막할 땐?

해커스텝스(**HackersTEPS.com**)에서
스타강사의 무료 동영상강의 보기!

Section 1 문제 유형별 공략

CHAPTER 01 빈칸에 문장의 일부 · 전체 넣기 (Part 1

글의 흐름이 자연스럽게 이어질 수 있도록 보기에서 문장의 일부 또는 문장 전체를 골라 지문의 빈칸에 넣는 유형이다. 이 유형은 Part 1에 8문제가 출제되어 Part 1의 대부분을 차지한다. 지문의 요지와 흐름을 이해하면 대부분 쉽게 해결할 수 있는 문제이다. 그럼 이 유형에 대해 자세히 알아보자.

■ 출제 경향

· 지문의 마지막 문장에 빈칸이 제시되는 문제가 가장 많이 출제되고, 지문의 처음 한두 문장과 중간에 빈칸이 제시되는 문제 순으로 이 출제된다.

· 지문 전체의 중심 내용을 담고 있는 주제문을 완성하는 문제가 주로 출제되고, 앞뒤 문맥에 맞는 내용을 채워 넣는 문제도 상당수 출 된다.

■ Step별 문제풀이 전략

Step 1 빈칸이 있는 문장을 읽고 지문의 소재를 파악하거나 무엇을 빈칸에 넣어야 할지 예상한다.

(ex) We can observe that the **human brain** _____.
> ▶ human brain(인간의 뇌)이 지문의 소재임을 파악하여 이와 관련된 내용이 빈칸에 올 것임을 예상한다.

(ex) **This suggests** that _____.
> ▶ This suggests(이것은 ~을 시사한다)를 통해 앞에서 언급한 내용의 결론이 빈칸에 올 것임을 예상한다.

Step 2 지문 앞부분부터 읽어 내려가며 지문의 중심 내용이나 흐름을 파악한다.

· 빈칸이 지문 마지막에 있는 경우, 빈칸이 있는 문장이 주제문이거나 지문의 흐름과 관련된 경우가 많다. 따라서 중심 내용이 자 등장하는 처음 한두 문장을 자세히 읽은 후, 아래의 표현들을 단서로 지문의 흐름을 파악한다.

지문의 흐름을 나타내는 표현

대조/전환	but 그러나	however 그러나	yet 그러나	on the other hand 반면에
인과	as a result 그 결과	because ~ 때문에	for this reason 이러한 이유로	that's why ~한 이유이다
결론	now 이제	so 따라서	then 그러면, 그 다음에	thus, therefore 그러므로

＊대조/전환을 나타내는 표현 뒤에는 정답의 단서가 되는 내용이 나오는 경우가 많으므로 뒤에 이어지는 내용을 주의 깊게 읽는다.

· 빈칸이 지문 앞부분에 있는 경우, 빈칸이 있는 문장이 대부분 주제문이므로 뒤에 나오는 세부 내용을 읽으며 지문의 중심 내용 파악한다.

· 빈칸이 지문 중간에 있는 경우, 지문의 흐름상 적절한 세부 내용을 빈칸에 넣어야 하는 경우가 대부분이므로 빈칸 앞뒤 문맥을 확히 파악한다.

Step 3 보기에서 정답을 선택한 후 빈칸에 넣어 문맥이 자연스러운지 확인한다.

빈칸이 지문 마지막에 있는 경우

August Wilson's personal experiences as a racially-mixed child growing up in an impoverished neighborhood had a profound effect on his plays. The black experience in the twentieth century a frequent theme. Wilson's work is not sentimental; **however,** ━ **Step 2** 지문의 중심 내용이나 흐름 파악하기

e strives for accuracy. His plays draw heavily on his research of earlier eras to give a voice to the minorities of the past. **Literary** ━ **Step 1** 빈칸이 있는 문장을 읽고, 소재나 빈칸에 넣을 내용 예상하기

itics see his plays as _____.

) limited to a certain audience

) well-informed but too idealistic

) both autobiographical and historical ━ **Step 3** 정답 선택하기

) relevant only to a bygone period

1 빈칸이 있는 문장을 통해, his plays(그의 희곡)가 지문의 소재이며, 문학 비평가들이 그의 희곡을 어떻게 여기는지 빈칸에 넣어야 함을 예상한다.

2 '개인적인 경험이 희곡에 영향을 끼쳤다'라는 내용이 나오다가 흐름의 전환을 나타내는 however(그러나) 다음부터는 '정확성을 위해 이전 시대에 대한 연구에 의존한다'라는 내용이 나온 것을 파악한다.

3 보기 (c)는 however 앞뒤 내용을 각각 autobiographical(자전적인)과 historical(역사에 바탕을 둔)이라고 나타내어 빈칸에 넣었을 때 자연스러운 문맥이 된다.

빈칸이 지문 앞부분에 있는 경우

recent study has shown that _____. ━ **Step 1** 빈칸이 있는 문장을 읽고, 소재나 빈칸에 넣을 내용 예상하기

ofessors from the University of Newcastle were researching the fects of the beverage upon those suffering from Alzheimer's, disease marked by serious memory impairments. One set of atients drank several cups of green tea daily, while another oup did not. The scientists were able to demonstrate that **the** ━ **Step 2** 지문의 중심 내용이나 흐름 파악하기

nzyme AChE, which breaks down the chemicals used by e brain to recall information, is inhibited in those who rank green tea.

) memory function is maintained in those drinking green tea ━ **Step 3** 정답 선택하기

) green tea can reverse the damage done by Alzheimer's disease

) the chemical structure of green tea is similar to AChE

) green tea is only effective if taken in copious amounts

1 빈칸이 있는 문장을 통해, recent study(최근의 연구)가 지문의 소재이며, 최근의 연구를 통해 나온 결과를 빈칸에 넣어야 함을 예상한다.

2 빈칸 이후의 문장을 읽으며 '녹차를 마신 사람들에게서 두뇌가 정보를 회상하기 위해 사용하는 화학 물질을 파괴하는 효소가 억제된다'라는 중심 내용을 파악한다.

3 보기 (a)는 지문 전체에 걸쳐 설명된 최근의 연구 결과를 '녹차를 마시는 이들에게서 기억 기능이 유지된다'라고 표현하여 빈칸에 넣었을 때 자연스러운 문맥이 된다.

해석 p.110

Hackers **Practice**

구문독해 연습 – 주어

구문독해를 익힌 후 주어진 문제를 풀어 보세요.

01 동명사 주어

Teaching students to enjoy the process of learning / should be / the most important goal of any school
학생들에게 학습 과정을 즐기도록 가르치는 것은   되어야 한다   모든 학교의 가장 중요한 목표가
that wishes to successfully educate children.
아이들을 성공적으로 교육시키기 원하는

위 문장에서 주어는 Teaching ~ learning이다. 이처럼 동명사 형태(동사 + ing)가 주어인 경우 '~하는 것은, ~하기는'으로 해석한다.

다음 문장이 바르게 paraphrase된 보기를 고르세요.

Cooking risotto to produce a creamy texture is possible if it is constantly stirred as it heats and kept at a reasonably low temperature.

(a) Risotto that is stirred often and cooked on low heat will have a creamy texture.
(b) A creamy texture can be achieved if risotto is stirred and then heated for a long period.

02 'What (+ 주어) + 동사' 형태의 주어

What I had never realized / is / that the band's song was the tale of a broken heart and not about
내가 전혀 깨닫지 못했던 것은   이다   그 밴드의 노래가 내가 처음에 생각했던 것처럼 사랑에 빠지는 것에 대한 이야기가 아니라 실연에 대한 이야기였다는 것
falling in love as I had originally thought.

위 문장에서 주어는 What I had never realized이다. 이처럼 'What (+ 주어) + 동사' 형태가 주어인 경우 '~가 ~하는 것은'으로 해석한다.

다음 문장이 바르게 paraphrase된 보기를 고르세요.

In my childhood, what I chose to eat in the morning consisted only of sugary breakfast cereals and the occasional plate of pancakes with maple syrup.

(a) The breakfast foods available in my youth were unhealthy.
(b) I only ate certain foods for breakfast as a youngster.

03 가짜 주어(It) – 진짜 주어(that · to부정사)

It / is suspected / that the gang is also responsible for several other unsolved crimes that have shocked
의심된다   그 갱단이 최근 지역 주민을 놀라게 했던 다른 몇 건의 미해결 사건에도 책임이 있다고
local residents as of late.

위 문장에서 진짜 주어는 It이 아니라 that the gang is ~ as of late이다. 이처럼 긴 주어를 대신해 가짜 주어 it이 쓰이며, 이때 뒤에 오는 that 절이나 to부정사가 진짜 주어이다. 이 경우 가짜 주어 it은 해석하지 않고, 뒤에 있는 진짜 주어를 it의 자리에 넣어 '~라고, ~하는 것은'으로 해석한다.

다음 문장이 바르게 paraphrase된 보기를 고르세요.

It was reasonable to predict Joe McNeil's eventual defeat by Sarah Bowman based upon the pre-election survey results.

(a) The survey results indicated that Sarah Bowman would win the election.
(b) Joe McNeil was expected to be the candidate who would win the election.

형 연습

을 읽고 빈칸에 알맞은 보기를 고르세요.

This afternoon marked the launch of California's largest-ever _____.
It has been suggested that the fall drought has created the conditions for the recent blazes,
which have killed several people and torched nearly a million acres of land in all. Governor
Schwarzenegger hopes that such efforts on behalf of the government will educate people about
the dangers of fire and how they can help to avert such catastrophes in the future.

(a) drought insurance scheme
(b) fire prevention program

Your workout routine may be at fault if you're not getting the results you've come to expect.
If you exercise the same muscle groups on consecutive days, you might be overworking those
parts of your body. What you need to realize is that muscles need ample rest to grow stronger
as opposed to continual, stressful work. A good policy is to work out each muscle group no
more than twice a week, and your muscles _____.

(a) will no longer become weaker
(b) will have enough time to recover

The earliest home video game console was released in North America in 1972. The Magnavox
Odyssey came with two controllers and could be connected to any television set. The display
capabilities of the Odyssey were very limited compared to the stunning images produced by
modern systems; furnishing buyers with a set of colored overlays to attach to the television set
was the company's solution to the Odyssey's monochromatic output. People enjoyed the simple,
easy-to-learn games, which thousands of families bought despite their poor graphics. Overall,
the Odyssey _____.

(a) differed greatly from current graphics-intensive game systems
(b) was innovative because of its visual overlay technique

정답 p.110

01

When it comes to automobiles, different countries _____.
The Japanese are known for making extremely reliable family cars, and companies like Honda and Toyota always top consumer satisfaction surveys. In fact, a 2006 study of the most reliable vehicles lists Japanese models in 39 of the top 47 positions. German cars are known for luxury, as brands like Mercedes-Benz, BMW, and Audi can attest. Italian automobiles are perceived as being sporty. If you ask any car aficionado to name the best sports cars, the names Ferrari, Lamborghini, and Alfa Romeo will surely be mentioned.

(a) are producing specialized cars to suit local tastes
(b) have a reputation for certain types of cars
(c) have divergent views about their cars' reliability
(d) are unlikely to surpass the quality of Japanese offerings

02

Face-to-face meetings have historically been the way business is conducted. This began to change in the 1800s, however, as a more efficient postal service made sending letters more feasible. Decades later, companies seeking instantaneous communication used the telephone system to accomplish this. Most recently, because of the popularity and lower cost of computers, the business trend has again shifted. Statistics show that, for business communication, _____.
Just as other means of communication enjoyed widespread use, the vast majority of companies now correspond with customers online.

(a) office workers are becoming more proficient with computers
(b) telephone usage is no longer decreasing at a high rate
(c) electronic mail has now become the prevailing method
(d) the postal service has gradually become obsolete

03

When you are running a race, blisters are your worst enemy. This is especially true for marathon runners, who can't afford to cover great distances with torn up feet. For this reason, CurrentSox running socks are what the leading runners wear. Our socks are webbed to separate the toes from one another, unlike conventional athletic socks. This prevents _____.
With CurrentSox, foot problems from chafing skin will never again be a concern.

(a) feet from getting sore due to ground contact
(b) toes from rubbing against one another
(c) toes from bending as you run
(d) feet from gathering too much moisture

The hyperactivity drug Ritalin _____. A significant number of pediatricians are criticizing the drug, designed to treat a condition called ADHD(Attention Deficit Hyperactivity Disorder). They insist the drug, currently used by one in ten children, is being overprescribed and that its dangerous side effects are being ignored by doctors. However, advocates of the drug argue that it has been proven to bring about calm behavior in usually hyperactive children, and should continue to be distributed at current rates.

(a) has been proven to be ineffective
(b) has recently started to be used on children
(c) is becoming a subject of debate
(d) is adversely effecting children's behavior

In an effort to design cheap and plentiful solar panels, researchers have been inspired by the process of photosynthesis, in which plants use naturally occurring chemicals to manufacture food from sunlight. Solar panels have traditionally been made of silicon, a mineral which is present in copious amounts in the earth's crust but expensive to extract and refine. Recently, New Zealand scientists have been engineering a more cost-effective way to create the panels by _____.

(a) outsourcing their production to other countries
(b) using substances that simulate photosynthesis
(c) finding a mineral that costs less to extract
(d) eliminating the need for electric light controls

Media coverage of video games generally focuses on the negative effects they have on children. Most arguments cited take issue with the positive in-game rewards children receive for the repetition of violent or negative behaviors, which many fear will encourage them to deal with emotional turmoil by repeating such antisocial behaviors in the real world. Despite this, Noah Stupak, a sociologist at Rochester University, insists that such concerns are misplaced. He suggests that violent video games _____.

(a) can persuade children to think that violence is acceptable
(b) teach children to find a solution to their problems
(c) cause an increasing amount of anger-related issues
(d) may provide children with an outlet for harmful emotions

07

Ever since the rediscovery of the lost city of Pompeii in 1748, archaeologists have struggled to determine what the city looked like before the eruption of Mt. Vesuvius buried it. This isn't because of damage done to the city's structures – in fact, several of them were well preserved in the volcanic ash. The problem is that the city was badly damaged in an earthquake fifteen years before the eruption. Information about subsequent reconstruction efforts and the extent of the damage can only be gleaned from conflicting historical records. Thus, even in modern times, _____ _____.

(a) fewer archaeologists are traveling to study the ruins
(b) envisioning the city before the eruption is difficult
(c) volcanoes still threaten the area around Pompeii
(d) structures from before the eruption no longer remain

08

At the current rate, China will be completely deforested within the next 10 years if disposable chopstick usage continues unabated. Every year, restaurants in China go through 45 billion pairs of disposable chopsticks, causing an annual loss of 25 million trees. For restaurants, the choice to use disposable chopsticks is financially motivated: the cost is somewhat less than the price of buying hundreds of sets of conventional chopsticks and the extra expense involved in washing them numerous times. As a result, these chopsticks are discarded after each meal. In short, _____ _____.

(a) single-use chopsticks create environmental problems in China
(b) washing wooden chopsticks would prevent deforestation
(c) people who dine at home are not affected by the issue
(d) disposable chopsticks are a waste of financial resources

09

Lou Stone's *A Guidebook to Western Thought* is a necessary part of any philosophy lover's book collection. The volume is written in a clear, lucid style that will appeal to any reader. It covers all eras of philosophical thought, from the Ancient Greeks all the way to Nietzsche, Marx, and Frege. Stone is able to put each philosophical trend into its social and scientific context to help the reader understand the factors that led to new ideas. The 900-page work is _____.

(a) a great biography of philosophers from the past
(b) effective at focusing on thoughts from Ancient Greece
(c) an ideal survey of Western philosophical developments
(d) designed for university students enrolled in philosophy

Genetic oncology is fast becoming an important area of medical research dealing with _____ _____. A major focus is on "Sox genes," which control the development of blood vessels in cancerous regions. When a tumor starts to form, Sox genes send a signal to cancer cells causing them to build up a stronger circulatory system in the area. Essentially, because of the greater blood flow, the cancer growth can receive more oxygen and continue to grow larger.

(a) how genes can affect cancerous growths
(b) why genes are important to stopping cancer
(c) what effect cancers have upon genetic development
(d) when cancers initially develop in humans

Dear Suzanne,

Our department received your suggestions for an updated advertising campaign, and we _____ _____. The head director expressed an understanding of your vision, but she feels images that better reflect our company's values are necessary. All the same, we feel that your submission has several merits, and we would like to invite you to a meeting with our advertising department to discuss how we can rework some of your ideas and implement them in our upcoming commercials. Please contact us at your earliest convenience.

Sincerely,

Robert Adams, Assistant Marketing Director

(a) wish to express our appreciation for your hard work
(b) regret that we cannot employ them as is
(c) decided to incorporate more visual details
(d) are interested in hiring you for our department

In pre-colonial times, New York City's Coney Island was known for its bunnies — the seaside was often teeming with rabbits. Later, this part of the city became known for its amusement park, which has quickly become run-down over the years. But recently, land developers are hoping to transform the area into one with upscale beach resorts and hotels to attract a different sort of visitor during the summer. They hope Coney Island will become known for _____.

(a) exciting attractions along with natural beauty
(b) chic accommodations as opposed to urban blight
(c) local wildlife together with improved facilities
(d) its extensive history instead of the recent renovations

13

The body needs both calcium and vitamin C to stay healthy, but it is important to ensure a balance between these two nutrients. Healthy amounts of calcium can regulate the production of stomach acid triggered by vitamin C, but too much calcium can lead to tissue calcification, a buildup of unabsorbed calcium that causes kidney stones and gallstones. Excess amounts of vitamin C, on the other hand, can lower calcium levels in the body, which may result in bone loss. Therefore, people should bear in mind the correlation between vitamin C and calcium, as failure to do so may _____.

(a) make the body susceptible to infections
(b) cause calcium and vitamin C deficiency
(c) have detrimental effects on health
(d) contribute to problems with digestion

14

Dear clients,

Brechin International Freight Limited would like to advise you _____. Starting July 1, all wooden pallets bound for Indonesian ports must be fumigated by accredited operators to ensure that the pallets are termite-free. Moreover, each wood pallet must bear a stamp verifying that it has been treated. These new policies are in line with a directive from the Indonesian Customs Department. For more information, please visit our website at www.brechinlimited.com.

Alex Marshall, Client relations officer

(a) that we no longer deliver wooden pallets to Indonesia
(b) that we are closing our Indonesian office for fumigation
(c) of new regulations involving shipments to Indonesia
(d) of revised guidelines for shipping hazardous chemicals

15

British actress Audrey Hepburn was one of the most influential Hollywood personalities of the 20th century. In 1967, despite her immense popularity as an actress, she left Hollywood to focus on humanitarianism. Although she had done work for UNICEF as early as the 1950s, Hepburn thought that she could contribute more to society by engaging in philanthropy full time. She visited underprivileged communities throughout the world and dedicated herself to helping impoverished children until her death in 1993. In leaving show business for charity work, Hepburn felt she _____ _____.

(a) was able to make more significant contributions to humanity
(b) became progressively focused on helping young actors
(c) lost many opportunities to appear in movies and TV shows
(d) achieved the peace she lacked at the height of her popularity

Play-Doh, the popular non-toxic modeling compound, was first used as a wallpaper cleaner. Noah McVicker concocted the substance for a family-owned soap company in the 1930s. More than two decades later, his nephew Joseph McVicker saw the rubbery product's commercial potential as a toy after learning that his sister's nursery class used it to make Christmas decorations. Joseph then added colorants to the cleaner, gave it a pleasant scent, and re-released it as a toy. Hence, before Play-Doh became popular among children, _____.

(a) the material had originally been intended for other purposes
(b) the cleaner was the soap company's best-selling product
(c) it could not be advertised as a wallpaper cleaner
(d) Joseph McVicker first introduced it to his nursery class

Following a hearing by the International Rugby Board, the Andorra national rugby team is now faced with the fact that_____. Andorra captain Dogan Mas was found guilty of misconduct after he made inappropriate comments about decisions made by referee Salvador Bofill in his team's recent friendly match against Botswana. The board handed Mas a six-month suspension, which means that he will miss his team's campaign in next month's Global Rugby Cup.

(a) it must appeal a recent decision by rugby's governing body
(b) it will have to do without a key player in upcoming matches
(c) it should have benched a player charged with misconduct
(d) it has to discipline a player for an on-field incident

The amount of precipitation that falls within an area_____. To be categorized as a rainforest, the area must receive no less than 1.7 meters of rainfall per annum. If an area does not receive as much rainfall, then it does not qualify as a rainforest. Regular forests are sometimes mistaken for rainforests, as both may have high density of trees and are home to a wide range of animal and plant species. Only after measuring the amount of rainfall in a forest can experts determine if it can be classified as a rainforest.

(a) factors into the classification of rainforests
(b) has nothing to do with the cataloging of rainforests
(c) highly depends on the location of rainforest
(d) ranges from heavy to light in tropical rainforests

정답 p.111

CHAPTER **02** 빈칸에 연결어 넣기 (Part 1)

글의 흐름이 자연스럽게 이어질 수 있도록 지문의 빈칸에 적절한 연결어를 보기에서 골라 넣는 유형이다. 이 유형은 Part 1의 마지막 9번, 10번에 2문제가 출제된다. 자주 나오는 연결어의 종류와 의미를 알고 있으면 쉽게 해결할 수 있는 문제이다. 그럼 이 유형에 대해 자세히 알아보자.

■ 출제 경향

· 주로 지문의 중간과 마지막 문장에 빈칸이 제시된다.

· 빈칸 앞뒤 문장의 관계만 파악하면 답을 찾을 수 있는 문제가 주로 출제되나, 글 전체의 흐름을 파악해야 해결할 수 있는 문제가 출제되는 경우도 있다.

■ Step별 문제풀이 전략

Step 1 빈칸 앞뒤에 있는 문장을 읽고, 그 문장들 간의 논리적 관계를 파악한다.

자주 나오는 논리적 관계에는 '대조/전환, 양보, 첨가/부연, 유사, 예시, 이유/결과, 결론/요약, 경과, 강조' 등이 있으며, 이 중 대조/전환과 첨가/부연이 가장 많이 나온다.

Step 2 파악한 논리적 관계를 나타내는 연결어를 보기에서 선택한다.

자주 등장하는 논리적 관계와 이에 해당하는 연결어는 다음과 같다.

대조/전환	however / but / (and) yet 하지만, 그러나 instead 그 대신 rather 오히려 otherwise 그렇지 않다면	in contrast / by contrast / conversely 대조적으로 on the other hand / on the contrary 반면에 that being said 그렇기는 하지만 alternatively 그 대신에
양보	in spite of that / even so / for all that / all the same / (that) notwithstanding / still / nevertheless / regardless / nonetheless / despite this 그럼에도 불구하고	
첨가/부연	in addition / besides / furthermore / moreover / what is more / on top of that 게다가 as such 그런 만큼, 그와 같이	
유사	similarly / likewise / in the same way / in the same vein 마찬가지로	
예시	for instance / for example / to illustrate 예를 들면	as an example / as an illustration 한 가지 예로서
이유/결과	for this reason / for these reasons 이러한 이유로 granted ~이므로	as a result 그 결과 given that fact 그 사실을 고려할 때
결론/요약	thus / hence / therefore / accordingly / consequently 그러므로, 따라서 in conclusion 결론적으로 in short / in brief / in sum 요약하면 ultimately / in turn 결국	all in all / overall 대체로 in other words / namely / that is / put another way 다시 말해 in this way 이렇게 해서, 이런 방식으로
순서/경과	to begin with / firstly 우선, 먼저 meanwhile 그러는 동안, 한편 subsequently / thereafter 그 후에	simultaneously / at the same time 동시에 eventually / in the end / after all 결국, 마침내
강조	in fact / in effect / in actuality 사실상, 실제로는 indeed 정말로 admittedly / to be sure 확실히	(more) specifically / especially / particularly / in particular in any case 어쨌든 not surprisingly 당연히

Step 3 선택한 연결어를 빈칸에 넣어 문맥이 자연스러운지 확인한다.

전략 적용

movie remake will never have the impact of the original. onetheless, directors continuously try to provide updated, odern interpretations to memorable films like *Charlie and the hocolate Factory* or *Titanic*. **Even in the hands of a capable** ← Step 1 빈칸 앞뒤 문장의 논리적 관계 파악하기
irector, these films will never leave the same impression
s the originals. _____, **occasionally a director will** ← Step 3 선택한 연결어 넣어 문맥 확인하기
ecreate a film in such a way that it completely departs
om the original and becomes a masterpiece in its own
ght.

) Yet ←————————————————————— Step 2 파악한 논리적 관계를 나타내는 연결어 선택하기
) Hence
) Consequently
) Meanwhile

1 빈칸 앞문장은 '리메이크된 영화가 원작과 같은 감동을 줄 수 없을 것이다'라는 부정적인 내용이고, 빈칸 뒷문장은 '리메이크된 영화가 걸작으로 재창조될 것이다'라는 긍정적인 내용이다. 따라서 앞뒤 문장의 논리적 관계가 '대조'임을 파악한다.

2 보기에서 '대조'를 나타내는 연결어로 (a) Yet(하지만)을 선택한다.

3 (a) Yet(하지만)을 빈칸에 넣으면, 지문 전체가 '리메이크된 영화가 원작과 같을 수는 없겠지만 때때로 걸작으로 재창조되기도 할 것이다'라는 자연스러운 문맥이 된다. 따라서 정답은 (a)이다.

Hackers **Practice**

구문독해 연습 – 목적어·보어

구문독해를 익힌 후 주어진 문제를 풀어 보세요.

01 목적어 · 보어 역할을 하는 의문사절(when / why / who / where / what / how)

> People / concerned about the environment / contemplate / what they can do to help prevent the
> 사람들은   환경을 걱정하는   숙고한다   지구의 파괴를 막는 것을 돕기 위해 그들이 무엇을 할 수 있는지
> destruction of the earth.

위 문장에서 목적어는 what ~ earth이다. 이처럼 '의문사 + 주어 + 동사'가 문장의 목적어나 보어인 경우 '~가 의문사(언제 / 왜 / 누가 / 어디서 / 무엇을(을) / 어떻게) ~ 한지(를)'로 해석한다.

다음 문장이 바르게 paraphrase된 보기를 고르세요.

The failing students learned what they did wrong on their projects to receive such low grades.

(a) The struggling students were taught how to correct the mistakes on their badly graded projects.
(b) The reasons for their poor project grades were explained to the underperforming students.

02 목적어 · 보어 자리에 오는 that 명사절

> The retiring workers / at the company / felt / that executives should have offered them a larger pension
> 퇴직 노동자들은   그 회사의   느꼈다   경영진들이 생계비를 지급하기 위해서 그들에게 더 많은 연금을 제공했어야만 했다고
> to provide for their living expenses.

위 문장에서 목적어는 that executives ~ living expenses이다. 이처럼 'that + 주어 + 동사 ~' 형태의 명사절이 목적어나 보어 자리에 오는 경우, '~가(이) ~하다는 것을(을)' 또는 '~가(이) ~하다고'라고 해석한다.

다음 문장이 바르게 paraphrase된 보기를 고르세요.

One of the most serious problems with the report is that none of the statistics the author mentioned have been confirmed by researchers.

(a) The lack of verified statistics is a major weakness of the report.
(b) The report needs a greater number of statistics to be included.

03 가짜 목적어(it) – 진짜 목적어(that절 / to부정사 / 의문사절)

> She / considers / it / important / that the project is completed soon / because she has already made
> 그녀는   여긴다   중요하고   그 프로젝트가 곧 완료되는 것이   그녀가 이미 장기간의 휴가를 갈 계획을 세웠기 때문에
> plans to go on an extended holiday.

위 문장에서 목적어는 it이 아니라 that the project ~ soon이며, important는 목적격 보어이다. 이처럼 긴 목적어를 대신해 가짜 목적어 it을 쓰며, 뒤에 오는 that절, to부정사, 의문사절 등의 긴 목적어가 진짜 목적어이다. 이때 it은 해석하지 않고, 뒤에 있는 진짜 목적어를 it의 자리에 넣어 해석한다.

다음 문장이 바르게 paraphrase된 보기를 고르세요.

Weather forecasters find it impossible to predict exact weather conditions more than a week in advance.

(a) It is not possible to predict the weather unless a forecaster is given advance notice.
(b) Forecasters can only predict the coming week's weather with accuracy.

형 연습

:을 읽고 빈칸에 알맞은 보기를 고르세요.

Shoe Savers, the area's largest women's shoe store, is relocating. The good news is we're liquidating our inventory, and this means discounts of up to 80 percent for customers! _____, since the sale began, our remaining stock has been selling quickly, so hurry and stop by before everything sells out. Our top-selling athletic shoes are priced from $19, sandals are just $6, and our Italian leather high-heeled shoes start at $25. This is one sale that you don't want to miss!

(a) Likewise
(b) However

Consumers know how fast food can be bad for their health and lacking nutritional value, but many chains want to convince them that their products aren't really so horrendous. Nearly every restaurant has reduced the quantities of fat and cholesterol in its dishes. New menu items are popping up, like spinach salads and stir-fried vegetables. The days of oversized meals are also coming to an end. _____, popular chains are opting for calorie-controlled set menus and reasonable portions.

(a) Otherwise
(b) Instead

The northern and southern regions of the United States were at odds with one another midway through the nineteenth century. They considered it problematic to find a compromise regarding their diverging opinions on slavery. _____, southern states felt that their constitutionally guaranteed rights were being eroded, which further distanced the two regions. South Carolina first made the split, formally withdrawing from the United States in 1860, and was followed soon after by several other states.

(a) In addition
(b) Nevertheless

정답 p.115

01

Performance-enhancing drugs give athletes taking them an unfair advantage in sports competitions, and those using them should definitely be punished. _____, baseball players found to be using steroids or other illegal medications should be banned from competing for at least three years. It is only fair to penalize these substance abusers as using these drugs negates the virtues of sportsmanship and fair play, while often putting an athlete's personal health at risk. This should not be tolerated, and it is therefore recommended that regulations be enhanced to prevent their use in sports.

(a) For instance
(b) Moreover
(c) However
(d) In other words

02

Recent surveys indicate that economic troubles are looming as middle-aged individuals, specifically those between 40 and 55, are experiencing foreclosures, loan defaults, and credit card debt in record numbers. _____, this demographic is increasingly susceptible to unsteady employment, as more layoffs occur and work is outsourced to other regions. Politicians hope that tax rebates and economic incentives will be enough to reverse the financial predicament the middle-aged currently face.

(a) Generally
(b) Moreover
(c) Thus
(d) Nevertheless

03

Anthem, a 1937 novella by Russian-American author Ayn Rand, depicted a futuristic society rooted in complete collectivism. The concept of the individual was forbidden, and the populace viewed themselves only as a single entity; this meant that relationships were not allowed. Children were taken from their parents at birth, and friendships were prohibited. _____, inhabitants were referred to numerically instead of by name, and jobs were assigned without any consideration of personal preferences. This created a society that functioned as a complete unit without internal dissension.

(a) Therefore
(b) Subsequently
(c) In addition
(d) Still

The presidency of Ferdinand Marcos marked a time of great upheaval in the Philippines. A period of martial law and accusations of corruption culminated in the People Power Revolution of 1986. Millions demonstrated in the streets and Marcos was forced to relinquish power. Visions of democratic politics, a stable government, and a stronger economy flashed through the minds of everyone in the nation. _____, political analysts assert that these ideals continue to elude the Philippines to this day.

(a) Nevertheless
(b) Furthermore
(c) In effect
(d) Therefore

We are pleased to announce the opening of the Helping Hands Soup Kitchen. The purpose of our charity is to provide the homeless and working poor in the local area with a warm, safe place to come and enjoy a meal. The soup kitchen will be open for lunch from 12:00 noon to 2:00 pm, and dinner will be served from 5:00 pm to 7:00 pm. Helping Hands is expected to attract several hundred visitors a day and will require a large staff. _____, we are soliciting the help of anyone interested in volunteering time for this noble cause.

(a) Likewise
(b) Otherwise
(c) Accordingly
(d) Meanwhile

Buying your new or used books through Nile Bookseller will save you loads of cash. Our prices are guaranteed to be the lowest in the industry, and standard shipping is offered free of charge on all orders totaling fifty dollars or more. _____, our selection of over three million titles is by far the largest of any bookseller worldwide. Head over to our Web site at nilebooks.com and place your order today!

(a) In short
(b) In other words
(c) In addition
(d) Indeed

07

The Ukrainian city of Chernobyl was a calm city of 55,000 situated near the border with Belarus. The city enjoyed mild weather compared to many other parts of the Soviet Union and boasted magnificent, heavily forested surroundings. _____, in 1986, a nuclear reactor malfunctioned and exploded in the town, releasing substantial amounts of radiation and causing the evacuation of all residents. Even today, the town is virtually abandoned, with the only residents being physicists, researchers, and government officials involved in investigating the aftermath of the disaster.

(a) Moreover
(b) Hence
(c) However
(d) Eventually

08

Transatlantic voyages in past centuries were often fraught with serious problems. Particularly during the times of North American colonization, disease and illness were rampant on ships due to the lack of space. Passengers and crew had very little room to move around and were unable to avoid coming in contact with sick passengers and animals. Maintenance issues, inclement weather, and accidents also put voyagers at risk. These transatlantic voyages were often dangerous and life-threatening. _____, the death rate for passengers and crew was as high as 10 percent.

(a) Furthermore
(b) Indeed
(c) However
(d) Likewise

09

Brazilian football retain young, developing players and aging footballers on the verge of retirement because they do not have the funds to pay the same salaries that the top clubs in Europe and the Middle East provide. _____, Brazil's brightest football stars are drawn in by lucrative contracts overseas and offer their talents to the highest bidder. As such, domestic football in Brazil has been declining in quality in recent years. The funds have been dwindling because of a history of widespread corruption in government and FIFA, resulting in a lack of support for Brazilian football.

(a) For instance
(b) Consequently
(c) Furthermore
(d) Nonetheless

The novelty song *Itsy Bitsy Teenie Weenie Yellow Polka Dot Bikini* hit number one on the Billboard Hot 100 less than a month after its release in June 1960. Aside from its chart success, the song is credited for changing the popular view of bikini bathing suits, which at the time were considered too risqué to be worn in public. The song prompted an increase in sales of the swimwear. _____, many people believe that bikini swimsuits would have remained unacceptable for much longer if it were not for the song.

(a) To illustrate
(b) That being said
(c) Even so
(d) Indeed

Research by the California Education Commission shows that students who attended kindergarten at a later age performed better academically than younger enrollees. The survey targeted students aged 8 to 16. According to the results, students who started kindergarten at age 5 or above showed greater reading ability once they reached elementary school than students who began kindergarten at age 4. _____, at the high school level, the late-starters had higher grade point averages than the students who started kindergarten early.

(a) Nonetheless
(b) Furthermore
(c) For instance
(d) That being said

Ethics Talk

Passing Down Prejudice

Children's social attitudes often mirror the attitudes held by their parents. For instance, if a child comes from a racist family, he or she will likely grow up with the same prejudices. _____, children who grow up in an open-minded family are more apt to possess a positive attitude towards multiculturalism. A person's attitude toward people of a different race is most certainly picked up at home rather in school. Setting an example at home can thus help children to learn to interact with people of different backgrounds.

(a) As a result
(b) Nevertheless
(c) Besides
(d) Conversely

CHAPTER **03** 어색한 문장 골라내기 (Part 2)

지문의 첫 문장에 이어서 나오는 4개의 보기 문장 중 지문의 흐름과 어울리지 않는 문장을 골라내는 유형으로 Part 2에 출제되는 2문제가 모두 이 유형에 속한다. 이 유형의 문제를 풀기 위해서는 모든 문장을 자세히 읽어야 한다. 하지만, 일단 지문의 중심 내용을 파악하고 나면 지문의 흐름상 어색한 문장을 비교적 쉽게 찾을 수 있다. 그럼 이 유형에 대해 자세히 알아보자.

■ 출제 경향

· 지문의 첫 문장 또는 중심 내용과 관련이 없는 문장이 정답이 되거나, 다른 보기와의 흐름이 어색한 문장이 정답이 되는 문제가 출제된다.

■ Step별 문제풀이 전략

Step 1 첫 문장의 내용을 정확히 파악한다.

첫 문장이 중심 내용을 담은 주제문인 경우가 대부분이고, 첫 문장과 관계없는 보기가 정답이 되는 경우가 많으므로, 첫 문장의 내용을 정확히 파악하여 기억해두는 것이 좋다.

Step 2 보기를 차례대로 읽으며 지문의 첫 문장 또는 중심 내용과 관련이 없거나 흐름상 어색한 보기를 정답으로 선택한다.

어색한 문장 골라내기 문제의 정답은, 대부분 첫 문장이나 앞뒤 문장에 있는 단어와 통일하거나 이와 연관된 단어를 사용하여 흐름이 자연스러운 것처럼 혼동하게 하는 경우가 많으므로 주의한다.

Step 3 선택한 문장을 제외하고 지문 전체를 빠르게 읽으며 흐름이 자연스러운지 확인한다.

전략 적용

There is no better way to see Paris than with a trip on the Bateaux Mouches. (a) Let us bring out the romance and splendid history of Europe's finest city. (b) Our guides can take you on a one-hour day trip, or you can enjoy the Seine River on a twilight dinner cruise. **(c) To become an on-board tour guide on the Bateaux Mouches, at least one year of experience and a knowledge of French are required.** (d) If you take a Bateaux Mouches tour, we promise you an unforgettable experience.

──Step 1 첫 문장의 내용 파악하기

──Step 2 첫 문장과 관련 없거나 흐름상 어색한 보기 선택하기

Step 3 선택한 문장을 제외하고 지문의 흐름 확인하기

Step 1 첫 문장이 '바토 무쉬 여행'이라는 파리 관광 방법을 소개하는 내용임을 파악한다.

Step 2 보기 (a)와 (b)는 바토 무쉬 여행의 특징, (d)는 바토 무쉬 여행을 권유하는 내용으로 첫 문장과 관련이 있다. 그러나 (c)는 '여행 가이드가 되기 위한 조건'에 대한 내용으로 첫 문장과 관련이 없음을 알 수 있다.

Step 3 보기 (c)를 제외하고 지문을 읽으면, 바토 무쉬를 이용한 파리 관광을 광고하는 내용이 되어 지문 전체가 자연스러운 흐름을 이룬다.

해석 p.118

구문독해 연습 – 비교 · 강조 · 동격

구문독해를 익힌 후 주어진 문제를 풀어 보세요.

01 최상급의 의미를 가진 'no other A as ~ as B'

No other international sporting event / is / as widely televised as the World Cup soccer tournament, /
어떤 국제 스포츠 행사도　　　　　않는다　　　　월드컵 축구 토너먼트 경기처럼 텔레비전으로 널리 중계되지

which takes place every four years in a different location.
다른 지역에서 4년마다 개최되는

....

'A as ~ as B'는 원급 표현으로 'A가 B만큼 ~한'으로 해석되지만, no other과 함께 쓰여 'no other A as ~ as B' 형태가 되면 '어떤 A도 B만큼 ~하지 않은', 즉 '어떤 A보다도 B가 가장 ~한'이라는 최상급의 의미가 된다. 따라서 위 문장은 '월드컵 축구 토너먼트 경기가 어떤 국제 스포츠 행사 보다 가장 널리 중계된다'라는 의미이다.

다음 문장이 바르게 paraphrase된 보기를 고르세요.

No other disease on record was as deadly as the bubonic plague, which was responsible for the death of nearly a third of Europe's population during the Middle Ages.

(a) The bubonic plague was the third disease outbreak to strike Europe's population since the Middle Ages.
(b) The most deadly disease outbreak ever was the bubonic plague, which struck Europe in the Middle Ages.

02 내용을 강조하는 It ~ that …

It / was / only with the help of my closest family and friends / that I was able to achieve the degree of
이었다　　　바로 오직 나의 가까운 가족과 친구들의 도움이 있었기 때문　　내가 즐길 수 있을 정도로 충분히 운이 좋은 성공을 이룰 수 있었던 것은

success I've been fortunate enough to enjoy.

....

위 문장에서 only with ~ friends가 It과 that 사이에 와서 강조되고 있다. 이처럼 It ~ that …은 It과 that 사이에 있는 내용을 강조하는 역할을 하며, '…한 것은 바로 ~이다'라고 해석한다.

다음 문장이 바르게 paraphrase된 보기를 고르세요.

The examinations, study sessions, and teachers are not what I remember from school; it is the times spent with my classmates that I reminisce about most.

(a) The ample time I spent with my classmates made me forget about educational concerns.
(b) Memories of my classmates are what I recall from school, as opposed to my academic pursuits.

03 동격을 나타내는 that절

The idea / that women are not capable of military service / has been disproven / by a rapidly growing
생각이　　　　　여성이 군복무를 할 수 없다는　　　　반증되어 왔다

number of brave female soldiers.
급격히 증가하는 용감한 여성 군인의 수에 의해서

....

위 문장에서 The idea와 that women ~ military service는 동격을 이루고 있다. 이처럼 that절이 idea, fact, news 등의 명사 뒤에 와서 명사와 동격을 이루는 경우 '~라는/~한다는 명사(생각, 사실, 소식 등)'라고 해석한다.

다음 문장이 바르게 paraphrase된 보기를 고르세요.

The fact that ground tremors pose a threat to high-rise buildings is a consideration of architects in every area where the chance of an earthquake happening exists.

(a) Architects take the threat of earthquakes into account when designing high-rises in vulnerable regions.
(b) Architects design every part of high-rise buildings to withstand an earthquake in case one happens.

형 연습

글을 읽고 글의 흐름과 어울리지 않는 보기를 고르세요.

There are various reasons why a couple might decide to deliver their baby at home. (a) First, many families want to be involved in the birth process and elect to attend to the mother. (b) Also, until recently, most deliveries took place in the confines of the couple's home. (c) Lastly, some families lack sufficient funds to cover the medical costs associated with a birth.

Freshly picked mushrooms are a nutritious food that can be a wonderful addition to any meal. (a) When finding fresh mushrooms in the wild, it is key to avoid toxic varieties which often resemble edible ones. (b) It is only mushrooms that contain high concentrations of copper, a mineral needed to maintain heart function. (c) A cup of fresh mushrooms also provides as the same amount of potassium as a large banana.

The fact that numerous artifacts were left behind by the Easter Island civilization after its decline has intrigued researchers for centuries. (a) Statues built by the society, known as moai, dot the island's landscape and many scientists have been continuously working on how they were made. (b) Dozens of stone tablets containing the native script are still being deciphered by linguists. (c) Several famous sociologists, including Jared Diamond, have written works about the Easter Island.

정답 p.118

01

After registering with Atlantic Airways' "Frequent Flyer Club," I am confident that I will never fly with another airline again. (a) I was able to get my flight reserved several weeks before the booking period available to travel agents and general customers. (b) This allowed me to get the specific flight I wanted, provided that I had planned my itinerary far enough in advance. (c) After flying, the airline contacted me through e-mail to provide special rates for return flights to the same destination. (d) Atlantic Airways offers flights to any of 200 destinations worldwide, all of which I wish to visit eventually.

02

Some animals are known to change their coloring in order to protect themselves from predators or disguise themselves from hunted prey. (a) The polar bear actually has black skin, but appears white because of the way light reflects off its translucent hairs. (b) Arctic foxes transform in fall and winter, shedding their usual gray hair and growing white hair to blend with snow. (c) Cuttlefish contain special chemicals that express certain colored skin pigments depending on what they see. (d) The nudibranch, another sea creature, changes color as a result of chemical substances in the type of coral it is eating.

03

The 1969 manned lunar mission was an important event in modern history. (a) International cooperatio was necessary to set up three equally distant antennas in Spain, Australia, and the United States.
(b) The intercontinental lunar mission was the first time human beings had stepped foot on the moon.
(c) Because of the varied receiver placements, data could be collected during the Earth's entire rotation.
(d) Without cross-border collaboration, communication between the astronauts and mission control would have been impossible.

Many people are familiar with the effects of asthma. (a) Current research indicates that approximately one in ten children develop asthma and experience breathing problems throughout their childhood and teen years. (b) It can sometimes result from problems at birth, or more likely from exposure to airborne pollutants. (c) Special air filtration masks worn by children should be inspected to make sure they fit snugly. (d) Thus, it is critical to protect your children from inhaling dangerous particles.

Film noir was a genre of filmmaking predominant in the 1940s and 1950s. (a) Films of this type were marked by a characteristic visual style and reflective of a pessimistic worldview. (b) Film noir movies tended to use low lighting to create stark contrasts and were usually shot in black and white. (c) Color moviemaking techniques were available since the 1920s, but didn't garner widespread usage until several decades later. (d) The story lines of these films also depicted people in difficult situations, often dealing with ambiguous moral questions and evoking a sense of despair.

In some occupations, people continue to use a special form of writing called shorthand. (a) Shorthand is designed for use in fast-paced situations, particularly when people have to quickly write down a great deal of information. (b) Many journalists, in their early years, are trained to use shorthand when conducting the interviews they will subsequently use to write their stories. (c) To some employers in the journalism field, the ability to write reports and press releases is considered just as critical as typing ability and research experience. (d) Its use is quickly decreasing, however, mainly on account of the widespread availability of handheld recording devices.

07

In 1974, a group of Chinese farmers digging a water well discovered an ancient emperor's burial ground containing over eight thousand replica warriors. (a) According to Sima Qian, a historian from the first century BC, the statues were built to decorate the tomb of Qin Shi Huangdi, the first emperor of the Qin dynasty. (b) The city of Xian, where the tomb is located, has been an architectural center since the Zhou dynasty. (c) Seven hundred thousand workers are believed to have worked on constructing the soldiers over a 38 year period. (d) The terra cotta warriors, as they are called, allegedly were built to help the emperor rule a separate empire in the afterlife.

08

Aspirin begins working soon after it is ingested. (a) The most common side effect of aspirin is gastric irritation, particularly noticeable in cases where large doses are taken. (b) It is directly absorbed by the lining of the intestines and stomach and, as with most medicines, circulated through the blood. (c) Aspirin reaches the body's organs and prevents the transmission of signals by the nerves. (d) The drug's main effect is to desensitize the brain, thereby preventing it from sensing headaches or bodily pain.

09

The wilderness was my only companion while hiking the picturesque Cascade Trail. (a) There were neither cars nor the din of construction noise detracting from the forest's natural bustle. (b) The trickle of small ravines and the calls of chirping birds were ever present. (c) Other than at the trailhead, I explored for hours without coming across another human being, which was a welcome experience for a city-dweller like myself, unaccustomed to the solitude of nature. (d) Trail maps and hiking guides were both available at the park office.

Now more than ever, the nation's youth are unconcerned with cultural differences. (a) Even children from racially homogeneous areas have no trouble relating to those from other backgrounds. (b) Recent polls suggest that two-thirds of the U.S. population have acquaintances from other ethnic groups. (c) This generation concentrates on the aspects they have in common with their peers instead of what sets them apart. (d) As expected, these individuals are the most likely of anyone to establish close friendships across ethnic lines.

The famous children's novelist Laura Ingalls Wilder was born in 1867. (a) Wilder attended school as a child, but had no particular education that hinted she would become a writer. (b) She married at the age of 18 and barely survived on income from a farm she owned with her husband. (c) Scholars are unsure, when she first embraced writing as a career. (d) All that is known about Wilder is that she published her first written work in 1911.

Political parties are a major part of the democratic process. (a) Political parties are different than most political organizations because political parties are concerned with electing specific candidates to government positions. (b) In America, political parties were initially formed to prevent one group from gaining too much power. (c) Ironically, these political parties now seem to prevent outsiders from gaining a political voice. (d) A majority of those who don't belong to a large political party become unelectable.

CHAPTER 04 중심 내용 문제 (Part 3, 4)

글의 주제나 요지, 글의 내용을 대표할 수 있는 제목, 또는 글을 쓴 목적 등 지문에서 나타내고자 하는 중심 내용을 적절하게 담고 있는 보기를 선택하는 유형이다. 이 유형은 평균적으로 Part 3의 초반에 4문제 정도 나오며, Part 4에는 2~3문제가량 출제된다. 지문에서 글쓴이가 궁극적으로 하고자 하는 말이 무엇인지 파악한다는 생각으로 접근하면 해결할 수 있는 문제이다. 그럼 이 유형에 대해 자세히 알아보자.

■ 질문 유형

주제나 요지를 묻는 유형이 가장 많이 나오고, 제목이나 목적을 묻는 유형도 가끔 출제된다.

주제 What is the passage **mainly about**? 지문은 주로 무엇에 관한 내용인가?
What is **mainly discussed** in the second paragraph? 두 번째 단락에서 주로 논의되는 것은 무엇인가?
What is the writer **mainly saying** about OOO? 글쓴이가 ○○○에 대해 주로 말하고 있는 것은 무엇인가?
What is the **main topic** of OOO? ○○○에 대한 주제는 무엇인가?
* 주제는 지문에서 중점적으로 논의되는 소재를 뜻하며 보기가 명사구로 제시된다.

요지 What is the **main idea** of the passage? 지문의 요지는 무엇인가?
What is the **main point** about OOO? ○○○에 대한 요지는 무엇인가?
* 요지는 지문에서 중심이 되는 의견이나 관점을 뜻하며 보기가 문장으로 제시된다.

제목 What is the best **title** for the passage? 지문의 제목으로 가장 적절한 것은 무엇인가?

목적 What is the **main purpose** of the letter? 편지의 주된 목적은 무엇인가?

■ Step별 문제풀이 전략

Step 1 지문 전체를 빠르게 읽으며 중심 내용을 파악한다.

· 중심 내용을 담고 있는 문장은 Part 3의 경우 주로 지문 앞부분이나 마지막에 나오거나, 앞과 마지막 모두에 나온다. Part 4의 경
주로 첫 번째 단락의 앞부분, 마지막 부분 혹은 지문 전체에 걸쳐 나온다. Part 4에서는 간혹 두 번째 단락에만 해당되는 중심 내
을 묻기도 한다.

· 중심 내용을 담고 있는 문장은 주로 다음과 같은 표현 뒤에 나온다.

결론	thus / so 그러므로 / 그래서	accordingly 따라서	This suggests that 이것은 ~을 나타낸다
대조/ 내용 전환	however / but / yet 그러나 instead 대신	contrary to ~에 반하여 in fact 사실상	on the contrary 반대로 rather 오히려
인용	according to ~에 따르면	Experts say that 전문가들은 ~라고 말한다	
연구 결과	Recent studies show[suggest / indicate] that 최근의 연구는 ~을 보여준다[제시한다 / 나타낸다] Researchers have found[proven] that 연구자들은 ~을 발견했다[증명해냈다] Researchers now concede that 연구자들은 이제 ~을 인정한다		

· 중심 내용을 담고 있는 문장을 찾기 힘들 경우, 지문 전체를 포괄할 수 있는 내용이나 지문에서 반복되는 내용을 파악한다.

Step 2 파악한 중심 내용을 바르게 표현한 보기를 선택한다.

지문의 세부 내용을 나타낸 보기, 중심 내용처럼 보이지만 한두 단어가 틀린 보기, 중심 내용과 반대되는 보기, 또는 지문에 언급되
않은 보기는 정답이 될 수 없다.

전략 적용

Researchers have proven that birds are able to mimic the ●——— Step 1 지문을 빠르게 읽고 중심 내용 파악하기
songs from other nearby species. To test this long-suspected
assumption, two birds were kept enclosed in a large patch of
forest protected by nets and scientists recorded their songs. Later,
a third bird was added to the group in order to record its songs.
After a brief learning period, the third bird was soon observed
whistling some of the songs used by the other two birds.

● What is the passage mainly about?

(a) A method of recording bird songs
(b) Birds' ability to learn other species' habits
(c) The unique nature of different bird songs
(d) Birds' capacity to imitate others' songs ●———— Step 2 중심 내용을 바르게 표현한 보기 선택하기

Step 1 연구 결과를 나타내는 표현 Researchers have proven that(연구자들은 ~을 증명해냈다) 뒤에 온 '새가 근처 다른 종의 노래를 흉내 낼 수 있다'라는
내용이 지문의 중심 내용임을 파악한다.

Step 2 파악한 중심 내용을 '다른 새의 노래를 모방하는 새의 능력'이라고 바르게 표현한 (d)가 정답이다.
(a) 지문에서 '새의 노래를 녹음하는 방법'은 중심 내용을 보충 설명하기 위한 세부 내용이므로 오답이다.
(b) 지문에 '습성(habits)'에 대한 내용은 언급되지 않았다.
(c) 지문에 '다양한 새 노래들의 독특한 특징'에 대해서는 언급되지 않았다.

Hackers **Practice**

구문독해 연습 - 분사

구문독해를 익힌 후 주어진 문제를 풀어 보세요.

01 명사를 수식하는 현재분사

Edward Steichen's photograph / depicting the moon rising through a narrow gap in a forest / was / one of
에드워드 스타이컨의 사진은   숲의 좁은 틈 사이로 떠오르는 달을 묘사하는   였다
the first color photographs taken.
최초로 촬영된 컬러 사진 중 하나

위 문장에서 depicting the moon은 명사 photograph를, rising ~ forest는 명사 moon을 꾸며 주는 수식어이다. 이처럼 '동사 + ing' 형태의
현재분사가 수식어 역할을 하여 앞의 명사를 꾸며 줄 경우 '~하는, ~하고 있는'으로 해석한다.

다음 문장이 바르게 paraphrase된 보기를 고르세요.

The race car driver leading at the moment appears in danger of being passed by several of the other racers
closing in behind him.

(a) The driver is about to pass several other cars and will take the lead for the moment.
(b) The driver will probably give up his lead to the cars that are currently behind him.

02 명사를 수식하는 과거분사

During her farewell concert at Seacrest Arts Center, / Alice Menty / solidified / her place / as frontrunner
Seacrest Arts Center에서의 그녀의 송별 콘서트 동안   Alice Menty는   확고히 했다   그녀의 입지를
for the best female vocalist award presented by the National Academy of Recording Arts and Science.
전미 레코딩 예술과학 아카데미에 의해 수여되는 최고 여가수상에 대한 유력한 후보로서

위 문장에서 presented ~ Science는 award를 꾸며 주는 수식어이다. 이처럼 '동사 + ed' 형태의 과거분사가 수식어 역할을 하여 앞의 명사를
꾸며 줄 경우 '~된, ~되어진'으로 해석한다.

다음 문장이 바르게 paraphrase된 보기를 고르세요.

If you are having trouble completing your tax return, it might be a good idea to take advantage of the
assistance provided by the National Tax Service's Web site.

(a) The National Tax Service's Web site is a good place to go if you need help with your taxes.
(b) Individuals facing delays when filing taxes can do so by using the National Tax Service Web site.

03 목적격 보어 역할을 하는 분사

Chris / watched / the waves / crashing / as he readied his surfboard for the first of many rides he would
Chris는   보았다   파도가   부딪치는 것을   그가 하루 동안 타게 될 많은 파도타기 중 첫 번째 파도타기를 위해 서프보드를 준비했을 때
take over the course of the day.

위 문장에서 crashing은 목적어 the waves를 보충 설명하는 보어 역할을 한다. 이처럼 분사가 목적격 보어인 경우 현재분사는 '~가 ~한'으로,
과거 분사는 '~가 ~된'으로 해석한다.

다음 문장이 바르게 paraphrase된 보기를 고르세요.

Remembering that chocolate desserts are his wife's favorites, Raymond had a gourmet chocolate cake baked
by a chef at the nearby bakery.

(a) Raymond and his wife had a chocolate cake that the chef had already made.
(b) Raymond ordered a special chocolate cake for his wife at the bakery.

유형 연습

지문을 읽고 질문에 바르게 답한 보기를 고르세요.

04

As the gap in incarceration rates has increased between the US and other countries, apprehension is mounting about the severity of the American criminal justice system. Many criticize the large list of crimes demanding imprisonment, including such minor offenses as writing bad checks and petty theft. However, other explanations have been proposed for the rise in the number of inmates, including the harsh sentences handed down by judges wishing to appear tough on crime.

Q What is the passage mainly about?

(a) The causes of the high prison population in America

(b) Things to be considered when sentencing criminals

05

Several political commentators have published glowing reviews of Dennis McClain's new book, but I am not one of them. His book attempting to detail the current health insurance crisis is full of arguments justified by several biased facts and assumptions. It describes the problems as being caused by the former administration, appeasing the current president's supporters and protecting him from blame. If the book gave a more evenhanded view of the situation, it might be a valuable piece of analysis.

Q What is the main idea about McClain's book in the passage?

(a) It gives an unbalanced view of the crisis.

(b) It gives a subjective view of the current administration.

06

Inspectors probing an industrial accident at a local shoe factory noticed waste escaping, which is causing concern because of the factory's proximity to the city's water supply. The prospect of waste products in the water alarmed those living nearby, as many of the adhesives used in the shoe manufacturing process have been proven to be cancer-causing if ingested. The mayor had local health officials investigate whether any residents were harmed by the incident, but no adverse health effects were discovered.

Q What is the best title for the article?

(a) Cause of Industrial Accident Investigated by Mayor

(b) Residents' Health Unaffected by Industrial Accident

정답 p.121

READING COMPREHENSION | 문제 유형별 공략

해커스 텝스 Reading

01

Dalton Trumbo, widely considered to be one of Hollywood's most talented screenwriters ever, was born in Colorado in 1905. His career started to take off in the 1940s, when Marxism was spreading to countries throughout the world. In this political climate, Trumbo became a member of the Communist Party. Despite the growing popularity of Marxism worldwide, there was a backlash in the United States against the movement. Trumbo was eventually blacklisted by Hollywood executives and forbidden to work in the film industry for several years due to his ideology.

Q What is the main idea of the passage?

(a) Trumbo's political viewpoint clashed with that of Hollywood.
(b) Trumbo's work was heavily shaped by Communism.
(c) Trumbo was legally denied employment in the film industry.
(d) Trumbo was admired by movie fans for his Marxist stance.

02

Vitamin E is an essential part of the human diet and occurs naturally in several chemical compounds. The vitamin's main function is to protect the body's cells against free radicals, which are molecules that attack cells and lead to genetic mutations. This protective role is important in preventing many forms of cancer caused by cell damage from free radicals. Vitamin E compounds are generally found in cooking oils, nuts, and certain green vegetables. Recently, doctors have been recommending these foods to heart patients because of their possible role in preventing heart blockage.

Q What is the main idea of the passage?

(a) Most people are unaware of how free radicals harm the body.
(b) Research shows that Vitamin E acts to stop cancer from developing.
(c) Found in natural sources, Vitamin E can help prevent serious diseases.
(d) A strong link between Vitamin E and heart disease exists.

03

Many people think that planets closer to the Sun are hotter than planets that are farther away. On the contrary, some faraway planets are hotter than closer ones. Most planets have a gaseous atmosphere that surrounds them. Venus, in particular, has the thickest atmosphere of any planet, leading to surface temperatures over 460 degrees Celsius. Even though Mercury is closer to the Sun and receives much more solar radiation, temperatures on Venus are much higher due to its heat-trapping atmosphere.

Q What is the passage mainly about?

(a) The effect of an atmosphere on planetary temperatures
(b) The relationship between planetary distance and mass
(c) The role of the Sun in creating a planet's atmosphere
(d) The reason for high temperatures on planets near the Sun

Public transportation in Southeast Asia is quite unpredictable, which makes it difficult for those who are traveling in the area to gauge the expected duration of a trip. As an example, a trip may typically take only 3 hours in the dry season. However, it may take 12 hours in the rainy season because dirt roads become nearly impassable in wet weather, lengthening travel times considerably. So, when traveling in the region, don't try to keep a strict schedule. It's also a good idea to have a book or music player with you.

Q What is the main point about travel in Southeast Asia?

(a) It is necessary to choose transportation appropriate for the season.
(b) People should travel only during the dry season.
(c) It is best to bring something to pass time while traveling.
(d) Travelers must be prepared for unexpected slowdowns during trips.

Sightseeing in Memphis

Memphis, Tennessee has a great reputation for sightseeing. In fact, Memphis is quickly becoming a very popular American travel destination, renowned for its music clubs and authentic blues bars. For those interested in music history, the city houses the birthplaces of Elvis Presley, B.B. King, and Johnny Cash. The National Civil Rights Museum is also an ideal place to learn about Memphis' role in the civil rights movement. The natural beauty of the area's parks and neighborhoods is not to be missed. Why not stop by for a weekend getaway?

For more information, contact us at 1-800-MEMPHIS.

Q What is mainly advertised about Memphis?

(a) Its interesting historical sites
(b) Its developing live music venues
(c) Its appeal as a travel destination
(d) Its reputation for famous musicians

06

Canadian scientists have achieved a major breakthrough in the battle against diabetes. While experimenting on diabetic mice, the scientists identified a substance secreted by pancreatic nerves used to control insulin production. This substance, dubbed "Substance P" by the scientists, is not adequately produced by diabetics, causing insulin amounts to drop. If the substance is directly injected into the pancreas, insulin production normalizes and the condition recedes. The researchers have proven that diabetes can occur due to problems with the nerves that produce Substance P.

Q What is the main topic of the passage?

(a) The role of the nervous system in the development of diabetes
(b) Features of substances invented to cure diabetes
(c) Treatment options available for those suffering from diabetes
(d) How Substance P was discovered and researched

07

Dear Professor Benjamin,

I have a big favor I'd like to ask of you. During my time at Lansing University, I was a student of yours in three different philosophy classes. I feel that you have the best understanding of my intellectual potential and my work ethic. Accordingly, I'd like to ask you to write a recommendation on my behalf. I'm trying to enroll in graduate school this fall, and I'd really appreciate your support in helping me achieve my goal. Please let me know if you are willing and able to help.

Sincerely, Gavin Ross

Q What is the main purpose of the letter?

(a) To request admission to a graduate school
(b) To seek the counsel of an old instructor
(c) To solicit a former teacher for assistance
(d) To update the professor on future plans

08

According to recent research, leprosy is not the highly contagious disease it was once considered to be. Scientists discovered that leprosy is actually transmitted via droplets from the lungs instead of by way of a skin-to-skin transmission mechanism as previously thought, meaning it less communicable to others. These droplets come from deep in the respiratory tract and are only exchanged if fluid from an infected person's lungs is breathed in by another individual.

Q What is the main idea of the passage?

(a) Leprosy is no longer a worldwide health concern.
(b) Those with leprosy can quickly spread the disease.
(c) Respiratory diseases are more dangerous than leprosy.
(d) Leprosy is not transmitted easily among people.

During the days of Soviet Communism, Stalin attempted to strengthen his grip on power through special political messages directed towards children. Songs, cartoons, and books were designed to express the virtues of the Communist movement and describe the behavior which was best suited to helping maintain the Communist regime. By using such indoctrination techniques, Stalin hoped to guarantee that future generations would passively submit to his authority, thereby securing his long-term control over the country.

Q What is the best title for the passage?

(a) Youth Propaganda Used to Maintain Rule
(b) The Role of Children During Soviet Communism
(c) Government Control Threatened by Media
(d) Using Politics to Critique Social Behavior

Truth: Then and Now

What is "truth"? To many, it is an objective construct, yet ultimately dependent on the scope of one's available knowledge. This symposium will investigate "truth" as an epistemological concept and examine how the definition of truth has morphed in the fields of religion and philosophy. Our dialogue will extend across society's intellectual history, from the conceptions of the ancient Greeks up through those of modern theorists. The works to be covered include those by Aristotle, Aquinas, Kant, Foucault, and Baudrillard.

Q What is the passage mainly about?

(a) A course on epistemology and philosophy
(b) A theoretical analysis of modern philosophers
(c) An examination of thought in ancient Greece
(d) A symposium on the development of religious thought

해커스 텝스 Reading

http://www.brighthavendaily.com/headline/Brighthaven-Election

Brighthaven Daily News

Latest Headline

Macintyre Loses Brighthaven Election to Alderson

Michael Clarkson

John Alderson of the Progressive Party triumphed in yesterday's midterm election in Brighthaven although Sarah Macintyre of the Conservative Party started the campaign as the overwhelming favorite. Commentators expected Alderson to lose by a wide margin as they assumed voters would opt for Macintyre's conservative policies. However, the recent revelations of misconduct on the part of Macintyre caused many voters to abandon her. According to Russex University chancellor Frederick Hoffman, Macintyre promised him that she would back an extension of the university's campus in exchange for her son's admission to a degree program.

Historically considered a conservative stronghold, Brighthaven now has a Progressive Party politician as its representative for the first time in almost 20 years. The fact that Alderson's win was not due to his popularity among the citizens of Brighthaven has led some political pundits to predict a rocky term for the new member of Congress. A post-election survey revealed that two-thirds of those voting for Alderson said they were more influenced by Macintyre's scandal than his policies. It is therefore doubtful whether Alderson will be able to win over the people of Brighthaven, particularly as many are expected to object to his proposed tax hike for high earners.

11. Q: What is the main idea of the passage?
   (a) Many expected the Conservative candidate to be victorious in the election.
   (b) A scandal caused Macintyre to lose her position as a representative.
   (c) Brighthaven announced that it will crack down on corrupt public officials.
   (d) A political underdog won the election thanks to an opponent's misconduct.

12. Q: According to the news report, why will John Alderson face opposition?
   (a) He is the first Progressive Party politician to represent Brighthaven.
   (b) He got two-thirds of the votes in his election triumph.
   (c) He would like wealthy members of society to pay more taxes.
   (d) He has policies that are too conservative for the Brighthaven population.

14

Gene therapy is a medical technique that targets disease-causing genetic mutations through the implantation of new genetic material. It is considered promising since it may be able to provide a cure for untreatable diseases, such as Alzheimer's. However, the procedure is still in an experimental stage and has a long way to go.

One of the main dangers of gene therapy is that the viruses used as vectors to carry genetic material could trigger an adverse response from the body's immune system, which could be fatal. In 1999, an 18-year-old boy died due to a reaction to a viral vector during a procedure to treat an enzyme disorder, halting all gene therapy trials in the United States for a time. Even though the procedure has advanced significantly since then and this type of tragedy is much less likely, doctors are still reluctant to test it on humans.

The question of which genetic conditions should be treated using gene therapy is also a contentious one, with some arguing that the ability to alter people's genetic makeup would give physicians too much power over patients' lives. Moreover, the likelihood that it could be used to edit genes before birth is, for many, profoundly worrying.

3. Q: What is the passage mainly about?

   (a) The creation of a genetic therapy procedure with a range of applications
   (b) The expectations that people have of new genetic therapy procedures
   (c) The legislative efforts to get gene therapy approved for certain conditions
   (d) The problems with the medical application of genetic therapy treatments

4. Q: Which of the following is correct about gene therapy according to the passage?
   (a) It is certain to provide a treatment for many incurable diseases.
   (b) It has yet to be tested on a single human patient.
   (c) It could provide doctors with excessive control over their patients.
   (d) It has attracted support for its uses during pregnancy.

정답 p.122

CHAPTER 05 육하원칙 문제 (Part 3, 4)

무엇을, 누가, 왜, 어떻게 하였는지 등 질문에서 묻는 특정한 세부 내용을 지문에서 확인하고, 이와 일치하는 보기를 선택하는 유형이다. 이 유형은 평균적으로 Part 3에 1~2문제 정도 나오고, Part 4에는 2~3문제가량 출제된다. 질문을 잘 읽고 묻는 내용이 무엇인지 정확히 파악하면 비교적 쉽게 해결할 수 있는 문제이다. 그럼 이 유형에 대해 자세히 알아보자.

■ 질문 유형

의문사 what을 사용하여 질문하는 문제가 가장 많이 나오고, how, why, who, when 등의 의문사 및 which를 사용하여 질문하는 형태로도 출제된다.

What is the most popular automobile according to the passage? 지문에 따르면 무엇이 가장 인기 있는 자동차인가?
According to the passage, **how** did the citizens react to the proposal? 지문에 따르면, 어떻게 시민들은 그 제안에 반응했는가?
According to the letter, **why** doesn't the university wish to admit the applicant?
편지에 따르면, 왜 대학은 그 지원자의 입학을 허가하지 않는가?
Who can apply for this job opening? 누가 이 일자리에 지원할 수 있는가?
When did movie rental stores begin providing films to customers online?
언제 영화 대여점은 온라인상으로 고객에게 영화를 제공하기 시작했는가?
Which of the following is NOT included in the fee? 다음 중 무엇이 요금에 포함되지 않는가?

■ Step별 문제풀이 전략

Step 1   질문의 의문사와 키워드를 파악한다.

(ex) **What** is **the most popular** automobile according to the passage? 지문에 따르면, 가장 인기 있는 자동차는 무엇인가?
　　　　의문사　　　　　보기의 키워드

Step 2   질문의 키워드와 관련된 부분을 지문에서 찾아 그 주변의 내용을 파악한다. 이때 질문의 키워드는 대부분 다른 말로 paraphrase되어 지문에 제시된다.

(ex) **the most popular** automobile. 가장 인기 있는 자동차
　　　　보기의 키워드

　　　　4-door sedans are still **the top sellers** for car companies. 문이 4개 달린 세단형 승용차가 자동차 회사에서 여전히 가장 잘 팔리는 상품
　　　　　　　　　　　　　　지문의 관련 부분

Step 3   지문의 내용과 일치하는 보기를 정답으로 선택한다. 이때 지문의 내용은 대부분 다른 말로 paraphrase되어 보기에 제시된다.

(ex) **4-door sedans** are still the top sellers for car companies. 문이 4개 달린 세단형 승용차가 자동차 회사에서 여전히 가장 잘 팔리는 상품
　　　　지문의 관련 부분

　　　　Cars with four doors 문이 4개 달린 자동차
　　　　정답으로 paraphrase된 보기

전략 적용

A special two-month showing of *The Life of Galaxies* will come to Abrams Planetarium. The first screening will take place on Monday, October 9, at 7:30 p.m. and will be shown every weekday at the same time. **Every Friday, we will offer a late-night encore showing after the 7:30 p.m. presentation.** The film will not be shown on Saturdays and Sundays, and the final evening screening, featuring a preview of the planetarium's next release, will take place Thursday, December 7. For ticketing information, please visit the box office.

———— Step 2 질문의 키워드와 관련된 부분 찾고 내용 파악하기

What days is the movie shown twice? ———— Step 1 질문의 의문사와 키워드 파악하기

(a) Every Monday
(b) Most Thursdays
(c) During the weekend
(d) On Friday evenings ———— Step 3 지문의 내용과 일치하는 보기 선택하기

Step 1 질문의 의문사가 What days(어느 날), 키워드가 shown twice(두 번 상영되는)임을 파악한다.

Step 2 질문의 키워드 shown twice(두 번 상영되는)를 지문의 관련 부분인 encore showing(재상영)과 연결하여 매주 금요일에 심야 재상영이 제공 된다는 내용을 파악한다.

Step 3 지문의 Every Friday(매주 금요일)를 On Friday evenings(매주 금요일 저녁)로 paraphrase한 (d)를 정답으로 선택한다.

해석 p.125

Hackers **Practice**

구문독해 연습 – 분사구문

구문독해를 익힌 후 주어진 문제를 풀어 보세요.

01 결과를 나타내는 분사구문

The power plant / was finally completed / after ten years of on-and-off work, / providing residents of the
발전소는　　　　　마침내 완공되었다　　　　　10년간의 간헐적인 작업 끝에　　　　　그리고 (그 결과) 마을 거주자들에게
village with electricity for the first time.
처음으로 전력을 공급했다

위 문장에서 분사구문 providing ~ first time은 수식어이다. 이처럼 분사구문이 문장 뒤에 올 경우, 종종 앞에 있는 절에 대한 결과를 나타내는데
이때 분사구문은 '그리고 (그 결과) ~하다'라고 해석한다.

다음 문장이 바르게 paraphrase된 보기를 고르세요.

The gym teacher loudly blew his whistle once he noticed that it was time for the class to end, startling the
students and causing them to jump.

(a) After noticing that class time was finished, the teacher suddenly blew his whistle and surprised the students.
(b) The teacher's whistle was blown to startle the jumping students and inform them that class was finished.

02 동시상황을 나타내는 분사구문

The player / who scored six goals last night, / helping the home team to win the game, / competed /
그 선수는　　　　　어젯밤에 6골을 기록한　　　　　홈팀이 그 게임을 이기도록 도움을 주면서　　　　　경쟁했다
fearlessly against the opponents.
상대편에 대항하여 두려움 없이

위 문장에서 helping ~ game은 수식어이다. 이처럼 분사구문이 주어와 동사 사이에 또는 문장 뒤에올 경우, 종종 동시에 일어나는 상황을
나타낸다. 이때 분사구문은 '~ 하면서'라고 해석한다.

다음 문장이 바르게 paraphrase된 보기를 고르세요.

The prominent environmental activist who spoke at the rally, urging the audience to start living more simply, dre
large cheers from the inspired crowd.

(a) The activist speaking at the environmental rally was applauded for his simple lifestyle.
(b) The activist who spoke to the crowd about living simply was greeted with applause.

03 이유를 나타내는 분사구문

Built sturdily with a variety of twigs and grasses, / often several meters high in a tree, / a basket nest /
다양한 가지와 풀로 튼튼하게 지어졌기 때문에　　　　　종종 몇 미터 높은 나무에　　　　　바구니 모양의 둥지는
helps / to protect a hummingbird's eggs.
도움이 된다　　　벌새의 알을 보호하는 데

위 문장에서 분사구문 Built sturdily ~ tree는 수식어이다. 이 경우 분사구문은 종종 뒤에 있는 절에 대한 이유를 나타내는데, 이때 분사구문은
'~하기 때문에'라고 해석한다.

다음 문장이 바르게 paraphrase된 보기를 고르세요.

Fashioning their products out of gold or silver, sometimes including a diamond or other precious stones, clas
ring manufacturers provide valuable mementos for many university students.

(a) University class rings are considered to be valuable mementos because of the high-quality materials used by
manufacturers.
(b) University students consider class rings very important, so they select manufacturers that use high-quality material

영 연습

의 내용과 일치하는 보기에는 T, 일치하지 않는 보기에는 F를 표시하세요.

The Hollywood Walk of Fame, immortalizing countless entertainment personalities via personalized star-shaped plaques, was constructed in 1960. Over two thousand blank stars were initially placed in the ground. By 1962, nearly 1,600 of the stars had been engraved with names. However, to prevent the Walk from becoming too quickly filled, a restriction on the number of stars that could be awarded per month was soon announced.

(a) The stars were initially placed in the ground in 1960. (   )
(b) Well-known stars funded the Hollywood Walk of Fame. (   )
(c) Two thousand of the stars included names by 1962. (   )
(d) A restriction on the frequency with which stars could be awarded was announced. (   )

Statistics show that over half of all people who get tattoos eventually wish to have them removed. Scientists, experimenting with unlikely materials and hoping to make semipermanent tattoos that can completely vanish, have created a special ink that is contained in microscopic plastic capsules. To wipe out any trace of the tattoo, lasers can be used to burst the ink-filled capsules, causing the materials to break down to be absorbed by the body. The only catch is that tattoos using the ink are more costly than conventional tattoos.

(a) Lasers are used to create the new tattoos. (   )
(b) The new tattoos can be removed in their entirety. (   )
(c) A majority of those with tattoos ultimately have them removed. (   )
(d) The special ink is more expensive than traditional tattoo ink. (   )

Repairing your car's engine can be a complicated process. It can be tricky to repair a crankshaft or to choose the spark plugs, especially when each vehicle model has a unique configuration of parts. That's why you need *Schwartz's Guide to Do-It-Yourself Automotive Repair*. Written with the novice repairperson in mind, often including detailed diagrams for each model, the guide provides you with the information you need to fix your car without resorting to the help of a mechanic.

(a) The reader is provided with thorough illustrations related to particular models. (   )
(b) The book can be understood even by those inexperienced with car repair. (   )
(c) The inconsistencies in engine design between models makes vehicle repair difficult. (   )
(d) The guide is a reference work originally designed for use by mechanics. (   )

해석 p.125

01

The Roman emperor Nero has been widely portrayed in popular literature and film. More often than not, these representations don't match much of what modern historians believe characterized his life. Although he achieved popularity for brokering peace treaties and improving the plight of freed slaves, he struggled with mental health issues. In most portrayals, this personality aspect becomes the focus, showing him as tyrannical and deranged. He is commonly believed to be like this, despite the existence of evidence that shows he was an effective policymaker who garnered considerable public support.

Q How do most works depict Nero according to the passage?

(a) As a successful legislator
(b) As an insane dictator
(c) As a popular ruler
(d) As a complex political figure

02

Attitudes after the collapse of the Soviet Union supported one of two ideologies: ethnic nationalism or centralism. Ethnic nationalists hoped the collapse would allow them to gain political control over traditionally-held ethnic territories. Centralists, on the other hand, feared that economically weaker regions would suffer because of the split. They wanted some semblance of central organization maintained and saw a continued need for a common market. In the end, the ethnic nationalists won out, and fifteen completely independent republics came to replace the Soviet Union by the end of 1991.

Q According to the passage, how did some Soviets respond to the collapse?

(a) They used it as an opportunity to overthrow the government.
(b) They hoped it would create greater ethnic diversity throughout the country.
(c) They wanted to expand the empire to control other nations.
(d) They felt that cooperation would need to be preserved among regions.

03

Airports have made great strides in the past hundred years. The first airport was established in College Park, Maryland in 1909 by Wilbur Wright. Initially, airports were only open to solo flyers and military pilots until Sydney Airport opened completely to commercial flights in 1920. In 1936, London's airport authority unveiled a new airport at Gatwick which included a passenger terminal and setup akin to modern airports. The airport in Tampa, Florida, opened the first inter-terminal monorail in 1991, similar to those found in cities throughout the world.

Q Which city's airport had the first configuration similar to the one found nowadays?

(a) College Park
(b) Sydney
(c) London
(d) Tampa

Britain first started to settle the Australian continent in 1788 by sending over a settlement party composed primarily of exiled convicts. In ensuing years, an increasing amount of settlers continued to make their way over. From 1829 to 1837, the rate of settlement in Australia reached its peak, with tens of thousands of convicted lawbreakers making the voyage each year. Eventually, in 1865, Britain finally put an end to the practice. At that time, they passed a law to restrict settlement in Australia to free individuals.

Q When did Britain restrict settlement in Australia?

(a) 1788   (b) 1829

(c) 1837   (d) 1865

The Everyday Gourmet

As with every recipe book in the ProChef series, the newly released *The Everyday Gourmet* contains recipes from dozens of top chefs containing only readily available ingredients. This new volume includes over 300 recipes selected to give even the most novice of cooks the opportunity to create delectable dishes without needing to procure any gourmet or specialty items. This is a key aspect of the book, which will allow anyone to create high-end cuisine with only a trip to the corner store.

Q What is the most important feature of *The Everyday Gourmet*?

(a) Its recipes were contributed by highly trained chefs.

(b) It contains a vast quantity of delicious recipes.

(c) Its recipes require only commonly found supplies.

(d) It is the most recent book in the ProChef series.

06

Visual problems are typically caused by a physical defect of the eyes. In myopic individuals, the eyeball is too long and light waves are incorrectly focused once they reach the retina. To rectify this, corrective lenses are used to diffuse the light more. In farsighted individuals, the eyeball is too short, so nearby images become blurred. Glasses or contact lenses concentrate light waves more so that they are focused over a smaller distance. The quality of vision at a given distance, and whether or not one needs to wear corrective lenses, is dependent upon the front-to-back diameter of the eyeball.

Q What determines the visual ability of an individual?

(a) The length of the eyeball
(b) The strength of the retina
(c) The power of their lenses
(d) The diffusion of light

07

Soy-based foods are becoming increasingly popular in the United States as a healthy alternative to meat and dairy products. In the $3.6 billion-a-year soy foods market, annual sales figures for the historically best-selling soy sauce were recently eclipsed by that of soy milk, which accounts for over $500 million in revenue. Neither of these products, nor the Asian favorite of tofu, accounts for the highest growth in sales among soy-based foods, however. Sales of TVP, or imitation meat, have more than doubled annually since 2001, making it the most rapidly expanding segment of the market.

Q Which type of soy-based food currently sells the most?

(a) Soy sauce   (b) Soy milk
(c) Tofu   (d) Imitation meat

08

During the middle part of the 20th century, China insisted on a government-controlled economy based upon socialist ideology. Such a system was at odds with the increasingly successful movement towards capitalism taking place in the rest of the world. Despite the financial gains being made in countries with private enterprise, the Chinese appeared unwilling to adopt a more open economic system. Nevertheless, after organizational changes in the Communist Party during the late 1970s and the rise to power of Deng Xiaoping, China began gradually implementing certain principles of capitalism to help resuscitate the economy.

Q According to the passage, how did the Chinese economy change?

(a) Capitalist ideas were adopted by the Chinese government.
(b) Deng Xiaoping took direct control over economic affairs.
(c) Government-run enterprises were completely replaced by private ones.
(d) The government ceased interference in economic matters.

Most dentists profess that a regular flossing regimen is effective in preventing cavities and gum disease. Last month, a study published by the Irish Dental Professionals Association shows that even those flossing once a month report a thirty percent reduction in emergency dental visits. According to the study, it's not the actual floss that makes a difference — it's the person using it. Author Taylor Simpson suggests, "It's a question of effort. If a person makes the effort to floss, even occasionally, it suggests they are more likely to brush hard-to-reach teeth and use mouthwash."

Q According to the study, why do floss users experience fewer dental problems?

(a) They remove plaque from between their teeth and gums.
(b) They perform a more complete oral care routine.
(c) They damage teeth less by using brushes with soft bristles.
(d) They visit the dentist's office on a more regular basis.

Lecture Notice

"The decisive moment," the point at which a perfect relationship between observer and observed in a scene is achieved, is what famous twentieth-century photographer Henri Cartier-Bresson attempted to capture with his prints. An upcoming lecture series bearing that name will analyze the philosophical approach of several prominent photographers when seeking an ideal shot. Guest speakers will also detail the technical aspects of their field, including the control of shutter speed and lighting conditions. The final session will include a workshop period where amateur photographers can solicit feedback from experts.

Q According to the passage, what will take place during the lecture series?

(a) Speeches discussing how to retouch and alter photos
(b) An examination of Henri Cartier-Bresson's famous work
(c) An analysis of the workshop methods used by experts
(d) Information sessions on the technical side of picture taking

[6:31 p.m.]

Simon:

Sarah, have you heard the news? All flights to Omaha have been canceled because of a storm. They are saying that the wind speeds make it too dangerous to land. So our business trip will have to be postponed. The Omaha branch office has suggested we reschedule the meeting for the first week of March, but that is the same week I'm supposed to get together with the potential contractors to discuss their bids for the project. Is it alright with you if we push the business trip back another week?

[6:55 p.m.]

Sarah:

Yes, I heard about the storm, and it seems like it will be a big one. Apparently Omaha has already had record levels of snowfall this winter. Moving the business trip to the second week of March is fine with me. But I am starting my maternity leave the week after, so I'd really like to get everything finished before that. If you could finish the report on the cost effectiveness of the design before your discussions with the contractors, that would be good. And I will complete the specifications before the meeting. Then, once we're back, we will meet and finalize the winning bid.

11. Q: Why has the business trip been delayed?

    (a) The local airport has decided to cancel all outgoing flights.

    (b) The potential contractors have not submitted their bids yet.

    (c) The weather makes it unsafe for planes to make a landing.

    (d) The Omaha branch has asked to reschedule the meeting.

12. Q: Which of the following is correct according to the passage?

    (a) Sarah will start her maternity leave in the second week of March.

    (b) The successful bid will be settled following the meeting in Omaha.

    (c) They plan to discuss the design's cost effectiveness before Sarah's leave.

    (d) The specifications should be finished by Simon before the meeting.

14

One of the most influential movements in European avant-garde art, Dadaism emerged in the early 20th century as a reaction to the violence of World War I and the conformity of bourgeoisie society. Dadaism, or Dada, foregrounded irrationality and nonsense as a means of rejecting the Enlightenment values of reason and rationality. The movement began in Zurich, as a small band of like-minded artists, many of whom were émigrés from other European countries, gathered at the Cabaret Voltaire nightclub. Disgusted by the society around them, they determined to make art that would shock, confuse, and frighten people.

Over the next decade, Dada spread to other cities, including Paris, where it flourished in the 1920s. There, the staging of Tristan Tzara's play *The Gas Heart* marked a turning point for the movement. During its premiere, a riot broke out when leading Dadaist André Breton began fighting with several people in attendance. This was because Tzara and Breton had disagreed over the future direction of Dada, with Breton believing performance art to be an ineffective means of unconscious expression. While the rift between Tzara and Breton heralded the end of Dada and the beginnings of surrealism, the influence of Dada on contemporary art continued to grow.

3. Q: What is the main topic of the passage?

(a) The role of artists in spurring early 20th century social movements
(b) The émigré figures who made up the Dadaist art collective
(c) The way in which Dada spread from Zurich to Paris
(d) The development of Dadaism and its influence on 20th century art

4. Q: What caused the violence during the staging of *The Gas Heart*?

(a) The Parisian audience's negative reception to Tzara's play
(b) The offensive parody of conventional society in Tzara's play
(c) A split between André Breton and those who opposed the play
(d) A conflict between Breton and Tzara over the future path of Dada

CHAPTER 06 Correct 문제 (Part 3, 4)

지문에 제시된 사실과 일치하는 내용을 보기에서 찾아 선택하는 유형이다. 이 유형은 평균적으로 Part 3에 4~6문제 정도 나오며, Part 4에는 2~4문제가량 출제된다. 이 문제를 풀기 위해서는 지문과 보기의 내용을 꼼꼼하게 대조하며 읽어야 하므로 다른 유형에 비해 시간이 많이 소요된다. 하지만 보기의 키워드만 잘 파악한다면 비교적 신속하고 정확하게 해결할 수 있다. 그럼 이 유형에 대해 자세히 알아보자.

■ 질문 유형

주로 correct를 사용하여 질문하는 형태로 출제된다.

Which (of the following) is **correct** according to the passage? (다음 중) 지문의 내용과 일치하는 것은?
Which of the following is **correct** about OOO (according to the passage)? (지문에 따르면) 다음 중 ○○○에 대한 내용과 일치하는 것은?

■ Step별 문제풀이 전략

Step 1 지문을 빠르게 읽으며 전체 내용을 간략하게 파악한다.

Step 2 보기의 키워드와 관련된 부분을 지문에서 찾아 하나씩 비교한다. 이때 보기의 키워드는 대부분 다른 말로 paraphrase되어 지문에 제시된다.

　　　　(ex) Their research resulted in a **major improvement**. 그들의 연구는 큰 발전을 가져왔다.
　　　　　　　　　　　　　　　　　└── 보기의 키워드

　　　　　　They made **great advances** in scientific research. 그들은 과학 연구에 있어 커다란 진보를 이루었다.
　　　　　　　　　　지문의 관련 부분

　　　　보기의 숫자나 고유명사를 키워드로 이용하면 지문에서 관련 부분을 빨리 찾을 수 있다.

　　　　(ex) It was developed in the **1860s**. 그것은 1860년대에 개발되었다.
　　　　　　　　　　　　　　　　└── 보기의 숫자

　　　　　　In the late **1860s**, city officials looking to decrease road congestion built a subway system.
　　　　　　　　　　　　지문의 관련 부분
　　　　1860년대 후반에, 교통 혼잡을 줄이는 방법을 찾던 시 공무원들은 지하철 시스템을 만들었다.

Step 3 지문의 내용과 일치하는 보기를 선택한다.

전략 적용

n the United States, one in every three deaths can be attributed o some sort of cardiovascular disease, making it the leading ause of mortality. In particular, the prevalence of the disease in women has been on the rise as of late. **Some cardiovascular** ◄━━ **Step 2** 보기의 키워드 관련 부분 찾아 비교하기 **diseases, like high blood pressure, are gradually becoming more widespread**, whereas reports of conditions like stroke have declined because of greater public awareness of associated health risks. Nevertheless, doctors are hopeful that a new ◄ **Step 1** 지문을 읽고, 전체 내용 간략하게 파악하기 generation of pharmaceuticals currently in the trial stage will help to reduce the onset of cardiovascular disease.

Which of the following is correct according to the passage?

(a) High blood pressure rates are slowly increasing. ◄━━━ **Step 3** 지문과 내용 일치하는 보기 선택하기
(b) One in every four Americans dies of cardiovascular disease.
(c) The prevalence of heart disease in women has been decreasing.
(d) Medicine to combat cardiovascular disease is on the market.

Step 1 지문 전체를 빠르게 읽으며, 지문이 '심혈관계 질환의 발병 추세'에 대한 내용임을 파악한다.

Step 2 보기 (a)의 키워드 High blood pressure rates(고혈압 비율)가 지문의 high blood pressure, are gradually becoming more widespread(고혈압, 점차 널리 퍼지고 있다) 부분과 관련이 있음을 알 수 있다. 나머지 보기도 키워드와 지문의 관련 부분을 찾는다.

Step 3 지문의 are gradually becoming more widespread(점차 널리 퍼지고 있다)가 are slowly increasing(천천히 증가하고 있다)으로 paraphrase된 (a)가 정답이다.
(b) 지문에서 '3명 중 1명'의 사망이 심장 혈관 질환에서 기인한다고 했으므로 '4명 중 1명'이라는 내용은 지문과 다르다.
(c) 지문에서 여성의 심장 질환 발병률이 '증가'하고 있다고 했으므로, '감소'하고 있다는 내용은 지문과 반대된다.
(d) 지문에서 '약이 시험 단계에 있다'라고 했으므로, '약이 시중에 나와 있다'라는 내용은 지문과 다르다.

Hackers **Practice**

구문독해 연습 - 관계절

구문독해를 익힌 후 주어진 문제를 풀어 보세요.

01 관계절 안에 또 다른 관계절이 있는 경우

Kidneys / are / the organs / which filter the waste products that are produced by the body / **while breaking**
신장은　　　이다　　　장기들　　　　　　　　몸에서 생산되는 노폐물을 걸러내는
down important life-sustaining molecules.
　　　생명을 유지하는 중요한 분자들을 분해하는 동안

위 문장에서 which filter ~ the body는 앞의 the organs를 꾸며 주는 수식어로 이 안에는 that are produced ~ the body라는 또 다른 수식어가 the waste products를 꾸며 주고 있다. 이처럼 'which/that/who (+ 주어) + 동사' 형태의 관계절이 앞의 명사를 꾸며 주는 수식어인 경우 '~하는'으로 해석한다.

다음 문장이 바르게 paraphrase된 보기를 고르세요.

Real estate agents are the ones who supervise the negotiations that take place between the owners of a house and the prospective buyers.

(a) Homeowners hire real estate agents to negotiate deals with possible buyers of a property.
(b) Negotiations between the buyer and seller of a property are managed by real estate agents.

02 that / which가 생략된 경우

Record companies / are rethinking / the outlets / they used to distribute their music to customers /
음반 회사들은　　　다시 생각하는 중이다　　판로를　　　그들이 고객들에게 음악을 제공하기 위해 사용했던
due to the exploding popularity of online music purchasing.
　　　온라인 음악 구매의 폭발적인 인기 때문에

위 문장에서 they ~ customers는 앞의 the outlets를 꾸며 주는 수식어로, 이 수식어 앞에는 목적격 관계대명사(that, which)가 생략되어 있다. 이처럼 목적격 관계대명사가 생략된 '주어 + 동사' 형태의 관계절이 앞의 말을 꾸며 주는 수식어인 경우 '~가 ~하는'으로 해석한다.

다음 문장이 바르게 paraphrase된 보기를 고르세요.

It is impossible to compare the achievements of basketball players from different eras because the training and practice methods coaches employed were unlike those current coaches use to prepare their players for competition

(a) A different set of standards is needed when comparing the performance of basketball coaches.
(b) The use of different training techniques prevents the comparison of past and present basketball players.

03 '관계대명사 + be동사'가 생략된 경우

The new chairman of the school board / predicted / that he could bring about the changes necessary
　　　학교 이사회의 새 의장은　　　　　　예상했다
for the improvement of schools by working together with community leaders.
　　　그가 공동체 대표들과 함께 일함으로써 학교의 발전을 위해 필요한 변화를 일으킬 수 있다고

위 문장에서 necessary ~ schools는 앞의 the changes를 꾸며 주는 수식어로, 이 수식어 앞에는 '관계대명사 + be동사'(which are)가 생략되어 있다. 이처럼 '관계대명사 + be동사'가 생략되어 형용사로 시작된 관계절이 앞의 말을 꾸며 주는 수식어인 경우 '~한'으로 해석한다.

다음 문장이 바르게 paraphrase된 보기를 고르세요.

An important thing to keep in mind when making a presentation is that successful speakers always make remarks suitable for the occasion.

(a) If you want to be a good speaker, it is important to keep the content of your speech appropriate.
(b) A successful speaker should always be used if you want a satisfactory presentation.

형 연습

의 내용과 일치하는 보기에는 T, 일치하지 않는 보기에는 F를 표시하세요.

The Vikings were a seafaring group originally inhabiting a part of northern Europe that comprises much of the land that currently makes up Denmark, Norway, and Sweden. They were renowned for their elegant, resilient boats. Almost always adorned with intricate carvings and dragon heads, the boats were visually appealing and well designed. They also featured a long, wide hull using a series of overlapping planks that guaranteed stability. The design of the boats would be imitated by other cultures for centuries to come.

(a) The Vikings were a nomadic people who lived throughout Europe. (   )
(b) Viking boats often featured carefully engraved images. (   )
(c) The Viking boat design was copied well into the future. (   )
(d) Viking boats were kept light to improve stability. (   )

Mitch Albom was a highly regarded sports reporter in the 1980s and 1990s before embarking on the motivational book writing career he is most well-known for. *Tuesdays with Morrie*, his first non-sports publication, appeared in 1997. The book was a best seller, and a made-for-TV version of the story won four Emmy Awards in 1999. Two more novels followed: *The Five People You Meet in Heaven* and *For One More Day*. The latter was released as a movie in 2007.

(a) Albom's book *Tuesdays with Morrie* was very well received. (   )
(b) *The Five People You Meet in Heaven* was awarded four Emmys in 1999. (   )
(c) *For One More Day* has been remade in film form. (   )
(d) Albom is more famous as a book writer than as a sports reporter. (   )

The taser is a gun-like electric weapon capable of physically incapacitating threatening individuals, used by police in cases where deadly force is not required. Since its development in 1993, thousands of American law enforcement agencies have purchased the weapons. Recent controversy involving the death of tasered individuals, however, has led police to reconsider their use. Several police departments have enacted restrictions on their use, whereas other departments in Indiana and Georgia have completely banned them.

(a) The use of tasers by American police is now prohibited. (   )
(b) Police use of tasers has led to several fatalities. (   )
(c) The first death of a tasered suspect occurred in 1993. (   )
(d) Tasers are designed to prevent individuals from moving. (   )

정답 p.129

01

DDT is a chemical pesticide that has been shown to be highly effective in killing insects. It was first synthesized in 1874, but didn't achieve widespread use until its applicability to agriculture was discovered during the middle of the twentieth century. It quickly became a popular pest control product, but its popularity was sharply reduced once it was linked with negative impacts on the environment and human health. Nowadays, the use of DDT has been banned in North America and Europe, while some countries like South Africa and Thailand use the chemical solely in their fight against malaria-carrying mosquitoes.

Q Which of the following is correct about DDT according to the passage?

(a) It was ineffective when used against disease-carrying mosquitoes.
(b) South Africa and Thailand have prohibited its use.
(c) It was initially used as an agricultural tool to protect crops from insects.
(d) Ecological damage has resulted from its application.

02

The Songhai empire thrived in Western Africa between the fourteenth and sixteenth centuries. A series of military victories led to a rapid expansion of the empire's territory, westward to the Atlantic Ocean and eastward across Mali and deep into the area that is currently part of Nigeria. The empire benefitted from several educational institutions including the celebrated Sankore University, home to Africa's largest library at the time. However, in 1592, the empire's capital city Gao was attacked and occupied by Moroccan forces, leading to the collapse of the Songhai empire.

Q Which of the following is correct according to the passage?

(a) The Songhai empire stretched into modern-day Nigeria.
(b) The Songhai empire boasted Africa's largest university.
(c) The Songhai empire began expanding in the sixteenth century.
(d) The Songhai empire defeated the Moroccan army in a battle.

03

Dear Luke,

I wanted to let you know about the family's financial situation. It's really taking a toll on all of us. You should be happy that you're working overseas and not having to deal with the same day-to-day realities that we must face. Dad still hasn't found a job yet, so we are surviving on unemployment compensation. The payments aren't that big, and they are set to run out next month. If that happens, I'm not sure we'll be able to make payments on the house. If there's any way you could send money home, it would really help.

Will

Q Which of the following is correct according to the letter?

(a) Luke hasn't been able to find a job.
(b) Unemployment compensation for the family will soon stop.
(c) Will has been working abroad for some time.
(d) The family is going to lose possession of their house.

Robert Hanssen, an employee of the Federal Bureau of Investigation, was arrested on February 18, 2001 while delivering classified information to Russian agents. The high-profile case of espionage was a surprise to most Americans, but government agents had been aware of a spy in their department for several months. Documents acquired by the United States government gave proof that Hanssen had been regularly providing information to the Russians since 1979, only pausing between 1991 and 1999 while establishing a new set of contacts after the fall of the Soviet Union.

Q Which of the following is correct according to the passage?

(a) Hanssen provided information to the Russians prior to 1979.
(b) Hanssen no longer worked for the FBI at the time of his arrest.
(c) Hanssen spied for the Russians before the fall of the Soviet Union.
(d) The FBI said Hannsen spied for Russia between 1991 and 1999.

Construction Notice 124

• Drivers should expect narrowed lanes along Camberwell Street from May 12 to 18. On Wednesday and Friday (9 a.m. to 6 p.m.), the road will be closed completely; on Thursday, there will be one lane only.

• Residents are asked to park in the Sugar Hill Car Park. Compensation can be claimed from the local council (details in the link below). Buses 353 and 212 will be rerouted to Bromley Drive for the entire week; the 164 and 156 will terminate at Camberwell Station.

• Residents of Ruskin Street can expect drilling noise and some flashing lights from Tuesday until Friday. Residents of Hollyhead Lane will find construction vehicles parked on their road.

For more information, visit www.localgov.news.com/maintenance.

Q Which of the following is correct according to the passage?

(a) Only one lane will be open on Camberwell Street on Wednesday.
(b) The 164 bus will stop at Bromley Drive rather than Camberwell Station.
(c) Camberwell Street will be inaccessible to cars on Friday at 3 p.m.
(d) Construction vehicles will be parked on Ruskin Street.

06

The Aborigines of modern-day Australia have the oldest continuously existing culture in the world. The Aborigines are believed to have arrived on the continent in 50,000 BC, and dating procedures done on stone tools and paint fragments found by archaeologists confirm this estimate. However, DNA evidence tracing the genetic drift between cultures is suggesting an even earlier arrival date for these indigenous Australians of around 70,000 BC. At peak levels, aboriginal Australia boasted a population of over 750,000, before being colonized by the British in the eighteenth century. During the early colonial period, disease and war caused the population level to drop nearly 80 percent.

Q Which of the following is correct according to the passage?

(a) Genetic evidence suggests an earlier date for the foundation of Aboriginal culture.
(b) Indigenous Australians have the oldest human culture to ever exist.
(c) DNA testing indicates the Aborigines arrived 20,000 years later than previously thought.
(d) The arrival of the British caused a jump in the population of Aborigines.

07

The new line of Nihone tires, the XG-45, is the result of several years of research by a team of automotive specialists. The XG-45 is formulated with a synthetic material that gives 53 percent more traction than standard rubber. The tires are designed for use across all weather conditions, including rain and snow, without any measurable decrease in performance. The best thing about the XG-45 is its use of run-flat technology, which allows drivers to travel up to 100km on a deflated tire while keeping the rim and suspension intact. The new Nihone XG-45 is available at tire retailers nationwide.

Q Which of the following is correct according to the advertisement?

(a) The tire is meant to be used exclusively in bad weather.
(b) The tire is made from high-traction natural rubber.
(c) The tire can only be bought at an authorized retailer.
(d) The tire can still be driven on if it becomes flat.

08

Monet was a devotee to the natural world and tried to paint in a manner that represented his feeling upon quickly glancing at a scene. His painting *Impression, Sunrise*, a morning seascape painted in 1872 at Le Havre, is a good example of the expansive strokes and pastel colors that he used to recreate such a sense. Muted color shades were used to portray the morning mist enveloping the scene. He also set out to give the reflection of sunlight on the water a choppy quality in the painting by using heavily weighted, rough slashing motions to achieve such a look.

Q Which of the following is correct according to the passage?

(a) *Impression, Sunrise* is characterized by the use of vibrant hues.
(b) Monet employed coarse strokes to depict light reflecting.
(c) *Impression, Sunrise* was produced using a precise technique.
(d) Monet studied a scene carefully before beginning to paint.

Rudyard Kipling began his professional career as a journalist and newspaper editor before eventually becoming a full-time author in England. Kipling enjoyed a celebrated writing career and, at 41, was the youngest writer ever to win the Nobel Prize in literature. Colonial themes were present throughout his literature, written during Britain's final stages of empire-building. The culture and legends of India, Kipling's childhood home, also formed the basis for many of his most famous works. His poems and stories are notable for their exploration of the relationships between British colonists and native inhabitants.

Q Which of the following is correct about Kipling according to the passage?

(a) He turned to newspaper editing after becoming an established author.
(b) He won the Nobel Prize at the end of his writing career.
(c) His works described his personal relationships with Indians.
(d) His literature was often rooted in the traditions of India.

Arts > What's new

Barcelona's Miró Museum Expands

Surrealist painter and sculptor Joan Miró's personal art collection – including his own sketches, paintings, and works by other artists – was donated to the Joan Miró Foundation Museum in Barcelona. Among these items were pieces bestowed upon Miró by fellow artists like Calder, Picasso, and Royo. Furthermore, 12 unsold paintings from the early part of his career were also donated to the museum and are being housed there on a permanent basis. These significant additions to the museum will undoubtedly help to further the public's understanding of this influential artist.

Q Which of the following is correct about Joan Miró according to the passage?

(a) He obtained several artworks from his contemporaries.
(b) His personal collection consists only of his sketches and paintings.
(c) Twelve paintings done early in his career have different owners.
(d) The paintings will be housed at the museum temporarily.

11

Bell's palsy, which affects forty thousand people annually, is a condition triggering partial paralysis of the face. This disorder has usually been treated by means of facial retraining, a form of physical rehabilitation. However, doctors are now using a new method of treatment to overcome the condition. Prednisolone improves muscular function by increasing the number of neurotransmitters, providing the patient with a greater degree of facial control. Those who have used the medicine were found to recover from their symptoms much more quickly than others. Patients who took the drug reportedly did not experience any serious side effects.

Q Which of the following is correct according to the passage?

(a) Prednisolone existed long before it began to be used medicinally.
(b) Those unaffected by Bell's palsy have a low number of neurotransmitters.
(c) Facial retraining ensures faster recovery than does the new medication.
(d) Prednisolone improves Bell's palsy patients through increased muscular control.

12

Evidence has been found that early chimpanzees were capable of using tools, including those made of stone and wood. These archaeological findings lend credibility to the idea that chimpanzees have a more advanced intelligence than previously thought. Scientists had believed that chimpanzees only learned to use tools very recently through interaction with human populations. In areas known to have been inhabited by chimpanzees, a variety of stones have been found with their edges sharpened, along with the shells of cracked-open nuts.

Q Which of the following is correct according to the passage?

(a) Modern chimpanzees are more intelligent than earlier ones.
(b) Chimpanzees needed tools for predation and self-defense.
(c) Early chimpanzees fashioned implements to help them find food.
(d) Tool usage was too advanced for chimpanzees to learn.

13

We would like to express our gratitude to everyone here at the Morse and White Incorporated office for helping us save paper, and we hope that you will continue supporting this campaign. We are happy to report that the office's use of paper has decreased by 25 percent since last month. Please remember that for every ton of paper we save, we are saving around 17 mature trees. Also, when we recycle paper or avoid using it unnecessarily, we help reduce the toxic byproducts that are produced when paper is manufactured.

Q Which of the following is correct according to the passage?

(a) The office has new restrictions on the purchase of office supplies.
(b) The consumption of paper in the office was reduced by half.
(c) Seventeen trees are cut down to produce a ton of paper products.
(d) Toxic byproducts are created when paper is disposed of.

Thoughts on Gun Control

For too long in America, gun control has been portrayed as a civil liberties issue, as if any attempt to cut down on firearms was an infringement of individual liberty. This has fostered an inability to limit firearms sales as there are few politicians brave enough to face this sort of criticism. However, as gun violence continues to rise, the pressure for reform is getting so intense that politicians will be forced to act. Gun deaths increased by 4,000 between 2015 and 2016, and the rate of mass shootings has skyrocketed, with 1,624 occurring in the last 1,870 days.

According to current estimates, there are 300 million guns in America — almost half of the civilian firepower in the world. It is therefore unsurprising that the US is responsible for 31 percent of the planet's mass shooters, despite making up only five percent of the global population. Gun homicides are also 25.2 times higher in the US than in comparable countries. These facts alone make it plain that America's love affair with weaponry is causing serious harm to our people. Politicians must question whether they can afford to continue ignoring this issue, knowing that if they do, more deaths from gun violence will result.

4. Q: What is the writer's main point about gun control?

   (a) It is an attack on civil liberties and infringes upon citizens' rights.
   (b) It will not prevent individuals from obtaining arms illegally.
   (c) It is an issue that politicians are in urgent need of addressing.
   (d) It has proven ineffective as the homicide rate has increased.

5. Q: Which of the following is correct according to the passage?

   (a) America is the number one country for mass shooters.
   (b) Nearly all of the guns in the world are produced in America.
   (c) Gun murders in countries similar to the US are far less common.
   (d) Politicians are becoming more willing to support gun ownership.

Is the World's Love of Chocolate Causing Deforestation?

In recent decades, the global demand for chocolate has taken a toll on the environment in the countries that supply cocoa beans. The majority of cocoa is grown in Africa, with the two biggest producers being Ivory Coast and Ghana, both of which have suffered rampant deforestation as a result of illegal cocoa production. Around 25 percent of the land in Ivory Coast was once covered in forest, but that figure is now 4 percent. If this trend continues, the country's forests could be completely exhausted by 2030.

While the major chocolate brands, such as Nestle, Mars, and Hershey, have pledged to only use cocoa from legitimate sources, experts believe that most chocolate products contain cocoa grown by farmers who have illegally cleared forests. One way of reducing this negative impact is to support local authorities in enforcing forest protection laws. At the same time, chocolate companies can make a difference by ensuring that cocoa farmers with legitimate operations are paid more for their labor. Providing a better wage for these farmers would make the operation of illegal farms, which are currently more lucrative, less financially worthwhile.

16. Q: What is the main purpose of the passage?

   (a) To argue for limits on the global trade in chocolate confectionery
   (b) To discuss the negative ecological impact of cocoa production
   (c) To suggest how African authorities can reduce environmental damage
   (d) To describe the effect cocoa production is having on African economies

17. Q: Which of the following is correct according to the passage?

   (a) About a quarter of the forest in Ivory Coast has been cleared.
   (b) Local authorities are well-equipped to deal with illegal deforestation.
   (c) Illegal farming would be less beneficial if legal operations had higher pay.
   (d) Legitimate farms are being pressured to produce beans at a faster rate.

19

http://www.prepresearch.org/topics/social-media-is-the-new-news/

Social Media is the New News

These days, the primary medium by which many people get their news is social media. In the US, two-thirds of adults stated that they use social media to keep up with the news, and social media sites now provide most of the traffic for the websites of traditional newspapers. As a result, these long-established papers have gained access to global audiences. This has led to a change in both the tone and style of their articles as they attempt to tailor their content to appeal to a broader audience.

Today's social media users prefer more succinct pieces of information since they can be both rapidly consumed and easily shared. For example, the "listicle," in which a topic is reduced to a list format, has become popular even on news websites. Meanwhile, social media's continuous nature rewards not the quality but the quantity of the content—to the extent that quality is often compromised. While some of these trends could be said to make news content more engaging, it is worth asking whether they also lead to a loss of nuance and, by extension, a less-informed public.

8. Q: Which of the following is correct according to the passage?

(a) Most Americans get their news from television rather than newspapers.
(b) Some traditional papers have given up print in favor of online publishing.
(c) Newspapers are struggling to make enough money from social media.
(d) Many adults reported getting their news through social media sites.

9. Q: Why are shorter pieces favored by social media users?

(a) People prefer visual information to reading essays or reports.
(b) Shorter articles are easier to read on a screen or handheld device.
(c) More concise content is easier to take in and distribute online.
(d) Articles that aren't too long are more nuanced and engaging.

정답 p.130

CHAPTER 07 추론 문제 (Part 3, 4)

지문에 드러나 있지 않은 내용을 바르게 유추한 보기를 선택하는 유형이다. 이 유형은 평균적으로 Part 3의 후반에 3문제 정도 나오며, Part 4에는 2~3문제가량 출제된다. 이 문제를 풀기 위해서는 지문의 내용을 이해하는 것뿐만 아니라, 이를 바탕으로 추론까지 해야 하므로 난이도가 높은 편이다. 하지만 모든 추론의 근거는 지문에 드러나 있으므로, 지문의 내용을 정확하게 파악하면 정답을 찾을 수 있다. 그럼 이 유형에 대해 자세히 알아보자.

■ 질문 유형

infer를 사용하여 질문하는 형태가 가장 많이 나오고, 글쓴이가 동의할 의견이나 이어질 내용을 묻는 문제도 가끔 출제된다.

infer가 사용된 유형

infer   What can be **inferred** from the passage? 지문에서 추론할 수 있는 것은 무엇인가?
         What can be **inferred** about the writer of the passage? 지문의 글쓴이에 대하여 추론할 수 있는 것은 무엇인가?
         What can be **inferred** about OOO from the passage? 지문에서 ○○○에 대하여 추론할 수 있는 것은 무엇인가?

infer가 사용되지 않은 유형

의견   Which statement would the writer most likely **agree with**? 글쓴이는 어떤 진술에 가장 동의할 것 같은가?
이어질 내용 What will most likely **follow** the passage? 다음에 이어질 내용은 무엇인가?

■ Step별 문제풀이 전략

Step 1   질문 유형을 확인한 후 지문 또는 보기를 읽는다.

· 질문에 infer가 사용된 유형인 경우, 전체 내용을 이해해야 답을 찾을 수 있는 경우가 많으므로 지문 전체를 빠르게 읽으며 중심 내용을 파악한다.

· 질문에 infer about ○○○가 사용된 유형인 경우, 질문의 키워드인 ○○○와 관련된 부분을 지문에서 찾아 그 주변의 내용을 파악한다.

· 질문에 infer가 사용되지 않은 유형인 경우, 보기를 빠르게 읽어 키워드를 파악한 후, 지문에서 각각의 키워드와 관련된 부분을 찾아 질문에 대한 답을 예상하며 지문을 읽는다.

Step 2   지문에 제시된 내용을 바탕으로 추론한 보기를 선택한다.

전략 적용

My son was on the city's youth basketball league championship team last year, and they hope to win a second time. As an ex-ballplayer myself, I am pleased with his love for sports. Nevertheless, **if they lose, I'm sure that he will be crushed. I know what it's like to lose big games as a youngster. It's horrible**, but as an adult I recognize how important experiencing failure is. He will learn to overcome disappointment and be better prepared for the future.

Q What can be inferred from the passage? ———————— Step 1 질문 유형 확인 후 지문 읽기

    (a) He is concerned about his son's youthful innocence. ———— Step 2 지문의 내용을 바탕으로 추론한 보기 선택하기

    (b) He doesn't want his son to play sports as an adult.

    (c) He thinks it is unlikely that his son's team will win.

    (d) He doesn't believe that his son is that good of a player.

Step 1 질문에 infer가 사용된 유형이다. 지문을 빠르게 읽어 아들이 실패를 경험해보는 것이 중요하다는 것이 중심 내용임을 파악한다.

Step 2 아들이 어리기 때문에 경기에 지면 크게 좌절할(crushed) 것이고, 끔찍할(horrible) 것이라는 지문의 내용을 바탕으로 '아버지가 아들의 젊은이다운 순수함에 대해 걱정한다'라고 바르게 유추한 (a)가 정답이다.

    (b) 지문에서 '아들이 어른이 되어 운동하는 것을 원하지 않는다'라는 내용은 유추할 수 없다.

    (c) 지문에는 팀의 승패에 대해 예측한 내용이 없으므로 '아들의 팀이 이길 수 없을 것'이라는 내용은 유추할 수 없다.

    (d) 지문에는 아들의 농구 실력에 대한 내용이 없으므로 '아들이 뛰어난 선수라고 생각하지 않는다'라는 내용은 유추할 수 없다.

해석 p.135

Hackers **Practice**

구문독해 연습 – 접속사

구문독해를 익힌 후 주어진 문제를 풀어 보세요.

01 and

The patient / was / very pleased / when the doctor said / that his illness wasn't life-threatening / and
그 환자는 했다 매우 기뻐 의사가 말했을 때 그의 병이 생명을 위협하지 않는다고 그리고

that he will only need to stay in the hospital for three more days.
그가 오직 3일만 더 병원에 있으면 될 것이라고

위 문장에서 and는 두 개의 that절, 즉 that his illness wasn't life-threatening과 that he will ~ more days를 연결하는 접속사이다. 이처럼 and가 긴 구나 절을 연결하는 경우 '그리고' 또는 '~와(과)'로 해석한다.

다음 문장이 바르게 paraphrase된 보기를 고르세요.

Erica Lundgren, the star in Joe Belluci's new film, predicts that the movie will earn favorable reviews from critics and that the film will become a box-office hit.

(a) Joe Belluci believes the film will be a critical and commercial triumph due to Lundgren's prediction.
(b) Erica Lundgren anticipates that Belluci's new film will be successful both critically and financially.

02 not A but B (= no longer A but B)

The flattering book review / in the literature magazine / was written / not by an independent reviewer
그 책에 대한 호평은 문학 잡지에 있는 쓰여졌다 독자적인 평론가에 의해서가 아니라

/ but by the author of the book herself.
그 책의 저자 자신에 의해서

위 문장에서 not ~ but은 by an independent reviewer와 by the author ~ herself를 연결하는 접속사이다. 이와 같은 not A but B 형태는 'A가 아니라 B'라고 해석하며, A에는 부정하는 내용, B에는 긍정하는 내용이 온다.

다음 문장이 바르게 paraphrase된 보기를 고르세요.

Analysts are no longer regarding the country's economic woes as natural occurrences but instead are viewing them as the consequence of overzealous market speculation.

(a) Economic problems in the country are caused by speculators and don't happen naturally, according to analysts.
(b) According to analysts, the nation's economic problems are a natural result of ambitious market speculation.

03 so ~ that …

The cold front / passing over the island / created / fog / which was so thick that it was impossible for the
한랭 전선은 그 섬을 지나가는 일으켰다 안개를 매우 짙어 어부들이 낚싯대의 끝을 보는 것이 불가능한

fishermen to see the tips of their fishing poles.

위 문장에서 so 다음에는 형용사(thick), that 다음에는 절(it was impossible ~ fishing poles)이 와 있다. 이와 같은 so ~ that … 형태는 '매우 ~해서 (그 결과) …하다'라고 해석하며, ~ 부분은 원인, … 부분은 결과를 나타낸다.

다음 문장이 바르게 paraphrase된 보기를 고르세요.

A large portion of the fruit being sold at the neighborhood fruit stand was so badly bruised that customers refused to purchase it.

(a) Because of the condition of the fruit at the stand, customers opted not to buy it.
(b) The fruit at the stand started to become bad because the customers were not buying it.

연습

을 읽고 추론할 수 있는 보기에는 ○, 추론할 수 없는 보기에는 ×를 표시하세요.

Jigme Singye Wangchuck, the king of Bhutan, maintained a ban on television in the kingdom until 1999. He thought that the technology was an invasive force and that it would undermine the values of the predominantly Buddhist country. Since the ban was lifted, changes have in fact come. Reports of violence, theft, and drug abuse have risen exponentially. A growing legion of critics is again questioning the damaging effects of television, but a reinstatement of the ban is unlikely.

(a) Television viewing was allowed once King Wangchuck stepped down. (　)
(b) Bhutanese society has been harmed by the introduction of television. (　)
(c) The advent of television has led to a decline in the practice of Buddhism. (　)
(d) Television programming will continue to be available to the Bhutanese. (　)

In recent times, more and more supermarket shoppers are focusing not on price but on safety when they buy fruits and vegetables. By selecting organically grown foods, consumers are making the statement that they do not want to consume genetically modified foods or those laden with chemical pesticides, even if they ultimately make groceries cheaper. The potential harm that such foods can do outweighs the greater cost associated with naturally grown organic products.

(a) Many shoppers consider personal health their primary concern. (　)
(b) Most shoppers don't believe that pesticides are harmful. (　)
(c) Organically grown foods are considered safer than regular foods. (　)
(d) Chemical pesticides and genetic modifications help lower food prices. (　)

As the demand for ivory continues unabated, the African elephant is being hunted so vigorously that some species are on the verge of extinction. Wildlife conservation groups worldwide are trying to determine the appropriate steps to take in order to stop this alarming trend. The creation of laws against poaching has been marginally successful, but conservationists are continuously looking for other solutions that might prove to be more effective at protecting the animals.

(a) Poaching laws have not effectively reduced animal killings. (　)
(b) Conservationists are unlikely to prevent elephant extinctions. (　)
(c) Many poachers kill elephants for the ivory in their tusks. (　)
(d) The extinction of African elephants is harming other animals. (　)

정답 p.135

01

Recent literacy statistics indicate that around eighteen percent of the world's total adult population is illiterate. The accuracy of this figure, however, is questioned by several experts who argue that the groups conducting the surveys only base their data on self-declaration, whereby respondents directly answer questionnaires themselves. Though this type of survey has been accurate for measuring things such as physical health, welfare, or wealth, it may be too subjective for intelligence measures. If literacy tests were used instead of questionnaires, the resulting figures could be higher.

Q What can be inferred from the passage?

(a) There are no international standards for measuring literacy.

(b) Literacy figures will be more accurate with reliable questionnaires.

(c) Some people may not answer census questionnaires truthfully.

(d) There are groups who manipulate the results of literacy survey.

02

Autism is a condition marked by repetitive behavior and difficulties with social interaction. In the past, people had many different ideas about what caused such behavior. Some thought autistics were mentally disabled, but many autistics have led successful careers in science, literature, and other fields. Others considered autistics mentally ill, even schizophrenic. However, autism is currently recognized as a genetic disorder. Scientists are gradually determining which genes are responsible, and doctors are increasingly able to support patients with the condition.

Q What can be inferred about those with autism from the passage?

(a) Autistic people have difficulties finding suitable employment.

(b) Science has transformed people's view of autistic individuals.

(c) Their social difficulties lead to mental illness in many cases.

(d) Recent research has led to a cure for those with autism.

03

The ocean floor is the site of a vast number of rarely observed aquatic creatures, specifically adapted to such an uncompromising environment. This ecosystem is home to a unique animal called the tube worm. Also known as "hydrothermal worms," they survive by absorbing sulfur from the water near hydrothermal vents at the bottom of the ocean. These large cracks in the ocean floor are typically the result of volcanic eruptions occurring beneath the surface of the earth. Although the presence of sulfur is unusual in oceans and seas, it can be released in substantial amounts through volcanic activity.

Q What can be inferred from the passage?

(a) Many creatures have adapted to survive in sulfurous water.

(b) Tube worms can be found within volcanoes on the ocean floor.

(c) Hydrothermal vents are present throughout the world's oceans.

(d) The sulfur ingested by tube worms comes from undersea volcanoes.

The new album by British rock group Stereofingers is the subject of intense interest due to delays hampering its release. *Hello Machine* is coming out nearly 18 months after its initial release date, which has left die-hard fans waiting impatiently. Despite the powerful lyrics and emotional depth that the group is known for, the songs are spoiled by poor instrumentation and lackluster production. The album will undoubtedly be panned by critics as it is certainly not the band's best release, but because of the long wait, fans are sure to be lined up at music stores everywhere.

Q What can be inferred about the album from the article?

   (a) The reviewer has yet to listen to the new album.

   (b) *Hello Machine* is the debut album from Stereofingers.

   (c) Album reviewers will criticize the album due to its delayed release.

   (d) The album is expected to sell a large number of copies.

Books > New Release

Shining a Light on the Life of Afghani Women

Khaled Hosseini's most recent novel follows the relationship that develops between two Afghani women, Mariam and Laila, both married to the same abusive husband. The women's situation offers the reader a view into the conditions in which many women live in Afghanistan's male-dominated society. The strongest quality of Hosseini's work is the down-to-earth manner in which he describes the setting. In depicting Kabul, the capital, Hosseini evokes a scene where "children pushed each other on swings and slapped volleyballs over ragged nets tied to tree trunks."

Q What can be inferred about Hosseini's latest book from the passage?

   (a) It realistically portrays the lives of Afghani people.

   (b) It critiques male-dominated Afghan society.

   (c) It is an excellent psychological profile of women in Afghanistan.

   (d) It provides the reader with a child's viewpoint of Kabul.

06

It increasingly seems that the conflict in the Middle East will never end. Who should be held accountable for the immeasurable violence in the region? Is it the Palestinians, who have resorted to violence after having their land taken from them without recourse? Or should Israel be held to blame, with its continued provocation of Palestine by building walls and sending settlers into Palestinian territory? Israeli governmental actions have raised the unemployment rate in Palestine to well over 50 percent, and two-thirds of Palestinians are living in poverty. The Palestinians are not the ultimate cause of instability in the region.

Q Which statement would the writer most likely agree with?

(a) Palestinians need to take drastic action to improve their economy.
(b) Israel should change its national policies to promote peace.
(c) Palestine should remain patient in order to gain their land back.
(d) Israelis need to continue building settlements in Palestinian territory.

07

Dear Editor:

The absurd opinions voiced by Joseph Irvin in last month's article on news broadcaster Gary Tisdale infuriated me. Despite what Irvin claims, I feel that Tisdale's recent pieces still bring to mind his earlier work. Just last month, Tisdale presented two phenomenal exposés: a story about food shortages in Egypt, and an investigation of government educational spending that led to several resignations. The quality of these reports rivaled that of even his best work.

Q What can be inferred from the passage?

(a) Irvin thought Tisdale's recent broadcasts fell short of his earlier ones.
(b) Gary Tisdale was a popular news broadcaster early in his career.
(c) There is nothing phenomenal about Tisdale's broadcasts.
(d) It was not Tisdale's objective to make government people resign.

08

The power of the earthquake causing the 2004 Asian tsunami was estimated at 9.0 on the Richter scale. However, according to researchers at Northwestern University, this measurement was determined from only short-distance waves detected by sensors located throughout the region and failed to include measurements from long-distance waves. Using information from long-distance waves, the scientists reached a conclusion that the earthquake was three times stronger, with a magnitude of 9.3.

Q What can be inferred from the passage?

(a) Long-distance waves have more magnitude than short-distance waves.
(b) The power of earthquakes is likely to become stronger in the future.
(c) The accuracy of the Richter scale will become a source of debate.
(d) The power of the 2004 earthquake was originally miscalculated.

Baroque architecture, popularized throughout Europe in the seventeenth and eighteenth centuries, was influenced by an assortment of previous architectural styles. One of the most noteworthy of these predecessors was Italian Renaissance architecture, which came to an end during the latter part of the sixteenth century. Arguably the most well-known Renaissance architect was Michelangelo, who was famous for his paintings and sculptures. Michelangelo's design for St. Peter's Basilica in Rome, a landmark example of Renaissance architecture, provided an obvious point of reference for Baroque architects.

Q What can be inferred from the passage?

(a) Like other architects in Rome, Michelangelo produced many paintings and sculptures.
(b) Michelangelo's building designs had a huge influence on Baroque architecture.
(c) Michelangelo accomplished more in art than in architecture.
(d) The Renaissance had a greater impact on art than the Baroque.

Commercialism in Sports

Looking at the state of professional sports, I am often dismayed by how they have become so business oriented. Organizations will not hesitate to trade long-tenured players considered past their prime, even those who have contributed to their teams by helping them win championships, for younger and more marketable ones. Similarly, many star athletes are always on the lookout for better deals, jumping ship when offered a more lucrative contract. It seems to me that loyalty to a person, organization, and fan base is a mere afterthought in the world of sports nowadays.

Q What can be inferred about the writer from the passage?

(a) He thinks star players are being offered too much money.
(b) He believes athletes should retire once they pass their prime.
(c) He feels making money has become the overriding concern in sports.
(d) He deems it necessary for teams to trade players to win championships.

One of the most significant economic changes of the post-war era was the Nixon Shock, a series of measures undertaken by President Nixon in 1971. At the time, the world economy was dominated by Bretton Woods, a monetary system in which dollars could be converted to gold at a fixed rate. This had been agreed upon by 44 nations at the United Nations Monetary and Financial Conference in 1944. As currencies around the world were pegged to the dollar, the Bretton Woods system guaranteed a measure of economic stability following the devastation of World War II.

However, by the late 1960s, some American politicians had started to blame the strict framework of Bretton Woods for the decline of the dollar and the perceived weakness of the American economy. Consequently, Nixon announced his "New Economic Plan," a package of policies that replaced Bretton Woods. Among its main objectives was the suspension of the direct conversion of US dollars into gold. While many Americans viewed this as a positive move, it was regarded as shockingly unilateralist overseas. The legacy of the Nixon Shock has likewise been mixed. Its flexibility has allowed the Federal Reserve Board to counter economic dips, but its reliance on a floating exchange rate has also led to increased economic volatility.

11. Q: Which of the following is correct according to the passage?

   (a) The Bretton Woods monetary system began to break down in 1944.
   (b) The international economy was less stable as a result of Bretton Woods.
   (c) Gold was exchangeable for dollars at a set price under Bretton Woods.
   (d) Economic improvement led to the establishment of Bretton Woods.

12. Q: Which statement would the writer most likely agree with?

   (a) Nixon's economic policies had both positive and negative outcomes.
   (b) The economic volatility caused by the Nixon Shock canceled out its benefits.
   (c) Suspending the conversion of dollars into gold harmed the American economy.
   (d) The policies of the Nixon Shock led to a far less lively global economy.

14

Claim for Reimbursement

• Employee Name	: Joseph Dylan
• Department	: Marketing Department
• Total Reimbursement Amount	: $195
• Purpose of Claim	: Marketing Conference
• Nature of Expense	: Self-development
• Company E-mail	: jdylan@ppcr.com
• Date Submitted	: March 14th

• Explanation for the Claim

The personnel department has just announced an expansion of the company's coverage of activities for self-development. As far as I am aware, employees can now claim up to $500 per quarter for courses taken for work purposes, and this change will go into effect on the first day of the coming month. Although there is no detailed information about the eligibility of marketing courses, I believe it should cover a conference I have recently preregistered for: the second Big Data and Marketing Conference at Southwest Beach. The conference will be held on May 1st, after the new policy starts, so I would like to put in this claim to have the registration fee reimbursed.

Attending this conference will be worthwhile as it will allow me to develop my knowledge of data in the context of marketing. Currently we focus on traditional marketing strategies, which do not utilize our customer data very effectively. This conference will be a chance to see how we could change that. The conference includes training in the most recent data management techniques, as well as analytics and digital software that would be essential if we were to focus on using data in our marketing strategy.

3. Q: When does the new self-development policy start?

   (a) February 1st
   (b) March 14th
   (c) April 1st
   (d) May 14th

4. Q: What can be inferred from the form?

   (a) Joseph Dylan specializes in using data and analytics in marketing.
   (b) Joseph Dylan's company is notable for providing self-development courses.
   (c) The company has found that digital marketing techniques are ineffective.
   (d) The conference provides instruction in unconventional marketing strategies.

정답 p.137

시험에 나올 문제를 미리 풀어보고 싶을 땐?

해커스텝스(**HackersTEPS.com**)에서
텝스 적중예상특강 보기!

Section 2 지문 유형별 공략

CHAPTER 08 실용문 1 - 편지 / 코멘트

편지/코멘트 지문은 매회 평균적으로 1~3개 정도 출제된다. Part 1, 3, 4에 주로 나오고 Part 2에 간혹 출제된다. 편지/코멘트는 상대방에게 특정한 용건을 전달하기 위해 쓰는 글이므로 목적 또는 요구 사항이 지문에 분명히 드러나고, 이를 파악하면 내용을 쉽게 이해할 수 있다. 그럼 이 유형에 대해 자세히 알아보자.

■ 출제 토픽

· 감사 / 사과	만족스러운 서비스 제공, 지원에 대한 감사 // 기계의 오류에 대한 사과, 대금 청구서의 오류에 대한 편지 등
· 통보 / 요청	졸업 요건 미달, 합병으로 인한 해고 통보 // 추가 근무에 대한 수당 지급, 행사 참석 여부 확인 요청 편지 등
· 동의 / 불만	기사에 대한 동의 // 기사에 대한 반대, 임금 삭감의 부당함에 대한 편지 · 코멘트 등
· 안부	가족, 친구, 직장동료에게 보내는 안부 편지 등

■ 빈출 문제 유형

· 문장의 일부 · 전체 완성하기	편지/코멘트를 쓴 배경 · 목적을 언급한 지문 앞부분이나, 맺음말이 나오는 지문 마지막 부분에 칸이 제시되는 문제가 주로 출제된다.
· 중심 내용 문제	편지/코멘트를 쓴 목적을 묻는 문제가 출제된다.
· 육하원칙 문제 · Correct 문제	편지/코멘트의 세부 내용과 일치하는 보기를 선택하는 문제가 출제된다.
· 추론 문제	편지/코멘트 내용을 통해 유추할 수 있는 내용을 선택하는 문제가 출제된다.

■ 예제 및 지문 flow

Dear Editor,

Last weekend, I was taking my dog for a walk along the beach and noticed several individuals disposing of garbage in the water.

편지/코멘트를 쓴 배경 · 목적

I think this behavior is part of a larger problem with the residents of our city. Recent statistics show that the beach's water quality has dropped sharply in the last five years due to waste. Also, our downtown area is becoming overwhelmed by trash — even Fitzgerald Park is not the same place it used to be.

세부 내용

As a citizen, I believe that _____.

맺음말 (요구 · 주장 / 끝인사)

Regards,
Ethel Williams

(a) laws against littering must be enforced
(b) Fitzgerald Park should be closed down

해석 p.140

해설 | 지문 마지막의 빈칸을 채우는 문제이다. 빈칸이 있는 문장을 통해 글쓴이가 생각하는 바를 빈칸에 넣어야 함을 알 수 있다. 쓰레기를 버리는 행위로 인해 해안의 수질이 크게 떨어졌고 도심지가 쓰레기로 매몰되고 있다는 세부 내용으로 보아, '쓰레기 투기에 대한 법이 시행되어야 한다'라는 내용의 (a)가 정답이다.

정답 | (a)

Hackers **Practice**

Dear Customer Service:

My wife's birthday was four months ago, and considering her love for the outdoors I thought that getting her a subscription to American Trail magazine would be something she would appreciate.

> 편지를 쓴 배경

Unfortunately, not a single issue has arrived yet. This is despite the fact that my credit card was billed for the one-year subscription fee just days after placing the order. The lack of prompt delivery has been quite irritating, and we no longer wish to receive the magazine.

> 세부 내용

With that being said, I wish _____.

> 끝인사

Sincerely,
Matthew Jackson

(a) to receive a refund of the subscription fee
(b) to extend my subscription period
(c) to submit a change of address form
(d) to get the first issue mailed to me soon

t III

Reader's Comment:

I agree with your editorial that the new bicycle path along the North Shore Canal will allow cyclists to avoid a risky route along the highway. But going ahead with this proposed new pathway is far too dangerous.

> 코멘트를 쓴 배경

The proposal will extend the walkways alongside the canal to supposedly enable pedestrians and cyclists to use them at the same time. However, the one-meter extension will make collisions inevitable, putting both cyclists and pedestrians at serious risk of being forced into the canal.

> 세부 내용

If the city truly cares about the safety of its residents, it will make the walkways at least twice as wide.

> 주장

Q Which of the following is correct according to the comment?

(a) Cyclists currently ride along an unsafe road.
(b) The path would increase the canal's width.
(c) Pedestrians would not be permitted on the path.
(d) Collisions have occurred on the cycle path often.

Chapter 08 실용문 1 – 편지 / 코멘트 **419**

READING COMPREHENSION | 지문 유형별 공략

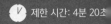
Part I Read the passage. Then choose the option that best completes the passage.

01

Dear Mrs. Reyes,

This letter is in response to your _____. If you believe the product has mechanical problems and is in need of service, you can contact an accredited technician using the enclosed information. Another option is to troubleshoot the issue yourself by logging on to the customer support forums on our Web site. The forums allow our company personnel to field any product-related questions that arise from users. We hope this information will be of assistance.

Jason Maxwell, Lightspeed Technology

(a) complaints regarding a mechanic's service
(b) inquiries about registering for our Web site
(c) question regarding a malfunctioning item
(d) posting on our Web site's forums

Part III Read the passage and the question. Then choose the option that best answers the question.

02

http://www.nynews.com/congestion-charge

National > N.Y. Local
Opinion: Drivers in Central New York Should Pay Charge

COMMENTS

user127   2 hours ago

I was disappointed that your article in favor of forthcoming congestion charge didn't mention the impact it would have on the livelihoods of thousands of ordinary New Yorkers. While the well-off residents living in the center of the city will be exempt, those who live on the outskirts and commute will have to pay the charge. Many of these commuters have very low wages and will struggle to afford the extra expense. Furthermore, the city's public transportation is an unmitigated disaster, something which will only be exacerbated by an influx of people avoiding the congestion charge.

Q What is the main topic of the passage?

(a) The disastrous state of New York City's public transportation
(b) The negative impact the fee will have on numerous New Yorkers
(c) The harmful effect of the congestion charge on traffic levels
(d) The inequality in New York City's distribution of housing

t IV Read the passage and the questions. Then choose the option that best answers each question.

-04

[11:35 a.m.]

Michelle:

Have you confirmed your holiday for our trip to Rome? I can go on any week in July, but it would be great to get the date fixed by the end of the month so I can plan my work schedule. By the way, shall we hire a travel agent to sort out the flights and hotel? My college classmate Jessica works for a travel company, so she can find us cheap flights. Or we can do it ourselves!

[12:01 p.m.]

Julie:

Yeah, I've got the second week of July off! I really had to beg my manager. You are so lucky that you work for yourself. I think that we should plan the trip ourselves. I had a bad experience with a travel agency when I went to a wedding in Spain with Michael. Plus, I have a lot of ideas already. I really want to show you some of Rome's lesser known attractions. How does that sound? Let me know soon!

03. Q: Which of the following is correct about Michelle?

(a) She confirmed her holiday after pleading with her manager.
(b) She prefers to go on an expensive holiday in July.
(c) She has an acquaintance who can get her inexpensive airline tickets.
(d) She made a reservation for the holiday with a travel agency.

04. Q: What can be inferred from the messages?

(a) Michelle is in charge of her own work timetable.
(b) Julie originally came up with the idea of going to Rome.
(c) Michael and Julie went to Spain for their honeymoon.
(d) Julie has never been to the Italian Capital before.

CHAPTER **09** 실용문 2 - 광고

광고 지문은 매회 평균적으로 2~3개 정도 출제된다. Part 1, 3, 4에 주로 나오고 Part 2에 간혹 출제된다. 광고는 상품이나 서비스를 홍보하여 상대방의 선택을 유도하는 글이므로 광고 대상의 특징이 지문에 분명하게 드러나고, 이를 파악하면 내용을 쉽게 이해할 수 있다. 그럼 이 유형에 대해 자세히 알아보자.

■ 출제 토픽

· 서비스 / 제품 / 상점 광고	원격 바이러스 검사, 요리 강좌 // 화장품, 제빵 기계, 의류 // 미술 용품점, 유치원 광고 등
· 관광지 / 관광 상품 광고	런던의 웨스트민스터 성당, 스키장 // 유람선 여행, 시티 투어 패키지, 화실 투어 광고 등
· 구인 / 행사 광고	대체 교사, 장기 기증자, 보모, 작가 모집 // 영화제, 백화점 할인 행사 광고 등

■ 빈출 문제 유형

· 문장의 일부 · 전체 완성하기	관심을 유발하는 내용이나 광고 대상 소개가 나오는 지문 앞부분이나, 이용 · 방문 권유 또는 광고 내용을 강조하는 내용이 나오는 지문 마지막 부분에 빈칸이 제시되는 문제가 주로 출제된다.
· 중심 내용 문제	광고 대상과 특징을 묻는 문제가 출제된다.
· 육하원칙 문제 · Correct 문제	광고 대상의 장점 · 특징과 일치하는 보기를 찾는 문제가 출제된다.
· 추론 문제	광고를 통해 유추할 수 있는 내용을 선택하는 문제가 출제된다.

■ 예제 및 지문 flow

Have you had a chance to try Vitality facial cream? It is your best defense against dryness, clogged pores, and excess oil.	관심 유발 / 광고 대상 소개
The product is made from shea butter and collagen, which leave your skin with a healthy glow. It also contains special additives to help protect against damage from the sun.	세부 광고 내용 (대상의 장점 · 특징)
The cream is available in cosmetic stores nationwide and comes in a variety of scents, including vanilla and lavender. Your face is special, so _____.	이용 · 방문 권유 / 광고 내용 강조

(a) make an effort to beautify your skin
(b) be sure to wear suncream at all times

해석 p.141

해설 | 지문 마지막의 빈칸을 채우는 문제이다. 빈칸이 있는 문장의 so(그러므로)를 통해 앞 내용에 대한 결론이나 결과를 빈칸에 넣어야 함을 알 수 있다. 화장 크림을 광고 대상으로 소개했으므로, 화장 크림의 효과를 언급하여 이용을 권유하는 '피부를 가꾸기 위해 노력하세요'라는 내용의 (a)가 정답이다.

정답 | (a)

t I

Does your firm need to find office space in a foreign city? If so, Schott Services can help.

관심 유발

Schott has the most comprehensive database of overseas commercial and industrial buildings, featuring thousands of properties located in hundreds of cities worldwide. Our locally resident specialists can recommend the perfect location to accommodate your expanding business and can take care of the paperwork and formalities required by local government authorities.

세부 광고 내용

Schott Services should be the first choice for those seeking _____ _____.

광고 내용 강조

(a) an experienced building construction company
(b) expertise on property regulations
(c) assistance with paperwork and formalities
(d) information about international real estate

t III

"A Taste of India" is a unique five-day program offered by the Indian Cultural Center where attendees will learn to prepare several of the area's diverse regional cuisines.

광고 대상 소개

A $65 fee will cover the costs of instruction by highly trained local chefs, the price of food and supplies, and a comprehensive recipe book that will allow you to prepare each dish at home.

세부 광고 내용

This special event will begin on Monday, January 23, and interested parties can reserve a spot by calling (876) 756-4298.

이용 권유

Q What is the advertisement mainly about?

(a) A cookbook release event at the Indian Cultural Center
(b) Details of a unique Indian tourist event itinerary
(c) The food sampling party at an Indian restaurant
(d) Information regarding an Indian cooking course

Hackers **TEST**

Part I Read the passage. Then choose the option that best completes the passage.

01

The scientists at GreenFuel Technologies are currently testing a new form of fuel made from a renewable resource: a type of algae that can produce massive amounts of oil. Because of algae's hardiness and rapid growth, it can produce eight times more fuel per acre of land than other methods of fuel production while producing close to zero pollution when burned. Our innovations in renewable energy are helping the world to live cleaner, healthier, and smarter. For more information about _____, visit us online at www.greenfueltech.com.

(a) energy production and healthy living
(b) renewable energy and pollution control
(c) algae growth and environmental protection
(d) algae harvesting and fuel composition

Part III Read the passage and the question. Then choose the option that best answers the question.

02

The Best in Modern Sportswear

United Threads is an industry leader in producing high-quality sportswear for men and women. For 11 years, we've designed, manufactured, and sold our products in hundreds of United Threads retail locations from coast to coast. Our production techniques are state-of-the-art, meaning that our products are free of the loose threads and misprinted logos that plague our competitors. Whether you're looking for a new yoga outfit or the latest in basketball gear, we are sure to have what you're looking for.

Q Which of the following is correct about United Threads?

(a) They make both casual and formal apparel.
(b) They have been the top selling brand for 11 years.
(c) They specialize in making team sports attire.
(d) They have eliminated manufacturing defects.

t IV Read the passage and the questions. Then choose the option that best answers each question.

-04

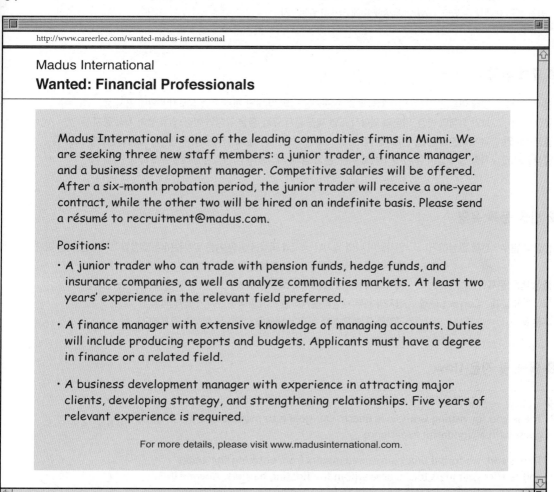

```
http://www.careerlee.com/wanted-madus-international
```

Madus International
Wanted: Financial Professionals

Madus International is one of the leading commodities firms in Miami. We are seeking three new staff members: a junior trader, a finance manager, and a business development manager. Competitive salaries will be offered. After a six-month probation period, the junior trader will receive a one-year contract, while the other two will be hired on an indefinite basis. Please send a résumé to recruitment@madus.com.

Positions:

- A junior trader who can trade with pension funds, hedge funds, and insurance companies, as well as analyze commodities markets. At least two years' experience in the relevant field preferred.

- A finance manager with extensive knowledge of managing accounts. Duties will include producing reports and budgets. Applicants must have a degree in finance or a related field.

- A business development manager with experience in attracting major clients, developing strategy, and strengthening relationships. Five years of relevant experience is required.

For more details, please visit www.madusinternational.com.

READING COMPREHENSION | 지문 유형별 공략

해커스 텝스 Reading

03. Q: What type of contract will the finance manager be offered?

　(a) A contract with a higher salary than the junior trader position

　(b) A contract with the option to renew after six months

　(c) A one year contract with a competitive salary and leave package

　(d) A permanent contract following the completion of a trial period

04. Q: Which of the following is correct according to the passage?

　(a) The junior trader will be responsible for carrying out commodities research.

　(b) The finance manager must be familiar with working on business strategy.

　(c) The business development manager applicants should have two years' experience.

　(d) The junior trader should have at least five years of experience in commodities.

정답 p.142

CHAPTER **10** 실용문 3 - 공지

공지 지문은 실용문 중 자주 출제되는 지문 유형으로 매회 평균적으로 2~3개 정도 나오며, Part 1~4에서 고루 출제된다. 공지는 특정한 사항을 공식적으로 전달하기 위한 글로서 이와 관련된 세부 내용이 지문에 분명하고 일관성 있게 제시되므로, 이를 파악하면 내용을 쉽게 이해할 수 있다. 그럼 이 유형에 대해 자세히 알아보자.

■ 출제 토픽

· **행사 공지**   연례 여름 밤 행사, 의과 대학의 20주년 기념 강의, 미술관 개관 기념 심포지엄 안내 공지 등
· **규정 공지**   보안 정책의 변경, 약국의 의학적 조언 제공 금지 규정, 환불 규정의 변경, 압류 절차 시작 공지 등
· **설명 / 조언**   피아노 관리 방법, 얼룩 제거법 등 // 보고서 작성, 재무 상태 점검을 위한 전문가 고용과 관련된 조언 등
· **양식 / 보고**   지출 결재 양식 등 // 보고서의 서문, 환경 범죄, 기업의 재정 안정성에 대한 보고서 등

■ 빈출 문제 유형

· **문장의 일부 · 전체 완성하기**   인사말이 나와 있거나 공지의 목적을 밝힌 지문 앞부분이나, 맺음말이 나오는 지문 마지막 부분에 빈칸이 제시되는 문제가 주로 출제된다.
· **중심 내용 문제**   공지의 목적이나 공지하고 있는 행사가 무엇인지 묻는 문제가 출제된다.
· **육하원칙 문제 · Correct 문제**   공지의 세부 사항과 일치하는 보기를 찾는 문제가 출제된다.
· **추론 문제**   공지를 통해 유추할 수 있는 내용을 선택하는 문제가 출제된다.

■ 예제 및 지문 flow

> Thank you for visiting Grandville Beach. Our goal is to provide every guest with a wonderful experience.   ⌉ 인사말 / 목적
>
> To this end, we forbid unaccompanied minors from entering the water and restrict swimmers to the area within the floating barriers. Anyone in violation of these rules will be asked to leave the beach. Any questions about our policies can be addressed to the lifeguards.   ⌉ 세부 사항
>
> By working together, we can _____.   ⌉ 맺음말
>
> (a) train the lifeguards to better do their jobs
> (b) ensure that everyone enjoys the beach safely

해석 p.143

해설 | 지문 마지막의 빈칸을 채우는 문제이다. 빈칸이 있는 문장을 통해 함께 협조함으로써 할 수 있는 것이 무엇인지를 빈칸에 넣어야 함을 알 수 있다. 손님들에게 해변에서 지켜야 하는 규정을 공지하고 있으므로 '모두가 해변을 안전하게 즐기는 것을 보장한다'라는 내용의 (b)가 정답이다.

정답 | (b)

t I

> We wish to inform you of the following rules concerning _____.   □ 목적
>
> If your booking was made with a credit card, then the card used in the
> transaction must be presented at the reception desk. One member of your
> party must possess photo identification that will be kept as a security deposit
> until checkout. If you desire a specific view or special accommodations, please   세부 사항
> inform the staff upon your arrival. Guests requiring the use of our airport
> shuttle service must contact the front desk in advance.
>
> We always strive to satisfy our customers, and thank you for choosing us.   □ 맺음말

(a) the airline's passenger regulations
(b) the hotel's check-in policy
(c) the restaurant's reservation system
(d) the car rental agency's procedures

t III

> The majority of the camp counselors at Silver Lake work the entire ten-week
> summer session. A limited number of positions also exist for those who wish
> to work a Friday evening to Sunday afternoon shift, which generally entails   목적
> organizing sports and social activities.
>
> Full-time workers share further duties such as nature education, cooking, and
> facility maintenance. Counselors begin their day at dawn and stay on site
> throughout the night. They are also responsible for personal transportation to   세부 사항
> and from the camp.

Q Which of the following is correct according to the passage?

(a) Counselors are expected to remain at the camp most of the time.
(b) Weekend workers prepare food and maintain the camp's facilities.
(c) The camp provides the transportation of workers to the site.
(d) All camp counselors are required to perform the same duties.

정답 p.143

Hackers **TEST**

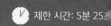 제한 시간: 5분 25초

Part I Read the passage. Then choose the option that best completes the passage.

01

The Lakeside Craft Club will _____. City residents of all ages are welcome to join us. Some experience with sewing, weaving, or needlepoint would be beneficial, but is not required. The classes will take place at the community center on Wednesday evenings and will continue for 8 weeks. A $50 fee is due before the first class to cover the cost of materials. In just a short time, you will be an expert with the help of our qualified instructors.

(a) recruit volunteers to teach crafts to kids
(b) hold a meeting about the upcoming craft show
(c) start offering instructional lessons for novices
(d) need several new teachers for their craft classes

02

Providing the utmost in customer service is a top priority for everyone working at Jacobsen's, and we expect all of our employees to act in accordance with this objective. A complete list of the company's corporate rules and regulations has been included in the employee manual. We fully expect our new employees to become acquainted with these policies. If an employee fails to comply with them, disciplinary action will be taken. As a member of the Jacobsen's team, you are _____

_____.

(a) expected to uphold company guidelines
(b) a valued and trusted employee to us
(c) entitled to receive an employee handbook
(d) required to always dress in business attire

Part III Read the passage and the question. Then choose the option that best answers the question.

03

Landmark Survey

The city's Urban Planning Commission is collecting information about early twentieth-century homes for potential inclusion in a newly created registry of historic landmarks. Please check the data we've included below and contact our secretary if any corrections must be made. It is important to inform us of any recent renovations or additions to your home: major design changes may disqualify you from receiving a historic home restoration grant from the city. We appreciate your help in supporting the city's heritage.

Q What can be inferred from the passage?

(a) The city has yet to designate any homes as historic landmarks.
(b) The secretary made mistakes when compiling the registry.
(c) Plans are being made to tear down the city's old buildings.
(d) Restoration grants are available to all of the city's homeowners.

IV Read the passage and the questions. Then choose the option that best answers each question.

05

London Literature Tour Application Guidelines

- Open to students who are currently enrolled as literature majors or are studying literature as a minor at Fernriver University
- Tour dates: from April 3rd until the 8th
- Application forms can be downloaded from the department website. Completed forms should be submitted to admin@engdept.fernuni.edu. Please include a photocopy of your passport photo page.
- Application deadline: February 12th (Applicants should demonstrate an academic interest in London's literature in their cover letter.)
- Costs: Flights and accommodation will be provided. Food, drink, and transportation in London should be covered by students. Theater tickets for one performance will be supplied. (Entrance to most galleries is free.)
- Activities:
  - Students must attend several literature lectures at King's College London and spend time researching in the British Library archives.
  - Essential group activities will include exploring landmarks related to writers, from Shakespeare's Globe Theatre to Charles Dickens's London house.
  - An optional excursion to the Sussex residence of author Virginia Woolf (two hours from London) will be organized.

Call the English Department on 504-765-3722 for more information.

English Department Office

---

04. Q: Which of the following is correct?

(a) Applicants must include a photocopy of their student ID.
(b) Tour participants must purchase meals with their own money.
(c) The trip is open to all students of Fernriver University.
(d) A scholarly concern for fiction from London is not essential.

05. Q: Which of these activities on the tour is NOT compulsory?

(a) A period of study in the British Library archives
(b) An excursion to a theater that is named after a writer
(c) A trip to visit the former house of a writer outside London
(d) A series of lectures on literature in a London university

정답 p.144

CHAPTER **11** 실용문 4 - 기사 / 논평

기사/논평 지문은 실용문 중 가장 자주 출제되는 지문 유형으로 매회 평균적으로 4개 정도 나오며, Part 1~4에서 고루 출제된다. 기사/논평은 특정한 사건을 전달하거나 구체적인 사안에 관한 의견을 표하는 글로서 지문의 앞부분에 중심 내용이 요약되어 있거나 지문의 소재가 제시되므로, 이를 파악하면 내용을 쉽게 이해할 수 있다. 그럼 이 유형에 대해 자세히 알아보자.

■ 출제 토픽

· **신문 기사** 콜롬비아의 정치적 상황, 기업의 해외 생산공장 건설 조치, 선거 결과 등
· **일기 예보** 플로리다의 이상 한파 예상, 시카고 지역의 꽃샘 추위 예보 등
· **논평** 정부 정책, 환경 문제, 새로운 연구 결과, 새로 출간된 소설에 대한 논평 등
· **설문 조사** 좋은 직장을 위한 이사와 관련된 직원 설문 조사 결과, 인터넷 이용자 설문 조사 결과 등

■ 빈출 문제 유형

· **문장의 일부 · 전체 완성하기** 사건 · 소식을 소개하는 지문 앞부분이나, 기사 · 논평 내용 정리 또는 현황 · 전망을 언급하는 지문 마지막 부분에 빈칸이 제시되는 문제가 주로 출제된다.
· **중심 내용 문제** 기사 · 논평의 중심 내용이나 제목을 묻는 문제가 출제된다.
· **육하원칙 문제 · Correct 문제** 기사 · 논평의 세부 내용과 일치하는 보기를 찾는 문제가 출제된다.
· **추론 문제** 기사 · 논평의 내용을 통해 유추할 수 있는 내용을 선택하는 문제가 출제된다.

■ 예제 및 지문 flow

Bus driver Tom Collins took full responsibility for last week's serious collision.
사건 · 소식 소개

On Friday evening, traffic bottlenecks in the city caused Collins' downtown commuter bus to be significantly behind schedule. Despite the flashing warning light at a train crossing, he attempted to cross the tracks before the train arrived. The bus could not accelerate quickly enough and several passengers situated in the rear of the bus were seriously injured.
세부 내용

Collins wept in front of journalists _____.
내용 · 의견 정리

(a) upon confessing to his role in the accident
(b) while pleading not guilty to the crime

해석 p.145

해설 | 지문 마지막의 빈칸을 채우는 문제이다. 빈칸이 있는 문장을 통해 Collins가 기자들 앞에서 흐느껴 울었다는 말에 연결되는 내용을 빈칸에 넣어야 함을 알 수 있다. Col 충돌 사고에 대한 전적인 책임을 졌다는 사건 소개에 이어서 사고 발생 상황이 자세히 묘사되었다. 따라서 '사고에서의 그의 책임을 시인하면서'라는 내용의 (a)가 정답이

정답 | (a)

Hackers **Practice**

rt I

> An eight-year-old Orlando boy is still in critical condition after being struck by a vehicle while playing in the residential street in front of his home.   사건 소개
>
> Citing privacy concerns, the family has requested that the boy's identity be withheld. According to investigative sources, no witnesses were present nearby when the accident occurred. A long set of skid marks was found at the scene, suggesting the driver attempted to stop but could not decelerate in time.   세부 내용
>
> The evidence indicates that _____.   내용 정리

(a) friends could not warn the child in time
(b) the delivery truck driver was asleep
(c) the vehicle was traveling at high speed
(d) an arrest will soon be made in the case

rt III

> Despite persistent water shortages, the state legislature has voted down a bill that would allow farmers to use waste water for irrigation by installing water purification systems.   소식 소개
>
> Currently, agriculture uses a third of the state's water, with farmers paying high irrigation fees to avoid the low yields and stunted produce that come with regular droughts. Meanwhile, most of the state's waste water is flushed away, even though it can be made safe for crops.   세부 내용
>
> If farmers are encouraged to use recycled water, our water usage will fall dramatically. To stop water supplies drying up completely, the state government must act now.   의견 정리

Q Which of the following is correct?

(a) Lower rainfall has led to limited growth for many farmed products.
(b) Droughts are expected to become less frequent in the coming years.
(c) Agriculture has become unprofitable due to much higher water bills.
(d) Farmers are reluctant to use waste water because of contamination.

Hackers **TEST**

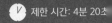
Part I Read the passage. Then choose the option that best completes the passage.

01

A middle school student in Vermont, claiming that his school violated his rights to free speech, triumphed in a lawsuit that has captured the attention of schools nationwide. The argument, which involved the student's right to wear clothing containing political or controversial subject matter, was carefully monitored by school districts concerned that the verdict might force a revaluation of student rights. Currently, many schools have restrictions in place regarding student apparel. However, the court's ruling is expected to _____.

(a) result in new laws regarding free speech
(b) expand the political content taught in schools
(c) prompt school officials to revise their regulations
(d) make students reconsider inappropriate clothing

Part III Read the passage and the question. Then choose the option that best answers the question.

02

TRANSPORTATION

Airlines Struggle Due to Rising Oil Prices

In light of the recent spike in oil prices that has hurt the revenues of airlines worldwide, many companies are increasing their fuel surcharges to compensate. The average international fare has increased 40 percent, and domestic ticket prices are up nearly 25 percent over the past 6 months. Airlines expected profits to return to previous levels as a result; this hasn't been the case, however. Instead of improving airline revenues, the change has actually caused customers to cancel their air travel plans, and airlines are now operating at a loss.

Q Which of the following is correct according to the passage?

(a) Airlines are amassing larger stocks of fuel.
(b) Ticket sales in the airline industry have decreased.
(c) Overseas airfares have risen by 25 percent.
(d) Profits in the airline industry have risen again.

The Monthly Standard

Child Poverty Reforms Don't Go Far Enough

The government has announced a range of policies aimed at reducing child poverty, including an increase in benefits for families in the lowest wage bracket. Although the policies represent necessary steps, they will merely scratch the surface of a profound problem.

According to a study conducted by the Social Science Research Council, 400,000 children have been forced into poverty in the past two years. This has primarily been the result of two government measures. First, the benefit cuts made by this very government have affected lower-class families the hardest. Second, a reduction in welfare payments to unemployed parents has made it even harder for such families to get by. Meanwhile, the new proposals being made to address these issues are expected to have minimal effect, as they make no provision for families where the parents are out of work.

Making allowances for parents on low salaries is a step in the right direction, but it ignores those who have no wages at all. Substantially reducing child poverty will be impossible unless further action is taken to assist families in the most dire of circumstances.

03. Q: What is the main idea of the passage?

(a) The positive role of the government in reducing child poverty

(b) The economic hardships being endured by the middle class

(c) The positions of government officials on the issue of poverty

(d) The insufficiency of the government's child poverty reform

04. Q: Which statement would the writer most likely agree with?

(a) The new policies will help the government reach its targets.

(b) The government has pushed many children into poverty with its cuts.

(c) The new policies are an effective means of assisting unemployed parents.

(d) The government cuts are a necessary measure to address child poverty.

정답 p.145

CHAPTER **12** 학술문 1 - 인문학

인문학 지문은 학술문 중 자주 출제되는 지문 유형으로 매회 평균적으로 5개 정도 나오며, Part 1~4에서 고루 출제된다. 인문학에는 역사, 예술, 언어 등의 주제가 포함되며, 인문학 지문 유형은 주로 주제 제시, 이를 뒷받침하는 세부 내용, 그리고 요약이나 결론으로 이어지는 흐름을 보인다. 그럼 이 유형에 대해 자세히 알아보자.

■ 출제 토픽

· **역사/종교**   미국 초기 정착민들의 삶, 일본의 메이지 유신 // 중세의 이동형 종교 재판소, 종교 중심지로서의 예루살렘 등
· **예술/문학**   앤디 워홀의 팝아트, 추상적 표현주의 // 점강법의 이해, 빅토르 위고의 소설에 포함된 에세이 등
· **언어/사상**   생성 문법 이론, 언어의 급속한 소멸 현상 // 불교 철학의 기원, 아리스토텔레스의 영혼론 등
· **교육/심리**   성인의 제2언어 학습, 교육의 실효성 // 청소년의 집단주의, 소득과 행복의 연관성 등

■ 빈출 문제 유형

· **문장의 일부·전체 완성하기**   역사적 사건, 사조, 작품, 인물 등에 대한 주제 또는 도입 문장이 나오는 지문 앞부분이나, 지문 내용을 요약하거나 결론을 도출하는 지문 마지막 부분에 빈칸이 제시되는 문제가 주로 출제된다.
· **중심 내용 문제**   지문에서 중점적으로 설명하거나 논의하는 내용을 파악하는 문제가 출제된다.
· **육하원칙 문제·Correct 문제**   주제나 소재와 관련된 비교, 연구, 묘사, 서술한 내용과 일치하는 보기를 찾는 문제가 출제된다.
· **추론 문제**   주제나 소재를 통해 유추할 수 있는 내용을 선택하는 문제가 출제된다.

■ 예제 및 지문 flow

British policies while ruling colonial America led to the Revolution of 1776.	주제/도입 (역사적 사건, 사조, 작품, 인물 등)
Despite each colony having a local government, the control over most economic and political decisions was firmly in the hands of the British Parliament. The levying of taxes on the American colonists by the British, while offering them very little in return, was considered unjust and angered the colonists. Americans were unwilling to pay money to a distant empire controlling them from across the world.	세부 내용 (비교, 연구, 묘사, 서술 등)
In essence _____.	요약·결론

(a) the American response to higher taxes was unjustified
(b) Britain prompted the American colonies to revolt

해석 p.146

해설 | 지문 마지막의 빈칸을 채우는 문제이다. 빈칸이 있는 문장의 In essence(본질적으로)를 통해 앞에 온 내용에 대한 결론을 빈칸에 넣어야 함을 알 수 있다. 영국의 정책이 미국 독립 혁명을 야기했다는 주제가 나온 후 미국 독립 혁명이 발생한 배경이 설명되었으므로 '영국이 미국 식민지들이 반란을 일으키도록 자극했다'라는 내용이 빈칸에 오는 것이 적절하다.

정답 | (b)

t I

Nineteenth century American author Henry David Thoreau, best known for his works discussing the virtues of nature, also wrote divisively about his government.

주제

Thoreau was an advocate of personal rights, and he disagreed with government policies on slavery, war with Mexico, and taxation. He went as far as to refuse to pay taxes, eventually spending a night in jail because he would not financially support principles with which he disagreed.

세부 내용

In this way, Thoreau used his voice as a writer to oppose _____ _____.

요약

(a) an end to war and the abolition of slavery
(b) a political ideology he considered unjust
(c) the collection of tax revenue from citizens
(d) a way of life that violated natural principles

t III

Because of his success at modernizing Russia and expanding its territory, Peter the Great is considered the most successful ruler in Russian history.

도입

Upon his ascent to the throne in 1696, Peter's goals were to advance the interests of the people and to make the country powerful in regional affairs. Between 1700 and 1721, Peter led the Russians in the Great Northern War, in which the Russians secured their only warm-water port, allowing them easy trade with the rest of the world.

세부 내용

By taking such steps, Peter was able to bring to Russia the innovations and advancements taking place worldwide.

결론

Q What is mainly discussed in the passage?

(a) Peter the Great's relationship with the northern countries
(b) The military conquests of Peter the Great
(c) How Peter the Great set the stage for Russia's success
(d) How Peter the Great ultimately came to power

정답 p.146

READING COMPREHENSION | 지문 유형별 공략

해커스 텝스 Reading

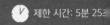
Part I Read the passage. Then choose the option that best completes the passage.

01

Director Stanley Kubrick's film *Dr. Strangelove* examines the Cold War through _____ _____. The movie's farcical plot is centered around the concept of mutually assured destruction, a Cold War policy guaranteeing nuclear war if either the United States or Soviet Union was directly attacked. In mocking the opinion of military officials who advocated war, Kubrick portrayed an unauthorized nuclear attack being launched against the Soviets by a rogue Air Force commander. The bizarre actions of several characters also represent Kubrick's condemnation of the male tendency towards violence.

(a) historically impartial accounts of battle
(b) the use of humor and critique
(c) an entertaining depiction of Soviet policy
(d) his dramatic storytelling ability

Part II Read the passage. Then identify the option that does NOT belong.

02

Cornish was the predominant language spoken in the Cornwall region of Britain until the eighteenth century. (a) English replaced Cornish in daily conversation as a result of the Act of Uniformity passed in 1549, which mandated the use of the language across Britain. (b) The last piece of prose written in Cornish was a 1776 letter written by William Bodinar. (c) By the beginning of the 1900s, all remaining native speakers of the language had died. (d) All two thousand speakers of the language currently alive learned Cornish strictly as a second language.

Part III Read the passage and the question. Then choose the option that best answers the question.

03

One of artist Marc Chagall's most well-known paintings is his piece entitled *I and the Village*. The painting alludes to the artist's upbringing in Belarus, including imagery of animals, Orthodox churches, and farm equipment. These images are embedded within a dreamlike scene involving a goat and a farmer face-to-face, painted in a manner that invokes the surrealism featured in paintings from the following decades. *I and the Village* was hailed by critics who were taken in by the innocent, childlike quality of the work.

Q What can be inferred from the passage?

(a) *I and the Village* was a precursor to surrealist paintings.
(b) Chagall had a conflicting positive and negative impression of his birthplace.
(c) Chagall is most well-known for autobiographic features in paintings.
(d) Art critics have purchased many of Chagall's works.

IV Read the passage and the questions. Then choose the option that best answers each question.

05

A Pioneering Humanitarian

Born in 1821 in Massachusetts, Clara Barton was taught the importance of humanitarian issues from a young age by her parents, who also encouraged her to take up a career in education. After becoming a teacher, she developed a commitment to social causes, such as providing education to impoverished children. Barton was instrumental in founding New Jersey's first free school, but when she discovered that a man had just been hired at twice her salary, she resigned in protest. At the outbreak of the Civil War, Barton began distributing supplies on the front lines and providing nursing care to wounded soldiers, despite having no formal nursing training.

In the years following the war, Barton went to Europe to recuperate from an extreme bout of exhaustion. When in Switzerland, she visited the International Red Cross, which encouraged her to open the American Red Cross. Under her stewardship, this institution helped to dispense medical care in the Spanish-American War, and provided relief for natural disaster victims during peacetime. Barton served in the Red Cross until she was 83, when she was forced to resign due to her egotistical leadership style. Nevertheless, she is remembered as a pioneering figure, both for her work with the organization and for breaking gender boundaries.

4. Q: Why did Clara Barton leave her position in the free school?

(a) She wanted to protest against the outbreak of the Civil War.

(b) Exhaustion prompted her to travel to Europe to recover.

(c) She learned her salary was half that of a recent hire.

(d) The school employed a man who she didn't approve of.

5. Q: What can be inferred from the passage?

(a) Most children in New Jersey were unable to afford schooling.

(b) There wasn't an American Red Cross during the Civil War.

(c) The Red Cross provided care to both Spanish and American soldiers.

(d) Barton's resignation from the Red Cross damaged her reputation.

CHAPTER 13 학술문 2 - 사회과학

사회과학 지문은 매회 평균적으로 2개 정도 출제된다. 주로 Part 3~4에서 나오고, Part 1~2에서 간혹 출제된다. 사회과학에는 경제, 문화, 정치, 법 등의 주제가 포함되며, 주로 사회적 현상 제시, 이를 뒷받침하는 세부 내용, 그리고 요약이나 결론으로 이어지는 흐름을 보인다. 그럼 이 유형에 대해 자세히 알아보자.

■ 출제 토픽

· **경제**   세계적 금융 위기, 마카오의 도박 산업, 케인스의 경제 이론, 마케팅 경향 분석 등
· **문화**   키스의 다양한 의미, 노출에 대한 문화적 차이, 인도의 카스트 제도, 이란의 명절 노우루즈 등
· **정치/법** 사회주의 정부의 붕괴, 유럽의 문화 정책 변화 // 미국의 사생활 보호법에 의한 초상권, 미국에서 파산법의 등장 배경 등

■ 빈출 문제 유형

· **문장의 일부 · 전체 완성하기**   사회적 현상에 대한 주제 또는 도입 문장이 나오는 지문 앞부분이나, 지문 내용을 요약하거나 결론을 도출하는 지문 마지막 부분에 빈칸이 제시되는 문제가 주로 출제된다.
· **중심 내용 문제**   사회적 현상에 대해 지문에서 중점적으로 설명하는 내용을 파악하는 문제가 출제된다.
· **육하원칙 문제 · Correct 문제** 주제나 소재와 관련된 연구, 조사, 통계, 사례, 문제점, 원인 등에 대한 내용과 일치하는 보기를 찾는 문제가 출제된다.
· **추론 문제**   주제나 소재를 통해 유추할 수 있는 내용을 선택하는 문제가 출제된다.

■ 예제 및 지문 flow

Many people believe that our society is dangerous and scary. If someone is a frequent television viewer, he or she is more likely to share such a view.	주제/도입 (사회적 현상)
This is the result of a steady stream of television content that sensationalizes everyday life in order to provide programs that will captivate the audience. Conflict, scandal, and violence absorb a viewer's attention and generate a series of emotional thrills. It helps add a sense of drama.	세부 내용 (연구, 조사, 통계, 사례, 문제점, 원인 등)
Thus, _____ if they habitually watch television.	요약 · 결론

(a) viewers tend to commit more violent act
(b) people develop a negative view of the world

해석 p.148

해설 | 지문 마지막의 빈칸을 채우는 문제이다. 빈칸이 있는 문장의 내용과 Thus(따라서)를 통해 습관적으로 TV를 시청하면 발생하는 결과를 빈칸에 넣어야 함을 알 수 있다. 자주 시청하는 사람이라면 우리 사회가 위험하고 무시무시하다고 생각하기 쉽다는 내용의 주제로 보아, '사람들은 부정적인 세계관을 키우게 된다'라는 내용의 (b)가 정답이다.

정답 | (b)

rt I

> The Internet allows for the distribution of important information, but can also create a public forum for individuals to make defamatory statements.
>
> 도입
>
> If an individual feels something you wrote is libelous, he or she may simply ask you to retract your comments. Otherwise, the victim can contact the owner of the Web site. Federal law authorizes stiff penalties for those guilty of publishing libelous material online, and Web sites wanting to keep clear of litigation will generally cooperate.
>
> 세부 내용
>
> In the end, if you create online content, be sure to avoid _____ _____.
>
> 결론

(a) Web sites that do not protect publishing rights
(b) distributing your content to a wide audience
(c) anything but the distribution of information
(d) making controversial remarks about others

rt III

> Citizens are expressing outrage at the country's contentious agricultural policies, which have resulted in higher grocery bills nationwide.
>
> 도입
>
> Many critics are complaining that the government mandate providing farmers with economic subsidies has driven up the prices of many staple crops. This is not the only basis for the price increases, however, as global weather conditions, which negatively affect a farm's production figures and thereby cut the supply of food available to stores, have also contributed to the problem along with restrictions on agricultural imports.
>
> 세부 내용

Q What is the main idea of the passage?

(a) Administrative strategies are designed to protect local producers.
(b) Government policies and climate conditions have resulted in higher food prices.
(c) Farm workers face difficulties because of the economic environment.
(d) The country is experiencing serious problems in agricultural trade.

Hackers **TEST**

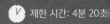

Part I Read the passage. Then choose the option that best completes the passage.

01

It is possible that the United States is not the melting pot it has long been thought to be. According to a recent study published by the Manhattan Institute for Policy Research, _____
_____. New arrivals to the country face many barriers to finding inclusion in the cultural, civic, and economic fabric of society. For them, seeking familiar surroundings in an ethnic neighborhood or engaging in business relationships with people from similar cultural backgrounds is an easier task than becoming assimilated into a new way of life.

(a) the country is becoming more ethnically diverse
(b) immigrants are not adapting to American life
(c) ethnic neighborhoods are growing in popularity
(d) foreigners operate many successful businesses

Part III Read the passage and the question. Then choose the option that best answers the question.

02

Market Sketch

A task force convened by federal trade regulators is examining the safety of China's manufactured goods after a series of product recalls has cast a spotlight on the country's production practices. Since the 1990s, nearly every major manufacturer has outsourced production to China in an attempt to capitalize on lower operating costs, which has proven profitable. However, safety issues related to the craftsmanship and materials used by suppliers have resulted in the loss of millions of dollars from products being pulled off store shelves.

Q What can be inferred from the passage?

(a) Companies are moving their manufacturing outside of China.
(b) Suppliers in China are no longer able to turn a profit.
(c) Consumers are boycotting the sale of Chinese products.
(d) The quality of Chinese-made goods is not up to safety standard.

t IV Read the passage and the questions. Then choose the option that best answers each question.

-04

Coffee is big business these days, with a number of chains dominating the high street, and a variety of artisanal products available for the more discerning drinker. The success of these chains is primarily down to the quality of their coffee and the welcoming atmosphere they create, but it is also due to the innovative marketing strategies they have employed. What they have in common is the establishment of a distinctive brand for each coffee chain, which allows them to compete in a segmented and saturated market.

One element of such a marketing strategy is the construction of a unique lexicon. This is clear in the wide array of terms that cafés nowadays deploy for their drink names, often types of coffee from Italy or France, such as a "Lungo" or an "Espresso Romano." This suggests to customers that the coffee being served is unique, rather than just black coffee. Another tactic that is apparent in all of the major chains is the setting up of loyalty programs. These can range from simple stamp cards to apps that automatically record purchases on customers' smartphones. The more varied and interactive these programs are, the more they convince customers to keep coming back.

03. Q: What is the main purpose of the passage?

(a) To explain how changing consumer tastes have led to innovations in the coffee industry
(b) To suggest that marketing is the most important factor of success
(c) To describe some highly effective approaches to publicity for café franchises
(d) To provide information on how to successfully open a coffee shop

04. Q: Which of the following is correct about loyalty programs according to the passage?

(a) They have a greater impact if they have diverse features.
(b) They are far more successful if they are automatic.
(c) They allow customers to purchase products with their phones.
(d) They help to establish the coffee chain's distinctive lexicon.

정답 p.148

CHAPTER 14 학술문 3 - 자연과학

자연과학 지문은 학술문 중 자주 출제되는 지문 유형으로 매회 평균적으로 8개 정도 나오며, Part 1~4에서 고루 출제된다. 자연과학에는 건강, 의학, 환경, 생물학 등의 주제가 포함되며, 자연과학 지문 유형은 주로 과학적 사실이나 개념 제시, 이를 뒷받침하는 세부 내용, 그리고 요약이나 결론으로 이어지는 흐름을 보인다. 그럼 이 유형에 대해 자세히 알아보자.

■ 출제 토픽

· **건강 · 의학**   식품 화학 첨가물의 부작용, 임신부에게 엽산 섭취의 중요성, 수면 패턴의 중요성 등
· **환경 / 생물학** 바다와 대기의 상호작용, 홍콩의 환경 오염 // 철새들의 이동 경로, 파리의 성장, 황제펭귄의 특징 등
· **천문학**   핼리 혜성, 화성의 생명체 존재 여부, 은하계에 대한 허블의 발견, 지구와 달의 지형이 다른 이유 등
· **기술**   에어컨의 소음, 두 종류의 바이오 연료 비교, 핵융합 원자로가 핵분열 원자로보다 안전한 이유 등

■ 빈출 문제 유형

· **문장의 일부 · 전체 완성하기**   과학적 사실이나 개념에 대한 주제 또는 도입 문장이 나오는 지문 앞부분이나, 지문의 내용을 요약하거나 결론을 도출하는 지문 마지막 부분에 빈칸이 제시되는 문제가 주로 출제된다.

· **중심 내용 문제**   과학적 사실이나 개념에 대해 지문에서 중점적으로 설명하는 내용을 파악하는 문제가 출제된다.
· **육하원칙 문제 · Correct 문제** 주제나 소재와 관련된 실험, 연구, 사례, 근거 등에 대한 내용과 일치하는 보기를 찾는 문제가 출제된다.
· **추론 문제**   주제나 소재를 통해 유추할 수 있는 내용을 선택하는 문제가 출제된다.

■ 예제 및 지문 flow

Pheromones, chemicals periodically released by animals, are used as a method of communication with other members of the species.

주제/도입
(과학적 사실 · 개념 등)

Ants are an example of an insect that uses them. If an ant is within a close enough range to be able to detect these chemicals from other ants, messages can be passed indicating mating opportunities, imminent danger, or the location of a nearby colony.

세부 내용
(실험, 연구, 사례, 근거 등)

This is because pheromones act as _____.

요약 · 결론

(a) a mechanism for transmitting various types of information
(b) a visual signal that cannot be detected by other species

해석 p.149

해설 | 지문 마지막의 빈칸에 문장의 일부를 넣는 문제이다. 빈칸이 있는 문장을 통해 페로몬의 어떤 작용이 앞에서 언급된 내용의 원인이 되는지를 빈칸에 넣어야 함을 알 수 있다. 페로몬이 의사소통 수단으로 사용된다는 주제가 나온 후 개미가 짝짓기 기회, 위험, 집단 서식지의 위치 등을 알리는 메시지를 전달할 수 있다는 사례가 나왔으므로, '다양한 유형의 정보를 전달하는 기제'라는 내용의 (a)가 정답이다.

정답 | (a)

Hackers **Practice**

rt I

The varying position of stars is the primary navigational clue used by nocturnally migrating birds when plotting their migratory course through the night sky.	주제
This was confirmed in an experiment done on warblers by German scientist Franz Sauer. Caged birds captured during migration season were put under a planetarium's ceiling, and Sauer moved the position of the stars on the ceiling each night to simulate the birds having traveled 300km in the direction they faced. The birds eventually "navigated" to the star pattern that would be seen at their migration site in central Africa.	세부 내용
This demonstrates that the night sky acts as _____.	결론

(a) a map that helps birds become oriented
(b) an obstacle to navigational instincts of birds
(c) a way for birds to calculate time flown
(d) a variable that was controlled experimentally

rt III

Recording small molecules has been a challenge to researchers because of their speed and random movement.	주제
Scientists trying to observe molecules could not predict the path a molecule would take, which prevented them from being studied deeply. This task became slightly easier with the discovery of carbon nanotubes, miniscule tubes scientists can construct to force molecules to travel in a single direction. However, complications still exist. Scientists are as yet unable to achieve a low enough molecular velocity – visible to the naked eye – to get a detailed picture.	세부 내용

Q What is the passage mainly about?

(a) The scientific merits of using carbon nanotubes
(b) The complications in observing molecular movement
(c) The methods used to track molecular motion
(d) The recently discovered characteristics of small molecules

Hackers **TEST**

Part I Read the passage. Then choose the option that best completes the passage.

01

An expansive network of roots absorbs water and nutrients from the soil and distributes them throughout the rest of the plant. Simultaneously, leaves take in carbon dioxide from the atmosphere through thousands of small holes called stomata. As chlorophyll-containing cells within the leaves absorb sunlight, a series of naturally occurring processes convert it to a molecule called ATP. Finally, the ATP molecules react with water and carbon dioxide present within the plant to produce energy the plant can use. In this way, _____.

(a) plants are able to survive and grow
(b) the body can use plants as food
(c) carbon dioxide and water are released
(d) the roots act as the site of metabolism

02

Nanomedicine is a promising field of medical research studying _____.
Nanotechnology, or the creation and control of objects on a molecular scale, is at the heart of this new approach to medicine. When scientists want a medical treatment only delivered to a specific part of the body or pharmaceuticals to affect only certain cells, they can take advantage of nanotechnology to create a microscopic device for achieving their objectives. Nanotechnology, it can be said, provides small scale solutions to big medical problems.

(a) the creation of medicines that are free of side effects
(b) medical treatment using molecules already in the body
(c) the use of miniature technology to improve health
(d) the application of microscopes in targeting certain diseases

Part III Read the passage and the question. Then choose the option that best answers the question.

03

Modern astronomers have no problems measuring the path, size, and distance of comets with a high degree of accuracy. In ancient times, however, most prominent thinkers considered a comet to be a foreboding omen, which more often than not would signal an upcoming disaster or a sudden burst of anger from heavenly gods. Contrary to the excitement that greets a comet sighting today, observers during previous civilizations did not experience such enthusiasm when a comet was observed streaking across the sky.

Q What can be inferred from the passage?

(a) Ancient civilizations held a special ceremony upon a comet appearing.
(b) Comets inspired a feeling of fear in ancient societies.
(c) In most instances comets are visible to the naked eye.
(d) Historians noted catastrophic events often preceding a comet sighting.

rt IV Read the passage and the questions. Then choose the option that best answers each question.

-05

The annual migration of birds from breeding to wintering grounds is one of the wonders of the natural world, but this activity is actually restricted to a minority of bird species. Only 1,800 of the world's 10,000 bird species are long-distance migrants. The rest stay largely in one environment and are known as sedentary birds. Avoiding the arduous yearly migration allows these birds to save energy, defend their territory, and spend more time nurturing their young. However, it also makes them more susceptible to localized threats, and therefore more vulnerable to extinction.

This was underlined by the findings of Stanford University biologist Cagan Sekercioglu, who, after analyzing a database of the world's bird species, discovered that non-migratory birds are 2.6 times more likely to be endangered than migratory birds. As these birds are reliant on conditions in their habitats, they are unable to adjust to disruption, either from climate change, deforestation, or habitat fragmentation. In contrast, whenever this occurs for migratory birds, they are able to search for alternative sites to breed or feed. As destruction to natural habitats increases, many of these endangered sedentary species are approaching a point of no return.

04. Q: What is the writer's main point about sedentary birds?

(a) They make up the vast majority of global bird species.
(b) They are unable to migrate due to environmental conditions.
(c) They are under more threat of dying out than migratory birds.
(d) They are much safer as they stay in the same location.

05. Q: What can be inferred from the passage?

(a) The nesting and eating grounds of migratory birds can be disrupted.
(b) There are no migratory birds that are presently at risk of extinction.
(c) The main threat to the habitats of sedentary birds is climate change.
(d) The majority of sedentary bird species were at one time migratory.

정답 p.150

READING COMPREHENSION | 지문 유형별 공략

해커스 텝스 Reading

혼자 하기 어렵고 막막할 땐?

텝스 실전모의고사

* Answer Sheet은 p.473에 수록되어 있습니다.

VOCABULARY & GRAMMAR

Part I Questions 1~10

Choose the best answer for the blank.

1. A: Aren't you taking Deegan Avenue to the hotel?
    B: Traffic may be heavy at this hour, so I'd rather _____ along a side street.

    (a) wing
    (b) curve
    (c) detour
    (d) waver

2. A: Is Dawn Lee a _____ friend of you and your wife?
    B: No, only my wife knows her personally.

    (a) genial
    (b) casual
    (c) mutual
    (d) habitual

3. A: You told me you'd be here an hour ago.
    B: It's not my _____ ! The traffic was heavy.

    (a) vice
    (b) guilt
    (c) fault
    (d) flaw

4. A: I heard your house was burglarized last weekend.
    B: Yeah, the thief _____ with most of my money and jewelry.

    (a) gave in
    (b) made off
    (c) copped out
    (d) booted up

5. A: You shouldn't have yelled at Ben.
    B: You're right. It was wrong to _____ my anger like that.

    (a) slip
    (b) haul
    (c) pass
    (d) vent

6. A: What do you think the _____ the case will be?
    B: The lawyers presented strong eviden against the suspect, so the jury will likely find him guilty.

    (a) grant
    (b) verdict
    (c) concept
    (d) mandate

7. A: I'm glad this hotel has an indoor poo and wireless Internet access.
    B: Yeah, this place has great _____

    (a) refinements
    (b) dexterities
    (c) increments
    (d) amenities

8. A: I think Sophia has a problem she's no telling us about.
    B: I'm sure she'll _____ when she's good and ready.

    (a) keep a straight face
    (b) rule with an iron fist
    (c) get it off her chest
    (d) put her foot in her mouth

9. A: That new video game *Delta-K* is a hit with the gamers.
    B: Yeah. They've given it _____ praise for its special effects.

    (a) scrupulous
    (b) unanimous
    (c) harmonious
    (d) anonymous

10. A: I heard Dean is recovering well from his injuries.
    B: Yes, but he won't be leaving the hospital until he's fully _____.

    (a) accelerated
    (b) modernized
    (c) recuperated
    (d) exhilarated

Choose the best answer for the blank.

. The workers complained to the labor board that they had not been given prior _____ before being laid off.

(a) homage
(b) notice
(c) order
(d) alibi

. Having no experience working with tools, Elizabeth could not _____ the shelf by herself.

(a) assemble
(b) compile
(c) amass
(d) gather

. Taking a _____ stand against piracy, France recently passed a stringent law that denies Internet access to frequent illegal downloaders.

(a) firm
(b) stout
(c) brisk
(d) static

. The government has _____ a campaign to raise awareness of lung disease, the country's fourth most common cause of death.

(a) initiated
(b) received
(c) departed
(d) animated

. In some Asian cultures, it is usually the eldest child who is designated to _____ the father in running the family business.

(a) remit
(b) herald
(c) conduct
(d) succeed

16. Fees at the spa include taxes and tips, but customers may provide an additional _____ if they are happy with the service.

(a) profit
(b) gratuity
(c) offering
(d) premium

17. The local government's concerted effort to cut costs is expected to result in a year-end budget _____.

(a) debit
(b) benefit
(c) surplus
(d) revenue

18. The research shows that violent television programs may _____ behavioral changes in young children.

(a) induce
(b) enchant
(c) convince
(d) simulate

19. Because Nadia and Tom were _____ about discussing their relationship, no one knew that they were dating.

(a) frivolous
(b) obdurate
(c) reticent
(d) austere

20. Because of the city's rising criminality, residents have been told to be _____ at all times.

(a) versed
(b) cordial
(c) susceptive
(d) vigilant

21. Bob was given _____ tickets to the premiere of the play after setting the stage.

    (a) stupendous
    (b) indecorous
    (c) temporary
    (d) complimentary

22. Marlon Brando was a talented performer whose career reached its _____ when he won the Academy Award for best actor in 1973.

    (a) chasm
    (b) eulogy
    (c) panegyric
    (d) pinnacle

23. The new CEO wasted no time and immediately _____ into the details of his plans for the company.

    (a) approbated
    (b) interjected
    (c) divested
    (d) delved

24. _____ to New Zealand, the Maori lived in the region hundreds of years before European settlers arrived in the 1600s.

    (a) Indigenous
    (b) Instinctive
    (c) Inherent
    (d) Intrinsic

25. Daisy sought to _____ her parents' concerns over her recent academic performance by staying home on the weekend to study for exams.

    (a) allay
    (b) laud
    (c) obtrude
    (d) tranquilize

26. Archaeologists were _____ by the mysterious, indecipherable carvings discovered at an excavation in Jerusalem.

    (a) mollified
    (b) parched
    (c) baffled
    (d) revered

27. The Black Sea is a _____ of a large but now extinct body of water called Tethys Ocean, which existed during the Mesozoic era.

    (a) plethora
    (b) remnant
    (c) snippet
    (d) morsel

28. I am unable to _____ what the author of this book is saying because he uses highly convoluted language.

    (a) muddle
    (b) tally
    (c) fathom
    (d) eschew

29. Health activist Dan Lee made a speech against cosmetic companies today, _____ their use of harmful chemicals in beauty products.

    (a) trifling
    (b) litigating
    (c) denouncing
    (d) squandering

30. Despite objections from the film's producers, the director was _____ about casting his daughter for the main role.

    (a) assailable
    (b) adamant
    (c) formidable
    (d) benignant

The Vocabulary section is complete. Please move on to the Grammar section.

Part I **Questions 1~10**

Choose the best answer for the blank.

A: Oh, the puppy is back from the vet.
B: Yeah. You _____ when dad came home with it.

(a) have been sleeping
(b) were sleeping
(c) have slept
(d) are sleeping

A: Did you have any trouble finding seats on the subway?
B: It was so crowded that I _____ barely even find a place to stand.

(a) might
(b) should
(c) need to
(d) could

A: How did the negotiations with the landlord go?
B: Great. Our lease _____ for another two years with no increase in rent.

(a) extended
(b) was extended
(c) has extended
(d) was being extended

A: Are you sure you can't join me in Ohio this summer?
B: Unfortunately, I can't. But I'm still hoping _____ their minds.

(a) to change for my parent
(b) for my parent change
(c) for my parents to change
(d) for my parents to changing

A: I need advice regarding adopting a child.
B: I know a lawyer _____ main focus is on family law.

(a) who
(b) which
(c) whose
(d) of whom

6. A: I'm disturbed by some of the articles that were published in the magazine.
   B: Then I would advise _____ your subscription.

   (a) discontinue
   (b) discontinuing
   (c) to discontinue
   (d) to be discontinuing

7. A: I've been thinking about _____ for some time now.
   B: I don't see any reason why you shouldn't go for it.

   (a) teaching at overseas
   (b) to teach overseas
   (c) teaching overseas
   (d) taught at overseas

8. A: I've quit drinking and smoking.
   B: Good. Indulging _____ vices only harms your body.

   (a) so
   (b) such
   (c) any of
   (d) much of

9. A: It's a shame Joe didn't pass his admissions exam.
   B: Yes. He was disappointed when he found out _____.

   (a) a bad news
   (b) all bad news
   (c) the bad news
   (d) any bad news

10. A: Have you heard that Ed quit his job to go traveling?
    B: Yeah. Only if I were younger _____ the same.

    (a) could I consider doing
    (b) could I doing consider
    (c) doing consider I could
    (d) I consider doing could

Part II   **Questions 11~25**

Choose the best answer for the blank.

11. Due to breakthroughs in research on spinal cord injuries, _____ were once considered untreatable cases are now curable.

(a) that
(b) what
(c) when
(d) which

12. Lydia is interested in art _____ her sister likes playing sports.

(a) either
(b) whether
(c) except
(d) whereas

13. The road repairs, _____ to finish in time for the town parade, recently commenced.

(a) scheduled
(b) scheduling
(c) schedule
(d) to be scheduled

14. Anti-piracy laws make it illegal _____ video cameras inside movie theaters.

(a) bring
(b) bringing
(c) to bring
(d) of bringing

15. Since filming for the television show's new season _____ a week ago, fans have been fervently awaiting its release.

(a) ends
(b) ended
(c) will end
(d) is ending

16. Facing mounting health problems, Mann passed the days without _____ hope for a speedy recovery.

(a) little
(b) a few
(c) many
(d) much

17. An ordinance banning cell phone use while driving is set _____ in May of next year.

(a) implemented
(b) implementing
(c) to be implemented
(d) to be implementing

18. The negative responses from people who tested the new computer compelled

_____.

(a) the company to rethink its design
(b) to rethink its design company
(c) the company rethinks its design
(d) rethinking the company to its design

19. Claiming all the responsibility for the outcome of a joint action is

_____ egocentric bias

(a) psychologists are calling
(b) what psychologists call
(c) psychologists are calling it
(d) what psychologists call it

20. _____ savings accounts and loans, Lodge Bank also offers an array of investment services.

(a) Beyond
(b) Upon
(c) Between
(d) Unlike

1. The city council was keen on _____ the mayor's proposal to preserve a historical landmark.

(a) support
(b) supporting
(c) be supporting
(d) be supported

2. Turkey's Hagia Sophia, _____ for its majestic architecture, is on the list of must-see sites in the Middle East.

(a) known
(b) knowing
(c) is being known
(d) has been knowing

3. Had it not been for several unavoidable delays, the case _____ earlier.

(a) will be tried
(b) has been tried
(c) will have been tried
(d) would have been tried

24. During the press conference, the mayoral candidate said the corruption allegations directed at him were _____

_____.

(a) preposterous as offensive as they were
(b) as preposterous as they were offensive
(c) preposterous and as they were offensive
(d) as preposterous and they were offensive

25. The parents requested that their child _____ leave class early because of an important appointment.

(a) be able to
(b) is able to
(c) was able to
(d) has been able to

Identify the option that contains an awkward expression or an error in grammar.

26. (a) A: Those are nice shoes you have there, Norah.
(b) B: Thanks. Would you believe I got them on sale for only $20?
(c) A: How is it that you always managing to find such great deals?
(d) B: Whenever I go shopping, I take my time and make sure I see everything on offer.

27. (a) A: Could we stop and rest a minute? I am exhausted from all this sightseeing.
(b) B: You didn't think we'd be walking this much?
(c) A: No, I would buy an all-day bus pass instead if I had known.
(d) B: Well, at least you're wearing a comfortable pair of shoes.

28. (a) French tennis player Markus Pontui is preparing for his comeback at this year's Madrid Open. (b) To have rested several months, Pontui says he has continuously worked on his tennis game after recovering from a wrist injury. (c) Despite his hiatus, sports analysts and fans alike remain optimistic about Pontui's upcoming performance on the court. (d) Aside from his steady ground strokes, Pontui is also known for his fast serve.

29. (a) Self-regulation, the process of which children gain control over their behavior, is a developmental milestone. (b) Children go through three phases before they reach this stage of personal growth. (c) During the two initial phases, occurring from birth until the twelfth month, children develop reflexes and the ability to adjust their actions in response to an event. (d) A third phase follows, during which children learn to act according to a caregiver's demands, before self-regulation starts to develop.

30. (a) The performance art of oriental dance originated in the Middle East. (b) Widely known by its misnomer "belly dance," it is characterized by fluid movements of the torso punctuated with rhythmic hip shaking. (c) In the West, it is often misunderstood being a dance of seduction, but in Middle Eastern cultures, it is simply a way to celebrate. (d) In fact, not only do Middle Eastern women perform the dance but men and children as well.

The Vocabulary and Grammar sections are complete. Do NOT start the Reading Comprehension section until instructed to do so. You are NOT allowed to open any of the other sections of the exam.

READING
COMPREHENSION

Part I **Questions 1~10**

Read the passage. Then choose the option that best completes the passage.

1. The advent of the information age introduced Internet blogging as a new avenue for advertising. So, how effective are blogs in generating leads that are convertible to sales? A study was recently conducted on how blogs affect purchasing decisions. In a survey of 1,000 regular Internet users living in the United States, 63 percent claimed that at least one purchasing decision in recent months had been influenced by blogs. It is clear that blogs can help move products. Judging by this trend, we can assume that _____

   (a) interest in blog marketing will continue
   (b) people's trust in bloggers has diminished
   (c) bloggers can generate negative publicity
   (d) blog readers ignore most online ads

2. The training department's goal this quarter is to _____
   Based on the recent quality assurance survey, most of our customers think our representatives are knowledgeable about our products and services. However, respondents also feel that our sales representatives lack friendliness. We all know that this could affect the image, and ultimately, the bottom line of the company. Thus, developing our employees' abilities to relate to customers should be everyone's main focus.

   (a) refresh our employees' product knowledge
   (b) teach our representatives new selling techniques
   (c) improve employees' rapport with our customers
   (d) inform staff of the revised quality standards

3. Census figures indicate that the divorce rate in the United States _____
   _____. From a peak of 5.3 divorces per 1,000 people in 1981, the rate has gradually decreased over the following three decades and now stands at 3.6 divorces annually per 1,000 persons. Such a low rate was last achieved in 1970 before the adoption of no-fault divorce, which allowed marriages to be dissolved without proving adultery or abuse.

   (a) hit a record high then steadily declined
   (b) decreased by 3.6 percent in the last decade
   (c) is on the rise due to the no-fault law
   (d) surpassed its previous peak in 1981

4. During election campaign periods, opinion polls are regularly conducted by independent, nonpartisan polling agencies to predict actual voting results. Though the surveys are impartial, their integrity can be compromised if individuals or organizations involved in a campaign skew the data to suit their own needs, often with the intention of deceiving the public. The results are most often misrepresented to discredit a particular candidate's campaign. Hence, the interpretation of election poll results _____

   (a) is an exercise that isn't always objective
   (b) should be overseen by the government
   (c) is the key to making accurate predictions
   (d) should be closely monitored by candidates

To whom it may concern,

I visited your salon yesterday, and I would like to tell you about _____ _____. Your receptionist, Jen, was very accommodating even though I was looking for a last-minute appointment. She offered to give me a call if she found an available stylist to cut my hair. Within an hour, she was able to schedule me for the afternoon. The stylist, Marco, also did a great job with my hair. He was very attentive, and I was able to get the exact look I described to him. I will definitely become a regular customer. Keep up the good work!

Regards,
Marilyn Stone

(a) the problems that I encountered getting an appointment
(b) how I feel about having my hair styled by Jen
(c) a suggestion I have to improve your salon's service
(d) the gratifying experience I had at your establishment

Finest Moments, one of the country's oldest photography studios, has begun to _____ _____. Having made a name for itself through traditional portraiture, the company has now ventured into themed photography, which caters to clients looking for a fun, creative photo shoot. Some of our most popular outfits are inspired by animated films like *Cinderella* and *Aladdin*. Another option is the celebrity shoot, in which customers can dress as their favorite movie, music, or sports stars. Clients wishing to evoke a bygone era can also choose from among our collection of period attire.

(a) allow on-location photography sessions
(b) provide clients with an array of costumes
(c) give clients the celebrity treatment
(d) cater to a younger set of customers

Most people think that pizza, one of the world's most popular food items, is strictly an Italian creation. On the contrary, pizza is an amalgam of regional culinary creations. The flat bread that has become the basis of most pizzas was actually Greek in origin. The bread was introduced to 16th century Naples, where the locals garnished it with tomatoes and cheese. As the dish's popularity spread to other Italian cities, people used their own local ingredients as pizza toppings. Therefore, despite its strong association with Italy, pizza _____ _____.

(a) is not exclusively of Italian origin
(b) was a staple of the Greek diet
(c) was initially despised by Neapolitans
(d) is more popular elsewhere in the world

8. Halitosis is often blamed on poor dental hygiene. Most people think that bad-breath-causing bacteria results from inadequate tooth and gum care or a pungent diet. This is sometimes the case, but halitosis may also be an indication of serious health problems. People who exhale noticeably unpleasant odors may have gastroesophageal reflux disease or lower respiratory tract infections, among other medical conditions. Hence, it is not necessarily correct to assume that people with halitosis _____.

   (a) observe proper habits of personal care
   (b) are not meticulous about oral hygiene
   (c) are required to seek medical attention
   (d) have underlying genetic preconditions

9. Merriam's kangaroo rats live in sandy areas with high temperatures in summer, like Southern California and Arizona, and they have some very unusual features. _____, they have long kangaroo-like hind feet, which allow them to hop around on their hind legs. To avoid predation, they leap high into the air or quickly change direction. The animals' tails are longer than the combined lengths of their heads and bodies, which helps counterbalance the jumping motion. Merriam's kangaroo rats also possess fur-lined cheek pouches, where they store seeds that they hoard during foraging trips. Additionally, they are capable of digesting the seeds they eat without drinking water.

   (a) Meanwhile
   (b) For example
   (c) That being said
   (d) As a result

10.

   ## Against the Odds

   Although Tim Page grew up struggling with a pervasive developmental disorder called Asperger's Syndrome, he is now among the most respected writers and music critics in the United States. Page obtained a college degree from Columbia University and became a classical music critic for prestigious newspapers such as *The New York Times* and *The Washington Post*. He would go on to write and edit more than a dozen books for which he achieved recognition, and _____, he was awarded a Pulitzer Prize in 1997 for his music criticism in *The Washington Post*.

   (a) after all
   (b) on the other hand
   (c) on top of that
   (d) in conclusion

Read the passage. Then identify the option that does NOT belong.

11. Research shows that women are more likely to suffer from insomnia than men. (a) A survey was conducted by the National Sleep Foundation in America to study the sleeping patterns of men and women. (b) Participants were asked to identify any symptoms of insomnia that they were experiencing and the frequency of their occurrence. (c) A majority of female respondents reported that they were going through emotional stress. (d) Results indicated that 63 percent of women experienced symptoms of insomnia at least a few times a week, while only 54 percent of men reported the same problem.

12. The indigenous Himba tribe in Namibia has a unique kinship system called bilateral descent. (a) In this practice, tribe members belong to both their father's and mother's clans. (b) Bilateral descent is practiced in only a few tribes in Africa, India and Australia, and on the islands of Melanesia and Polynesia. (c) Although they live with their father's kin, tribesmen receive their inheritance from their maternal families, specifically from their mother's brothers. (d) This is in contrast to the customs of other African tribes, which strictly trace kinship to either the paternal or maternal clan.

Part III **Questions 13~25**

Read the passage and the question. Then choose the option that best answers the question.

13. A crucial element for survival, water plays a part in many belief systems. Among Christian sects, water is central to baptismal rites, which are said to purge the soul of past sins. In the same way, for Hindus, water is originally endowed with cleansing properties and is considered more potent if it comes from a sacred river such as the Ganges. In fact, Hindu holy places are often found near sources of water. In Islam, people must perform ablution rituals before praying, and running water is available outside every mosque for just this purpose.

Q: What is the passage mainly about?

(a) Water's role in the spread of religion
(b) How water is used in spiritual customs
(c) The role of water in creation myths
(d) Why temples are built near bodies of water

14.

HEAVY METAL HORROR

Unlike most writers who prefer to work in quiet places, Stephen King, one of the most prolific horror writers known today, listens to heavy metal music when he writes. For many, loud music makes concentration difficult, but the music of bands like Metallica and Anthrax produces in King a creative state of mind. He says the music inspires him and helps him write as long as the songs are familiar enough that listening to the lyrics is no longer a distraction.

Q: What is the main topic of the passage?

(a) The favorite music genres of Stephen King
(b) The role of music in Stephen King's writing routine
(c) How Stephen King uses song lyrics to create stories
(d) Why Stephen King's characters are influenced by music

Telling stories to children involves more than the simple act of reading a book out loud. Unlike adults, children find it difficult to concentrate for long periods of time. Therefore, they must be constantly reminded to focus their attention on the storyteller. Luckily, several tried and tested techniques have been found to engage young audiences. Speaking in a theatrical voice, using animated facial expressions and exaggerated actions, and employing props and illustrations all help to keep a child's attention firmly fixed on the reader.

Q: What is the main point of the passage?

(a) Storybooks help improve children's attention spans.
(b) Children who cannot focus need intervention.
(c) Engagement is important when reading to children.
(d) Reading in front of people must be learned early.

It is our business at Jeans Infinity to make sure that you're always in a perfect pair of denim jeans. From skinny to baggy, flare to boot cut, and anything in between, we'll make a pair especially for you. Once you've selected the style, wash, buttons, and other add-ons, our expert tailors will get your exact measurements, and in two weeks' time, you'll receive your custom-made Infinity jeans. So, visit the Jeans Infinity store nearest you and design your own pair of denim jeans.

Q: What is mainly being advertised?

(a) The latest fashion trends in jeans
(b) A special sale at Jeans Infinity
(c) A store offering made-to-order attire
(d) A newly opened tailoring establishment

In the US, the number of interracial marriages is at a record high, with one out of seven new marriages being interethnic. Such marriages have been on the rise ever since the US Supreme Court declared in 1967 that laws banning such unions are unconstitutional. Moreover, the steady influx of immigrants and increasing globalization has made the phenomenon more commonplace. One positive effect of this social reality is its ability to chip away at long-standing racial barriers. However, it can also lead to homogeneity and the loss of ethnic identities.

Q: Which of the following is correct according to the passage?

(a) Interethnic unions can undermine racial uniqueness.
(b) In 1967, one out of seven marriages was interethnic.
(c) Interracial marriages are expected to decline in the US.
(d) Racial barriers are exacerbated by interracial unions.

18. Thank you for purchasing City Life: Road Life. This expansion pack adds more functionalit to the City Life 3 video game by upgrading the lineup of cars available to characters. Following installation, please register as part of the City Life Community by clicking on the "register now" button on the game launcher. The unique code you received upon purchase the game must be provided. Once the information is verified, vehicle upgrades will be available to players from the "garage" menu.

Q: Which of the following is correct according to the passage?

(a) City Life: Road Life offers players more characters.
(b) The "register now" button is on the game's website.
(c) The expansion pack can be downloaded for free.
(d) The cars become available after a product code is entered.

19.

Tom's Bakery
One Day Baking Class

On Saturday the 23rd of March at 11 a.m., come to Tom's Bakery for a one day baking class taught by Tom Stafford, an internationally renowned baker. Participants will learn how to make three types of bread: sourdough, rye, and pita, using recipes from Tom's bestselling cook book *The Baking Bible*.

- Registration Fee: $10, materials and utensils inclusive
  *Attendees must bring their own aprons; hairnets will be provided.
- Exclusive offers: all attendees will get a 10 percent discount on our regular classes.

Go to www.tomsbakery.com to reserve a spot.

Tom's Bakery
21 Pearl Street, Boston
Massachusetts, 03521

Q: Which of the following is correct?

(a) Participants should bring Tom Stafford's popular baking cook book.
(b) All the ingredients and cooking tools are covered by the class fee.
(c) Class participants are expected to have their own hairnets and aprons.
(d) One-day-class attendees will get a $10 discount on regular classes.

Pit bulls, a group of several dog breeds belonging to the molosser category, are mistakenly feared for their temperament. They are perceived as more dangerous to humans than other canines because of the severe physical injuries they can cause. Pit bulls can inflict serious damage, as they are predisposed to bite, hold, and shake their victims with their powerful jaws during attacks. A study shows, however, that pit bulls are on par with, or even superior to, other dogs when it comes to stability, aggressiveness, and friendliness during human interactions. It is only when they are trained by irresponsible owners that they become a vicious threat to people.

Q: What has a study of pit bulls revealed about their character?

   (a) They have more powerful jaws than other dog breeds.
   (b) They have a tendency to bite humans and cause serious harm.
   (c) They are less friendly and stable than any other dog breed.
   (d) They are not any more violent than other types of dog.

After Apple-Picking is one of Robert Frost's most anthologized poems and one of the few he composed in free verse. Known for his mastery of traditional meter, Frost rarely employed the style, as he found its looseness too lacking in form, comparing it to playing tennis without a net. *After Apple-Picking*, which describes a tiring day of picking apples but likewise alludes to death, is perhaps Frost's finest example of a free verse poem, with its varying patterns of long and short lines and unorthodox rhyming scheme.

Q: Which is correct about Robert Frost according to the passage?

   (a) He considered the format of free verse to be too unstructured.
   (b) Many of his poems employed unconventional rhyming patterns.
   (c) *After Apple-Picking* directly refers to mortality.
   (d) *After Apple-Picking* was a masterpiece of standard verse.

22.

Beachfront Property

Posh Holdings, the number one real estate company in the country, has put a beachfront cottage on Morey Beach up for sale. The 130-square-meter, two-story house was built in 1961 and has only been owned by one family. Despite having been renovated in 1995, this quaint beach house manages to retain its old-world charm. It has three bedrooms, two fully appointed bathrooms, living and dining areas, and a second-floor deck that overlooks the beach. Prospective buyers living outside Morey can take a video tour of the property at www.posh.com/morey.

Q: Which is correct about the cottage according to the advertisement?

(a) It was recently renovated in preparation for the sale.
(b) Its ownership has passed from one family to another.
(c) It may be virtually explored by clients online.
(d) Its living and dining areas overlook the beach.

23. The Age of Discovery, from the 15th to the 17th centuries, was a defining moment in world history. As Europeans explored the world, they discovered new crops, such as maize and potatoes, which they brought back to Europe. At the same time, the explorers also introduc Old World plants like dandelions and wheat to the territories they colonized. The importec species thrived in their new environments, increasing the biodiversity on both sides of the globe. While the crop exchange is often overlooked in discussions of this era, its benefits are still being reaped today.

Q: Which statement would the writer most likely agree with?

(a) The crop exchange solved food shortage problems around the world.
(b) Global exploration led to unprecedented ecological developments.
(c) The New World became overrun with imported species.
(d) The prolific exchange of crops defines the Age of Discovery.

4. Colic, described as the frequent and prolonged excessive crying of an otherwise healthy infant, usually causes anxiety for parents. There's no reason for worry, though, as colic is a normal and temporary condition. It generally occurs within the first four months of birth. While its real cause is still unknown, colic is often attributed to intestinal gas. The gas causes the baby discomfort, which can be eased by burping or massaging the child's stomach. If accompanied by fever or other symptoms, however, the condition may be due to illnesses, so medical care must be sought in such cases.

Q: What can be inferred from the passage?

   (a) Colic can accompany more serious conditions.
   (b) The crying fits frequently occur in the middle of the night.
   (c) Medication must be given if colic persists for four months.
   (d) Intestinal gas can be caused by overfeeding.

5.

Shoes on Trial

Footwear giant Zerc is being sued for false advertising in a class action suit filed by plaintiff Anna Moore. Last year, to stay ahead of the competition, the shoe manufacturer released its Contour line, claiming that the footwear was designed to help tone calf muscles even by just walking—a first in the industry. Moore, however, accuses Zerc of deceptive advertising, as she claims the product failed to deliver on its supposed benefit. Though the company won a similar lawsuit against its Soar line in 2005, law experts believe that Zerc may be hard-pressed to win this time.

Q: What can be inferred from the news report?

   (a) The complainant suffered minor injuries from wearing the footwear.
   (b) Zerc was the first to feature a specific innovation in shoe design.
   (c) A new advertising campaign will be created for the Contour.
   (d) The Contour line was temporarily recalled from the market.

Read the passage and the questions. Then choose the option that best answers each question.

Questions 26-27

Wanted: Engineer

Washington State's Highway Maintenance Department is looking for a skilled engineer to help maintain the high standards of the road system throughout the state.

Job Description:

• Duties include managing highway construction, road maintenance, and traffic system repair; monitoring traffic reports and replying to regular complaints from drivers about the highways.

• Other responsibilities include hiring and managing teams of contractors, communicating with stakeholders, and overseeing the bidding process for major works.

• Successful candidates must be reliable, professional, and highly accurate in the work they carry out.

• A full driving license and experience driving a van is essential.

• Candidates should have three years of relevant experience, those with experience working for state-level transportation departments favored.

• A bachelor's degree is required, engineering majors are preferred.

Send a completed application form, along with a full résumé, a copy of your diploma, and the contact details of two recent references to highways@washingtonstate.com. The deadline for applications is August 10.

26. Q: What will the engineer be responsible for dealing with?

(a) Communications from the public about the bidding process for works
(b) Complaints from pedestrians about the road surfaces in towns
(c) Messages from drivers who have been in accidents along the highways
(d) Issues with the highways raised by people driving vehicles

27. Q: What can be inferred from the passage?

(a) Driving across country will be a regular duty for the engineer.
(b) The stakeholders are responsible for overseeing the bidding process.
(c) Candidates do not need an engineering degree to be qualified.
(d) The department hires contractors to carry out all construction work.

http://www.oregongazette.com/editorial/goverment-housing-policy

Oregon Gazette

Editorial: Government Housing Policy

COMMENT

user925   15 hours ago

You appear to be oblivious to the fact that this state has been mired in a housing crisis for almost half a decade. How can you be so ignorant? This crisis has led to record rates of homelessness and more people on the waiting list for public housing than the state could ever accommodate. Given this situation, the argument that the emergency measures for housing are a waste of taxpayers' money is demonstrably false. Contrary to your belief, the market will not sort out this problem by itself.

In the last few decades, the housing market has undergone a massive boom, with rents rising at three times the rate of average income. For those making the minimum wage, this is frankly unsustainable. Although the government has made many mistakes in public housing, its actions to curb the excesses of this market are laudable. Its policy of forcing landlords to pay tenants' relocation fees if they raise rents by 10 percent or more has helped tenants to find a new rental property instead of being forced onto the street. Otherwise, former tenants would have had to join the legions of the working homeless who are already there.

Q: What is the main purpose of the comment?

(a) To criticize the local government's various public housing policy failures
(b) To explain why homelessness has become such a major contemporary problem
(c) To support the government's policies to limit the housing crisis
(d) To highlight the disparity between average rental prices and average incomes

Q: Which of the following is correct according to the comment?

(a) The waiting list for public housing has been reduced in recent years.
(b) There are many people who have a job but are currently homeless.
(c) Landlords must cover relocation costs whenever tenants move out.
(d) The emergency provision for housing has yet to come into effect.

Science Note

The tongue of the butterfly is one of its most distinctive features. Curved, thin, and in some cases as long as its body, this unique appendage is used like a straw, to suck up sweet nectar from a flower. Considered a type of proboscis, this tongue was thought to be a result of the insect's evolutionary adaptation to feed from flowers. However, new research from Utrecht University in the Netherlands has revealed that this may not be the case, as the butterfly's unique tongue appears to have predated the evolution of flowers by millions of years.

The scientists at Utrecht were analyzing the scales of ancient butterflies to determine their evolutionary links to today's butterfly species. Their scales were hollow, like those of the Glossata group of butterflies, all of which have proboscises. This finding implies that butterflies have had proboscises since at least the Triassic-Jurassic period, around 200 million years ago, while flowers did not evolve until around 140 million years ago. Now, many scientists are questioning what purpose these tongues have had if, as this study suggests, they did not coevolve with flowers.

30. Q: How do the findings of the Utrecht University researchers contradict earlier theories?

    (a) They show how butterflies used their proboscises in the Triassic-Jurassic period.
    (b) They reveal that Glossata butterflies had hollow scales.
    (c) They suggest how the butterfly has evolved to have a proboscis.
    (d) They show how the butterfly could not have evolved with the flower.

31. Q: What can be inferred about Glossata butterflies from the passage?

    (a) They are the oldest subspecies of butterfly in existence.
    (b) They are descended from ancient hollow-scaled butterflies.
    (c) They are currently the dominate species of butterfly.
    (d) They do not use their proboscises to feed from flowers.

Built throughout America in the 19th century, poorhouses were municipal institutions that took in people who couldn't support themselves. In doing so, they were designed to help these poverty-stricken individuals. They initially offered the indigent shelter in exchange for labor on a farm or in a factory, but these institutions became increasingly restrictive as their punitive aspect developed. This was a reflection of the prejudice surrounding poverty, which equated it with moral failure. Poorhouses were thus seen as places where the poor were disciplined for their failings.

The destitute individuals that entered these facilities, either voluntarily or involuntarily, paid a high price for the shelter and food the poorhouses provided. Residents, known as inmates, were subjected to draconian controls on what they ate, wore, and did. Moreover, conditions in the poorhouses were usually dismal; individuals and families lived and worked in disease-ridden, cramped rooms. Although poorhouses were abolished in the 20th century, the idea that the poor are to blame for their poverty persists in some contemporary institutions, as well as in many of the government's social welfare policies.

2. Q: What is the main point of the passage?

(a) Poorhouses were usually effective measures of helping the poor.
(b) The problem of poverty should be controlled by the government.
(c) People staying in poorhouses lived in very unhygienic conditions.
(d) Poorhouses for aiding the poor ended up stigmatizing them.

3. Q: Which of the following is correct according to the passage?

(a) Poorhouses enforced strict rules on various aspects of residents' lives.
(b) The people in poorhouses faced severe discipline if they tried to escape.
(c) Children were often separated from their parents in poorhouses.
(d) Residents of poorhouses were paid a small salary in exchange for their work.

READING COMPREHENSION

BRUXI Times

Zika virus affects 52 local people

Sarah Ralph

An outbreak of the Zika virus has affected 52 people, health officials today revealed. Of the 52 who were infected, 19 have recovered, while 33 are still being treated. Doctors believe that the sudden appearance of the disease can be traced to a single individual who picked up the virus on a recent business trip to Southeast Asia.

There is not thought to be any risk of the infection spreading further, but officials say they will remain vigilant. The virus, which is usually mosquito-borne, can also be spread through blood transfusions.

While it is rarely deadly for adults, the Zika virus can cause serious harm to unborn children. If a woman becomes infected during pregnancy, the infection can result in the fetus developing brain defects, such as microcephaly, a condition that leads to babies being born with undersized craniums.

Most sufferers of the Zika virus experience flu-like symptoms, such as fever, joint pain, redness of the eyes, and headache. However, if the virus is contracted by someone who is infirm or has a pre-existing health condition, then it can be fatal. Health officials have warned people to remain alert and to avoid any possible sources of infection.

34. Q: Which of the following is correct according to the passage?

(a) Over half of the infected people have already recovered.
(b) The Zika virus is typically contracted through an insect bite.
(c) The Zika virus is only fatal to people with pre-existing conditions.
(d) Pregnant women with the Zika virus are more likely to miscarry.

35. Q: What can be inferred from the passage?

(a) The vast majority of Zika cases are not life threatening.
(b) Most people who have the Zika virus were infected it in hospitals.
(c) People with the Zika virus remain contagious for a number of weeks.
(d) The first cases of the Zika virus were detected in Southeast Asia.

정답 p.15

The Reading Comprehension section of the exam is complete. Please stay in your seat until the proctor tells you to leave. You are NOT allowed to open any of the other sections of the exam.

Seoul National University

성명
Name
한글
한자

교시실란 Room No.

주민등록번호 National ID No.

좌석번호 Seat No.

비밀번호 Password

수험번호 Registration No.

청해 Listening Comprehension

어휘 & 문법

어휘 Vocabulary

문법 Grammar

독해 Reading Comprehension

본인은 필기구 및 기재오류와 답안지 훼손으로 인한 책임을 지고, 부정행위 처리규정을 준수할 것을 서약합니다.

서 약

답안작성시 유의사항

1. 답안 작성은 반드시 컴퓨터용 싸인펜을 사용해야 합니다.
2. 답안을 정정할 경우 수정테이프(수정액 불가)를 사용해야 합니다.
3. 본 답안지는 컴퓨터로 처리되므로 훼손해서는 안되며, 답안지 하단의 타이밍마크(▮▮▮)를 찢거나, 낙서 등으로 인한 훼손시 불이익이 발생할 수 있습니다.
4. 답안은 문항당 정답을 1개만 골라 ● 와 같이 정확히 기재해야 하며, 필기구 오류나 본인의 부주의로 잘못 표기한 경우에는 당 관리위원회의 OMR판독기의 판독결과에 따르며, 그 결과는 본인이 책임집니다.

Good ●   Bad ◐◖◑◯⊗∅

5. 감독관의 확인이 없는 답안지는 무효처리됩니다.

Answer Sheet 473

텝스 문법·어휘·독해의 기본서

해커스 텝스 READING

개정 3판 15쇄 발행 2024년 8월 12일

개정 3판 1쇄 발행 2018년 5월 3일

지은이	David Cho | 언어학 박사, 前 UCLA 교수
펴낸곳	(주)해커스 어학연구소
펴낸이	해커스 어학연구소 출판팀

주소	서울특별시 서초구 강남대로61길 23 (주)해커스 어학연구소
고객센터	02-537-5000
교재 관련 문의	publishing@hackers.com
동영상강의	HackersIngang.com

ISBN	978-89-6542-251-8 (13740)
Serial Number	03-15-01

텝스 전문 포털,
해커스텝스(HackersTEPS.com)

텝 해커스텝스

외국어인강 1위,
해커스인강(HackersIngang.com)

텝 해커스인강

· 본 교재 무료 동영상강의
· 매달 업데이트되는 스타강사의 **텝스 무료 적중예상특강**
· 매일 실전 텝스 문제 및 **텝스 단어시험지 자동생성기** 등 무료 학습 콘텐츠

· 텝스를 분석 반영한 **온라인 실전모의고사**
· 텝스 시험에 나올 어휘를 정리한 **단어암기장** 및 **단어암기 MP3**
· 해커스 스타강사의 본 **교재 인강**

1위 해커스의 노하우가 담긴
해커스텝스 무료 학습자료

1 매일 업데이트되는 텝스 실전문제로 시험 대비

매일 텝스 풀기

2 베스트셀러 1위 해커스 텝스 리딩의 학습효과를 2배로

최신 텝스 리딩 무료강의

청해 장원 문법 이나진 독해 김형일

3 1위 해커스 스타 강사진의 텝스 적중예상특강으로 고득점 달성 가능

텝스 적중예상특강

4 텝스 필수 기출 어휘 학습

매일 텝스 어휘

5 텝스 최신 기출 어휘를 꼼꼼하게 복습

해커스 텝스 기출 보카 TEST